CHILDHOOD AND ADOLESCENCE IN SOCIETY

SELECTIONS FROM CQ RESEARCHER

SAGE
Los Angeles | London | New Delhi
Singapore | Washington DC

For information:

SAGE Publications, Inc.
2455 Teller Road
Thousand Oaks, California 91320
E-mail: order@sagepub.com

SAGE Publications Ltd.
1 Oliver's Yard
55 City Road
London, EC1Y 1SP
United Kingdom

SAGE Publications India Pvt. Ltd.
B 1/I 1 Mohan Cooperative Industrial Area
Mathura Road, New Delhi 110 044
India

SAGE Publications Asia-Pacific Pte. Ltd.
33 Pekin Street #02-01
Far East Square
Singapore 048763

Printed in the United States of America

Library of Congress Cataloging-in-Publication Data

Childhood and adolescence in society : selections from CQ Researcher.
p. cm. -- (Global issues)
Includes bibliographical references.
ISBN 978-1-4129-9434-7 (pbk.)
1. Child development. 2. Children and violence. 3. Child soldiers. 4. Bullying. 5. Child welfare. 6. Adolescence. 7. Teenagers--Social conditions. 8. Teenage pregnancy. I. Congressional Quarterly, inc.
HQ767.9.C4453 2012
362.70973--dc22 2010051835

This book is printed on acid-free paper.

11 12 13 14 15 10 9 8 7 6 5 4 3 2 1

Acquisitions Editor: Christine Cardone
Associate Editor: Julie Nemer
Editorial Assistant: Sarita Sarak
Production Editor: Laureen Gleason
Typesetter: C&M Digitals (P) Ltd.
Cover Designer: Candice Harman

Contents

CHILD AND ADOLESCENT RIGHTS

SOCIAL ISSUES

Annotated Contents

GLOBAL ISSUES

Rescuing Children: Is the Global Community Doing Enough?

The numbers are grim: Every day more than 25,000 children under age 5 — the equivalent of 125 jetliners full of youngsters — die from hunger, poverty or easily preventable illnesses, such as diarrhea and malaria. Millions of others are abandoned, trafficked into prostitution, forced into armed conflict or used as child laborers — mostly in sub-Saharan Africa, Asia and Eastern Europe. While governments and nongovernmental organizations struggle to help, aid cutbacks due to the world economic crisis could trigger 200,000-400,000 additional child deaths each year. Meanwhile, experts and policy makers disagree over how best to combat AIDS among children, and whether more foreign aid would do more harm than good. Others question whether the United States should ratify the U.N. Convention on the Rights of the Child. The United States is the only nation besides Somalia that hasn't adopted the treaty.

Child Soldiers: Are More Aggressive Efforts Needed to Protect Children?

Since the mid-1990s, the world has watched in horror as hundreds of thousands of children and young teenagers have participated in nearly 50 wars, mostly in Africa and Asia. Children as young as 5 or 6 have served in combat, and thousands of abducted young girls were forced into sexual slavery. Some terrorist groups even strap explosive-rigged vests onto children and send them off as suicide bombers. Others have been recruited, sometimes forcibly, into the official armed forces or paramilitary units of several dozen countries. U.N. treaties prohibit the use of child soldiers, and the Security Council "names and shames" persistent violators. But only four former guerrilla commanders have been convicted by international tribunals, and some human-rights advocates urge more aggressive prosecution of perpetrators. However, some peace negotiators say threats of prosecution can obstruct cease-fire negotiations and prolong the fighting. In the U.S., where children under 18 serve in the military in non-combat roles, Congress is considering laws to combat the use of child soldiers overseas.

VIOLENCE AND BULLYING

Youth Violence: Are "Get Tough" Policies the Best Approach?

Several recent violent crimes by youths, including the vicious beating death of a Chicago honor student by a mob of teenagers, have sparked a new look at urban youth violence. Despite a steep overall drop in youth crime in recent years, researchers say many urban areas continue to be plagued by homicide and other violence involving young offenders. Some experts say tougher sentencing laws and a greater focus on parental responsibility are the best ways to fight the violence, while others argue for more federal money for social programs and anti-violence efforts. In some cities, collaborative approaches involving police, educators, community leaders and neighborhood groups are aimed at pressing youths to forsake violence while offering them a path toward redemption. Meanwhile, two competing proposals are being considered on Capitol Hill, and major foundations are funding programs to help youths in trouble.

Cyberbullying: Are New Laws Needed to Curb Online Aggression?

Child advocates say a growing epidemic of "cyberbullying"—the use of computers, cell phones, social-networking sites and other technology to threaten or humiliate others—is putting young people at risk, sometimes with deadly consequences. The Centers for Disease Control and Prevention has labeled "electronic aggression" an "emerging public-health problem." Court precedents on school discipline and students' First Amendment rights provide limited guidance to educators grappling with the emerging world of cyber communication, especially transmissions originating off school grounds. Nonetheless, many states and school districts are taking strong steps aimed at curbing cyber abuse. In Congress, bills to provide new funding for online-safety programs have been introduced, but conflicts have arisen over how federal money for such efforts should be spent.

Domestic Violence: Do Teenagers Need More Protection?

On a typical day in the United States, three women are murdered by their spouses or partners, and thousands more are injured. While men are also victims of domestic violence, women are at least five times more likely to suffer at the hands of a loved one. Young people between the ages of 16 and 24 are most at risk. The victims include teens who are abused by their parents as well as young parents who assault each other or their children. Moreover, teen-dating violence touches more than 30 percent of young men and women. The good news is that domestic violence against women has dropped dramatically in recent years. Now Congress has just approved a measure that advocates say will provide much-needed funding to try to stop domestic violence before it starts. Meanwhile, some fathers'-rights and conservative groups say too many domestic-violence programs demonize men, promote a feminist agenda and do not try hard enough to keep families together.

Bullying: Are Schools Doing Enough to Stop the Problem?

The nation received a shocking wake-up call about bullying when investigators revealed that the Columbine killers and other school shooters had been repeatedly bullied by classmates. On a typical school day today three out of 10 American youngsters are involved in bullying as perpetrators, victims or bystanders, and an estimated 160,000 children skip school for fear of being harassed. Bullied students are more prone to suicide, depression and poor school performance; bullies have a far higher likelihood of committing crimes as adults. At least 16 states have passed laws requiring schools to provide anti-bullying programs, but many states and school districts have been slow to act. Their reluctance may stem in part from opposition by conservative Christians, who argue that anti-bullying legislation and programs aimed at reducing sexually oriented teasing promote homosexuality and impinge on Christian students' freedom of speech.

CHILD AND ADOLESCENT RIGHTS

Student Rights: Have Courts Gone Too Far or Not Far Enough?

The Supreme Court introduced a new era in public education in the United States in 1969 by declaring that students do not shed their constitutional rights at the schoolhouse gate. Four decades later, state and federal court dockets are dotted with suits by students or parents challenging disciplinary decisions and school policies and practices. The Supreme Court, which has upheld random drug testing of students, is currently considering whether an Arizona school district violated a teenaged girl's rights by strip-searching her because of what proved to be an unfounded accusation that she was carrying a prescription-strength pain reliever. Student-speech cases often pose difficult issues as administrators, principals and teachers seek to reconcile students' free-speech rights with the need to prevent disruption, maintain discipline and protect rights of teachers and other students. In recent years, judges appear to be giving more deference to schools — a trend applauded by many educators but criticized by student-rights advocates.

Juvenile Justice: Are Sentencing Policies Too Harsh?

As many as 200,000 youths charged with crimes today are tried in adult courts, where judges tend to be tougher and punishments harsher —including sentencing to adult prisons. But with juvenile crime now on the decline, youth advocates are seizing the moment to push for major changes in iron-fisted juvenile justice systems nationwide. Above all, they want to roll back harsh state punishments — triggered by the crack cocaine-fueled crime wave of the late 1980s and early '90s — that sent thousands of adolescents to adult courts and prisons. Many prosecutors say the get-tough approach offers society the best protection. But critics say young people often leave prison more bitter and dangerous than when they went in. Moreover, recent brain studies show weak impulse control in young people under age 18, prompting some states to reconsider their tough punishments. Prosecutors respond that even immature adolescents know right from wrong.

Child Welfare Reform: Will Recent Changes Make At-Risk Children Safer?

The U.S. child welfare system is designed to protect the nation's children, but in recent years it has been rocked by horror stories of children who were physically and sexually abused and even murdered. More than 900,000 children were maltreated in 2003 — and some 1,300 died. But a nationwide reform movement offers hope for the future. Welfare agencies across the country are focusing more on keeping families together and quickly moving the nation's 500,000 foster children into permanent homes. Although the foster care rolls are dropping, unadopted foster teens still must struggle with a lonely transition to adulthood after leaving the system. No state program has passed a federal review, but states are hitting improvement targets in follow-up checks. Meanwhile, social workers continue to complain that they are underpaid and overworked. And Congress is divided over a Bush administration plan that would give states more flexibility in using federal funds but end the guarantee of federal support for every foster child.

SOCIAL ISSUES

Teen Pregnancy: Does Comprehensive Sex-Education Reduce Pregnancies?

After dropping steeply for a decade-and-a-half, America's teen birth rate began edging upwards in the past few years. Analysts aren't sure whether the trend will last and say there are numerous causes. A significant factor, however, is a drop-off in contraceptive use that began in the early 2000s, as better HIV/AIDS treatments diminished fear of the disease. In 2009, the Obama administration ended the Bush administration policy of federally funding only sex-education programs with abstinence until marriage as the primary focus. Instead, most funding will now go to programs that have been demonstrated in large, randomized trials to be effective for pregnancy prevention. Critics say the plan will unfairly eliminate funding for abstinence programs, which they contend have not been adequately evaluated by researchers and are the only ones that consistently teach the value of committed relationships.

Teen Spending: Are Teenagers Learning to Manage Money Wisely?

Teenage American consumers spent a mind-boggling $159 billion last year on everything from movies and French fries to clothes and iPods. Experts say teens are spending more than ever before because they have more to spend. About 10 percent of teens have credit cards, nearly twice that number have debit cards and about 20 percent get money simply by asking their parents for it. Consumer advocates — as well as rappers and professional football players — say kids aren't learning how to use "plastic" wisely. In fact, parents themselves are setting poor examples. Credit card loan delinquencies are at record levels, while Americans' saving rate is at an all-time low. Critics say the credit card industry is too aggressive in marketing to younger and younger kids. The Bush administration and some members of Congress are pushing for more financial-literacy courses earlier in schools. Meanwhile, only a few states require schools to teach personal finance.

Teen Driving: Should States Impose Tougher Restrictions?

More teenage drivers are involved in car crashes every year — and more are killed — than any other age group. And the number of deaths is rising, even though overall fatalities of teen drivers and passengers have decreased substantially in the last 25 years. Still, some 6,000 teens die in accidents annually — more than 15 a day. Teens are the least likely age group to use seat belts and the most likely to drink and drive. Moreover, the presence of teenage passengers strongly increases the risk that a teen driver will crash, as does driving at night or on weekends. Graduated driver licensing programs have helped bring down teen crash statistics in many states, but safety experts and advocates say more needs to be done, including imposing tougher limits on teen driving. Some say driver education programs are ineffective; others argue that state laws need to be better enforced. Almost all agree, however, that parents need to be more involved in training and monitoring teenagers behind the wheel.

Youth Suicide: Should Government Fund More Prevention Programs?

This year, about 2,800 young people will kill themselves, including about 1,600 in the emotionally volatile 15-to-19-year-old age group. Suicidal tendencies are so common that about one in five high school students seriously considers suicide. To reduce the teen suicide rate, mental health experts say it is vital to identify and treat at-risk youngsters. But suicidal youths are difficult to identify. Some experts worry that talking about suicide may actually exacerbate the problem. Others point to studies indicating antidepressant drugs, increasingly prescribed for children, may trigger suicide in certain cases. Meanwhile, limited government funds have been allocated for the problem, few schools have screening or counseling programs and many states lack comprehensive suicide-prevention plans.

Preface

Are new laws needed to curb cyberbullying? Are "get tough" policies the best approach to addressing youth violence? Do teens need more protection from domestic violence? These questions — and many more — are at the heart of the study of childhood and adolescence in society. How can instructors best engage students with these crucial issues? We feel that students need objective, yet provocative examinations of these issues. This collection aims to promote in-depth discussion, facilitate further research and help readers formulate their own positions on crucial issues. Get your students talking both inside and outside the classroom about *Childhood and Adolescence in Society*.

This first edition includes thirteen key reports by *CQ Researcher*, an award-winning weekly policy brief that brings complicated issues down to earth. Each report chronicles and analyzes executive, legislative, and judicial activities at all levels of government.

CQ RESEARCHER

CQ Researcher was founded in 1923 as *Editorial Research Reports* and was sold primarily to newspapers as a research tool. The magazine was renamed and redesigned in 1991 as *CQ Researcher*. Today, students are its primary audience. While still used by hundreds of journalists and newspapers, many of which reprint portions of the reports, the *Researcher's* main subscribers are now high school, college and public libraries. In 2002, *Researcher* won the American Bar Association's coveted Silver Gavel award for magazine excellence for a series of nine reports on civil liberties and other legal issues.

Researcher staff writers — all highly experienced journalists — sometimes compare the experience of writing a Researcher report to drafting a college term paper. Indeed, there are many similarities. Each report is as long as many term papers — about 11,000 words — and is written by one person without any significant outside help. One of the key differences is that writers interview leading experts, scholars and government officials for each issue.

Like students, staff writers begin the creative process by choosing a topic. Working with the *Researcher's* editors, the writer identifies a controversial subject that has important public policy implications. After a topic is selected, the writer embarks on one to two weeks of intense research. Newspaper and magazine articles are clipped or downloaded, books are ordered and information is gathered from a wide variety of sources, including interest groups, universities and the government. Once the writers are well informed, they develop a detailed outline, and begin the interview process. Each report requires a minimum of ten to fifteen interviews with academics, officials, lobbyists and people working in the field. Only after all interviews are completed does the writing begin.

CHAPTER FORMAT

Each issue of *CQ Researcher,* and therefore each selection in this book, is structured in the same way. Each begins with an overview, which briefly summarizes the areas that will be explored in greater detail in the rest of the chapter. The next section chronicles important and current debates on the topic under discussion and is structured around a number of key questions, such as "Should the federal government do more to combat domestic violence?" or "Are schools and governments doing enough to prevent youth suicide?" These questions are usually the subject of much discussion among practitioners and scholars in the field. Hence, the answers presented are never conclusive but detail the range of opinion on the topic.

Next, the "Background" section provides a history of the issue being examined. This retrospective covers important legislative measures, executive actions and court decisions that illustrate how current policy has evolved. Then the "Current Situation" section examines contemporary policy issues, legislation under consideration and legal action being taken. Each selection concludes with an "Outlook" section, which addresses possible regulation, court rulings, and initiatives from Capitol Hill and the White House over the next five to ten years.

Each report contains features that augment the main text: two to three sidebars that examine issues related to the topic at hand, a pro versus con debate between two experts, a chronology of key dates and events and an annotated bibliography detailing major sources used by the writer.

ACKNOWLEDGMENTS

We wish to thank many people for helping to make this collection a reality. Tom Colin, managing editor of *CQ Researcher,* gave us his enthusiastic support and cooperation as we developed this edition. He and his talented staff of editors and writers have amassed a first-class library of *Researcher* reports, and we are fortunate to have access to that rich cache. We also wish to thank our colleagues at CQ Press, a division of SAGE and a leading publisher of books, directories, research publications and Web products on U.S. government, world affairs and communications. They have forged the way in making these readers a useful resource for instruction across a range of undergraduate and graduate courses.

Some readers may be learning about *CQ Researcher* for the first time. We expect that many readers will want regular access to this excellent weekly research tool. For subscription information or a no-obligation free trial of *CQ Researcher,* please contact CQ Press at www.cqpress.com or toll-free at 1-866-4CQ-PRESS (1-866-427-7737).

We hope that you will be pleased by this edition of *Childhood and Adolescence in Society.* We welcome your feedback and suggestions for future editions. Please direct comments to Chris Cardone, Acquisitions Editor, SAGE Publications, 2455 Teller Road, Thousand Oaks, CA 91320, or christine.cardone@sagepub.com.

—The Editors of SAGE

Contributors

Thomas J. Billitteri is a *CQ Researcher* staff writer based in Fairfield, Pennsylvania, who has more than 30 years' experience covering business, nonprofit institutions and public policy for newspapers and other publications. He has written previously for *CQ Researcher* on "Domestic Poverty," "Curbing CEO Pay" and "Mass Transit." He holds a BA in English and an MA in journalism from Indiana University.

Marcia Clemmitt is a veteran social-policy reporter who previously served as editor in chief of *Medicine & Health* and staff writer for *The Scientist.* She has also been a high-school math and physics teacher. She holds a liberal arts and sciences degree from St. John's College, Annapolis, and a master's degree in English from Georgetown University. Her recent reports include "Climate Change," "Health Care Costs," "Cyber Socializing" and "Prison Health Care."

John Felton is a freelance journalist who has written about international affairs and U.S. foreign policy for nearly 30 years. He covered foreign affairs for the *Congressional Quarterly Weekly Report* during the 1980s, was deputy foreign editor for National Public Radio in the early 1990s and has been a freelance writer specializing in international topics for the past 15 years. His most recent book, published by CQ Press, is *The Contemporary Middle East: A Documentary History.* He lives in Stockbridge, Massachusetts.

John Greenya is a freelance writer in Washington, D.C., who has written for *The Washington Post, The New Republic, The New York Times* and other publications. He teaches writing at George Washington University and is the author of several books, including *Silent Justice: The Clarence Thomas Story* and *P.S. A Memoir,* written with the late Pierre Salinger. He holds an AB in English from Marquette University and an MA in English literature from The Catholic University.

David Hosansky is a freelance writer in Denver who specializes in environmental issues. He previously was a senior writer at *CQ Weekly* and the *Florida Times-Union* in Jacksonville, where he was twice nominated for a Pulitzer Prize. His recent *Researcher* reports include "Invasive Species" and "Food Safety."

Kenneth Jost graduated from Harvard College and Georgetown University Law Center. He is the author of the *Supreme Court Yearbook* and editor of *The Supreme Court from A to Z* (both CQ Press). He was a member of the *CQ Researcher* team that won the 2002 ABA Silver Gavel Award. His recent reports include "Democracy in the Arab World" and "Religious Persecution."

Peter Katel is a *CQ Researcher* staff writer who previously reported on Haiti and Latin America for *Time* and *Newsweek* and covered the Southwest for newspapers in New Mexico. He has received several journalism awards, including the Bartolomé Mitre Award for coverage of drug trafficking from the Inter-American Press Association. He holds an AB in university studies from the University of New Mexico. His recent reports include "The New Philanthropy" and "War in Iraq."

Robert Kiener is an award-winning writer whose work has appeared in the *London Sunday Times, The Christian Science Monitor, The Washington Post, Reader's Digest, Time Life Books, Asia Inc.* and other publications. For more than two decades he lived and worked as an editor and correspondent in Guam, Hong Kong, England and Canada and is now based in the United States. He frequently travels to Asia and Europe to report on international issues. He holds a MA in Asian Studies from Hong Kong University and an MPhil in International Relations from Cambridge University.

Pamela M. Prah is a *CQ Researcher* staff writer with several years previous experience at Stateline.org, Kiplinger's Washington Letter and the Bureau of National Affairs. She holds a master's degree in government from Johns Hopkins University and a journalism degree from Ohio University. Her recent reports include "War in Iraq," "Methamphetamines" and "Disaster Preparedness."

Tom Price is a Washington-based freelance journalist who writes regularly for *CQ Researcher*. Previously he was a correspondent in the Cox Newspapers Washington Bureau and chief politics writer for the *Dayton Daily News* and *The Journal Herald*. He is the author of two Washington guidebooks, *Washington, D.C., for Dummies,* and the *Irreverent Guide to Washington, D.C.* His work has appeared in *The New York Times, Time, Rolling Stone* and other periodicals. He earned a BS in journalism at Ohio University.

William Triplett covered science and the arts for such publications as *Smithsonian, Air & Space, Nature, Washingtonian* and *The Washington Post* before joining the *CQ Researcher* staff. He also served as associate editor of *Capitol Style* magazine. He holds a BA in journalism from Ohio University and an MA in English literature from Georgetown University. His recent reports include "Search for Extraterrestrials" and "Broadcast Indecency."

1

Rescuing Children

Is the Global Community Doing Enough?

Robert Kiener

AFP/Getty Images/Munir Uz Zaman

A young boy works at a balloon factory in Dhaka, Bangladesh, one of the world's poorest countries. Worldwide, about 158 million children under age 14 were working in 2006, according to the most recent U.N. statistics.

From *CQ Global Researcher*, October 2009.

As she sits on a swing in a children's shelter outside Phnom Penh, the dark-eyed 7-year-old Cambodian girl rarely smiles. Her wounds are still too raw.

A year earlier, Srey Tok (not her real name) was rescued from a brothel where she had been raped by men who believed sex with a virgin could cure them of AIDS. When she fought back, she was locked in a small cage for days at a time. If Srey still resisted, her captors would cut her arms and put salt into the wounds, or pull her hair out. Several times they hit her in the head with a nail-studded board. As she parts her hair to show a visitor the scars, she whimpers.

"Those men were monsters," says shelter founder Somaly Mam, a former child prostitute herself, as she wraps her arms around Srey. "It will take years for her to heal. Perhaps she never will."

Still, Mam says, Srey is "one of the lucky ones" — she was rescued. "Thousands of other little girls in Southeast Asia have been sold into prostitution" — as Srey was by her mother — "but they have disappeared," explains the 36-year-old Mam. "They have been raped, beaten, tortured and simply thrown away." Estimates range from 10,000 to 20,000 child prostitutes under age 16 in Cambodia alone, according to Mam.

Children's-rights activists say millions of children around the world are in crisis situations of one kind or another, including a staggering 1 million youngsters who are forced into prostitution every year. Some activists say 10 million children at any one time are working as prostitutes.[1] Children routinely are trafficked across international borders, enslaved, kidnapped and forced to become soldiers or are otherwise caught in war's crossfire.

Africa Has Highest Child Death Rates

Of the 25,000 children under age 5 who die every day in developing countries — most from preventable causes such as malaria and diarrhea — nearly half are in sub-Saharan Africa (map). While under-5 mortality rates overall in developing countries have dropped 27 percent since 1990, some regions have made more progress than others. Latin America and Central and Eastern Europe, for instance, have seen their rates decline by 55 percent, compared to a 22 percent drop in sub-Saharan Africa (bottom graph).

Under-5 Mortality Rates, 2007

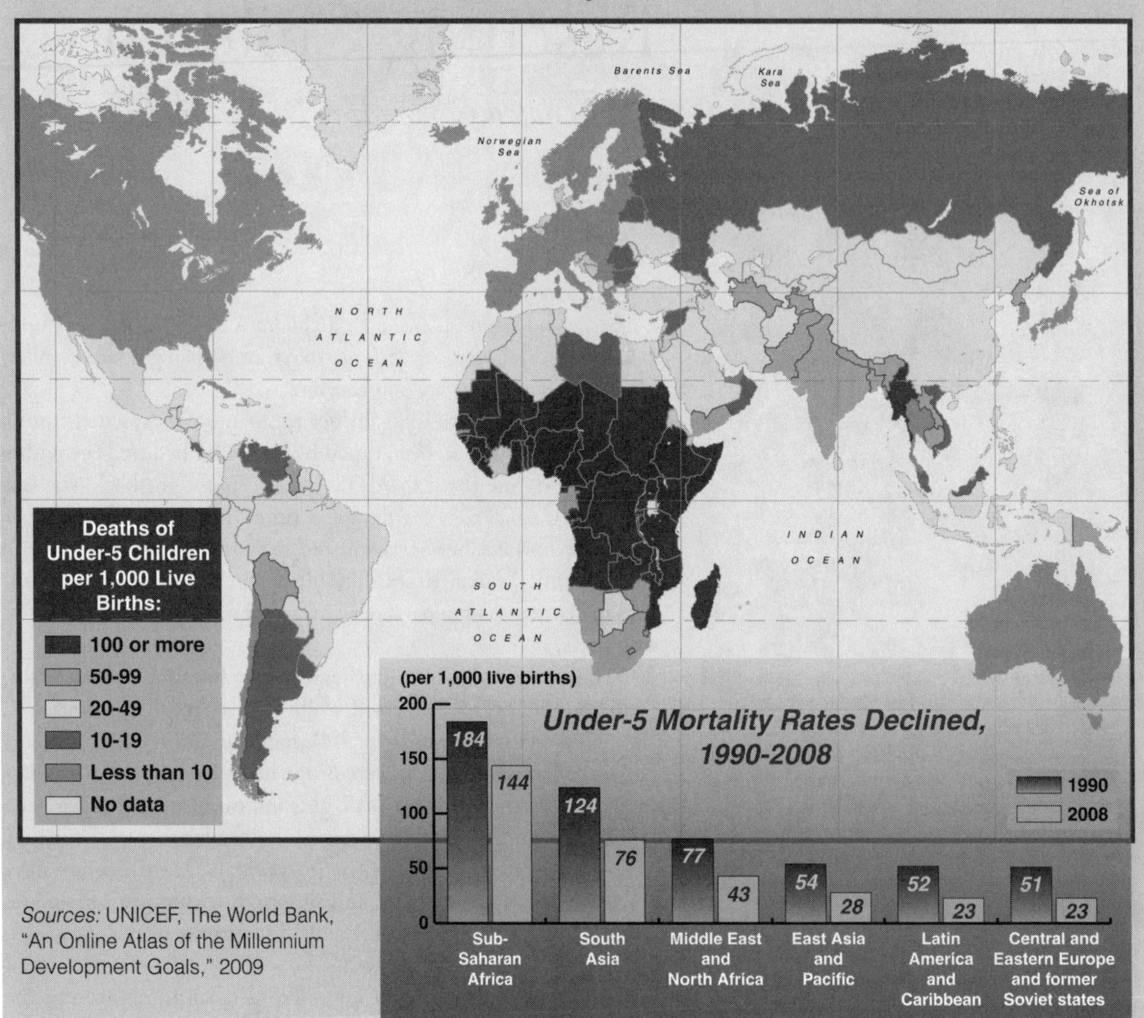

Sources: UNICEF, The World Bank, "An Online Atlas of the Millennium Development Goals," 2009

"An estimated 300 million children are subjected to violence, exploitation and abuse," according to UNICEF (the United Nations Children's Fund).[2]

Every day, 25,000 children under age 5 — the equivalent of 125 jetliners full of youngsters, or one every 3.5 seconds — die from hunger, easily preventable diseases and other poverty-related causes.[3]

"It is a tragedy that the world needs to know more about and help solve," says Charles MacCormack, director of Save the Children. The Connecticut-based organization, dedicated to helping needy children around the world, recently launched its "Survive to Five" campaign to reduce the death toll among young children.[4]

But as horrific as today's under-5 death toll is, it's a vast improvement over the rate in 1990. The death rate for children under 5 in developing countries has fallen 27 percent since 1990, with some regions — Latin America and Central and Eastern Europe — seeing even more dramatic declines. (*See graph, p. 2.*) And children's lives have improved in other respects as well. Until the worsening global economy resulted in more food shortages, some developing nations, such as Malawi, were reducing malnutrition.[5] The world is close to eradicating polio, and from 1999 to 2005 child deaths from measles fell 60 percent worldwide and 75 percent in Africa. Insecticide-treated mosquito nets are helping to combat malaria, and zinc pills promise to cut diarrhea deaths. (*See story, p. 10.*) Many countries are close to enrolling all young children in primary school — both boys and girls.[6] Meanwhile, celebrities, nongovernmental organizations (NGOs), wealthy governments and foundations — including the Bill & Melinda Gates Foundation, rock star Bono and the U.S. government — have raised or committed billions of dollars in recent years to eradicate malaria and HIV-AIDS.

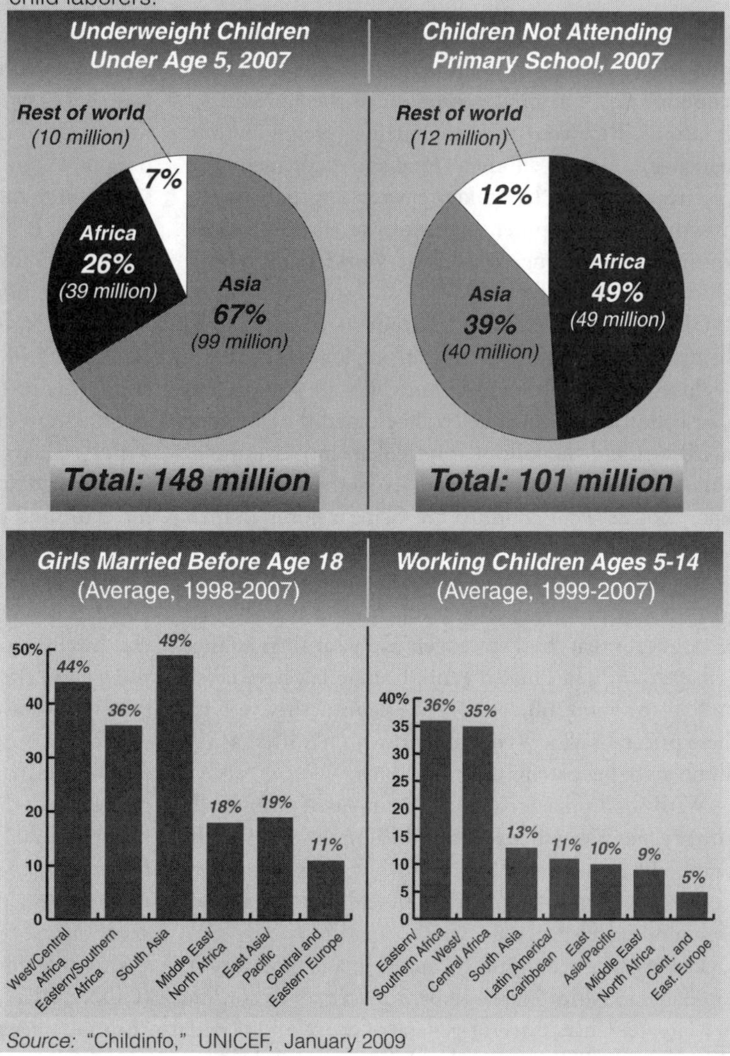

Source: "Childinfo," UNICEF, January 2009

And just last month, on Sept. 23, British Prime Minister Gordon Brown announced a $5.3 billion financing package that will help provide free healthcare to some 10 million people — mostly women and children — in Africa and Asia.[7]

But horrific troubles still confront the world's children, including:

- An estimated 100-150 million children live on the streets — many of them runaways or abandoned — and their numbers are rising, partly due to the global economic crisis.[8]
- About 112 million children are malnourished; 9 million die before age 5.[9]

- Some 158 million children ages 5 to 14 were working in 2006, 30 percent of them in the world's poorest countries.[10]
- About 250,000 children are involved in armed conflicts, serving either as combatants, messengers, spies, porters, cooks or sex slaves.[11]

Although malaria, tuberculosis, AIDS and other diseases have claimed young lives for decades, the global economic downturn has compounded their precarious situations. Rich countries are cutting foreign aid and reducing money for children's food and medicines.

The recession "has taken a wrecking ball to the growth and development gains of the world's poorest countries," according to a recent World Bank report, which notes that the world's gross domestic product (GDP) — or total economic output — is expected to shrink 1.7 percent this year after rising for eight years.[12]

Prices for food, fuel and commodities are soaring, and poor countries — which generally escaped the subprime meltdown and the fallout from collapsing investment banks — are now facing recession. As another World Bank report noted: "Poor countries are facing a slump in their exports, [and] government budgets are badly stretched."[13]

As governments struggle, so do children who have no government programs to rely on. A drop in recycling prices means that child scavengers' daily earnings at huge garbage dumps in Phnom Penh, Cambodia, have fallen by half (to about 60 cents). "We cannot survive with these prices," says a 9-year-old girl who has lived at the dump since her parents abandoned her.

With food prices rising, the number of chronically hungry people will exceed 1 billion in 2009.[14] In Cambodia alone, the WFP already has stopped a school feeding program for some 450,000 children because of high food prices.[15]

During past economic collapses, infant mortality in sub-Saharan Africa increased by 3 percent.[16] According to Margaret Chan, director-general of the World Health Organization (WHO), the global downturn could cause the deaths of between 200,000 to 400,000 children each year, or up to 2.8 million additional child deaths by 2015.[17] "There is no reason [to] doubt that this will happen if we fail to act," she told the *London Times.* "More children will die because of lack of food or immunization or poor water or sanitation."[18]

And the recession is plunging more children into prostitution and child labor. "The recent economic downturn is set to drive more vulnerable children and young people to be exploited by the global sex trade," said Carmen Madriñán, executive director of the Bangkok-based End Child Prostitution, Child Pornography and Trafficking of Children for Sexual Purposes.[19]

The worldwide economic crisis has also decimated foreign-aid coffers. Donors, both governmental and private, have cut back on funding to charities, nongovernmental organizations and philanthropic humanitarian programs. For example, Catholic Relief Services, which serves more than 100 million people in more than 100 countries, is planning to reduce child-aid programs in various regions after a 13 percent drop in private donations in the first half of 2009.

Other NGOs are similarly affected. Oxfam, the London-based international charity, is planning layoffs, and CARE is trimming its budgets.[20] "There's no question these are challenging times, and we have to do more with less," says Save the Children's MacCormack.

Some aid officials criticize governments for not doing more to fund children's programs or keep aid promises. Many also fault the United States for failing to ratify the Convention on the Rights of the Child (CRC), adopted 20 years ago by the U.N. General Assembly to promote child well-being. Since then 193 countries have ratified the treaty; the United States and Somalia remain the only hold-outs.

According to the Paris-based Organisation for Economic Co-operation and Development (OECD), representing the industrialized nations, foreign aid from Europe in 2007 fell from 0.41 percent of gross national income to 0.38 percent.[21] "European governments' failure to meet aid pledges is nothing short of disgraceful," said Olivier Consolo, director of the European Confederation of Relief and Development NGOs (CONCORD), representing more than 1,600 NGOs. "Europe likes to see itself as a world leader in development assistance, but these figures show that governments are taking a step backward."[22]

Graça Machel — Nelson Mandela's wife and founder of the Mozambique-based Foundation for Community Development — said human lives should get precedence over bank bailouts and military spending. "I don't believe the issue is money," she told a recent AIDS conference in

Cape Town, South Africa. "The issue is the consciences of the people we elect. Human life is priceless; you should never bargain when it comes to saving lives."[23]

As children's-rights advocates face the daunting prospect of doing more with less, here are some of the questions they are asking:

Are rich nations giving enough aid to help children in poor countries?

How much aid is enough? In 1970 the United Nations recommended that developed nations donate 0.7 percent — less than 1 percent — of their gross national incomes to poor nations. Since then, only a handful of countries — notably Denmark, Norway and Sweden — regularly meet the 0.7 percent target. Others have fallen woefully behind. (*See graphs, p. 6.*)

Although total donations have regularly increased, the 0.7 percent target is a distant goal for most. For example, the United States usually gives more total dollars than any other country, but it has habitually been among the lowest when the amount is viewed as a percentage of gross income.

Although the world's 23 major donor countries gave a record $19.8 billion in 2008 — a 10.2 percent jump — it represented only 0.3 percent of GNI, a whopping $260 billion less than if all rich countries gave 0.7 percent.[24]

"Rich countries can come up with the money when they want to," said Max Lawson, head of development finance at Oxfam, citing the U.S. government's recent bailout of giant insurance company AIG, which then gave out huge executive bonuses. "AIG's executive bonuses alone could have paid for enough teachers for 7 million children in Africa. We need to . . . rescue babies not just bankers."[25]

But few believe that economically battered donor nations will donate more anytime soon. Not surprisingly, as money has become tight, debates over foreign aid's effectiveness have intensified, often centering on Africa.

Dambisa Moyo, a Zambia-born former Goldman Sachs economist who wrote *Dead Aid: Why Aid Is Not Working and How There Is a Better Way for Africa*, calls aid to Africa a "Band-Aid solution" at best. The more than $1 trillion in development-related aid that rich countries have sent to Africa has "made the poor poorer, and the growth slower," she wrote. "The insidious aid culture has left African countries more debt-laden, more inflation prone, more vulnerable to the vagaries of the currency market and more unattractive to higher-quality investment."[26]

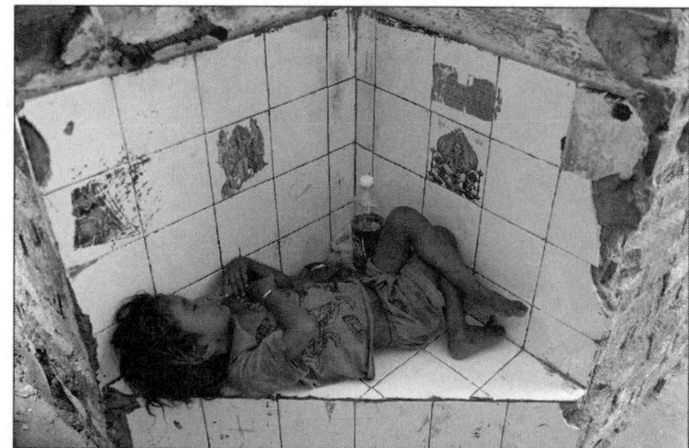

AFP/Getty Images/Manan Vatsyayana

AFP/Getty Images/Ramzi Haidar

Children of the Streets

A homeless Indian girl sleeps in New Delhi on June 16, 2009 (top). Iraqi orphans in Baghdad smoke cigarettes and "huff" glue, a common and deadly practice of street children worldwide (bottom). An estimated 100-150 million children live on the streets — many of them runaways or abandoned by their families — and their numbers are rising, partly as a result of the global economic downturn.

William Easterly, an American economist at New York University and author of *White Man's Burden: Why the West's Efforts to Aid the Rest Has Done so Much Ill and so Little Good*, is even harsher. "The West already spent $2.3 trillion on foreign aid over the last five decades and still had not managed to get 12-cent medicines to children to prevent half of all malaria deaths," he told the Senate Foreign Relations committee.[27]

Aid Hits Record But Fails to Meet Target

The world's wealthiest countries gave a record $119.8 billion in overseas development assistance (ODA) in 2008. But that represented an average of only 0.3 percent of the countries' gross national income (GNI), or less than half of the U.N.'s 0.7 percent target set in 1970. Only Denmark, Luxembourg, the Netherlands, Norway and Sweden met the 0.7 percent target (bottom graph). Aid to Africa, the world's poorest continent, declined as a proportion of total assistance.

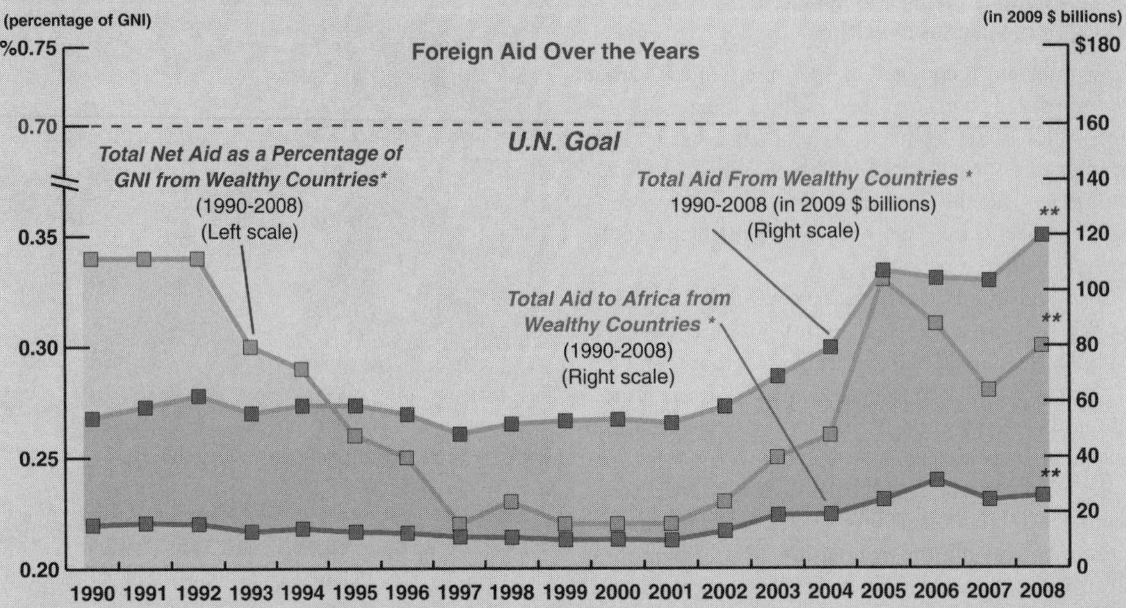

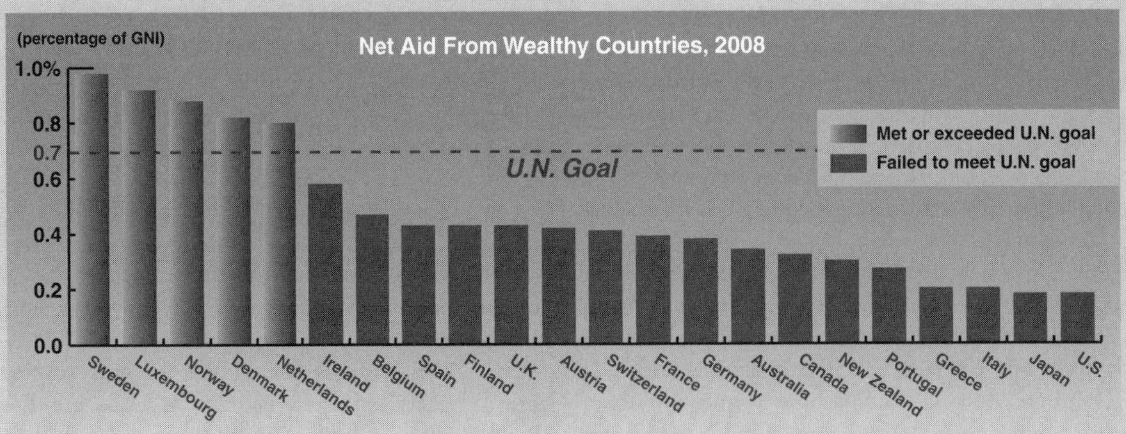

* The 22 countries and the European Commission that are members of the Organisation for Economic Co-operation and Development's Development Assistance Committee

** Preliminary data

Source: Organisation for Economic Co-operation and Development, March 30, 2009

James Shikwati, a Kenyan, who is director of the Nairobi-based Inter Region Economic Network, says aid often does more harm than good, especially when countries are flooded with emergency food aid that causes local crop prices to plummet, discouraging farmers from planting.

"In the 1990s, drought aid actually killed local production in parts of Africa and increased dependency," he says. "It's a model we see time and time again."

Corruption and poor governance also block Africa's progress, he says. "Aid money is subsidizing these corrupt, ineffective governments and keeping Africans poor," he says. The governments feel more accountable to their aid donors than to their own citizens, he adds.

Other foreign-aid critics agree. "Aid . . . makes [African] politicians much more oriented toward what will get them more money from the West than it does to making them meet the ends of their own people, which is really a scandal," said Easterly.[28]

For foreign aid to produce results, countries must develop stable governments with solid infrastructures and end official corruption. "The most obvious criticism of aid is its links to rampant corruption," wrote Moyo. "Aid flows destined to help the average African end up supporting bloated bureaucracies in . . . poor-country governments and donor-funded nongovernmental organizations."[29]

But proponents of increased aid, like U.S. economist Jeffrey Sachs — director of the Earth Institute at Columbia University and special advisor to U.N. Secretary-General Ban Ki-moon — cite examples in which aid has helped millions survive. For instance, foreign aid helped to bring Rwanda back from the brink of collapse, he says. "The government's own development efforts have been very important, of course," he wrote, "but without the aid backing them, none of the recovery to date would have been possible."[30]

Others point to measles vaccination and antimalarial campaigns as proof that outside aid can accomplish goals that local governments cannot. "If outside governments and NGOs had not addressed, and funded, health issues such as maternal health, child nutrition and HIV treatment, very, very few governments of poor nations would have done it on their own," says Laurie Garrett, senior fellow for global health at the Council on Foreign Relations, a New York-based think tank. "For decades, money went to defense budgets, and little ended up at ministries of health."

Save the Children's MacCormack says governments can only do so much, while "charities and NGOs have a real duty to engage the public, provide the citizen commitment and help in the field from the ground up."

Sachs, whose 2006 book *The End of Poverty* suggests how to end extreme poverty by 2025, believes developed nations must do more for Africa, especially when preventable diseases like malaria and diarrhea take so many lives. "How can we go another day when 20,000 children are going to be dying of these stupid reasons that are utterly preventable?" Sachs asked. He'd like Western governments to double their aid to Africa to $50 billion.[31]

Should the United States ratify the U.N. Convention on the Rights of the Child?

November 20 is the 20th anniversary of the adoption of the U.N. Convention on the Rights of the Child (CRC) — the most widely and rapidly ratified human-rights treaty in history. It spells out children's rights to survival and protection from abuse and exploitation, as well as their right to develop to the fullest and to participate in family, cultural and social life.

"The convention protects children's rights by setting standards in health care, education and legal, civil and social services," UNICEF says.[32]

Only the United States and Somalia, which has no functioning national government, have not ratified the treaty. Although U.S. representative to the U.N. Madeleine Albright signed the treaty on Feb. 16, 1995, the Clinton administration, under pressure from treaty opponents in the GOP-controlled Senate, never submitted it to the Senate for approval.

The United States did ratify two optional supplemental protocols, however — one banning child prostitution, pornography and trafficking and the other prohibiting the compulsory military recruitment of children under 18. The United States included a caveat, however, explaining that it permits voluntary recruitment of 17-year-olds.

Many believe America's failure to adopt the CRC undermines its international leadership role in protecting children. During his presidential campaign Barack Obama confessed he found it "embarrassing" that the United States had not ratified the treaty.

During Susan Rice's confirmation hearings to become ambassador to the United Nations, CRC proponent Sen. Barbara Boxer, D-Calif., asked, "How can we be proud of our country when we haven't ratified it? In this case, the only other country, as I understand it, that hasn't ratified is Somalia. . . . We're standing with Somalia. . . . What has happened?"

Replied Rice: "The president-elect, Secretary [of State Hillary] Clinton and I share a commitment to the objectives of this treaty and will take it up as an early question."[33]

Kul Chandra Gautam, former assistant secretary-general of the United Nations and deputy executive director of UNICEF, said the U.S. handling of the treaty "baffles" many non-Americans and Americans alike. Ratification, according to Nepal-born Gautam, would be tantamount to "sticking up for the rights of the underdog." Protecting children's rights in democratic societies, he says, is urgent. "Most other problems can wait — children cannot."[34]

Meanwhile, alarmed that the CRC may again be placed on the Senate's table, opponents are reviving the same arguments espoused in 1995 to block the treaty. For instance, they say, the CRC's Geneva-based Committee on the Rights of the Child, which reviews children's rights in nations that have ratified the treaty, would usurp Americans' parental rights.

The treaty "clearly undermines parental rights in the United States," U.S. Rep. Pete Hoekstra, R-Mich., has said. He has moved to block any approval of the treaty by introducing a bill to amend the U.S. Constitution codifying a set of parents' rights.[35]

Other opponents agree. Famously, the late Sen. Jesse Helms, R-N.C., described the treaty as "a bag of worms" and a threat to the U.S. Constitution. Other critics say it would enable children to sue their parents or participate in a religion of their choosing.

Michael Smith, president of the Home School Legal Defense Association (HSLDA), in Purcellville, Va., said the CRC "would drastically weaken the United States' sovereignty over family life, which would have a substantial impact on every American family."[36]

Stephen Groves, a fellow at the Heritage Foundation, said the CRC would erode American sovereignty by giving "a group of unaccountable so-called experts in Switzerland . . . a say over how children in America should be raised, educated or disciplined."[37]

Some CRC critics have gone so far as to claim the treaty could bar U.S. parents from spanking their children or could allow children to get abortions without parental consent. "If the American public is informed on this, there's no chance it will be ratified," said the HSLDA's founder, Michael Farris.[38]

Nonsense, say the treaty's proponents. "This treaty can never usurp the national sovereignty of the United States," says Martin Scherr, vice chair of the Campaign for U.S. Ratification of the Convention on the Rights of the Child. "No treaty the United States has signed ever has. If we object to anything in it we can simply exclude those parts. And there is nothing in the treaty that would give children rights over [their] parents. Indeed, quite the contrary is true; Article Five of the treaty reinforces the right of the parent to nurture his or her child."

"Name me one country that has seen a diminution in parents' rights," says Marjorie Newman-Williams, chief operating officer at the Washington, D.C.-based Children's Defense Fund. "The rest of the world seems to be very pleased with the treaty." Nowhere in the treaty, for example, are children given the right to sue their parents.

Says Caryl M. Stern, president and CEO of the U.S. Fund for UNICEF: "In all my travels I have never heard a single person complain that the CRC has caused any such problems. On the other hand, I get asked all the time why the U.S. is one of only two nations in the world *not* to ratify the CRC."

Thomas Miller, former U.S. ambassador to Greece and now president of the United Nations Association of the USA, points out that there are no enforcement mechanisms or penalties associated with the CRC. "Critics scare people by claiming we would be invaded by United Nations' 'blue beret nannies,' " adds Scherr, "but that's ridiculous." The treaty provides for an 18-member committee that simply "monitors" children's rights.

Although the Obama administration appears interested in getting the CRC ratified, few believe that will happen anytime soon. The administration has too much on its plate now to risk another fight, especially one that has the potential for becoming a drawn-out, polarizing "family values" debate.

As the world examines America's reluctance to ratify the bill, many wonder how U.S.-based treaty opponents can overlook how the CRC has strengthened national children's rights institutions around the world. Numerous countries — such as Italy and Sweden, where the CRC has given birth to children's ombudsmen — have strengthened children's rights while preserving the rights of parents.

"It is in the USA's interest that we ratify the CRC. It would win us support from those whose support we need in the world," says Save the Children's MacCormack. "By not ratifying it we have everything to lose and nothing to gain. The rest of the world is wondering why a nation that calls itself a world leader has not ratified it."

Should AIDS prevention be emphasized more than treatment?

The first sentence of a recent report on the effects of AIDS on children pulls no punches: "Today's youth is today's AIDS generation."

The chilling report points out that today's children have never known a world without the devastating disease and now "bear the greatest burden of the disease."[39]

Indeed, the numbers are terrifying:

- More than 33 million people live with HIV/AIDS; 2.5 million of them children under 15.
- Every day about 1,150 children become infected with HIV, mostly due to mother-to-child transmission.
- Eight children die of AIDS-related illness every 15 minutes.
- More than 13 million children have lost a parent to AIDS, a figure expected to exceed 25 million for 2010 alone.
- Nearly 90 percent of all HIV-positive children live in sub-Saharan Africa.[40]

When AIDS strikes, it destabilizes families and entire societies. "There's a knock-on effect when AIDS takes a parent," says Save the Children's MacCormack. "Children are left to take on the burdens of the family. Millions also become orphans," less than 10 percent of whom receive any public support.

AIDS is powerfully linked to poverty. "AIDS can intensify poverty, forcing families to make difficult choices between short-term necessities and long-term investments in children," notes UNICEF. A Cambodia study showed that families affected by AIDS were more likely to sell off assets and ration medical care than their unaffected neighbors. In Nigeria, families with AIDS lost about 56 percent of their income compared with healthy families.[41]

The developed world has not neglected the global AIDS epidemic. Indeed, in 2003 President George W. Bush pledged to spend $15 billion over five years to fight AIDS abroad, and Congress recently reauthorized the President's Emergency Plan for AIDS Relief (PEPFAR) to the tune of $48 billion. Other countries also have poured billions into AIDS programs, and wealthy individuals like American billionaire and CNN founder Ted Turner have earmarked millions of dollars to combat AIDS. Thanks to all that effort and generosity — plus the 1996 invention of a combination antiretroviral drug "cocktail" that successfully treats HIV — millions of people with HIV/AIDS around the world are still alive.

But, as the disease continues to spread, many are asking if too much is being spent on AIDS treatment and not enough on prevention. "There is a dangerous trend in the AIDS establishment that wants to shift — or eliminate — funding for HIV vaccine research and prevention programs in favor of HIV treatment," says Garrett, of the Council on Foreign Relations. "Treatment should be seen as a stop-gap measure, until we can completely stop the spread of HIV. We need both treatment and prevention."

For many, the treatment/prevention question comes down to simple economics. Expensive treatments cannot be sustained, they point out, given the global economic crisis. In Africa, for example, a year of treatment typically costs $1,000 per patient. Because of the high cost of antiretroviral treatment, programs for 61 percent of the world's AIDS sufferers are now at risk, according to the World Bank.[42]

Helen Jackson, a South Africa-based HIV adviser at UNAIDS, told a recent AIDS conference in Nairobi, Kenya, "If each person who has HIV progresses to AIDS, the financial burden of sustaining treatment becomes enormous, and the only way to make sure it is sustainable is to turn off the tap of new infections. Otherwise, down the line, no countries are going to be able to afford treatment."[43]

Meanwhile, Botswana and Mozambique are among the many nations cutting back or canceling treatment programs due to lack of funding.[44]

Diarrhea: Deadly No More?

A cheap, new pill helps cure a disease that kills 5,000 children a day.

In a village in sub-Saharan Africa, a mother is wailing. Her toddler, who came down with a fever and stopped eating days ago, is losing weight quickly. His belly is distended, he is dehydrated and listless. His life is literally slipping away. In days the child will die from an easily preventable disease that kills more children than either malaria or AIDS — diarrhea.

Diarrhea is the second-leading cause of death of children under 5, killing nearly 2 million children a year — or 5,000 a day.[1] Only pneumonia kills more children.

"In villages across Asia and Africa, diarrhea is still a feared killer," explains Save the Children CEO Charles MacCormack. "For centuries, those villagers have become resigned to the fact that they may lose loved ones to diarrhea."

Without proper sanitation facilities, food and water easily become infected with *E. coli*, rotavirus, salmonella or other intestinal bugs. If left untreated, diarrhea can cause the intestines to stop absorbing water and nutrients, quickly stealing a small child's life.

In the 1980s and '90s, however, an inexpensive mixture of sugar, salts and water — oral-rehydration therapy (ORT) — helped to slash the disease's mortality rate by half. But the disease then was largely ignored because many believed the problem had been solved. In addition, some victims saw ORT as only a stop-gap measure and stopped using it. Funding was cut, and other diseases, such as AIDS and malaria, garnered the world's attention.

"The top killer of children ended up at the end of the agenda," said vaccine specialist John Wecker.[2]

Recently, another promising cure has come to light. Several aid organizations, including Save the Children and the Bill & Melinda Gates Foundation, have been distributing zinc tablets to treat diarrhea. The results have been dramatic. The tablets have reduced diarrheal deaths in children by 13 to 21 percent.[3] The pills, which cost as little as 38 cents for a 10-14 day supply, not only stop diarrhea but also reduce the chance it will recur in the next two to three months, apparently by building up the body's immune system.[4]

"It's incredible that we can cure this disease by just pennies a day," says MacCormack. "It's a no-brainer."

The word is spreading fast. Pilot programs have begun in several African nations, and more firms are manufacturing the tablets. Mali's Ministry of Health recently added zinc supplements to its list of essential medications.[5] With a new vaccine for rotavirus, another cause of diarrhea, being tested, many are optimistic that the killer illness can be eradicated.

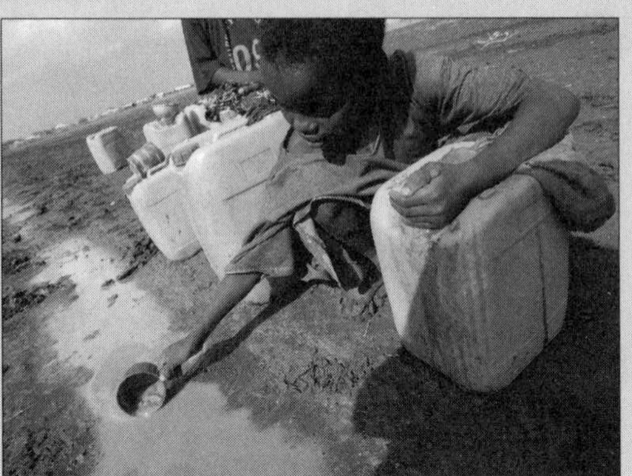

AFP/Getty Images/Mohamed Dahir

A boy collects rainwater from a puddle in Somalia in March 2009. The lack of clean water is a major cause of diarrhea — the second-leading cause of child deaths — but cheap, new zinc tablets are helping to cure the disease.

For many around the world there's no time to lose. A mother in Mali told *Time* magazine that after she lost one son to diarrhea she was terrified when another son developed the same symptoms. However, after giving the 2-year-old zinc tablets, he "came back to life."[6]

---

[1] "Save the Children Targets the Second Leading Cause of Death for Children Under 5," *Save the Children*, August 2009, www.savethechildren.org/programs/health/child-survival/survive-to-5/survive-zinc.html.

[2] Martha Dodge, "Experts: Diarrhea Neglect Killing Millions of Children," *One World US*, May 14, 2009, http://us.oneworld.net/article/362901-experts-diarrhea-neglect-killing-millions-children.

[3] "First Zinc Treatment Produced in Africa Aims to Reduce Child Deaths from Diarrhea," Academy for Educational Development, June 21, 2007, www.pshi.aed.org/news_pouznprtz.htm.

[4] "Save the Children Targets. . . ," *op. cit.*

[5] *Ibid.*

[6] Vivienne Walt, "Can One Pill Tame the Illness No One Wants to Talk About?" *Time*, Aug. 17, 2009, www.time.com/time/magazine/article/0,9171,1914655,00.html.

Even in Uganda, long hailed as a model in the AIDS battle for reducing its HIV rate from double digits to 5 percent in 2001, many patients are no longer receiving free antiretroviral drugs due to cutbacks from donors.[45] And such changes are only the tip of the iceberg, some observers warn.

Some donors are demanding that aid recipients establish effective prevention programs. "Donors want to be assured that rates of new infections are declining," says Garrett.

Others agree that prevention should get more attention. In a letter to *The Washington Post*, the Rev. Sam L. Ruteikara, co-chair of the Uganda National AIDS Prevention Committee, wrote, "In Uganda, we have a proverb: 'You cannot continue mopping the floor while the broken tap is still running.' Every $1 spent on treatment is $1 unspent on effective prevention."[46]

Huge disagreements exist, however, over what constitutes effective prevention. In many societies the use of condoms is taboo, and some groups reject the "ABC" ("Abstain, Be Faithful, Use a Condom") prevention message promoted by the Bush administration over sex education and condom distribution. Also, sex education does not always produce the anticipated results. In Nairobi teenagers say they were becoming "overloaded" with sex education that "makes us want to know what sex is, we want to experience it."[47]

MacCormack agrees that prevention programs must be "ramped up" before treatment costs become prohibitive, but adds, "Treatment is saving lives, and we cannot lessen our emphasis on that aspect of the issue."

Other experts say the call for more prevention is symptomatic of a "two-tiered" strategy, or an "economic caste system" regarding HIV/AIDS. It is fine for developed nations to call for more prevention programs while millions of people are dying around the world, they say. "A strategy that emphasizes prevention to the exclusion of treatment offers no hope to these tens of millions of human beings. In fact, it passes a death sentence on them," write Harvard researchers Alexander Irwin, Joyce Millen and Dorothy Fallows.[48]

While prevention is more cost effective, lives are more important than dollars, say treatment proponents. "It's relatively simple to say that dollar for dollar prevention is more cost-effective," said Chris Collins, director of the AIDS Vaccine Advocacy Coalition. "The more complex point is: What happens in societies where one in five or one in three people in the professional class are wiped out?"[49]

BACKGROUND

Industrial Revolution

For years, the West owed its searing image of child laborers to 19th-century British novelist Charles Dickens, whose harrowing descriptions of sweatshops, foul-tempered bosses and horrific conditions reflected first-hand knowledge. When he was just 12, Dickens worked 10 hours a day in a shoe-polish factory and later used that experience to alert the world to the horrors of child labor in such books as *David Copperfield* and *Oliver Twist.*

But children had been forced into labor long before Dickens' powerful novel shined a light on the problem. More and more workers shifted from farm and home-based jobs to factory work in burgeoning cities as the Industrial Revolution created booming industries in Britain and then later in the United States.[50] Children — some as young as 4 — worked long hours operating dangerous machines in factories and underground coal mines. Children were preferred because they were cheaper, easier to manage than adults and were less apt to strike.[51] In 1788, children comprised more than 60 percent of the workforce in British and Scottish textile mills.[52]

By the early 1800s thousands of children were working for pittance wages in both Great Britain and the United States. Britain's Factory Act of 1833 set a minimum age of 9 for factory workers, but employers regularly ignored it. Indeed, very young British boys and girls, small enough to climb up and down chimneys, were often employed as chimney-sweep apprentices under horrific conditions:

"Some were forced to sleep in cellars on bags of soot, and washing facilities rarely existed. Cancer of the testicles was a common illness amongst the boys and was contracted from the accumulated soot. There was no safety clothing or safety regulation to protect the boys, and there are instances recorded where they were choked and suffocated to death by dust inhalation whilst trying to clean the chimneys. They often became trapped in the narrower flues or fell from the rotten stack to their death."[53]

In British coal mines children were enlisted to work as "trappers," stationed in damp, dark mines to open the

CHRONOLOGY

1800s *Child labor abuses in Great Britain and the United States during the Industrial Revolution spark reform movements.*

1802 Britain's factory acts limit work by women and children.

1833 Britain prohibits working in textile mills for children under 9.

1842 Massachusetts limits children's workday to 10 hours; several states follow.

1870 U.S. Census reports 250,000 children ages 10-15 are non-farm workers.

1880 Britain's Elementary Education Act makes school mandatory until the age of 10.

1900s *Number of U.S. child laborers tops 2 million; reform efforts intensify.*

1900 About 12 percent of Mexican textile workers are children.

1904 Britain's Prevention of Cruelty to Children Act authorizes interventions to protect children from abuse. . . . U.S. group forms to ban child labor in United States.

1916 Congress bans interstate commerce in products made by children; law is declared unconstitutional two years later.

1937 India bans children under 14 from factory or mining work.

1938 U.S. Fair Labor Standards Act prohibits child labor in products sold in interstate commerce.

1940s-1950s *United Nations embraces aid to children.*

1946 UNICEF is created to aid Europe's refugee children after World War II.

1950 UNICEF, other groups begin aiding children in the developing world.

1959 U.N. General Assembly adopts Declaration on the Rights of the Child.

1960s-1980s *Children face new challenges as urbanization, industrialization spread through developing world.*

1972 Children Act of 1972 requires British children to stay in school until 16.

1977 Geneva Conventions establish 15 as minimum age for combat soldiers.

Late 1970s HIV/AIDS begins to spread throughout sub-Saharan Africa.

1989 U.N. General Assembly adopts Convention on the Rights of the Child (CRC); U.S., Somalia haven't ratified it.

1990s-Present *Despite progress in many areas, child prostitution, trafficking and other problems abound.*

1990 World Summit for Children sets 10-year goals for children's health, nutrition and education.

1995 U.S. ambassador to the U.N. Madeleine Albright signs CRC, but President Bill Clinton does not send it to the Senate.

1998 Coalition to Stop the Use of Child Soldiers is formed in London.

1999 More than 25 million people in sub-Saharan Africa have HIV/AIDS, many of them children.

2000 U.N.'s Millennium Declaration is signed by 189 countries, establishing goals for ending poverty by 2015.

2002 International Labour Organization estimates that 19 percent of children 5-14 in Asia and the Pacific are engaged in child labor.

2008 A total of 193 nations have ratified the CRC.

2009 U.N. prepares to celebrate 20th anniversary of the Convention on the Rights of the Child on Nov. 20. . . . Number of under-5 children dying annually falls below 9 million for the first time. . . . Experts fear global recession could cause 200,000 to 400,000 more under-5 deaths each year — or up to 2.8 million additional deaths by 2015.

trap doors for coal-filled carts. Mining would not be regulated until 1842, when Britain's *First Report on Children in Mines* exposed the horrible conditions. The report led to girls being banned from the mines, along with boys younger than 10.[54]

But other children were forced into factory work by their parents, who obtained falsified permits showing their children were older than they really were. Others were sold or indentured to factory owners. The government aided and abetted the owners by turning over thousands of young orphans to work in the factories and live in crowded, often-drafty barracks.

Beatings, for working too slowly or being late, were common. In 1832 a worker testified to a British Parliamentary committee: "When I was 7 years old, I went to work at Mr. Marshall's factory at Shrewsbury. If a child was drowsy, the overlooker touches the child on the shoulder and says, 'Come here.' In a corner of the room there is an iron cistern filled with water. He takes the boy by the legs and dips him in the cistern, and sends him back to work."[55]

The United States imported the concept of child labor from across the Atlantic. By 1820 nearly a quarter of the workers in the Northeast were under 16. In some cotton mills half the workers were children.[56] By the 1900s, according to historian Roger Butterfield, more than 1.7 million American children under 16 were working 13-hour days in the nation's cotton mills — 25 percent of them under 12.[57]

As in Great Britain, owners flouted minimum-age laws. When inspectors arrived, children were hidden or sent away, or investigators were told that the children were there to visit their mothers. Child-protection laws often did not apply to immigrants, and dozens of immigrant girls, some as young as 12, died in the infamous Triangle Waist Factory fire (commonly called the Triangle Shirtwaist Factory fire) in New York City in 1911, which killed 146 workers.[58]

Because Canada industrialized later than the United States, child labor abuses were not as prevalent there until the early 1900s. Demand for child labor in Europe reached its peak during the pre-industrial and industrialized periods of those economies.

"The belief that idle children are immoral children who will adopt deviant behavior and commit crimes was widespread in Europe," a book reviewer noted. "This led to a social policy of putting orphaned and pauper children to work in French hopitaux, in English Hospitals or Workhouses, Danish Bornehus, Swedish barnhus, and Russian state-sponsored hospitals . . . . This paved the way for poor and working-class families to send their children to work in the new factories, mills and mines."[59]

Child Labor Reforms

In the early 19th century, reformers sought to end some of the most egregious child labor practices. In 1802 England passed its first child labor legislation, but the measure applied only to "pauper apprentices" and was not widely enforced. From 1819 to 1878 various "Factory Acts" raised minimum work ages and shortened working hours. In 1836 children were prohibited from working in textile mills, and in 1840 no one under 21 could work as a chimney sweep. Both laws, however, were abused for decades. Indeed, the minimum working age in the United Kingdom was not raised to 14 until 1933.

The United States was even slower to reform. Although organizations like the National Consumer's League and the National Child Labor Committee worked to ban child labor and end sweatshops, the Fair Labor Standards Act wasn't passed until 1938. It instituted firm restrictions on child labor, raising the minimum hourly wage to 40 cents and banned children under 16 from hazardous industries. It also prohibited children from working during school hours.

Concern about children's rights grew throughout the world in the first half of the 20th century. During its first session in 1946, the U.N. General Assembly voted to establish the U.N. International Children's Emergency Fund (UNICEF) to provide short-term relief to children in war-ravaged Europe. Between 1947 and 1950, UNICEF distributed approximately $87.6 million in aid to 13 European countries.[60]

The needs were so great, however, that UNICEF's brief was broadened in 1950 to include children in developing countries. In 1953 that mandate became a permanent part of the U.N. One of its first global campaigns was against yaws, a disease affecting millions that is easily cured with penicillin. Campaigns against tuberculosis, trachoma and malaria followed.

UNICEF continued to expand, eventually becoming a model for bringing humanitarian and economic aid to the developing world. By the mid-1950s, UNICEF was

The Unspeakable Horror: Child Rape

Some blame the "virgin cure" myth for rise in attacks.

Growing numbers of children — some just tiny infants — are being raped every day across the globe. In Zimbabwe sexual violence against children increased by more than 40 percent between 2005 and 2008.[1] In the northern Nigerian city of Kano child rape cases soared 50 percent between 2007 and 2008.[2] It's also reportedly on the rise in Afghanistan's northern provinces.[3]

But South Africa is the epicenter of child rape, with the world's largest number of recorded child sexual assaults — some 60 a day — and children's advocates believe thousands more go unreported.[4]

Reports of men raping infants outraged South Africans since an infamous 2001 case involving a 9-month-old girl. The country was also shocked when a study by the Red Cross Children's Hospital in Cape Town showed that the average age of children brought in for reconstructive surgery following a rape was 3 years old. In a recent horrific case, a 16-month-old toddler who was raped in Delft had to undergo extensive reconstruction surgery.[5]

Many blame the rise in child rapes on the mistaken belief that sex with a virgin protects a man from HIV-AIDS or can actually cure the deadly disease — the so-called "virgin cure." Mamelato Leopeng, an AIDS counselor in Johannesburg, says about a third of the HIV-infected men she meets at her clinic believe sex with a virgin will cure them, and that using a condom will void the cure.[6] Africa's traditional healers reportedly perpetuate the myth, often explaining that the blood of a virgin will "wash away" the HIV virus.

As South African rape survivor, journalist and activist Charlene Smith explained, "I was working with a 9-year-old child whose mother took her to the mother's boyfriend who was HIV-positive, and the mother watched while he raped the child. The rapist admitted this because he believed he could save himself."[7]

The belief in the healing powers of virgins' blood is not a new idea. In 19th-century England some men believed having sex with a virgin could cure venereal disease.

While experts differ on how much belief in the "virgin cure" leads to child rape, there is an undeniable link. "It is hard to find a virgin of 16 nowadays, so men are turning to babies under 10," said Leopeng, "They are looking for clean blood. It is all based on ignorance and a lack of education."[8]

The "virgin cure" myth is also perpetuated in other developing regions as well, including India and Southeast Asia. In Cambodia, for instance, a man will spend a year's wages or more to buy — and rape — a virgin.

"They are animals," says Cambodian children's-rights activist Somaly Mam. "They are ruining so many young lives."

Mam has rescued scores of girls — some as young as 5 — who have been raped in an effort to cure AIDS. The belief is so widespread in Cambodia, she says, that brothel owners and pimps will have girls who have been raped

active in 100 countries, but the United Nations had not established guidelines or recommended minimum ages for child workers.[61]

21st-Century Problems

By the mid-20th century, developing countries were shaking off their colonial yokes and beginning to transform their economies. As the world's population began shifting from the countryside to huge, industrialized cities, familiar children's problems arose, including labor abuses, poverty and exploitation. Children throughout the developing world were often forced to work in dangerous, low-paid jobs to supplement their families' incomes.

The developed world took notice, determining that the key to saving the world's children was lifting their countries out of poverty. "For this they needed aid from their richer neighbors in the form of funds and technical expertise to help them industrialize," notes a UNICEF historian.[62]

Organizations, institutions and citizens in the developed world also took notice. Images of underage children working in American or British textile mills have been replaced by scenes of young children working long hours surgically sewn up repeatedly — an extremely painful procedure — so they can be sold and violated again.

Besides being traumatized by the rape itself, the young rape victims will likely contract AIDS, thus spreading the disease to a group of otherwise sexually inactive girls.[9]

Education is considered the best weapon against the practice, and some countries are launching public health education campaigns. In Zambia, for example, roadside billboards feature a picture of a young girl with the message, "Sex with me doesn't cure AIDS!"[10] And traditional healers in Zimbabwe also are being educated. But surveys show that from 18-30 percent of African men still believe the myth.[11]

Some governments are strengthening child-abuse laws. Zimbabwe, Swaziland, South Africa and Zambia have all begun to establish child-friendly courts for abused children. South Africa's Sexual Offences Act imposes harsher jail sentences for rape and allows victims to demand rapists take HIV tests. In 2000 Namibia passed the Combating of Rape Act, which ensures that victims and survivors will be informed of trial dates and any bail applications of the accused rapist.

But much more has to be done to wipe out the unspeakable crime, says Mam. "Part of the problem is that too many people are still embarrassed to talk about sex matters," she says. "Meanwhile, children are being raped and given a death sentence. The world has to wake up."

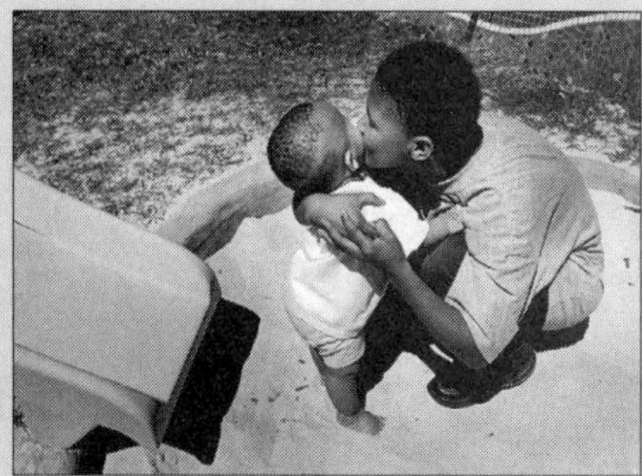

Getty Images/Per-Anders Pettersson

Patricia Lincoln, 16, comforts her daughter, known as "Baby Thsepang." The child was raped when she was 9 months old by her mother's HIV-positive boyfriend, triggering outrage across South Africa.

[1] "Trying to understand the unspeakable crime," IRIN, March 12, 2008, www.aegis.com/news/IRIN/2008/IR080312.html.

[2] "Child Rape on the Rise in North Nigerian City: Officials," *The Body*, Jan. 4, 2008, www.thebody.com/content/whatis/art44632.html.

[3] Aryn Baker, "Afghanistan's Epidemic of Child Rape," *Time*, Aug. 17, 2008, www.time.com/time/world/article/0,8599,1833517,00.html.

[4] "South Africa: child raped every three minutes," News24.com, Sept. 6, 2009, www.news24.com/Content/South Africa/News/1059/f3fc05773cf6402cad1cf-ba0da4b5428/03-06-2009%2009-06/Child_raped_every_3_min_-_report.

[5] Sibongile Mashaba, "Shocking child abuse statistics," *Sowetan*, Sept. 17, 2009, www.sowetan.co.za/News/Article.aspx?id=1066487.

[6] Adriana Stuijt, "Child rapes soared in South Africa this month," *Digital Journal*, Dec. 21, 2008, www.digitaljournal.com/article/264259.

[7] Carolyn Dempster, "South African trial brings rape into public view," newsfromafrica.org, May 2, 2006, www.newsfromafrica.org/newsfromafrica/articles/art_10669.html.

[8] *Ibid.*

[9] "Child rape survivor saves 'virgin myth' victims," CNN, June 5, 2009, www.edition.cnn.com/2009/LIVING/06/04/cnnheroes.betty.makoni/index.html.

[10] "Myths and Misconceptions about HIV/AIDS," The AIDS Pandemic, April 7, 2008, www.the-aids-pandemic.blogspot.com/2008/04/myths-and-misconceptions-about-hivaids.html.

[11] Dempster, *op. cit.*

at looms in Pakistan, Bangladesh and elsewhere. Underage cotton pickers may have vanished from the American South, but they still work in the cotton fields of Africa and India.

"In our country we think of these as 19th-century problems, but these are 21st-century problems," said Sandra Polaski, deputy undersecretary for international affairs in the U.S. Department of Labor.[63]

In 1979 the world focused on children's issues by celebrating The International Year of the Child. Studies spotlighted issues ranging from poor nutrition to polio and homelessness. In the 1980s, alarmed that after decades of humanitarian work millions of children under 5 were still dying each year from preventable causes, organizations like UNICEF launched massive immunization and "child survival" nutrition programs.

NGOs began to lobby for officially recognizing children's rights. With rapid industrialization in the developing world putting increasing stress on families, more and more children were living on city streets, being exploited, abused and deprived of their futures.[64]

In 1989 the U.N. General Assembly adopted the Convention on the Rights of the Child, the first legally binding international instrument to incorporate the full

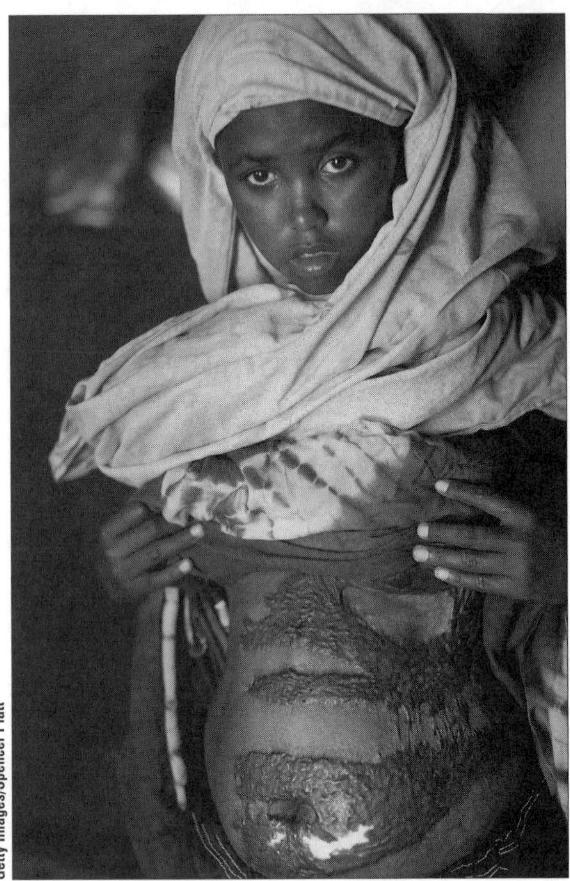

Getty Images/Spencer Platt

Naib Naema Abde Mohamed shows the scars from wounds she suffered when a shell hit her home in Mogadishu, Somalia. Having lost her two brothers and her father to the decade-long conflict in her home country, the 14-year-old now lives with her mother in the world's largest refugee complex, in Dadaab, Kenya. Besides injuries, armed conflict causes increased poverty, illiteracy, homelessness, early mortality and malnutrition among children.

range of human rights — civil, cultural, economic, political and social. It says the world's children have the right to survive, develop to their fullest potential, be protected from harmful influences, abuse and exploitation and to participate fully in family, cultural and social life.

Article 32 says children have the right to be protected from economic exploitation and from performing work that is hazardous or will interfere with the child's education or that will harm the child's health or physical, mental, spiritual, moral or social development. The convention became law on Sept. 2, 1990 — faster than any other human rights convention — and by 2009 had been ratified by 193 countries.

'Brilliant Purpose'

Children's rights were again center stage in 1990 at the U.N. Millennium Summit, the largest gathering of world leaders in history. In the summit's final declaration the international community pledged to end global poverty and spelled out eight Millennium Development Goals (MDG), six of which relate directly to children and all of them still used to measure progress in the global war on poverty. (*See box, p. 17.*)

Progress in meeting the MDGs has been uneven. More than half of the goals are progressing too slowly and have been further stalled by the global recession, says a 2009 U.N. report. Some countries like China are on track, but many sub-Saharan nations are woefully behind. Meeting the goals would lift 300 million children out of abject poverty, the report says, but that goal is still a long way off.[65]

While some critics bemoan the lack of progress, others praise the goals for publicizing the plight of children. "Thanks to these goals, not only U.N. agencies but the world at large knows the key measures of poverty, hunger, health and education," billionaire philanthropist Bill Gates, co-chair of the Bill & Melinda Gates Foundation, told the U.N. last year. "Some of the numbers are good and some are not. But the fact that the world is focusing on the numbers is excellent. It means people see where things are going well, and understand how we can spread those successes. They see where we're falling short, and they see the need to apply more effort and do things differently. That is the purpose of these goals, and it's a brilliant purpose."[66]

CURRENT SITUATION

Deadly Birthdays

Although many developing countries are making dramatic progress at reducing child mortality, in sub-Saharan Africa 1,500 babies die each day within the first 24 hours after they are born — most from birthing complications, neonatal tetanus, malaria and other conditions.

Infant death is so common in the region that many parents "postpone naming their baby for at least a month, until they are certain they will survive infancy," says Save the Children's MacCormack.

"Throughout the developing world, the most dangerous day in a child's life is the day the child is born," he adds. Twenty-five percent of all child deaths in sub-Saharan Africa — more than 1 million annually — occur during the first month of life.[67]

Most of the deaths are preventable and would rarely claim the life of a child in a wealthy country. For example, neonatal tetanus, one of the major killers of newborns, can be prevented by a 50-cent vaccine. Pneumonia, a disease that kills nearly 1 million people a year, can be treated with antibiotics that cost less than one dollar a patient.[68] Diarrhea, another lethal killer, can be cured for pennies a day. (*See sidebar, p. 10.*)

While the under-5 mortality rate in northern Africa — Algeria, Egypt, Morocco, Libya and Tunisia — has plummeted by up to 56 percent since 1990, child survival trends in sub-Saharan Africa are still grim. In 2007 roughly one in every seven sub-Saharan children failed to reach their fifth birthday — the world's highest under-5 mortality rate.[69]

But there are some bright spots. Malaria, which kills 800,000 people annually, is being fought with insecticide-dipped nets, with dramatic results in countries like Ethiopia, Niger, Mali and Zambia.[70] Malawi has reduced its under-5 mortality rate from 210 per 1,000 live births in 1990 to 111 per 1,000 in 2007.[71]

One of the Millennium Development Goals aims to reduce by two- thirds the under-5 mortality rate by 2015. While some countries have come close to being on track, most are still falling short. To meet that goal, emphasis must be placed on the poorest, most marginalized countries and regions, such as sub-Saharan Africa. "Business as usual will be grossly insufficient to meet these Millennium Development goals," notes a UNICEF spokesperson. "We have to redouble our efforts."

At the United Nations, the fate of child mortality once again earned worldwide attention in late September. The world must help children in crisis, President Obama said: "What happens to the hopes of a single child — anywhere — can enrich our world, or impoverish it."

U.N. Goals Could Aid 300 Million Children

Three hundred million children would be lifted out of abject poverty if the world were to meet the U.N.'s eight Millennium Development Goals (MDGs) — adopted in 1990. But according to a 2009 U.N. report, progress is slow on more than half of the goals, which have been further stalled by the global recession.

The eight MDGs are to:

- ***Eradicate extreme poverty and hunger*** — To halve, by 2015, the proportion of people whose income is less than $1 a day and the proportion of people suffering from hunger.
- ***Achieve universal primary education*** — Ensure that by 2015 children everywhere — girls as well as boys — will be able to complete primary schooling.
- ***Promote gender equality and empower women*** — Eliminate gender disparity in primary and secondary education by 2005 and at all education levels by 2015.
- ***Reduce child mortality*** — Reduce the 1990 under-5 mortality rate by two-thirds by 2015.
- ***Improve maternal health*** — Reduce the maternal mortality ratio by three-quarters between 1990 and 2015.
- ***Combat HIV/AIDS, malaria and other diseases*** — Halt and start reversing the spread or incidence of HIV/AIDS, malaria and other major diseases by 2015.
- ***Ensure environmental sustainability*** — Integrate sustainable development principles into country policies and programs and reverse the losses of environmental resources. Cut in half by 2015 the proportion of people without sustainable access to safe drinking water. Achieve a significant improvement in the lives of at least 100 million slum dwellers by 2020.
- ***Develop a global partnership for development*** — Help developing countries achieve the other seven MDGs through additional development assistance, improved access to markets and debt relief.

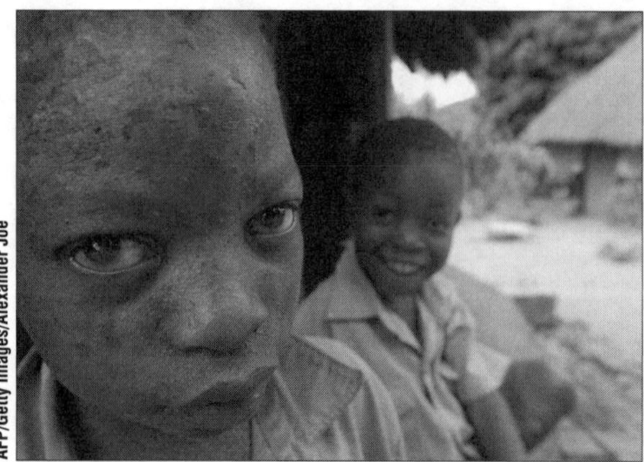
AFP/Getty Images/Alexander Joe

AIDS-infected orphans Evans Mahlangu (left), 13, and his brother Edmond, 8, walked across a mountain range in Zimbabwe and jumped the border to obtain free antiretroviral drugs at a hospital in neighboring Mozambique. They are among the 2.5 million children under age 15 suffering from AIDS, 90 percent of them in sub-Saharan Africa.

But words must be backed up by actions. As Obama spoke, thousands of children across the Horn of Africa were starving to death, and millions more were facing a similar fate — victims of what Save the Children calls "East Africa's worst food crisis in decades."

How severe is the global child mortality crisis? In the time it took to read the last paragraph 10 children died from mostly preventable causes.

Child Slavery

Human-rights advocates say millions of children around the world are being enslaved today in a variety of ways — and some are tortured into submission.

"If I refused to sleep with a client, the brothel owners would take me to the dungeon in the basement and tie me to a bed. Then they would shock me with a live electric cord," says Sina, a former child prostitute in Phnom Penh, Cambodia. Kidnapped from Vietnam at 13, Sina endured years of rape and, like many others who refused to submit, was tortured.

Cambodian children's rights activist Mam remembers her own experience: "We were enslaved. If I disobeyed I was tortured in just such a dungeon. Brothel owners would tie me to a chair and throw live snakes on me."

According to UNICEF 1.2 million children are trafficked every year, and 100 million girls are involved in child labor worldwide, says the International Labour Organization. An estimated 120 million children live on the streets, and 8.4 million children work as slave laborers, sex slaves or soldiers.[72]

In the Balkans, for instance, girls as young as 8 are kidnapped, forced to beg on the streets and become prostitutes. In Afghanistan, young boys are forced to work in dangerous coal mines for just $3 a day. In India, as exemplified in the Oscar-winning movie "Slumdog Millionaire," children are deliberately maimed and forced to beg on the streets.[73]

In nearly every big city throughout the developing world children live on the streets. From New Delhi to Lagos to Bogotá, these "street kids" scratch out a living with no hope of being rescued by the social safety net that rescues children in more prosperous countries. In Eastern Europe, a "lost generation" of vulnerable children have been abandoned by their parents — many of whom have sought work abroad — including 350,000 such children in Romania who eke out a living by working for minimal wages, begging, stealing or prostituting themselves.[74]

Much of the slavery involves virgin girls and is exacerbated by tough economic times. For example, an Iraq-based human-rights activist recently told *Time* magazine that Iraqi virgins as young as 11 and 12 can be sold for anything from $2,000 to $30,000. She explained, "The buying and selling of girls in Iraq, it's like the trade in cattle . . . . I've seen mothers haggle with agents over the price of their daughters."[75]

Global recession inevitably leads to an increase in forced child labor and trafficking. "Growing poverty is making people more vulnerable to both labor and sex trafficking, boosting the supply side of human trafficking all over the world," says the U.S. State Department's 2009 "Trafficking in Persons Report." It quoted an International Labour Organisation report, which said, "Vulnerable workers — particularly migrants, including young women and even children — are more exposed to forced labor, because under conditions of hardship they will be taking more risks than before."[76]

Child slavery and trafficking occurs in rich countries as well. The State Department recently decided to include data about its investigations of such practices in the United States in its annual human trafficking report. According to the New York-based Foundation for Child Development,

AT ISSUE

Is more aid the best way to help the world's children?

YES

Ann M. Veneman
Executive Director, United Nations Children's Fund (UNICEF)

Written for *CQ Global Researcher*, October 2009

Aid effectiveness can — and must — be measured in positive and sustainable results. While experts debate the impact aid has on development, wide consensus exists about the importance of investing in children.

Where strategic, targeted and effective interventions have increased, positive results have followed. Recent UNICEF figures show a 28 percent decline in the rate at which children die before their fifth birthday — from 90 deaths per 1,000 live births in 1990 to 65 deaths per 1,000 in 2008. Thus, compared to 1990, 10,000 fewer children are dying every day.

Key health interventions — such as immunizations, anti-malarial bed nets and Vitamin A supplementation — all have contributed. Increased measles vaccinations in sub-Saharan Africa have achieved a 91 percent reduction in measles mortality in just six years. The distribution of insecticide-treated bed nets to prevent malaria has increased more than threefold since 2000.

Early childhood lays the foundation for a lifetime. If a child suffers from malnutrition, particularly under the age of two, the child is likely to have difficulty learning in school and earning as an adult — contributing to the intergenerational cycle of poverty.

Research shows that every $1 spent on vitamin A and zinc supplementation creates more than $17 worth of benefits. Each $1 invested in girls education returns $12 in productivity. For instance, when a girl in the developing world receives seven or more years of education, she marries four years later, on average, and has 2.2 fewer children. And for every year a girl spends in secondary school, her earnings increase by an estimated 15 to 20 percent.

But to have the maximum impact on our collective future, some things must change about foreign aid. Ineffective governance and even corruption undermine aid utilization and effectiveness. Good data about where to invest and about what delivers the best results are essential to improving aid efficiency and results. Although data collection, analysis and availability have improved, more needs to be done.

Aid can be used to leverage improved national investment decisions. One UNICEF study, costing only around $12,000, so effectively identified the causes of adolescent school dropouts that the national government invested an additional $40 million in secondary education.

Properly targeted and employed, aid can help build the foundation for poverty alleviation, enhanced national capacity and sustainable growth. It also helps save countless lives.

NO

James Shikwati
Founder and Director, Inter Region Economic Network
CEO, The African Executive magazine

Written for *CQ Global Researcher*, October 2009

In Africa, conventional economic statistics are used to depict an otherwise resource-rich continent as poor. This not only drives inhabitants to lose confidence in their abilities and opportunities but also promotes a culture of dependence on external assistance. Consequently, African children are born into a cycle of artificial dependency.

The global market system that denies parents from poor countries a chance to be productive and participate in the marketplace is as dangerous to children as disease, malnutrition and the effects of war. A skewed market system that dangles money as a solution assaults parents' noble role by turning them into procreators who surrender their children's upbringing to outsiders loaded with money.

Tackling the reasons why individuals and institutions fail to provide a good environment for raising children should be a priority for everyone. Children looking into the eyes of their mothers or fathers should draw inspiration. Parents, on the other hand, should demand that institutions they built and paid for deliver better services to their children.

Aid money can never replace an environment that promotes the adoption of scientific and rational ideas. The world needs to reward parents and innovators who provide solutions to diseases, malnutrition, poor shelter, insecurity and poor education and a multitude of other problems that hamper children's optimum development.

With people in poor countries trapped in a global market system that denies them an opportunity to be industrious, some well-intentioned projects use mosquito bed-nets as a lure to encourage parents to have their children vaccinated. As an unintended consequence, some children have died from vaccine overdoses because their poor parents had them vaccinated repeatedly in order to get extra bed-nets. The quest to be industrious is exemplified by poor people's readiness to convert anti-mosquito bed-nets into fishing nets and wedding dresses.

It is tempting to push for money as a solution to save an estimated 3 million children who die annually of preventable diseases; to educate the 75 million who miss school and to rescue millions of children affected by war. However, this does not explain why parents in these scenarios are incapable economically to address the challenges their children encounter.

More aid money won't help the world's children. The freedom to exercise individuals' ingenuity and, within acceptable standards, share the fruits of their energy with society will help them more.

AP Photo/Heng Sinith

The global recession is driving food prices up while forcing reductions in the amount of food aid being offered. In Cambodia, for instance, U.N. World Food Programme school meals — like these offered near Phnom Penh in 2008 — have been discontinued for 450,000 children this year. The number of chronically hungry people worldwide is projected to exceed 1 billion this year.

American children's quality of life is expected to decline through 2010 due to the financial crisis. Soon one in five American children will be "living in poverty," according to the foundation.[77]

For many children trapped in slavery around the world, there is little hope. But NGOs, government agencies and others are working to rescue children. As more and more nations and organizations like the United Nations expose child labor and trafficking abuses, countries are forced to act. "These kids have been traumatized," explains Scott Neeson, founder of the Cambodian Children's Fund, an NGO that has rescued more than 400 children from child labor and poverty in Phnom Penh. "They need security, lodging and education."

There is hope. After announcing a crackdown on child trafficking in April, China investigated more than 700 cases in a little over a month, rescuing 1,000 children and women.[78] Thirty-six children between the ages of 5 and 15 were recently rescued in Ghana after being sold into slavery by their parents. They received no pay or schooling while "enslaved" in the local fishing industry.

Although similar rescue stories occur regularly around the world, the problem of child trafficking is growing every day. Cambodian children's rights activist Mam, who was sold into prostitution while still a child, says, "Although this is a fight we may never win, we have no choice but to keep battling. Children's lives are hanging in the balance."

Children and Conflict

Kon Kelei, a former child solider from Sudan, is not sure how old he was when he was kidnapped by rebels and taken to a rebel military camp, where he was trained to fight. He just knows he was too little to carry a rifle.

"I was four or five," he told the Inter Press Service news agency. "An AK-47 is not made for a kid."[79]

Kelei is one of the lucky ones; he has been rehabilitated and is helping to establish the Global Network of Young People Formerly Affected by War (NYPAW), which promotes the rehabilitation and empowerment of former child soldiers.[80]

According to some estimates, 250,000 children are serving in armed conflicts around the world as soldiers, suicide bombers, sex slaves or spies.[81] As soldiers, children are considered cheap, easily controllable and expendable.

And increasingly, children are being used as suicide bombers. A recent CNN report detailed how the late Baitullah Mehsud, a top Taliban leader in Pakistan, had been "buying and selling children" — some as young as 11 — to train as suicide bombers. "He has been admitting he holds a training center for young boys, for preparing them for suicide bombing," said a Pakistani army spokesman. Once trained, the children are sold to other Taliban officials for $6,000 to $12,000.[82]

Wars also have indirect consequences on children, such as the loss of sanitation services, interruption of their education and an uptick in poverty and malnutrition. "Armed conflict perpetuates poverty, illiteracy and early mortality," explains UNICEF Executive Director Ann M. Veneman.

Children's scars from armed conflict are not always as evident as a bullet wound or a lost limb, she points out. In war-torn Madagascar, for instance, a child recalls, "Every time I hear shooting, my heart beats out of control and I start to shake. My thoughts go to what might happen, and what I would do if members of my family died."[83]

Researchers studying Madagascar's conflict noted, "One long-term consequence of this crisis is the difficulty for young people to distinguish what is 'correct' and what is 'incorrect;' what is 'true' and what is 'false,' as traditional grounding values have been radically altered by recent events."[84]

Girls are especially vulnerable in armed conflicts. Some have referred to their plight as a "double tragedy," explaining that even after a war ends they still suffer from sexual harassment, physical attacks and even forced marriages to armed forces commanders. And in recent years, rape — often coupled with the maiming of young girls so they can never conceive — has increasingly been used as a weapon of war.[85]

Even though enlisting children under 15 is now officially a war crime (due to a 1977 amendment to the Geneva Conventions and the International Convention on the Rights of the Child), the practice continues to flourish, especially among nongovernmental forces. While the United Nations has been publicizing the plight of child soldiers, armed groups continue to use children, especially in Asian, African and Middle Eastern battle zones. Last year Iraqi insurgents strapped explosives to a young girl and remotely detonated the bomb at an army command post in Yousifiyah. A 13-year-old girl blew herself up at a checkpoint in Ba'qubah, Iraq. Last May, 85 children were among the 212 suspected rebels rounded up in Chad.[86]

A recent U.N. report blames "non state actors" in Afghanistan, Burundi, Chad, Burma, Nepal, the Philippines, Somalia, Uganda and elsewhere for recruiting and using child soldiers.[87] In Chad, despite promises from both rebel groups and the government to stop recruiting child warriors, rebel groups have reportedly stepped up the recruitment of children in recent months. UNICEF says Chad currently has up to 10,000 child soldiers.[88]

Until such practices are banished, the words of one Madagascar child scarred by war will haunt everyone who hears them: "Who cares if I die? I am not alive anyway."[89]

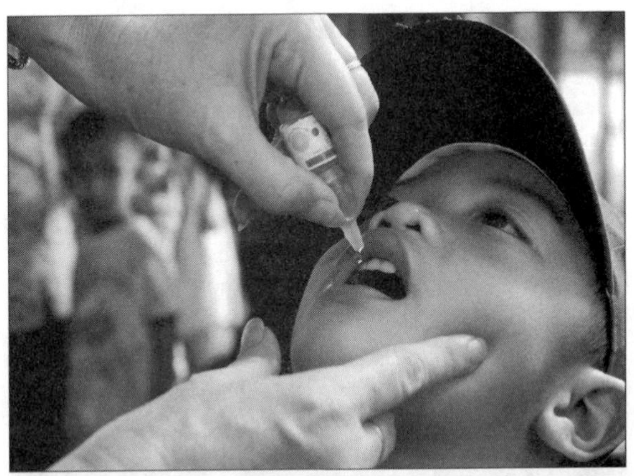

AP Photo/Tatan Syuflana

Robert Kiener

Getting Help

A girl receives polio vaccine drops in Jakarta, Indonesia (top). Global immunization programs have nearly eradicated the crippling disease. But children still face horrific man-made dangers, such as forced child labor and sex trafficking — which are on the increase due to the global recession. Two of these three Cambodian girls rescued from a Phnom Penh brothel were sold to pimps when they were just 6 years old (bottom). They are now living in a shelter run by former child prostitute Somaly Mam. An estimated 10,000 to 20,000 child prostitutes under 16 are in Cambodia. Children's-rights activists say 1 million youngsters around the world are forced into prostitution every year.

OUTLOOK

Half-Full Glass

A list of problems confronting the world's children reads like way stations on a journey through hell: infant mortality, HIV/AIDS, homelessness, child soldiers, trafficking, prostitution. And given the added impact of the global economic crisis, climate change and armed conflicts, experts say children are in greater danger than ever.

But veteran activist MacCormack of Save the Children takes a longer view. "On the whole, things are getting better," he says. "I started in this business in the 1950s, when children in South Korea and Taiwan couldn't get enough to eat. Look at them today. The pattern has repeated itself in other regions. Sure, many children are in peril, but things are constantly improving. I am an optimist."

The world will be a different place in 20 years, MacCormack says, noting that about half of the children

AFP/Getty Images/Mauricio Lima

A ruined hut is all that remains of a girl's home after authorities bulldozed her shantytown near São Paulo, Brazil, on Aug. 26, 2009. World leaders pledged at a 1990 U.N. summit to meet eight Millennium Development Goals, which would help lift 300 million children out of abject poverty. But achieving that aim is still a long way off, say experts, partly because of lack of funds and political will.

in crisis today live in China and India, where they will inevitably benefit from the robust economic growth those countries are experiencing.

"In 20 years their lot will have improved dramatically," he says. "That will allow us to put even more of our resources into places like sub-Saharan Africa."

Thanks to the efforts of countless child advocates, the state of the world's children is improving. Since 1990 deaths of children under 5 have decreased steadily worldwide.[90] The absolute number of child deaths has declined from 12.5 million in 1990 to 8.8 million in 2008.[91] In Egypt, for instance, child mortality fell by a whopping 68 percent during that period. By promoting basic procedures such as vaccinations, oral rehydration therapies and improving health services, Egypt now leads the developing world in efforts to save the lives of its children.[92]

"Compared to 1990," said UNICEF Executive Director Veneman, "10,000 fewer children are dying every day" around the world. But, she quickly adds, "While progress is being made, it is unacceptable that each year 8.8 million children die before their fifth birthday."[93]

Much work remains to be done to attain the U.N. Millennium Development Goals, which have produced mixed results so far. At least 980 million children under 18 still lack access to improved sanitation, millions of children are victims of violence and one-fourth of children in developing countries are underweight.[94]

To solve such problems, UNICEF plans to expand its Accelerated Child Survival and Development Initiative (ACSD) to other countries in Africa and Asia. The initiative has proven how a set of well-designed interventions can transform the fate of a nation's children. Custom designed for each community's needs, a typical ACSD package contains vitamin A tablets to strengthen children's immune systems, antimalaria mosquito nets, oral rehydration therapy kits, antibiotics, anti-retroviral drugs for HIV-infected mothers and more. In pilot programs in West Africa, the packages have helped to slash child mortality rates by an average of 20 percent — at a cost of only $500 to $1,000 per life saved.[95]

Although a weakening economy may tempt richer countries to cut their aid budgets, development experts say it is more important than ever to invest in the world's children. "It is important to recognize the moral imperative to act," said the London-based Overseas Development Institute. "A major share of the cost of the financial and economic crisis will be borne by hundreds of million of people who have not shared in the benefits of recent growth."[96]

Melinda Gates, co-chair of the Gates Foundation, has overseen the distribution of billions of dollars of aid money and visited scores of developing countries. "On my side of the mat," she wrote, "when my kids are sick, they get antibiotics. On the other side of the mat, when their children get sick, they may be receiving a death sentence. Those of us in the wealthy countries must try to put ourselves on the other side of the mat."[97]

NOTES

1. "Child Prostitution a Global Problem," *The Body*, April 22, 2002, www.thebody.com/content/whatis/art22944.html.
2. "Child Protection From Violence, Exploitation and Abuse," UNICEF, May 2009, www.unicef.org/media/media_45451.html.
3. "The State of the World's Children 2009," UNICEF, December 2008, www.unicef.org/sowc09/docs/SOWC09-FullReport-EN.pdf.

4. "Survive to Five," Save the Children, www.savethechildren.org/programs/health/child-survival/survive-to-5.

5. "The State of Food Insecurity in the World, 2008: High food prices and food security — threats and opportunities," Food and Agriculture Organization, 2008, www.fao.org/docrep/011/i0291e/i0291e00.htm.

6. Alula Berhe Kidani, "Children and the MDGs, Progress Towards A World Fit for Children," *Sudan Vision*, April 8, 2009, www.sudanvisiondaily.com/modules.php?name=News&file=print&sid=33567.

7. "Great leap forward on free healthcare," IRIN, Sept. 24, 2009, www.irinnews.org/report.aspx?ReportId=86280.

8. "Children and Human Rights," Amnesty International, www.amnesty.org/en/children.

9. "Global: WHO Snapshot of Global Health," IRIN, July 10, 2009, www.irinnews.org/Report.aspx?ReportId=85235.

10. "Child Protection From Violence, Exploitation and Abuse," *op. cit.*

11. *Ibid.* For background, see John Felton, "Child Soldiers," *CQ Global Researcher*, July 2008, pp. 183-211.

12. "Averting a Human Crisis During the Global Downturn," World Bank 2009, foreword, http://siteresources.worldbank.org/NEWS/Resources/AvertingTheHumanCrisis.pdf.

13. "The Economic Crisis and the Millennium Development Goals," The World Bank, April 24, 2009, http://web.worldbank.org/WBSITE/EXTERNAL/NEWS/0,,contentMDK:22154703~pagePK:64257043~piPK:437376~theSitePK:4607,00.html.

14. *Ibid.* For background on the 2008 food crisis, see Marcia Clemmitt, "Global Food Crisis," *CQ Researcher*, June 27, 2008, pp. 553-576.

15. Rosalind Ryan, "Call for global action to tackle food crisis," *Guardian*, April 22, 2008, www.guardian.co.uk/politics/2008/apr/22/development.internationalaidanddevelopment.

16. "Africa: Mortgages and mortality," IRIN, March 6, 2009, www.irinnews.org/Report.aspx?ReportId=83344.

17. "The Economic Crisis and the Millennium Development Goals," *op. cit.*

18. Sam Lister, "Downturn could kill 400,000 children, warns Margaret Chan," *Times* (London), March 14, 2009, www.timesonline.co.uk/tol/life_and_style/health/article5904637.ece.

19. Quoted in "Global recession boosts child prostitution and trafficking," IRIN, Sept. 29, 2009, www.irinnews.org/report.aspx?Reportid=86335. Also see "Financial Crisis and Human Trafficking," U.S. Department of State, 2009, www.state.gov/g/tip/rls/tiprpt/2009/124798.htm.

20. "Less money for more work — the NGO double whammy," IRIN, April 21, 2009, www.irinnews.org/Report.aspx?ReportId=84023.

21. The gross national income is the total net value of the goods and services produced by a country, including wages, profits, rents, interest and pensions.

22. "Scandalous lack of progress in EU development aid," Global Movement for Children, April 10, 2008, www.gmfc.org/index.php/gmc6/content/view/full/815.

23. "Save lives not banks, says Machel," IRIN, July 23, 2009, www.plusnews.org/Report.aspx?ReportId=85410.

24. "Development aid at its highest level ever in 2008," Organisation for Economic Co-operation and Development, March 3, 2009, www.oecd.org/document/35/0,3343,en_2649_34487_42458595_1_1_1_1,00.html. Also see www.globalissues.org/article/35/us-and-foreign-aid-assistance.

25. "Aid still at 1993 level despite increase," OXFAM, March 30, 2009, www.oxfam.org/en/pressroom/pressrelease/2009-03-30/aid-still-1993-level-despite-increase.

26. Dambisa Moyo, "Why Foreign Aid Is Hurting Africa," *The Wall Street Journal*, March 21, 2009, www.online.wsj.com/article/SB123758895999200083.html.

27. William Easterly, "Multilateral Development Banks: Promoting Effectiveness and Fighting Corruption," testimony before the Senate Committee on Foreign Relations, March 28, 2006, www.nyu.edu/fas/institute/

dri/Easterly/File/oral_testimony_senate_foreign_relations_committee.pdf.

28. John Stossel and Patrick McMenamin, "Will More Foreign Aid End Global Poverty?" ABC News, May 12, 2006, www.abcnews.go.com/2020/Story?id=1955664&page=1.
29. Moyo, *op. cit.*
30. William Wallis, "Is aid working?" *Financial Times Blog*, June 1, 2009, www.blogs.ft.com/arena/2009/06/01/is-aid-working/.
31. Stossel and McMenamin, *op. cit.*
32. "Convention on the Rights of the Child," UNICEF, August 2008, www.unicef.org/crc/.
33. Andie Coller, "Parental rights: The new wedge issue," *Politico*, April 8, 2009, www.politico.com/news/stories/0409/21041.html.
34. Sakun Akhtar, "Gautam, 72, examines child health," *The Dartmouth.com*, Feb. 3, 2009, www.thedartmouth.com/2009/02/03/news/gautam.
35. *Ibid.*
36. Michael Smith, "Home schooling: U.N. treaty might weaken families," *The Washington Times*, Jan. 11, 2009, www.washingtontimes.com/news/2009/jan/11/un-treaty-might-weaken-families/.
37. Joseph Abrams, "Boxer seeks to ratify UN treaty that may erode US rights," Fox News, Feb. 25, 2009, www.foxnews.com/politics/2009/02/25/boxer-seeks-ratify-treaty-erode-rights/.
38. David Crary, "Children's rights treaty stirs debate," The Associated Press, May 2, 2009, www.ajc.com/news/content/printedition/2009/05/02/currents0502.html.
39. "Youth In Crisis," IRIN In-depth, February 2007, p. 23, www.irinnews.org/InDepthMain.aspx?InDepthId=28&ReportId=69981.
40. "What is child survival and why does it matter?" Global Action for Children, www.globalactionforchildren.org/issues/child_survival1/.
41. "Children, AIDS and the economic crisis," UNICEF, April 2009, www.uniteforchildren.org/files/AIDSandFinancialCrisis_June_5_2009.pdf.
42. "Averting a human crisis during the global downturn," *op. cit.*
43. Daniel Ooko, "Health forum calls to avert new HIV/AIDS infections," *China View*, Feb. 24, 2009, http://english.peopledaily.com.cn/90001/90777/90855/6600165.html.
44. Vidya Krishnan, "Now, meltdown hits HIV/AIDS treatment, prevention," *Indian Express*, July 22, 2009, www.indianexpress.com/news/now-meltdown-hits-hiv-aids-treatment-preve/492360/.
45. Elvis Basudde, "Uganda: HIV/AIDS: no more free drugs," *The New Vision*, Aug. 30, 2009, www.allafrica.com/stories/200908310829.html.
46. Sam Rutekiara, "Africa's Real AIDS Priority: Prevention," *The Washington Post*, April 16, 2008, www.washingtonpost.com/wp-dyn/content/article/2008/04/15/AR2008041502738.html.
47. "Youth In Crisis," *op. cit.*, p. 24.
48. Alexander Irwin, Joyce Millen and Dorothy Fallows, "Myth Four: Prevention vs. Treatment?" *The Body*, April 2003, www.thebody.com/content/art13662.html.
49. Rachel Zimmerman and Mark Schoofs, "World AIDS Experts Debate Treatment vs. Prevention," *The Wall Street Journal*, July 2, 2002, www.aegis.com/news/wsj/2002/WJ020702.html.
50. For more details see Charles S. Clark, "Child Labor and Sweatshops," *CQ Researcher*, Aug. 16, 1996, pp. 721-744.
51. "Child Labor in U.S. History," Child Labor Public Education Project, www.continuetolearn.uiowa.edu/laborctr/child_labor/about/us_history.html.
52. "History of Child Labor," www.buzzle.com/articles/history-of-child-labor.html.
53. "A Brief History of Chimney Sweeping," www.a1specialistservices.co.uk/history.htm.
54. "Library — Children's Employment Commission Part II," The Origins Network, www.originsnetwork.com/help/popup-aboutbo-galleryemploy.htm.
55. "Punishment in Factories," www.spartacus.schoolnet.co.uk/IRpunishments.htm.
56. Robert Whaples, "Child Labor in the United States," www.eh.net/encyclopedia/article/whaples.childlabor.
57. Quoted in "Children," The World Affairs Blog Network, www.children.foreignpolicyblogs.com/.

58. "The Triangle Factory Fire," www.ilr.cornell.edu/trianglefire/.

59. Carolyn Tuttle, "Centuries of Child Labour: European Experiences from the Seventeenth to the Twentieth Century; Book Reviews," Eh.net, November 2005, www.eh.net/bookreviews/library/1008.

60. See Brian Hansen, "Children in Crisis," *CQ Researcher*, Aug. 31, 2001, pp. 657-688.

61. David Koch, "About UNICEF: Who we are," www.unicef.org/about/who/index_37404.html.

62. "1946-2006: Sixty Years for Children," UNICEF, p. 11, www.unicef.org/publications/files/1946-2006_Sixty_Years_for_Children.pdf.

63. Marcy Nicholson, "Child, forced labor behind many products: study," Reuters, Sept. 10, 2009, www.reuters.com/article/domesticNews/idUSTRE5896QD20090910.

64. "1946-2006: Sixty Years for Children," *op. cit.*, p. 21.

65. "The Millenium Development Goals Report, 2009," United Nations, www.un.org/millenniumgoals/pdf/MDG_Report_2009_ENG.pdf.

66. "Bill Gates Addresses the UN General Assembly," Sept. 25, 2008, www.gatesfoundation.org/speeches-commentary/Pages/bill-gates-united-nations-2008.aspx.

67. "28 Days to save a life," IRIN, June 16, 2009, www.irinnews.org/report.aspx?ReportId=84869.

68. *Ibid.*

69. "Briefing for the day of the African Child," Save the Children, June 16, 2009, www.savethechildren.org/countries/africa/Briefing-Day-of-the-African-Child2.pdf.

70. For background, see Jason McClure, "Ethiopia Takes on Malaria," in "The Troubled Horn of Africa," *CQ Global Researcher*, June 2009, pp. 149-176.

71. "Briefing for the day of the African Child," *op. cit.*

72. "Trafficked children and child slaves," Global Angels Foundation, www.globalangels.org/pages/4686/Trafficked_Kids_&_Child_Slaves.htm.

73. See Andrew Malone, "The real Slumdog Millionaires: Behind the cinema fantasy, mafia gangs are deliberately crippling children for profit," *The Mail Online*, Jan. 24, 2009, www.dailymail.co.uk/news/worldnews/article-1127056/The-real-Slumdog-Millionaires-Behind-cinema-fantasy-mafia-gangs-deliberately-crippling-children-profit.html#ixzz0SRUGLsTY.

74. "Orphans, child slaves, street kids and trafficked children," Global Angels Foundation, www.globalangels.org/pages/3660/Orphans,_Child_Slaves,_Street_Kids_and_Trafficked_Children.htm.

75. Rania Abouzeid, "Iraq's unspeakable crime: mothers pimping daughters," *Time*, March 7, 2009, www.time.com/time/world/article/0,8599,1883696,00.html.

76. "Financial Crisis and Human Trafficking," U.S. Department of State, www.state.gov/g/tip/rls/tiprpt/2009/124798.htm.

77. "Child Well-Being Index (CWI) 2009, Annual Release and Special Focus Report on Anticipating the Impacts of a 2008-2010 Recession," Foundation for Child Development, May 2009, www.fcd-us.org/resources/resources_show.htm?doc_id=906348.

78. Wang Qian, "Cops crack 700 trafficking cases," *China Daily*, June, 2009, www.chinadaily.com.cn/cndy/2009-06/02/content_7961144.htm.

79. See "War Child," NYPAW, www.warchildholland.org/nieuws/1561/nypaw.html.

80. Mirela Xanthaki, "Rights: Former Child Soldiers Work to Save Those Left Behind," IPS, Nov. 26, 2008, www.ipsnews.net/news.asp?idnews=44865.

81. *Ibid.*

82. Nic Robertson, "Pakistan: Taliban buying children for suicide attacks," CNN, July 7, 2009, www.edition.cnn.com/2009/WORLD/asiapcf/07/07/pakistan.child.bombers/index.html.

83. "Madagascar: A shell-shocked youth," IRIN, June 24, 2009, www.irinnews.org/report.aspx?ReportId=84988.

84. *Ibid.*

85. Natassia Hoffet, "Rights: Girl Soldiers Used Up, Then Thrown Away," IPS, March 12, 2009, www.ipsnews.net/news.asp?idnews=46085.

86. "Chad: Scores of children among rebels rounded up in east," IRIN, May 27, 2009, www.irinnews.org/Report.aspx?ReportId=84581.

87. Thalif Deen, "Rights: Recruiters of Child Soldiers Defy U.N. Pressure," April 29, 2009, www.ipsnews.net/news.asp?idnews=46669.
88. "Chad: Instability Threatens Demobilisation of Child Soldiers," IRIN, April 16, 2009, www.allafrica.com/stories/200904160862.html.
89. "Madagascar: A shell-shocked youth," *op. cit.*
90. Celia W. Dugger, "Child Mortality Rate Declines Globally," *The New York Times*, Sept. 10, 2009, www.nytimes.com/2009/09/10/world/10child.html.
91. "UNICEF: Global child mortality continues to drop," Sept. 10, 2009, www.unicef.org/media/media_51087.html.
92. Amny Radwain, "Egypt leads in cutting infant deaths," *Time*, May 16, 2007, www.time.com/time/world/article/0,8599,1621812,00.html.
93. *Ibid.*
94. "What is child survival and why does it matter?" *op. cit.*
95. "What Is the Accelerated Child Survival and Development Initiative (ACSD)?" UNICEF, www.unicefusa.org/about/faq/what-is-acsd.html.
96. Caroline Harper, Nicola Jones, Andy McKay and Jessica Espey, "Children in times of economic crisis," Overseas Development Institute, March 2009, www.odi.org.uk/resources/download/2865.pdf.
97. Melinda French Gates, "The other side of the mat: uniting for maternal, newborn and child survival and health," UNICEF, www.unicef.org/sowc08/docs/sowc08_panel_5_2.pdf.

BIBLIOGRAPHY

Books

Aronowitz, Alexis, *Human Trafficking, Human Misery: The Global Trade in Human Beings, Praeger*, 2009.
A criminologist in the Netherlands provides a scholarly examination of the worldwide problem of human trafficking.

Mam, Somaly, *The Road of Lost Innocence, Spiegel & Grau*, 2008.
A noted Cambodian children's advocate recounts how she went from being sold into prostitution as a child to founding and running a world-famous foundation that rescues children from a similar fate.

Moyo, Dambisa, *Dead Aid: Why Aid is Not Working and How there is a Better Way for Africa*, Farrar, *Straus and Giroux*, 2009.
A Zambia-born former Goldman Sachs economist argues that aid to Africa is largely ineffective and has fostered dependency, corruption and poverty.

Sachs, Jeffrey, *The End of Poverty: Economic Possibilities for our Time, Penguin*, 2006.
The celebrated Columbia University economist defends aid to developing nations and explains his plan to eliminate extreme poverty around the world by 2025.

Articles

Garrett, Laurie, "The Wrong Way to Fight Aids," *International Herald Tribune*, July 30, 2008, www.cfr.org/publication/16875/wrong_way_to_fight_aids.html.
A noted health researcher examines the HIV/AIDS "prevention versus treatment" debate.

Heilprin, John, "Obama seeks to join Global Rights of Child pact," *Associated Press*, June 23, 2009, www.cnsnews.com/news/article/49953.
Controversy is likely to accompany proposed U.S. ratification of the Convention on the Rights of the Child.

Shikwati, James, "Divorce Africa from the World Bank and IMF," *Inter Region Economic Network*, March 31, 2009, www.africanexecutive.com/modules/magazine/articles.php?article=4267.
A Kenyan economist argues that much aid to Africa benefits donors more than the recipients.

Walt, Vivienne, "Diarrhea: The Great Zinc Breakthrough," *Time*, Aug. 17, 2009, www.time.com/time/magazine/article/0,9171,1914655,00.html.
Reporter Walt describes how inexpensive zinc tablets are helping to eradicate the scourge of diarrhea in Mali.

Reports and Studies

"2009 Trafficking in Persons Report," *U.S. Department of State*, June 2009, www.state.gov/g/tip/rls/tiprpt/2009/.
The State Department's annual report details how 12.3 million adults and children worldwide are victims of human trafficking.

"Averting a Human Crisis During the Global Downturn," *The World Bank*, 2009, www.siteresources

.worldbank.org/NEWS/Resources/AvertingThe Human Crisis.pdf.
The international development institution examines how the global economic crisis is affecting foreign aid.

"Children and Conflict in a Changing World," ***UNICEF*****, April 2009, www.unicef.org/publications/files/Machel_Study_10_Year_Strategic_Review_EN_030909.pdf.**
A follow-up to a groundbreaking 1996 report on how armed conflict impacts children describes how millions still suffer due to war every year.

"Home Truths: Facing the Facts on Children, AIDS and Poverty," ***Joint Learning Initiative on Children and HIV/AIDS*****, February 2009, www.jlica.org/protected/pdf-feb09/Final%20JLICA%20Report-final.pdf.**
An international network of AIDS experts provides a thorough, wide-ranging investigation into the world's response to children affected by HIV/AIDS.

"In-Depth: Youth in Crisis: Coming of Age in the 21st century," ***IRIN*****, July 2009, www.irinnews.org/IndepthMain.aspx?IndepthId=28&ReportId=70140.**
The U.N.'s independent news agency reports on how children are being affected by issues ranging from illegal forced marriage to deteriorating education systems.

"The State of the World's Children 2009," ***UNICEF*****, January 2009, www.unicef.org/sowc09/docs/SOWC09-FullReport-EN.pdf.**
The aid agency's annual report examines maternal and neonatal health and identifies actions and interventions needed to save lives.

Harper, Caroline, ***et al.*****, "Children in Times of Economic Crisis: Past lessons, future policies,"** ***Overseas Development Institute*****, March 2009, www.odi.org.uk/resources/download/2865.pdf.**
A London-based think tank examines how the global economic downturn is affecting children around the world.

For More Information

CARE, 151 Ellis St., N.E., Atlanta, GA 30303; (800) 521-CARE; www.care.org. Global antipoverty organization.

Catholic Relief Services, 228 W. Lexington St., Baltimore, MD 21201-3413; (888) 277-7575; www.crs.org. Aids people in more than 100 countries.

ChildFund International, 2821 Emerywood Pkwy., Richmond, VA 23294; (800) 776-6767; www.childfund.org. Works in 28 countries on critical children's issues.

Coalition to Stop the Use of Child Soldiers, P.O. Box 22696, London, U.K. N4 3ZJ; (44 20) 726-0606; www.child-soldiers.org. Works to prevent governments and insurgency groups from using children as soldiers.

Defence for Children International, P.O. Box 88, CH 1211, Geneva 20, Switzerland; (41 22) 734-0558; www.defenceforchildren.org. Investigates sexual exploitation of children and other abuses.

Human Rights Watch; 350 Fifth Ave., New York, NY 10118; (212) 290-4700; www.hrw.org. Largest U.S. human-rights organization; investigates abuses around the world, including those against children.

International Labour Organization, 4, route des Morillons, CH-1211, Geneva 22, Switzerland; (41 22) 799-6111; www.ilo.org. Sets and enforces worldwide labor standards.

Save the Children, 54 Wilton Rd., Westport, CT 06880; (203) 221-4000; www.savethechildren.com. Helps children and families in 47 developing countries improve health, education and economic opportunities.

Somaly Mam Foundation, P.O. Box 4569, New York, NY 10163; (917)-388-9623; www.somaly.org. Cambodia-based foundation that rescues and rehabilitates child prostitutes in Southeast Asia.

United Nations Children's Fund (UNICEF), 3 United Nations Plaza, New York, NY 10017; (212) 326-7000; www.unicef.org. Helps poor children in 160 countries.

World Vision International, 800 West Chestnut Ave., Monrovia, CA. 91016; (626) 303-8811; www.wvi.org. Christian relief and development organization working to promote the well-being of all people — especially children.

2

Child Soldiers

Are More Aggressive Efforts Needed to Protect Children?

John Felton

AFP/Getty Images/Jack Guez

Former child soldier Ishmael Beah addresses a 2007 international conference on child soldiers. His best-selling autobiography about his horrific experiences in Sierra Leone has raised public awareness of the use of children in armed conflicts.

From *CQ Global Researcher*, July 2008.

Ishmael Beah kept on the move in the bush for months with some of his friends to escape the chaos of war-torn Sierra Leone in the early 1990s. Their greatest fear was ending up in the clutches of rebel groups who abducted young boys to join them in fighting against the government and raping, murdering and mutilating civilians. Instead, they wound up in the hands of government soldiers, which wasn't much better.

"We were told that our responsibilities as boys were to fight in this war or we would be killed," he told a U.S. Senate committee last year. "I was 13 years old."[1]

Then, recalling his first day in battle, Beah told the panel that after less than a week of training in how to use AK 47s, M16s, machine guns and rocket-propelled grenades, the adult soldiers led him and his friends into the forest to ambush rebels. "My squad had boys who were as young as 7 . . . dragging guns that were taller than them as we walked to the frontlines."

At first, "I couldn't shoot my gun," he remembered. "But as I lay there watching my friends getting killed . . . I began shooting. Something inside me shifted and I lost compassion for anyone. After that day, killing became as easy as drinking water." For the next two years, Beah said, "all I did was take drugs, fight and kill or be killed."

Children always have been among the first victims of warfare, usually as innocent bystanders. Indeed, in most conflicts, more women and children die — from a combination of disease, starvation or violence — than soldiers. Children also have been pressed into service occasionally as fighters, often as the last, desperate resort of losing armies.[2]

Dozens of Countries Use Child Soldiers

Tens of thousands of children under age 18 — some as young as 5 — serve as soldiers or spies for rebel groups, government-linked paramilitary militias or government armed forces. Most are recruited or conscripted in Africa and Asia. Government armed forces in several industrialized countries induct under-18-year-olds but don't use them in combat.

Countries That Use Child Soldiers
(Between April 2004-October 2007)

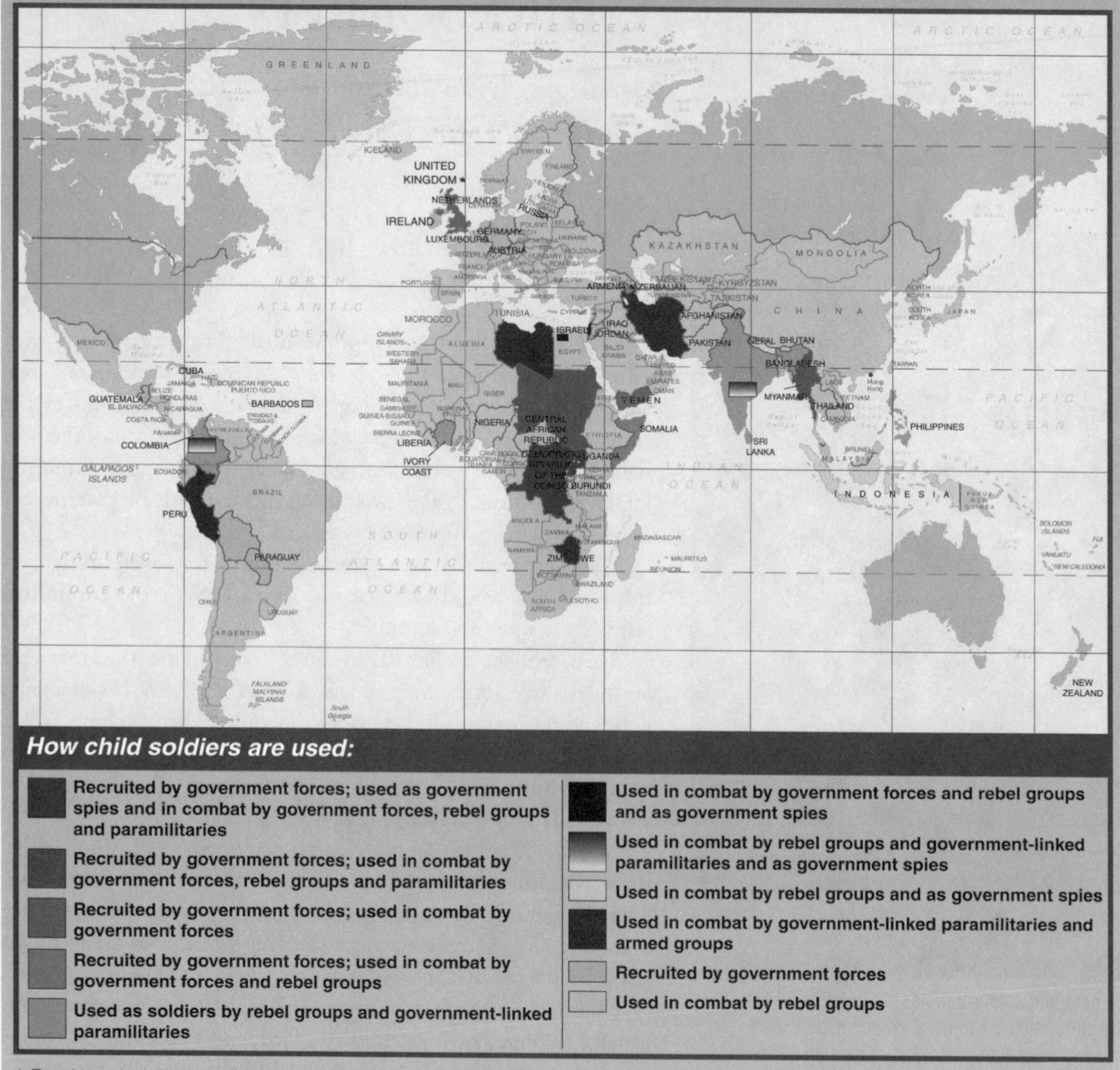

* Deployed children under 18 to Iraq, where they were exposed to risk of hostilities.

Source: "Child Soldiers: Global Report 2008," Coalition to Stop the Use of Child Soldiers

Laws and Resolutions Dealing with Child Soldiers

Several United Nations treaties make it illegal under international law for governments or rebel groups to recruit and use children in warfare, including:

- **Additional Protocols to the Geneva Conventions (1977)** — Establishes age 15 as the minimum for participation in armed combat by government forces or nongovernmental groups; applies both to international and domestic conflicts.
- **Convention on the Rights of the Child (1989)** — Prohibits the recruitment and use of children under 15 by armed groups; a compromise is reached after objection by the United States, Britain and the Netherlands to an 18-year-old standard. The United States and Somalia are the only countries that have not ratified it.[1]
- **Rome Statute (1998)** — Creates the International Criminal Court and defines as a war crime the recruitment or use in combat of children under 15.
- **Worst Forms of Child Labour Convention (1999)** — Adopted by member states of the International Labor Organization; defines a child as anyone under 18 and says child labor includes "forced or compulsory recruitment of children for use in armed conflict."
- **Optional Protocol to the Convention on the Rights of the Child (2000)** — Raises to 18 the minimum age for using children in conflicts, prohibits compulsory recruitment by governments or non-state groups of anyone under 18; allows governments to recruit 16- and 17-year-olds for military service if the recruitment is voluntary and approved by the parents or legal guardians. The United States ratified it in 2002.[2]

Since 1999, the U.N. Security Council has adopted six resolutions pertaining to children in armed conflict:

- **Resolutions 1261 (1999) and 1314 (2000)** — Calls on all parties to respect international law concerning the protection of children, including girls, in armed conflict.
- **Resolution 1379 (2001)** — Asks the U.N. secretary-general to create a blacklist of those who recruit child soldiers.
- **Resolutions 1460 (2003) and 1539 (2004)** — Calls for children to be included in programs designed to help former soldiers disarm, demobilize and reintegrate into society; suggests implementation of country-specific, targeted measures.
- **Resolution 1612 (2005)** — Creates a mechanism for monitoring and disseminating information on six types of child-rights violations; creates a Security Council Working Group to recommend measures on a per-situation basis; urges those using children in conflict to establish action plans for their release and reintegration.

---

[1] Available at www.unhchr.ch/html/menu2/6/crc/treaties/crc.htm.

[2] Available at www.unhchr.ch/html/menu2/6/crc/treaties/opac.htm.

But in recent times tens of thousands of children like Beah have been actively and regularly used in warfare. Since the closing decades of the 20th century, rebel groups and even government armies routinely have used children in combat or supporting roles throughout Africa, Asia, Europe and Latin America.

Many of these children were forced to participate in or witness acts almost beyond comprehension, including:

- The 1994 genocide in Rwanda during which at least 800,000 people were slaughtered within a few weeks, many hacked to death with machetes;
- Sierra Leone's civil war in which children were forced to kill their parents and cut off the hands and feet of civilians;
- Indiscriminate guerrilla attacks on noncombatants in Colombia and Sri Lanka;
- The forced murders of their own family members and neighbors, perpetrated at the direction of the Lord's Resistance Army (LRA), a rebel group led by fanatical recluse Joseph Kony in northern Uganda and neighboring countries.
- The use of children, in some cases preteens, as suicide bombers by several groups, including the Tamil

19 African Commanders Charged with Using Child Soldiers

A total of 19 former and current commanders — all from Africa — have been charged with enlisting children under age 15 as soldiers. Four are serving time in prison after being convicted. Six are on trial, while six have been charged but never captured. Most were accused of other war crimes as well, including murder, rape, abductions, forced labor and looting. No commanders from other countries have been charged for using child soldiers.

Country	Commander	Military Group*	Status
Democratic Republic of the Congo			
Lubanga	Thomas Lubanga Dyilo	Union of Congolese Patriots	International Criminal Court trial indefinitely suspended 6/2008; his release is pending appeal
Katanga	Germain Katanga	Patriotic Forces of Resistance	ICC pre-trial hearings began 5/27/2008
	Mathieu Ngudjolo Chui	Front for National Integration	ICC pre-trial hearings began 5/27/2008
	Kyungu Mutanga	Mai-Mai	In Congolese custody
	Jean-Pierre Biyoyo	Mudundu 40	Sentenced to 5 years by Congolese military tribunal 3/2006; escaped
	Bosco Ntaganda	Union of Congolese Patriots	ICC warrants issued 8/22/2006
Liberia			
Taylor	Charles Taylor	Former president, Liberia	Trial continues at Special Court of Sierra Leone
Sierra Leone			
	Alex Tamba Brima	Armed Forces Revolutionary Council	Convicted, serving 50 years
	Brima Bazzy Kamara	Armed Forces Revolutionary Council	Convicted, serving 45 years
	Santigie Borbor Kanu	Armed Forces Revolutionary Council	Convicted, serving 50 years
	Allieu Kondewa	Civil Defense Forces	Convicted, 8-year sentence increased to 20 years, 5/2008
	Issa Hassan Sesay Morris Kallon Augustine Gbao	Revolutionary United Front Revolutionary United Front Revolutionary United Front	Joint trial in Special Court of Sierra Leone expected to conclude in August
Uganda			
Kony	Joseph Kony	Lord's Resistance Army	ICC warrant issued 7/8/2005
	Vincent Otti	Lord's Resistance Army	Reportedly killed in 2007
	Raska Lukwiya	Lord's Resistance Army	Killed, 2006
Otti	Okot Odiambo	Lord's Resistance Army	ICC warrant issued 7/8/2005
	Dominic Ongwen	Lord's Resistance Army	ICC warrant issued 7/8/2005

* The accused were serving with these groups at the time of their alleged crimes. Some are in other groups now.

Sources: United Nations; Human Rights Watch; Special Court of Sierra Leone, www.sc-sl.org/RUF-Casesummary.html

Tigers in Sri Lanka, the Taliban in Afghanistan and the Palestinian groups Hamas and Islamic Jihad.

Thousands of other children raided and burned villages, shouldered automatic weapons in combat or served as porters, spies or decoys. The girls were often forced to satisfy the sexual appetites of the guerrillas.

The U.N.'s Special Representative for Children and Armed Conflict, Radhika Coomaraswamy, says there are at least 250,000 child soldiers worldwide.[3] But other experts say the nature of civil conflicts makes it difficult to compile accurate records.

"It's absolutely impossible to determine the number of child soldiers with any accuracy," says Victoria Forbes Adam, executive director of the London-based Coalition to Stop the Use of Child Soldiers. "We think it is in the many tens of thousands, but that is a complete guesstimate." Leaders of armed groups, particularly rebels fighting in the bush, generally refuse to open their rosters to international inspection, she explains, and "children come in and out of conflicts, they die of illness, they die of injuries, or they may simply be missing from their communities."

However, many more children are recruited by official national armies than by rebel groups, according to some studies. About 500,000 under-18-year-olds serve at any given time in government armies and paramilitary groups in about 50 countries, according to P.W. Singer, a senior fellow at the Brookings Institution think tank in Washington, D.C., who has written widely on the problem. (*See map, p. 30.*) Most serve in reserve units until they are called into combat, Singer writes.[4]

The United Nations and human rights groups have accused some countries of forcibly recruiting children for their armies. The military government of Myanmar, for example, allegedly rewards recruiters with money and bags of rice for luring children into the army, according to Human Rights Watch (HRW).[5]

The presence of children in combat can make conflicts more persistent because conflicts involving children "are easier to start, more difficult to end, and more likely to resume," says Singer. Children are so readily available, cheap and expendable — from the viewpoint of leaders of armed groups — that using them can be an incentive to start conflicts and keep fighting even if success seems futile, he says.

AFP/Getty Images/Guido Benschop

Former Liberian President Charles Taylor, in handcuffs, arrives in the Netherlands in 2006 for his war crimes trial before the Special Court of Sierra Leone in The Hague. Taylor is accused of sponsoring and aiding rebels who carried out murders, sexual slavery, mutilations and the conscription of child soldiers during the civil war in Sierra Leone. The trial continues.

Defining a "child soldier" is a complex issue. Who is a child? And who is a soldier? As set out in several U.N. treaties since World War II, a child is anyone under 18. The most recent legal definition is contained in the 2000 Optional Protocol to the Convention on the Rights of the Child on the Involvement of Children in Armed Conflict — known as the "Optional Protocol." It allows governments to recruit 16- and 17-year-olds but prohibits them from serving in combat. The United States and 25 other countries recruit under-18-year-olds into their armed services, according to the Coalition to Stop the Use of Child Soldiers.[6] Under the Optional Protocol, "non-state actors" such as rebel groups, may not recruit anyone under 18.

But many rebel leaders around the world either ignore the prohibition or claim not to know the ages of their recruits. "They say, 'The children come to us without any birth certificates, so how are we to know how old they are?'" says U.N. Special Representative Coomaraswamy,

Former Girl Soldiers Get Little Aid

Many programs often ignore their needs

When she was 12 years old, Lucy Aol was abducted by the Lord's Resistance Army (LRA), a rebel group in northern Uganda. They made her walk several hundred miles to a hideout in southern Sudan.

"We were used like slaves," she recently recalled. "We used to work in the fields or collect firewood from 7 in the morning until 5 in the evening, and we were given no food. If you made a mistake or refused, they would beat us," she said. "The three girls who were taken from my village with me were beaten to death."

A year after she was abducted, Aol was forced to become the "wife" of a rebel commander. She and her "husband" later fled the rebel group together, but he was killed, and she discovered she was pregnant, and at age 16 she gave birth to a daughter. Now 21, Aol is studying environmental health at a college in Uganda.[1]

Similar stories could be told by thousands of girls in recent decades. Up to 40 percent of the children serving in some armed groups are girls.[2] A 2004 study found that girls served in 38 regional conflicts between 1990 and 2003 and were fighters in all but four.[3] Yet, the plight of young girls forced to join armed groups still isn't on the radar screens of many governments and world leaders — or even those working to reintegrate former male child soldiers into society.

Only in the last few years have aid programs taken girls' needs into consideration, and they still are not being given as much attention or help as the boys. Many girls also avoid official postwar reintegration programs for fear of being stigmatized.

"Boys might be called rebels, but girls are not just rebels. They may have been raped, they may feel spiritually polluted or unclean, and if they are mothers they may be called the mothers of rebel children, and so they are isolated," says Michael Wessells, a professor of psychology at Randolph-Macon College in Virginia who has aided former child soldiers in Africa and Asia for three decades. "But all they want is to be like other children."

"In many parts of the world, if you are female and you're not a virgin, you are not marriageable," says Neil Boothy, a professor at Columbia University who has developed and studied aid programs for former child soldiers for two decades. "And marriage remains the economic pathway for most women in most societies."

Only a few postwar integration programs, however, provide vocational training for both girls and boys. One exception is a program in northern Uganda run by local organizations supported by the Anglican Church. It allows both girls and boys who had been in armed groups to attend a technical school where they learn basic business skills and agricultural trades, such as beekeeping.

who has negotiated with many rebel leaders in Africa and Asia.

Perhaps the most precise definition of a child soldier was produced at a conference of scholars and representatives of various child-protection agencies, organized in 1997 by the United Nations Children's Fund (UNICEF). Convening in Cape Town, South Africa, the group developed the so-called Cape Town Principles, which define a child soldier as anyone under 18 "who is part of any kind of regular or irregular armed force" in any capacity, including cooks, porters, messengers and non-family members accompanying such groups. Also included were girls recruited for sexual purposes and those forced into marriage.[7]

However, David M. Rosen, a professor of anthropology and law at Fairleigh Dickinson University in Madison, New Jersey, argues that the age "when the young are fit to be warriors" varies from culture to culture.[8] In some societies, he wrote in a provocative 2005 book, "young people are deliberately socialized into highly aggressive behavior, and both individual and collective violence are highly esteemed." Other societies, he added, put more emphasis "on peaceful resolution of disputes." Rosen contends the United Nations and international humanitarian organizations have used the subject of child soldiers to advance their own agendas, including, in his view, protecting post-colonial governments in Africa and Asia against internal rebellion and denouncing

A recent study of former LRA girl soldiers focused on several thousand girls and young women who had been forced to "marry" rebel commanders.[4] The study said the presence of forced wives in rebel units "served to bolster fighter morale and support the systems which perpetuate cycles of raiding, looting, killing, and abduction." Thus, says study co-author Dyan Mazurana, forcing girls to become commanders' wives is an integral part of how many armed groups conduct their business — not an incidental factor that can be ignored by governments and aid groups in their postwar negotiations with rebels.

Reuters/Ahmed Jadallah

A Palestinian policeman teaches a girl how to use an AK-47 assault rifle in a Gaza refugee camp in southern Gaza Strip. Palestinian extremist groups reportedly have used children as suicide bombers.

The leaders of local communities often argue that the best way to deal with the forced wives of rebels after a war "is for them to stay with their captors," she continues. But the young women overwhelmingly reject that idea.

Grace Akallo — abducted by the LRA in 1996 but who escaped after seven months — says she "can't imagine" any girl wanting to stay with her captors. "We were all so anxious to get away from them, we would do anything to get away from them," says Akallo, now a college student in the United States.

Complicating the situation, says Wessells, are girls who joined armed groups voluntarily to avoid abusive parents, to escape arranged marriages or in hopes of finding a better life. These girls are often more reluctant than abducted girls to return to their communities after the war, so they are unlikely to seek help from official aid programs, Wessells says.

[1] "In the Tragedy of Child-soldiering in Africa, a Girl's Story Finds a Happy Ending," The Associated Press, Aug. 25, 2007.

[2] Hilde F. Johnson, deputy executive director, UNICEF, address to the Ministerial Meeting on Children and Armed Conflict, Oct. 1, 2007, a follow-up to the Paris Principles and Paris Commitments, formulated in February 2007, www.unicef.org/protection/files/Final-Paris-Principles-1Oct07-HFJ-speech.pdf.

[3] Susan McKay and Dyan Mazurana, "Where are the Girls? Girls in Fighting Forces in Northern Uganda, Sierra Leone, and Mozambique. Their Lives During and After War," International Centre for Human Rights and Democracy, Montreal, 2004, pp. 22, 25.

[4] Kristopher Carlson and Dyan Mazurana, "Forced Marriage within the Lord's Resistance Army, Uganda," Feinstein International Center, Tufts University, May 2008.

Israel for its attacks on Palestinians while ignoring terrorist attacks perpetrated by Palestinian child soldiers.

Children end up in armies and rebel groups for a variety of reasons, depending on the circumstances. All too often, children are abducted from their villages or displaced-person camps or — like Beah — are swept up by government armies. Leaders of armed groups often use narcotics to dull the fears of their child soldiers or to stimulate them for combat. Beah's experiences were similar to those of Albert, a former child soldier who told Amnesty International he was forced to join a rebel group in the Democratic Republic of the Congo when he was 15.

"[T]hey would give us 'chanvre' [cannabis] and force us to kill people to toughen us up," he recalled. "Sometimes they brought us women and girls to rape. . . . They would beat us if we refused."[9]

Many young children join armed groups voluntarily because their families can't support them, or they're lured by the prospect of carrying a gun and wearing a snazzy uniform. Others are enticed by recruiters who make extravagant promises to the children and their families that they have no intention of keeping.

The child soldier problem has captured the world's attention intermittently over the past two decades — most often when children are found to engage in atrocities. Conflicts in the West African nations of Liberia and Sierra Leone during the 1990s seemed to represent the quintessential use of child soldiers in brutal circumstances.

Abducting Girls Is Most Widespread in Africa

Girls were abducted into either official armed forces or non-state armed groups in 28 countries between 1990 and 2003 — 11 of them in Africa.

Countries Where Girls Were Abducted into Armed Groups (1990-2003)

Africa	***Americas***	*Sri Lanka*
Angola	*Colombia*	*Timor-Leste*
Burundi	*El Salvador*	
Democratic Republic of the Congo	*Guatemala*	***Europe***
Ethiopia	*Peru*	*Federal Republic of Yugoslavia*
Liberia		*Germany*
Mozambique	***Asia***	*Northern Ireland*
Rwanda	*Myanmar*	
Sierra Leone	*Cambodia*	***Middle East***
Somalia	*India*	*Iraq*
Sudan	*Indonesia*	*Turkey*
Uganda	*Nepal*	
	Philippines	

Source: Susan McKay and Dyan Mazurana, "Where are the girls?" Rights & Democracy, March 2004

In Liberia, Charles Taylor rose to power at the head of a rebel army composed substantially of young fighters whom he sent out to rape, pillage and murder. In neighboring Sierra Leone, the Revolutionary United Front (RUF) — a rebel group armed and supported by Taylor — forced its child soldiers to mutilate victims in one of the most depraved civil conflicts in modern times. These wars spawned other conflicts in the region, notably in Guinea and the Côte d'Ivoire, sometimes involving child soldiers who crossed borders to keep fighting because it was the only life they knew.

Beah, who was fortunate enough to be removed from the Sierra Leone conflict by UNICEF, recounted his story in the gripping 2007 bestseller, *A Long Way Gone: Memoirs of a Boy Soldier.*[10] The book, and Beah's engaging media appearances, quickly drew more public attention to the child soldier issue than stacks of U.N. reports and resolutions had done.

Besides being an appealing advocate for child soldiers, Beah, now in his late-20s, shows that child soldiers can return to a normal life once they're removed from conflict and receive appropriate assistance from groups specializing in protecting children. Admittedly, as a ward of the U.N. system for several years, Beah had opportunities few other former soldiers enjoy. Even so, child-protection experts emphasize that even after committing heinous acts or suffering deep psychological or physical injuries, former child soldiers can be rehabilitated.

As governments and international organizations around the globe wrestle with the problem of child soldiers, here are some of the questions being addressed:

Does "naming and shaming" help prevent the use of child soldiers?

In his most recent report on children and armed conflict, released in January, United Nations Secretary-General Ban Ki-moon identified 40 governments or rebel groups, in 13 conflicts, that recruited and used child soldiers.[11] This report was a key component of the U.N.'s policy of publicly identifying those who recruit and use child soldiers — and condemning them for it. The U.N. has been in the "naming and shaming" business since November 2001, when the Security Council adopted Resolution 1379, asking the secretary-general to identify governments and groups that engaged in the practice.[12]

Secretary-General Kofi Annan submitted his first such report in 2002, and subsequent reports have been filed each year.

Human-rights advocacy groups, such as Amnesty International and HRW, also have made naming and shaming an important part of their campaigns to draw attention to the use and abuse of child soldiers. These groups issue their own reports on specific conflicts, and a collaboration of such groups, the Coalition to Stop the Use of Child soldiers, periodically publishes a comprehensive assessment of the use of child soldiers worldwide. The coalition's most recent report, "Child Soldiers Global Report 2008," was published in May.[13]

In his 2007 report, Secretary-General Ban said naming offending parties "has proven to have a deterrent effect" and has allowed the U.N. and other agencies to maintain political pressure and take action against those who are "persistent violators of child rights."[14]

U.N. Special Representative Coomaraswamy says it's also significant that the child soldier problem is the only "thematic issue" regularly addressed by the Security Council — as opposed to specific crises in individual countries. The council has established a "working group" that meets every two months to discuss the secretary-general's reports. On behalf of the Security Council, the working group condemns those who continue using child soldiers and praises those who agree to stop the practice.

"People do listen to the Security Council," Coomaraswamy says. "They may not always act in ways we wish they would, but they do listen, and this should not be dismissed."

Jo Becker, child rights advocacy director of HRW, agrees naming and shaming has had some impact, but mostly on governments. For example, she notes, governments in Chad, the Democratic Republic of the Congo and Myanmar have pledged to stop using child soldiers due to international pressure. And while these and other governments haven't always kept their promises, at least they have taken the first step of forswearing their use, she says.

Some rebels have responded to international pressure, such as the Tamil Tigers of Sri Lanka, who "promote themselves as a reputable group and rely very heavily on contributions from the international diaspora of Tamils," Becker points out. According to the U.N., the group has released some child soldiers — but certainly not all of them — and continued recruiting children well into 2007, although in lower numbers than in previous years.[15]

However, leaders of many other groups — such as Kony, of the Lord's Resistance Army — appear to have little or no regard for how they are seen internationally and are not swayed by having their names published in U.N. reports. "Kony's name was already mud and could hardly get any worse," says Christopher Blattman, an assistant professor of political science and economics at Yale University who has done extensive research on Kony.

An even more skeptical view comes from Singer at Brookings, who says most of those who use child soldiers see it as a purely pragmatic rather than a moral issue. "You can't shame the shameless," Singer says, "but you can create some sense of accountability by figuring out what their interests are, what drives their calculations and how you can alter their calculations." Prosecuting and imposing sanctions are more effective parts of a "cost structure" that can be imposed on those who use child soldiers, Singer says.

Some experts argue that naming and shaming can be useful in some cases but counterproductive in others. "If you are . . . trying to use communication and negotiations channels [with rebels] to get the release of child soldiers, it can be undermined by strident or hostile criticism of the group," says Michael Wessells, a professor of psychology at Randolph-Macon College in Virginia, who has worked with programs to aid child soldiers for nearly three decades. "The door closes, and the lives of children are damaged even further."

For instance, Blattman says pending International Criminal Court (ICC) indictments of Kony and four of his commanders may have helped persuade Kony to authorize aides to enter into peace negotiations with the Ugandan government in hopes the indictments would be lifted. But the court's insistence on maintaining the indictments "could now be an impediment to peace because it doesn't offer them [Kony and his commanders] much of an option," Blattman says. If Kony faces a choice of prison or lifetime exile, he probably will choose exile and continued conflict, Blattman adds, prolonging his two-decade-long war well into the future.

Nevertheless, Wessells says, it is "profoundly important to make clear that it is not OK for leaders of armed groups to say they can do whatever they want." Reflecting concerns about the potential negative consequences of naming and shaming, an international forum of experts on child soldiers, meeting in Switzerland in 2006, called for more research on the effectiveness of naming and shaming.[16]

Should the United States prosecute alleged child soldiers detained at Guantánamo Bay?

An alleged terrorist captured in Afghanistan when he was 15 could be the first person tried for war crimes

AFP/Getty Images/Ravi Manandhar

Girl soldiers serve with Maoist rebels near Kathmandu. According to a recent U.N. report, the group refuses to release its child soldiers on a regular basis despite signing an historic peace pact with the Nepalese government.

committed as a child. Omar Ahmed Khadr, now 21, is facing trial by a military commission after spending nearly six years in prison at the U.S. military base at Guantánamo Bay, Cuba.

The son of a financier for the al Qaeda Islamic terrorist group, Khadr is charged with murder, spying against the United States and other crimes. He allegedly threw a grenade that killed a U.S. soldier and injured others in Afghanistan on July 27, 2002.[17] Khadr was seriously wounded during the fighting and was transferred to Guantánamo in November 2002, where he was placed under the jurisdiction of the U.S. military commission created after the Sept. 11, 2001, terrorist attacks.

The commission in late 2007 and early 2008 rejected several motions filed by Khadr's attorneys challenging the proceedings, including one contending Khadr had been illegally recruited by his father into working as a translator at al Qaeda training camps in Afghanistan. Col. Peter Brownback, the commission's judge, dismissed that motion on April 30 on the grounds that Congress did not set a minimum age for defendants when it authorized the military commissions in 2006.[18] Khadr's trial is scheduled to begin in October.

HRW and other groups have denounced the government's handling of Khadr, noting that he was treated as an adult despite his age when he allegedly committed the crimes and has been held in "prolonged" periods of solitary confinement for more than five years.[19] In an *amicus curiae* brief submitted to the commission on Jan. 18 on behalf of 23 members of Canada's parliament and 55 legal scholars from Canada, Sarah H. Paoletti, clinical supervisor and lecturer at the Transnational Legal Clinic at the University of Pennsylvania School of Law, argued that Khadr's prosecution "is in stark opposition to longstanding and well-established precedent under international law protecting the rights of children unlawfully recruited into armed conflict."[20]

Paoletti's brief said recent treaties and agreements suggest that former child soldiers should be offered rehabilitation and reintegration back into their communities rather than prosecution. For instance, the 1998 Rome Statute, which created the ICC, denied the court jurisdiction over anyone younger than 18 at the time of the alleged crime. This ban does not apply to courts or tribunals established by national governments.[21]

Similarly, a set of "principles" negotiated by representatives of countries and nongovernmental organizations in Paris last year suggested that former child soldiers should not be prosecuted but rather treated as "victims of offences against international law, not only as perpetrators. They must be treated in accordance with international law in a framework of restorative justice and social rehabilitation, consistent with international law, which offers children special protection through numerous agreements and principles."[22]

David M. Crane, former chief prosecutor at the U.N.-backed Special Tribunal for Sierra Leone, is one of the most prominent opponents of Khadr's prosecution. He says he decided not to prosecute child soldiers — even those who had committed "horrendous crimes" — because adults were the responsible parties. "Even if a child willingly goes along, he really has no choice in the matter, and this certainly appears to be true in the case of Khadr," who was under the influence of his father, Crane says.

The U.N.'s Coomaraswamy has appealed to the United States to halt the prosecution, saying "children should not be prosecuted for war crimes." She is pleased that Khadr's military lawyers are fighting the prosecution "tooth and nail."

The Pentagon has defended its prosecution on the grounds that none of the international treaties dealing with children and armed conflict expressly forbid a national government from prosecuting alleged child soldiers. In fact, a prosecution motion in the case argued that the Optional Protocol obligated the government to take legal action against Khadr. Al Qaeda itself violated that treaty by recruiting Khadr, the prosecution said, so dismissing the charges against him — as his defense lawyers argued — "would effectively condone that alleged violation by allowing Khadr to escape all liability for his actions and would further incentivize such actions."[23]

In another government defense of the Khadr case, the Pentagon official in charge of detention policy, Sandra L. Hodgkinson, told a U.N. committee on May 22 that the U.S. detention of Khadr and other juveniles in Afghanistan and Iraq reduces the threat that they will be used to carry out suicide bombings and other attacks. "If there is a sense that juveniles cannot be removed from the battlefield, there is a valid concern that the tactic of recruiting children will be further utilized against coalition forces and innocent civilians in Iraq and Afghanistan," she said.[24]

Although Khadr is a Canadian citizen by birth, Canada has refused to intervene on the grounds that he has been charged with a serious crime. Even so, the Canadian Supreme Court on May 23 denounced the early stages of the U.S. handling of his case. In a unanimous opinion, the court said U.S. legal processes at Guantánamo in 2002-03 "constituted a clear violation of fundamental human rights protected by international law." Moreover, the court said the Canadian government erred in turning over to U.S. authorities information about interviews with Khadr conducted by the Canadian intelligence service in 2003; Khadr's defense lawyers were entitled to see some of these documents, the court said.[25]

In a follow-up to that decision, a lower-court judge in Canada ruled on June 25 that Khadr's lawyers could be given a document and recordings describing alleged mistreatment of him by U.S. officials at the Guantánamo prison in 2004.

Another alleged child soldier held at Guantánamo, Mohammed Jawad, was captured in Afghanistan in December 2002 when he was either 16 or 17 and charged last January with attempted murder and intentionally causing bodily harm. The military alleges he threw a hand grenade into a vehicle carrying two U.S. soldiers and their Afghan interpreter.[26] Jawad's case is still in the early stages of consideration by a military commission at Guantánamo.

Hearings on both the Khadr and Jawad cases continued in mid-June despite a major Supreme Court ruling on June 12 that Guantánamo prisoners could challenge their detentions in U.S. federal court. The decision didn't directly go to the actions of the military commissions, but defense lawyers already have said they will use it to challenge a broad range of government actions concerning the detainees.

Should Congress pass legislation to combat the use of child soldiers overseas?

The child soldier issue has reached the U.S. Congress, which is considering two bills intended to put some force behind American criticisms of the use of child soldiers. The House-passed Child Soldier Prevention Act would bar U.S. military aid or arms sales to governments that recruit or use child soldiers (defined as children under 16 voluntarily recruited into an official army or under 18 forced to join an army). The U.S. president could waive the ban by declaring that it is in America's national interest to provide aid or sell weapons to governments that use child soldiers.

The Senate, meanwhile, passed the Child Soldiers Accountability Act, which would make it a crime under U.S. law for anyone, anywhere, to recruit a child under 15 into an armed group or use a child in combat. The measure also prohibits entry into the United States of anyone who recruits or uses child soldiers under 15.

Sen. Richard L. Durbin, D-Ill., one of the bill's sponsors, said it would help "ensure that the war criminals who recruit or use children as soldiers will not find safe haven in our country and will allow the U.S. government to hold these individuals accountable for their actions."[27] Senate aides say there has been no active opposition so far to either measure.

The House-passed measure potentially could prove controversial, however, because the national police force in Afghanistan — a key U.S. ally — has been accused of forcibly recruiting children under 18. The State Department cited the allegations in its 2007 human rights report on the country.[28]

Afghanistan was scheduled to receive about $8 million in military aid in fiscal 2008, according to the Center for Defense Information, a liberal think tank in Washington.

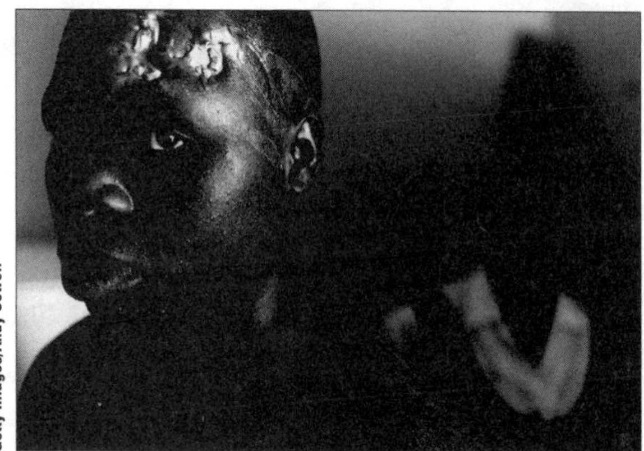

Getty Images/Andy Sewell

Simon, now 19, spent eight years as a child soldier with the Lord's Resistance Army (LRA) after being abducted from his home in northern Uganda. During that time he saw hundreds of people killed, including some who were hacked to death in front of him, and he was forced to kill other child abductees who tried to escape. Besides his psychological wounds, he is struggling to recover form a head wound received during combat. The LRA is led by Joseph Kony, a notorious, self-styled prophet who was indicted by the International Criminal Court in 2005 but remains at large.

The center said the bill could affect military aid to six other countries unless the president waived the provisions. The center compared the State Department's 2007 human rights reports — which dealt with child soldiers for the first time — and the administration's allocations of military aid as well as its arms sales to foreign countries. The six other countries that used child soldiers in some official capacity while receiving U.S. military aid were Chad, the Democratic Republic of the Congo, Somalia, Sri Lanka, Sudan and Uganda. Most of the aid programs were small and included only military training — generally considered the stepping stone to a broader relationship between the U.S. and foreign militaries.[29]

Sen. Durbin said the bill "would ensure that U.S. taxpayer dollars are not used to support this abhorrent practice by government or government-sanctioned military and paramilitary organizations." The United States could continue military aid if the president chose to do so, Durbin added, "but it would be used only to remedy the problem by helping countries successfully demobilize their child soldiers and professionalize their forces."[30]

Neither of the two measures has encountered any formal opposition in either chamber of Congress. Although the Bush administration has taken no formal position on either bill, congressional aides and lobbyists favoring the proposals say they expect the White House to oppose them as a matter of course because legislation limiting a president's flexibility in foreign policy is generally resisted.

BACKGROUND

Child Armies Proliferate

An explosion of civil conflicts around the globe during the last half of the 20th century was accompanied by several developments that ensured children would bear much of the burden of war. Chief among them was the invention of simple-to-use, lightweight weapons — especially automatic rifles and rocket launchers. Even a 10-year-old can carry and use the world's most ubiquitous weapon: the Kalashnikov assault rifle, or AK-47.

After the collapse of communism in Eastern Europe and the Soviet Union between 1989-91, millions of Kalashnikovs and other Soviet weapons fell into the hands of unscrupulous arms dealers, who sold them to rebel leaders and warlords around the world. They often paid with narcotics, diamonds or other resources plundered from their own countries.

Rebels claiming to be fighting for social justice or a host of other causes found they could easily fill their ranks with children. An official of the Chadian military explained their advantages: "Child soldiers are ideal because they don't complain, they don't expect to be paid and if you tell them to kill, they kill."[31]

Children also are easy to abduct or force into military service, especially if they live in unprotected villages or communal facilities, such as refugee camps, where they are often protected only by mothers and unarmed humanitarian workers. "All the boys in the village were asked to join the army," a former child soldier told author Singer. "There was no way out. If I left the village I would get killed by the rebels who would think that I was a spy. On the other hand, if I stayed in the village and refused to join the army, I wouldn't be given any food and would eventually be thrown out, which was as good as being dead."[32]

Social and economic conditions in many poor countries, such as poverty and lack of educational and job opportunities, make children susceptible to the call of combat. "Demagogues, warlords, criminals and others

CHRONOLOGY

1980s *Civil conflicts in Africa and Asia begin to use children in combat.*

1983 Tamil Tiger insurgency erupts in Sri Lanka. The group later gains notoriety for its use of suicide bombers and thousands of child soldiers.

1987 Joseph Kony's Lord's Resistance Army in Uganda begins abducting children for use as soldiers.

1989 U.N. General Assembly adopts Convention on the Rights of the Child, which establishes 15 as the minimum age for recruiting children into armed forces. Eventually, 190 countries ratify the treaty; the United States refuses to ratify it.

1990s *Genocide in Rwanda focuses global attention on child soldiers.*

1994 Thousands of children take part in Rwandan genocide.

1996 UNICEF's Landmark "Impact of Armed Conflict on Children" report focuses international attention on child soldiers.

1997 Zaire's dictator Mobutu Sese Seko is ousted by Laurent Kabila's rebel group, which uses several thousand child soldiers. Kabila's backers in Rwanda and Uganda later turn against him, setting off a war using tens of thousands of child soldiers. . . . Ugandan diplomat Olara Otunu becomes the U.N.'s first Special Representative for Children and Armed Conflict.

1998 Human-rights organizations form Coalition to Stop the Use of Child Soldiers.

1999 First U.N. resolution on child soldiers, Resolution 1261, condemns abduction and recruitment of children for combat.

2000s *U.N. steps up efforts to combat use of child soldiers.*

2000 U.N. "Optional Protocol" sets 18 as the minimum age for children in combat and bars non-state armed groups from recruiting or using children under 18.

2001 U.N. Security Council asks secretary-general to identify parties recruiting or using children in armed conflicts.

2002 U.S. Senate ratifies Optional Protocol.

2003 U.N. Secretary-General Kofi Annan submits first report listing groups recruiting and using children in armed conflicts. Security Council asks secretary-general to report on actions being taken by armed groups cited in his report to stop the use of children.

2004 Security Council calls for "action plans" to stop use of child soldiers.

2005 Security Council establishes monitoring and reporting mechanism on children and armed conflict. . . . International Criminal Court (ICC) issues war crimes arrest warrants for Lord's Resistance Army leader Kony and four commanders for forced recruitment and use of child soldiers in Uganda.

2006 ICC charges Thomas Lubanga Dyilo, leader of the rebel Union of Congolese Patriots, with using child soldiers.

2007 UNICEF and the French government sponsor a conference in Paris on preventing the use of child soldiers and aiding children in post-conflict situations. . . . *A Long Way Gone: Memoirs of a Boy Soldier*, by Ishmael Beah, becomes worldwide bestseller and focuses new attention on child soldiers. . . . Four former militia leaders are convicted by a U.N.-backed special tribunal on charges that they recruited and used child soldiers during the war in Sierra Leone — the first time an international court has addressed the use of child soldiers. . . . Former Liberian President Charles Taylor goes on trial at the Special Court of Sierra Leone (at The Hague) on 11 charges of war crimes and crimes against humanity, including conscripting children into the armed forces and using them in combat.

2008 Cease-fire agreement signed in January offers a potential end to fighting in eastern Congo, where the use of child soldiers is common. . . . ICC temporarily halts its first-ever case, against Congolese rebel leader Lubanga because of a dispute over the handling of confidential evidence.

Former Child Soldiers Can Become Good Citizens

But reintegration must be handled carefully by aid agencies

"My parents ran away when they saw me. I had to follow them; they thought I would abduct them."

— Former girl child soldier, 15[1]

"We feel different because of the way other children look at us; it seems as if we are not children born from this land. They view us as though we come from a different place."

— Former boy child soldier, 17[2]

For many child soldiers, the end of a war can be nearly as traumatic as the conflict itself. Some cannot remember anything but warfare and have little concept of what normal civilian life is like. Others suffered serious physical wounds, and most endure at least short-term psychological problems, and sometimes drug addiction.

Returning child soldiers often find that one or both parents have been killed or may have moved elsewhere. Parents also are sometimes reluctant to accept a returning child whom they no longer know or understand, especially if the child was forced to commit atrocities — sometimes even against his own family.

Because their schooling has been interrupted, most former child soldiers have few job skills appropriate to civilian society. Governments and international aid agencies often include provisions for child soldiers in official programs to disarm, demobilize and reintegrate rebel fighters. But several experts in the field say many of these so-called DDR programs are underfunded, badly managed or lack appropriate resources to meet the special needs of children.

Many researchers consider economic opportunity as the greatest need faced by former child soldiers. "When they go home, their struggles are going to be largely economic — as much, if not more so, than mental health or some other concerns," says Neil Boothby, director of the Program on Forced Migration and Health at Columbia University. "They need to learn how to make a living in a peaceful and useful way. Their fights will be against poverty as much as to maintain mental health."

Boothby and other experts say research also refutes public perceptions — fostered by some news accounts — that former child soldiers are so deranged they cannot adapt to civilian life. At least two studies have found that former child soldiers tend to be good citizens once they are integrated back into their home communities. A long-term study of nearly 40 former child soldiers in Mozambique — all of them demobilized in 1988 — showed they have "turned out quite well," co-author Boothby says.[3] "They are perceived by their communities to be good neighbors, a high percentage are active in the equivalent of the PTA and many are leaders in their communities. It dispels the notion that there are lost generations" of former child soldiers. "The only time you lose generations is when you don't help them after a crisis."

Another study — of young Ugandans abducted by the notorious Lord's Resistance Army (LRA) — also found "a greater propensity toward engaged citizenry, including voting at higher rates and being more involved with community leadership" than their counterparts.[4] Christopher Blattman, a co-author of that study and an assistant professor from Yale University, says only a small minority of youth abducted by the LRA were so traumatized they could no longer function in society.

Grace Akallo, who was abducted at 15, says her personal experience demonstrates that children can overcome their past so long as they get help. "I suffered a lot in the LRA, but I went back to school and my family, and I am fine now. So long as a child gets an opportunity for a future, that child can be OK."

Experts who have assisted or studied former child soldiers say several important lessons have been learned during recent post-conflict experiences, including:

- Governments and aid agencies administering post-war reintegration programs should be cautious about making cash payments to former child soldiers. Giving returnees clothing, food, job training, medical aid and psychological counseling is appropriate, experts say, but in many circumstances giving them cash is not. "We know from many different contexts that when young people in these situations are given cash, bad things happen," says Michael Wessells, a psychology professor from Randolph-Macon College in Virginia, who has helped and studied child soldiers in Africa and Asia. "Commanders sometimes grab the cash and use it to recruit other children, so it runs counter to the intended purpose." A cash payment also can be seen as a reward for serving in an armed group, which is counterproductive, he says. On the other hand, Boothby says cash payments can help in some circumstances if they are carefully monitored to ensure the money benefits the children.

- Girls who have served with armed groups have different needs from boys, particularly if they return from the bush with children. Child soldier aid programs recently have begun to consider girls' special needs, such as child care, assistance with reproductive health matters and psychological aid to deal with the potential stigmatization in their home communities, where the girls are considered "unclean" because of their forced sexual relationships with rebel commanders.
- Reintegration programs should consider the needs of local communities, and community members should be involved in the process. Programs designed by officials in aid agencies or even by government officials in the conflict country often fail because they ignore local situations.
- Donor countries and aid agencies that fund reintegration programs should commit for the long haul. In several recent cases, money ran out before the bulk of former fighters returned from the bush, leaving thousands of youths feeling angry and betrayed. U.N. officials say that after the long war in the Democratic Republic of the Congo, for example, only about half of former child and adult fighters received assistance.[5]
- Targeting aid exclusively or primarily to former members of armed groups risks stigmatizing them and fostering jealousy among their neighbors. Thus, aid programs should be directed at entire communities, not just individuals, Wessells says. Moreover, all children who have served with armed groups — whether as porters, spies or as "wives" of commanders — should be eligible for reintegration aid, not just the fighters, experts say.

AFP/Getty Images/Sena Vidanagama

Former Sri Lankan Tamil Tiger fighters Velayutham Chuti, 18, (left) and 14-year-old Pulidha Logini (right) celebrate with their families after being released by a rival rebel group. The Hindu Tamil Tigers reportedly have used thousands of children in their long battle against the predominantly Buddhist government, making the Tigers one of the world's most persistent users of child soldiers.

---

[1] "Returning Home: Children's Perspectives on Reintegration: A Case Study of Children Abducted by the Lord's Resistance Army in Teso, Eastern Uganda," Coalition to Stop the Use of Child Soldiers, February 2008, p. 14.

[2] *Ibid.*, p. 16.

[3] N. Boothby, J. Crawford and J. Halperin, "Mozambique Child Soldier Life Outcome Study: Lessons Learned in Rehabilitation and Reintegration," *Global Public Health*, February 2006.

[4] "Making Reintegration Work for Youth in Northern Uganda," The Survey of War Affected Youth, www.sway-uganda.org.

[5] "Report of the Secretary General on Children and Armed Conflict in the Democratic Republic of the Congo," June 28, 2007, pp. 14-15.

Congo Reintegrates the Most Child Soldiers

More than 104,000 child soldiers have been demobilized and reintegrated into society worldwide, including 27,000 in the Democratic Republic of the Congo — more than any other country. UNICEF estimates up to 33,000 children were involved in the long-running Congolese war — the biggest and deadliest since World War II. Uganda, where the Lord's Resistance Army notoriously relied on abducting children, has reintegrated 20,000 former child soldiers into their communities. Outside Africa, Sri Lanka has reintegrated more child soldiers than any other country.

Number of Child Soldiers Reintegrated Into Society
(since 1998)

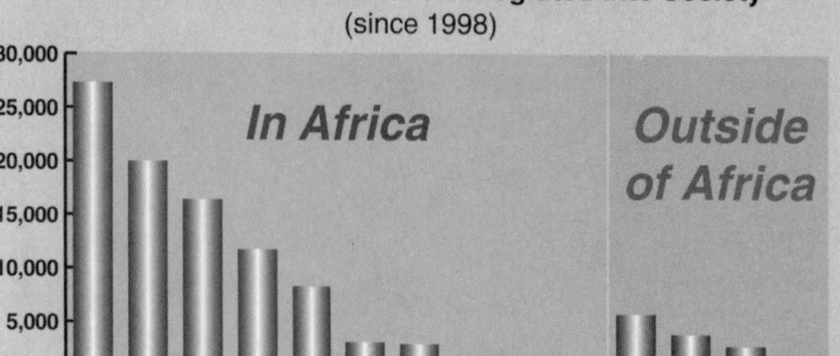

Source: U.N. Integrated Disarmament, Demoblisation and Reintegration System; UNICEF

find it easier to recruit when a large population of angry, listless young men fill the street," Singer said.[33]

Impressionable children also can find military life alluring. When a recruiter from the army or a rebel group shows up and offers an impoverished child the opportunity to wear a uniform and make himself feel powerful by carrying a gun, the sales pitch is often difficult to resist.

U.N. Roles

The task of curtailing the use of under-age fighters has fallen largely to the United Nations, which has had only limited success. The U.N. has taken a two-pronged approach: getting a treaty enacted making it illegal for governments and armed groups to use children under 18 in combat and establishing a system for identifying armed groups that recruit and use child soldiers. The Security Council has threatened to sanction more than a dozen persistent violators of the law but has taken that step only once, in Côte d'Ivoire in West Africa.

Several treaties and regulations adopted by the U.N. after World War II created a legal structure offering theoretical protection to children and discouraging their use in warfare, including the 1948 Universal Declaration of Human Rights, the Geneva Conventions of 1949 and Additional Protocols to those conventions adopted in 1977 and the 1989 Convention on the Rights of the Child. These treaties were strengthened substantially in 2000 with adoption of the Optional Protocol, which specifically barred non-state armed groups from recruiting or using any children under 18 but allowed governments to recruit children 16 or 17 as long as they weren't used in combat until they turned 18. In essence, the treaty made it illegal under international law for anyone to use a child under 18 in combat. In addition, the 1998 Rome Statute — which went into effect in 2002 and created the International Criminal Court — defined as a "war crime" the conscription or use in war of any child under 15.

Since 1996 the Security Council also has adopted six resolutions dealing specifically with children and armed conflict. The last four of these (Resolution 1379 adopted in 2001, Resolution 1460 adopted in 2003, Resolution 1539 adopted in 2004, and Resolution 1612 adopted in 2005) created a system under which U.N. officials monitor the impact of armed conflicts on children and publicly identify countries and groups that illegally recruit and use children in combat.

In some cases, when confronted by the U.N. with solid evidence about their use of child soldiers, warlords have promised to release them. Some have kept their promises, notably the leaders of three groups in Côte d'Ivoire who were subjected to Security Council sanctions in 2006.[34] Most others broke their promises. In Somalia, for example, the Union of Islamic Courts, which briefly held power in 2006, told U.N. officials they would stop using child soldiers, but didn't.[35]

Children at War

The United Nations, nongovernmental groups and academic experts have identified nearly 50 civil conflicts since World War II that have involved children, mostly in sub-Saharan Africa. The following examples are representative of recent or ongoing conflicts involving heavy use of child soldiers:

Colombia — The long-running, multifaceted civil conflict in Colombia has featured the most extensive use of child soldiers in the Americas. According to various estimates, 11,000 to 14,000 Colombians under 18 have been recruited into the country's armed groups.[36] Most are members of the two leftist guerrilla factions, the Revolutionary Armed Forces of Colombia (FARC) and the National Liberation Army (ELN). Several thousand underage fighters also have been associated with right-wing paramilitary groups aligned with the government, the military and major landowners; the largest paramilitary force is the United Self-Defense Forces of Colombia (AUC).[37]

The Colombian army also used under-18-year-olds as fighters until 2000, when it reportedly halted the practice after domestic and international protests. But there have been reports about the army's continued use of children. American journalist Jimmie Briggs said the army still recruits soldiers under 18 but assigns them to non-combat duty until they turn 18.[38] In its "2008 Global Report," the Coalition to Stop the Use of Child Soldiers cited the army for using captured children for intelligence-gathering.[39]

Significantly, since 1999 more than 3,300 former child soldiers (mostly from the FARC) have gone through the government-sponsored demobilization, disarmament and reintegration process — one of the few major demobilization efforts ever conducted during an ongoing conflict.[40]

Democratic Republic of the Congo — The Congolese war — the biggest and deadliest since World War II — took place in the former Zaire from about 1998 until 2003. It involved more than a dozen guerrilla groups and, at various points, the armies or paramilitary groups from Angola, Burundi, Rwanda, Uganda and Zimbabwe. The International Rescue Committee has estimated that up to 5.5 million people — about one-tenth of the Congo's population — may have died as a result of the conflict.[41]

Many of the armed groups used children as fighters or in support roles. In 2002, as part of the war was ending, UNICEF estimated that about 33,000 children were involved in the fighting — or 20 percent of active combatants.[42] In June 2007, U.N. Secretary-General Ban told the U.N. Security Council that 29,291 children had been released by armed groups during the previous three years under a U.N.-sponsored demobilization program. However, due to alleged mismanagement of the program and a failure by donor nations to fulfill their funding pledges, only about half of the former child soldiers had received aid to reintegrate into their communities, the report found.[43]

Although peace agreements were signed in 2002 and 2003, fighting has continued in parts of eastern Congo, where renegade Tutsi commander Laurent Nkunda leads a militia in fighting the Congolese army. Nkunda claims his group is protecting Congo's minority Tutsi population — an ethnic group that was slaughtered by the hundreds of thousands during the 1994 genocide in Rwanda.

The U.N. has accused Nkunda of forcibly recruiting hundreds, and possibly several thousand, children.[44] Nkunda, along with other rebels, signed a cease-fire agreement on Jan. 23, 2008, pledging to end the fighting.[45] Reports since then have suggested the cease-fire merely reduced the level of fighting rather than stopping it.[46] Government security forces also used child soldiers, at least through 2007, according to the U.S. State Department.[47]

Liberia — From the early 1990s until President Charles Taylor was ousted from power in 2003, Liberia was a focal point for several civil conflicts in West Africa, all involving child soldiers. During the early 1990s, Taylor led a rebel army, composed in large part of children, which controlled much of Liberia. After he became president in 1997, he also backed rebel groups in neighboring Côte d'Ivoire, Guinea and Sierra Leone.

AFP/Getty Images/Esdras Ndikumana

Former child soldiers at a demobilization camp in Burundi wait to be reintegrated back into society. About 104,000 children worldwide have been reintegrated into their communities after serving in various rebel or government armed forces.

Taylor's support for the notorious Revolutionary United Front in Sierra Leone — in exchange for access to diamonds and other natural resources in rebel-controlled areas — was the basis for his indictment on 11 war-crimes charges by a U.N.-sponsored tribunal. His trial, which began in July 2007, is still under way. The regional impact of the war in Liberia and Taylor's sponsorship of neighboring rebel armies continued at least until 2005. According to the Coalition to Stop the Use of Child Soldiers, rebel groups in Guinea and Côte d'Ivoire were still recruiting child soldiers (and former child soldiers who had reached age 18) from Liberia.[48]

Myanmar — The U.N., HRW and other organizations say the secretive military government of Myanmar (formerly Burma) makes widespread use of children in its army even though the minimum recruitment age is 18.[49] According to HRW, government recruiters force boys under 18 to lie about their ages or falsify induction forms to meet quotas.[50] The government began recruiting children extensively in the 1990s, when it more than doubled the size of the army — from 200,000 to 500,000 — to combat an upsurge in a decades-old separatist insurgency in Karen state in southeastern Myanmar, the group said.[51]

Responding partly to pressure from the U.N., the government in 2004 created a committee to prevent the military recruitment of under-18-year-olds. Since then, government representatives have insisted the army has no under-age soldiers. However, Secretary-General Ban wrote in a November 2007 report that recruitment continued unabated, with recruiters still rewarded with cash and a bag of rice for each new soldier they produced, regardless of his age.[52]

U.N. and HRW officials do not know how many children now serve in the Myanmar military because the government severely restricts international access to the country. However, the HRW report quoted several former soldiers as estimating that 20 to 50 percent of the soldiers in their units had been underage.[53]

Many of the country's non-state military groups also use underage soldiers, but the extent is unknown, according to both the U.N. and HRW.[54]

Sri Lanka — The Liberation Tigers of Tamil Eelam (LTTE), better known as the Tamil Tigers, reportedly has used thousands of children in the Hindu group's long battle against the majority Sinhalese (mostly Buddhist) government, making it one of the world's most persistent users of child soldiers. A breakaway rebel faction, known as the Karuna group, which in recent years has been aligned with the government, also reportedly has used child soldiers.[55] A cease-fire negotiated by Norwegian diplomats in February 2002 helped reduce violence for more than three years, but several incidents in 2005 and 2006 led to an escalation of fighting, particularly in the north, which continues today. The cease-fire essentially collapsed in 2006, and the government formally withdrew from it in mid-January 2008. The U.N. had estimated a year earlier that at least 67,000 people had died in the quarter-century of conflict.[56]

The total number of children caught up in the conflict is unknown. However, a UNICEF database showed that between 2002 and 2007 the Tigers recruited 6,248 children, and up to 453 children were recruited by the Karuna group during the last three years of that period. UNICEF said these figures most likely understate the actual use of child soldiers, because the agency relies on voluntary reporting by parents and community leaders, who often withhold information because they fear retaliation.[57] Whatever the actual total, the Tamil Tigers have used children actively in fighting, including as suicide bombers — a technique the group introduced to the world in the 1980s.

U.N. officials and human rights groups have accused the government of complicity in the Karuna group's use of child soldiers and even allowing the group to recruit or abduct children in government-controlled areas. In some cases army units allegedly have participated actively in forcibly recruiting children.[58] The government has denied these accusations.

The Tamil Tigers pledged in 2007 to stop recruiting child soldiers and release all of those in its custody by the end of that year. As of January 2008, however, UNICEF listed 1,429 cases in which a recruited child soldier had not been released, including at least 168 children who were still under 18.[59]

Sudan — Africa's largest country has experienced two major conflicts and several smaller ones in recent years — all involving child soldiers. Secretary-General Ban reported in 2007 that more than 30 armed groups operated in Sudan.[60]

Ban's report and independent human rights groups have found that children have been recruited and used as soldiers by the government's Sudan Armed Forces, by the pro-government militias known as the Janjaweed (which operate in the western region of Darfur), by the main Darfur rebel groups — the Justice and Equality Movement (JEM) and the Sudan Liberation Army (SLA), which have both splintered into factions — and by armed groups in southern Sudan, including the region's main rebel group, the Sudan People's Liberation Army (SPLA).[61]

The Security Council's Working Group on Children and Armed Conflict has repeatedly — most recently in February 2008 — condemned the "continuous recruitment and use of children" by the government and armed groups in Sudan and demanded that the children be released so they could be reintegrated into their families and communities.[62]

In southern Sudan, the government and the SPLA signed a peace agreement in January 2005 ending a 20-year conflict. The agreement called for creation of a "government of national unity," but real unity has been elusive, as the Khartoum government and the former rebels continue to bicker about many of the same issues that fueled the war, including control over oil production in the region.[63]

Between 2001 and early 2006 the SPLA demobilized about 20,000 former child soldiers, but the Coalition to Stop the Use of Child Soldiers reported that as of late 2007 about 2,000 children remained under the militia's control.[64] Secretary-General Ban reported in August 2007 that the SPLA had made "significant progress" by releasing at least 47 children in one of its units, but two armed groups associated with the government's army had not fulfilled their promises to release children.[65]

AFP/Getty Images/Sonia Rolley

The use of child soldiers, like these, by the Chadian military was officially prohibited in May 2007, but as a government official explained, using children is "ideal" because "they don't complain, they don't expect to be paid and if you tell them to kill, they kill."

In Darfur, the fighting remains well below the peak of the conflict in 2002-03, but serious violence continues despite the presence of a U.N. peacekeeping mission. Ban's report found that nearly all armed groups in Darfur, including the Sudanese army and its related militias, continued to recruit and use children as fighters.[66]

The conflict in Darfur also has spilled into neighboring conflicts in Chad and the Central African Republic, where government armies and rebel groups (some supported by the Sudanese government) have recruited and used child soldiers. The Chadian government, in turn, reportedly participated in the forced recruitment in 2006 of nearly 5,000 Sudanese refugees, including several hundred children, by one of the Darfur rebel groups.[67]

Uganda — As in Sierra Leone, the use and abuse of child soldiers has reached a depraved level in Uganda, largely due to the fanatical Kony's Lord's Resistance Army. The United Nations has estimated that Kony, a violent, self-styled prophet, abducted or forced nearly 25,000 children into his army between 1986 and 2005.[68] However, independent experts have said the U.N. estimate counts only former LRA members who later turned themselves into Ugandan government reception centers. Researchers at Tufts University in Boston estimate that the LRA abducted at least 60,000 boys and girls, and that 15-20 percent of the boys and 5 percent of the girls died during the war, said Yale's Blattman, one of the researchers.

Human rights groups say the LRA continues to abduct children, although in lower numbers than earlier.[69] Blattman says his team believes the LRA now has fewer than 1,000 people — adults or children — in its ranks. The International Criminal Court in July 2005 issued arrest warrants for Kony and four of his aides, charging them with war crimes, including the use of child soldiers; at least one of the aides reportedly has since died.[70]

The LRA was one of several Ugandan groups that took up arms in 1986 against the new government of Yoweri Museveni, himself a former rebel leader who had used large numbers of child soldiers during a five-year war against President Milton Obote. Kony claimed to be fighting on behalf of his own ethnic group in northern Uganda, the Acholi people, but ultimately the Acholi became the principal victims in the two-decade-long war between the LRA and the government.[71] Kony reportedly claims his fight is ordained by God. At a 2006 meeting with Ugandan officials, Kony denied that his forces had committed atrocities and insisted "the tragedy that was taking place in Uganda was done by the Uganda government."[72]

The war developed a critical international dimension in the mid-1990s, when Sudan armed Kony's forces to help in its own war against the SPLA in southern Sudan. Kony used southern Sudan as a base from which to launch attacks against both the SPLA and the Ugandan army. He later established bases in the Democratic Republic of the Congo and the Central African Republic.[73]

The conflict in northern Uganda peaked after March 2002, when the Ugandan government launched an offensive against the LRA, which responded by targeting civilians as well as government forces. Over the next two years Kony increased the pace of abductions of children, forcing many of them to endure beatings and to carry out atrocities against each other and against civilians, sometimes even members of their own families. Girls were forced into virtual slavery, the youngest ones as servants and the older ones as "wives" of LRA commanders, says Grace Akallo, who was abducted at 15 and held for seven months until she escaped. Fearing such abductions, thousands of children living in rural villages trudged long distances every evening to sleep in larger towns considered safe. Known as "night commuters," the children became the most visible symbols to the outside world of the horrors in northern Uganda.[74] Despite denials, the Ugandan government also recruited children into its army and local pro-government militias called the UPDF, according to U.N. officials and human rights groups.[75]

The fighting slowed significantly in 2005, when Sudan signed a peace accord with the rebels in southern Sudan and, reportedly, ended much of its support for Kony — a development that led to efforts to end the war in northern Uganda. Peace talks between Uganda and LRA representatives began in Juba, southern Sudan, in 2006. A cease-fire signed in August that year generally has held, resulting in the longest sustained period of peace in northern Uganda in more than two decades.[76] Although the LRA is no longer operating in northern Uganda, it is still present in the Central African Republic, Congo and Sudan and reportedly has continued abducting children well into 2008, according to a June 23 report by Secretary-General Ban.[77]

A diplomat negotiating on Kony's behalf initialed a peace agreement in February 2008, but Kony himself failed to show up for much-publicized signing ceremonies in April and May, reportedly fearing he might be arrested to face war crimes charges.[78] Uganda has offered to request that the charges against Kony be dropped so he could be tried in a local tribunal, but so far this has not been enough incentive for him to turn himself in.

CURRENT SITUATION

"Empty Threats"

United Nations officials and independent human rights groups say the U.N. Security Council risks losing credibility because of its failure to follow through on repeated threats to impose sanctions against governments and armed groups that persist in recruiting and using child soldiers.

In its last two resolutions on child soldiers — Resolution 1539 in 2004 and Resolution 1612 in 2005 — the Security Council threatened to impose "targeted measures" (primarily sanctions) against armed groups that defy international demands to stop using children in combat, but so far it has not taken any action. The council "needs to show that the threats they make are not empty threats," says Becker, of Human Rights Watch.

Top U.N. officials in recent months also have called on the council to follow through on its threats to punish those who use child soldiers. In his annual report on children and armed conflict, published in January, Secretary-General Ban suggested the council impose various measures, including banning the export or supplying of weapons, banning military assistance, imposing travel restrictions on government officials or leaders of armed groups, preventing armed groups and their leaders from accessing the international financial system and referring violators to the ICC for possible war-crimes punishment.[79]

And on Feb. 12, Special Representative Coomaraswamy confronted the council directly on the issue, pointing out that U.N. reports over the past five years had identified 16 "persistent violators" of international law, some of whom were "making efforts" to comply with the law, while others "remain in contempt of the council and its resolutions."[80]

She doubts the council will impose sanctions anytime soon, however, which she finds frustrating. "You have to realize that [imposing sanctions] is the most extreme action the Security Council can take in any context," she says. "And this is the Security Council, where there are always strong political considerations, and they are very cautious, so I think it will be some time down the road before they agree on sanctions."

Her comments reflect the fact that all actions by the Security Council require extensive compromise among countries with often-conflicting viewpoints, and the council cannot act unless there is unanimous agreement among all five of its permanent, veto-wielding members (Britain, China, France, Russia and the United States). In recent years China and Russia have been the most reluctant of the so-called "permanent five" to intervene in what they consider the domestic affairs of member states.

On the same day Coomaraswamy called for Security Council action, the council said it was "gravely concerned by the persistent disregard of its resolutions on children and armed conflict by parties to armed conflict." The council also said it "reaffirms its intention to make use of all the tools" provided in its previous resolutions. However, it did not mention sanctions nor did it take any specific action — either then or in subsequent months.[81]

AFP/Getty Images/Simon Maina

A young Congolese Patriotic Union soldier totes his rifle in the Democratic Republic of the Congo. In addition to rebel groups, Congo's government also uses child soldiers. Congo is one of seven countries — including Afghanistan, Chad, Somalia, Sri Lanka, Sudan and Uganda — that have used child soldiers while receiving U.S. military aid. Legislation pending before Congress would bar military aid to any country that uses child soldiers.

As Becker's comments suggest, independent human-rights groups are equally frustrated with the Security Council's lack of action. In two reports last January, the Watchlist on Children and Armed Conflict (a coalition of human rights groups) detailed several cases in which the council suggested it would act against violators but did not.[82] Becker says the council's reluctance to act

AT ISSUE

Should the U.S. prosecute alleged child soldiers at Guantánamo?

YES

David B. Rivkin, Jr.
Partner, Baker Hostetler LLP, Washington, D.C.
Former Justice Department official and associate White House counsel during the Reagan and George H.W. Bush administrations

Written for *CQ Global Researcher*, June 2008

In a challenge to the laws of war employed by the United States since 9/11, critics claim the military commission prosecution of Omar Ahmed Khadr is illegitimate. A Canadian national, Khadr is accused of committing war crimes while fighting with al Qaeda in Afghanistan when he was 15. His lawyers argue he is a "child soldier" and thus immune from liability. These claims have no legal or policy merit.

Although the Optional Protocol to the Convention on the Rights of the Child bars recruitment and use of juveniles for combat, terrorist groups are not likely to comply with the protocol or worry about potential liability for their non-compliance. But this is irrelevant to Khadr's liability.

As presiding Judge Peter Brownback has properly ruled, the Military Commissions Act of 2006 gave the commission jurisdiction to try war-related offenses committed by juveniles, and nothing in U.S. law or the Constitution contradicts that. He also has properly concluded that no international treaty, convention or customary law norm establishes age as a bar to war-crimes prosecutions. Indeed, Khadr's lawyers have not cited any international law supporting their extraordinary claim of legal immunity.

This leaves the United States with a choice of whether to continue with Khadr's prosecution or exercise prosecutorial discretion and dismiss all charges against him — even if his prosecution is legally permissible. But first one must ask whether prosecuting him makes policy sense or is fair and just. Would we not be better served by sending Khadr home to be reunited with his family?

The answer is no. The gravity of the alleged offenses and the fact that he chose to join al Qaeda, an unlawful enemy entity, strongly mitigate against granting him immunity. Plus, he performed these actions at 15 — an age old enough to assess the moral and legal implications of his behavior.

Moreover, proponents of immunity fail to see that it would only further incentivize the continued recruitment of child soldiers and the use of children in the commission of war crimes. This result would neither benefit juveniles involved nor help their victims, who usually are civilians.

More broadly, granting him immunity would further debase international laws against war crimes — laws that have taken centuries to develop and are absolutely necessary if 21st-century warfare is not to descend into unbridled barbarism and carnage, to the detriment of the civilized world.

NO

Jo Becker
Advocacy director, Children's Rights Division, Human Rights Watch;
Founding chairman, Coalition to Stop the Use of Child Soldiers

Written for *CQ Global Researcher*, June 2008

Since 2002 the United States has held at least 23 detainees who were under 18 at the U.S. military base at Guantánamo Bay, Cuba. Two of them, Omar Khadr and Mohammad Jawad, are being prosecuted before U.S. military commissions for allegedly throwing grenades at American soldiers in Afghanistan. Khadr was 15 when he reportedly killed U.S. Army Sgt. First Class Christopher Speer and injured other soldiers in a July 2002 firefight. Jawad was 16 or 17 in December 2002 when he allegedly tossed a grenade into a military vehicle and injured two U.S. soldiers and an Afghan translator.

During the more than five years that Khadr and Jawad have been detained at Guantánamo, the United States has ignored their juvenile status. In violation of international juvenile-justice standards, the two have been incarcerated with adult detainees, subjected to prolonged solitary confinement, denied direct contact with their families and refused educational opportunities or rehabilitation.

Under juvenile-justice standards and international guidelines for the treatment of former child soldiers, children should be treated according to their unique vulnerability, lower degree of culpability and capacity for rehabilitation. Although international law does not preclude prosecution of child soldiers for serious crimes, their rehabilitation and reintegration into society must be paramount.

America's treatment of Jawad and Khadr cannot be construed as rehabilitative. They are confined in small cells for 22 hours a day, with little more than a mattress, the Koran and toilet paper. Their attorneys say Jawad and Khadr have been tortured. Khadr says his interrogators shackled him in painful positions, threatened him with rape and used him as a "human mop" after he urinated on the floor during one interrogation session. Jawad was moved from cell to cell and deprived of sleep. Eleven months after arriving at Guantánamo, Jawad tried to hang himself with his shirt collar. His lawyer says he suffers from severe depression and appears to have lost touch with reality.

Under juvenile-justice principles, cases involving children must be resolved quickly and their detention be as short as possible. But Khadr and Jawad were held for more than three years before even being charged. Now, five years after their apprehension, there is no foreseeable end to their ordeal.

Guantánamo, with its flawed military commissions, is no place for children. The United States should either transfer their cases to U.S. federal court and apply fundamental standards of juvenile justice, or release them for rehabilitation.

means that "as long as governments and commanders of these groups know they can recruit and use child soldiers without serious consequences, in particular to them personally, they will do it. But if their visas are denied or their assets are frozen or they suffer some real penalties, they will at least think twice about it."

U.N. officials say they repeatedly have confronted government officials and leaders of armed groups with evidence of their use of child soldiers, often to be greeted with outright denials or with vague pledges to stop the practice. "Their justification is, 'We don't go out and recruit,' which of course is not true," says Coomaraswamy, who often meets with leaders of armed groups using child soldiers. "They say, 'The children are hanging out at the gates, they want to join, many of them are orphans, how can I send them away?' This is usually the line, along with, 'We give them food, they are so happy,' that kind of thing."

Prosecuting Violators

The international community has another, stronger weapon against government leaders and military commanders who use child soldiers: Prosecution for war crimes. So far 19 commanders — all from Africa — have faced charges or prosecution either at the International Criminal Court or in special war crimes tribunals. Five have been convicted; the others are either on trial, awaiting trial, still at large or have reportedly died.

Four of the five convictions were handed down by the U.N.-supported special tribunal on war crimes committed during the brutal civil war in Sierra Leone, which raged from 1991 to 2002. The Hague-based Special Court for Sierra Leone in June 2007 convicted and sentenced three members of the Armed Forces Revolutionary Council — Alex Tamba Brima, Brima Bazzy Kamara and Santigie Borbor Kanu — on charges the rebel group committed war crimes and recruited and used child soldiers. It was the first time an international tribunal had ruled on the recruitment of child soldiers. "These convictions are a ground-breaking step toward ending impunity for commanders who exploit hundreds of thousands of children as soldiers in conflicts worldwide," Human Rights Watch said at the time.[83] The three men were sentenced to prison terms ranging from 45 to 50 years, and those sentences were affirmed in February by the court's appellate division.

A fourth man, Allieu Kondewa, a member of the Civil Defense Forces militia, was convicted in August 2007 on several charges, including recruitment of child soldiers.[84] He was sentenced to eight years in prison, which has since been increased to 20 years.[85]

Crane, the Syracuse University law professor who was the first prosecutor at the Sierra Leone court, says those convictions established important precedents. "This tells the leaders of these kinds of groups all over the world, 'If you are committing international crimes like abducting children and making them kill people, you can be convicted and sent to prison for the rest of your life.' "

A tribunal in the Democratic Republic of the Congo in March 2006 convicted Jean-Pierre Biyoyo, former commander of the Mudundu 40 armed group, on charges of recruiting and using child soldiers. Although he was sentenced to death, the sentence was reduced to five years' imprisonment.[86] Three months later he escaped from prison and eventually joined rebel leader Nkunda in North Kivu province, according to the U.S. State Department.[87]

Among the dozen other officials and warlords charged with war crimes for using child soldiers, the most prominent defendant is Taylor of Liberia, who currently is on trial before the Special Court for Sierra Leone on 11 charges of war crimes and crimes against humanity, including the use child soldiers.[88]

The International Criminal Court has charged three former Congolese guerrilla leaders with various war crimes, including the use of child soldiers. Thomas Lubanga Dyilo, leader of the Union of Congolese Patriots, had been scheduled to be the first person ever tried by the court. He was charged in 2006 with enlisting, recruiting and using child soldiers during the long and bloody fighting in Ituri region in eastern Democratic Republic of the Congo.[89]

However, the case appeared on the verge of collapse in early July as the result of a dispute between the U.N. and the ICC judges over U.N. documents that the prosecution had used to develop its charges. The U.N. had given the documents to the prosecution on a confidential basis. The court's judges indefinitely halted the Lubanga case on June 13 because the documents contain "exculpatory material" that should have been made available to the defense. An initial attempt to work out a compromise failed, and the trial judges on July 2 ordered Lubanga's eventual release as the "logical consequence" of the earlier decision. The prosecution appealed the decision to halt the case, and the ICC's appellate chamber said on July 7 that Lubanga should remain in prison until it had ruled on that appeal. News reports said ICC officials were still hoping for a compromise on the documents issue.

Human Rights Watch expressed disappointment over the legal wrangling, saying the failure of the case would deny justice to the alleged victims of Lubanga's actions. "The victims are the ones who suffer as a result of these embarrassing legal difficulties at the ICC," HRW counsel Param-Preet Singh says. Even so, she adds, denying Lubanga a fair trial "would also be an injustice, and the ICC cannot afford that, either."[90]

The possible collapse of the Lubanga case also came as a disappointment to the U.N., which had expected the case to establish legal doctrines on punishing those who recruit and use child soldiers. In a statement after the June 13 decision to halt the trial, U.N. Special Representative Coomaraswamy urged that the trial "not be compromised for technical reasons" and noted that the case "is considered a major milestone in international attempts" to eradicate the practice of using child soldiers."

U.S. Legislation

Both of the U.S. bills concerning child soldiers have made some progress but are still pending, with time running out for action during an election year. The House approved the Child Soldier Prevention Act — which would bar military aid and arms sales to countries using child soldiers — on Dec. 4, 2007. It was included in a measure to reauthorize a 2000 anti-human-trafficking law.[91] The vote on the underlying bill was 405-2, with no opposition to the child soldier provisions. The Senate, by contrast, has passed the Child Soldiers Accountability Act, which criminalizes the use of child soldiers and bars entry into the United States by anyone using child soldiers. The measure was approved by unanimous consent on Dec. 18, 2007.

Senate sponsors combined both bills into one measure, the Child Soldier Accountability and Prevention Act of 2008 (S 3061), introduced on May 22 by Joseph R. Biden, D-Del., and Sam Brownback, R-Kan. The measure is pending before the Senate Judiciary Committee, after markup was delayed on June 26 by an unnamed Republican senator who put a hold on the bill.

OUTLOOK

Child Terrorists?

Some of the recent conflicts that have involved the most widespread and notorious use of child soldiers have ended with formal peace agreements or dwindled into low-level, sporadic fighting. Among them were the interrelated conflicts in West Africa; the huge, pan-African war in the Democratic Republic of the Congo; and civil wars in the Balkans, El Salvador and Indonesia. The latest global survey by the Coalition to Stop the Use of Child Soldiers said the number of countries where children were directly involved in conflicts declined from 27 in 2004 (when the group issued its previous report) to 17 by the end of 2007.[92]

Becker, of Human Rights Watch, says the decline is good news but does not mean the child-soldier problem has disappeared. "Some conflicts are ending, but that does not mean that children are no longer being used in war," she says. "When armed conflicts occur, children are almost inevitably involved." As examples, Becker cites new, or newly revived conflicts in the past two years in the Central African Republic, Chad and Somalia — all involving extensive use of children.

Moreover, new conflicts can be expected because the underlying conditions that led to most of the world's civil conflicts remain unresolved. "It's not like we have fewer poor kids today, fewer orphans who can be recruited by warlords," says Singer of the Brookings Institution. "You still have these problems on a global scale."

Specialists in the field, as well as government officials worldwide are particularly concerned about what appears to be the increasing use of children as terrorists, including as suicide bombers. The Tamil Tigers developed the tactic two decades ago, even fashioning suicide bomb vests in small sizes for children, according to some sources.[93]

Suicide bombing as a terrorist tactic has spread in recent years to other parts of South and Central Asia — including Afghanistan, India and Pakistan — to Colombia and to the Middle East, including extremist Palestinian factions, and Iraq.[94] Children in their early- and mid-teens have carried out, or attempted, suicide attacks in nearly all these places, sometimes causing large-scale fatalities. In Iraq, U.S military officials have said insurgents often use children to place the roadside bombs, known as "improvised explosive devices," that typically kill American troops.

Singer does not expect terrorism and the use of children by terrorists to diminish anytime soon, despite the efforts of the U.S. "war" against terrorism. In fact, he says, "we could see the use of children as terrorists globally, if you put yourself in the position of the planners of these attacks and how they might be looking to expand their operations."

As for combating the more conventional use of children in civil conflicts, the U.N.'s Coomaraswamy is optimistic the world is ready to act more decisively. "This is an issue on which you have a near-global consensus on the need for action, not just rhetoric," she says. "Not that we will be able to stop all recruitment and use of child solders, but I think we can lessen it quite a bit in the next decade."

She and other experts had hoped that the two most prominent cases involving use of child soldiers — the ongoing Taylor tribunal and the ICC case against Lubanga — would produce ground-breaking convictions demonstrating that the use of children in war will be punished.

The dismissal of the Lubanga case could give added importance to the Taylor trial, where Crane, the former special prosecutor in Sierra Leone, expects a guilty verdict. "That will have an incredible ripple effect, particularly on the dictators and warlords of the world," he says. "It says that the lives of their citizens matter. In particular, it shows Africans themselves that their lives matter."

NOTES

1. Testimony of Ishmael Beah, Senate Judiciary Subcommittee on Human Rights and the Law, hearing on "Casualties of War: Child Soldiers and the Law," April 24, 2007, http://judiciary.senate.gov/testimony.cfm?id=2712&wit_id=6387.
2. P. W. Singer, *Children at War* (2006), p. 23.
3. "Some 250,000 children worldwide recruited to fight in wars — UN official," United Nations Department of Public Information, Jan. 30, 2008, www.un.org/apps/news/story.asp?NewsID=25450&Cr=children&Cr1=conflict#.
4. Singer, *op. cit.*, p. 30.
5. "Sold to be Soldiers: The Recruitment and Use of Child Soldiers in Burma," Human Rights Watch, October 2007, www.hrw.org/reports/2007/burma1007/burma1007web.pdf.
6. "Child Soldiers Global Report 2008," Coalition to Stop the Use of Child Solders, p. 29, www.childsoldiersglobalreport.org/files/country_pdfs/FINAL_2008_Global_Report.pdf.
7. "Cape Town Principles and Best Practices," April 1997, UNICEF, p. 8, www.unicef.org/emerg/files/Cape_Town_Principles(1).
8. David M. Rosen, *Armies of the Young: Child Soldiers in War and Terrorism* (2005), p. 4.
9. "Childhood Denied: Child Soldiers in Africa," Amnesty International, available online under the title "Democratic Republic of Congo: Children at War," on p. 7, at www.amnesty.org/en/library/asset/AFR62/034/2003/en/dom-AFR620342003en.pdf.
10. Ishmael Beah, *A Long Way Gone: Memoirs of a Boy Soldier* (2007).
11. "Children and Armed Conflict, Report of the Secretary General," Dec. 21, 2007, pp. 40-45.
12. U.N. Security Council Resolution 1379, www.securitycouncilreport.org/atf/cf/{65BFCF9B-6D27-4E9C-8CD3-CF6E4FF96FF9}/CAC%20SRES%201379.pdf.
13. "Child Soldiers Global Report 2008," *op. cit.*
14. "Children and Armed Conflict," *op. cit.*, p. 33.
15. "Report of the Secretary General on Children and Armed Conflict in Sri Lanka," Dec. 21, 2007, pp. 3-7.
16. "International Forum on Armed Groups and the Involvement of Children in Armed Conflict: Summary of Themes and Discussion," Coalition to Stop the Use of Child Soldiers, August 2007, p. 16, www.child-soldiers.org/childsoldiers/Armed_groups_forum_report_August_ 2007_revision_0ct07.pdf.
17. "Military Commission Charges Referred," U.S. Department of Defense news release, April 24 2007, www.defenselink.mil/releases/release.aspx?releaseid=10779. For background, see David Masci and Kenneth Jost, "War on Terrorism," *CQ Researcher*, Oct. 12, 2001, pp. 817-848; also see Peter Katel and

Kenneth Jost, "Treatment of Detainees," *CQ Researcher*, Aug. 25, 2006, pp. 673-696.

18. "Ruling on Defense Motion for Dismissal Due to Lack of Jurisdiction Under the MCA in Regard to Juvenile Crimes of a Child Soldier," *United States of America v. Omar Ahmed Khadr*, April 30, 2008, www.defenselink.mil/news/d20080430Motion.pdf.
19. "Letter to U.S. Secretary of Defense Robert Gates on Omar Khadr," Human Rights Watch, April 2, 2008, www.hrw.org/english/docs/2008/02/01/usint17956.htm.
20. *Amicus curiae* brief contained in the April 30 ruling, note 19 above, pp. 108-146.
21. Rome Statute of the International Criminal Court, United Nations Doc. A/CONF.183/9, July 17, 1998.
22. "The Paris Principles: Principles and Guidelines on Children Associated with Armed Forces or Armed Groups," February 2007, section 3.6, www.diplomatie.gouv.fr/en/IMG/pdf/Paris_Conference_Principles_English _31_January.pdf.
23. "Government's Response to the Defense's Motion for Dismissal Due to Lack of Jurisdiction under the MCA in Regard to Juvenile Crimes of a Child Soldier," Jan. 25, 2008. p. 9, footnote 3.
24. Deputy Assistant Secretary of Defense Sandra L. Hodgkinson, testimony to the U.N. Committee on the Rights of the Child Concerning U.S. Implementation of the Optional Protocol on Children in Armed Conflict, May 22, 2008, p. 26, www2.ohchr.org/english/bodies/crc/docs/statements/48USA Opening_Statements.pdf.
25. Randall Palmer, "Top Court Says Canada Complicit in Guantánamo Base," Reuters, May 23, 2008.
26. "Military Commission Charges Referred," U.S. Department of Defense, Jan. 31, 2008, www.defenselink.mil/releases/release.aspx?releaseid=11655.
27. *Congressional Record*, Dec. 18, 2007, p. S15941.
28. "Country Reports on Human Rights Practices: Afghanistan," U.S. State Department, March 11, 2008. www.state.gov/g/drl/rls/hrrpt/2007/100611.htm.
29. "U.S. Military Assistance to Governments and Government-Supported Armed Groups Using Child Soldiers, 2002-2008," Center for Defense Information, April 2, 2008, p. 1, www.cdi.org/PDFs/CS_MilAssist08.pdf.
30. "Casualties Of War: Child Soldiers and The Law," Sen. Dick Durbin, April 24, 2007, http://durbin.senate.gov/showRelease.cfm?releaseId=280883.
31. "Report of the Secretary General on Children and Armed Conflict in Chad," United Nations, July 3, 2007, p. 7; also see "Early to War: Child Soldiers in the Chad Conflict," Human Rights Watch, July 2007, www.hrw.org/reports/2007/chad0707/.
32. Singer, *op. cit.*, p. 63.
33. *Ibid.*, p. 41.
34. "Security Council committee concerning Côte d'Ivoire issues list of individuals subject to measures imposed by Resolution 1572 (2004)," SC/8631, U.N. Department of Public Information, Feb. 7, 2006.
35. "Report of the Secretary General on Children and Armed Conflict in Somalia," May 7, 2007, p. 13, www.unhcr.org/cgi-bin/texis/vtx/refworld/rwmain?docid=4850fe4e2.
36. Jimmie Briggs, *Innocents Lost: When Child Soldiers Go to War* (2005), p. 41.
37. "Child Soldiers Global Report 2008," *op. cit.*, pp. 101-103; "Overcoming Lost Childhoods: Lessons Learned from the Rehabilitation and Reintegration of Former Child Soldiers in Colombia," YCare International, 2007, p. 4; "You'll Learn Not to Cry: Child Combatants in Colombia," Human Rights Watch, September 2003, www.hrw.org/reports/2003/colombia0903/.
38. Briggs, *op. cit.*, p. 56.
39. "Child Soldiers Global Report 2008," *op. cit.*, p. 101.
40. *Ibid.*, p. 102.
41. "Mortality in the DRC: An Ongoing Crisis," International Rescue Committee, January 2008, www.theirc.org/media/www/congo-crisis-fast-facts.html.
42. "Child soldier recruitment continues," United Nations Integrated Regional Information Network, Feb. 19, 2007.
43. "Report of the Secretary General on Children and Armed Conflict in the Democratic Republic of the Congo," June 28, 2007, pp. 14-15, http://daccessdds.un.org/doc/UNDOC/GEN/N07/390/16/PDF/N0739016.pdf?OpenElement.

44. *Ibid.*, pp. 3-6.

45. "MONUC welcomes the success of the Goma conference and the signing of its acts of engagement," United Nations Mission in the Democratic Republic of the Congo, Jan. 23, 2008, www.monuc.org/News.aspx?newsId=16531.

46. "After two key deals, what progress towards peace in North Kivu?" United Nations Integrated Regional Information Network, May 14, 2008, www.reliefweb.int/rw/rwb.nsf/db900sid/KKAA-7EN5EQ?OpenDocument&rc=1&cc =cod.

47. "Report on Human Rights, Democratic Republic of the Congo, 2007," U.S. Department of State, www.state.gov/g/drl/rls/hrrpt/2007/100475.htm.

48. "Child Soldiers Global Report," *op. cit.*, p. 212.

49. "Report of the Secretary General on Children and Armed Conflict in Myanmar," Nov. 16, 2007, pp. 4-5.

50. "Sold to be Soldiers," *op. cit.*

51. *Ibid.*, pp. 25-26.

52. "Report of the Secretary General on Children and Armed Conflict in Myanmar," *op. cit.*, pp. 5-6.

53. "Sold to be Soldiers," *op. cit.*, p. 60.

54. *Ibid.*, p. 94.

55. "Report of the Secretary General on Children and Armed Conflict in Sri Lanka," Dec. 21, 2007.

56. "United Nations Concerned by Civilian Deaths in Sri Lanka," U.N. Department of Public Information, Jan. 2, 2007, www.un.org/News/Press/docs/2007/iha1248.doc.htm.

57. "No Safety, No Escape: Children and the Escalating Armed Conflict in Sri Lanka," Watchlist on Children and Armed Conflict, April 2008, p. 5.

58. "Complicit in Crime: State Collusion in Abductions and Child Recruitment by the Karuna Group," Human Rights Watch, January 2007, www.hrw.org/reports/2007/srilanka0107/.

59. "Press Conference on Children and Armed Conflict in Sri Lanka," U.N. Department of Public Information, April 14, 2008, www.un.org/News/briefings/docs/2008/080414_Children.doc.htm.

60. "Report of the Secretary General on Children and Armed Conflict in the Sudan," Aug. 29, 2007, p. 4, www.cfr.org/publication/11358/report_of_the_secretary general_on_children_and_armed_conflict_in_the_sudan.html.

61. *Ibid.*, pp. 5-6.

62. "Conclusions on Parties in the Armed Conflict in the Sudan," Working Group on Children and Armed Conflict, U.N. Security Council, Feb. 5, 2008, p. 1.

63. "Report of the Secretary General on the Sudan," Jan. 31, 2008, p. 2.

64. "Child Soldiers Global Report 2008," *op. cit.*, p. 319.

65. "Report of the Secretary General on Children and Armed Conflict in the Sudan," *op. cit.*, pp. 2, 5.

66. *Ibid.*, p. 6.

67. "Child Soldiers Global Report 2008", *op. cit.*, pp. 89, 93.

68. "Report of the Secretary-General on Children and Armed Conflict in Uganda," May 7, 2007, p. 3.

69. "Child Soldiers Global Report 2008," *op. cit.*, p. 347; "Uganda: LRA Regional Atrocities Demand Action," Human Rights Watch, May 19, 2008, www.hrw.org/english/docs/2008/05/19/uganda18863.htm.

70. "Report of the Secretary-General on Children and Armed Conflict in Uganda," *op. cit.*, p. 4.

71. "Child Soldiers Global Report 2008," *op. cit.*, p. 347.

72. "The Shadows of Peace: Life after the LRA," IRIN news service, Sept. 18, 2006.

73. "Optimism prevails despite setback in peace talks," IRIN news service, April 18, 2008.

74. "Stolen Children: Abduction and Recruitment in Northern Uganda," Human Rights Watch, March 2003, www.hrw.org/reports/2003/uganda0303/.

75. "Report of the Secretary-General on Children and Armed Conflict in Uganda," *op. cit.*, pp. 2, 5.

76. "Living with the LRA: The Juba Initiative," IRIN news service, May 1, 2008.

77. "Additional report of the Secretary-General on children and armed conflict in Uganda," United Nations, p. 3, June 23, 2008, http://daccess-ods.un.org/access.nsf/Get?OpenAgent&DS=s/2008/409&Lang=E.

78. Charles Mpagi Mwanguhya, "Peace Deal Dissolves," Institute for War and Peace Reporting, May 19, 2008, www.iwpr.net/?p=acr&s=f&o=344708&apc_state=henh.

79. "Report of the Secretary-General on Children and Armed Conflict," Dec. 21, 2007, p. 37.
80. "Statement in the Security Council by Special Representative of the Secretary General for Children and Armed Conflict Radhika Coomaraswamy," Feb. 12, 2008.
81. "Statement by the President of the Security Council," Feb. 12, 2008, http://daccess-ods.un.org/access.nsf/Get?Open&DS=S/PRST/2008/6&Lang=E&Area=UNDOC.
82. "Getting it Done and Doing It Right: A Global Study on the United Nations-led Monitoring and Reporting Mechanism on Children and Armed Conflict," Watchlist on Children and Armed Conflict, January 2008, www.watchlist.org/reports/pdf/global-v8-web.pdf; and "The Security Council and Children and Armed Conflicts: Next Steps towards Ending Violations Against Children," Watchlist on Children and Armed Conflict, January 2008.
83. Christo Johnson, "Sierra Leone tribunal issues historic verdicts," *The Independent* (London), June 21, 2007.
84. "Report of the Special Representative of the Secretary General for Children and Armed Conflict," Aug. 13, 2007, p. 5; Coalition to Stop the Use of Child Soldiers, www.child-soldiers.org/childsoldiers/legal-framework.
85. See www.sc-sl.org/CDF-Timeline.html.
86. "Report of the Secretary General on Children and Armed Conflict in the Democratic Republic of the Congo," *op. cit.*, p. 27.
87. "Report on Human Rights, Democratic Republic of the Congo, 2007," U.S. State Department, www.state.gov/g/drl/rls/hrrpt/2007/100475.htm.
88. "Report of the Special Representative of the Secretary General for Children and Armed Conflict," *op. cit.*
89. "The Prosecutor v. Thomas Lubanga Dyilo," International Criminal Court, www.icc-cpi.int/cases/RDC/c0106/c0106_doc.html.
90. "International Criminal Court's Trial of Thomas Lubanga 'Stayed,' " Human Rights Watch, http://hrw.org/english/docs/2008/06/19/congo19163.htm.
91. For background, see David Masci, "Human Trafficking and Slavery," *CQ Researcher*, March 26, 2004, pp. 273-296.
92. "Child Soldiers Global Report 2008," *op. cit.*, p. 12.
93. Singer, *op. cit.*, p. 118.
94. *Ibid.*, pp. 117-119.

BIBLIOGRAPHY

Books

Beah, Ishmael, *A Long Way Gone: Memoirs of a Boy Soldier*, *Sarah Chrichton Books*, 2007.
A former child soldier tells his compelling story of being recruited into one of Sierra Leone's rebel groups at age 13.

Briggs, Jimmie, *Innocents Lost: When Child Soldiers Go to War*, *Basic Books*, 2005.
A New York journalist provides first-hand reports about child soldiers in Afghanistan, Colombia, Sri Lanka and Uganda.

Rosen, David M., *Armies of the Young: Child Soldiers in War and Terrorism*, *Rutgers University Press*, 2006.
An American anthropologist examines legal and political issues surrounding the use of child soldiers.

Singer, P. W., *Children at War*, *University of California Press*, 2006.
A senior fellow at the Brookings Institution provides a comprehensive overview of the use of child soldiers.

Wessells, Michael, *Child Soldiers: From Violence to Protection*, *Harvard University Press*, 2006.
A professor of psychology at Randolph-Macon College examines issues involving child soldiers, drawing on his own three decades of experiences reintegrating former child soldiers into their former communities.

Articles

Boustany, Nora, "Report: Brokers Supply Child Soldiers to Burma," *The Washington Post*, Oct. 31, 2007, p. A16.
Burma's military government has been forcibly recruiting child soldiers through brokers who buy and sell boys to help the army deal with personnel shortages, according to a detailed report by Human Rights Watch.

Pownall, Katy, "In the Tragedy of Child-Soldiering in Africa, a Girl's Story Finds a Happy Ending," *The Associated Press*, Aug. 25, 2007.
A former female child soldier in Uganda is now studying environmental health at a university.

Reports and Studies

"Child Soldiers: Global Report 2008," *Coalition to Stop the Use of Child Soldiers*, May 2008, www.childsoldiersglobalreport.org/.
A nongovernmental organization offers its latest report on the use of child soldiers, including assessments of how well the United Nations and others are combating the problem.

"Children in Conflict: Eradicating the Child Soldier Doctrine," *The Carr Center for Human Rights Policy, Kennedy School of Government, Harvard University*, www.hks.harvard.edu/cchrp/pdf/ChildSoldierReport.pdf.
The center recommends international action to combat the use of child soldiers.

"Getting it Done and Doing It Right: A Global Study on the United Nations-led Monitoring and Reporting Mechanism on Children and Armed Conflict," *Watchlist on Children and Armed Conflict*, January 2008, www.watchlist.org/news/reports/pdf/global-v8-web.pdf.
A watchdog group critiques the U.N. Security Council's system of monitoring the impact of armed conflict on children, including child soldiers.

"Making Reintegration Work for Youth in Northern Uganda," *The Survey of War Affected Youth*, November 2007, www.sway-uganda.org/SWAY.ResearchBrief.Reintegration.pdf.
This report summarizes two phases of a long-term study of the economic, educational, social and other needs of former child soldiers in the Lord's Resistance Army in northern Uganda.

"The Security Council and Children and Armed Conflicts: Next Steps towards Ending Violations Against Children," *Watchlist on Children and Armed Conflict*, January 2008, http://watchlist.org/docs/Next_Steps_for_Security_Council_-_Child_Soldiers_Coalition_and_Watchlist_-_January_2008.pdf.
The watchdog group recommends that the U.N. Security Council take tougher measures against those who continue to use child soldiers.

"Soldiers of Misfortune: Abusive U.S. Military Recruitment and Failure to Protect Child Soldiers," American Civil Liberties Union, May 2008, www.aclu.org/intlhumanrights/gen/35245pub20080513.html.
A civil rights organization critiques U.S. policies toward the use of child soldiers, including voluntary recruitment of teenagers under 18 and detention of under-18-year-old alleged terrorists by the military.

U.N. Reports

"Children and armed conflict: Report of the Secretary-General," *U.N. Security Council*, Dec. 21, 2007, http://daccessdds.un.org/doc/UNDOC/GEN/N07/656/04/PDF/N0765604.pdf?OpenElement.
In his latest annual report to the U.N. Security Council, Secretary-General Ban Ki-moon listed 40 groups in 13 countries around the world that continue to use child soldiers. A complete list of other U.N. reports on conflicts affecting children is at www.un.org/children/conflict/english/reports.html.

For More Information

Amnesty International, 1 Easton St., London WC1X 0DW, United Kingdom; 44-20-7413-5500; http://web.amnesty.org. Actively advocates on a wide range of human rights issues, including child soldiers.

Child Rights Information Network, c/o Save the Children, 1 St. John's Lane, London EC1M 4AR, United Kingdom; 44-20-7012-6866; www.crin.org. Advocates for enforcement of international legal standards protecting children; associated with Save the Children-UK.

Coalition to Stop the Use of Child Soldiers, 4th Floor, 9 Marshalsea Road, London SE1 1EP, United Kingdom; 44-20-7367-4110/4129; www.child-soldiers.org. A coalition of international human rights groups that sponsors conferences and issues regular reports on child soldiers in armed conflicts.

Human Rights Watch, 350 Fifth Ave., 34th Floor, New York, NY 10118-3299; (212) 290-4700; http://hrw.org/campaigns/crp/index.htm. One of the most active international groups pushing governments, the United Nations and other agencies to stop using child soldiers.

International Committee of the Red Cross, 19 avenue de la Paix, CH 1202 Geneva, Switzerland; 41-22-734-6001; www.icrc.org/web/eng/siteeng0.nsf/html/children!Open. Advocates on behalf of all victims of war, including child soldiers.

United Nations Children's Fund (UNICEF), UNICEF House, 3 United Nations Plaza, New York, NY 10017; (212) 325-7000; www.unicef.org. Monitors the impact of war on children, including the recruitment and use of child soldiers.

United Nations Special Representative of the Secretary-General for Children and Armed Conflict, United Nations S-3161, New York, NY 10017; (212) 963-3178; www.un.org/children/conflict/english/home6.html. The primary U.N. official dealing with children and armed conflict; works with governments and armed groups to develop action plans for releasing child soldiers and easing the burden of children in conflict; issues regular reports on the world's most serious conflicts.

War Child International, 401 Richmond St. West, Suite 204, Toronto, Ontario, Canada M5V3A8; (416) 971-7474; www.warchild.org/index.html. A coalition of groups advocating on behalf of children caught in armed conflicts.

Watchlist on Children and Armed Conflict, c/o Women's Commission for Refugee Women and Children, 122 East 42nd St., 12th Floor, New York, NY 10168-1289; (212) 551-3111; www.watchlist.org. Publishes studies and advocates strong international action to aid children caught up in armed conflict.

3

Youth Violence

Are "Get Tough" Policies the Best Approach?

Thomas J. Billitteri

AP Photo/Chicago Police

Eighteen-year-old Eugene Riley is among five young men ages 14-19 who face murder charges in the vicious beating death last September of 16-year-old Chicago honor student Derrion Albert. Among young people ages 10 to 24, homicide is the leading cause of death for African-Americans and second-highest cause for Hispanics, according to the Centers for Disease Control and Prevention.

From *CQ Researcher*, March 5, 2010.

It was a typical day after school last fall for Derrion Albert, a 16-year-old honor student from Chicago's far South Side. As he made his way to a bus stop, he suddenly found himself in the middle of a mob of fighting teenagers. He was clubbed in the head with a piece of wood, then pushed down and stomped — all recorded on a cellphone video. Derrion died from the beating, and five suspects, ages 14 to 19, have been charged in his death.[1]

The violence was shocking, but hardly unique:

- In Seattle, a surveillance video aired on the Internet shows a teenage girl on a subway platform in late January viciously kicking another girl in the head as security personnel nearby take no action.[2]

- In Pompano Beach, Fla., a YouTube video shows three teenagers attacking and dragging a homeless man.[3]

- In Richmond, Calif., six males ages 15 to 21, plus a 43-year-old, are accused of participating in an attack in which a teenage girl was beaten, robbed and sexually assaulted for hours outside a homecoming dance last October.[4]

Youth violence today "is much more serious, much more complex and it's spreading," says Carl Taylor, a Michigan State University sociologist who has studied the phenomenon for decades. Once limited largely to hard-core street gangs, he says, the problem now is "transcending race, class and gender."

"Youth violence isn't a Chicago problem, any more than it is a black problem or a white problem," U.S. Attorney General Eric

Illinois Has Highest Violent-Crime Arrest Rate

Illinois leads the nation in juvenile arrests for violent crime, with 1,000 arrests per 100,000 persons ages 10 to 17. Five states — Maine, New Hampshire, South Dakota, Vermont and West Virginia — had arrest rates below 100.

Juvenile Arrest Rate for Violent Crime, 2008

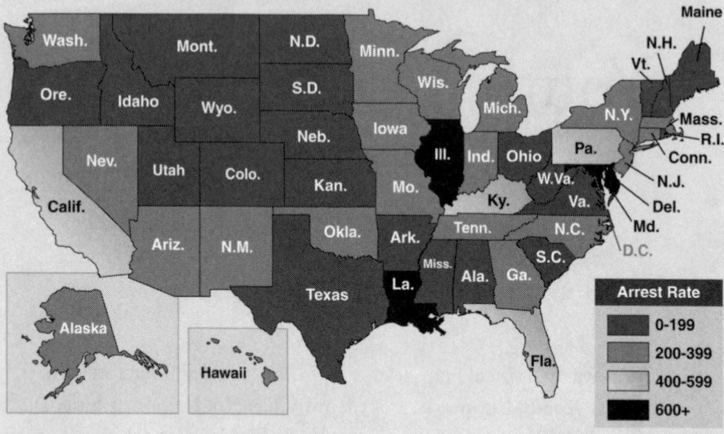

Note: While juvenile arrest rates in part reflect juvenile behavior, many other factors can affect these rates. For example, jurisdictions that arrest a relatively large number of nonresident juveniles would have higher arrest rates than jurisdictions where resident youth behave in an identical manner. Therefore, jurisdictions that are vacation destinations or regional centers for economic activity may have arrest rates that reflect more than the behavior of their resident youth. Other factors that influence arrest rates in a given area include the attitudes of its citizens toward crime and the policies of the jurisdiction's law enforcement agencies.

Source: Charles Puzzanchera, "Juvenile Arrests 2008," U.S. Department of Justice, December 2009

Holder said after Albert's death. "It's something that affects communities big and small, and people of all races and colors."[5]

Indeed, an Urban Institute study found, for example, that low-income black adolescents are less likely than low-income white adolescents to sell drugs or destroy property.[6] Holder pointed to a Justice Department survey showing that more than 60 percent of respondents age 17 and younger had been exposed to violence, directly or indirectly, over the past year. Nearly half said they had been assaulted at least once in that time.[7]

Charting statistical trends in youth violence is tricky, however. In many respects the news is positive. Juvenile crime is down sharply from the mid-1990s, when it spiked dramatically and some predicted an impending wave of adolescent "super-predators."[8] The Justice Department says, for example, that the juvenile murder arrest rate in 2008 was 74 percent less than its peak in 1993.[9]

But such data don't tell the whole story. Youth violence tends to be concentrated in certain neighborhoods, and it most often is committed not by juveniles but young adults, experts say.

"Serious violence, both in terms of those who commit it and the victims, is a young man's problem," says David M. Kennedy, director of the Center for Crime Prevention and Control at John Jay College of Criminal Justice in New York City and co-chair of the National Network for Safe Communities. "The peak years are late adolescence into the mid-20s. People often think this is a juvenile issue, but it's not. The offending rate for the 20-24 cohort is consistently much more severe than for actual juveniles."

What's more, youth violence disproportionately affects minorities. Among young people 10 to 24 years of age, homicide is the leading cause of death for African-Americans and second-highest cause for Hispanics, according to the Centers for Disease Control and Prevention.[10]

"What we're talking about is not remotely evenly socially distributed," says Kennedy. "It is far worse among minorities than among whites, and among African-Americans than other minorities. It is very heavily concentrated in particular neighborhoods, and in those neighborhoods, at a time when the national homicide rate is around five per 100,000 population, young black men are dying at a rate of over 500 per 100,000. It's astronomical."

In a 2008 study, James Alan Fox, a nationally known Northeastern University criminologist, found that homicides involving black male juveniles as victims rose 31 percent and as perpetrators 43 percent from 2002 to

2007. The picture was even grimmer for gun killings.[11]

"It's not race itself that's the issue," Fox says. "It's the socioeconomic conditions associated with race. There are longstanding problems that the black community has faced, and it's related to the inferior schools that many of these kids attend and the lack of supervision they receive — partly because of the large number of single-parent families or two-career homes where both parents are working — and the attraction of gangs that pervade these neighborhoods."

Finding solutions to youth crime and violence is not easy. In some circles, says Taylor, a "you do me, I'll do you" way of resolving conflict has become so deeply rooted, and the use of firearms so trivialized, that violence has become "almost a playful, recreational outlet."

"It's going to take a lot more than policies and police," said 28-year-old Miesha Houston, who grew up near Albert's school. "It's the poverty, drugs, rap music, the media. There are a lot of single-parent homes and parents on drugs, so the kids don't want to be home. And when they go outside, there's trouble."[12]

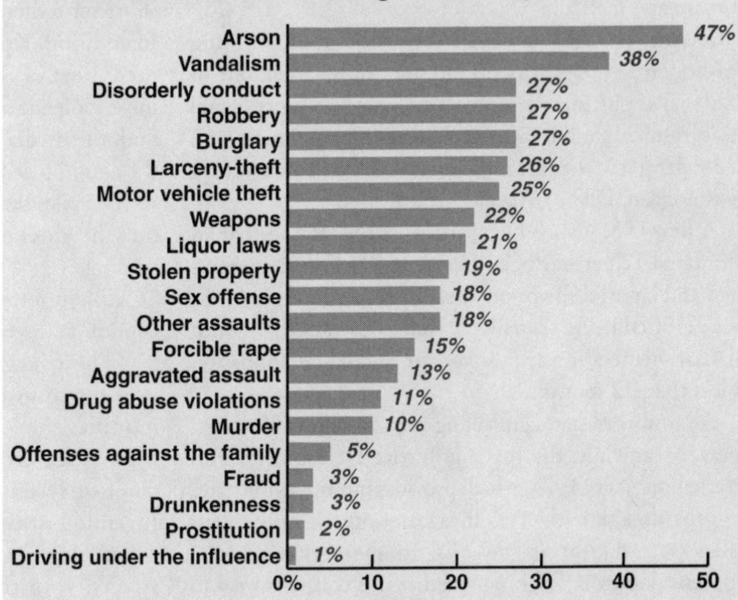

Source: Charles Puzzanchera, "Juvenile Arrests 2008," U.S. Department of Justice, December 2009

And that trouble can have a profound impact on young people who experience it, according to James J. Mazza, a professor at the University of Washington College of Education and director of its school psychology program. He studied the psychological effects of community crime and violence, including chronic drive-by shootings, gang activity, physical assaults and illegal drug sales on elementary-school students in Brooklyn's Bedford-Stuyvesant neighborhood and in Seattle. He found that the more violence the youngsters experienced, the greater the severity of their mental-health problems, including anxiety, depression, conduct disorders and risk of suicidal behavior.

Experts say some collaborative intervention approaches are making inroads into the youth-violence problem. For example, Operation Ceasefire, devised by Kennedy, forms partnerships among law enforcement officials, social-service agencies and community figures to engage with serious offenders, set clear standards against violence, offer help to those who want it and explain ahead of time the legal consequences for those who continue with crime.

On Capitol Hill, Congress has been considering several bills that offer competing approaches for dealing with youth crime. The $1.2 billion Youth Prison Reduction Through Opportunities, Mentoring, Intervention, Support and Education Act (Youth PROMISE Act) focuses on community-based prevention and intervention strategies. The Gang Abatement and Prevention Act, on the other hand, would set tough federal penalties for gang activity and provide more than $1 billion over five years for enforcement and other anti-gang efforts.

The renewed focus on juvenile crime comes amid harsh scrutiny of the juvenile-justice system. Child advocates and criminologists argue that while some juvenile crimes demand stringent punishment, too many youths are subjected to draconian incarceration, often for so-called status offenses such as truancy, running away, curfew violations and underage drinking, that is both abusive and ineffective.

Despite changes in some states, thousands of young delinquents (not status offenders) are incarcerated in adult jails, putting them at risk of physical and sexual assault, suicide and increased chances of being rearrested, according to the Campaign for Youth Justice, a Washington, D.C., advocacy group.[13]

A new U.S. Justice Department survey found that an estimated 12 percent of adjudicated youth in state-operated and large locally or privately operated juvenile facilities reported being sexually victimized by another youth or staff member in the past year or since their admission if less than 12 months.[14]

A number of states are taking steps to reform their systems. Meanwhile, the Juvenile Justice Delinquency and Prevention Act of 1974, which provides incentives for states to provide alternatives to incarceration for nonviolent offenders, is due for congressional reauthorization. And the Supreme Court is weighing whether it is constitutional to impose life sentences without parole for non-homicide crimes committed as juveniles. (*See sidebar, p. 68.*)

As cities wrestle with youth violence, here are some issues under discussion:

Is youth violence on the upswing?

To read the news in recent months it would be easy to think the nation is in the grip of a new youth crime wave. In Patchogue, on Long Island, seven teens were charged in a fatal assault on an Ecuadorian immigrant, and prosecutors alleged a pattern of teen violence against Hispanics in the area.[15] In Texas, two young men, 19 and 21, were charged with a church fire, and authorities said they may face charges in nine others.[16]

But Barry Krisberg, former president of the National Council on Crime and Delinquency and now a distinguished senior fellow at the University of California, Berkeley, law school, says youth crime "is way down from the peak in the middle 1990s." Since then, he adds, "it leveled off a little bit, and the latest numbers suggest it's down again. There's hardly a surge of it at any level."

In testimony last year to a congressional hearing, Krisberg said much of the public's perception of rising youth crime is based on the way news outlets report on crime.

A study conducted in Dallas, Washington, D.C., and San Mateo County, Calif., found that the media consistently reported increases in juvenile crime — if they were short-term increases — but not crime decreases, he said. In addition, Krisberg said, the media consistently attributed most of the violence problems to youth whereas most violence was committed by young adults. And, he said, the media often failed to offer context: "They don't do a good job of answering the 'why' questions."[17]

The relentless airing of incidents over the Internet has only heightened the public's view that youth crime is surging.

Still, in some cities, and in some neighborhoods, perception and reality can be one.

"These [aggregate crime] data are numbers from all over the country put into a blender, and in some communities the levels are very low, and in other communities they are crazy high," says Melissa Sickmund, chief of systems research at the National Center for Juvenile Justice. "You can't go into a community that's experiencing a real problem in their world, on their streets, with their kids ending up dead or their kids ending up behind bars because they committed these crimes, and tell them nationally stuff is down, it's not a problem."

In Pittsburgh, an informal survey of students ages 9 to 18 in urban neighborhoods found that almost 80 percent have had family members or friends wounded or killed by gun violence.[18] In South Philadelphia, parents, teachers and activists testified recently at a public hearing on school violence in the wake of several highly publicized incidents, including the fatal shooting of a high school football star.[19]

Jeffrey Butts, a criminologist who this spring will become executive director of the Criminal Justice Research and Evaluation Center at the John Jay College of Criminal Justice, points out that while aggregate youth crime has not been going up nationally, it can seem that way. Crime, he says, is "very local," meaning crime rates may vary among neighborhoods a few blocks from each other.

"If you're living in a poor, disadvantaged neighborhood with no infrastructure and lots of gang activity, it can seem that [crime] has gotten lots worse in the last couple of years," he says. Criminologists are only now developing reliable techniques to measure crime trends at the neighborhood level, he says.

Butts says violent youth crime generally has been fluctuating in a narrow range near what may turn out to be the bottom of a trough formed over the last dozen or so years. While youth crime is "not going up" he says, "I can't imagine it will go down a whole lot more, especially given what's going on in the economy."

Whatever the direction of overall trends, youth violence continues to plague pockets of many big cities, with minorities often the heaviest victims. "There remains an extraordinary and unconscionable persistent problem of extremely high violent criminal victimization," says Kennedy of John Jay College. "This is peer-on-peer stuff. . . . It's extremely densely concentrated among young black men in particular neighborhoods."

The crime is typically perpetrated by what Kennedy calls "a very small population of high-rate offenders involved in high-rate-offending groups like gangs, drug crews, neighborhood sets, and so on. . . . Most of the serious violent crime in these communities is perpetrated by members of these standout groups."

In Cincinnati, where an Operation Ceasefire program is under way, "there are about 60 of these identifiable offending groups, and they have a totality of about 1,500 people in them," Kennedy says. "They are associated — as victims, offenders or both — with 75 percent of all the killings in Cincinnati. Those identified by name — and therefore open to criminal-history background checks — average 35 prior charges apiece." Still, Kennedy points out, those 1,500 and all the groups associated with the killings represent a tiny fraction of the metro area's overall population.

Fox, the Northeastern University criminologist, says that in updating his study on homicides and gun killings among black youth, he found an improvement in the latest data, for 2008. Still, he says, "I don't think it changes the overall argument and overall findings that this plummeting crime rate we've been seeing in this country is not across the board and that we still have rates among certain segments, particularly young black males, that remain elevated.

"These things can vacillate from year to year. Unless we see these numbers go down for several more years, I'm still very concerned about what's happening among some Americans in some cities. And I'm concerned that there's very little attention paid toward it because overall things are better."

Are minority youths singled out for arrest and detention?

In the Pittsburgh area this year, three white undercover police officers were suspended with pay while the city investigated accusations that they severely beat a black Creative and Performing Arts High School student as he walked between his mother's and grandmother's house at night.

A criminal complaint said the 18-year-old resisted after officers confronted him. He seemed to be "sneaking around" a house with an object in his coat that the officers believed was a weapon. Police said the object turned out to be a bottle of Mountain Dew. The student alleged the officers attacked him without cause. His mother said he was attacked because he is black.[20]

However the case turns out, it highlights a longstanding debate over whether the criminal-justice system deals differently with minority youths than with whites.

"There's a lot of evidence to suggest that white youth and minority youth who commit the same crime are treated differently," says Ashley Nellis, research analyst at The Sentencing Project, a research and advocacy group in Washington.

David Muhlhausen, a senior policy analyst at the conservative Heritage Foundation think tank, sees the issue differently. "It's unfortunate, but a lot of young minorities commit a lot of crime compared to young, white males," he says. "We can argue about the reasons, but the fact is, young black males and young Hispanics have far higher rates of criminal activity than other groups. People who think the criminal-justice system is being discriminatory sort of have a false notion that the offending rates of all groups are equal, and that's simply not true."

Criminal-justice researchers point to data showing an overrepresentation of minorities in the juvenile-justice system — a phenomenon experts call "disproportionate minority contact."

For instance, a 2007 report by the National Council on Crime and Delinquency said that from 2002 to 2004, African-Americans constituted 16 percent of the American youth population but 28 percent of juvenile arrests, 35 percent of youths judicially waived to

AP Photo/Nam Y. Huh

One of Derrion Albert's cousins stands vigil beside a poster of the slain youth at the high school he had attended, Christian Fenger Academy, on Chicago's South Side. Prosecutors said Albert was an "innocent bystander" who was on his way to his bus stop when he ended up in the middle of a street fight between two factions of students. When youth violence occurs, it tends to be concentrated in certain urban neighborhoods, and it most often is committed not by juveniles but young adults, experts say.

criminal court and 58 percent of youths admitted to state adult prisons.[21]

"While public attention has tended to focus on the disproportionate number of youth of color in confinement," the report said, "this overrepresentation is often a product of actions that occur at earlier points in the juvenile-justice system," including the decision to make an initial arrest.

Interpreting juvenile-justice data can be extremely tricky. Consider Justice Department data on disproportionate minority contact showing that in 2005, the arrest rate among white youths ages 10 to 17 was 49.1 per 1,000; for black youths it was 101 per 1,000.

"This means that the black arrest rate in 2005 was more than double the white rate, documenting a racial disparity at arrest," the report notes. But, it continues, "Does this imply a racial bias in the arrest process? Not necessarily. There could be many reasons other than racial bias that produced this racial disparity at arrest." Data on relative rates of contact with the system say only "that disparity [exists] and additional exploration is needed to determine the source of the bias."[22]

Indeed, criminologists say it can be unclear why disparities exist. Possibilities range from outright bias to higher crime rates in some minority neighborhoods to the idea that more people are arrested in minority neighborhoods because, as criminologist Butts says, "that's where the police are."

"If you're a police department and you have 100 patrol cars, you don't fan them out across your area equally. You focus on the high-probability areas. Part of that could be the reality of crime, and part of it could be old-fashioned discrimination. It's just really hard to tease out."

Butts also cautions against simply reciting arrest rates for various ethnic or racial groups and not taking into account the hard realities facing many youths in impoverished urban neighborhoods, including the notions that gangs often hold sway over vulnerable teens, housing may be dangerous and substandard and job opportunities may be few. "It would be nice if we could eliminate economic and housing disparities and then see what racial disparities are left over," Butts says, "but we can't."

Nellis of The Sentencing Project says several recent trends have contributed to racial disparities in juvenile arrest and detention data. One, she says, is the presence of police officers in schools, a practice that has grown with the introduction of zero-tolerance discipline policies in recent years.[23]

"Whereas altercations used to be handled by the school, now police are called in, and it's considered an assault rather than just a scuffle. It's more likely to happen in low-income school districts in urban areas, where there are more minority youth." And once minority youths get a police record, she says, "they're more likely to get another record and penetrate the [criminal-justice] system further."

Nellis also says behavior such as drug and alcohol use that families in majority-white communities might handle through private therapists or social-service agencies are more likely dealt with in the criminal-justice system in low-income minority communities. Often, she says, minority youths are inappropriately placed in juvenile facilities in order to receive services not otherwise available in their communities.

Sometimes, criminology experts say, minority youth are targeted by police not because their basic offenses are different from those committed by whites but because of the location of the offenses. Drug sales can be an example. Illegal street-corner transactions in low-income neighborhoods typically get more police attention than does drug distribution carried out circumspectly in

Sexual-Victimization Survey Names 13 Youth Facilities

Thirteen out of 195 juvenile facilities surveyed by the National Survey of Youth in Custody had more than a 20 percent — or "high" — sexual-victimization rate. Six of the 13 had rates of 30 percent or above. Indiana, Texas and Virginia each had two facilities on the list.

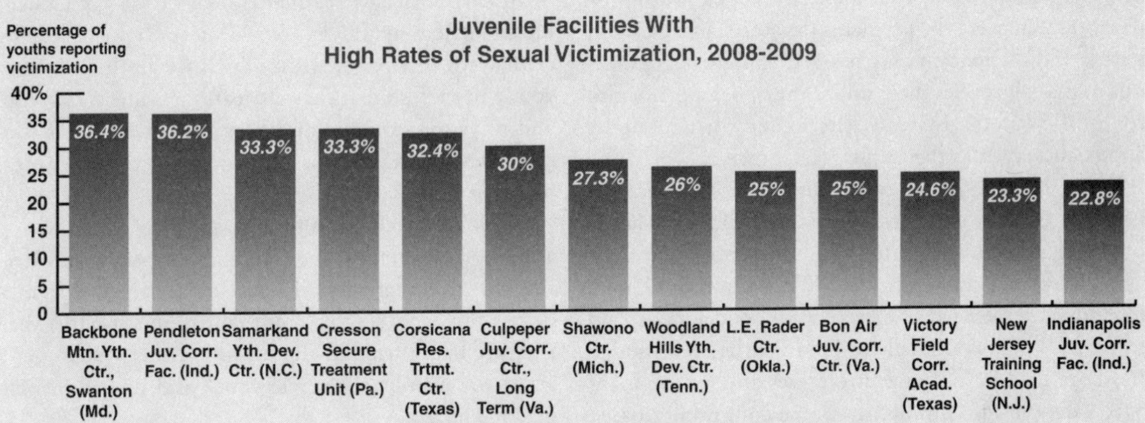

Source: Allen J. Beck, et al., "Sexual Victimization in Juvenile Facilities Reported by Youth, 2008-09," Bureau of Justice Statistics, January 2010

wealthier white neighborhoods, says Sickmund of the National Center for Juvenile Justice.

"If there were unlimited police resources, they might have the luxury of observing what goes on in the suburban community," says Sickmund. "A lot of white kids do drugs, but they're being passed out at school or in a car or at home, so there's less of an outcry."

Are "get tough" policies the best approach for fighting youth crime?

Beginning this year, Connecticut raised, from 16 to 17, the age at which youths accused of crimes are automatically tried in adult courts. (The age rises to 18 in July 2012.) That left only two states — New York and North Carolina — that set the bar at 16.[24]

Connecticut's move reflects a broad national trend of easing away from "get tough" juvenile-justice strategies instituted during the 1980s and '90s, when many feared the onset of a massive new crime wave.[25]

Still, many say the juvenile-justice system remains in need of wholesale reform. Among the deepest concerns is the potential for abuse. "Most of our juvenile facilities, with very few exceptions, are abusive places," the University of California's Krisberg says. "We have an epidemic of abuse in juvenile facilities" that ranges from subjecting youths to isolation and seclusion to using excessive force. "These tend to be dangerous, gang-ridden environments. So the more kids we put in these places, the worse the situation gets."

Sexual abuse is a prime concern. In its study of the issue in juvenile prisons, the Justice Department said six facilities had victimization rates of 30 percent or higher.[26]

Sexual abuse of youths in prison "is one of those hidden closets of the system," Bart Lubow, director of the Juvenile Justice Strategy Group for the Annie E. Casey Foundation, recently told *USA Today.* The abuse rates at the worst juvenile prisons are "so high they're stunning," he said. "I am, on the other hand, never surprised as people peel the layers of the youth corrections onion and expose more and more things that make you cry."[27]

Physical cruelty also is a worry. In New York State, a U.S. Justice Department report last August cited abuse by staff at four juvenile prisons.[28] "Anything from sneaking an extra cookie to initiating a fistfight may result in a full prone restraint with handcuffs," the report stated. "This one-size-fits-all approach has . . . led to an alarming number of serious injuries to youth, including concussions, broken or knocked-out teeth and spinal fractures."[29]

In December, a state-appointed panel in New York concluded that the kind of abuse cited in the federal investigation prevailed throughout the state's youth prisons. So severe were the problems that the state agency in charge of the detention centers asked family-court judges not to place juveniles there unless they pose a major risk to public safety. Instead, the agency urged other approaches, such as therapeutic foster care.[30]

Many juvenile-justice experts argue that incarceration not only is costly and leaves youths vulnerable to abuse but often also leads them toward more serious crimes.

The Justice Policy Institute, a Washington think tank that advocates less use of incarceration, said states spend some $5.7 billion annually to hold youths even though most are held for nonviolent offenses and can be managed safely in the community. Some community-based programs have cut recidivism rates as much as 22 percent, it said.[31]

Gladys Carrión, commissioner of New York's Office of Children and Family Services and a reform advocate, said a longitudinal study in New York State found that 85 percent of boys and 65 percent of girls who are incarcerated are convicted of a felony as adults.[32]

"We have to recognize that incarceration of youth per se is toxic, so we need to reduce incarceration of young people to the very small dangerous few," Krisberg says. "And we've got to recognize that if we lock up a lot of kids, it's going to increase crime. Nothing could be more dramatic than California, where we moved our youth prison population from 10,000 inmates to 1,500 in a decade, and crime went down."

While child advocates say the juvenile-justice system has a long way to go before it is safe for youthful defendants and effective at keeping them from falling deeper into crime, a number of jurisdictions have been taking steps — both big and small — toward rethinking the way they treat young offenders.

In Missouri, for example, they are assigned to small cottage-style facilities staffed by highly trained adults called facilitators. The so-called Missouri Model stresses "rehabilitation in small groups, constant therapeutic interventions and minimal force," according to a recent profile in *The New York Times*. "Perhaps most impressive," it added, "Missouri has one of the lowest recidivism rates in the country."[33]

"What Missouri does is to say, look, what's important is not just that we have programs that meet individual needs and deficits, like a GED program or mental health treatment or drug [treatment]," says John Jay College President Jeremy Travis. "What's important is that we change the environment in which we are imprisoning young people, so that they are learning some social skills and ways to get along and how to manage their own impulses so that when they get out they're better prepared."

Illinois, which in 2006 separated its juvenile and adult correctional systems, changed a nearly four-decade-old law under which 17-year-olds charged with misdemeanors were sent to adult court. Starting this year, they are being tried in the juvenile court system, with access to rehabilitative services such as drug and mental-health counseling.[34]

In Florida, the state Supreme Court in December barred the widespread practice of shackling juveniles in court, saying it is "repugnant, degrading [and] humiliating." The court said handcuffs and leg shackles should be permitted only if a judge determines a youth will likely become violent.[35]

In Wisconsin, where 17-year-old criminal defendants are automatically tried as adults, a handful of bills have been introduced aimed at changing the way juvenile offenses are handled. For example, a measure that would require a judge to order a psychological assessment when a juvenile claimed a mental illness, developmental disability or substance-abuse problem passed 3-2 along party lines in December in the Senate Judiciary Committee.[36]

A joint legislative council said in 2008 that Wisconsin should send more youthful offenders into the juvenile system, citing a 48 percent recidivism rate among juveniles placed in the adult system — triple that of those in the juvenile system.[37]

BACKGROUND

Early Reforms

Youth violence is by no means a uniquely modern problem. Youth gangs, for instance, date back to the dawn of the Republic.

CHRONOLOGY

1900-1960s *Juvenile-court system comes under scrutiny as legal reformers seek constitutional protections for juveniles accused of wrongdoing.*

1924 Fourteen-year-old Bobby Franks is killed by two wealthy teenagers in Chicago "thrill" killing.

1925 All but two states have juvenile courts or probation services.

1953 Senate Subcommittee to Investigate Juvenile Delinquency urges more federal aid for state delinquency prevention and treatment programs.

1961 President John F. Kennedy signs Juvenile Delinquency and Youth Offenses Control Act, authorizing $30 million over three years for prevention and research.

1962 Youths under 18 are involved in more than 50 percent of car-theft arrests, half of larceny and burglary arrests and 8 percent of murder arrests.

1966-1970 Supreme Court extends constitutional due-process rights to defendants in juvenile courts.

1970s-1980s *Crack-cocaine epidemic spurs crime wave, leads to strict, new laws on youth crime.*

1974 Congress amends Juvenile Crime and Delinquency Prevention Act of 1968 to require states receiving grants under the law to bar detention for "status" offenses, such as curfew violations and other acts that would not be crimes if committed by adults, and to separate juveniles from adult inmates in jails and prisons.

1978 Murders by 15-year-old Willie Bosket Jr. lead to tough, new juvenile-crime law in New York.

1982 In *Eddings v. Oklahoma*, Supreme Court limits death penalty for juveniles.

1987 As crack epidemic takes off, youth murder arrests begin to climb.

1988 In *Thompson v. Oklahoma*, Supreme Court declares executions of youths under 16 as unconstitutional, but the next year, in *Stanford v. Kentucky*, the court upholds executions of 16- and 17-year-old defendants.

1990s *Youth violence soars in mid-decade but then falls even as states pass new laws allowing more juveniles to be tried as adults.*

1992 Forty-seven states and the District of Columbia pass laws over the next five years to make juvenile-justice systems stricter.

1993 Juvenile-arrest rate for murder peaks at more than 14 per 100,000 juveniles ages 10-17, but then begins a steep decline, to about 4 per 100,000 in 2000.

1997 Forty-five states have made transferring juveniles to the criminal system easier.

2000s-Present *Supreme Court abolishes death penalty for juveniles and weighs life-without-parole sentences.*

2005 In *Roper v. Simmons*, Supreme Court abolishes death penalty for juvenile offenders.

2006 Illinois separates its juvenile and adult correctional systems.

2007 Connecticut raises the age at which youths can be tried as adults from 16 to 18, leaving two states — New York and North Carolina — remaining with 16 as the threshold age.

2009 High-profile killing of Chicago honor student Derrion Albert leads Obama administration to call for more focus on youth violence; more than 60 percent of youths responding to Justice Department survey say they had been exposed to violence.

2010 Justice Department estimates 12 percent of youths in state juvenile facilities and large, non-state facilities reported at least one incident of sexual victimization by another youth or facility staff member in past year. . . . Supreme Court scheduled to decide whether it is constitutional to impose life sentences without the possibility of parole for non-homicide crimes committed by juveniles.

Defendants Seek Review of Life Sentences

Supreme Court to decide in two Florida cases involving former teenagers.

Five years ago the U.S. Supreme Court abolished the death penalty for defendants who murder as juveniles, saying in the 5-4 ruling that execution violates "the evolving standards of decency that mark the progress of a maturing society."[1]

This term the court faces another monumental decision: whether sentencing a defendant to life in prison without the chance of parole for a crime committed as a juvenile in which nobody was killed violates the Eighth Amendment's ban on cruel and unusual punishment. (*See "At Issue," p. 75.*)

Before the court is a pair of Florida cases. Joe Sullivan, who is mentally disabled, was sentenced to life without parole in 1989 after a conviction for sexual battery of an elderly woman at age 13. Terrance Graham was convicted of armed burglary at age 16 and was on probation when, at 17, he participated in a home invasion.

While the Supreme Court's decision may be significant, its reach could also be limited. Ashley Nellis, a research analyst at The Sentencing Project, a criminal-justice research and advocacy group, says that only 109 inmates are currently serving life-without-parole sentences for crimes they committed as minors in which no one died. And only two — including Sullivan — were 13 when they committed their crimes, she says.

That still leaves some 2,000 youthful offenders serving life without parole in cases involving homicides, Nellis says.

A bill sponsored by U.S. Rep. Bobby Scott, D-Va., chairman of the Subcommittee on Crime, Terrorism and Homeland Security, addresses the broad issue of life sentences for juvenile offenders.[2]

The legislation would, among other things, require states to grant juvenile offenders serving life the opportunity for parole or supervised release at least once during their first 15 years of incarceration and at least once every three years after that. It also would require the U.S. Attorney General to put in place an early-release system for juvenile offenders serving life sentences in federal prison.

So far, the bill has garnered only four co-sponsors in the House, all Democrats.

Critics argue that life-without-parole sentences are draconian, out of step with international law and fail to take into account scientific research showing that adolescents' capacity for reasoning and impulse control are not fully mature. But others say life sentences for some juvenile offenders are an appropriate way to protect public safety, deter crime and hold perpetrators accountable.

"While other countries have abolished this practice, we continue to impose this sentence at alarming rates," Scott declared at a hearing last year on his proposed bill.

In 14 states, Scott said, children as young as 8 can be sentenced to life without parole. African-American youths receive such sentences 10 times more often than white youths, on average, with disparities even greater in states such as Pennsylvania and California, he added. What's more, Scott said, most juvenile life-without-parole sentences stem from mandatory-minimum sentencing guidelines.

"In 29 states, once a youth is convicted of certain crimes, the court must impose life and cannot give consideration at sentencing to either the child's age or life history."[3]

Shay Bilchik, director of the Center for Juvenile Justice Reform at the Georgetown University Public Policy Institute, says "every case should be analyzed individually.

"To say that an offense committed when someone is a juvenile leads to a life-without-parole sentence is basically saying his life is over, there's no possibility of redemption, and I just don't believe that to be true. It's too strict a sentencing parameter to not reflect the understanding we have about the development of young people."

"The earliest record of their appearance in the United States may have been as early as 1783, as the American Revolution ended," the Justice Department noted. While experts debate when and why youth gangs first appeared, "[t]hey may have emerged spontaneously from adolescent play groups or as a collective response to urban conditions in this country," it said.

And by the early 1800s, it added, "gangs appear to have spread in New England . . . as the Industrial Revolution gained momentum in the first large cities in the United States: New York, Boston and Philadelphia."[38]

As is the case today, some youths fell into serious crime, but many more found themselves in trouble for minor misdeeds. In the 19th century, those offenses might have

Marc Mauer, executive director of The Sentencing Project, makes a similar argument. "To assume that we can know on the day of sentencing what a 15-year-old will be like in 10, 20 or 30 years — it's just ludicrous," he says. "To deny even the possibility of permitting a reconsideration of the case seems foolish not only on compassionate grounds, but on the grounds of cost-effectiveness, too. It doesn't help any of us to incarcerate a 50-year-old who's no longer a public safety threat when those funds could be better used to deal with teenagers who are beginning to get into trouble and need some kind of intervention."

But others argue that life sentences fit some crimes.

"An overwhelming national consensus exists that a life-without-parole sentence is appropriate and constitutional for juvenile offenders who show an exceptional disregard for human life," the National Organization of Victims of Juvenile Lifers argued in a brief filed in the Supreme Court case.

"Courts, legislatures and American people have strongly approved of these sentences as an effective and lawful device to deter juvenile crime and protect law-abiding citizens. These institutions understand that violent crimes are no less traumatizing to victims because the offenders are underage. A criminal-justice system which categorically denies constitutional and proper sentences for juvenile offenders perpetuates no justice at all."[4]

Charles D. Stimson and Andrew M. Grossman of the conservative Heritage Foundation argued in a report last year that a life-without-parole sentence "for the very worst juvenile offenders is reasonable, constitutional and (appropriately) rare. In response to the Western world's worst juvenile crime problem, U.S. legislators have enacted commonsense measures to protect their citizens and hold these dangerous criminals accountable."[5]

In testimony in support of Scott's bill, Mark William Osler, a former federal prosecutor and a professor at Baylor Law School, said that while the measure would not allow children who commit serious crimes to escape prosecution or long sentences, "it would . . . give them hope that someday, perhaps in middle age, they might see something other than the inside of a prison. Life with the possibility of parole would be both a reasonable and a principled incremental change."[6]

But James P. Fox, a district attorney in California and chairman of the National District Attorneys Association, called the bill an "overly broad and one-sided attempt to require state legislatures to revise juvenile codes across America to make it more difficult to prosecute juvenile offenders as adults for egregious crimes and to punish juvenile offenders less seriously for their criminal behavior solely because of their perceived immaturity."[7]

And Rep. Louie Ghomert, R-Texas, ranking member of the crime subcommittee, said the bill "violates the principles of federalism." He said, "It is inappropriate at best and unconstitutional at worst for Congress to seek to regulate the manner in which states determine appropriate sentences for state crimes committed and prosecuted within their jurisdiction."[8]

— ***Thomas J. Billitteri***

---

[1] *Roper v. Simmons*, 543 U.S. 551 (2005)

[2] Rep. Scott's bill is HR 2289.

[3] Statement of Rep. Robert C. "Bobby" Scott, hearing on the Juvenile Justice Accountability and Improvement Act of 2009, House Subcommittee on Crime, Terrorism and Homeland Security, June 9, 2009, http://judiciary.house.gov/hearings/printers/111th/111-47_50141.pdf.

[4] National Organization of Victims of Juvenile Lifers, Amici Curiae brief in support of State of Florida, Sept. 21, 2009, pp. 12-13, accessed at www.abanet.org/publiced/preview/briefs/pdfs/07-08/08-7412_RespondentAmCuNOVJL.pdf.

[5] Charles D. Stimson and Andrew M. Grossman, "Adult Time for Adult Crimes," Aug. 17, 2009, www.heritage.org/research/crime/sr0065.cfm.

[6] Written testimony of Mark William Osler, House Subcommittee on Crime, Terrorism and Homeland Security, *ibid.*

[7] Written testimony of James P. Fox, House Subcommittee on Crime, Terrorism and Homeland Security, *ibid.*

[8] Comments of Rep. Louie Gohmert, hearing on the Juvenile Justice Accountability and Improvement Act of 2009, House Subcommittee on Crime, Terrorism and Homeland Security, June 9, 2009.

been petty stealing, street begging or even less serious acts such as loitering, partly a manifestation of the widespread poverty resulting from massive European immigration to American cities in the 1800s.

Yet back then, the United States had no separate justice system for dealing with juvenile offenders. Children and adolescents accused of crimes were tried in adult courts and, if found guilty, could be jailed alongside adults.

Reformers began to set up separate institutions for the confinement of juveniles, with "houses of refuge," reform schools and "industrial schools" among the approaches. Yet, as law professor Lawrence M. Friedman noted, "Despite all these institutional changes, children could still be arrested, detained, tried and sent to prison in many states. In 1870, there were 2,029 minors in jail in Massachusetts; 231 of them were under 15. And even in states with specialized institutions . . . the trial process for juveniles was the same as for adults."[39]

That began to change at the turn of the 20th century with the formation of the nation's first juvenile court, in 1899 in Cook County (Chicago), Illinois. The basic philosophy behind the emerging juvenile-justice system was that the state could exercise guardianship over children who found themselves in trouble with the law, treating them not as criminals but as youngsters who needed care and direction of the sort a parent gives a child.

"Courts focused on what was in the best interests of the child instead of concerning themselves solely with issues of criminal guilt or punishment," a recent book on youth justice explained. "The underlying principle was that children were different and could be rehabilitated if given a second chance."[40]

As Judge Julian Mack, among the new juvenile court's first judges, wrote: "Why is it not just and proper to treat these juvenile offenders, as we deal with the neglected children, as a wise and merciful father handles his own children whose errors are not discovered by the authorities? Why is it not the duty of the state, instead of asking merely whether a boy or girl has committed a specific offense, to find out what he is physically, mentally, morally, and then if it learns that he is treading the path that leads to criminality, to take him in charge, not so much to punish as to reform, not to degrade but to uplift, not to crush but to develop, not to make him a criminal but a worthy citizen."[41]

By 1910, juvenile courts and/or probation services were established in 32 states, and by 1925 they were in all but two states.[42] Still, as researcher John L. Hutzler wrote, "the new weapons of diagnosis and treatment with which the [juvenile court] campaign began never achieved their anticipated accuracy or effectiveness, and the monetary resources needed to pursue the new strategy effectively were never provided. The failure of the movement to achieve its ultimate objective — the solution to juvenile misbehavior — eventually began to erode public confidence in the juvenile court."[43]

Even as the nation sought to address the challenges of juvenile justice and delinquency, it was not immune to instances of wanton violence committed by teens and young adults. One of the most notorious cases involved the 1924 Chicago "thrill" killing of 14-year-old Bobby Franks. Richard Loeb, the 18-year-old son of a retired Sears Roebuck vice president, and his 19-year-old partner, Nathan Leopold, a law student, were convicted of the murder and sentenced to life in prison.[44]

Rising Delinquency

In the post-World War II period, government officials and private citizens began to grow increasingly worried about rising levels of teenage delinquency and the potential for youth violence.

Data from the era underscore the trend. In 1962, for example, arrests of juveniles under 18 had risen at a pace that was more than three times that of their population growth in the previous six years. Youths under 18 were involved in more than 60 percent of car-theft arrests, roughly half of larceny and burglary arrests, a fourth of robbery arrests, 19 percent of forcible rape arrests, 13 percent of aggravated assault arrests and 8 percent of murder and non-negligent manslaughter arrests. All together, juveniles accounted for 45 percent of arrests for those crimes.[45]

As anxiety was growing over serious juvenile crime, confidence also was eroding in the juvenile-justice rehabilitation and treatment model devised at the turn of the 20th century. Many believed the approach simply wasn't working effectively to reduce youth crime. Conversely, some argued that too many young people were being swept up in the justice system without being afforded proper legal rights.

Starting in the 1960s, the Supreme Court began to weigh in on the issue of juvenile rights. It rendered a series of rulings that granted juveniles greater constitutional protections but also drew the juvenile-justice system further from the paternalistic one created at the turn of the century and closer to that used for adult defendants. For example, in the landmark 1967 case *In re Gault*, involving a 15-year-old boy accused of making a prank phone call, the court declared that juveniles have basic constitutional rights in hearings that can lead to their confinement in an institution, including the right to question witnesses, the right against self-incrimination and the right to legal counsel.[46]

In the 1970s, new laws and policies emphasized community-based programs and other approaches designed to minimize incarceration of juveniles involved in noncriminal offenses, such as truancy and underage drinking. But starting in the late 1970s and early '80s, the public mood began to shift toward a less tolerant view of juvenile crime and delinquency, fueled by a perception that serious youth crime was on the upswing.

"Although there was substantial misperception regarding increases in juvenile crime, many [s]tates responded by passing more punitive laws," a Justice Department report noted. "Some laws removed certain classes of offenders from the juvenile-justice system and handled them as adult criminals in criminal court. Others required the juvenile-justice system to be more like the criminal-justice system and to treat certain classes of juvenile offenders as criminals but in juvenile court."[47]

The move toward a stricter law-and-order approach was spurred partly by street crime arising from the sale and use of crack cocaine and other illegal drugs. Beginning in 1987, violent crimes, including rapes, robberies, aggravated assaults and homicides, committed by juveniles and young adults began to escalate dramatically, reaching a peak in the mid-1990s. In 1994, juvenile arrests for violent crimes were 40 percent higher than the 24-year average, and in 1993 victim reports were more than 50 percent higher.[48] The juvenile arrest rate for murder rose 110 percent from 1987 to 1993, with roughly 14 arrests per 100,000 juveniles ages 10 to 17 in 1993.[49]

As youth crime moved toward its mid-1990s peak, states began to pass strict new laws, including provisions allowing more and more juveniles to be tried in the adult system. Between 1992 and 1997, a total of 47 states and the District of Columbia passed laws making their juvenile-justice systems stricter. Forty-five states made it easier to transfer juveniles to the criminal system. In 31 states, laws allowed criminal and juvenile courts to expand their options for sentencing juveniles. And 47 states made juvenile proceedings and records more open, undercutting confidentiality provisions that had been a hallmark of the traditional juvenile-justice system.[50]

As laws grew more stringent, incarceration rates soared. From 1985 to 1997, the one-day count of state prisoners younger than 18 rose 135 percent, about the same as for older inmates.[51] The average daily population in juvenile detention facilities more than doubled in that time span, to 28,000, according to data cited by the Annie E. Casey Foundation.[52]

Helping Hands

While overall crime and violence has fallen sharply since the mid-1990s, it remains a scourge in some inner-city neighborhoods, and the consequences for young people who experience it are grave, experts say.

Timothy Brezina, an associate professor of criminal justice at Georgia State University, says research he and others have conducted on the attitudes of young offenders shows that children exposed to violence often become perpetrators themselves as they get older.

Often, youngsters become desensitized to violence and come to believe it is normal, Brezina says. What's more, he says, being a victim can breed a desire for retaliation or revenge. And "to prevent becoming a victim, people may arm themselves, not just with guns but other weapons, for self protection, which increases the likelihood that future altercations may result in violence or injury."

In interviews with young offenders in Atlanta, Brezina says he found a strong sense of "futurelessness" — a feeling of hopelessness, heightened by the violence and economic disparity around them, which sometimes leads them to flout the law or otherwise ignore the consequences of their actions.

"Without having certainty that you have a stable future to look forward to, future planning didn't seem to make a lot of sense" to the youths, Brezina says. "Or avoiding certain things because you didn't want to jeopardize your future — that didn't seem to register with a lot of these young men, because the future for them is something they didn't necessarily count on or could count on. Many suggested that surviving this day is the challenge, and five years from now might seem like another century to them."

That view has policy implications, Brezina says. "The idea of being apprehended, convicted and serving a long sentence — that assumes you have a future that can be jeopardized by being wrapped up in the criminal-justice system," he says. But "if you don't have a stable future to look forward to, there's less reason to defer or delay gratification, to be cautious or careful. That may help to explain why deterrence-based strategies alone [haven't been] a solution for youth violence"

That, Brezina says, points to the need for the juvenile-justice system to focus more strongly on the underlying causes of youth violence. "I'm not suggesting it's an easy problem," he says. "But to focus on deterrence and not deal with some of the root causes has done little to address the problem."

Intervention approaches that seek to give young offenders a path away from trouble have made some inroads into the youth-crime problem.

When Offenders and Victims Sit Down and Talk

"Restorative Justice" provides an alternative to the courtroom.

Like many victims of violent crime, Phyllis Lawrence ended up in a courtroom. But when she later heard about a unique alternative to the judicial process — in which the victim and perpetrator sit down and talk — "it sounded like what was missing for me in the whole courtroom process," Lawrence says.

The process is called restorative justice, and it encourages offenders to take responsibility for their actions, such as by apologizing to the victim, repaying money or participating in community service. Lawrence is a lawyer and has been a consultant in restorative justice and victim issues in Alexandria, Va., for the past 15 years. Typically used in juvenile criminal cases, restorative justice brings the offender and victim of a crime together with a facilitator as well as their respective "support systems" — usually friends or family members — to openly discuss what happened. The fundamental idea behind the process is to provide support for victims while holding offenders accountable.

"When I started 15 years ago, you could practically name every program," Lawrence says.

There are now more than 290 restorative justice programs throughout the United States.[1] The Community Conferencing Center of Baltimore (CCC), which uses restorative justice and community conferencing practices in cases ranging from petty theft and neighborhood disputes to murder, has handled over 10,000 cases since its founding in 1998. Lauren Abramson, an assistant professor of psychology at Johns Hopkins University and founder of the CCC, estimates that 90 percent of the cases the center handles involve young people, many of them dealing with assault. Abramson said that the CCC has not handled a murder case with a juvenile offender.

"I think it's a process that's very effective with human beings regardless of the age," Abramson says. "Our society just seems more comfortable using this with young people before we start using it with adults."

Especially in the case of juveniles, restorative justice allows many people to substitute conferencing for the legal system, in what is called a diversion case — usually involving first or second-time offenders.

Lawrence says that every case operates differently. In diversion cases, restorative justice is used in place of going to court. The starting point is often a local court-services unit that will talk to courts that use the restorative justice approach about deferring a case to a restorative justice organization. For cases involving severe violence, conferencing is often used in conjunction with the court system, as a rehabilitation tool for offenders after sentencing.

In a community conference session, everyone involved in a crime or dispute sits in a circle and talks about how everyone in the circle has been affected by what happened and what can be done to fix it. Participants are prepared for the meeting by the facilitator, who talks to them individually beforehand to decide what they want to get out of the discussion.

"The key to the restorative justice process is preparation," says Lawrence. "People who watch sessions are often shocked at how quiet they are. That's because a lot of anger and fear has been expressed in the preparation process."

At the end of most conferences, participants compose a written agreement about how to resolve the situation, usually addressing what the offenders will do to change their behavior. Abramson says almost all of her conferences result in an agreement and that they have a 98 percent compliance rate.

One approach is Operation Ceasefire. Kennedy of John Jay College says it began as a way to deal with high rates of gun homicides in Boston and now is being used in Chicago, Cincinnati and more than 40 other cities to address violence and sometimes open-air drug dealing. He says the program has helped to cut homicides by 35 to more than 50 percent across cities where it operates.

Because most homicides and other serious crimes are committed by "a very small population of high-rate offenders," Kennedy says, it is possible to identify them by name and engage them personally.

In the case of gangs, probation and parole authorities direct one or two members of each gang to come to a meeting. There, people in the gangs' community, such as ex-offenders and mothers of murdered children, tell the gang members that their own community needs the violence to stop. Social-service providers explain how the gang members can get special access to a wide range

However, in a diversion case, if the conferencing doesn't work out, the case is handled as it normally would be through the court system.

According to the CCC, recidivism rates for juveniles who go through community conferencing are 60 percent lower than rates for youths who go through the juvenile justice system.

In addition to being more effective in holding offenders accountable, Lawrence says the process also provides sensitivity toward the victim's experience that is often lacking in a courtroom.

"When you hear how you hurt the victim, it's much more effective in hitting them at the core than having a judge talk to you," Lawrence says.

"I think it's a pretty strong underground movement in this country," says Abramson. "The hope is that it will eventually be funded at the level it should be because it's getting far better social outcomes at about one-tenth of what current court proceedings cost."

Restorative justice advocates say the technique also has the potential to save some of the taxpayer money that is poured each year into prison upkeep. According to a July 2009 report by The Sentencing Project, there are 2.3 million people in prisons or jails in the United States, a 600 percent increase since 1972.[2] If implemented on a large scale, restorative justice practices could greatly decrease the number of prisoners in the United States while also helping to rehabilitate criminals, the group says.

Restorative practices are also being used to solve conflict within schools. Abramson and the CCC have started school-community conferencing programs and say they have worked with about 70 percent of the schools in Baltimore.

"Especially in our work in schools, we notice that so many serious fights were a result of poor social skills and poor relationship management skills," says Abramson. "So we started an in-class dialogue process with teachers for them to facilitate with students called the Daily Rap."

The CCC has provided three-hour training sessions for about 1,500 teachers, supplying them with a classroom-management tool that allows students and teachers to sit down regularly to discuss issues that concern them, in order to be proactive in avoiding conflict and miscommunication.

"I think it's vital that we start in the schools," says Lawrence, who currently volunteers with Northern Virginia Mediation Services, which works with Fairfax County schools.

This type of mediation has proven successful in reducing violence as well as fostering better relationships between teachers and students. When West Philadelphia High School implemented what the faculty and students call "circles," they quickly saw positive results.

"Before we had circles at our school there were a lot of fights, riots, problems," said Ashai Peterson, a student at West Philadelphia High School, in a video documenting the school's transformation. "It was just a lot of confusion."[3]

The school had consistently been on the city's "persistently dangerous" school list. Within a year of starting the "circles," crime rates dropped 52 percent.[4]

"We need these kinds of structures in our culture that provide a chance for people to talk to each other," says Abramson. "In doing so we increase our chances of survival as a species."

— ***Dagny Leonard***

---

[1] Barron County Restorative Justice Programs, Inc., www.bcrjp.org/victim_off.html.

[2] "No Exit: The Expanding Use of Life Sentences In America," The Sentencing Project, July 2009, http://sentencingproject.org/doc/publications/publications/inc_noexitseptember2009.pdf.

[3] "The Transformation of West Philadelphia High School: A Story of Hope," The International Institute for Restorative Practices, 2009, www.youtube.com/watch?v=HatSl1lu_PM.

[4] *Ibid.*

of services, and law enforcement officials explain that a killing or shooting by any member of their gang will lead to focused police attention around, for instance, street drug dealing, on all members.

"You have a message of standards and redemption" and accountability, Kennedy says, "a message of help and of uncompromising community standards that violence is wrong and will not be tolerated. Law enforcement says, 'we would like you to listen to your own and put your guns down — we don't want to lock you up. But at the end of the day, this is not negotiable.' "

The approach does several things, Kennedy says. "You're giving people a way out" by providing them help. In addition, "you are articulating these very, very powerful, simple community standards that say violence is not OK. You're directly undercutting the street rules that drive the violence. You are reversing the dynamic within the group that promotes the violence by creating this collective accountability for it."

Another collaborative approach — this one in Philadelphia — is the 11-year-old Youth Violence Reduction Partnership (YVRP). Its goal is to redirect youths ages 14 to 24 who are at the highest risk of killing or being killed away from violence and toward productive lives.

YVRP provides juveniles and young adults who are already on probation for serious offenses with "intense supervision and support," says Wendy S. McClanahan, vice president for research at Public/Private Ventures, a national nonprofit organization that evaluates the program's results. Now working in six violence-prone police districts in Philadelphia, the program is a collaboration among law enforcement officials, probation officers, child-welfare agencies, nonprofit community groups, district attorney offices, school districts and others.

It uses a carrot-and-stick approach. It has a zero-tolerance policy for guns, uses a system of graduated sanctions for noncompliance and holds youths accountable with "swift sanctions" if they get into further trouble, McClanahan says. Probation officers work in teams with a system of "street workers," with the probation officers mainly supervising the youths and the street workers serving as mentors to them and linking them to community resources for everything from childcare and drug and alcohol therapy to employment counseling.

The street workers are not social workers following a formal case-management approach, but rather "paraprofessionals" who may or may not have been in trouble themselves, McClanahan says. All, however, come from backgrounds similar to that of the youths they work with, she adds.

McClanahan said an evaluation of the program's effects on individual participants is in the final stages of completion, but that fewer murders have occurred among youths in the police districts where it has operated.

While punishment is necessary when youths commit crimes, particularly violent ones, McClanahan says, policy makers must also use collaborative approaches to address the needs of urban youths at risk of committing or being victimized by violence.

"When we think about youth violence, we cannot forget that these are kids," she says. Many youths in big-city urban cores, particularly males, "are really at risk for violence and for being murdered. . . . There are just so many stressors for them: poverty, being surrounded by violence, perhaps lack of employment opportunities, not good schools and not the safety net that middle-class and upper-class kids have. . . . When you think about public opinion, I don't feel there is a lot of discussion about the fact that these are kids. And what does that mean for how we try and solve this problem?"

CURRENT SITUATION

Action on Capitol Hill

In the wake of Derrion Albert's killing in Chicago last September, Attorney General Holder criticized the way youth violence has been handled in the past.

"Our responses to this issue . . . have been fragmented," he said at a news conference. "The federal government does one thing, states do another, and localities do a third. We need a comprehensive, coordinated approach to address youth violence, one that encompasses the latest research and the freshest approaches."

Holder said the Obama administration is committed to putting such strategies into practice, noting that it asked for $24 million in next year's budget for community-based crime prevention programs.[53]

Still, the ballooning federal deficit doesn't help. President Obama's fiscal 2011 budget request would sharply reduce federal spending on overall juvenile-justice programs, upsetting reform groups.

"While children as a whole stand to benefit from Obama's proposed budget, America's most vulnerable youth — those at risk of involvement in the juvenile-justice system — continue to be ignored," stated Nellis of The Sentencing Project. "Federal spending on juvenile justice has dropped steadily since 2002 and needs to be restored at least to these 2002 levels to give at-risk juveniles a fair chance."

On Capitol Hill, ideas on how to attack youth crime and violence are contained in a pair of competing bills making their way through Congress.

The Youth PROMISE Act, introduced by Rep. Bobby Scott, D-Va., and Mike Castle, R-Del., emphasizes prevention and intervention approaches in communities most challenged by youth crime and gangs.[54] The measure would provide $1.2 billion over five years to help locally based collaborative councils of police, schools, social-service agencies and community groups implement "evidence-based"

AT ISSUE

Should juveniles be sentenced to life without parole for non-homicide crimes?

YES

National District Attorneys Association

From amicus curiae brief in support of State of Florida

Sentencing a juvenile to life imprisonment without the possibility of parole is a weighty matter. Prosecutors do not seek such punishment lightly, nor do courts impose it without careful consideration and compelling reasons. But youthful offenders sometimes commit heinous crimes — rapes, kidnappings, and violent robberies and assaults that may leave the victim maimed for life, or worse. Many do so with full knowledge of the wrongfulness of their actions, and with callous disregard of both the demands of the law and the rights of their victims. And many are already repeat offenders with histories of recidivism.

Such offenses cannot be chalked up to "youthful indiscretion."

It is in these rare and tragic cases of heinous crimes committed by already-hardened and violent juvenile offenders that a State can and must be allowed to impose the severe sanction of life imprisonment without parole.

The crimes committed by juveniles, like those committed by adults, vary in severity. And individual juvenile offenders, like adult criminals, have different levels of maturity, culpability, and potential for rehabilitation. But [the] petitioners would have this Court impose a categorical rule that the imposition of a life sentence without parole on a juvenile is always "cruel and unusual punishment" — regardless of the nature and severity of the crime, the individual defendant's maturity and criminal history, or the procedural safeguards the State has put in place to avoid grossly disproportionate sentences.

This one-size-fits-all approach is not mandated by the Constitution. Indeed, it runs squarely afoul of this Court's holding that for non-capital punishments, the Eighth Amendment "forbids only extreme sentences that are 'grossly disproportionate' " to the individual crime. . . . As the Court has recognized, such cases are "exceedingly rare." . . . To proportionately punish the guilty, adequately protect the public, and deter future crimes, prosecutors and judges must have the flexibility to ensure that violent crimes committed by the most dangerous juvenile offenders may be met with an appropriately severe sanction. . . .

Prosecutors (and courts) recognize that life without parole is a severe sanction that should be imposed on a youthful offender only in extreme circumstances, and as a consequence, the penalty is rarely imposed. But that does not mean that the Constitution bars such punishment on those rare occasions when it is necessary to protect society.

** The cases (*Graham v. Florida and Sullivan v. Florida*) involve appeals by two men sentenced to life without parole: Terrance Jamar Graham, who was sentenced after participating in a home invasion committed at age 17, and Joe Harris Sullivan, convicted of raping an elderly woman at age 13.*

NO

Marc Mauer
Executive Director, The Sentencing Project

Written for *CQ Researcher*, March 2010

Children are different than adults. That's why we don't permit 15-year-olds to drink, drive, vote or join the military, because children lack the maturity of adults. For the same reason it should be unconscionable to permit juveniles who commit non-homicide offenses to be sentenced to life without parole.

Unfortunately, though, 109 children currently are serving such sentences in the United States, the only nation in the world that engages in this practice. It's not that kids in other nations don't commit serious crimes. Some do, but no other country believes in routinely denying any possibility of release.

The limited capacity of children is not just a function of inexperience, but of immature brain development as well. In particular, those areas of the brain that control reasoning and risk taking are less developed than in adults, contributing to poor impulse control. As any parent knows, few teenagers are thinking about the long-term consequences of their actions. As a result, they are particularly immune to any deterrent effect of sentencing policies.

Children also differ from adults with regard to their propensity to develop and change. Looking back, most adults now regret some of their actions as teenagers, some of which were merely foolish, others illegal. But the vast majority outgrow those behaviors as they take on adult roles and responsibilities. Such transitions are equally true for incarcerated children. None of us can predict whether a 15-year-old today will be dangerous or law-abiding at the age of 30 or 40. By imposing a sentence of life without parole we exclude any opportunity to account for a youth's reformed behavior and lifestyle.

Some juveniles commit serious offenses, and they should certainly be held accountable for their actions. And there may be some youths who are not capable of change and will present a long-term threat to public safety. But this is why we need professional parole boards to make such determinations, and to avoid a "one-size-fits-all" approach to sentencing.

Ultimately, a policy of life without parole impedes efforts to promote public safety. By incarcerating many juveniles long past the time they present a threat to the public, we are diverting resources and attention from investments in strengthening families and communities that would be more effective in preventing crime. Moreover, carving out an exception to life without parole for juvenile non-homicide offenses is a minimum standard for maintaining a humane and fair justice system.

strategies that proponents say are built upon sound research. The bill also would help police gain more expertise in dealing with juveniles.

"In a nutshell, it would treat the problem of juvenile crime much earlier in the process, rather than just respond to crime after kids have gotten into trouble and exhibited a whole variety of symptoms," says Nellis.

Scott, chairman of the House Judiciary Committee's Subcommittee on Crime, Terrorism and Homeland Security, has said the bill would ultimately save money but not eliminate current tough anti-crime laws. "While it is understood that law enforcement will still continue to enforce those laws, research tells us that no matter how tough we are on the people we prosecute today, unless we are addressing the underlying root causes of criminal activity, nothing will change," Scott's office said.[55]

The measure has garnered 234 co-sponsors in the House, including some 18 Republicans, and in December was approved by the House Judiciary Committee.

Companion legislation in the Senate, sponsored by Sens. Bob Casey, D-Pa., and Olympia J. Snowe, R-Maine, has a dozen cosponsors. The act also has the support of more than 200 national and state juvenile-justice, education and religious groups as well as the U.S. Conference of Mayors and cities including Los Angeles, Philadelphia, Pittsburgh and Richmond, Va.[56]

But the act also faces opposition. In testimony last summer before Scott's subcommittee, Muhlhausen of the Heritage Foundation raised a variety of objections to the bill, including its federal approach for dealing with local crime. "Establishing grant programs . . . that subsidize the routine responsibilities of state and local governments is a misuse of federal resources and a distraction from concerns that are truly the province of the federal government," he said.

Muhlhausen also questioned the measure's promotion of "evidence-based" prevention strategies, arguing that "there is not enough emphasis on evaluating programs implemented in the real world."[57]

A competing approach, the Gang Abatement and Prevention Act, sponsored by Sen. Dianne Feinstein, D-Calif., takes a harder line. It would set strict new federal penalties for illegal street-gang activity. The bill has 14 Senate co-sponsors and endorsement from law-enforcement groups.[58]

In endorsing the measure, the National Sheriffs' Association said that while prevention and intervention programs are important, legislation that "fails to include strong enforcement measures falls short of dealing with highly organized and violent gangs, and should not be offered as a solution to the rising violent gang crimes across the country."

Like the Youth PROMISE Act, the Gang Abatement bill has raised concerns about federalization. "Basically, it's taking ordinary crimes and making them federal crimes," Muhlhausen says.

While Congress mulls the proposed crime bills, it also faces reauthorization of the Juvenile Justice and Delinquency Prevention Act of 1974. A bill sponsored by Sen. Patrick J. Leahy, D-Vt., chairman of the Senate Judiciary Committee, would authorize more than $4 billion over five years, most of it for Justice Department grants to state and local governments for programs to reduce juvenile delinquency and improve the juvenile-justice system.[59]

One aim of the bill is to push states to move away from incarcerating juveniles in adult prisons. "After years of pressure to send more and more young people to adult prisons, it is time to seriously consider the strong evidence that this policy is not working," Leahy said in introducing the measure last March.[60] The bill also seeks to curb the detention of runaway, homeless and other "at risk" youths for status offenses.

In addition, the measure would encourage states to identify reasons for minority overrepresentation in the juvenile-justice system and work with the federal government and localities to address the problem.

But the bill would not require states to reduce overrepresentation, says Nellis of The Sentencing Project. She says the bill's lack of an enforcement mechanism on the issue is a "major flaw" in the legislation. Earlier reauthorizations of the act, going back to 1988, have included provisions urging states to study the issue, but the problem of overrepresentation has gotten worse in many places, she says.

Private Reform Efforts

As Congress considers ways to push states toward reforms in juvenile justice, private groups are continuing efforts of their own. Among the most active are the Chicago-based John D. and Catherine T. MacArthur Foundation and the Baltimore-based Annie E. Casey Foundation.

MacArthur's "Models for Change" program supports reform efforts in 16 states. In its core states of Illinois,

Pennsylvania, Louisiana and Washington, it has been focusing on such issues as community-based alternatives to incarceration for juveniles and ways to coordinate the juvenile-justice system with other community groups, such as education, child-welfare and mental-health systems.

MacArthur also has special "action network" programs in a variety of states focusing on racial and ethnic disparities in the juvenile-justice system, mental health needs of youths in the system and indigent defense — making sure that poor youths have adequate legal counsel.[61]

The Casey Foundation's Juvenile Detention Alternatives Initiative (JDAI), started in the early 1990s, aims to reduce the reliance on incarceration of juveniles, with a key focus on safely reducing detention of youths in the early stages of the process as they await trial or placement in a correctional program. Reducing racial disparities in the juvenile-justice system also is a key priority. [62]

Through technical support and other aid, Casey helps local entities — among them juvenile courts, probation agencies, prosecutors, defenders and community groups — form collaborations aimed at reducing detention levels and instituting broader juvenile-justice reforms in their locality.

The Casey initiative is now active in 110 sites in 27 states and the District of Columbia, says Lubow, director of Casey's Juvenile Justice Strategy Group. On average, participating JDAI sites reduced their detention populations by 35 percent, and a significant number reported declines of 50 percent or more, Lubow says. "These decreases in detention population did not result in decreases in public safety and in fact most JDAI sites report significant improvements in public safety," he says.

The program is "an effort to create a smarter, fairer and more effective juvenile-justice system using detention as the entry [point] for system reform," Lubow says. "Unnecessary and inappropriate detention," he says, poses a "grave risk to children and public safety and represents a huge public expenditure."

Lubow points to research showing that juvenile detention makes behavior problems worse rather than better.

For example, a recent Canadian study that tracked 779 low-income Montreal boys into adulthood found that the deeper the involvement in the juvenile-justice system, the greater the likelihood of being arrested as an adult, according to a summary in *Youth Today*.[63]

"The study joins a stream of recent research indicating that, both here and abroad, juvenile-justice systems are more likely to exacerbate delinquency than cure it, especially when young people are incarcerated or placed into group treatment programs where they interact with other troubled and trouble-making teens," *Youth Today* said.[64]

OUTLOOK

'Cautious Optimism'

Many youth-crime experts hope that new approaches and new insights into adolescent behavior will lead to further strides in curbing youth crime rates.

"The overall picture is one of cautious optimism," says Marc Mauer, executive director of The Sentencing Project. "In lower-income minority communities, where the rates have historically been higher, those communities are safer today than 15 years ago, but not as safe as more well-off communities. Certainly there are very significant problems that need to be addressed."

At the same time, he says, "there's growing interest and attention in trying to look at more collaborative models of how to address these problems. . . . Punishment per se is increasingly viewed as of only limited value in terms of preventing or deterring kids from engaging in violence and crime."

The Obama administration's attention to youth violence in the days following the Derrion Albert murder has given youth advocates reason for optimism, though the administration has said little on the subject since then. Still, the massive budget deficit, which has led the administration to seek a freeze on much of the government's domestic outlay, is likely to hold down spending on juvenile-justice programs, making a return to the levels of the early 2000s less likely anytime soon.

At the same time, anti-terrorism efforts are competing for Justice Department funds, even as concern about gang violence and other organized criminal activity grows in some urban areas.

Meanwhile, the deep recession is likely to continue to play a role — both positive and negative — in the outlook on youth crime. In some neighborhoods, economic pressure could lead some young people to engage in violent behavior. What's more, cash-strapped local and state governments are under pressure to cut spending, which could result in further cuts in prevention and intervention programs aimed at deterring youth crime.

On the other hand, states and localities seeking to save money are reducing prison construction, incarcerating fewer people and looking for less expensive ways to stem crime, such as collaborative prevention and intervention programs. That bodes well for programs such as Ceasefire, says Kennedy, the John Jay College criminologist.

"What I'm seeing in a strange way is the reverse" of budget cuts posing a problem, he says. "Economic restraint is making people look very seriously at the utility of the money they're spending, and because most money that goes at this issue doesn't work, it's raising the profile of cheap things that do work."

NOTES

1. "No bond for fifth suspect in fatal Fenger High beating," *Sun-Times Media Wire*, WBBM, Jan. 20, 2010, www.wbbm780.com/pages/6163265.php?.
2. Mark Rahner and Jennifer Sullivan, "Teen beaten in transit tunnel; Metro reviews policies," *Seattle Times*, Feb. 9, 2010, http://seattletimes.nwsource.com/html/localnews/2011027703_webbeating09m.html.
3. Diana Moskovitz, "3 teens arrested in attack on homeless man in Pompano Beach," *The Miami Herald*, Oct. 28, 2009, www.miamiherald.com/2009/10/28/1303472/3-teens-arrested-in-attack-on.html.
4. Malaika Fraley, "Richmond man pleads not guilty in gang rape case," *San Jose Mercury News*, Feb. 3, 2010, www.mercurynews.com/breaking-news/ci_14325694.
5. "Attorney General and Education Secretary Call for National Conversation on Values and Student Violence," press release, U.S. Department of Education Oct. 7, 2009, http://ed.gov/news/pressreleases/2009/10/10072009.html.
6. Marla McDaniel and Daniel Kuehn, "Vulnerable Youth and the Transition to Adulthood: Low-Income African American Youth," Urban Institute, 2009, www.urban.org/publications/411949.html.
7. David Finkelhor, *et al.*, "Children's Exposure to Violence: A Comprehensive National Survey," Office of Juvenile Justice and Delinquency Prevention, U.S. Department of Justice, October 2009, www.ncjrs.gov/pdffiles1/ojjdp/227744.pdf. See also "Justice Department Releases Survey Findings of the Nature and Extent of Children's Exposure to Violence," press release, Oct. 7, 2009, www.ojp.gov/newsroom/pressreleases/2009/ojjdp09162.htm.
8. For background see Peter Katel, "Juvenile Justice," *CQ Researcher*, Nov. 7, 2008, pp. 913-936, and Brian Hansen, "Kids in Prison," *CQ Researcher*, April 27, 2001, pp. 345-376.
9. Charles Puzzanchera, "Juvenile Arrests 2008," Office of Juvenile Justice and Delinquency Prevention, U.S. Department of Justice, December 2009, www.ncjrs.gov/pdffiles1/ojjdp/228479.pdf.
10. "Youth Violence: Facts at a Glance," Centers for Disease Control and Prevention, summer 2009, www.cdc.gov/violenceprevention/pdf/YV_DataSheet_Summer2009-a.pdf.
11. James Alan Fox and Marc L. Swatt, "The Recent Surge in Homicides involving Young Black Males and Guns: Time to Reinvest in Prevention and Crime Control," December 2008, www.jfox.neu.edu/Documents/Fox%20Swatt%20Homicide%20Report%20Dec%2029%202008.pdf. For a criticism of Fox's methodology, see: Steven D. Levitt, "The Latest on Homicide Rates," Freakonomics Blog, *The New York Times*, Dec. 30, 2008, http://freakonomics.blogs.nytimes.com/2008/12/30/the-latest-on-homicide-rates/?scp=1&sq=%22the%20latest%20on%20homicide%20rates%22&st=cse.
12. Quoted in Peter Slevin and Kari Lydersen, "In Violent Chicago, 'It's Tough to Be a Kid,' " *The Washington Post*, Oct. 6, 2009, p. 3A.
13. "Jailing Juveniles: The Dangers of Incarcerating Youth in Adult Jails in America," Campaign for Youth Justice, November 2007, www.campaign4youthjustice.org/Downloads/National ReportsArticles/CFYJ-Jailing_Juveniles_Report_2007-11-15.pdf.
14. "12 Percent of Adjudicated Youth Report Sexual Victimization in Juvenile Facilities During 2008-2009," press release, Department of Justice, Jan. 7, 2010, www.ojp.usdoj.gov/newsroom/pressreleases/2010/BJS10037.htm.

15. Anne Barnard, "Youth Charged With More Attacks on Latinos," *The New York Times*, Jan. 29, 2009, www.nytimes.com/2009/01/29/nyregion/29patchogue.html.

16. Derrick Henry, "2 Men Charged in Texas Church Fire," *The New York Times*, Feb. 21, 2010, www.nytimes.com/2010/02/22/us/22webchurch.html?ref=us.

17. Testimony before House Judiciary Subcommittee on Crime, Terrorism and Homeland Security, Feb. 11, 2009, http://judiciary.house.gov/hearings/hear_090211.html.

18. Sally Kalson, "Survey finds gun violence affects youth," *Pittsburgh Post-Gazette*, Jan. 20, 2010, www.post-gazette.com/pg/10020/1029497-53.stm. The written survey of 455 students was a project of the Metro-Urban Institute of the Pittsburgh Theological Seminary and several other organizations.

19. Dafney Tales, "Violence has students attending in fear," *Philadelphia Daily News*, Jan. 29, 2010.

20. Sadie Gurman, "3 officers accused in beating suspended with pay," *Pittsburgh Post-Gazette*, Feb. 2, 2010, www.post-gazette.com/pg/10033/1032746-53.stm.

21. "And Justice for Some: Differential Treatment of Youth of Color in the Justice System," National Council on Crime and Delinquency, January 2007, www.nccd-crc.org/nccd/pubs/2007jan_justice_for_some.pdf.

22. See "2005 Case Processing Summary, Relative Rates for Person Offenses," *National Disproportionate Minority Contact Databook*, National Center for Juvenile Justice, Office of Juvenile Justice and Delinquency Prevention, www.ojjdp.ncjrs.gov/ojstatbb/dmcdb/asp/display.asp?year=2005&offense=1&displaytype=rri&cmdRun=Show+Table.

23. For background see Thomas J. Billitteri, "Discipline in Schools," *CQ Researcher*, Feb. 15, 2008, pp. 145-169.

24. See Stephanie Chen, "States rethink 'adult time for adult crime,'" CNN, Jan. 15, 2010, www.cnn.com/2010/CRIME/01/15/connecticut.juvenile.ages/index.html.

25. Katel, *op. cit.*

26. Allen J. Beck, Paige M. Harrison and Paul Guerino, "Sexual Victimization in Juvenile Facilities Reported by Youth, 2008-09," U.S. Department of Justice, January 2010, http://bjs.ojp.usdoj.gov/content/pub/pdf/svjfry09.pdf.

27. Quoted in Martha T. Moore, "Study: Youths sexually abused in juvenile prisons," *USA Today*, Jan. 7, 2010, www.usatoday.com/news/nation/2010-01-07-juvenile-prison-sexual-abuse_N.htm.

28. Nicholas Confessore, "4 Youth Prisons in New York Used Excessive Force," *The New York Times*, Aug. 25, 2009, www.nytimes.com/2009/08/25/nyregion/25juvenile.html?scp=1&sq=%224%20Youth%20Prisons%20in%20New%20York%20Used%22&st=cse.

29. Quoted in *ibid.*

30. Nicholas Confessore, "New York Finds Extreme Crisis in Youth Prisons," Dec. 14, 2009, www.nytimes.com/2009/12/14/nyregion/14juvenile.html?scp=3&sq=task%20force%20and%20juvenile%20justice%20and%202009&st=cse.

31. "The Costs of Confinement: Why Good Juvenile Justice Policies Make Good Fiscal Sense," Justice Policy Institute, May 2009, www.justicepolicy.org/images/upload/09_05_REP_CostsOfConfinement_JJ_PS.pdf.

32. Julia Dahl, "Throw-Away Children: Juvenile Justice in Collapse," Guggenheim Special Report, *The Crime Report*, Feb. 9, 2010, http://thecrimereport.org/2010/02/09/throw-away-children-juvenile-justice-in-collapse/.

33. Solomon Moore, "Missouri System Treats Juvenile Offenders With Lighter Hand," *The New York Times*, March 27, 2009, www.nytimes.com/2009/03/27/us/27juvenile.html?_r=1&scp=1&sq=%22missouri%20system%20treats%20juvenile%20offenders%20with%20lighter%20hand%22&st=cse.

34. "New Illinois Law Offers 17-Year-Olds Charged With Misdemeanor Chance in Juvenile Court," Juvenile Justice Initiative, Feb. 10, 2009, www.jjustice.org/pdf/sb2275%20Press%20Release%20Feb%2010%2009.pdf. See also "Our Opinion: Young offenders get a better deal," *State Journal-Register*, Feb. 20, 2009, www.sj-r.com/editorials/

x286843903/Our-Opinion-Young-offenders-get-a-better-deal.

35. Carol Marbin Miller, "Florida Supreme Court limits 'degrading' shackles for juveniles," *The Miami Herald*, Dec. 18, 2009, www.miamiherald.com/news/5min/story/1388214.html.

36. Dee J. Hall and Tim Damos, "State reviewing juvenile crime law," *Wisconsin State Journal*, Jan. 21, 2010, http://host.madison.com/wsj/news/local/crime_and_courts/article_d20521e2-070f-11df-95a8-001cc4c03286.html.

37. *Ibid.*

38. James C. Howell, "Youth Gangs: An Overview," Office of Juvenile Justice and Delinquency Prevention, *Juvenile Justice Bulletin*, August 1998, www.ojjdp.ncjrs.gov/jjbulletin/9808/contents.html.

39. Lawrence M. Friedman, *Crime and Punishment in American History* (1993), p. 165.

40. Maryam Ahranjani, Andrew G. Ferguson and Jamin B. Raskin, *Youth Justice in America*, CQ Press (2005), p. 16.

41. Julian W. Mack, "The Juvenile Court," *Harvard Law Review 23*, 1907, pp. 104 and 106, quoted in Ahranjani, *et al.*, *op. cit.*, p. 15.

42. Howard N. Snyder and Melissa Sickmund, "Juvenile Offenders and Victims: 1999 National Report," Office of Juvenile Justice and Delinquency Prevention, September 1999, p. 86, www.ncjrs.gov/html/ojjdp/nationalreport99/toc.html.

43. John Hutzler, "Canon to the left, canon to the right, Can the juvenile court survive?," *Today's Delinquent*, July 1982, pp. 25-38, quoted in James C. Howell, *Juvenile Justice and Youth Violence*, Sage Publications (1997), p. 15.

44. See Douglas O. Linder, "The Leopold and Loeb Trial: A Brief Account," University of Missouri-Kansas City School of Law, www.law.umkc.edu/faculty/projects/ftrials/leoploeb/leopold.htm.

45. *American Peoples Encyclopedia 1964 Yearbook* (1964), p. 192.

46. Snyder and Sickmund, *op. cit.*, pp. 90-91. In *re Gault*, 387 U.S. 1 (1967).

47. *Ibid.*, p. 88.

48. Snyder and Sickmund, "Juvenile Offenders and Victims: 2006 National Report," Office of Justice Programs and Office of Juvenile Justice and Delinquency Prevention, March 2006, p. 64, www.ojjdp.ncjrs.gov/ojstatbb/nr2006/downloads/NR2006.pdf.

49. *Ibid.*, p. 133.

50. Snyder and Sickmund, *ibid.*, 1999 report, p. 89.

51. Snyder and Sickmund, *ibid.*, 2006 report, p. 238.

52. "Two Decades of JDAI," Annie E. Casey Foundation, 2009, p. 5, www.aecf.org/KnowledgeCenter/Publications.aspx?pubguid={245B4489-CC0E-41DA-8D0F-A2A51017487D}. The source of the figure is the Census of Public and Private Juvenile Detention, Correctional and Shelter Facilities, 1985-1995, and the Office of Juvenile Justice and Delinquency Prevention Statistical Briefing Book, *Census of Juveniles in Residential Placement Databook*, 1997.

53. "Attorney General Eric Holder Speaks at News Conference on Youth and School Violence," Oct. 7, 2009, www.justice.gov.

54. H.R. 1064.

55. "The Youth Promise Act," accessed at www.bobbyscott.house.gov/images/stories/ypa_white_paper.pdf.

56. Lauren Victoria Burke, "Anti-crime bill picks up cosponsors, momentum," *The Hill*, June 23, 2009, http://thehill.com/homenews/house/47267-anti-crime-bill-picks-up-cosponsors-momentum.

57. Testimony of David B. Muhlhausen, "The Youth PROMISE Act: Outside the Scope and Expertise of the Federal Government," Aug. 5, 2009, www.heritage.org/Research/Crime/tst080509a.cfm.

58. See "Combating Criminal Street Gangs," Office of Sen. Dianne Feinstein, http://feinstein.senate.gov/public/index.cfm?FuseAction=IssueStatements.View&Issue_id=5b8ee71d-7e9c-9af9-79af-591842260dfe&CFID=35647380&CFTOKEN=97961746.

59. "S. 678, Juvenile Justice and Delinquency Prevention Reauthorization Act of 2009," Congressional Budget Office Cost Estimate, Jan. 26, 2010, www.cbo.gov/ftpdocs/110xx/doc11010/s678.pdf.

60. Statement of Sen. Patrick Leahy, http://leahy.senate.gov/press/200903/032409b.html.

61. For background on the MacArthur program, see "Models for Change: Systems Reform in Juvenile Justice," December 2008, www.macfound.org/atf/cf/%7BB0386CE3-8B29-4162-8098-E466FB856794%7D/INFO-MODELSFORCHANGE.PDF.
62. For background on Casey's Juvenile Detention Alternatives Initiative, see, "Two Decades of JDAI," Annie E. Casey Foundation, 2009, www.aecf.org/KnowledgeCenter/Publications.aspx?pubguid={245B4489-CC0E-41DA-8D0F-A2A51017487D}.
63. Dick Mendel, "In Juvenile Justice Care, Boys Get Worse," *Youth Today*, Feb. 1, 2010. See also Maia Szalavitz, "Why Juvenile Detention Makes Teens Worse," *Time*, Aug. 7, 2009, www.time.com/time/health/article/0,8599,1914837,00.html. The study is Uberto Gatti, Richard E. Tremblay and Frank Vitaro, "Latrogenic Effect of Juvenile Justice," *Journal of Child Psychology and Psychiatry* 50:8, 2009, pp. 991-998.
64. Mendel, *op. cit.*

BIBLIOGRAPHY

Books

Ahranjani, Maryam, Andrew G. Ferguson and Jamin B. Raskin, *Youth Justice in America*, *CQ Press*, 2005.
Legal scholars provide a useful mix of material from criminal-law cases and expert commentary on crime and youth rights.

Loeber, Rolf, and David P. Farrington, eds., *Serious & Violent Juvenile Offenders*, *SAGE Publications*, 1998.
The authors present research by various experts and conclude that anti-violence prevention efforts are "never too early" and intervention efforts for serious and violent juvenile offenders "can never be too late."

Rich, John A., *Wrong Place, Wrong Time: Trauma and Violence in the Lives of Young Black Men*, *Johns Hopkins University Press*, 2009.
A medical doctor, founder of Boston's Young Men's Health Clinic and recipient of a MacArthur Foundation "Genius Grant," explores the emotional and psychological effects of violence against urban victims.

Articles

Dahl, Julia, "Throw-Away Children: Juvenile Justice in Collapse," *The Crime Report*, Feb 9, 2010, thecrimereport.org/2010/02/09/throw-away-children-juvenile-justice-in-collapse/.
The United States spends $5 billion annually on juvenile courts, but studies suggest the money isn't helping juveniles who need help the most.

Moore, Martha T., "Youth Prison System Under Pressure," *USA Today*, Feb. 2, 2010, www.usatoday.com/news/nation/2010-02-02-youth-prison-juvenile_N.htm.
The Justice Department has conducted at least 11 probes into juvenile facilities since 2000, consistently finding problems of overreliance on physical restraint and insufficient mental-health services.

Moore, Solomon, "Missouri System Treats Juvenile Offenders With Lighter Hand," *The New York Times*, March 27, 2009, www.nytimes.com/2009/03/27/us/27juvenile.html?scp=1&sq=%22missouri%20system%20treats%20juvenile%20offenders%20with%20lighter%20hand%22&st=cse.
The so-called Missouri Model for dealing with juvenile offenders — in which youths are placed in small groups with minimal force and constant therapeutic interventions — is among the most promising reform movements.

Szalavitz, Maia, "Why Juvenile Detention Makes Teens Worse," *Time*, Aug. 7, 2009, www.time.com/time/health/article/0,8599,1914837,00.html.
A study finds that juvenile detention in Montreal, Canada, makes the behavior of troubled youths worse.

Reports and Studies

Bell, James, *et al.*, "The Keeper and the Kept: Reflections on Local Obstacles to Disparities Reduction in Juvenile Justice Systems and a Path to Change," *W. Haywood Burns Institute*, December 2009, www.burnsinstitute.org/downloads/BI%20Keeper%20Kept.pdf.
In its second report on the juvenile-justice system, the nonprofit institute argues that "states spend approximately $5.7 billion each year imprisoning youth, even though the majority are held for non-violent offenses"

and that "most youth could be supervised safely in the community with alternatives that cost substantially less than incarceration and that could lower recidivism by up to 22 percent."

Fox, James Alan, and Marc L. Swatt, "The Recent Surge in Homicides Involving Young Black Males and Guns: Time to Reinvest in Prevention and Crime Control," ***Northeastern University*****, December 2008, www.jfox.neu.edu/Documents/Fox%20Swatt%20 Homicide%20Report%20Dec%2029%202008.pdf.**
Criminal-justice scholars at Northeastern University provide data showing that "while overall homicide levels in the United States have fluctuated minimally in recent years, those involving young victims and perpetrators — particularly young black males — have surged."

Jucovy, Linda, and Wendy S. McClanahan, "Reaching Through the Cracks: A Guide to Implementing the Youth Violence Reduction Partnership," ***Public/ Private Ventures*****, 2008, www.ppv.org/ppv/publications/assets/241_publication.pdf.**
The report draws on lessons from a Philadelphia program dedicated to steering young people who are at risk of killing or being killed away from violence and toward productive lives.

Puzzanchera, Charles, "Juvenile Arrests 2008," ***U.S. Department of Justice*****, December 2009, www.ojjdp.ncjrs.gov/publications/PubAbstract.asp?pubi=250498.**
The Office of Juvenile Justice and Delinquency Prevention report summarizes juvenile-crime data from the FBI and shows a 3 percent decline in overall juvenile arrests from 2007 to 2008, and a 2 percent drop in juvenile arrests for violent offenses during the same period.

Stimson, Charles D., and Andrew M. Grossman, "Adult Time for Adult Crimes," ***Heritage Foundation*****, Aug. 17, 2009, www.heritage.org/research/crime/sr0065.cfm.**
The authors argue that life without parole for violent youths is "reasonable, constitutional and (appropriately) rare."

For More Information

Campaign for Youth Justice, 1012 14th St., N.W., Suite 610, Washington, DC 20005; (202) 558-3580; www.campaignforyouthjustice.org. Seeks to end the practice of trying, sentencing and incarcerating youths under age 18 in the adult criminal-justice system.

John Jay College of Criminal Justice, 899 10th Ave., New York, NY 10019; (212) 237-8000; www.jjay.cuny.edu. Research and academic institution that focuses on criminal justice and is part of the City University of New York.

Justice Policy Institute, 1012 14th St., N.W., Suite 400, Washington, DC 20005; (202) 558-7974; www.justicepolicy.org. Research and policy group focusing on prison and incarceration issues.

National Center for Juvenile Justice, 3700 S. Water St., Suite 200, Pittsburgh, PA 15203; (412) 227-6950; www.ncjj.org. Provides research and data on juvenile justice and is the research division of the National Council of Juvenile and Family Court Judges.

National Council on Crime and Delinquency, 1970 Broadway, Suite 500, Oakland, CA 94612; (510) 208-0500; www.nccd-crc.org. Conducts research and makes policy recommendations on criminal justice, juvenile justice and child welfare.

Office of Juvenile Justice and Delinquency Prevention, U.S. Department of Justice, 810 7th St., N.W., Washington, DC 20531; (202) 307-5911; www.ojjdp.ncjrs.gov. Helps states, localities and tribal jurisdictions develop effective programs for juveniles.

The Sentencing Project, 514 10th St., N.W., Suite 1000, Washington, DC 20004; (202) 628-0871; www.sentencingproject.org. Conducts criminal-justice research and advocacy.

4

Cyberbullying

Are New Laws Needed to Curb Online Aggression?

Thomas J. Billitteri

AP Photo/Mary Ann Chastain

After cyberbullies drove his son Ryan to suicide, John Halligan created a Web page devoted to the 13-year-old, who had been harassed for months by classmates in Essex Junction, Vt., including instant messages calling him gay. "He just went into a deep spiral in eighth grade," said his father, who advocates a state law forcing schools to develop anti-bullying policies. "He couldn't shake this rumor."

From *CQ Global Researcher*, May 2008.

The episodes are hurtful, ugly — and sometimes deadly. In Lakeland, Fla., a group of teenagers records the beating of another teen and threatens to show the video on the Internet. The local sheriff says the attack was in retaliation for online trash-talking by the victim.[1]

At a high school near Pittsburgh, an anonymous e-mail list features sexually explicit rankings of 25 female students, names and photos included.[2]

In suburban Dardenne Prairie, Mo., near St. Louis, 13-year-old Megan Meier hangs herself after receiving cruel messages on the social-networking site MySpace. She thinks the messages are from a boy she met online, but the messages are a hoax.[3]

In Essex Junction, Vt., 13-year-old Ryan Patrick Halligan kills himself after months of harassment, including instant messages calling him gay. "He just went into a deep spiral in eighth grade," said his father, who advocates a state law forcing schools to develop anti-bullying policies. "He couldn't shake this rumor."[4]

The cases, albeit extreme, highlight what school officials, child psychologists, legal experts and government researchers argue is a fast-spreading epidemic of "cyberbullying" — the use of the Internet, cell phones and other digital technology to harass, intimidate, threaten, mock and defame.

Experts say cyberbullying has become a scourge of the adolescent world, inflicting painful scars on youngsters and vexing adults unable to stop the abuse. While many instances are relatively harmless, others can have serious, long-lasting effects, ranging from acute emotional distress, academic problems and school

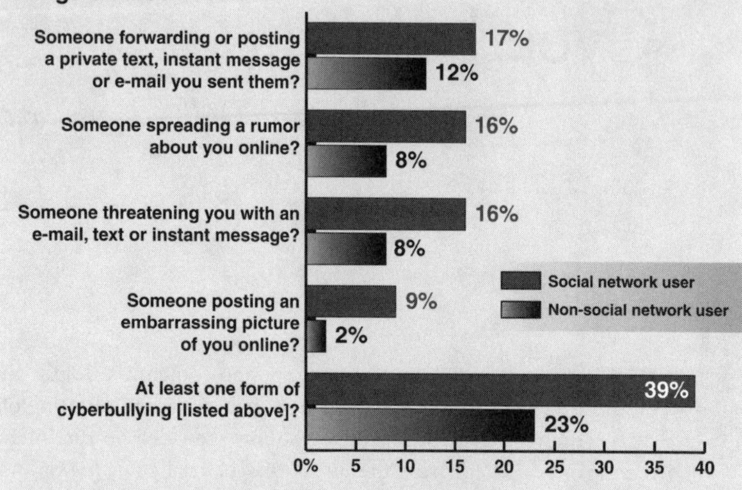

Source: Amanda Lenhart and Mary Madden, Pew Internet & American Life Project, Jan. 3, 2007

absenteeism to violence, a desire for revenge and vulnerability to sexual predation.

Studies show cyberbullying affects millions of adolescents and young adults and can be more prevalent among girls than boys, especially in the earlier grades. The Centers for Disease Control and Prevention last year labeled "electronic aggression" — its term for cyberbullying — an "emerging public-health problem."[5] Still, a reliable profile of cyberbullying is difficult to construct. Research is in its infancy, experts who measure online abuse define it in different ways and many incidents are difficult to tally accurately. Studies leave little doubt, however, that cyberbullying is growing, as the following small sampling of recent research makes clear:

- Roughly a third of teens who use the Internet said they'd received threatening messages, had e-mail or text messages forwarded without consent, had an embarrassing picture posted without consent, had rumors about them spread online, or experienced some other kind of online harassment, according to the Pew Research Center.[6]
- About 9 percent of respondents ages 10 through 17 said they were victims of threats or other offensive behavior, not counting sexual solicitation, that was sent online to them or about them for others to see, according to a 2005 University of New Hampshire survey. That rate was up 50 percent from a similar survey five years earlier.[7]
- More than 70 percent of heavy Internet users ages 12 through 17 — mostly girls — said they had experienced at least one incident of online intimidation via e-mail, cell phones, chat rooms and other electronic media in the previous year, according to a national survey posted on a teen Web site in 2005 by Jaana Juvonen, a psychology professor at the University of California at Los Angeles. A fifth of respondents reported seven or more incidents.[8]

Some cyberbullies are angry loners or misfits, sometimes seeking revenge for having been bullied themselves. But experts say it is common for online abusers to be popular students with plenty of self-esteem who are trying to strengthen their place in the social hierarchy. They do it by intimidating those they perceive to have less status.

"It's not really the schoolyard thug character" in some cases, says Nancy Willard, executive director of the Center for Safe and Responsible Internet Use, a research and professional development organization in Eugene, Ore. "It's the in-crowd kids bullying those who don't rank high enough."

What fuels cyberbullying is "status in schools — popularity, hierarchies, who's cool, who's not," says Danah Boyd, a fellow at the Berkman Center for

Internet and Society at Harvard Law School who studies teens' behavior on MySpace, Facebook and other social-networking sites. Peer pressure for status is further aggravated by adult pressure on teens to succeed, which can breed a cruel game of one-upmanship, Boyd says. "That pressure exerted by parents and reinforced and built out in peer groups is sort of the Petri dish for bullying."

Of course, bullying itself is nothing new. In some respects, cyberbullying is simply a new manifestation of a problem that in earlier days played out chiefly in playground dustups and lunch-money shakedowns.

What's new is the technology. More than 90 percent of teens are online.[9] More than half of online teens have profiles on social-networking sites.[10] And cell phones — many with photo and instant-messaging capabilities — are ubiquitous. The rise of networking sites, personal Web pages and blogs brimming with the minutiae of teen antics and angst has helped to create a rich climate for cyber mayhem: locker-room photos snapped with cell phones and broadcast on the Internet, fake profiles created on social-networking sites, salacious rumors spread in chat rooms, threats zapped across town in instant messages.

Child advocates also tie the increase in cyberbullying to a rise in incivility in the broader culture, from gratuitous insults on popular TV shows like "American Idol" to cynical sniping on the presidential campaign trail.

"I think the culture is angrier," says Mark Weiss, education director of Operation Respect, a nonprofit group in New York City founded by folk singer Peter Yarrow (a member of the legendary trio Peter, Paul and Mary) that promotes safe and compassionate educational climates. While kids have always picked on each other, Weiss says "the virulence is greater" today than in past generations.

"It's more intense, it might be more widespread, and I think you see more of it. The things on TV, the laugh tracks of situation comedies, it's all about making fun of each other and putting each other down, and reality TV is all about humiliation."

Cyberbullying has impelled lawmakers, especially at the state level, to either pass anti-bullying laws that encompass cyberbullying or add cyberbullying to existing statutes. Some laws are propelled by a mix of concern about electronic bullying and online sexual predators.

But using laws and courts to stop cyberbullying has been tricky and sometimes highly controversial. "There's a big conflict in knowing where to draw the line between things that are rude and things that are illegal," says

Older Girls Typically Create Profiles

Girls ages 15-17 are far more likely to create profiles on social-networking sites than any other age or gender group. Disparities aren't as significant across economic and racial lines.

Percentage of Online Teens Who Create Profiles Online

Sex	
Boys	51%
Girls	58
Age	
12-14	45
15-17	64
Age by Sex	
Boys 12-14	46
Girls 12-14	44
Boys 15-17	57
Girls 15-17	70
Household income	
Under $50,000	55
Over $50,000	56
Race/ethnicity	
White, non-Hispanic	53
Non-white	58

Source: Amanda Lenhart and Mary Madden, Pew Internet & American Life Project, Jan. 3, 2007

Parry Aftab, an Internet privacy and security lawyer who is executive director of wiredsafety.org, an Internet safety group in Irvington-on-Hudson, N.Y., that bills itself as the world's largest.

School officials, for instance, must negotiate the treacherous shoals of cyberbullying content transmitted by a student who is off school grounds. Legal precedents on student expression allow educators to suppress speech that substantially disrupts the educational process or impinges on the rights of others. Some argue that school officials' authority to regulate cyber communication stops at the schoolhouse door, while others say they should regulate it when it affects the school climate. (*See "At Issue," p. 100.*)

"Even when it's off campus, the impact is coming to school in the form of young people who have been so tormented they are incapable of coming to school to study, which leads to dropouts, fights, violent altercations and suicide," says Willard, a former attorney and former teacher of at-risk children. "It has an incredibly long-lasting effect on the school community."

But the law on that question can be confusing, and the U.S. Supreme Court has yet to decide a case involving student Internet speech. Trying to regulate what students do or say on their home computers or in text messages sent from the local mall could wind up trampling students' constitutional rights or the rights of parents to direct their children's upbringing as they see fit, say free-speech advocates.

"There are more questions than answers in this emerging area of law," David L. Hudson Jr., research attorney for the First Amendment Center, a free-speech advocacy group, noted recently.[11]

As cyberbullying grows, here are some of the questions educators and legal experts are asking:

Are new laws needed to curb cyberbullying?

Jane Clare Orie, a state senator in Pennsylvania and majority whip for the Republican Caucus, says criminal laws have failed to keep up with the technological revolution, including the onset of cyberbullying.

A former prosecutor, Orie has introduced a bill that would leave both minors and adults open to potential criminal charges for cyberbullying a student or school employee.[12]

Bullying "has risen to a level so much further than what we grew up with," Orie says. "Anything done in a computer lasts forever."

But civil libertarians and others express concerns about the wave of new cyberbully laws. Some argue that educating students and parents on the harmful consequences of online abuse, instituting school-based prevention programs and promulgating clear school policies on harassment are more effective than passing laws.

Cyberbullying is "a big deal," with serious consequences for victims, says Justin W. Patchin, an assistant professor of criminal justice at the University of Wisconsin-Eau Claire who has done extensive research on the phenomenon. But he adds, "I don't know if it's something that we can legislate away."

Boyd, the Berkman Center fellow at Harvard, says highly publicized cases like the Megan Meier suicide are "absolutely horrible," but rare. Most cyberbullying occurs among peers jockeying for status, and much of the electronic bullying takes the form of taunting and jokes taken too far, she says. Technologies from social-networking sites to cell phones are also used to extend everyday bullying beyond the schoolyard.

Legislators are overreacting, Boyd says. "These laws aren't doing anything. What we desperately need is education and discussion," along with greater attention from parents and other adults to the heavy pressures and expectations weighing on adolescents.

Still, many lawmakers are moving to add provisions to existing anti-bullying laws or writing new codes. Legislatures including Iowa, Maryland, Minnesota, New Jersey and Oregon have passed cyberbullying laws recently, and a number of others are considering such statutes.[13]

"Those who bully and harass stand in the way of learning and threaten the safety of our children," said Matt Blunt, the Republican governor of Missouri, Megan Meier's home state, after the state Senate passed a cyberbullying bill in March.[14]

In Florida, Republican state Sen. Stephen Wise (Jacksonville), chairman of the Education Pre-K-12 Appropriations Committee, relented this year and let the committee consider a bill named after a 15-year-old boy who killed himself after enduring cyberbullying by a classmate. The bill would require all school districts to develop anti-bullying and harassment policies and let school districts punish students who use an electronic device to bully or harass their peers, even if the acts take place off campus and during non-school hours.[15]

Wise said he had opposed the measure because he thought existing law offered protections.[16] But proponents said it sends a message about bullying's gravity and potential harm. The Florida bill "provides a more formalized and transparent process for dealing with bullying situations, for the schools, the parents and for the student," said Republican state Rep. Gary Aubuchon (Cape Coral), a cosponsor. "By making it law rather than school board policy, we are adding an extra layer of emphasis on how important it is to protect our children at all times."[17]

Thomas Hutton, senior staff attorney for the National School Boards Association, says that while it may be acceptable for legislatures to require school districts to formulate cyberbullying policies, laws mandating that school districts deal with cyber abuse in a specific way are "missing the boat."

The desire of school districts to base policy decisions on "local conditions" makes specific directions to school districts a bad idea, Hutton says. Moreover, he says, "a lot of the real action [on cyberbullying] is happening in the courts."

Judicial rulings are evolving quickly, Hutton says, and state laws can create confusion among school districts as to the scope of their power to control online bullying. A new court ruling might limit what a school can do, putting administrators who act more broadly in legal jeopardy, he says. On the other hand, a court might broaden the power of schools to fight cyberbullying beyond what legislators contemplated when they passed a state cyberbullying law.

"Let's say a state attempts to read what the courts have said thus far and boil it down to a statute," Hutton says. "Then we get a ruling saying, 'We're going to allow [school districts] a little more leeway.' Now the statute has locked in place a more restrictive" approach.

Aftab, the Internet privacy and security lawyer, argues that more state laws are unnecessary because states already have cyber stalking and harassment laws on the books. What is needed, she says, is uniformity in those laws "so we know that what's illegal in one state is illegal in the next." Moreover, she says, "prosecutors need to know what laws are on the books."

Getty Images/F. Micelotta/American Idol

Child advocates see a link between the increase in cyberbullying and the rise in incivility in the broader culture, such as gratuitous attacks on popular TV shows like "American Idol" and cynical sniping on the presidential campaign trail.

Aftab also argues that schools can fight cyberbullying using a little-known federal anti-stalking provision that President George W. Bush signed into law in 2006 as part of the reauthorization of the Violence Against Women Act. It makes it a crime to anonymously "annoy, abuse, threaten or harass" someone over the Internet.[18] Critics have said the law is vague and subjective.[19]

Aftab says she has a surefire way for school districts to attack cyberbullying, whether it originates at school: write a policy that covers cyberbullying wherever it occurs among students, then ask all students and parents to sign the policy at the beginning of the school year. Once that happens, Aftab argues, the document becomes a binding contract that gives the school legal authority to take action.

Of course, a student or parent could always wind up challenging a school's interpretation of a particular incident or its definition of cyberbullying. Many experts expect the same thing to occur with the raft of state laws hitting the books. So far, case law provides uneven guidance on what constitutes electronic harassment.

"The rub in almost all these statutes is that when you try to regulate speech, [the challenge is] writing a statute that singles out bullying and distinguishes it from legitimate expression," says Dale Herbeck, who teaches communications and cyber law at Boston College. "The way to solve it is to write a statute that is very, very, very specific. The problem is that a lot of the behavior you think is bullying doesn't qualify as bullying. I'm aware that a lot of states have kind of stepped up on this," he says. "But I'm not aware of these laws being challenged."

Do cyberbully laws violate constitutional rights?

In 2003, New Jersey eighth-grader Ryan Dwyer created and briefly maintained a Web site from home that included criticism of his school and postings by others in a "guest book." Some visitors ignored his plea that they not use profanity or threats in their postings. The principal "is a fat piece of crap," one declared. "He should walk his fat a— into oncoming traffic."[20]

School officials punished Dwyer, but the American Civil Liberties Union (ACLU) helped him and his parents sue, claiming violation of his constitutional rights. In a settlement, the district apologized and agreed to pay $117,500 in damages and attorney fees.[21]

"I'm hopeful this will help ensure that free-speech rights of students aren't trampled on again," Dwyer said.[22]

The case points to the difficult legal terrain surrounding abusive cyber expression, especially when it originates away from school. "Schools have a growing concern about the problem, and their concern is whether they can discipline students and how far the bullying has to go before they can get involved," said Kim Croyle, a lawyer in Morgantown, W.Va., who represents several school boards and lectures on cyberbullying.[23]

Under a legal standard set by the Supreme Court in 1969 in *Tinker v. Des Moines Independent Community School District*, educators can prohibit student speech if it causes substantial interference with school discipline or the rights of others.[24] *Tinker* remains the chief yardstick in cyberbullying cases, but it can be tricky to apply.

If, for example, a student is afraid to go to school because of a cyberbullying incident, a school might be hard-pressed to justify harsh action under the *Tinker* ruling. What constitutes substantial interference can be in the eye of the beholder.

The fact that *Tinker* isn't the sole yardstick for deciding students' First Amendment rights further complicates matters. For example, the Supreme Court has said that "true threats" are not protected by the First Amendment.[25] And it has allowed educators to crack down on vulgar student speech at school and to exert control over school-sponsored expression such as school newspapers.[26]

Perhaps the most nettlesome circumstance is cyberbullying that is transmitted at home or the local mall or skating rink, but that nonetheless causes disruption at school.

"There's always the legal discussion of 'if it doesn't happen at school, can a district take action?' " said Joe Wehrli, policy-services director for the Oregon School Boards Association. "If a student is harassed for three hours at night on the Web and they come to school and have to sit in the same classroom with the student that's the bully, there is an effect on education, and in that way, there is a direct link to schools."[27]

But free-speech advocates say educators sometimes punish students whose speech is protected by the First Amendment.

"Off-campus behavior that is not connected to the school in any way — no use of school computers, no transmission of messages in school — is not within the purview of school officials," contends Joan Bertin, executive director of the National Coalition Against Censorship, an advocacy group in New York. "It may have some play-out within school, but the actual speech took place in a protected zone. The school can't go after the speech, but it can go after the behavior that occurs on campus" as a result of the speech.

An exception would be speech that constitutes a true threat, Bertin says, but true threats must meet a high standard, she says. "A kid e-mailing another kid saying, 'I'm going to knock your brains out' or 'I wish this teacher were dead' — these are not, in my opinion, true threats."

Still, most courts would say the school could address any "speech that constitutes the equivalent of stalking or harassment, which would potentially fall under the criminal code," she continues, especially if it is directed at fellow students, teachers or the administration.

Bertin acknowledges that cyberbullying can be a "terrible problem" and understands why teachers and parents are concerned about childhood cruelty. But on the other hand, "There are limits about what schools can and should do," she argues. "Punitive, censorious response tends to be the first line of attack" by state lawmakers. "If people sat down in a more thoughtful, dispassionate way and thought about what they're trying to achieve, they might well reconsider that response."

Some argue, though, that the ability of cyber communication to quickly spread far and wide demands that school officials step in even when the bullying is generated off school grounds. Rumors spread by cell phone or embarrassing photos posted online can often create a disruptive buzz at school and sometimes lead to other problems, including absenteeism or violence.

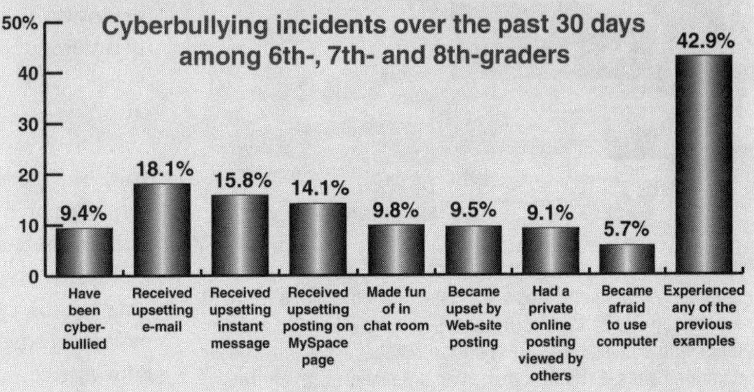

In Bethesda, Md., at Walt Whitman High School, known for its high academic achievement, students got into fist fights twice in April to settle disputes that arose on Facebook. The incidents prompted Principal Alan Goodwin to ask parents to monitor their children's postings on the site. "I am becoming increasingly frustrated by negative incidents at school that arise from students harassing other students on Facebook," he wrote. Goodwin told *The Washington Post* that the students involved "had not been involved in such things before, and we could have prevented [the fights], I think, if we had known."[28]

In Washington, D.C., last month, Francis Junior High School Principal Stephannie Crutchfield spent two class periods counseling a group of seventh-grade students who began arguing at school as a result of a conflict over "boyfriend-type stuff" that started on MySpace over the weekend. The parents of one girl had called Crutchfield, concerned that her child had been threatened. When the spat turned ugly in the school hallways, Crutchfield didn't hesitate to move in.

"I cannot discipline what a child has written off campus, but if the end result is a behavior infraction inside the school, then that's what I have to deal with," Crutchfield says. "Disorderly conduct or whatever behavior in my building is what I address."

The University of Wisconsin's Patchin argues that "just about everything kids do on or off campus ultimately will come back to the school," and therefore "school officials absolutely must do something." But that doesn't necessarily mean having to take punitive measures, he says. Schools should be proactive in teaching students about cyberbullying and its consequences and in promoting safe school climates, Patchin says. "We advocate doing the brunt of the work ahead of time."

Sometimes it is not civil libertarians but school officials themselves who argue that off-campus cyber expression is outside their purview. They might be concerned, for example, that if they begin to regulate speech that occurs off school grounds, their liability grows if they fail to catch a specific off-campus incident ahead of time and violence ensues.

But schools shouldn't back away from confronting cyberbullying that impinges on school order and safety, some experts contend.

"Schools want to say cyberspace is beyond our control, but you can't be in denial," says Juvonen, the UCLA researcher. "You can't be saying this is not our business. It is the schools' responsibility to address it when it is so closely connected to what goes on at school."

Willard, at the Center for Safe and Responsible Internet Use, strongly advises educators to step in even

CQ Press/Screenshot

Cyberbullying is fueled by "status in school — popularity, hierarchies, who's cool, who's not," says Danah Boyd, a fellow at the Berkman Center for Internet and Society at Harvard Law School who studies teens' behavior on MySpace and other social-networking sites. Early this year, in an agreement with attorneys general from 49 states and the District of Columbia, MySpace said it would develop technology and work with law-enforcement officials to improve children's protection.

when cyberbullying occurs away from school if the clear potential exists that it would affect students and the educational climate. Even so, she says the manner in which administrators act is important.

"They may impose discipline if . . . they're protecting the school's ability to deliver instruction, the security of students coming to school and [to avert] violence," she says.

But she also says that excessive discipline frequently exaggerates a problem. It can undermine feelings of remorse among bullies and also lead to vicious online retaliation by victims. "I strongly encourage an approach that helps bring the students to a greater level of understanding of the true harm caused by these online activities," she says.

Some administrators err by coming down hard on a student not because the speech endangers school order or safety but simply because it angers or upsets the school officials, Willard says.

"I would remind school administrators that the founders of our country called King George a tyrant."

Should parents be held liable for cyberbullying offenses?

When juveniles do commit serious online abuses, the question often arises: Where were the parents?

Shouldn't they be held accountable, or at least share the blame?

"The question isn't 'should,' the question is 'can,' and the answer is 'yes,' " says Willard. Under parental-liability statutes or parental-negligence standards, parents may be held liable for the harm caused by their children, she says.

Willard says she hopes cases don't reach that point. Still, "the fact that there is the potential for liability can help get parents motivated" to monitor their children's actions, she says.

In the civil-litigation system, "financial consequences for cyberbullying are now serious enough to make even the most lenient parent of a bully sit up and take notice," Millie Anne Cavanaugh, a family-law attorney in Los Angeles, wrote recently on the Web site of a group that provides programs for troubled adolescents. "In addition to liability against the cyberbully himself on theories such as defamation, invasion of privacy, disclosure of private information and intentional infliction of emotional distress, parents could now [be] held accountable for their child's cyberbullying if they failed to properly supervise the child's online activity."[29]

The University of Wisconsin's Patchin sees the issue in a similar light as vandalism cases. "If a parent knows it's going on or creates the opportunity where they're unwilling to supervise the behavior of their kids, certainly we should consider holding them responsible as well," he says.

But Patchin is cautious on the subject. "If you've got a 16- or 17-year-old kid who's logging on at a friend's house" and the parent is unaware of what's going on, "then I don't know. A lot of parents simply don't know much about computers and may be unwilling to educate themselves. Is that deliberate indifference? I don't know."

Experts say parents are often clueless about their children's online activity and that adolescents tormented by cyberbullies often hide their victimization from parents for fear of losing their computer and cell phone privileges.

Researchers say both situations — victims' silence and parents' obliviousness — help cyberbullying to grow.

Aftab, of wiredsafety.org, who speaks regularly to middle- and high-school students, says 45,000 students — 85 percent to 97 percent of her audiences — reported having been victims of cyberbullying last year. Yet, "only 5 percent will tell a trusted parent or adult," she says.

"We've found that over 90 percent of kids did not tell their parents about these incidents," echoes Juvonen, the UCLA researcher. Among 12- to 14-year-old girls, almost half were concerned about their parents restricting their Internet access if they revealed they were victimized, she says. Half of the adolescents Juvonen surveyed wanted to deal with incidents of cyberbullying by themselves rather than seeking help from adults.

"We're very concerned about this belief and the fear of parental restrictions," Juvonen says. "It's what is making cyberbullying so very dangerous."

Susan Limber, a Clemson University psychologist who studies bullying, says many adolescents in focus groups say parents and teachers don't seem to talk enough with them about online behavior. "Kids on the one hand say parents should be a little more involved," Limber says. "But as one kid said, they want supervision, not 'snoopervision.' "

In other words, Limber says, "They want appropriate rules, but they don't want parents poking into every last e-mail or text message. But that's a fine line."

Parents can have an especially difficult time keeping track of what adolescents are posting on social-networking sites. Some child advocates say parents should create their own accounts so they can monitor what their children are doing on the sites.

The sites allow people to post online pages featuring personal facts, photos, gossip and other information for others to read. Social scientists say such sites can serve a useful, and even vital, purpose by helping adolescents build friendships, learn tolerance for others' views and form a sense of self-identity. But critics say the sites have the potential to be incubators for cyber abuse, magnets for sexual predators and embarrassing archives of a student's immature behavior that college admissions officials or employers may wind up seeing.

"Putting something on the Internet is a whole lot different than whispering it on the playground," says Witold "Vic" Walczak, legal director of the ACLU in Pennsylvania.

Many parents and other responsible adults often neglect to impart that message to youngsters.

Weiss, of Operation Respect, says engaging adolescents in "conversation around moral issues" like cyberbullying "is really important for kids" but that many adults — teachers among them — don't know how to do so.

"We're not having this conversation enough," he says. "If we did, it would be the strongest thing we could do."

BACKGROUND

Students' Rights

Inflammatory speech by young people is nothing new, and neither is adults' desire to suppress it. In 1908, the Wisconsin Supreme Court ruled that school officials could suspend two students who ridiculed their teachers in a poem in a local newspaper.[30] Seven years later, a California appellate court said a student could be suspended for criticizing school officials in an assembly.[31]

Courts gradually broadened students' rights, but those liberties remain limited.

In 1969, the Supreme Court said in the watershed *Tinker* case that school officials had no right to suspend students for wearing black armbands to protest the Vietnam War. "It can hardly be argued that either students or teachers shed their constitutional rights to freedom of speech or expression at the schoolhouse gate," Justice Abe Fortas wrote.

Yet, students do shed some rights. Under the *Tinker* standard, school officials can discipline students whose speech disrupts school activities or interferes with the rights of others. Other rulings allow schools to suppress students' lewd speech and punish those who make credible threats.[32]

Cases involving cyberbullying can be especially difficult for school officials and judges to weigh, however. Distinguishing true threats and defamation from harmless adolescent high jinks can be a matter of debate.

In a decision last year, a federal judge ruled that a Pennsylvania school district violated a student's First Amendment rights when it punished him for creating on his grandmother's computer a parody profile on MySpace that crudely made fun of his principal.[33] Still, the judge called the decision, which is being appealed, a "close call."

The school district had based its defense partly on an earlier Pennsylvania case in which the state Supreme Court upheld the expulsion of an eighth-grader — whose initials were J.S. — who created a "Teacher Sux" Web site containing derogatory material aimed at an algebra teacher and the principal. The court said the site created a substantial disruption of school activities.[34]

"[T]he advent of the Internet has complicated analysis of restrictions on speech," Justice Ralph J. Cappy wrote in the J.S. case. "Indeed, *Tinker's* simple armband, worn silently and brought into a Des Moines, Iowa, classroom, has been replaced by J.S.'s complex multimedia Web site, accessible to fellow students, teachers and the world."

Growing Phenomenon

Judges aren't the only ones who struggle to distinguish juvenile antics from truly troublesome behavior.

"I have been teaching in public schools for 13 years. I am not sure what bullying is," a reader responded to a newspaper blog on anti-bullying legislation in Georgia last year. "Is it when a child calls another child's mama ugly or fat? Is it breaking in line after recess? . . . Children are cruel to each other, and they always have been. If a child does smell to high heaven, kids are going to talk about it. When did all this become 'bullying'? I am just asking."[35]

Some experts say that in many ways, face-to-face bullying remains more problematic than online abuse, but that teachers and parents often perceive cyberbullying as more of a threat because it is delivered through new and perhaps bewildering technology. Still, researchers say cyberbullying affects so many youngsters that it cannot be taken lightly.

An anonymous survey of nearly 4,000 middle-school students by Limber and fellow Clemson University psychologist Robin Kowalski found that 18 percent reported being bullied at least once in the previous two months through e-mail, instant messaging, chat rooms, Web sites and cell-phone text messaging. Girls were roughly twice as likely as boys to be victims. Eleven percent of the students — slightly more girls than boys — admitted bullying someone else.[36]

The University of Wisconsin's Patchin says in a random-sample study of about 2,000 middle-school students in 30 schools in a major school district, he and his colleagues found that less than 10 percent of youngsters said they had been victims of cyberbullying — defined as repeated abuse — in the previous 30 days. But when asked about specific types of online harassment and aggression, nearly 43 percent said they had experienced at least one incident in the previous 30 days, such as receiving an e-mail or instant message that made them upset, having something upsetting to them posted on their MySpace site or being made fun of in a chat room.

Because cyberbullying does not require physical confrontation and is often anonymous, it can appeal more to girls than boys, researchers say. "Girls have really taken on a bullying role that has changed in the last couple of years with the electronic age," said Kristy Hagar, a neuropsychologist at Children's Medical Center in Dallas.[37]

Aftab of wiredsafety.org says she has noticed that online bullying is growing, especially among second- and third-graders, and that "by the fourth grade it is institutionalized."

"Fourth-graders use extortion as a form of cyberbullying: 'If you don't do this, I will tell,' " Aftab says. "Sometimes they think it's funny and say they don't mean it." By middle school, she says, cyberbullying can get "more malicious." In high school, many students will claim cyberbullying doesn't exist — not because that's true, Aftab says, but because high-school students don't want to admit that someone else may have power over them and can hurt their feelings.

"Bullying is for babies — that's just stuff that happens," Aftab says she hears high-school students say.

Aftab says cyberbullying is most prevalent among 13- and 14-year-olds. A Harris Poll found that the incidence is highest among 15- and 16-year-olds, particularly girls.[38]

Impact of Technology

The pell-mell expansion in the use of technology has fueled cyberbullying's growth. Nearly half of online youths ages 12-17 have uploaded photos where others can see them (though many restrict access to the pictures), and 14 percent have posted videos online, according to the Pew Research Center.[39]

Technology can make cyber abuse an especially potent form of bullying. For one thing, transmission is instantaneous to a potentially limitless audience — including recipients in the next state or even overseas. "It's not like being called 'four eyes,' " Herbeck of Boston College says. "It's being blasted across cyberspace."

CHRONOLOGY

1960s-1970s *Supreme Court upholds students' rights to free speech and due process; computers take root in American society.*

1969 Supreme Court rules in *Tinker v. Des Moines Independent Community School District* that school officials violated students' First Amendment rights by suspending them for wearing armbands to protest the Vietnam War.

1975 Supreme Court rules in *Goss v. Lopez* that suspended students are entitled to a hearing.

1976 Apple computer is founded.

1980s *Supreme Court limits students' rights in speech and discipline cases; computers continue to gain a foothold in society.*

1981 IBM introduces its personal computer.

1985 Supreme Court rules in *New Jersey v. T.L.O.* that school officials do not need to get a search warrant or show probable cause before they search students at school.

1986 Supreme Court rules in *Bethel School District No. 403 v. Fraser* that school officials did not violate the First Amendment rights of a student suspended for delivering a vulgar speech to a school assembly.

1988 Supreme Court rules in *Hazelwood School District v. Kuhlmeier* that school officials can limit school-sponsored student expression if they have a legitimate educational reason.

1990s *Internet becomes big part of American life, spurring Congress to protect juveniles and others from online abuses.*

1997 Supreme Court rules in *Reno v. ACLU* that Internet speech merits First Amendment protection.

1998 Congress passes Child Online Protection Act in bid to limit access by minors to adult-oriented Web sites, but the law runs into court challenges.

2000-Present *Growth of technology and advent of social-networking sites present school and law-enforcement officials with new challenges in fighting adolescent bullying.*

2000 Children's Online Privacy Protection Act takes effect, giving parents the power to decide whether and what information can be collected online from children under 13.

2002 U.S. Secret Service says bullying played a significant role in some school shootings.

2002 Friendster, a global social-networking site, is launched, followed by MySpace (2003) and Facebook (2004).

2003 Ryan Halligan, a Vermont 13-year-old, commits suicide after online harassment.

2006 Suicide of Missouri teenager Megan Meier prompts calls for tougher laws on Internet harassment.

2007 Supreme Court rules in *Morse v. Frederick* that school officials can punish student speech that can be interpreted as advocating illegal drug use; the case involved a student who held up a "Bong Hits 4 Jesus" banner outside school grounds. . . . House passes bill to provide grants to fight online crime, including cyberbullying; Senate proposes separate measure. . . . Centers for Disease Control and Prevention calls "electronic aggression" among adolescents an "emerging public-health problem." . . . MySpace agrees to give states information on convicted sex offenders with accounts on the site.

2008 In an agreement with attorneys general from 49 states, MySpace says it will take additional steps to protect children from online abuses. . . . Eight Florida teens are charged as adults with battery and kidnapping in an attack on another teen that was videoed and posted on the Internet. . . . Consumer officials in New Jersey announce investigation of college-gossip Web site Juicy Campus. . . . AOL enters into agreement to acquire global social-networking site Bebo. . . . Florida Senate on April 30 is scheduled to consider an anti-cyberbullying measure, the Jeffrey Johnston Stand Up for All Students Act, named after a Cape Coral, Fla., teenager who killed himself in 2005 after enduring two years of cyberbullying by a classmate.

Suicide Uncovers Adult Role in Internet Shaming

Controversial practices include attacks on sex offenders.

Cyberbullying isn't just a problem among adolescents. Adults engage in it, too. From online vigilantism and angry blogs to e-stalking and anonymous ranting on newspaper Web sites, grownups can be as abusive as the meanest schoolhouse tyrant.

The suicide of 13-year-old Megan Meier in 2006 thrust adult cyberbullying into the open. The Dardenne Prairie, Mo., girl killed herself after receiving cruel messages on MySpace from imposters posing as a 16-year-old boy named "Josh Evans."

Lori Drew, the mother of one of Megan's friends, was accused of participating in the hoax along with her teenage daughter and a former teenage employee. Drew has denied sending messages to Megan.[1] While questions remain about Drew's role, the case has left no doubt that the Internet is rife with adult cyber passion.

After the suicide came to light, an outraged mother several states away ferreted out Drew's identity and posted it on a blog.[2]

Soon, "an army of Internet avengers . . . set out to destroy Lori Drew and her family," forcing them from their home and "vowing them no peace, ever," newspaper columnist Barbara Shelly wrote. "Who are these people who have made it their business to destroy her? They are a jury with laptops, their verdict rendered without insight into the dynamics of two families or the state of mind of a fragile 13-year-old girl or even a complete explanation of what actually occurred."[3]

Internet shaming is a growing cultural phenomenon, but Daniel Solove, a professor of law at George Washington University and author of the 2007 book *The Future of Reputation: Gossip, Rumor and Privacy on the Internet*, says it can backfire.

"Internet shaming is done by people who want actually to enforce norms and to make people and society more orderly," he said. But instead, "Internet shaming actually destroys social control and makes things more anarchic, and it becomes very hard to regulate and stop it."[4]

Among its many controversial uses, online technology is employed by some citizens to track or expose sex offenders — including those who themselves use the Internet to exploit others.

Perverted-justice.com is famous for its efforts, sometimes in combination with televised sting operations, to expose online predators. In 2006, a former Texas district attorney committed suicide when police tried to arrest him on a warrant linked to a child-predator sting that was a joint operation between Perverted Justice and NBC's "Dateline."[5]

While some criticize such stings as a form of vigilantism, others worry about those who use state online sex-offender registries to pursue their own brand of justice.

In a report last year of U.S. sex-offender policies, Human Rights Watch, an advocacy group in New York, concluded that unfettered public access to online sex-offender registries left former offenders open "to the risk that individuals will act on this information in irresponsible and even unlawful ways. There is little evidence that this form of community notification prevents sexual violence."[6]

In a section of the report on "vigilante violence," Human Rights Watch wrote: "A number of convicted sex offenders have been targets of violence from strangers who

And cyberbullies can avoid witnessing the damage they inflict. Researchers say adolescents often don't grasp that a vulnerable human being is on the receiving end of hateful words and images. "A lot of kids who engage [in cyberbullying], when confronted, say, 'I didn't mean it' or 'I didn't know the outcome,' " Wisconsin's Patchin says. "If I am bullying in real life, I can see the effect immediately."

Moreover, bullies tend to think their messages can't be traced back to them — often a faulty assumption. "They may think they have achieved anonymity," says Willard of the Center for Safe and Responsible Internet Use, "but they're really bad at hiding their identity."

Cyberbullying also has staying power. Words and images in the virtual world can exist in perpetuity in cyberspace. That means victims may review tormenting take it upon themselves to 'eliminate' sex offenders from communities. In April 2003, Lawrence Trant stabbed one New Hampshire registrant and lit fires at two buildings where registrants lived. When he was arrested, police found a printout of New Hampshire's sex-offender Internet registry, with checkmarks next to the names of those already targeted."

Cyber vigilantism also can occur in the realm of global terrorism. Some experts say that private citizens who seek to monitor and close down terror-linked Web sites are hurting the government's own investigations.[7]

"It is very unlikely they will find something of significance on the Internet that the government doesn't already know," said Michael Radu — a senior fellow at the Foreign Policy Research Institute, a think tank in Philadelphia — who studies revolutionary and terrorist groups. "They are redundant at best."[8]

Sometimes it's an adult's private blog, podcast or video that gets others the most upset. In April, Tricia Walsh Smith, being divorced by Philip Smith — president of the Shubert Organization, Broadway's biggest theater chain — put a video on YouTube containing derogatory information about their sex life.[9]

Yet, just as adolescents may learn to ignore the online gossip and cyber belittling that course through their cell phones and MySpace pages, adults may tire of what some call "net-venting."

Getty Images/Bruce Glikas/FilmMagic

Actress Tricia Walsh Smith, who is being divorced by Philip Smith, president of the biggest theater chain on Broadway, posted a video on YouTube containing derogatory information about their sex life.

"Most people who confront Web sites devoted to 'getting back' at other people for social sins may find them entertaining at first, but will tire of the novelty of electronic trash talk," David A. Furlow, a Houston attorney, wrote in a recent commentary. "Folk wisdom suggests that one should not wrestle with a pig, both because the wrestler gets dirty and the pig likes the challenge. The best response to the venom and vitriol of spite speech is to ignore it."[10]

---

1 Kim Zetter, "Cyberbullying Suicide Stokes the Internet Fury Machine," *Wired*, Nov. 21, 2007.

2 Rebecca Cathcart, "MySpace Is Said to Draw Subpoena in Hoax Case," *The New York Times*, Jan. 10, 2008, p. A19.

3 Barbara Shelly, "Online avengers perpetuate the problem," *Kansas City Star*, Dec. 7, 2007, p. 9B.

4 Quoted in Zetter, *op. cit.*

5 Richard Abshire, Marissa Alanis and Jennifer Emily, "Sex sting leads to suicide for former Kaufman D.A.," *Dallas Morning News*, Nov. 6, 2006.

6 "U.S.: Sex Offender Laws May Do More Harm Than Good," Human Rights Watch, Sept. 12, 2007. The report, "No Easy Answers: Sex Offender Laws in the United States," http://hrw.org/reports/2007/us0907/.

7 See, for example, Carmen Gentile, "Cyber Vigilantes Track Extremist Web Sites, Intelligence Experts Balk at Effort," Fox News, March 22, 2008, www.foxnews.com.

8 Quoted in *ibid.*

9 Leslie Kaufman, "When the Ex Blogs, the Dirtiest Laundry Is Aired," *The New York Times*, April 18, 2008, p. A1.

10 David A. Furlow, "Net-Venting: Should a Server or a Speaker Face Civil Liability for Spite Speech on the World Wide Web?," *Privacy Litigation Reporter*, September 2007, www.tklaw.com/resources/documents/PRV0501_FurlowComm.pdf.

---

words and images again and again. In fact, in charting cyberbullying incidents, some researchers wrestle with whether to count only the initial transmission or the number of times a victim views it.

Effect on Students

While experts contend that cyberbullying is a large and growing social problem, it is too new for definitive data on its effects to have been collected. Nonetheless, Clemson University's Limber says some clues can be drawn from past studies on traditional bullying.

In the short term, children who are victims of traditional, face-to-face bullying are more likely than their peers to have lower self-esteem and higher rates of anxiety, she says: "One can hypothesize that there may be similar short-term effects of cyberbullying," she adds, but "there

Bettmann/Corbis

Iowa high-school students Mary Beth and John Tinker, shown in 1968, were suspended along with three other students for wearing black armbands to oppose the Vietnam War. In 1969, the Supreme Court said in the watershed *Tinker v. Des Moines School District* case that school officials had no right to suspend the students. "It can hardly be argued that either students or teachers shed their constitutional rights to freedom of speech or expression at the schoolhouse gate," Justice Abe Fortas wrote. However, under *Tinker* school officials can discipline students whose speech disrupts school activities or interferes with the rights of others.

are elements of cyberbullying that may make it even more disturbing for kids. In many cases kids don't know the identity of the individual doing the bullying. That can create higher rates of anxiety."

More than half of adolescent girls responding to a survey by Patchin and two colleagues reported no negative effects from cyberbullying, but others "reported a wide variety of emotional effects . . . including feeling 'sad,' 'angry,' 'upset,' 'depressed,' 'violated,' 'hated,' 'annoyed,' 'helpless,' 'exploited' and 'stupid and put down.' Some girls described how the victimization made them feel unsafe." Many girls responded to the bullying by retaliating or "cyberbullying back," the study found.[40]

Jean Sunde Peterson, an associate professor of educational studies at Purdue University, in West Lafayette, Ind., studies the effects of bullying on gifted students, a group that she says is generally highly sensitive, acutely perceptive and disinclined to seek help. While her work has not focused on cyberbullying per se, she says many of her findings apply to it.

When Peterson and doctoral student Karen E. Ray asked 432 gifted eighth-graders in 11 states if they had experienced name-calling, pushing, hitting, teasing or other abuses during their school years, 67 percent said yes. Among the effects the respondents reported: depression, unexpressed rage and absenteeism from school.[41]

"You're really talking about post-traumatic stress and school phobia," Peterson says.

Gifted students may not be used to aggression, Peterson adds. When a bully strikes, they can feel betrayed, especially if the bully is part of their close social network, she says. "It's about what is real versus what is unreal. You can think something is real, like a friendship, and all of a sudden it's not." One casualty can be a student's self-identity, particularly if a rumor spreads about the victim's sexuality, she says.

While Peterson's research focuses on regular bullying, she says cyberbullying "kind of hits you without warning and [thus] might even have more impact."

One reason for cyberbullying's growth, experts say, is adults' unfamiliarity with the alien landscape of chat rooms and social networking, allowing online abuse to slip by unnoticed.

"Parents are kept in the dark intentionally by the kids," says Aftab of wiredsafety.org. "Even the victims hide from parents. The only time they tell is if they're under 10."

Patchin of the University of Wisconsin says teens often refrain from reporting cyberbullying because they don't think adults can or will do anything about it. School administrators frequently say they can't address off-campus behavior, Patchin points out, and police and prosecutors typically go after only the most egregious or threatening kinds of cyber harassment. In deciding not to tell adults, Patchin says, many young victims conclude: "What's really going to change?"

Sometimes adults respond to cyberbullying in what many experts say is the wrong way: by trying to ban teens' access to technology. For example, the Deleting Online Predators Act, which sailed through the then-Republican-controlled U.S. House of Representatives in 2006, would have required schools and libraries receiving special federal technology funds to block minors from accessing chat rooms and social-networking sites like MySpace. The bill apparently has stalled.

"I'm concerned that this [crackdown] is going to be as simplistic and thoughtless as the drug programs out there, which is 'Just say no,' when that is not a feasible, meaningful way to go about it," says UCLA's Juvonen.

Juvonen says that used properly, technology can help adolescents navigate through periods of angst and insecurity. "Online communication with even an unknown peer can alleviate the temporary stress of feeling rejection," Juvonen says. "The online world enables them to connect even from that lonely bedroom at home. It would be a pity if parents restrict all communication without better understanding how rich this world is. It has its pluses and negatives."

Potential Solutions

Child advocates and researchers continue to look for ways to curb cyber abuse. One approach encourages young people to police themselves. Social-networking sites offer tools to help them do that, including safety tips, settings to block unwanted communications and protect users' privacy and admonitions to report hateful or harassing content.

For example, Bebo, a San Francisco-based social-networking site aimed at users 13 and older, has an online "safety" tab that includes anti-bullying animations, resources for schools and advice for parents.[42]

Schoolwide programs designed to change a school environment to reduce or prevent behavior problems are also being used to fight cyberbullying. The Olweus Bullying Prevention Program, for instance, founded by Dan Olweus, a European researcher who has studied bullying for more than three decades, is being used by about 2,000 elementary and middle schools in the United States, according to Clemson University's Limber, who leads its U.S. implementation.

The approach includes training programs for teachers and administrators, surveys of students, classroom discussions about the effects of traditional and online harassment, efforts to raise community awareness of bullying, and when needed, individualized intervention with victims or perpetrators.

The program's effectiveness at fighting cyberbullying remains unclear, Limber says, because questions to assess cyberbullying were added only in the past year. But schools using the program to fight traditional bullying often see a 20 percent reduction in incidents, she says.

Limber acknowledges that some cases of cyberbullying call for strong action by school authorities and that online abuse that occurs off-site can create havoc at school.

Still, she says, "there is a lot a school and school personnel can do to raise kids' and kids' parents' awareness about cyberbullying even if it does happen off school grounds. It's important to focus on prevention and intervention. I'm more a proponent of the carrot than the stick."

CURRENT SITUATION

Action in Congress

Moves to improve online safety have been building in Congress and the states for years, spurred in part by concerns over the vulnerability of children to online predators and pornography. For example, the Children's Online Privacy Protection Act, which took effect in 2000, gives parents the power to decide whether and what information can be collected online from children under 13 and how the information can be used.

A bill sponsored by Sen. Ted Stevens, R-Alaska, would direct the Federal Trade Commission to carry out a public-awareness campaign focusing on the safe use of the Internet by children.[43] It also would substantially increase fines for Internet service providers, or those who provide computers for Internet access, such as café owners, who fail to report online child pornography.[44] In addition, it would require schools receiving special federal "E-Rate" technology funds to educate students about cyberbullying and "appropriate online behavior," including interaction with others on social-networking sites and in chat rooms.[45]

Congressional efforts to fight Internet crime are not without controversy, though.

In November 2007, for example, the House passed a bill sponsored by Rep. Linda Sanchez, D-Calif., who has proposed several anti-bullying measures in Congress. The bill would authorize grants for educational programs to fight Internet crime, including cyberbullying, sexual exploitation and privacy violations.[46]

Specifically, the measure would authorize the appropriation of $50 million over five years, half to i-SAFE — a nonprofit group in Carlsbad, Calif., that provides Internet safety programs in all 50 states — and half for a competitive grant program under which online-safety groups could vie for funding.

A coalition of online safety groups criticized the bill, saying it was funneling too much money to i-SAFE and would suppress competition and innovation in cyber-protection programs.[47]

Abusive Online Gossip Thrives on College Campuses

Juicycampus.com allows anonymous postings.

Librarian Graham Mallaghan wondered why students at the Kent University library in Canterbury, England, would laugh at him and sometimes take his picture. After a suggestion from a colleague, Mallaghan went to Facebook.com and found out why. On the site he found a page titled "For Those Who Hate the Little Fat Library Man," with hateful comments from many of the students he had disciplined in the library, telling them to stop eating or not to make noise.

After Mallaghan notified school authorities, his bike's brakes were cut and he was threatened with violence while leaving work. When the students responsible for the page had their computer access suspended, they simply passed on the password and user information to other students, who continued the abuse.

Mallaghan says he was so troubled that he sought therapy over the abuse and became underweight. The site eventually was removed.

At George Washington University in Washington, D.C., an argument between two female roommates led one of the young women to post negative comments on Facebook about her roommate, who had accused her of using drugs. The roommate complained about the mean-spirited comments to campus authorities, but the school said it did not have the authority to act. Facebook eventually stepped in, however, threatening to block the bullying roommate from using the social-networking site if she continued to run the page.

One of the latest and most abusive gossip sites is eight-month-old Juicycampus.com, now being used at some 60 campuses nationwide, including the U.S. Naval Academy and West Point.[1] The site promises posters complete anonymity. Many of the comments posted about sorority girls, football players and professors are sexist, homophobic, racist or anti-Semitic. Juicycampus postings at such schools as Loyola Marymount University in Los Angeles, Colgate University in New York state and the University of North Carolina at Chapel Hill have included students threatening shooting rampages, a fake "sex tape" of murdered UNC student-body President Eve Carson and a crude "photo-shopped" picture of a female Vanderbilt University student.

"For students who have been identified by name on Juicy Campus, the results can be devastating," wrote Richard Morgan recently in *The New York Times.* "In a tearful phone conversation, a 21-year-old junior at Baylor who majors in public relations recounted her experience when her name surfaced on the site in a discussion about the "biggest slut" on campus. " 'I'm trying to get a job in business,' she said. 'The last thing I need or want is this kind of maliciousness and lies about me out there on the Internet.' "[2]

The coalition expressed support instead for a Senate measure introduced by Sen. Robert Menendez, D-N.J., that calls for a $50-million competitive grant program for Internet education through 2012.[49]

"There are many good Internet safety organizations working hard in our schools and communities, and we feel that all organizations should have an equal opportunity to receive funding through an open and transparent grant process," said Judi Westberg-Warren, president of Web Wise Kids, an online safety group in Santa Ana, Calif.[49]

Willard, of the Center for Safe and Responsible Internet Use, criticized i-SAFE's approach and called the Sanchez legislation "a very bad bill that, if passed in its current form, will ensure mediocrity in the delivery of Internet safety education for years."[50]

But Sanchez stood up for her bill. "Authorizing i-SAFE ensures that this program, which has already helped over 3 million children in all 50 states, will be able to continue its work," she said, adding that the group has a "proven track record for teaching kids how to be safe on the Internet."[51]

Likewise, Teri Schroeder, founder and president of i-SAFE, defends her group and its curriculum, which is distributed free to schools. She says the House bill is more comprehensive than the Senate's and would protect the

Andy Canales, student body president at Pepperdine University in Malibu, Calif., opposes the juicycampus.com gossip site.

As of late April, Juicy Campus had not been banned on any campus, but student governments at several schools, including Pepperdine, Columbia and Yale universities, have called for school administrators to block the sites. At the University of California at Berkeley, Panhellenic Council President Christina Starzak urged sorority leaders in an e-mail not to use the site. Students at Pepperdine asked campus administrators to block the site from campus servers, but administrators declined on free-speech grounds. Some administrators, however, say that blocking Juicy Campus will force them to regulate hundreds of other offensive sites. Additionally, administrators and students simply hope the sites will eventually become less popular and fade away.[3]

Attorneys general in New Jersey and Connecticut, meanwhile, have recently subpoenaed the records of Juicycampus.com in hope of shutting down the site using consumer fraud statutes.[4]

"Me, I'm waiting for a horrific tragedy to happen — followed by a huge lawsuit (or 20) that cuts into the profits of Juicycampus.com," wrote columnist Debra J. Saunders in the *San Francisco Chronicle.* "I'll be rooting for the plaintiff's attorneys. There have to be some advantages to living in an overly litigious society."[5]

For his part, Facebook victim Mallaghan says his experience with cyberbullying has made one thing clear to him: Children must be taught that things "could get worse by staying quiet about Internet abuse. You need to find someone you trust to take you to the authorities. If nobody knows, nobody can protect you."

— *Kristina Ryan*

[1] Richard Morgan, "A Crash Course in Online Gossip," *The New York Times*, March 6, 2008.

[2] *Ibid.*

[3] Debra J. Saunders, "Tawdry, Not Juicy," SF Gate (the online edition of the *San Francisco Chronicle*), March 25, 2008, www.sfgate.com/cgi-bin/article.cgi?file=/c/a/2008/03/24/EDCPVPK55.DTL.

[4] "California Scrutinizes Juicy Campus Web Site for Potential Legal Violations," California Attorney Lawyers Web site, http://attorney-2california.com/california-scrutinizes-juicy-campus-web-site-for-potential-legal-violations/.

[5] Saunders, *op. cit.*

federal government's investment in i-SAFE, which has totaled $13 million since 2002.

The i-SAFE approach faces several financial pressures, Schroeder says. It has received no federal money for the past year-and-a-half but will nonetheless educate 6 million youths this year in Internet safety, relying on money raised from donors, she says. Moreover, she says, the federal government this year allocated federal funds through a competitive-bid process to other grantees besides i-SAFE to disseminate i-SAFE's program materials, putting an additional financial burden on i-SAFE. If Congress doesn't authorize new money to keep i-SAFE's programs current and available, those programs would be at risk, Schroeder says.

Social-Networking Sites

Cyber safety continues to draw close attention in the states, and no online mechanisms are drawing more scrutiny than social-networking sites.

MySpace agreed last year to hand over to state officials the names, addresses and online profiles of thousands of known convicted sex offenders with accounts on the networking site. It also said it had deleted the online profiles of 7,000 convicted sexual predators.[52]

And early this year, in an agreement with attorneys general from 49 states and the District of Columbia, MySpace said it would develop technology and work with

AT ISSUE

Should schools be able to regulate off-campus cyberbullying?

YES

Nancy Willard
Executive Director, Center for Safe and Responsible Internet Use

Written for *CQ Researcher*, April 2008

Two high-school students have created a racist profile on a social-networking site, including racist language and cartoons about lynching. Other students are linking to the site and have posted ugly comments. Teachers report that many of the school's minority students are frightened.

At another high school, students created a "We Hate Ashley" profile that includes crude sexual innuendos and cracks about their classmate's weight. Ashley is no longer willing to come to school, and her grades have plummeted. Her parents report she is under psychological care and on suicide watch.

Do school officials have the authority to impose discipline in response to harmful off-campus online speech? Should they? This is a major challenge facing school administrators today.

The problem is grounded in the fact that the most harmful incidents of cyberbullying occur when students post or send material while they are off-campus, because they have more unsupervised time. But the harmful impact is at school, because this is where students are physically together. Cyberbullying incidents lead to school avoidance and failure, youth suicide and school violence.

Studies on cyberbullying reported in the December 2007 *Journal of Adolescent Health* reveal that both perpetrators and targets of cyberbullying report significant psychosocial concerns and increased rates of involvement in off-line physical and relational aggression. Targets of cyberbullying were eight times more likely than other students to report bringing a weapon to school. The concerns for student safety are very real. Students who do not believe school officials can help them may seek their own revenge — or refuse to come to school.

Courts have consistently ruled that school officials can respond to off-campus student speech if that speech has caused — or a reasonable person would anticipate it could cause — a substantial disruption at school or interference with the rights of students to be secure. Situations that have met this standard include violent physical or verbal altercations, a hostile environment interfering with the ability of students to participate in school activities and significant interference with school operations and delivery of instruction.

School officials do not have the authority to respond to off-campus speech simply because they find the speech objectionable or repugnant. Response to such speech is a parent's responsibility. But when off-campus speech raises legitimate concerns about student safety and well-being, school officials must have the authority to respond — because every student faces the potential of harm.

NO

Witold J. Walczak
Legal Director, American Civil Liberties Union of Pennsylvania

Written for *CQ Researcher*, April 2008

If a school principal observed two students bullying another student at the local park or mall, she might speak to the children, alert the parents or, if really serious, call the police. Most likely she would not, however, contemplate using her principal's authority to suspend or otherwise discipline the bullies. Like most people, she would think that's outside of school and beyond her authority. The same standard should apply to cyberbullying.

School officials act *in loco parentis* (in place of a parent) when children are in school or in school-sponsored activities. Teachers are given leeway to instruct, direct and discipline to ensure a safe environment conducive to learning. And while students don't shed all their constitutional rights at the schoolhouse gate, courts have given administrators some leeway to restrict students' free speech, privacy and other rights while in school custody.

Once students leave the school's custody, they not only reacquire their full constitutional rights, but their parents or guardians regain theirs too, including their right to direct and control their children's upbringing. Parents' values and families' dynamics differ. Some parents prefer to turn the other cheek while others promote an eye for an eye. School officials have their own values and ways of addressing problems, and those may differ from the parents'. When it comes to their children's out-of-school behavior, parents have the right to decide if and how to discipline.

Limiting schools' disciplinary authority for out-of-school speech does not preclude school officials from taking steps, short of discipline, to address problems. Parents typically don't know everything their children do, and that's particularly true for Internet activity. Most parents would probably want school officials to alert them to bullying activity but leave disciplinary decisions to them. And for bullying that may cross the line into criminal behavior, contacting the police might be appropriate.

Finally, while school officials need to recognize that legally they have no authority over students' out-of-school speech, students should understand that Internet speech often carries real-world consequences. Unlike intemperate and stupid things uttered at the mall, speech posted on the Internet endures and is more widely accessible. Colleges, universities and prospective employers increasingly tend to uncover those mean and stupid Internet postings.

In sum, school officials have latitude to discipline students for bullying, cyber or otherwise, that occurs in school, but only parents (or police if necessary) have the authority to handle such matters off campus.

law-enforcement officials to improve children's protection. "Our responsibility is to show the way for social-networking sites," said Hemanshu Nigam, MySpace's chief security officer.[53]

The plan includes a police hotline to report suspicious behavior, automatically making the default setting "private" for profiles of 16- and 17-year-olds, allowing parents to submit their children's e-mail addresses to block them from establishing a MySpace profile and creating a separate section of MySpace for users younger than 18.[54]

MySpace also created a task force to explore how children can avoid unwanted contact and content when using it and other online sites. The task force will be run by Harvard's Berkman Center for Internet and Society, but the center's executive director said the group will operate independently. Recommendations by the task force will be non-binding.[55]

Connecticut Attorney General Richard Blumenthal called the agreement with MySpace "a profoundly significant step towards social-networking safety." He wrote that MySpace "commendably agreed to create and lead a task force of social-networking sites, technology companies and others to explore and develop age- and identity-verification technology." But, he warned, "If the task force fails to deliver, or if other social-networking sites decline to join, attorneys general stand ready to take aggressive steps, including litigation or legislative initiatives, if appropriate."[56]

Yet critics say it is easy for children to circumvent MySpace's safeguards by passing themselves off as adults, and for adults to manipulate MySpace by pretending to be adolescents. Texas Attorney General Greg Abbott, the lone holdout in signing the agreement, said he could not support the pact unless MySpace takes action to authenticate users' ages.

"We do not believe that MySpace.com — or any other social-networking site — can adequately protect minors" without an age-verification system, he said. "We are concerned that our signing the joint statement would be misperceived as an endorsement of the inadequate safety measures."[57]

Age-verification systems are difficult to implement and can lead to problems, some experts point out. Aftab, of wiredsafety.org, a task-force member, characterized the agreement as a good first step but said it could have unforeseen consequences.[58] "Age verification requires that you have a database of kids," she said, "and if you do, that database is available to hackers and anyone who can get into it."[59]

Still, Aftab said the task force will be "looking to see if age-verification or any other technology is out there that we don't know about that will help." The 20-member group includes such companies as Google, Microsoft, Yahoo and Verizon as well as networking sites Facebook, Xanga and Bebo (recently acquired by AOL), she said.

But Keith Durkin, chairman of the Department of Psychology and Sociology at Ohio Northern University, in Ada, said an effective age-verification system is nearly impossible. A predator or child could use a pre-loaded credit card to circumvent a system that uses credit cards to verify age and identity. And, he said, no hardware or software solutions will be effective unless they are expensive, intrusive and violate current privacy laws — something that would turn a law-enforcement problem into a political controversy.[60]

"You can't monitor your kids 24/7," he said. "Parents need to have a conversation with their children at an early age."[61]

Actions in States

Along with efforts to monitor social-networking sites, anti-bullying measures proposed or passed by state lawmakers are also stirring debate.

In Washington state, for example, legislators last year amended the state's anti-bullying statute, calling on school officials to develop policies barring harassment, intimidation or bullying by electronic means but limiting the scope to actions by students "while on school grounds and during the school day."[62]

The Center for Safe and Responsible Internet Use's Willard is critical of the law, saying it prevents school officials from responding to cyberbullying that originates off campus, even if the abuse causes disruption at school or threatens student safety.

In Oregon, Willard's home state, an anti-bullying statue was amended to include cyberbullying. The law defines bullying as any act that "substantially interferes" with a student's education and occurs "on or immediately adjacent to school grounds," at school-sponsored activities, on school-provided transportation or at school bus stops. The law's language creates the potential for incidents arising off campus to be off-limits, Willard says.[63]

Some states have adopted laws with broadened scopes. Arkansas, for example, last year added cyberbullying to its anti-bullying policies and included provisions for schools to act against some off-campus activities. The measure applies to actions originating on or off school grounds "if the electronic act is directed specifically at students or school personnel and is maliciously intended for the purpose of disrupting school, and has a high likelihood of succeeding in that purpose."[64]

In Maryland, lawmakers approved a bill in April that requires public schools to develop a policy barring cyber-bullying and other kinds of intimidation.[65] The bill says that even if the bullying occurs off school grounds, administrators can report it if it "substantially disrupts the orderly operation of a school."[66]

But Hudson, the research attorney for the First Amendment Center, said the school's power to reach off campus creates a "bit of tension in the First Amendment arena as to just how far school jurisdiction extends. There's no doubt that [the bill] is well-intentioned, but the question is whether it's going to sweep too much speech within its reach."[67]

In Kentucky, state Rep. Tim Couch, R-Hyden, filed a bill this year that would require anyone who contributes to a Web site to register a real name, address and e-mail address on the site. The name would then be used whenever the person posted a comment. Couch's intent was to call attention to anonymous cyberbullying.[68] "Some nasty things have been said about high-school kids in my district, usually by other kids," he said. "The adults get in on it, too."[69]

But Couch said because the measure is "probably unconstitutional," he isn't pursuing it.[70]

That's a good thing, opined the conservative *Washington Times*, citing what it called the bill's "bald violation of First Amendment rights."

"We're all concerned about cyberbullying," the newspaper said, "but we're more concerned when a lawmaker threatens our civil liberties and wastes public dollars on dim-witted legislation."[71]

OUTLOOK

Guidance Needed

As technology gets faster, cheaper and more far-reaching, cyberbullying is sure to grow, many experts say.

And that growth will demand clearer guidance from courts and policymakers on the responsibilities of schools, law-enforcement officials and online-network providers.

With state lawmakers and lower courts now focusing more on issues of defamation and cyberbullying, it may be only a matter of time before the Supreme Court rules on those issues. Still, it may be a while before the justices render guidance in a case involving adolescent cyberbullying.

"The cyber laws are emerging," says Boston College's Herbeck, noting that the initial cases involved pornography, followed by those on privacy and file-sharing issues.

In Congress, bills such as the Sanchez and Stevens measures "are raising the profile" of the cyberbullying issue, says Kim Mills, a spokeswoman for the American Psychological Association. The association is "pleased to see the recognition of cyberbullying as a serious issue," Mills says. But, she adds, "it's hard to know in this climate what the prospects are" for such legislation. It's an "election season," she notes, "and people's minds are focused on a number of other things, such as the economy and war."

Boyd, at Harvard's Berkman Center, is less than sanguine about the likelihood of finding solutions to cyber-bullying through legislation. Lawmakers, she says, continue to "focus on the extreme cases" and "Band-Aid the issue" without addressing the root cause of cyber abuses: social pressures that drive adolescents to compete for status and the lack of adequate attention to those pressures from busy or distracted parents and other adults.

Cyberbullying and other abuse can be expected to get worse among adolescents "because kids are so stressed," Boyd says. The most obvious source of that stress, she says, "is the pressure to get into college." But "anything that increases pressure for status increases bullying."

And that includes a change in the financial standing of a youth's family, Boyd says, noting that the nation's shaky economy could increase the pressure for status and validation among adolescents' peers.

NOTES

1. Billy Townsend, "High Bail Set In Beating Case," *Tampa Tribune*, April 12, 2008.
2. Mary Niederberger and Nikki Schwab, "Explicit ranking of high school girls sparks outrage; Mt. Lebanon's 'Top 25' List Details Students' Looks, Bodies," *Pittsburgh Post-Gazette*, April 26, 2006, p. 1A.

3. Kathleen Haughney, "Cyberbullies could face penalties," *St. Louis Post-Dispatch*, March 24, 2008.
4. Justin Norton, "Some states pushing for laws to curb online bullying," The Associated Press, Feb. 25, 2007, www.pantagraph.com/articles/2007/02/24/news/doc45df611de8ca0765543652.txt.
5. Corinne David-Ferdon and Marci Feldman Hertz, "Electronic Media, Violence, and Adolescents: An Emerging Public Health Problem," *Journal of Adolescent Health* 41, 2007.
6. Amanda Lenhart, "Data Memo: One in three online teens have experienced online harassment," Pew Internet & American Life Project, June 27, 2007, www.pewinternet.org/pdfs/PIP%20Cyberbullying%20Memo.pdf.
7. Janis Wolak, Kimberly Mitchell and David Finkelhor, "Online Victimization of Youth: Five Years Later," National Center for Missing & Exploited Children, 2006, www.missingkids.com/en_US/publications/NC167.pdf.
8. Publication of the study by Juvonen and Elisheva Gross is forthcoming in the *Journal of School Health*. The survey was posted on bolt.com, a popular teen Web site, in fall 2005, and responses were invited. Among the 1,454 respondents, half reported daily e-mail use, and 60 percent reported daily instant-messaging. Also see Marcia Clemmitt, "Cyber Socializing," *CQ Researcher*, July 28, 2006, pp. 625-648.
9. Alexandra Rankin Macgill, "Data Memo: Teens are more likely than their parents to say digital technology makes their lives easier," Pew Internet & American Life Project, Oct. 24, 2007, www.pewinternet.org/pdfs/PIP_Teen_Parents_data_memo_Oct2007.pdf. Also see John Greenya, "Bullying," *CQ Researcher*, Feb. 4, 2005, pp. 101-124.
10. Amanda Lenhart and Mary Madden, "Teens, Privacy & Online Social Networks," Pew Internet & American Life Project, April 18, 2007, www.pewinternet.org/pdfs/PIP_Teens_Privacy_SNS_Report_Final.pdf.
11. David L. Hudson Jr., "Student Online Expression: What Do the Internet and MySpace Mean for Students' First Amendment Rights?" First Amendment Center, posted Dec. 19, 2006, www.firstamendmentcenter.org/PDF/student.internet.speech.pdf.
12. The bill, SB 1329, was introduced on April 8, 2008, and referred to the state Senate Judiciary Committee.
13. See, for example, Abbott Koloff, "States push for cyberbully controls," *USA Today*, Feb. 6, 2008.
14. Ryan Bowling, "Missouri Senate passes new cyberbullying law," *Christian County Headliner News*, March 30, 2008, www.ozarksnewsstand.com.
15. Jason Wermers and Betty Parker, "Bully bill breakthrough: Senate committee chairman relents, lets panel consider measure," *News-Press*, March 11, 2008.
16. *Ibid.*
17. *Ibid.*
18. Richard Willing, "Cyberstalking law opens debate on what's annoying," *USA Today*, Feb. 14, 2006.
19. *Ibid.*
20. *Dwyer v. Oceanport School District, et al.*, U.S. District Court, District of New Jersey, Civ. No. 03-6005 (SRC), March 31, 2005.
21. Press release, "ACLU-NJ Announces Settlement in 8th Grade Webmaster Case," Nov. 6, 2005, www.aclu-nj.org/news/aclunjannouncessettlementi.htm.
22. *Ibid.*
23. Tresa Baldas, "As 'Cyber-Bullying' Grows, So Do Lawsuits," *The National Law Journal*, Dec. 10, 2007.
24. *Tinker v. Des Moines School District* (1969).
25. *Watts v. United States* (1969)
26. *Bethel School District No. 403 v. Fraser* (1986) and *Hazelwood School District v. Kuhlmeier* (1988), respectively.
27. Quoted in Anne Marie Chaker, "Schools Act to Short-Circuit Spread of 'Cyberbullying,' " *The Wall Street Journal Online*, Jan. 24, 2007.
28. Daniel de Vise, "Schoolyard Face-Offs Blamed on Facebook Taunts," *The Washington Post*, April 27, 2008, p. 1C.
29. Millie Anne Cavanaugh, "Cyberbullying Can Have Deadly Consequences," Aspen Education Group, 2007, www.aspeneducation.com/Article-cyberbulling-consequences.html.
30. "Does the First Amendment apply to public schools?" First Amendment Center, www.firstamendmentschools.org. The case is *State ex rel. Dresser v. Dist. Bd. of Sch. Dist. No. 1*, 135 Wis. 619, 116 N.W.

31. *Ibid.* The case is *Wooster v. Sunderland*, 27 Cal. App. 51, 148 P. 959 (Cal. App. 1915).
32. Last year in *Morse v. Frederick*, 439 F. 3d 1114, the Supreme Court upheld a principal's right to punish a student who displayed a "Bong Hits 4 Jesus" banner across the street from school during a parade. The court construed the parade as a school-sanctioned event at which the school district's discipline rules applied.
33. *Layshock v. Hermitage School District, et al.*, U.S. District Court, Western District of Pennsylvania, 2007.
34. *J.S. v. Bethlehem Area School District*, 807 A.2d. 803 (Pa. 2002), summarized at www.firstamendmentschools.org/freedoms/case.aspx?id=1687.
35. Bridget Gutierrez, "Get Schooled: Getting Tough on Bullying," *Atlanta Journal-Constitution*, March 7, 2007, www.ajc.com/blogs/content/shared-blogs/ajc/education/entries/2007/03/07/bully_this.html#comments.
36. Robin M. Kowalski and Susan P. Limber, "Electronic Bullying Among Middle School Students," *Journal of Adolescent Health* 41, 2007.
37. Quoted in Katie Menzer, "Boy Scouts preparing for a new threat: bullies handbook addresses how to deal with aggressive teasing — both online and face-to-face," *Dallas Morning News*, Jan. 20, 2008, p. 1B.
38. "Teens and Cyberbullying: Executive Summary of a Report on Research Conducted for National Crime Prevention Council," Harris Interactive, Feb. 28, 2007, http://vocuspr.vocus.com/VocusPR30/Newsroom/ViewAttachment.aspx?SiteName=NCPCNew&Entity=PRAsset&AttachmentType=F&EntityID=99295&AttachmentID=57d58695-7e1d-404c-a0f0-d5f6d0b18996.
39. Amanda Lenhart, Mary Madden, Alexandra Rankin Macgill and Aaron Smith, "Teens and Social Media," Pew Internet & American Life Project, Dec. 19, 2007, www.pewinternet.org/pdfs/PIP_Teens_Social_Media_Final.pdf.
40. Amanda Burgess-Proctor, Justin W. Patchin, and Sameer Hinduja, "Cyberbullying: The Victimization of Adolescent Girls," www.cyberbullying.us/cyberbullying_girls_victimization.pdf.
41. Press release, "Study: Gifted children especially vulnerable to effects of bullying," Purdue University, April 6, 2006.
42. www.bebo.com. See also the "Safety Tips" link on www.myspace.com.
43. The bill is S 1965.
44. Kathryn A. Wolfe, "Bill Outlines Program to Help Children Stay Safe Online," *CQ Today*, Sept. 26, 2007.
45. *Ibid.*
46. The bill is HR 4134.
47. Andy Carvin, "Debating Federal Funding for Online Safety Curricula," PBS Teachers, learning.now weblog, Dec. 7, 2007, www.pbs.org/teachers/learning.now/2007/12/debating_federal_funding_for_o_1.html. Carvin is founding editor of the Digital Divide Network, an online community of Internet activists seeking to bridge the digital divide.
48. The bill is S 2344.
48. Quoted in Andrew Noyes, "Bill's Passage Divides Child-Safety Groups," *National Journal's Technology Daily*, Nov. 16, 2007, http://techdailydose.nationaljournal.com/2007/11/bills_passage_divides_childsaf.php.
50. *Ibid.*
51. *Ibid.*
52. Brad Stone, "MySpace to Share Data With States on Offenders," *The New York Times*, May 22, 2007.
53. Quoted in Eric Benderoff and Kristen Kridel, "MySpace steps up security," *Chicago Tribune*, Jan. 15, 2008, p. 1C.
54. *Ibid.*
55. "MySpace picks Harvard to study Internet safety," *Chicago Tribune*, Feb. 29, 2008, p. 10.
56. Richard Blumenthal, "Our agreement is a big step," *USA Today*, Jan. 23, 2008, p. 12A.
57. Quoted in Clare Trapasso, The Associated Press, "MySpace agrees to new safety measures," *USA Today*, Jan. 14, 2008.
58. The Associated Press, "MySpace promises safeguards for youths," *Newsday*, Jan. 15, 2008, p. 8A.
59. *Ibid.*
60. Roy Bragg, "Texas AG's refusal to sign deal with MySpace called right move," *San Antonio Express-News*, Jan. 16, 2008, p. 1A.
61. Quoted in *ibid.*

62. The bill is SB 5288.
63. "State action on cyber-bullying," *USA Today*, Feb. 6, 2008.
64. *Ibid.*
65. The bill is HB 199.
66. Kathleen Fitzgerald, "Md. legislators approve bill aimed at curbing cyberbullying," Student Press Law Center, April 9, 2008, www.splc.org/newsflash.asp?id=1734&year.
67. *Ibid.*
68. John Cheves, "Anonymous Web postings targeted," *Lexington Herald Leader*, www.kentucky.com/454/v-print/story/338489.html.
69. Quoted in *ibid.*
70. Joanne Kaufman, "If You Don't Have Anything Nice to Post . . . ," *The New York Times*, March 17, 2008, p. 4C.
71. "Kentucky Roadkill," *The Washington Times*, March 20, 2008, p. A18.

BIBLIOGRAPHY

Books

Kowalski, Robin M., Susan P. Limber and Patricia W. Agatston, *Cyber Bullying: Bullying in the Digital Age*, Blackwell Publishing, 2008.
Two Clemson University psychology professors and a professional counselor provide an up-to-date overview of electronic abuse. "As bullying over the Internet becomes more commonplace," they write, "educators must become equally prepared to address this new form of bullying."

Solove, Daniel J., *The Future of Reputation: Gossip, Rumor, and Privacy on the Internet*, Yale University Press, 2007.
A law professor at George Washington University writes that "as social reputation-shaping practices such as gossip and shaming migrate to the Internet, they are being transformed in significant ways."

Willard, Nancy E., *Cyberbullying and Cyberthreats: Responding to the Challenge of Online Social Aggression, Threats, and Distress*, Research Press, 2007.
A lawyer and expert on technology in schools explores the legal, social and technical aspects of electronic aggression and offers a useful compendium of cyberbullying definitions.

Articles

Areheart, Bradley A., "Regulating Cyberbullies Through Notice-Based Liability," *Yale Law Journal Pocket Part 41*, 2007, http://thepocketpart.org/2007/09/08/areheart.html.
An attorney argues that the government should provide recourse for cyberbully victims by curbing the nearly absolute immunity Internet service providers enjoy and implementing a "notice and take-down scheme" in certain cases of wrongdoing.

Barry, Dan, "A Boy the Bullies Love to Beat Up, Repeatedly," *The New York Times*, March 24, 2008, p. A1, www.nytimes.com/2008/03/24/us/24land.html?scp=2&sq=dan+barry+and+bullies&st=nyt.
A newspaper columnist profiles Billy Wolfe, a high-school sophomore in Fayetteville, Ark., who has been the target of bullies since age 12.

Collins, Lauren, "Friend Game: Behind the online hoax that led to a girl's suicide," *The New Yorker*, Jan. 21, 2008, www.newyorker.com/reporting/2008/01/21/080121fa_fact_collins.
A journalist provides a revealing look at the suicide of Megan Meier and offers a close-up look at the personalities and neighborhood atmosphere behind a notorious cyberbullying case.

David-Ferdon, Corinne, and Marci Feldman Hertz, "Electronic Media, Violence, and Adolescents: An Emerging Public Health Problem," *Journal of Adolescent Health 41*, 2007, pp. S1-S5.
Two experts from the Centers for Disease Control and Prevention provide an overview of a series of articles that examine the benefits and risks of adolescents' access to new communications technology. The articles can be accessed at www.jahonline.org/issues/contents?issue_key=S1054-139X%2807%29X0249-0.

Reports and Studies

Englander, Elizabeth, and Am M. Muldowney, "Just Turn the Darn Thing Off: Understanding

Cyberbullying," Proceedings of Persistently Safe Schools: The 2007 National Conference on Safe Schools and Communities, Hamilton Fish Institute, The George Washington University, http://webhost.bridgew.edu/marc/marc%20research/hamfish%20paper.pdf.
Two researchers from the Massachusetts Aggression Reduction Center provide a useful overview of the available research on cyberbullying and help to shed light on the characteristics of its perpetrators.

Hudson, David L., Jr., "Student Online Expression: What Do the Internet and MySpace Mean for Students' First Amendment Rights?" First Amendment Center, Dec. 19, 2006, www.firstamendmentcenter.org/PDF/student.internet.speech.pdf.
A First Amendment scholar explores the legal terrain of student electronic expression and recommends that educators adopt clear policies, open lines of communication with parents and students and teach students that their postings can return to haunt them. But he recommends against punishing online expression simply because school officials don't like it.

Lenhart, Amanda, *et al.*, "Teens and Social Media," Pew Internet & American Life Project, Dec. 19, 2007, www.pewinternet.org/pdfs/PIP_Teens_Social_Media_Final.pdf.
One of a series of studies on teens and digital technology, this survey-based study found that more than 90 percent of teens use the Internet, "and more of them than ever are treating it as . . . a place where they can share creations, tell stories and interact with others."

Thierer, Adam, "Social Networking and Age Verification: Many Hard Questions; No Easy Solutions," The Progress & Freedom Foundation, March 2007, www.pff.org/issues-pubs/pops/pop14.5ageverification.pdf.
The director of the market-oriented think tank's Center for Digital Media Freedom argues that proposals to impose age-verification rules on social-networking sites "raise many sensitive questions with potentially profound implications for individual privacy and online freedom of speech and expression."

For More Information

Center for Safe and Responsible Internet Use, 474 W. 29th Ave., Eugene, OR 97405; (541) 344-9125; www.cyberbully.org. Provides guidelines, research and other resources for educators, parents and children to encourage safe use of the Internet, including avoiding cyber threats.

i-SAFE Inc., 5900 Pasteur Ct., Suite 100, Carlsbad, CA 92008; (760) 603-7911; www.isafe.org. A nonprofit foundation dedicated to educating students on how to avoid inappropriate and unlawful online content; various services include the i-Learn Online program and the i-Mentor network to provide an "On Demand" learning experience.

Internet Crime Complaint Center; www.ic3.gov. Enables victims of Internet-related crimes to file complaints, which are then referred to law-enforcement and regulatory agencies.

National Crime Prevention Council, 2345 Crystal Dr., Suite 500, Arlington, VA 22202; (202) 466-6272; www.ncpc.org/newsroom/current-campaigns/cyberbullying. Educates the public about cyberbullying and strategies for protection against Internet harassment. The NCPC's Web site links to publications and other organizations for research on cyberbullying.

NetSmartz Workshop, 699 Prince St., Alexandria, VA 22314; (703) 274-3900; www.netsmartz.org. Created by the National Center for Missing and Exploited Children and the Boys and Girls Clubs of America, the interactive workshop offers a wide variety of resources warning parents, teens, educators and law-enforcement officials about the dangers that exist on the Internet. The site links to videos, CyberTiplines and personal accounts of Internet exploitation.

Take a Stand. Lend a Hand. Stop Bullying Now!, 5600 Fishers Lane, Rockville, MD 20857; 1 (888) 275-4772; http://stopbullyingnow.hrsa.gov. The Health Resources and Services Administration campaign educates children and adults about cyberbullying and improving community prevention efforts.

WiredSafety, 1 Bridge St., Suite 56, Irvington-on-Hudson, NY 10533; (201) 463-8663; www.wiredsafety.org. The online safety group offers educational and help services to victims of cybercrimes like cyberbullying, hacking, identity theft and child pornography. In conjunction with WiredKids.org and WiredTeens.org, the group promotes safe and responsible technology use.

5

Domestic Violence

Do Teenagers Need More Protection?

Pamela M. Prah

AP Photo/Mary Ann Chastain

Supporters of tougher domestic-violence legislation demonstrate in Columbia, S.C., on April 27, 2005. Congress recently reauthorized the Violence Against Women Act, adding more funding for youth programs and prevention.

From *CQ Global Researcher*, January 2006.

Domestic violence doesn't seem to get much attention until a celebrity comes along like O. J. Simpson, the former football star and admitted wife beater who was accused of murdering his ex-wife and her male companion in a fit of jealous rage. Also grabbing headlines was the case of Lorena Bobbitt, the abused Virginia woman who cut off her husband's penis while he slept.*

Yet, on a typical day in the United States, three women are murdered by their spouses, ex-spouses or partners — and thousands more are raped or injured.[1]

They are women like Yvette Cade, 31, from Clinton, Md., who was doused with gasoline and set on fire by her estranged husband. And Jessica Wickiewicz, of Garden City, N.Y., whose boyfriend started punching and kicking her when she was a senior in high school. And Maria, a pregnant 15-year-old from Los Angeles whose boyfriend hit her so hard when she was pregnant that she had to have her baby delivered by cesarean.[2]

Violence against women has been reported since ancient Roman times and has been commonplace in America since Colonial times. But in the last decade, the rate of domestic violence against women has dropped more than 50 percent.[3] And the number of men

---

* Simpson was acquitted of the murders of Nicole Brown Simpson and her friend Ronald Goldman, but in a civil trial he was found liable for their deaths and ordered to pay the Goldman family $8.5 million in compensatory damages. A jury in Manassas, Va., acquitted Bobbitt of malicious wounding in January 1994.

Partner Violence Against Women Plummeted

The number of female victims of so-called intimate-partner violence dropped nearly 50 percent — from 1.1 million incidents in 1993 to 588,490 incidents in 2001. Women make up 85 percent of all victims of abuse by either a spouse or ex partner.

Rates of Non-Fatal Violence by an Intimate Partner*
(per 1,000 persons of each gender; includes rape, sexual assault, robbery and simple or aggravated assault)

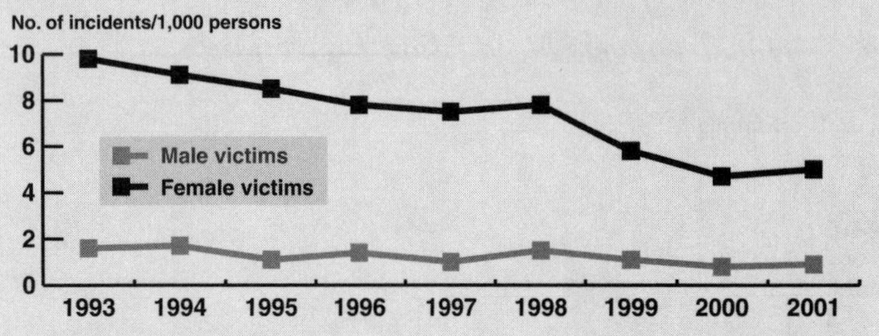

* Intimate partners include current or former spouses, boyfriends or girlfriends.

Source: Bureau of Justice Statistics, U.S. Department of Justice, February 2003

murdered by their wives, girlfriends and former partners has declined even more dramatically — by some 70 percent since 1976.

Many experts credit the changes to the billions of dollars spent in recent years on shelters, hotlines and legal help for victims and training sessions for police, prosecutors and judges. With more help available, abused women, in particular, recognized they no longer had to resort to violence to get out of a bad relationship.

Despite the positive trends, experts say the true scope of the domestic-violence problem is hard to gauge, because researchers and government agencies use different definitions for the term. Fourteen states, for example, do not include dating violence as a form of domestic violence. Nonetheless, the latest figures from the Department of Justice (DOJ) show more than 588,000 women and more than 100,000 men were physically assaulted, raped or robbed by their "intimate partners" in 2001.[4] And more than 1 million women are stalked.[5]

Researchers are now finding that young people ages 16 to 24 are most at risk.[6] Some teens are exposed to violence at the hands of their parents, while others are young parents themselves and are beating each other and/or their children.

Moreover, teen-dating violence is more prevalent than most parents suspect, since young people usually do not tell their parents about the abuse. Wickiewicz, for example, blamed her high school bruises on cheerleading and hid them under baggy jeans. "It was all a big secret," she said.[7]

While girls and women are much more likely to suffer at the hands of a loved one, men and boys are often victims as well. For 13 years, for example, Karen Gillhespy of Marquette, Mich., brutally abused her husband. Indeed, she broke his ribs, ripped patches of his hair out, beat him with a baseball bat and scratched, bit and kicked him — but he never hit back or filed charges.[8]

In fact, a federal study showed that high school boys are nearly as likely as girls to get hit, slapped or physically hurt by their partners. After surveying youths in Chicago, Dallas, Milwaukee, San Diego and Washington, D.C., the study found that 10 to 17 percent of girls are hit by their boyfriends, and almost the same number of boys — 10 to 15 percent — are abused by their girlfriends.[9]

The fact that researchers are studying dating violence reflects the recent sea change in how the nation views and deals with domestic violence. Forty years ago, there were no shelters or hotlines for battered women. Police often responded to a domestic-violence call by telling the batterer, typically a man, to walk around the block to cool off. Doctors and health-care providers rarely screened their patients for domestic violence.

But the women's liberation movement of the 1970s shined a spotlight on domestic violence — triggering a wave of state laws dealing with the problem. Much later, the 1994 Violence Against Women Act (VAWA) provided billions of federal dollars to help victims of domestic violence, including funds for legal services and for building local shelters.

The sweeping law — which Congress expanded in December 2005 — also created the National Domestic Violence Hotline and made it a federal crime to cross state lines with the intent of stalking or committing domestic violence. VAWA funding has been used to set up domestic-violence courts as well as specially trained "response teams" to deal with sexual-assault victims.

"Although violent crime has decreased nationwide, it still devastates the lives of many women," says Diane M. Stuart, director of the DOJ's Office on Violence Against Women, who in the 1980s ran a shelter for battered women in Utah. "We have much more work to do."

Today 2,000 shelters provide refuge for victims and information on how to obtain restraining orders against their abusers. Rape-victim advocates offer support in many hospitals, and state courthouses often provide special programs to help guide victims through the legal process.

Simple Assault Is Most Common Crime

Nearly three-quarters of the intimate-partner crimes against women and nearly half of those against men were simple assaults.

Types of Violence by Intimate Partners

Violent Crime	No. of female victims	Rate/1,000 females	No. of male victims	Rate/1,000 males
Simple Assault	421,550	3.6	50,310	0.5
Aggravated Assault	81,140	0.7	36,350	0.3
Robbery	44,060	0.4	16,570	0.1
Rape/Sexual Assault	41,740	0.4	---	---
Total	**588,490**		**103,230**	

Source: Bureau of Justice Statistics, U.S. Department of Justice, February 2003

Businesses also are becoming active on the domestic-violence front, partly because it's the right thing to do and partly because domestic violence costs society, particularly employers. Victims annually lose nearly 8 million days of work, the equivalent of more than 32,000 full-time jobs.[10] In 1995, researchers estimated that domestic violence costs the country more than $5.8 billion — more than $8.3 billion in today's dollars — primarily for medical and mental health care.[11]

In 2005 the DOJ formally kicked off the president's Family Justice Center Initiative, modeled after a San Diego program that brings legal and social services under one roof with victim-support and counseling programs. At the one location, victims can undergo forensic exams, obtain legal advice and even restraining orders against their abusers, speak with a chaplain and meet with a victim's advocate.

"It's a one-stop process. Everything that a person who has been victimized needs is right there," says Stuart.

Advocates and women's groups hope the recent VAWA expansion will usher in a new era that focuses on preventing domestic violence from ever beginning in the first place, rather than treating the victims and punishing the abusers afterward.

"Many programs today focus on helping adult victims, and prevention has a lesser emphasis, if it is addressed at all," says Esta Soler, president of the Family Violence Prevention Fund, an advocacy group that sponsors campaigns, in partnership with the Advertising Council, to raise awareness about family violence. She says adolescents, young adults and the poor particularly need more attention.

Prevention is key because children who grow up in homes where domestic violence or dating violence occur are more likely to become victims or perpetrators of domestic or dating violence themselves.[12] Abuse also tends to lead to other problems. Young people and adults abused by their spouses or partners are more likely to abuse alcohol or drugs, suffer from eating disorders and engage in risky behavior, such as having unprotected sex. They also are more apt to have mental and physical health problems that make it difficult for them to hold jobs.

Some fathers'-rights and conservative groups, however, say many domestic-violence programs demonize men and promote a feminist and leftist agenda. "The Violence Against Women Act is gender-driven politics being operated through the public purse," says Michael McCormick, executive director of the American Coalition for Fathers and Children. "We're spending nearly $1 billion a year to reinforce in the public's mind that men are indiscriminately attacking women."

As Congress, researchers and advocates debate how best to combat domestic violence, here are some of the questions being asked:

Should the federal government do more to combat domestic violence?

Women's groups say federal programs have contributed to remarkable gains in curtailing domestic violence, sexual

Office for the Prevention of Domestic Violence

A high-school student in New York state submitted the winning poster in a statewide contest to increase awareness of teen-dating violence.

assault and stalking. But they say the programs should be expanded to provide more housing options and focus more on prevention. Meanwhile, some fathers'-rights and conservative groups say the programs at the local level that get funds from the federal government demonize men and promote a radical feminist agenda.

In the decade after Congress passed the Violence Against Women Act in 1994, domestic violence dropped more than 50 percent, according to government figures. "VAWA has had a huge impact," says Jill Morris, public policy director of the National Coalition Against Domestic Violence. "It has changed attitudes. It's a great success."

Besides providing billions of dollars to help victims of domestic violence and sexual assault, VAWA forced the issue out into the open. "People are now talking about it in newspapers and in Congress," Morris says.

While lauding VAWA, the coalition and other women's groups say more federal funds should be targeted to help minorities, the disabled, the elderly, victims in rural areas, Native Americans, young people, gays and immigrants who fear being deported. And rape crisis centers should be guaranteed additional federal funds to help counsel victims of sexual assault.

Several states, including Illinois, Massachusetts and Pennsylvania, have waiting lists of sexual assault victims needing counseling, and in many states "rural areas have no services at all," said Mary Lou Leary, executive director of the National Center for Victims of Crime.[13]

Victims also need more housing options, say advocates. "Homelessness does not cause domestic violence, but rather the opposite," according to Lynn Rosenthal, president of the National Network to End Domestic Violence. Half of homeless women and children are fleeing domestic violence, and 38 percent of domestic-violence victims become homeless at some point in their lives, she estimated.[14]

Advocates say victims who live in public housing need protection from their abusers — and sometimes from their landlords. A 39-year-old North Carolina woman, for example, was evicted from her apartment because she was "too loud" after her ex-boyfriend shot her and she jumped from her apartment's second-story balcony to escape his attack.[15] A Michigan woman was evicted because of "criminal activity" in her apartment after her ex-boyfriend returned and attacked her.

Conservative and fathers'-rights groups, however, say VAWA ignores men who are abused. The Safe Homes for Children and Families Coalition and other groups want to rename the law as the Family Violence Prevention Act. They also have pressed for new VAWA language making clear that the law includes programs for men.

"It's a blatant lie to say that new language is not necessary," says David Burroughs, legislative consultant to the coalition. Burroughs says he was denied a VAWA grant because his proposal targeted men and also was rejected for a federal grant to pay for hotel stays for male victims wanting to leave their homes for a cooling-off period. He helped mount a billboard campaign at the Wilmington, Del., Amtrak station to remind Sen. Joseph Biden Jr., D-Del. — lead sponsor of VAWA — that men are abuse victims, too.

VAWA advocates argue, however, that all of the law's provisions are gender neutral. "Nothing in the act denies services, programs, funding or assistance to male victims of violence," says Morris.

Government figures show women overwhelmingly are the victims of domestic violence, with men making up only 15 percent of the victims.[16] But men's groups say more than 100 studies show that men and women are equally likely to initiate domestic violence, adding that 99 percent of the federal funding should not go to programs that help only women.

Abused men have a hard time finding legal help and shelters — services that get federal funds under VAWA, Burroughs says. About 20 percent of the victims who apply for free legal services are men, but they receive less than 1 percent of the pro bono services, he says, adding that only a handful of domestic-violence shelters nationwide are open to men.

VAWA should be scrapped altogether, says McCormick of the American Coalition for Fathers and Children, although he acknowledges, "the political reality is that it's not going to be withdrawn." The coalition opposes violence against anyone, but McCormick says VAWA funds "a one-sided agenda driven by people who really don't want to see families stay together," namely, feminists and left-wing organizations.

VAWA breaks up families and increases the number of fatherless children, McCormick says, because it funds programs that push couples into divorce instead of trying to get the victim and abuser into counseling.

Lisa Scott, a Bellevue, Wash., attorney specializing in family law, agrees. "VAWA is not about stopping violence," Scott wrote. "It is about greedy special interests slopping at the federal trough, perpetuating gender supremacy for women. If proponents were truly concerned about helping victims, they would demand that all intervention and funding be gender neutral and gender inclusive."[17]

Are judges and police doing enough to protect domestic-violence victims?

Forty years ago, a wife beater would not be arrested unless police actually saw the incident or had a warrant. Police and judges would routinely dismiss the problem as a "family matter."

Things have changed, particularly in the last decade, as police officers, judges and prosecutors have received VAWA-funded training on how to deal with domestic violence. But women's advocates say much still needs to be changed, both in the courtroom and on the police beat.

For instance, Yvette Cade might never have been burned if Judge Richard Palumbo had not dismissed her request for a protective order against her estranged husband. Three weeks later Mrs. Cade's husband walked into the store where she worked, poured gasoline on her and set her on fire. Cade suffered third-degree burns over much of her body. Advocates said Palumbo has a pattern of dismissing temporary protective orders and making flip remarks about domestic violence.* In one instance, he told an abused woman to speak up, even though he had been told her husband had attacked her and crushed her voice box.[18]

"There are judges, for whatever reason, who still don't get it," says Billie Lee Dunford-Jackson, co-director of the Family Violence Project at the National Council on Juvenile and Family Court Judges. But, she quickly adds, "most judges now readily recognize [domestic violence] as a crime and will take steps to protect the victim."

She points to intensive three-day training sessions for judges that the National Judicial Institute on Domestic Violence has sponsored since 1998, largely funded by VAWA. Judges are taught what makes a batterer batter, why victims stay and how to identify and overcome their own biases and blinders when it comes to the problem.

Nationwide, more than 300 judicial systems have established specially designed "domestic-violence courts."[19] Some states have created courts that handle only domestic violence, while others have staff trained who provide support to victims, Dunford-Jackson explains. New York uses both approaches, with more than 30 domestic-violence courts plus special units that include victims' advocates and staff members who monitor those convicted of domestic violence to ensure they are complying with the terms of their sentence.

Law students also are getting training. As of 2003, most law schools offered educational programming on domestic violence, says Robin R. Runge, director of the American Bar Association's Commission on Domestic Violence.

However, there are still gaps in the system. Most states require volunteers on domestic violence hotlines to complete 40 to 50 hours of training but don't require

---

* Palumbo's actions led to his temporary removal from the bench and reassignment to administrative duties on Oct. 26, 2005.

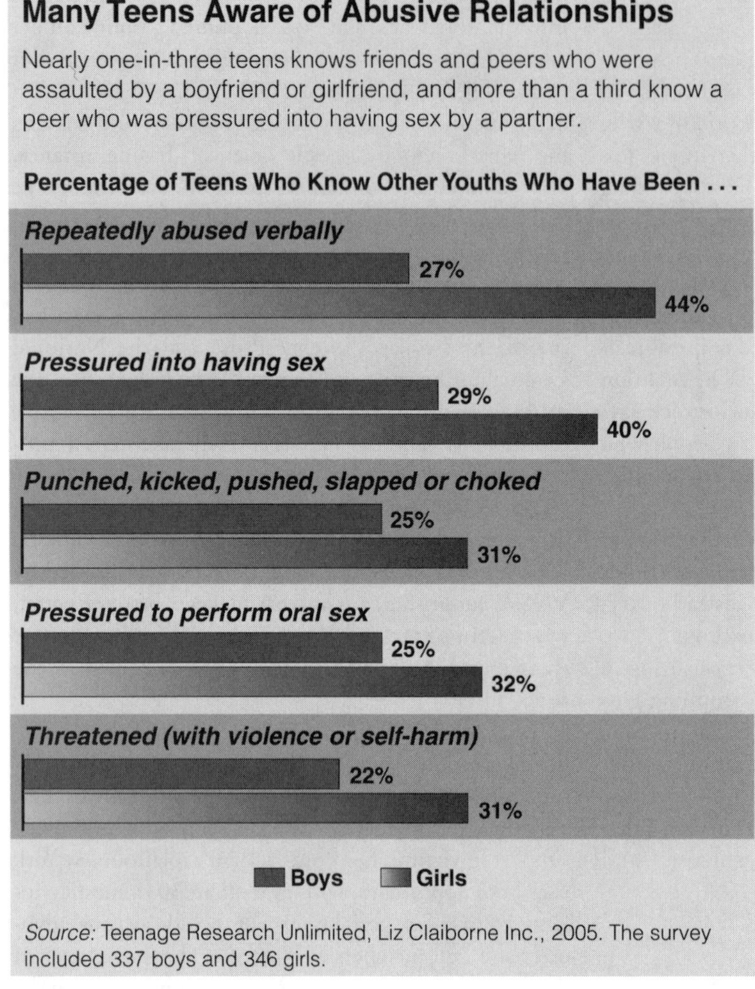

Source: Teenage Research Unlimited, Liz Claiborne Inc., 2005. The survey included 337 boys and 346 girls.

training for police, judges or lawyers. Even with VAWA, 80 percent of domestic-violence victims are without lawyers to guide them through the process, Runge says. "We've seen the difference having lawyers available" can make, she says. For example, lawyers can help abused women file the legal paperwork more quickly to obtain protection orders, which prohibit their abusers from coming into contact with them.

However, some men's groups say the training given to judges, police and attorneys reinforces the notion that only women are victims. "They are being taught garbage," says Burroughs, of the Safe Homes for Children and Families Coalition.

Some conservatives also argue that women who seek help from domestic-violence legal programs get an edge in their custody or divorce proceedings. VAWA "has little to do with violence and much to do with divorce court," family-law attorney Scott wrote.[20] McCormick of the American Coalition for Fathers and Children says abused women who turn to shelters do not get counseling first but instead are directed to the courthouse to get a restraining order, which helps them in a divorce or child custody case because judges will view the man as abusive and dangerous even if he is not.

Meanwhile, feminists and some domestic-violence experts are backing away from the "mandatory arrest" laws that they pushed states to enact 20 years ago. At least 23 states require police officers to make an arrest when responding to a domestic-violence complaint. But police on the scene often cannot tell the victim from the aggressor, so they arrest both.

States began passing mandatory-arrest laws after a 1984 Minnesota study found that few people arrested under such laws repeated their crimes. But researcher Lawrence Sherman says that states acted too hastily after his first study. His follow-up research showed that mandatory arrests only work in middle-class communities with low unemployment rates, but for some reason, he says, "the new findings got buried."

The new findings showed that unemployed people or those without ties to the community have less to lose by getting arrested and often become angrier. In such cases, mandatory arrest "causes more violence than it prevents," according to Sherman, director of the Jerry Lee Center on Criminology at the University of Pennsylvania.

In any event, even when mandatory-arrest laws are in effect, many police officers are reluctant to respond

Female Teens at Risk for Partner Violence

Females ages 16-24 were the most vulnerable to intimate-partner violence in 1999.

Number of Women Abused by Intimate Partners, 1999*
(by age)

Victims' Age	No. of Victims
12-15	9,000
16-19	119,630
20-24	144,100
25-34	182,070
35-49	194,380
50 or older	21,030

* Includes assault, robbery and rape/sexual assault

Source: Bureau of Justice Statistics, U.S. Department of Justice, 2001

quickly to domestic-violence cases because they are considered so potentially dangerous, with either the abuser or the victim — or both — liable to turn on the officer. Although studies have yet to prove that family disputes are more dangerous to police officers than other incidents, so many officers believe it to be true they often wait for backup before responding to such calls.[21]

However, John Terrill, a spokesman for the National Association of Police Organizations, denies that police treat domestic violence any differently than other cases and supports mandatory-arrest laws.

Some women's groups say a June 2005 U.S. Supreme Court decision undercut efforts to beef up enforcement of mandatory-arrest laws and restraining orders. In *Town of Castle Rock, Colorado v. Gonzales*, the court ruled that a woman did not have the right to sue a police department for failing to enforce a court-ordered restraining order against her husband.[22] Women's groups fear that police departments now will have less incentive to aggressively enforce such orders.

"Mandatory restraining orders aren't worth the paper they're printed on if police officers are not required to enforce them," said Eleanor Smeal, president of the Feminist Majority Foundation. The organization said the decision jeopardizes women's lives and potentially lets police departments off the hook for failing to enforce mandatory orders.[23]

Terrill says police "try to the best of their ability to enforce restraining orders," but sometimes they "get pushed down on the list" of calls police officers must handle. "You can't keep an officer stationed outside the door 24 hours a day."

Should the government do more to protect teens?

The recent expansion of VAWA provides millions of dollars to help teen victims of domestic violence, including dating violence.

Dating violence represents an "epidemic of monumental proportions" among today's youth, says Juley Fulcher, director of public policy at Break the Cycle, a Los Angeles-based group that provides information and legal help to young people experiencing domestic violence. Fulcher points to Justice Department data showing that girls and young women between the ages of 16 and 24 experience the highest rate of non-fatal "intimate-partner" violence, or attacks by a spouse, partner or former spouse or partner — 16 incidents per 1,000 women in this age group compared to six incidents per 1,000 for all women.[24]

"Not enough attention has been paid to finding ways to stop the intimate-partner violence that pervades and sometimes shapes the lives of adolescents and young adults," says Soler, of the Family Violence Prevention Fund.

In 2005, a Gallup survey found that one-in-eight teens ages 13 to 17 knows someone in an abusive relationship with a boyfriend or girlfriend.[25] Another 2005 youth survey, commissioned by Liz Claiborne Inc., the clothing maker, found that one-in-three 13-to-18-year-olds had a friend or peer who had been hit, punched, kicked or slapped by a partner.[26] And up

Safe Homes for Children and Families Coalition

Members of the Safe Homes for Children and Families Coalition call for changes in the Violence Against Women Act during a rally at the U.S. Supreme Court in July 2005. Congress in December 2005 addressed some of their concerns.

to 18 percent said their partners had threatened to harm themselves if the couple broke up, making the victim feel trapped.

In many cases, teens exposed to violence have fewer options than adults. Many shelters for battered women do not admit their teenage sons. And few shelters accommodate teenage mothers and their children. Teen mothers can be particularly vulnerable to domestic violence. A 2001 study found that a quarter of teen mothers experience violence by their boyfriends or husbands before, during or just after their pregnancies.[27]

Advocates successfully pushed Congress in 2005 to revise the Violence Against Women Act to provide federal money for new programs targeting teens, including programs to educate people working with teens on how to recognize, respond to and provide services to teen victims of domestic and dating violence. Women's groups also wanted middle and high schools to train teachers, coaches and administrators to recognize and address issues related to dating violence and sexual assault.

"Teens must be taught what is healthy and what is not, and services must be offered to help them through this transition," says Fulcher, noting that many teens are dating for the first time and are unsure of the differences between a healthy relationship and an abusive one. A 2003 federal study of schools in Alabama, Idaho, Oklahoma and Utah found that between 11 and 16 percent of female students — and between 4.5 and 7 percent of males — reported being forced to have intercourse.[28]

Fulcher and other women's groups want the federal government to pay for education programs that involve courts, law-enforcement agencies and youth-based community groups. Only a handful of states — Minnesota, Oklahoma, Utah, Washington and Wyoming — allow minors ages 16 and older to petition for an order of protection without an adult, according to the National Coalition Against Domestic Violence. Moreover, only one county in the United States — Santa Clara, Calif. — has a domestic-violence court just for juveniles.

VAWA already provides grants to reduce sexual assault, rape and other violent crimes on college campuses. "There isn't a university in the country that doesn't have this problem," says Stuart, of the Office on Violence Against Women. Some universities, for example, provide information to all incoming freshmen about sexual assault and other crimes, she says. The programs also "help universities understand that a rape or sexual assault on campus isn't something that can be handled within the university," she says. "It's a crime."

Stuart says she would also like to see secondary schools become more involved, allowing community leaders to come into the schools to share their expertise.

But McCormick, of the American Coalition for Fathers and Children, says the federal government is already too deeply involved in private matters and that talk of domestic violence in the classroom "is not in line with public education." He is particularly concerned that the "education" would in fact be "propaganda" that reinforces feminists groups' one-sided message that men are always the perpetrators.

Burroughs, of the Safe Homes for Children and Families Coalition, says domestic violence is an appropriate topic for schools, even though many school boards may be reluctant to address it because it is a family-related issue and involves sex and sexuality. "We'd be doing young people a favor by teaching them what healthy relationships are," he says, as long as the education doesn't "inject bias" that only women are victims.

Getty Images

Former NFL star O. J. Simpson was revealed as a wife beater during his trial for the murders of his ex-wife Nicole Brown Simpson and her friend Ronald Goldman. Simpson was acquitted but in a civil trial was found liable for their deaths and ordered to pay the Goldman family $8.5 million.

BACKGROUND

Women as Property

Well into the 19th century, U.S. laws were influenced by the 1768 English "rule of thumb" law, which allowed a husband to beat his wife as long as the stick was no thicker than his thumb.[29]

Early in America's history, women were viewed as the property of men, much like children or slaves, who could be punished physically for not obeying orders. The Mississippi Supreme Court in 1824 upheld a husband's right to use corporal punishment on his wife, even as women were fighting for equal rights and the right to vote.

Suffrage and temperance movement leaders in the 19th and early 20th centuries saw wife beating as one of society's scourges. The first women's-rights convention was held in Seneca, N.Y., in 1848, and by the 1870s, wife beating was becoming unacceptable, at least legally. In 1871, courts in Alabama and Massachusetts overturned the right of a husband to beat his wife. This change coincided with growing concern over child abuse, which expanded to women's issues.

Maryland became the first state to outlaw wife beating, in 1883, but it took the turbulent 1960s and the women's movement of the 1970s to fundamentally change how Americans viewed domestic violence.[30]

The race riots, violent protests and assassinations of President John F. Kennedy, Sen. Robert F. Kennedy, D-N.Y., and the Rev. Martin Luther King Jr. during the 1960s prompted creation of the President's Commission on the Causes and Prevention of Violence. The panel's national survey gave researchers invaluable — and troubling — data. For instance, about a quarter of all adult men said they could think of circumstances in which it was acceptable for spouses to hit one another.[31]

While abhorring violence in the streets, many Americans still viewed domestic violence as a private matter between family members. For example, after a young woman in New York City named Kitty Genovese was stabbed repeatedly in an alley in 1964 — and her neighbors ignored her screams — many concluded that Americans had become inured to violence. But upon closer examination, the witnesses said they didn't get involved because they thought it was a man beating his wife and felt it wasn't their business to get involved.[32]

Police and judges also were reluctant to intervene in family matters that turned violent. For example, in 1967 the International Association of Police training manual said that "in dealing with family disputes, arrest should be exercised as a last resort."

Slow Progress

The women's-rights movement of the 1970s helped to change such attitudes about handling domestic violence. It led to establishment of telephone hotlines, support groups and shelters for rape victims — all of which helped battered women admit that they were being beaten at home. The first shelter for battered women opened in 1974 in St. Paul, Minn., and the National Organization for Women created a task force to examine wife beating in 1975.

The judicial and law-enforcement communities also began to step in. In 1977 Oregon became the first state to enact a mandatory-arrest law for domestic-violence incidents. The next year Minnesota became the first state to allow domestic-violence arrests without warrants. By 1980, all but six states had domestic-violence laws. And in 1981, Massachusetts and New Jersey supreme courts ruled that a husband could be criminally liable for raping his wife.

But progress was slow. By the mid-1980s, 22 states still barred police from making arrests without a warrant in domestic-violence cases unless an officer had actually witnessed the battering.

In many cases, police departments beefed up their domestic-violence activities in order to protect against lawsuits. In 1984, a jury awarded a $2.3 million judgment against the Torrington, Conn., police department for failing to protect a woman and her son from her husband's repeated violence.[33] Indeed, while the police were at her house, Tracy Thurman's husband stabbed her 13 times and broke her neck, leaving her partially paralyzed.

That same year, Congress passed the Family Violence Prevention and Services Act and the Victims of Crime Act, which, for the first time, provided money for states to set up shelters for battered women and a national, toll-free hotline for victims of domestic violence. The amount of money provided, however, was "but a trickle," wrote Richard J. Gelles, now dean of the School of Social Work at the University of Pennsylvania and an expert in the field.[34]

By 1987, more than half of the nation's major police departments had adopted "pro-arrest" policies requiring officers to make arrests in domestic-violence cases unless they could document a good reason not to.

Two widely reported cases in the 1980s dispelled the notion that domestic violence affected only the poor or uneducated. In 1985, President Ronald Reagan forced the resignation of John Fedders, a top official at the Securities and Exchange Commission, when Fedders' wife cited 18 years of repeated beatings as grounds for divorce.

Two years later, New York City lawyer Joel Steinberg was convicted of beating his 8-year-old adopted daughter Lisa to death.* During the trial it was also disclosed that Steinberg also routinely beat his companion, Hedda Nussbaum, who hadn't tried to stop the child's abuse. Photos of Nussbaum's badly injured face and vacant stare introduced the nation to "battered women's syndrome," suffered by women living in abusive relationships. Its symptoms include loss of self-esteem, fear, passivity and isolation.

While data suggest that fewer battered women are resorting to violence against their abusers, no one really knows how many women are in prison today for killing or assaulting their abusive partners, says Sue Osthoff, director of the Philadelphia-based National Clearinghouse for the Defense of Battered Women. Recent Justice Department data don't track how many violent crimes committed by women involve spouses or intimates, although a 1991 Justice Department survey of 11,800 female prisoners found that nearly 20 percent were incarcerated for a violent offense committed against an intimate.

Only 125 battered women from 23 states have received clemency since 1978, according to the clearinghouse. Osthoff says many governors and pardon boards are leery of giving battered women a break on their sentences because much of the public opposes early releases for anyone convicted of violent crimes, including battered women. In addition, many believe victims could have avoided violence by turning to today's array of domestic-violence programs.

In the early 1990s the medical community got more involved in domestic violence. The Joint Commission on Accreditation of Hospitals in 1991 required that all emergency room personnel be trained in identifying battered women. The next year the American Medical Association (AMA) and the U.S. surgeon general encouraged the screening of all women patients for domestic abuse.

Few medical organizations, however, supported requiring health-care workers to report patients who were apparent

* Charlotte Fedders was granted a divorce in 1985. In 1987 John Fedders sought a financial share of his ex-wife's book about her experiences, *Shattered Dreams,* which became a made-for-TV movie; a circuit court judge rejected Fedders' claim. He was never criminally prosecuted and still practices law in Washington. Steinberg was convicted of first-degree manslaughter in 1989 and sentenced to up to 25 years in prison; he was released in 2004. Murder charges against Hedda Nussbaum were dropped after prosecutors concluded she had been too severely battered to protect Lisa. She now works at My Sisters' Place, an organization that helps battered women.

CHRONOLOGY

19th Century *Family violence becomes an issue for charitable organizations. By the 1870s, most states declare wife beating illegal, but there are few services and no shelters to help battered women.*

1824 Mississippi Supreme Court says a husband can beat his wife.

1871 Courts in Alabama and Massachusetts overturn the right of a husband to beat his wife.

1960s *Most police and judges view marital violence as a private affair. In most areas, a husband cannot be arrested for wife beating unless police see the incident or have a warrant.*

1967 International Association of Chiefs of Police training manual says arrests should be made only as a last resort in family disputes.

1970s *Feminist movement identifies spousal assault and rape as major women's issues, and shelters for battered women are established.*

1971 First hotline for battered women is started in St. Paul, Minn.

1977 Oregon becomes first state to require mandatory arrests in domestic-violence incidents.

1978 Minnesota becomes first state to allow arrests without warrants in domestic-violence incidents.

1980s *All states pass domestic-violence legislation, and most mandate or permit the arrest of batterers.*

1981 Massachusetts and New Jersey supreme courts say a husband can be charged with raping his wife.

1984 Congress passes Family Violence Prevention and Services Act and the Victims of Crime Act, providing federal funds for domestic-violence programs and shelters.

1985 President Ronald Reagan forces John Fedders, a top Securities and Exchange Commission attorney, to resign after his wife cites 18 years of repeated beatings as grounds for divorce. . . . U.S. surgeon general identifies domestic violence as a major health problem.

1990s *High-profile celebrity cases focus on domestic violence, leading to a new federal law providing money for services to help victims and train officials to deal with domestic violence.*

1991 Joint Commission on Accreditation of Hospitals in 1991 requires emergency-room personnel to be trained to identify battered women.

1992 American Medical Association and surgeon general suggest that all women patients be screened for domestic abuse.

1994 Spousal assault gets national attention during the trial of Lorena Bobbitt, a battered woman who cut off her sleeping husband's penis. . . . O. J. Simpson, a sports broadcaster and former football star, is charged with murdering his estranged wife and a male companion. Bobbitt and Simpson are both acquitted.

1994 Congress passes Violence Against Women Act (VAWA), establishing community-based programs for domestic violence, training for police and court officials and a national 24-hour hotline for battered women. The law also makes it a federal crime to cross state lines to commit domestic violence.

2000s *Supreme Court limits the types of lawsuits domestic-violence victims can file; Congress targets dating violence and prevention.*

2000 Supreme Court says victims of rape and domestic violence cannot sue attackers in federal court. . . . Congress reauthorizes VAWA to include dating violence and stalking.

2005 Supreme Court says a domestic-violence victim cannot sue a police department for failing to enforce a restraining order. . . . Congress updates VAWA to include teen dating and more prevention funds.

Domestic Violence Gets Military's Attention

Master Sgt. William Wright strangled his 32-year-old wife, Jennifer Gail, and buried her in a shallow grave in a North Carolina field. She was among four wives killed in a six-week period in 2002 by their husbands, all soldiers stationed at Fort Bragg, N.C. Three had recently returned from fighting in Afghanistan.[1]

The murders drew considerable media attention and prompted the Pentagon to modify its handling of domestic violence, says Anita Sanchez, spokeswoman for the Miles Foundation, a Connecticut-based advocacy group that deals with domestic violence in the military.

Among other things, the military started requiring troops returning from long deployments to complete a mental health checklist — promptly dubbed the "don't kill your wife survey" by troops. They quickly learned "what to check" to avoid raising red flags, Sanchez says, adding that few services are provided for families on what to expect from their returning soldiers. And with so many troops in Iraq and Afghanistan, many military families are strained and anxious.

Even before the four slayings, concern about domestic violence in the military had prompted lawmakers on Capitol Hill to require the Pentagon to establish a Defense Task Force on Domestic Violence. Established in 1999, it issued several reports and some 200 recommendations before disbanding in 2003.

Maj. Michael Shavers, a Pentagon spokesman, says the Defense Department has made "substantial progress" implementing the task force's recommendations and improving the military's response to domestic violence. For example, the department has funded 22 domestic-violence training conferences over the past two years for commanding officers, judge advocates, law-enforcement personnel, victims' advocates, chaplains, health-care providers and fatality-review team members. The Pentagon also is working with the Family Violence Prevention Fund and the National Domestic Violence Hotline to develop public-awareness campaigns encouraging the military community "to take a stand against domestic violence," Shavers says.

In the last five years, the Miles Foundation reports a dramatic spike in its caseload. In October 2001, the foundation was handling 50 cases a month. Now it has 147 a week, Sanchez says, attributing the increase to greater public awareness of the issue as well as to the confidentiality and privacy the foundation can offer that the military cannot.

Military life, by its very nature, is stressful, making some family members especially vulnerable to domestic violence. Frequent relocations and high unemployment for military spouses, for example, make them more dependent on their service-member partner for income, health care and housing. Moreover, long deployments can cause some soldiers to worry that their spouses are having extramarital affairs. And easy

victims of domestic violence to the police or social services, as they are required to do in cases of suspected child abuse.

"Reporting does not ensure that a victim will have access to necessary resources and safeguards, nor does it guarantee prosecution, punishment or rehabilitation of abusers," says Peggy Goodman, director of violence-prevention resources at East Carolina University's Brody School of Medicine in Greenville, N.C. "In fact, [reporting] can further escalate an abusive situation and further endanger the life of the patient," she says. Thus, she says the American College of Emergency Physicians, the AMA and the American College of Obstetrics and Gynecology all oppose mandatory reporting by health-care workers.

The 1990s also ushered in a series of domestic-violence cases that either involved celebrities or made celebrities out of the parties involved because the trials were televised. In 1992, heavyweight boxer Mike Tyson was convicted of raping an 18-year-old beauty-pageant contestant, drawing national attention to date rape. A year later, the issue of spousal assault got national attention when Bobbitt cut off her husband's penis with a knife.

Then, in 1994, O. J. Simpson was arrested and charged with murdering his ex-wife, Nicole Brown Simpson, and her friend, Ronald Goldman. Simpson had pleaded no contest in 1989 to charges that he beat his wife and was fined $700 and sentenced to two years' probation. Police records also showed that Mrs. Simpson had frequently made emergency calls to police to report that her husband was beating her.

Congress Acts

Experts say the Simpson case helped prod Congress to approve the Violence Against Women Act in 1994, which proponents call a turning point in the fight against access to weapons also has been shown to be a risk factor in domestic-violence homicides.

Abuse victims in military families are often reluctant to report incidents of abuse because they know it could jeopardize the spouse's career, along with the family's paycheck, housing and health care.

"Imagine, in the civilian world, that calling a local shelter or confiding in your doctor automatically caused your batterer's employer to find out about his acts of violence and abuse," Judith E. Beals, a member of the Defense Task Force on Domestic Violence, wrote in the group's 2003 report.[2]

Victims' advocates say, however, that in recent years the military has lagged behind the nation in dealing with domestic violence. When the military created its Family Advocacy Programs (FAP) more than 20 years ago, the programs were considered progressive. But over time, experts say, FAP stayed the same while the civilian world changed the way it dealt with domestic violence.

In terms of domestic-violence programs, "the military today is where the country was in the 1980s," Sanchez says. For example, in the 1980s, many civilian hospitals were beginning to make sure they had registered nurses on staff — called SANEs (sexual assault nurse examiners) — trained to examine sexual-assault victims. But Camp Lejeune, a big Marine Corps base in North Carolina, didn't get its first SANE until 2002, Sanchez says. Until recently, sexual-assault victims on some military bases had to be transferred to civilian hospitals to obtain treatment.

Advocates had hoped to persuade Congress in 2005 to add military-specific provisions to the Violence Against Women Act but were told the bill would have to go through the Armed Services and other committees with jurisdiction over military issues, possibly delaying or derailing the entire bill.

Meanwhile, the DOD and the Justice Department's Office on Violence Against Women in 2005 kicked off two domestic-violence demonstration projects that use the "coordinated community response" approach. The projects involve the U.S. Army at Fort Campbell, Ky., and the communities of Hopkinsville, Ky., and Clarksville, Tenn., and the U.S. Navy and the city of Jacksonville, Fla. The projects are expected to provide "lessons learned" and serve as a guide for other military installations.

"There really isn't a set model for coordinating the military and civilian response to domestic-violence incidents, so hopefully we can create one," said Connie Sponsler-Garcia, the Military Projects Coordinator and coordinator of the Jacksonville project.[3]

[1] Fox Butterfield, "Wife Killings at Fort Reflect Growing Problem in Military," *The New York Times*, July 29, 2002, p. A9, and "Rash of Wife Killings at Ft. Bragg Leaves the Base Wondering Why," The Associated Press, July 27, 2002.

[2] Judith E. Beals, "The Military Response to Victims of Domestic Violence," 2003. The report comes from the Battered Women's Justice Project, which provides technical advice to the Department of Justice's Office on Violence Against Women.

[3] Kaylee LaRocque, "New Program Will Help Navy Deal with Domestic Violence Cases," *Navy NewsStand*, March 4, 2005.

domestic violence. President Bill Clinton, who as a child had witnessed his own mother being beaten by his stepfather, was a strong supporter of VAWA, which was attached to Clinton's crime bill.

The legislation reworked several areas of federal criminal law. It created penalties for stalking or domestic abuse in which an abuser crossed a state line and then physically harmed the victim in the course of a violent crime. VAWA also set new rules of evidence specifying that a victim's past sexual behavior generally was not admissible in federal civil or criminal cases regarding sexual misconduct. The law also allowed rape victims to demand that their alleged assailants be tested for HIV, the virus that causes AIDS.

VAWA encouraged local governments to create "coordinated community responses" bringing together criminal-justice agencies, social-services systems and local shelters and other nonprofits. The strategy is often called the "Duluth model," after the northern Minnesota city where it was developed over a 15-year period. Researchers say the ideal coordinated community response should also involve health-care providers, child-protection services, local businesses, the media, employers and clergy. Health-care providers, in particular, can be important since doctors, nurses and emergency-room workers may see and treat women who don't or can't seek other kinds of assistance.

States in the 1990s also began experimenting with ways to help victims and alternatives to penalizing perpetrators. New Haven, Conn., for example, launched a pilot program that included weekend jail stays combined with counseling. The approach allowed offenders to keep their jobs while remaining behind bars on weekends, when batterers often drink and become abusive. Illinois and Oregon were among the states that put domestic-violence counselors in

Killings of Men Dropped

The number of men killed by so-called intimates dropped by 71 percent between 1976 and 2001.* Experts say women now feel they don't have to resort to violence because there are safer shelters and tougher laws to protect them from domestic violence.

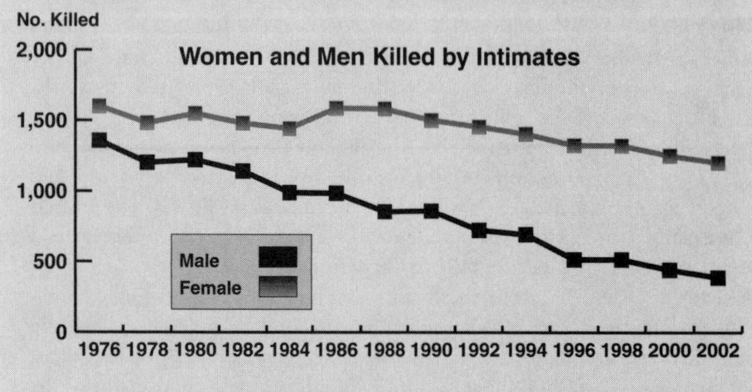

* "Intimates" includes spouses, ex-spouses, boyfriends and girlfriends.

Source: Bureau of Justice Statistics, U.S. Department of Justice, 2003.

welfare offices. Washington became the first state to allow battered women to set up confidential addresses their abusers couldn't locate.

Congress updated VAWA in 2000, adding "dating violence" to the definition of domestic violence and urging grant programs to address it. The revised law also created penalties for anyone traveling across state lines with the intent to kill, injure, harass or intimidate a spouse or intimate partner. The revised law also laid out special rules for battered immigrant spouses and their children, allowing them to remain in the United States. Under the old law, battered immigrant women could be deported if they left their abusers, who usually are their sponsors for residency and citizenship in the United States.

Also in 2000, the U.S. Supreme Court invalidated portions of the law permitting victims of rape and domestic violence to sue their attackers in federal court for damages. Ruling in *United States v. Morrison*, the justices said those provisions were unconstitutional under the Commerce and Equal Protection clauses. Victims could still bring damage suits in state courts. In addition, the court said, such violence does not substantially affect interstate commerce and noted that the Equal Protection clause is directed at government actions, not private. The high court's ruling did not affect any VAWA grant programs.[35]

Although the VAWA amendments passed in 2000 with nearly unanimous support, the law had its share of critics. Most of the criticism came from those who complained that violence was a problem of both men and women but that VAWA addressed only the needs of female victims.

CURRENT SITUATION

Reworking VAWA

Working until the early-morning hours of Dec. 17, 2005, Congress updated and expanded VAWA, kicking off several new initiatives, including a focus on young people and prevention.

Sen. Biden, the lead sponsor of both the original VAWA and the 2005 updated law, called passage of the new bill "a major victory," saying it "provides cities and towns with the tools they need to combat domestic violence, assist victims and go after abusers when it occurs."[36]

The updated legislation sets aside federal grant money for programs that help teen domestic-violence victims — including those in abusive dating relationships — and focuses more on children exposed to domestic violence at home. It also provides funds to combat domestic violence, sexual assault and dating violence in middle and high schools and expands services for rape victims and rape crisis centers, homeless-youth shelters and homes for runaways.

Targeting federal funds to younger victims "makes sense since we know that the highest rates of intimate-partner violence affect those in the 16-to-24 age group," says Kiersten Stewart, director of public policy at the Family Violence Prevention Fund, which lobbied Congress to enact the original Violence Against Women Act and many of the key revisions in 2005.

Stewart lauded Congress for continuing existing domestic-violence programs and for adding new ones, particularly those that focus on young people. "We're very pleased," she says.

The updated VAWA also includes money for programs to help domestic-abuse victims who are over age 60. It is difficult to say how many older Americans are abused, neglected or exploited, in large part because the problem remains "greatly hidden," says the National Center on Elder Abuse, a Washington, D.C., group that receives funds from the U.S. Administration on Aging. A 1998 federal study estimated that in 1996 some 450,000 Americans 60 and over were victims of physical, emotional or sexual abuse, neglect or financial exploitation. In 90 percent of the cases, a family member was the perpetrator, the study found.[37]

Experts fear that as the U.S. population ages, the number of elder-abuse cases will grow. "It's a hidden epidemic," Daniel Reingold, president and chief executive officer of the Hebrew Home for the Aged in Riverdale, N.Y., told *AARP* magazine.[38] That's largely because older victims are ashamed to report the abuse, because they feel they are old enough to know better than to be victimized. Reingold compares the current attention to elder abuse to the domestic-violence and child-abuse movements 25 years ago.

Is Your Relationship Healthy or Abusive?

Break the Cycle, a nonprofit organization helping young people create lives free of abuse, suggests teens ask themselves the following questions to determine if their relationships are healthy. If teens answer yes to any of these questions, they may be in an abusive or potentially abusive relationship, the organization says.

Does the person I am with:

- Get extremely jealous or possessive?
- Accuse me of flirting or cheating?
- Constantly check up on me or make me check in?
- Tell me how to dress or how much makeup to wear?
- Try to control what I do or whom I see?
- Try to keep me from seeing or talking to my family and friends?
- Have big mood swings — being angry and yelling at me one minute, and the next being sweet and apologetic?
- Make me feel nervous or like I'm "walking on eggshells?"
- Put me down or criticize me and make me feel like I can't do anything right or that no one else would want me?
- Threaten to hurt me?
- Threaten to hurt my friends or family?
- Threaten to commit suicide or hurt himself or herself because of me?
- Threaten to hurt my pets or destroy my things?
- Yell, grab, push, shove, shake, punch, slap, hold me down, throw things or hurt me in any way?
- Break things or throw things when we argue?
- Pressure or force me into having sex or going farther than I want to?

Source: Break the Cycle, www.breakthecycle.org

The expanded VAWA also funds programs to educate health-care professionals on how to identify and serve victims of domestic violence. A 2005 report from researchers at Harvard Medical School found that nearly one-third of doctors surveyed fail to document patients' reports of domestic violence, and only 10 percent offer information about domestic abuse to their patients.[39]

The National Network to End Domestic Violence says VAWA's new housing provisions are of particular importance, since 92 percent of homeless women have experienced severe physical or sexual abuse. The new law protects victims of domestic violence or stalking from being evicted from public housing and provides grants for transitional housing for domestic-violence victims.

"The reauthorization of VAWA shows that Congress recognizes domestic violence as a devastating social problem," said network President Rosenthal.[40]

The updated law fails to make the Violence Against Women Act gender neutral, as some men's groups had requested, but contains language specifying that men can't be discriminated against. Rep. James Sensenbrenner Jr., R-Wis., chairman of the House Judiciary Committee and

Innovative Programs Fight Domestic Violence

A host of programs around the country are dedicated to fighting and preventing domestic violence. Among those that have been found to work well are:

- **Coaching Boys into Men** — This program from the Family Violence Prevention Fund recognizes the mentoring role coaches have with their athletes and provides training tools to encourage disciplined and respectful behaviors. (www.endabuse.org) A similar effort comes from New York Yankees' Manager Joe Torre, who founded the Joe Torre Safe at Home Foundation to prevent others from suffering as he did as a child. Growing up, he stayed away from home, fearful of his own father, who abused his mother. (www.joetorre.org)
- **Cut it Out** — Originally a statewide program created by The Women's Fund of Greater Birmingham and the Alabama Coalition Against Domestic Violence, this program went national in 2003, training hair salon professionals to recognize the signs of domestic abuse and to encourage suspected victims to get help. The project is cosponsored by *Southern Living At Home* magazine, the National Cosmetology Association and Clairol Professional. (www.cutitout.org)
- **Domestic Violence Prevention Enhancement and Leadership Through Alliances (DELTA)** — These state demonstration projects get funds from the U.S. Centers for Disease Control and Prevention to focus on preventing violence between intimate partners. A program at John Dickenson High School in Wilmington, Del., involves an interactive play for ninth-graders, weekly "healthy relationship" lessons during health class and a weekly after-school club called "Teens Talking About Relationships." Delaware Gov. Ruth Ann Minner (D) awarded the club the 2004 Outstanding Youth Volunteer Service Award. (www.cdc.gov/ncipc/DELTA/default.htm)
- **Family Justice Center, San Diego, Calif.** — Opened in 2002, this program provides "one-stop shopping" for legal, social service and some medical services in downtown San Diego, avoiding the need for abuse victims to go to different locations on different days. It is considered the gold standard for a compact community with good access to mass transit. But researchers have found that such programs are not as efficient for rural areas or spread-out cities that are more auto-dependent. It's a model for President Bush's Family Justice Center program. (www.familyjustice-center.org)
- **Greenbook Demonstration Initiative** — Named for the report's green cover, this program was launched in 2001 and brings a closer collaboration between child-abuse and domestic-violence services. The project took place in six counties: San Francisco and Santa Clara counties in California; Grafton County, N.H.; St. Louis County, Mo.; El Paso County, Colo.; and Lane County, Ore. Among the key lessons from the Greenbook project: Mothers should not be accused of neglect for being victims of domestic violence, and separating battered mothers and children should be the alternative of last resort.[1] (www.thegreenbook.info/)
- **Judicial Oversight Demonstration Initiative** — This Justice Department program, which began in 1999, establishes closer working relationships between the courts, police departments, district attorneys' offices, probation departments and batterer intervention and victim services. The program was launched in Milwaukee, Wis., Dorchester, Mass., and Ann Arbor, Mich. (www.vaw.umn.edu/documents/1jod/1jod.html)
- **Victim Intervention Program (VIP)** — This program at Parkland Hospital at the University of Texas in Dallas provides staff caseworkers to help determine the health-care and social-service needs of patients who are victims of abuse and provides referrals for other services. Ellen Taliaferro, an emergency physician, founded the program in 1999. (www.parklandhospital.com)

---

1 "The Greenbook Demonstration Initiative: Interim Evaluation Report," Caliber Associates, Education Development Center and the National Center for State Courts, Dec. 16, 2004.

AT ISSUE

Did Congress improve the Violence Against Women Act?

YES

Jill J. Morris
Public Policy Director, National Coalition Against Domestic Violence

Written for the *CQ Researcher*, January 2006

Since Congress passed the bipartisan and groundbreaking Violence Against Women Act (VAWA) in 1994, the criminal-justice and community-based responses to domestic violence, dating violence, sexual assault and stalking have significantly improved. Ten years of successful VAWA programs have helped new generations of families and justice professionals understand that society will not tolerate these crimes.

Congress improved VAWA when it reauthorized it in December 2005. Since 1994, lawmakers have authorized more than $5 billion for states and local programs under VAWA. This relatively small amount has had a huge impact on local communities. For example, the number of women murdered by an intimate partner declined by 22 percent between 1993 and 2001. Also, more women came forward to report being abused in 1998 than in 1993.

VAWA is not only good social policy but also sound fiscal policy. A 2002 university study found that money spent to reduce domestic violence between 1995 and 2000 saved nearly 10 times the potential costs of responding to these crimes. The study estimated that $14.8 billion was saved on medical, legal and other costs that arise from responding to domestic violence. On an individual level, VAWA saved an estimated $159 per victim.

VAWA has fostered community-coordinated responses that for the first time brought together the criminal-justice system, social services and private, nonprofit organizations. With VAWA reauthorized, our local communities can continue to provide life-saving services such as rape prevention and education, victim witness assistance, sexual-assault crisis intervention and legal assistance.

Additionally, VAWA grants help reduce violent crimes on college campuses and provide services for children who witness violence, transitional housing, supervised visitation centers and programs for abused seniors and victims with disabilities.

The updated VAWA will expand programs to fill unmet needs, such as fostering a more community-based response system and addressing housing discrimination, preventing violence, promoting healthy relationships and engaging male allies to encourage positive roles for young men and boys.

The 2005 reauthorization of VAWA was one of the few pieces of legislation that was overwhelmingly supported by members of Congress on both sides of the aisle. Together, Democrats and Republicans agreed that passing VAWA showed that Congress was willing to recommit federal resources to programs that save lives, save money and help future generations of Americans live free from violence.

NO

Michael McCormick
Executive Director, American Coalition for Fathers and Children

Written for the *CQ Researcher*, January 2006

Violence perpetrated against others should be unacceptable regardless of the initiator's sex. But as many lawmakers privately confide, the Violence Against Women Act (VAWA) is not good law. Unfortunately, it has become the third rail of politics: Legislators acknowledge that it is political suicide to oppose passage of the bill. As one chief of staff aptly stated, "You do not want to be one of the few congressmen returning to your district having voted against this legislation, regardless of your reservations."

As a result, VAWA funds a political agenda that addresses domestic violence from a myopic viewpoint. It expands government encroachment into the private sphere of citizens' lives without adequate safeguards to those running afoul of the law and the domestic-violence industry.

Congress had a chance to address the law's shortcomings but failed to do so. For example, therapeutic approaches aimed at preserving the relationship and developing conflict-resolution skills still receive lower priority than law enforcement and relationship-dissolution options. This focus is at odds with stated public-policy objectives of building and maintaining strong, intact families. Congress should have changed this policy and did not.

Congress was correct to include language making clear that VAWA programs cannot discriminate against male victims, but it is still too early to tell whether male victims and their children will indeed get the help they need. Men and their children are not recognized as an underserved population, even though numerous studies indicate men are likely to be victims and suffer injury 15-30 percent of the time.

Even further, Congress made the right move by mandating that the Government Accountability Office study the issue, including the extent to which men are victims of domestic violence. This study will be balanced and give a better idea of how many men are abused and have access to services.

The biggest problem, however, is that VAWA does not recognize the role women play in domestic violence. The updated VAWA reinforces and statutorily codifies the notion that women are victims and men are abusers — a sure-fire way to assure half-baked solutions to a multi-faceted problem. This simplistic view of domestic violence ignores the vast storehouse of data indicating a small minority of both men and women are equally likely to initiate and engage in domestic violence.

Until such fundamental concerns are addressed, VAWA will continue to support a one-sided approach to dealing with domestic violence. Gender politics has no business being funded through the public purse.

Break the Cycle

Youths from Los Angeles plan programs to publicize and prevent domestic violence against teens at a meeting of Break the Cycle's Youth Voices program.

lead VAWA sponsor in the House, said after the bill's passage that the reauthorization "specifies that programs addressing these problems can serve both female and male victims."[41]

It is widely speculated on Capitol Hill that gay men, who have been excluded from men's groups, could be the biggest beneficiaries of making sure VAWA funds help abused men. While numbers are hard to come by, domestic-violence groups say gays are frequent victims of abuse. "Clearly, it would benefit gay men if the act was gender neutral," Sean Cahill, director of the National Gay and Lesbian Task Force's Policy Institute, told *CQ Weekly*.[42]

McCormick, of the American Coalition for Fathers and Children, is still troubled that the updated law focuses too much on the criminal aspect of domestic violence and not the social problems associated with it. "It still resorts to the nuclear option of blowing up a family," arresting and incarcerating someone who could be falsely accused without even seeing whether counseling could keep the family together, he says.

But McCormick says he's glad the new law authorizes the Government Accountability Office to study the issue, including the extent to which men, women, youths and children are victims of domestic violence, dating violence, sexual assault and stalking. The study will be balanced and provide a better idea of how many men are abused and have access to services, McCormick says.

Finding What Works

While Congress debated reworking VAWA, the Bush administration's Office on Violence Against Women was launching the president's Family Justice Center Initiative. Fifteen centers will get federal funds to provide one-stop help for victims, including legal, medical and social services.

In 2005 family-justice centers opened in Brooklyn, N.Y.; Bexar County, Texas; Alameda County, Calif.; Ouachita Parish, La., and Nampa, Idaho. Additional centers are slated to open in 2006 in St. Louis, Tulsa, Boston and Tampa. The DOJ's Stuart says the centers are examples of approaches that are working. (*See sidebar, p. 122.*)

Meanwhile, 14 states are working with the U.S. Centers for Disease Control and Prevention (CDC) to prevent domestic violence in the so-called DELTA (Domestic Violence Prevention Enhancement and Leadership Through Alliances) program.*

Each state project is a little different, since domestic violence and social programs differ from state to state, says Corinne Graffunder, branch chief of the CDC's National Center for Injury Prevention and Control. She says all 14 are innovative because they focus on prevention, not treating the victim or punishing the perpetrator. "That is new," she says.

In Valdez, Alaska, for example, the DELTA program is developing a healthy-relationships curriculum for the local high school. Mayor Bert Cottle proclaimed December 2005 as "White Ribbon Campaign Month" and encouraged all citizens, particularly men, to wear white ribbons in support of preventing domestic violence. And Dane County, Wis., provides programs and discussions for young men about sexual assault and domestic violence. The CDC expects to be able to evaluate the effectiveness of the programs in about three years, Graffunder says.

In New York state, Republican Gov. George Pataki and his wife Libby have spearheaded campaigns targeting teen-dating violence, including a statewide contest in which students were invited to submit posters, songs and music videos to raise awareness of the problem's seriousness. As part of Domestic Violence Awareness month in October 2005, New York kicked off its new "If It Doesn't Feel Right, It Probably Isn't" education campaign and distributed information packets — including copies of the 2005 winning poster — to all high schools in the state. (*See photo, p. 110.*)

---

* The 14 states are Alaska, California, Delaware, Florida, Kansas, Michigan, Montana, New York, North Carolina, North Dakota, Ohio, Rhode Island, Virginia and Wisconsin.

"This campaign will serve as a powerful platform to raise awareness about teen dating violence and will let all of New York's teens know that there are resources available to help if they are suffering from abuse," Pataki said.[43]

States also are using welfare offices to help victims of domestic violence, but the efforts have been spotty. Studies have indicated that up to 50 percent of welfare recipients are, or have been, victims of domestic violence and all but three states — Maine, Oklahoma and Ohio — screen welfare recipients for signs of domestic violence. Most states will waive some federal welfare rules pertaining to work, the five-year lifetime limit on cash assistance and child-support requirements for victims of domestic violence. But a recent Government Accountability Office report found that state requirements varied widely and that few welfare recipients received waivers.[44]

The Center for Impact Research, a Chicago anti-poverty research group, found that workers in a local welfare office "overwhelmingly" did not refer welfare recipients to domestic-violence services, says Lise McKean, the center's deputy director. Part of the problem was a cumbersome form that welfare recipients had to fill out and overburdened caseworkers who didn't have the time or interest to pursue the matter.

"The vision of the [welfare] office as the public agency with access to poor women that can identify individuals living with domestic violence and help them gain access to domestic violence services may be unrealistic," the center concluded.[45]

Rather than welfare offices, McKean suggests putting domestic-violence services at employment-service agencies — an approach the center tried in Houston, Chicago and Seattle.[46] Having a domestic-violence counselor on site was key, she says. The case manager did not have to worry whether clients would follow up because the manager could escort them directly to the counselor. Plus, adding domestic violence to a case manger's list of concerns was not a big burden since a specialist was available to handle it.

Experts say domestic violence also should be addressed in marriage and responsible-fatherhood programs. Recent federally funded research found that many of the widely available marriage-education programs were designed and tested with middle-income, college-educated couples and do not address domestic violence.[47]

Some states, such as New York, argue that programs designed to encourage healthy relationships have the positive benefit of reducing the likelihood of both physical and emotional abuse. The Oklahoma Marriage Initiative addresses domestic violence implicitly by focusing on communication and conflict resolution and has recently created a handout telling couples how to identify domestic violence and where to obtain help.[48]

Businesses and nonprofits also are stepping in. Liz Claiborne Inc., Break the Cycle and the Education Development Center, Inc., have created curriculums for ninth- and 10th-graders on dating violence. And 19 schools are participating in the "Love is not abuse" program, which formally began in October 2005.

"Our hope is that this curriculum will help educate teens on how to identify all forms of relationship abuse and understand what types of actions are and are not acceptable in a healthy dating relationship," said Jane Randel, vice president of corporate communications at Liz Claiborne.[49] (*See questionnaire, p. 121.*)

Kraft Foods has sponsored several studies, including the Center for Impact Research's project that looked at how domestic violence affects women's job training and employment.[50] Verizon Wireless has donated more than $8 million to shelters and prevention programs nationwide. Kaiser Permanente has stepped up its efforts to train counselors to perform domestic-violence evaluations and provides resources for patients who need help. The Blue Shield of California Foundation offers free consultations to any employer in California interested in setting up a domestic-violence prevention program in the workplace.[51]

OUTLOOK

Focus on Prevention

Most experts say the country has made significant headway in viewing domestic violence as a crime instead of merely a private family matter. But most agree that more focus should be placed on prevention.

"True primary prevention is the next real area on the horizon," says the CDC's Graffunder.

"We're just now beginning to scratch the surface," says Soler, of the Family Violence Prevention Fund. "We can't just intervene after the fact."

"All the recent emphasis has been on the criminal aspect of domestic violence," says Jeffrey L. Edelson, director of the Minnesota Center Against Violence and Abuse at the University of Minnesota. "This is a public health epidemic" that must be tackled in both the courts and public health agencies. "The prevention piece is important."

Until now, prevention has not been a top priority because the immediate concern has been helping victims in crisis and making sure batterers were held accountable and got counseling, says Graffunder. And, she adds, while advocates fighting domestic violence like to envision a day when violence no longer destroys families and lives, "We still have a lot of work to do."

Research and funding still lag behind the needs, advocates say. "We have a pretty good idea what works, but we need documentation by researchers to back it up," says Stuart, of the Justice Department's Office on Violence Against Women. For example, she says, research is particularly lacking on stalking. "Right now, it's hidden. We really don't know how much stalking is out there."

Dunford-Jackson, of the Family Violence Project, also sees a dearth of data. She says judges are always asking for statistics on successful programs and techniques. "We're still in the infancy of domestic-violence research," she says.

Researchers expect to know more from the CDC's DELTA prevention programs once results are in. Advocates are also trying to figure out best practices from several other demonstration projects, such as the "Greenbook" program that provides closer collaboration between child-custody and domestic-violence agencies.

Burroughs of the Safe Homes for Children and Families Coalition is confident that in the coming years male victims of domestic violence will get more attention and federal funds. Soler of the Family Violence Prevention Fund likewise sees a bigger role ahead for men — as major players in prevention.

"Men — as fathers, coaches, teachers and mentors — are in a unique position to influence the attitudes and behaviors of young boys," Soler says. The Family Violence Prevention Fund has two major initiatives aimed at boys, Founding Fathers and Coaching Boys Into Men, which are funded by foundations and private donors.

Fulcher of Break the Cycle says it's critical that more prevention programs target teens. "Now is the time to tell the youth of our nation that we are done pretending, that we will lead them into healthy adulthoods, that we won't tolerate violence and neither should they."

Advocates, however, worry that the budget crunch in Washington caused by Hurricane Katrina and the war in Iraq will mean less money for state and local social and domestic-violence programs, jeopardizing the progress made so far.

"As resources are strained, the decisions that people have to make at the local, community and state levels just get harder and harder," says the CDC's Graffunder. "Prevention doesn't traditionally fare well in those environments."

NOTES

1. U.S. Department of Justice, Bureau of Justice Statistics, "Intimate Partner Violence, 1993-2001," February 2003.
2. Prepared testimony of Juley Fulcher and Victoria Sadler before the U.S. Senate Judiciary Committee, July 19, 2005; Allison Klein and Ruben Castaneda, "Md. Burn Victim Told Judge of Fears," *The Washington Post*, Oct. 13, 2005, p. B7 (Cade); Pat Burson, "The Dark Side of Dating," *Los Angeles Times*, June 20, 2005, p. F6 (Wickiewicz).
3. U.S. Department of Justice, Bureau of Justice Statistics, "Family Violence Statistics," June 12, 2005.
4. U.S. Department of Justice, *op. cit.*, February 2003.
5. Testimony of Diane M. Stuart, director, U.S. Department of Justice Office on Violence Against Women before Senate Judiciary Committee, July 19, 2005.
6. Family Violence Prevention Fund, "Promoting Prevention, Targeting Teens: An Emerging Agenda to Reduce Domestic Violence," 2003.
7. Burson, *op. cit.*
8. Becky Beaupre, "Spotlight on female abuser: For 13 years, he never hit her back," *The Detroit News*, April 20, 1997.
9. Centers for Disease Control and Prevention, "Youth Risk Behavior Surveillance — United States 2003," *Surveillance Summaries*, May 21, 2004.
10. Centers for Disease Control and Prevention, National Center for Injury Prevention and Control, "Intimate Partner Violence: Fact Sheet," updated October 2005.
11. Wendy Max, *et al.*, "The economic toll of intimate partner violence against women in the United States," *Violence and Victims 2004*; 19(3), pp. 259-72.

12. Miriam K. Ehrensaft and Patricia Cohen, "Intergenerational Transmission of Partner Violence: A 20-Year Prospective Study," *Journal of Consulting and Clinical Psychology*, Vol. 71, No. 4, August 2003, pp. 741-753.
13. Prepared testimony, Senate Judiciary Committee, July 19, 2005.
14. Prepared testimony of Lynn Rosenthal, president, National Network to End Domestic Violence, Senate Judiciary Committee, July 19, 2005.
15. *Ibid.*
16. U.S. Department of Justice, *op. cit.*, February 2003.
17. Lisa Scott, "Pending federal DV law has little to do with violence and much to do with divorce court, attorney says," *The Liberator*, fall 2005.
18. Allison Klein and Ruben Castaneda, "Character in a Courtroom Drama," *The Washington Post*, Nov. 17, 2005, p. B1.
19. Kristin Little, "Specialized Courts and Domestic Violence," National Center for State Courts, May 2003.
20. Scott, *op. cit.*
21. Harvey Wallace, *Family Violence: Legal, Medical and Social Perspectives* (2002, 3rd ed.), p. 221.
22. *Town of Castle Rock v. Gonzales*, 542 U.S. ___ (2005).
23. "Supreme Court Decision Weakening Restraining Orders Short-Shrifted in the News," *Feminist Daily News Wire*, June 28, 2005.
24. U.S. Department of Justice, Bureau of Justice Statistics, "Special Report: Intimate Partner Violence and Age of Victim, 1993-1999," 2001.
25. Gallup Poll, "Adolescents Not Invulnerable to Abusive Relationships," May 24, 2005.
26. "Liz Claiborne Inc. Omnibuzz Topline Findings: Teen Relationship Abuse Research," February 2005; www.loveisnotabuse.com.
27. Sally Leidermann and Cair Almo, "Interpersonal Violence and Adolescent Pregnancy: Prevalence and Implications for Practice and Policy," Center for Assessment and Policy Development and National Organization on Adolescent Pregnancy, Parenting and Prevention, 2001.
28. Centers for Disease Control and Prevention, *op. cit.*, May 21, 2004.
29. Background drawn from Richard J. Gelles and Claire Pedrick Cornell, *Intimate Violence in Families* (1990) and Harvey Wallace, *Family Violence* (2002).
30. For background see Sarah Glazer, "Violence Against Women," *CQ Researcher*, Feb. 26, 1993, pp. 169-192.
31. Gelles and Cornell, *op. cit.*, p. 39.
32. *Ibid.*
33. *Thurman v. City of Torrington*, 595 F.Supp. 1521 (Conn. 1984).
34. Gelles and Cornell, *op. cit.*
35. *United States v. Morrison*, 529 U.S. 598 (2000).
36. Statement, Dec. 19, 2005.
37. "National Elder Abuse Incidence Study, Final Report," Administration for Children and Families and the Administration on Aging, U.S. Department of Health and Human Services, September 1998; www.aoa.gov/eldfam/Elder_Rights/Elder_Abuse/ABuseReport_Full.pdf.
38. David France, "And Then He Hit Me," *AARP The Magazine*, January/February 2006, p. 81.
39. Megan Gerber, "How and why community hospital clinicians document a positive screen for intimate partner violence: a cross-sectional study," *BMC Family News*, Vol. 6, p. 48, Nov. 19, 2005.
40. Statement, Dec. 17, 2005.
41. *Congressional Record*, Dec. 17, 2005, p. H12122.
42. Jill Barshay, "Men on the Verge of Domestic Abuse Protection," *CQ Weekly*, Sept. 5, 2005, p. 2276.
43. Press release, Office of New York Gov. George Pataki, "Governor Promotes Awareness of Teen Dating Violence," Sept. 23, 2005.
44. Government Accountability Office, "TANF: State Approaches to Screening for Domestic Violence Could Benefit from HHS Guidance," August 2005.
45. Center for Impact Research, "Less Than Ideal: The Reality of Implementing a Welfare-to-Work Program for Domestic Violence Victims and Survivors in Collaboration with the TANF Department," February 2001.

46. Lise McKean, Center for Impact Research, "Addressing Domestic Violence as a Barrier to Work," October 2004.
47. Government Accountability Office, *op. cit.*
48. *Ibid.*
49. Liz Claiborne Inc., "Love is not abuse" curriculum, Oct. 11, 2005.
50. McKean, *op. cit.*
51. Available at www.endabuse.org/workplace/display.php?DocID=33018.

BIBLIOGRAPHY

Books

Gelles, Richard J., *Intimate Violence in Families,* SAGE Publications, 3rd ed., 1997.
Gelles, the then-dean of the University of Pennsylvania's School of Social Work, looks at the myths that hinder understanding of family violence, such as the belief that domestic violence is a lower-class phenomenon.

Gosselin, Denise Kindschi, *Heavy Hands, An Introduction to the Crimes of Domestic Violence,* Prentice-Hall, 2000.
A Massachusetts State Police trooper who developed domestic-violence prevention courses for Western New England College examines different kinds of family violence and legal responses, with each chapter providing review questions on domestic violence.

Wallace, Harvey, *Family Violence, Legal, Medical and Social Perspectives,* 3rd ed., Allyn & Bacon, 2002.
The director of California State University's Justice Center examines medical and legal responses to domestic violence, particularly among homosexuals and rural victims.

Articles

Beaupre, Becky, "Spotlight on female abuser: For 13 years, he never hit her back," and "No place to run for male victims of domestic abuse," *The Detroit News,* April 20, 1997.
Male victims of domestic violence are sometimes turned away from aid agencies.

Burson, Pat, "The Dark Side of Dating," *Los Angeles Times,* June 20, 2005, p. F6.
The author examines teen-dating violence, giving examples of teens in abusive relationships and how few turn to their parents for help.

Young, Cathy, "Ending Bias in Domestic Assault Law," *The Boston Globe,* July 25, 2005, p. A11.
A libertarian *Reason* magazine editor argues that the Violence Against Women Act helped enshrine a one-sided approach to family violence and that it should be more gender neutral.

Reports and Studies

"Full Report of the Prevalence, Incidence, and Consequences of Violence against Women: Findings from the National Violence Against Women Survey," U.S. Department of Justice, November 2000; www.ncjrs.org/txtfiles1/nij/183781.txt.
The survey quantifies the pervasiveness of domestic violence and its impact on women and society.

"The Greenbook Demonstration Initiative: Interim Evaluation Report," Caliber Associates, Education Development Center and the National Center for State Courts, Dec. 16, 2004.
An innovative pilot program aims to improve coordination between public agencies that deal with domestic violence and child welfare.

"Intimate Partner Violence: Fact Sheet," National Center for Injury Prevention and Control, U.S. Centers for Disease Control and Prevention, updated October 2005.
This backgrounder includes the latest research on domestic violence.

"Intimate Partner Violence, 1993-2001," Bureau of Justice Statistics, U.S. Department of Justice, February 2003.
A federal domestic-violence study looks at abusive relationships involving spouses, boyfriends, girlfriends and ex-spouses and partners.

"Less Than Ideal: The Reality of Implementing a Welfare-to-Work Program for Domestic Violence Victims and Survivors in Collaboration with the TANF Department," February 2001, and "Addressing Domestic Violence as a Barrier to Work," October 2004, Center for Impact Research.
Providing domestic-violence services at welfare agencies does little to help battered women, but putting such services

in employment agencies can be beneficial because they help battered women achieve economic independence.

"Liz Claiborne Inc. Omnibuzz Topline Findings: Teen Relationship Abuse Research," February 2005, www.loveisnotabuse.com.
A survey sponsored by the clothing manufacturer shows that more than half of teens surveyed knew friends who had been physically, sexually or verbally abused.

"Promoting Prevention, Targeting Teens: An Emerging Agenda to Reduce Domestic Violence," Family Violence Prevention Fund, 2003.
An advocacy group concludes that the next generation of work in the domestic-violence field must target teens and young parents and emphasize prevention.

Ehrensaft, Miriam, and Patricia Cohen, "Intergenerational Transmission of Partner Violence: A 20-Year Prospective Study," ***Journal of Consulting and Clinical Psychology*****, Vol. 71, No. 4, August 2003, pp. 741-753.**
Children raised in homes where domestic or dating violence occurs are more likely to become victims or perpetrators of such violence.

For More Information

American Coalition for Fathers and Children, 1718 M St., N.W., Suite 187, Washington, DC 20036; (800) 978-3237; www.acfc.org. Argues that the Violence Against Women Act destroys families and funds an anti-male, pro-feminist ideological agenda.

Break the Cycle, P.O. Box 64996, Los Angeles, CA 90064; (888) 988-TEEN; www.breakthecycle.org. An advocacy group that educates and empowers youth to build lives and communities free from dating violence and domestic abuse.

Family Violence Prevention Fund, 383 Rhode Island St., Suite 304, San Francisco, CA 94103-5133; (415) 252-8900; www.endabuse.org. Sponsors education campaigns on family violence and was instrumental in lobbying Congress to enact the Violence Against Women Act.

National Coalition Against Domestic Violence, 1633 Q St., N.W., Suite 210, Washington, DC 20009; (202) 745-121; www.ncadv.org. Serves as a national information and referral center for battered women and their children as well as the public, media and allied agencies and organizations.

National Network to End Domestic Violence, 660 Pennsylvania Ave., S.E., Suite 303, Washington, DC 20003; (202) 543-5566; www.nnedv.org. Represents state domestic-violence coalitions and lobbies for stronger domestic-violence measures.

National Resource Center on Domestic Violence, (800) 537-2238; www.nrcdv.org. Provides comprehensive information and resources, policy development and assistance to enhance community response to and prevention of domestic violence.

National Sexual Violence Resource Center, 123 N. Enola Dr., Enola, PA 17025; (877) 739-3895; www.nsvrc.org. Provides information and technical assistance to local and national organizations and the public.

Safe Homes for Children and Families Coalition, 185 Springfield Dr., North East, MD 21901; (410) 392-8244. Advocates for gender-neutral federal legislation regarding domestic violence.

Stalking Resource Center, 2000 M St., N.W., Suite 480, Washington, DC 20036; (800) 394-2255); www.ncvc.org/src. Part of the National Center for Victims of Crime; serves as an information clearinghouse and peer-to-peer exchange program on stalking.

U.S. Centers for Disease Control and Prevention, National Center for Injury Prevention and Control, Mailstop K65, 4770 Buford Highway, N.E., Atlanta, GA 30341-3724; (770) 488-1506; www.cdc.gov/ViolencePrevention/intimatepartnerviolence/index.html. Studies ways to prevent intimate-partner and sexual violence.

U.S. Department of Justice, Office on Violence Against Women, 800 K St., N.W., Suite 920, Washington, DC 20530; (202) 307-6026; www.usdoj.gov. Handles legal and policy issues regarding violence against women and administers Violence Against Women Act grants.

6

Bullying

Are Schools Doing Enough to Stop the Problem?

John Greenya

AP Photo/Noah Burger

Thirteen-year-old Jacob Rubin, of Oakland, Calif., says students teased him throughout sixth grade because his hair was long and called him "gay," "faggot" and "homo." His mother, background, intervened when she found out he had been beaten up. A third of all students nationwide report being bullied, and an estimated 160,000 children skip school every day to avoid bullying.

Bullies made sixth grade a "living hell" for Jacob Rubin, an honor student in Oakland, Calif., but he kept silent. The daily insults gave him stomachaches and affected his grades, but it was only after several boys beat him up that his mother finally realized what had been happening.[1]

- Chris and Kim Brancato also finally realized their 12-year-old son had been suffering in silence from savage bullying at his middle school in Fork Union, Va., when they saw marks around his neck from a suicide attempt.[2]
- At Tonganoxie Junior High in Kansas, bullies who targeted a quiet seventh-grade boy even wrote their taunts on classroom blackboards. After three years of asking school authorities to stop the bullying, his parents sued the school board. The boy dropped out.[3]
- After Brittni Ainsworth, 16, a cheerleader in Plainfield, Ind., told a television reporter that other girls bullied her and damaged her car, she testified last year before state senators considering anti-bullying legislation.

Today, bullying is widely regarded as a serious problem in the United States. Ron Stephens, executive director of the National School Safety Center, calls bullying "one of the most enduring problems" in schools.[4] Up to 75 percent of American children have been victims of bullying, according to the National Crime Prevention Council.[5] On an average school day, three out of 10 American youngsters in grades six through 10 are involved in

From *CQ Researcher*, February 4, 2005.

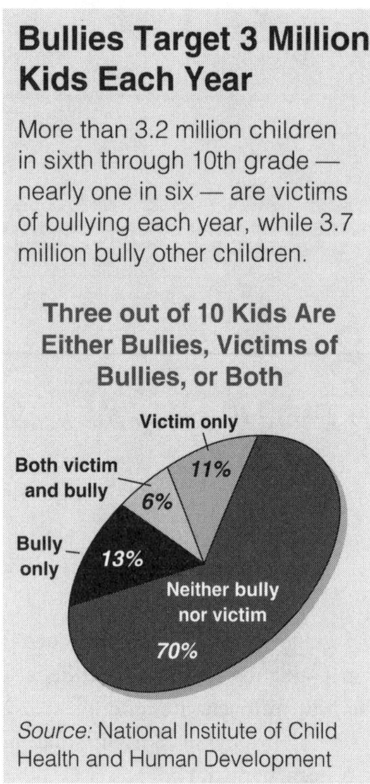

Source: National Institute of Child Health and Human Development

bullying — as perpetrators, victims or both — according to a National Institute of Child Health and Human Development (NICHD) study.[6]

But for many educators — and anguished parents — it took the horror of Columbine to awaken the nation to the seriousness — and pervasiveness — of bullying.

After Columbine High School students Dylan Klebold and Eric Harris massacred 12 students and a teacher and then killed themselves at their school in the affluent Denver suburb of Littleton in 1999, parents told investigators that bullying had been rampant at Columbine.

Shari Schnurr, the mother of a student injured at Columbine, told the Governor's Columbine Review Commission she had discussed bullying at the school with her daughter, who was a peer counselor. "There was just across-the-board intolerance [of others]," Schnurr said.

Several witnesses, including the aunt of slain Columbine student Isaiah Shoels, testified that Principal Frank DeAngelis had discounted their concerns about bullying. Several parents also testified that students and others were unwilling to come forward with their stories for fear of retaliation.[7]

In fact, bullying was also cited as a factor in subsequent school killings, according to a U.S. Secret Service study.[8] Concern about bullying has prompted at least 16 states to adopt legislation recommending or requiring schools to institute programs to help kids unlearn bullying behavior.[9] At least one such measure was introduced in Congress last year as well (*see p. 148*).

Most bullying begins in elementary school. "The thought of children barely old enough to read singling out and tormenting other youngsters is disturbing and uncomfortable to contemplate," Sandra Feldman, president of the American Federation of Teachers (AFT), wrote recently. "Yet researchers have found that bullying begins among preschool children and peaks in grades six through eight."[10]

During her first year of junior high school, a young woman recalls, "There were a bunch of them, and they were older than me. They took my backpack and kicked it along the ground like a soccer ball, and when I tried to stop them they kicked me. One boy pulled my hair so hard a big clump came out."[11]

Bullying in high school has a different name, says Ralph Cantor, the Safe and Drug Free Schools Coordinator for the Office of Education in Alameda County, Calif. "It's called harassment," particularly when it has sexual overtones, he says, and a "hate crime" if it involves bullying based on sexual orientation.

Indeed, experts say that much bullying revolves around taunts about other youths' sexuality. Gay, lesbian and bisexual youths (GLB) are five times more likely than their peers to miss school because they feel unsafe, according to a recent study.[12] And for good reason: Studies show that one-third of gay students are physically harassed due to their sexual orientation, one in six is beaten badly enough to need medical attention and gay teens are four times more likely to be threatened with a weapon at school than straight kids.

Jaana Juvonen, a psychologist at the University of California, Los Angeles (UCLA) who studies school culture, says bullying "may be particularly problematic in American schools." According to student surveys, she says, U.S. schools rank roughly on a par with those in the Czech Republic as among the least friendly in the Western world.[13]

Overweight Teens Are Bullied the Most

Overweight children are picked on the most, followed by kids who are gay or thought to be gay, according to a 2002 survey of schoolchildren ages 12 to 17.

How often are the following types of students teased or bullied in your school?

Kids who are:	Percentage of students who answered "all the time," "most of the time" and "some of the time"
Overweight	85%
Gay or thought to be gay	78
Dress differently	76
Have disabilities	63

Source: National Mental Health Association, "What Does Gay Mean? Teen Survey," December 2002

Some experts say American culture in some ways may condone, or even support, abusiveness as an acceptable way to get ahead — and not just on the playground. Television shows like "Scrubs," "House," and "ER," for instance, feature successful — albeit arrogant and rude — doctors frequently verbally humiliating and abusing underlings. Teen movies portray the most popular kids — cheerleaders and football players — as the most likely to bully. One of the regular cartoon characters on the "Simpsons," Nelson Muntz, is a bully who regularly picks on Bart.

Studies even confirm that school bullies are often star athletes or class leaders, popular with students, teachers and administrators who are often reluctant to discipline them. "Classmates are not keen to affiliate with a bully, but they recognize that these people have social capital and power," Juvonen said.[14]

Others say the enormous size of today's public schools may contribute to the problem by providing long, unmonitored hallways or stairwells where vulnerable students can be victimized with impunity. And some teachers and parents may be reluctant to intervene — perhaps unintentionally encouraging the practice by their inaction — either because they see bullying as a natural part of childhood or because they fear adult intervention will exacerbate the situation. According to Juvonen, teachers intervene only about 10 percent of the time.[15]

The U.S. Department of Education's Office of Safe and Drug Free Schools defines bullying as: "intentional, repeated, hurtful acts, words, or other behavior committed by one or more children against another; it may be physical, verbal, emotional, or sexual in nature."

The National Education Association (NEA) says bullying can be direct — such as teasing, hitting or threatening — or indirect, involving exclusion, the spreading of untrue rumors or psychological manipulation. The NICHD study said "belittling insults about looks and speech" were a common form of bullying, and that girls were more likely to spread rumors or make sexual remarks, while boys would slap, hit or push their victims.[16]

But even if bullying doesn't escalate into horrific Columbine-level violence, both the victims and the perpetrators suffer in other, less-obvious ways, along with society as a whole. Bullying not only begets depression and suicide but also serious crime, researchers say, not to mention poor academic performance, truancy and higher dropout rates.

"Parents and schools recognize that bullying is a problem that will not go away of its own choice — it's not a faddish thing," says Ted Feinberg, assistant executive director of the National Association of School Psychologists (NASP). "This is something that has been long overdue in terms of it being addressed by responsible agencies."

"When you and I were at school, mom or dad would say, 'Well, just ignore it and it will go away,' " recalls Rob Beaumont of Safe Schools, Safe Students. "Or, 'Stand up and fight for yourself.' Unfortunately, the level of violence has increased to the point where standing up and fighting back or ignoring it is not really an option," he said. Parents and teachers need to get involved right at the beginning."[17]

Anti-bullying programs are being conducted by schools and nonprofit organizations across the country, including the American Association of University Women (AAUW), the American Psychological Association and the Ford and Kaiser Family foundations.

Many programs say the role of the bystander is crucial. "Bystanders to bullying often play a key role in determining whether bullying will occur and escalate — or be prevented," wrote psychologist and bullying expert Ronald G. Slaby, developer of "Aggressors, Victims and Bystanders," a popular anti-bullying program. Slaby is a research scientist with the Education Development Corp. in Newton, Mass., and a lecturer in the Harvard Graduate School of Education and the Harvard School of Public Health. "Bystanders often directly fuel bullying encounters by setting up or cheering on the aggressor and victim," Slaby adds.[18]

Meanwhile, legislation and anti-bullying programs that seek to reduce sexually oriented teasing are encountering strong opposition from conservative Christians, who claim they promote homosexuality and impinge on Christian students' freedom of speech.

"When harassment based on sexual orientation is explicitly banned, school staff and students are inevitably trained that the reason such harassment is wrong is not because all harassment is wrong or because all people should be treated with respect, but because there is nothing wrong with being gay or lesbian," Peter Sprigg, senior director of policy studies at the conservative Family Research Council, testified before the Maryland House Ways and Means Committee, Feb. 19, 2003.

Although much is being done to reduce bullying, many parents say their children's schools are not responding quickly or aggressively enough. "I called everyone I thought could help me, and I just couldn't get it stopped," said the father of a boy who says he was bullied from the age of 12 until he dropped out of high school at 16. "It's like my son didn't matter."[19]

The boy's father has joined a growing list of parents and students who have sued their schools and school districts for not protecting their children. And in a new wrinkle, in July 2004 a teenager from Fredericksburg, Va., Joe Golden, sued three former high school classmates, alleging they shoved his head into a plastic bag and threatened to kill him; that teachers ridiculed him and that school administrators did nothing to stop the bullying. He is seeking $450,000 in damages.[20]

Daniel Fisher, 17, a senior at Chancellor High School who played recreational soccer with Golden, said he was picked on because he was "an average kid" — not from a family with a lot of money or part of a "cool" social group. Golden was also very friendly with teachers, Fisher said, something that would immediately make him a target. "He was just the perfect specimen for bullies to pick on."[21]

As legislators, school officials and parents confront the bullying problem, here are some of the questions being debated:

Is bullying a serious problem?

Before Columbine, few Americans would have drawn a connection between bullying and schoolyard massacres. But as Gerald Newberry, director of the NEA's Health Information Network, points out, "The kids who pulled the trigger weren't who we thought they were. They were not the bullies — they were the kids who had been bullied. That's what changed the focus of the schools and the nation."

In the next several years, gun-related school killings occurred in Conyers, Ga., Fort Gibson, Okla., Santee, Calif., New Orleans, La., and Red Lion, Pa. Suddenly a nationwide debate was raging over the causes and consequences of bullying on the victims, perpetrators and even bystanders.

A Bureau of Justice Statistics survey found that 86 percent of high school students said teenagers resort to violence in school because of "other kids picking on them, making fun of them, or bullying them."[22] The Secret Service's National Threat Assessment Center and the Department of Education found that in two-thirds of 37 school shootings over the last 25 years the attackers had felt "bullied, persecuted, or injured by others" before the attack and that the bullying was often "longstanding and severe."[23]

The findings strongly suggested that bullying could no longer be considered just a relatively harmless phase that children must go through to get toughened up for life. "Being bullied is not just an unpleasant rite of passage through childhood," says Duane Alexander, director of the NICHD. "It's a public health problem that merits attention. People who were bullied as children are more likely to suffer from depression and low self-esteem, well into adulthood, and the bullies themselves are more likely to engage in criminal behavior later in life." (*See graph, p. 137.*)

James C. Backstrom, county attorney of Minnesota's sprawling Dakota County, frequently speaks at local elementary and middle schools about bullying in an effort to "get to kids before they move up to a larger school setting." When parents and school officials ask why a county prosecutor is interested in bullying, Backstrom has a simple answer: "Bullying prevention is crime prevention."

Backstrom urges students to be part of the solution. "If they see other children being bullied, the worst thing is to start laughing," he says. Instead, he urges kids to "stand up and be a hero. Do the right thing: Tell an adult."

Yet, there are still those who think adolescent bullying is necessary for children to learn to make it in a tough world. Cantor, the Safe and Drug Free Schools program coordinator in California, says, "I've heard parents — usually the male parents — say, 'People just need to toughen up some. I went through this, and I've just got to teach my kid to defend himself.' "

Parry Aftab, executive director of WiredSafety.org, a group that combats online bullying, agrees that the attitude is common. "You often hear, 'Big deal; all of us were bullied,' " Aftab says. "Americans have this sense that they're supposed to be tougher. The country has a macho mindset."

Ray Lora, a school board member and a former high school teacher, said that Golden — the Virginia youngster who sued his alleged high school bullies — should have been able to get beyond the torment without filing a lawsuit. "I'm sad that he hasn't gotten over that," he said. "Every kid has a rough time, but you have to overcome it."[24]

Estimates of the prevalence of bullying vary widely. The U.S. Department of Education's Office of Safe and Drug Free Schools says 7 million school bullying incidents occur each year.[25] A recent Department of Justice survey found that in any given month a quarter of U.S. students are bullied.[26] The Kaiser Family Foundation found that 55 percent of 8-to-11-year-olds and 68 percent of 12-to-15-year-olds thought bullying and teasing were the "big problems" in their schools — bigger problems than drugs, alcohol, racism, AIDS or pressure to have sex.[27] The study also found that fully 86 percent of youngsters ages 12 to 15 thought that students at their school get teased or bullied.

AP Photo/ Lowell Mendyk

A kindergarten student adds her name to an anti-bullying poster at Grapevine Elementary School in Madisonville, Ky. Researchers say bullying often begins in preschool and peaks in grades six through eight.

In April 2001, the first large-scale national survey of bullying in U.S. schools among students in grades six through 10 was published. Conducted before Columbine, it found that bullying was a problem that needed immediate nationwide attention. "This is a serious problem that we should not ignore," Tanja Nansel, an investigator at NICHD and the lead author of the study, said. "In the past, bullying has simply been dismissed as 'Kids will be kids,' but the findings from this study suggest that it should not be accepted as a normal part of growing up."[28]

Effective Programs Stress Adult Intervention

One of the most successful anti-bullying programs used in American schools was developed in the 1980s by a Norwegian educator, Professor Dan Olweus, after three adolescent Norwegian boys committed suicide — probably because of severe bullying by their classmates.

The Olweus [Ol-VEY-us] Bullying Prevention Program, which is used in several hundred U.S. schools, has been found to reduce bullying by 20 percent in U.S. schools where it has been adopted, while bullying increased in schools without the program.[1]

Schools adopting the Olweus program usually first conduct a survey to determine the seriousness of the problem, followed by a training period for teachers, administrators and selected students, parents and other school personnel. Anti-bullying rules — and consequences for rule-breakers — are established before the school year starts. In addition, adult supervision is established in places where bullying is known to occur, and the monitors are charged with intervention, not just supervision.

Intervention — a major component of the process — also includes sessions with individual bullies (and their parents) and their victims. "The goal is to ensure that the whole school, and not just a few teachers, will come together and act to make sure students know that 'bullying is not accepted in our class/school, and we will see to it that it comes to an end.' "[2]

The program has been praised by the University of Colorado's Center for the Study and Prevention of Violence and the federal Substance Abuse and Mental Health Services Administration.

Two other highly regarded programs are LIFT (Linking the Interests of Families and Teachers) and The Incredible Years.

LIFT is a 10-week anti-aggression intervention program that takes place on three levels: the classroom; the home (parents attend six training sessions to learn how to implement the program at home); and the playground, where adults monitor the behavior and reward or warn the students.

According to Fight Crime: Invest in Kids, a national anti-crime group based in Washington, D.C., LIFT's goal is to "instill social coping strategies in the students and to create an environment that surrounds each child with parents, teachers and peers who are working together to help prevent aggression and bullying. The playground becomes the practice field for these new techniques, and the children come to prize their good-behavior armbands."

The Incredible Years was designed initially for dealing with highly aggressive children ages 2 to 8. It trains both parents and their children in "non-aggression social skills."

Carolyn Webster-Stratton of the University of Washington says the program has stopped "the cycle of aggression for approximately two-thirds" of the families in the program. In certain Head Start settings, 80 percent of the kids tested within an acceptable range for problem behaviors within a half hour; only 48 percent of the children not in the program were within the acceptable range.[3]

Several other anti-bullying programs are expected to show good results as soon as evaluations are concluded, including the Aggressors, Victims, and Bystanders program, which the U.S. Department of Education has chosen as a "Promising Program" for its Safe and Drug Free Schools program.[4] It has been shown to significantly reduce "bystander support for aggression."

Operation Respect, founded by the famed folk-singing group Peter, Paul and Mary, also is considered effective with elementary schoolchildren.

[1] The program reportedly has been found to reduce bullying by up to 50 percent in Norway.

[2] D. Olweus, *et al.*, "Bullying Prevention Program," in D. S. Elliott, series ed., *Blueprints for Violence Prevention: Book Nine* (1999), Center for the Study and Prevention of Violence.

[3] Webster-Stratton, *et al.*, "The Incredible Years" Parent Teacher and Child Training Series, in D. S. Elliott, *ibid.*

[4] U.S. Department of Education, *Safe, Disciplined, and Drug-Free Schools Expert Panel* (2002).

Nansel and her colleagues found bullying hurts both bullies and the bullied. Victims of bullies are lonely and have trouble making friends; they are five times more likely than their peers to be depressed. Bullied boys are four times more likely than their peers to be suicidal, and girls eight times more likely, according to the study.[29]

The bullies, meanwhile, were more likely to smoke, drink alcohol and get poor grades. Most troubled of all were those who had both been bullied and had bullied others: They not only reported being lonelier and having more trouble making friends but also did poorly in school, smoked cigarettes and used alcohol.

The negative effects of bullying can last a lifetime, Nansel says. "Your junior high and lower high-school years are when you develop your identity," she says. "When people get the message during those very important years that they're not worthwhile, it certainly makes sense that it can have lasting effects. Similarly, for the bullies, if you learn that the way you gain enjoyment or pleasure is by doing something hurtful to another person, that's a very dangerous thing."

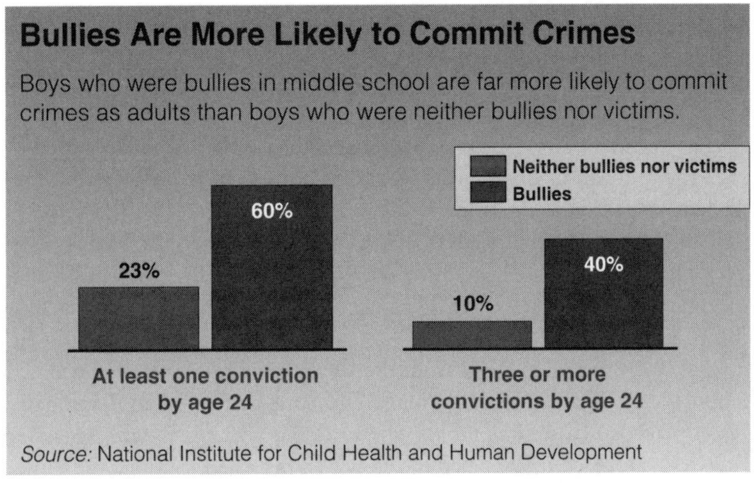

Indeed, society at large suffers from bullying. According to the NICHD, nearly 60 percent of boys who were bullies in middle school had at least one criminal conviction by age 24, and 40 percent had three or more convictions.[30]

"Bullying is an early warning that bullies may be headed toward more serious antisocial behavior," says Sanford A. Newman, president of Fight Crime: Invest in Kids, a crime-prevention organization of more than 2,000 police chiefs, sheriffs, prosecutors and crime survivors.[31]

Bullying also can affect school attendance, academic achievement and dropout rates. The National Association of School Psychologists (NASP) found that fear of being bullied may keep as many as 160,000 students out of school on any given day. And those who go to school are often too upset to concentrate.[32]

"He can't learn anything if he's scared to death," said Betty Tom Davidson, a school board member and parent in Orange County, N.C., who sought to pull her son out of class because bullying by an older student made him depressed and caused his grades to fall.[33]

Nonetheless, the NASP's Feinberg says he still sees schools that don't address the problem. "There are still some systems that deny the reality that is all around them," he says. "That's foolish thinking."

Is enough being done to curtail bullying?

There is considerable resistance to anti-bullying programs in many states and school districts, but nonetheless, many have joined with parents to fight bullying, and some programs have been running for three and four years.

"When I first started working on bullying five years ago, I used to hear from schools and parents that the bullying issue was blown out of proportion, but I haven't heard that in a long time," says Gaye Barker, coordinator of the NEA's National Bullying Awareness Campaign. "Now everyone is talking about the issue, and almost every state — if not every school district — is dealing with it. There are always going to be some groups that are slower to respond than others."

In fact, only 16 state legislatures have passed laws requiring school districts to implement anti-bullying programs, according to the National Conference of State Legislatures. Legislation is under consideration, however, in at least a dozen more states. Not surprisingly, some of the best programs are in schools that have had the biggest problems. In Colorado, for instance, school and governmental officials instituted the multilevel Bullying Prevention Program (BPP). Developed by the University of Colorado's Center for the Study and Prevention of Violence, BPP utilizes comprehensive measures at the student, class and staff levels to ensure that the entire school community is working together to stop bullying.

While many schools have responded to bullying aggressively, experts say an anti-bullying program is only as good as a school administrator's resolve to implement it.

"We tried for years and years to fix this problem, and at every turn this administration has refused to acknowledge the problem or do anything about it," said Patrice Anibal, a parent in Old Greenwich, Conn., who charged in a suit against school officials that they failed to protect her daughter from schoolyard bullies despite five years of parental pleas. "We felt we had no choice. We don't want this to happen to another family."[34]

Davidson finally resigned from the Orange County school board after it refused to deal with her son's bullies. "Complacency is unacceptable," she said. The board later acknowledged it had acted too slowly in her child's case and adopted an anti-bullying policy.[35]

In fact, fewer than one in four schools has any real bullying-prevention programs, says Newman of Fight Crime: Invest in Kids. "It's clear that not enough is being done. There are still 3.2 million kids being bullied each year in America and 3.7 million who are bullying other children."

Moreover, experts say, some schools are trying to "reinvent the wheel" by creating their own programs, rather than adopting proven measures. (*See sidebar, p. 136.*) Others are moving in another wrong direction, Newman says: "They are either blaming the victim — asking the kid why he doesn't just stand up for himself or quit provoking the bullies — or they are merely suspending or expelling the bullies."

Under zero-tolerance programs adopted by many school systems in the mid-1990s, youngsters were suspended or expelled the first time they broke a school disciplinary rule. When gun carrying or drug use were involved, the zero tolerance approach was often federally mandated.[36]

Newman opposes suspending or expelling a bully for two reasons: "It can feel like a vacation or a reward for the bully, and it squanders the early warning we've been given that a kid is headed for trouble later on." Noting that bullies are four times more likely to become repeat criminals later in life, he says that instead of sending the offending child home, schools should "work with the bully (along with his family) in a firm but effective way to get him back on track."

Teachers and administrators, however, are sometimes reluctant to address bullying, Newman says, fearing it will add to their workload and distract from efforts to improve student academic performance, mandated by the federal No Child Left Behind law.[37] But the fear is shortsighted, he says, because eliminating bullying reduces truancy and allows kids to concentrate better in class rather than worrying about being bullied at recess.

"Principals feel that they're under such pressure to deliver on academics that they don't have time to deal with bullying," says psychologist Slaby, who is a senior scientist at Health and Human Development Programs, an educational research organization in Newton, Mass. He has been studying bullying since the mid-1980s and has developed the widely used bullying-prevention program Aggressors, Victims and Bystanders. "[Principals] don't fully understand that academics suffer if you don't have a safe, bullying-free school. Even if you are only interested in academics and not the child's welfare and freedom from violence, you would do well to have bullying-prevention programs in the school."

"You hear from teachers, 'Don't ask me to do one more thing; I have more than I can handle already,' " the NEA's Barker says. "But when we explain that our program will save them time in terms of class disruptions and absenteeism, they are typically very positive."

However, some religious groups, as well as lawmakers and school officials, say that parents — not the government or schools — should be worried about disciplining and training children. And in some states, conservative Christian groups have sought to derail efforts to pass anti-bullying bills, arguing that when schools teach kids to tolerate classmates' racial, religious and sexual-orientation differences, the schools condone homosexuality and infringe on Christian kids' free-speech rights to oppose gay behavior.

Others also worry that basic discipline decisions are being taken out of the hands of the educators and placed in legislatures. Darcy Olsen, president of the Goldwater Institute in Phoenix, and former director of education and child policy at the Cato Institute, a libertarian think tank, says that anti-bullying legislation will undermine the authority of school administrators and teachers. "This is feel-good legislation," she said. "It is worthless. It will only burden them with more paperwork. Administrators and teachers don't need more training. They need to be able to get rid of students if they need to."[38]

Are school anti-bullying programs effective?

A wide range of anti-bullying information has become available over the last five years, including self-help books, parents' guides, teachers' manuals, informational pamphlets, Web sites and even interactive CDs.

Experts say it is important to identify programs that have been sufficiently tested and have shown meaningful results. The most successful anti-bullying programs, experts say, are both well-structured and well-enforced.

"The challenge," said Julie Thomerson, a policy analyst at the National Conference of State Legislatures, "is there is not enough research to point to specific, effective approaches. It's not that programs are bad, it's that many of them are too new to have been evaluated."[39]

Bullying Linked to Depression, Suicide

Girls who are bullied frequently are eight times more suicidal than other girls. Bullied boys are five times more likely than their peers to suffer depression.

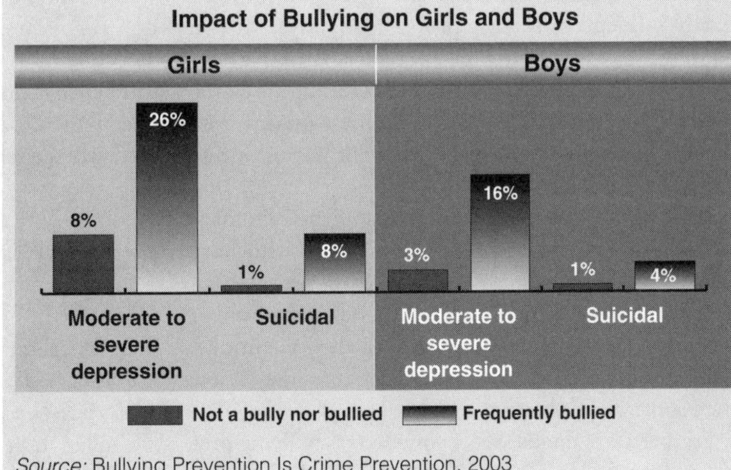

Source: Bullying Prevention Is Crime Prevention, 2003

Susan Limber, a professor at Clemson University's Institute on Family and Neighborhood Life who studies bullying, says zero-tolerance policies, group treatment, peer mediation and too-simple solutions, such as a single school assembly, are commonly used by schools, but are all ineffective.

Instead, she endorses a sustained, comprehensive effort to change school norms — like the renowned Olweus Bullying Prevention Program developed in Norway, which includes a prevention-coordinating committee, regular classroom meetings on bullying and immediate intervention and incident follow-up. Successful programs might also administer a questionnaire to assess bullying and teacher monitoring of areas where bullying usually occurs. Many of the schools that have used this program have reduced bullying by up to 50 percent and have achieved significant reductions in vandalism, fighting, and theft.[40]

But not all experts are convinced that bullying can be reduced that much, especially among older kids. In a study released in November 2004, Ken Rigby, an associate professor of social psychology at the University of South Australia, found that anti-bullying programs were less effective than previously had been thought, although still effective.[41] "It is comparatively rare to obtain a reduction in bullying of greater than 20 percent," Rigby says, quickly adding that a 20 percent reduction is still a substantial improvement. Moreover, he notes, nearly all the programs showed some results, especially in schools where the programs had been thoroughly implemented.

"Where there is improvement, it tends to be among younger children; the secondary schools generally show much less," Rigby says.

The American Association of University Women found that while the number of in-school anti-bullying programs and policies had increased, the incidence of sexual harassment and bullying had not declined. "You can change policies, but to actually change the behaviors takes time," says Leslie Annexstein, AAUW's director of legal advocacy. "Research indicates that there hasn't been enough emphasis on training teachers, counselors and administrators on how to deal with this issue."

The most successful programs, Rigby says, stress early intervention, helping potential victims protect themselves (because they are more motivated to change behavior than those who bully) and teaching kids to "problem-solve" — which is at least as effective as punishing the bullies, he says.

Slaby's "Aggressors, Victims and Bystanders" program, among several, focuses on changing the behavior of bystanders. "Bystanders are the most pivotal group of bullying influencers, especially since youth are so heavily influenced by their peers," Slaby says. "If you stand by and watch bullying, then you're letting it happen in your community. But if you stand up, then the bullies don't even have a chance. Bullies wouldn't even consider harassing others if they thought it wouldn't go over well."

Slaby says he has many reports of students who have been trained in the bystander curriculum who have helped defuse threatening situations. "Kids are speaking up to police officers or to teachers when they hear about something that ought to be brought to their attention," he says. "Kids are the best metal detectors. They know when something is happening."

Feinberg says the NASP's two-year anti-bullying program, "Stop Bullying Now and Lend a Hand," has been "an overwhelming success" both in increasing public awareness and preventing bullying because it teaches kids that bullying is not simply a rite of passage. Successful programs teach kids "that there are acceptable codes of conduct and . . . that there are consequences for violating those codes. [But] there will be little or no change in the behavior of school bullies unless the culture within the school is changed."

Experts agree that no matter what program is used, its effectiveness depends on school administrators' level of commitment. "There are a lot of schools with good-sounding programs," says former teacher Derek Randel of Wilmette, Ill., who became a "parenting coach" and specializes in dealing with bullying. "Words on paper are wonderful, but . . . they don't mean anything without a commitment to what they stand for."

For instance, he says, "In some very affluent neighborhoods, the schools take a 'We don't want to get the parents mad at us' approach. Frankly, many of these parents are dysfunctional parents and by bringing that dysfunction into the schools they're ruining the schools. I've seen a number of lawsuits brought by parents whose kids have been disciplined for bullying. You almost have to feel sorry for the schools, which then have to defend themselves."

Faced with confusing data on the effectiveness of various programs and vague anti-bullying laws that don't tell schools what they should do, some administrators resist confronting the problem. Some districts also lack the necessary funds, training and enforcement.

"We have a long way to go and a lot more work to do," Rigby says. "Success is not dependent upon the correct content of the programs. What does seem to make a difference is how thoroughly the program is supported and implemented, and a lot of work is still needed to motivate the schools to address this."

BACKGROUND

Early Research

A major theme of recorded history is the exploitation of the weak by the strong," Rigby writes in his 2002 book, *New Perspectives on Bullying.*[42]

Bullies have long been stock characters in movies, television, books and even cartoons, perhaps because they are so much a part of real life. In the early 18th century, novelist Henry Fielding featured a bully in *Tom Thumb.* On stage, bullies have been featured in works ranging from the intentionally humorous melodramas of the Golden Age to the unforgettable bellowing of Stanley Kowalski in Tennessee Williams's "A Streetcar Named Desire." Popular modern novelists such as S. E. Hinton, Robert Cormier and Walter Dean Myers often feature bullies.

The first scientific paper on bullying was published in 1897, when Norwegian researcher Fredic Burke's "Teasing and Bullying" explored why children bully, what effects bullying had on victims and how bullying could be reduced.[43]

However, bullying did not fully emerge as a field of scientific inquiry for social scientists until the 1970s, when a few articles were published. Then in 1978 came the publication in English of *Aggression in the Schools: Bullies and Whipping Boys,* by Norwegian psychologist Dan Olweus, one of the "founding fathers" of research on bullying and victimization.

In the 1980s, social scientists in Britain and the United States took an active interest in bullying. "Here was an issue that not only intrigued and challenged empirical researchers, counselors and theoreticians in psychology,

CHRONOLOGY

Before 1970 *Researchers pay little attention to bullying.*

1897 Norwegian social scientist F. L. Burk writes the first academic treatment of "bullying and teasing."

1970s-1980s *School bullying remains a low-key issue, although a sprinkling of journal articles discuss the problem. Norwegian school and government officials begin addressing the problem of bullying in schools, but officials in England and the United States begin to focus on the issue only late in the era.*

1978 Norwegian psychology Professor Dan Olweus, widely considered the father of social science research on bullying, publishes the English edition of *Aggression in the Schools: Bullies and Whipping.*

1982 After three unrelated suicides by children in Norway, a Nationwide Campaign Against Bullying is begun in all of the country's 3,500 schools.

1990-2000 *A string of schoolyard massacres in the United States — many committed by victims of bullies — prompts scientists, law enforcement and government officials to study the causes and negative effects of bullying.*

1993 Olweus publishes his landmark work, *Bullying: What We Know and What We Can Do About It.*

Feb. 2, 1996 Barry Loukaitis, 14, kills two students and a teacher in Moses Lake, Wash., later telling officials he was tired of being called a "faggot."

Feb. 19, 1997 Evan Ramsey, 16, kills his principal and another student in Bethel, Alaska, later complaining that school officials had failed to stop the bullying he was encountering at school.

Oct. 1, 1997 Luke Woodham, 16, kills two classmates and wounds seven in Pearl, Miss., after passing a note to friends stating "I killed because people like me are mistreated every day . . . . Push us and we will push back."

Dec. 1, 1997 Michael Carneal, 14, kills three students and injures five others at his West Paducah, Ky., high school. He later says he felt that going to prison would be better than continuing to endure the bullying he was subjected to in school.

Dec. 15, 1997 Joseph Colt Todd, 14, shoots and wounds two students at his Stamps, Ark., high school, later complaining that he was tired of being bullied.

April 20, 1999 Columbine High School students Dylan Klebold and Eric Harris shoot and kill a teacher and 12 students at their Littleton, Colo., school and then turn their guns on themselves; 23 students are wounded. The 18-year-old shooters had been favorite targets of bullies.

2000-Present *Schools across the United States adopt anti-bullying programs; the number of bullying incidents in some districts reportedly decreases by more than 20 percent. At least 16 state legislatures pass legislation requiring schools to adopt anti-bullying programs.*

May 2002 A study of school shooters by the U.S. Secret Service and U. S. Department of Education reveals that in two-thirds of 37 school shootings over the last 25 years the attackers had felt "bullied, persecuted, or injured by others" before the attack.

2004 Parents in Kansas and Connecticut sue their children's schools and school districts for failing to protect students from being bullied despite repeated complaints from the families. Parents in Virginia sue the alleged bullies of their child.

February 2005 Responding to a television report on widespread school bullying, the Indiana Senate is expected to pass a bill calling for statewide anti-bullying programs in schools.

education and sociology but also offered some kind of hope to thousands of people for whom bullying was a grim, everyday reality," Rigby wrote.[44]

When Rigby would tell fellow scientists what he was studying, they thought it "a curious thing to be researching," even though studies on aggression in animals and

Technology Gives Bullies a New Weapon

Hallie Fox, a high school senior in McLean, Va., was in seventh grade when her friends suddenly began giving her the silent treatment. Confused and upset, Fox went online that night to chat with some other girlfriends, who asked her why she had been picking fights through nasty instant messages and e-mails.

In fact, she hadn't. She had been cyberbullied. The culprit was a former friend who had hacked into her e-mail and instant message accounts.

Teasing and bullying are nothing new to youngsters. But modern technology enables bullies to follow kids far off school grounds, into their homes and bedrooms.

Cyberbullying includes sending malicious, sometimes threatening, e-mails, instant messages and cell phone text messages; creating humiliating Web sites that include stories and pictures; posting malicious gossip and comments on Web logs (blogs); and breaking into e-mail accounts to send vicious material to others.

The anonymity of the Internet allows bullies to flourish with increased viciousness and little fear of consequence.

"Kids don't have to look someone in the face when they're cyberbullying; they don't have to take responsibility for their actions," says Kristin Franke, of the Empower program, a Washington-based nonprofit group that works to prevent bullying.

She says that more than 40 percent of kids have been bullied online, according to a 2004 survey by i-SAFE, a nonprofit foundation that educates kids to use the Internet safely.[1] Moreover, as with traditional bullying, kids often bear the burden alone. In 2004, almost 60 percent of kids did not tell their parents or an adult about hurtful online messages, according to i-SAFE.

"Americans are realizing that the issue of kids hurting and harassing other kids is a big one," says Parry Aftab, executive director of WiredSafety.org, another Internet safety group. "We have to teach our kids to be good people when they're online just as we do offline."

A 2001 Department of Justice study found that approximately 14 percent of adolescents admitted to making rude or nasty comments to someone online during the past year.[2] But in 2004, the number increased to 53 percent.[3]

To combat the problem, kids need to be educated about the fingerprints they leave when using Internet, Aftab says, warning that each time the Internet is used, an Internet address is established that can be used to trace all electronic communications on that computer.

While educating kids about the harms and consequences of cyber-harassment is necessary for its prevention, bullying experts say that parents, law enforcers and school administrators also need to be on the alert.

"Schools have to take responsibility for cyberbullying because it can affect a student's ability to concentrate and learn while in class, and that impacts the school just as much as the schoolyard bully does," says

humans were well-established and respectable. "Few, however, had undertaken to study such a 'common' thing as bullying."

Olweus identified the characteristics of both bullies and their victims. In his 1993 book, *Bullying at School: What We Know and What We Can Do*, he found that bullies have a strong need to dominate and subdue other students and to get their own way; are impulsive and easily angered; are often defiant and aggressive toward adults, including parents and teachers and show little empathy toward students who are victimized. If they are boys, he observes, they are physically stronger than other boys in general.[45]

According to Olweus, victims generally are cautious, sensitive, quiet, withdrawn and shy, and are often anxious, insecure, unhappy and have low self-esteem. They also are depressed and "engage in suicidal ideation" much more often than their peers. "Often they do not have a single good friend and relate better to adults than to peers. If they are boys, they may be physically weaker than their peers. These characteristics are likely to be both a partial cause and a consequence of the bullying."

Another, smaller group of victims, called provocative victims or bully-victims, often has reading and writing problems and attention deficit-hyperactivity disorder characteristics.[46] "The behavior of the bully-victims tends to elicit negative reactions from many students in the classroom, and the teacher often dislikes them also," Olweus writes.

As all the experts have pointed out, the rash of school violence in the 1990s — punctuated by the Columbine

Katy Otto, Empower's director of grants and community outreach.

However, educators and administrators have little jurisdiction over events that happen outside of school grounds, often preventing schools from punishing online bullies, Aftab says. Most cyberbullying cases are not serious enough to warrant police involvement, she adds, further limiting a school's options.

A California-based Web site — schoolscandals.com — showed just how insidious and hurtful online bullying can be. In 2003 parents and school administrators discovered the site had become a breeding ground for hate speech and harassment. Parents and school administrators called for the site's closure, but had little luck. Police were unable to take action. Eventually the site was taken down after a radio station got involved and put enough pressure on the people running the site.[4]

But schoolscandals2.com is already up and running, and kids have already begun using it to cyberbully. "She wears like the same shorts everyday, dresses like a guy and has the ugliest face ever. She has a guy's voice, too! Yuck," wrote a Southern California middle-school student in May 2004.[5]

Similarly, in Chappaqua, N.Y., a wealthy New York City suburb, two senior boys created a Web site with offensive, personal information about students in 2001. Principal Kathy Mason called local police and suspended the boys for five days. But prosecutors said that while the site was "offensive and abhorrent," it did not meet the legal definition of harassment; to widespread community outrage criminal charges against the boys were dropped.[6]

To combat cyberbullying and the limits of school jurisdiction, some schools require students to sign an agreement at the beginning of the year obligating them to use e-mail and the Internet ethically. "Signing a contract is an excellent way to get the point across to the kids," Franke says. "We also recommend that schools get the contracts notarized so that students understand the severity and importance of what they are signing."

Students at Fox's high school must sign a contract each year, and the school monitors its wireless network for cyber offenses. "Last year, about 20 freshman girls were caught spreading rumors through e-mail," Fox says.

In the final analysis, however, most experts agree that fighting cyberbullying isn't that different from standing up to traditional bullying: Teach kids to report incidents to adults and not to respond to the bully's taunts. "If kids are going to have the power of the technology, they have to have the judgment to go with it," Aftab says. "They must learn how to use the filter between their ears to think before they click."

— Kate Templin

[1] i-SAFE America, www.isafe.org.

[2] David Finkelhor, *et al.*, "Highlights of Youth Internet Safety Survey," U.S. Department of Justice, March 2001.

[3] *Ibid.*

[4] Erika Hayasaki and Jia-Rui Chong, "Parents Rally to Stop 'Cyber Bullying," *Los Angeles Times*, April 17, 2003, p. B1.

[5] www.schoolscandals2.com.

[6] Amy Benfer, "Cyber slammed," *Salon.com*, July 3, 2001.

shootings — focused public attention on the problem and prompted a burst of new research on the dangers of bullying.

"In the wake of Columbine and a lot of other high-profile incidents," NICHD's Nansel says, "people wanted to know how much of a problem was posed by [students] who were victimized becoming violent." The study Nansel and her colleagues released in 2003 found that, while bullying victims were slightly more likely than other students to carry a weapon to school and exhibit other risk factors, the bullies themselves showed a much higher rate of violent behavior than either their victims or uninvolved people.

Nansel's group concluded — as have virtually all of the social scientists who've studied the problem in recent years — that bullying is a significant problem that despite all the sound and fury still has not received sufficient attention.[47]

Changing Society

Some experts blame bullying on the changes that have transformed society over the last few generations. For example, the anonymity provided by modern schools — often featuring large, unmonitored common areas — is frequently cited as a major reason bullies feel they can get away with abusive behavior. And the extra demands that education-reform measures have imposed on teachers often keep them too busy to be monitors.

"We used to think teachers stood in the hallway," Nansel says, "but now that doesn't really happen, because

Getty Images/Jacob Silberberg

Miss America Erika Harold says that when she was a teenager, teachers and school officials ignored her pleas for help in dealing with bullies. She devoted her reign in 2003 to representing the anti-bullying program Fight Crime: Invest in Kids.

teachers are so stressed about what they need to accomplish in the classroom. It leaves kids a lot of time when [they] are on their own."

Others blame deeper cultural forces, specifically a society that seems to condone or reward rudeness and/or abusiveness by successful people. In some "reality" television shows, for instance, those who shout at their peers and are the most manipulative and backstabbing are often the ones who triumph.

Indeed, teenage bullies are often the most popular kids in school, according to a study published in 2003 in *Pediatrics*. After surveying students and teachers in ethnically diverse urban schools, the researchers concluded that teenage bullies — contrary to some stereotypes — "do not feel depressed, anxious, or lonely" because they enjoy "high social status within their peer collective." But classmates would rather not spend time with them, the survey found, indicating that perhaps "the social prestige of bullies is motivated in part by fear."[48]

However, the authors continued, "When bullies are considered the 'coolest,' bullying behavior is encouraged" — underscoring the need to address bullying as a systemic problem that involves the entire school community.

Other research has found that comprehensive, school-wide, anti-bullying programs are most effective when they raise the awareness of how bystanders contribute to the bullying problem and aim to change peer dynamics that encourage the practice. Even when bystanders simply provide an audience of onlookers, they indirectly support bullying by providing the public acceptance that supports its perceived legitimacy and importance," researcher Slaby wrote. In a recent study, bystander peers were present in 88 percent of childhood bullying episodes, but a bystander intervened in less than one-fifth of the cases.[49]

Many anti-bullying programs, such as County Attorney Backstrom's in Minnesota, focus on teaching bystanders the importance of intervening, and how to do it. Many children and adolescents who become bystanders to bullying don't know what to say or do to stop the abuse. Or they may be reluctant to break a perceived "code of silence" or fearful of becoming victimized themselves. In some schools, bullies and their supporters directly intimidate bystanders into silence by stating, "snitches get stitches," according to Slaby.

Recent research has also shed light on how bullying affects those who both get bullied and bully others. Compared with bullies and their victims, bully-victims seem to have the worst of both worlds and a unique risk profile, UCLA's Juvonen and her colleagues have found. "Their high levels of social avoidance, conduct problems and school difficulties suggest that they are a particularly high-risk group," said the study. Other studies have shown that bully-victims are most vulnerable to psychiatric disorders and best fit the profiles of seriously violent offenders.[50]

Learned Behavior

It is now thought — contrary to the beliefs of several decades ago — that bullies are made, not born.

"The majority of bullies come from homes that are abusive and violent, where parents are authoritarian, inconsistent, negative or indifferent," and where there is "too little love and too much rejection," writes Delwyn

Tattum, an anti-bullying expert at the University of Wales Institute, in Cardiff.[51]

But outside of the home, bullies' "teachers" are everywhere, says Colman McCarthy, a former *Washington Post* columnist and founder of the Center for Teaching Peace, who has conducted classes in non-violent conflict resolution in high schools, colleges, universities and law schools for more than 20 years. "Like all types of violence, bullying is a learned behavior," McCarthy continues. "And there are many types: physical bullying, which people associate with schoolchildren; verbal bullying, which especially occurs in marriages; international bullying, when a powerful, militaristic nation bullies other nations; and there's environmental bullying, when corporations dominate a community. But it's usually associated with schoolyard bullies, who often learn it from a male figure in their lives, at home, and then there are gangs' teaching-the-initiate type of bullying."

But humans are not born with a propensity to bully, McCarthy contends. "I do a lot of death penalty-type work, and I've interviewed many killers. Almost all of them come from highly dysfunctional backgrounds," he says. "They learn how to be violent from all kinds of places, but we teach it in very subtle ways."

Andrea Cohn and Andrea Canter at the National Association of School Psychologists, agree. Bullying is "learned through influences in the environment, such as the home, school, peer groups and even the media, which means that it can also be unlearned or, better yet, prevented," they write.[52]

Is Your Child Being Bullied?

Children who are bullied often tell no one about their misery out of shame, fear of retaliation or feelings of hopelessness. Experts say parents should be aware of the following signs of victimization:

- Subtle changes in behavior (withdrawn, anxious, preoccupied, loss of interest in school and favorite activities)
- Comes home from school with bruises and scratches, torn or dirtied clothing or with missing or damaged books and property
- Loss of appetite
- Excessive trips to the school nurse
- Inability to sleep, bad dreams, crying in sleep
- Repeatedly loses clothing, money, or other valuables
- Appears afraid or reluctant to go to school in the morning
- Repeated headaches or stomachaches — particularly in the morning
- Chooses a roundabout or strange route to and from school
- Feels lonely
- Sensitive or withdrawn when asked about his or her day
- Big appetite after school (perhaps because lunch or lunch money was taken)
- Reluctant to take the school bus

Source: Tara L. Kuther, National PTA, accessed online Jan. 31, 2005

CURRENT SITUATION

Christian Opposition

Hoping to teach children to reject bullying behavior, at least 16 states have adopted legislation aimed at recommending or requiring schools to institute anti-bullying programs.

Besides Colorado, Washington and Oregon were among the first states to react after the Columbine incident, followed by Michigan, Massachusetts and others. Several states have required more adult oversight of lunchrooms and playgrounds, hired "school climate" directors and established procedures for reporting bullying. The "Dignity in All Schools Act" requires New York City schools to get more accurate reporting about the problem.

In the beginning, not all of these efforts went smoothly. Legislators had to deal with the problem that bullying "has been around for a long time and can be defined in a number of different ways," the NCSL's Thomerson said.[53]

In Providence, R.I., for instance, the school board in March 2004 redefined bullying after the American Civil Liberties Union (ACLU) said the school board's original definition was vague and could endanger free speech. The new rule now says: "Bullying occurs when a student, while at school, intentionally assaults, batters, threatens, harasses,

AP Photo/Tom Strattman

Brittni Ainsworth, a high school sophomore in Plainfield, Ind., hopes that proposed state legislation requiring schools to adopt anti-bullying policies will stop the girls who bullied her and others.

stalks, menaces, intimidates, extorts, humiliates or taunts another student; verbal abuse to include teasing, name-calling and harmful gossip; emotional abuse to include humiliation, shunning and exclusion."[54]

Conservative Christian groups, however, have mounted stiff resistance to anti-bullying programs. In northeastern Kentucky, for instance, hundreds of students either refused to attend tolerance training sessions or skipped school the day the program was offered because they felt the anti-harassment workshops were intended to promote acceptance of homosexuality.[55]

Similarly, conservative Christians opposed Washington state's anti-bullying legislation on the grounds that it would promote homosexuality and threatened free speech — specifically students' rights to condemn homosexuality. "[The proposed law] looked like it could be [used against] people who might speak out against behavior," Rick Forcier, director of the Christian Coalition of Washington, said. The legislation might lead to homosexual sensitivity training in schools, he added.[56]

Similar objections were raised when Maryland tried in 2003 to require local school boards to prohibit harassment based on any distinguishing characteristic, including sexual orientation. Supporters — including the Free State Justice Coalition and the Gay, Lesbian and Straight Education Network — described numerous incidents of taunting, name-calling and intimidation, by teachers as well as students, based on sexual orientation. The legislation, they argued, would make it clear that such activity is wrong.

But the nonpartisan group TakeBackMaryland — which seeks to return Maryland to "biblical foundations" — said the bill went too far. "What are we going to do? Go after every kid who says something some other kid doesn't like?" asked Tres Kerns, the group's chairman.[57]

Maryland Pastor David Whitney argued that such tolerance training "is not the jurisdiction of the government."[58] Republican Gov. Robert Ehrlich eventually vetoed the bill, saying its requirement that county school boards report incidents of harassment and intimidation would create more paperwork for administrators without making schools safer.[59]

Sprigg, at the Family Research Council, says his organization agrees that students should never be subjected to "unprovoked violence or to the use of abusive epithets for any reason — including sexual orientation." Such behavior should be prohibited by school disciplinary codes, which should be strictly enforced, he says. However, explicitly banning harassment based on sexual orientation teaches that "there is nothing wrong with being gay or lesbian," he says. Thus, anti-bullying rules "are being used as a Trojan horse to get to a larger pro-homosexual agenda."

Most anti-bullying legislation, he says, appears to punish thoughts or motivation behind behavior instead of focusing on actions. "An expression of opinion — saying we believe that homosexual behavior is wrong — is treated as a form of name calling or bullying."

For example, he says, one student opposed to homosexuality wore a T-shirt emblazoned with the slogan "straight pride" to school during a week in which the school's gay students were engaging in "gay pride" activities. The boy was punished and forced to change his shirt by administrators who said the slogan was offensive. "That's not an equal treatment of equal viewpoints," Sprigg says. "The words 'straight pride' are not a vulgar epithet, but they were treated as such."

Newman, of Fight Crime: Invest in Kids, defends anti-bullying programs, saying, "It's one thing to engage in legitimate debate. It's another thing to harass other students. Harassment and bullying shouldn't be tolerated regardless of the grounds."

AT ISSUE

Do anti-bullying programs promote homosexuality?

YES

Peter Sprigg
Senior Director of Policy Studies, Family Research Council

From testimony before House Ways and Means Committee, Maryland House of Delegates, Feb. 19, 2003.

Pro-homosexual activists contend that our schools have large numbers of students who are gay, lesbian, bisexual or transgendered (GLBT) and are frequent victims of verbal or physical harassment or even acts of violence. They argue, therefore, that victims of harassment or violence targeted for their real or perceived "sexual orientation" should be singled out for specific protection under school disciplinary codes.

Yet there is evidence that harassment of gay teens may neither be as frequent, as severe, nor as disproportionate, as some pro-homosexual rhetoric would suggest. The majority of gay teens (58 percent), according to a Gay, Lesbian and Straight Education Network (GLSEN) survey, reported no incidents of "physical harassment" in the past year (only 15 percent claimed to have experienced this "frequently" or "often").

Pro-family groups such as the Family Research Council agree wholeheartedly that no student should ever be the victim of unprovoked violence (or taunting) — for their sexual orientation or for any other reason. We believe that such behavior should be prohibited by school disciplinary codes, and that those codes should be strictly enforced.

However, singling out "sexual orientation" for special protection cannot be justified on logical grounds, and it could have consequences not clear at first glance. Lumping "sexual orientation" together with "race, color, national origin, sex and disability" for special protection is illogical because the latter qualities are inborn (except for some disabilities), involuntary, immutable and innocuous — none of which is true of homosexuality, despite the claims of its advocates.

Evidence that homosexuality is inborn (that is, unalterably determined by genetics or biology) is ephemeral at best; while same-sex attractions may come unbidden, homosexual behavior and adoption of a "gay" identity are clearly voluntary; the existence of numerous "former homosexuals" proves that homosexuality is changeable; and the numerous pathologies associated with homosexuality demonstrate how harmful it is.

If all forms of harassment are wrong, then all forms of harassment — without distinction — should be banned. When harassment based on sexual orientation is explicitly banned, school staffs and students are inevitably trained that the reason such harassment is wrong is not because all harassment is wrong or because all people should be treated with respect, but because "there is nothing wrong with being gay or lesbian."

NO

James Garbarino, Ph.D.
E. L. Vincent Professor of Human Development, Cornell University

Written for *The CQ Researcher*, January 2005

About 10 percent of Americans are gay and lesbian, and research shows that other than their sexual orientation there is little or nothing to differentiate them from the other 90 percent. What is more, the scientific consensus is that sexual orientation is a biologically based trait. That alone should be enough to sustain the claim to full human rights for gay and lesbian kids. Anti-bullying programs don't promote homosexuality. What they promote is basic respect for human rights.

Why pay special attention to the bullying of gay and lesbian kids? Research shows that gay and lesbian kids are disproportionately victimized by peers: five times more likely to miss school because they feel unsafe, four times as likely to be threatened with a weapon at school and three times as likely to be hurt so badly in a fight that they need medical treatment, according to a recent study.

The fact that adult bias and religious fundamentalism sustain and validate homophobic attacks is all the more reason to make efforts to deal with them as part of any community's initiative to protect children from harm at school. In fact, they should fall under the No Child Left Behind Act's provisions concerning the right to be protected in "persistently dangerous" schools: Studies of school shooters compiled by the FBI and Secret Service, among others, document that bullying (and particularly homophobic bullying) has been a contributing factor in severe school violence.

As our national consciousness of human rights issues evolves, we naturally include more and more people in our circle of caring. African-Americans were once outside the circle. Now no one but the most retrograde racist will tolerate overt racial discrimination in the form of verbal slurs, exclusionary policies and hateful assault aimed against children and youth.

Currently, gay and lesbian individuals are singled out for special negative treatment in American public life — such as being the target of state and national legislation and constitutional amendments to prevent them from exercising the basic human right of marriage (a right denied on racist grounds in the not-too-distant past when racially mixed marriages were prohibited).

Fifty years from now, we will experience the same regret for opposition to programs protecting gay and lesbian kids that all good-hearted people do now when they consider our racist past.

Kids Call Bullying the Biggest Problem

Two-thirds of the older children and more than half the younger ones say bullying and teasing are the biggest problems at their schools, according to the Kaiser Family Foundation.

Percentage of Children Who Say Each of the Following Is a Big Problem in School

	Ages 8 to 11	Ages 12 to 15
Teasing and bullying	55%	68%
Discrimination	41	63
Violence	46	62
Alcohol or drugs	44	68
Pressure to have sex	33	49

Source: Kaiser Family Foundation, "Talking With Kids About Tough Issues"

James Garbarino, a professor of human development at Cornell University and coauthor of the 2002 book *And Words Can Hurt Forever: How to Protect Adolescents From Bullying, Harassment, and Emotional Violence*, says rules giving special consideration to the bullying of homosexuals are needed because gays are disproportionately victimized by their peers. A student survey conducted by the National Mental Health Association found that gay kids — and those thought to be gay — are bullied more than any other group except overweight kids. Nine out of 10 respondents said they hear other kids use words like "fag," "homo," "dyke," "queer" or "gay" at least once in a while, with 51 percent hearing them every day.[60]

Gay students are also three-to-seven times more likely to attempt suicide; five times more likely to miss school because they feel unsafe; four times as likely to be threatened with a weapon at school, and three times as likely to be hurt so badly in a fight that they need medical attention, according to Garbarino. (*See "At Issue," p. 147.*)

Federal Law

While anti-bullying legislation has been primarily a state and local affair, in summer 2004 Reps. John Shimkus, R-Ill., and Danny Davis, D-Ill., proposed the first federal law to address the problem. Although the bill failed to advance in the last Congress, Shimkus says he will reintroduce it this session.

The bill required schools that receive funds under the Safe and Drug Free Schools Act to create bullying and harassment-prevention programs. Currently, those funds can be used to promote school safety but are not specifically earmarked for anti-bullying programs.

The bill did not authorize any new funds for bullying-prevention programs, but law enforcement officials say anti-bullying programs could be a cost-effective way to reduce school violence because they help nip violence in the bud. "Bullying creates a cycle of violence," says Newman of Fight Crime: Invest in Kids. "Bullies are six times more likely to be convicted of crime later on."

Nearly every school district has a Safe and Drug Free Schools coordinator, Newman's organization points out, each of whom could be trained as an anti-bullying trainer for their school district at a one-time cost of $4,000. By comparison, the group says, every high-risk juvenile prevented from adopting a life of crime could save the country between $1.7 million and $2.3 million.[61]

Other groups, such as the AAUW, are using another federal law — Title IX of the Education Amendments of 1972 — to address bullying. Title IX prohibits sexual harassment of female students, which AAUW calls a "close cousin" of bullying, so the AAUW is encouraging schools to make sure their Title IX coordinators are aware of the connection between sexual harassment and bullying.

"As far as bullying and sexual harassment are concerned, it's difficult to talk about one without talking about the other," AAUW's Annexstein, says. The group views sexual harassment primarily as a college and workplace issue but defines bullying as a K-12 issue. "We're seeing evidence of bullying at very young ages, and that's troubling on a lot of levels."

However, she says, most parents of bullied kids do not yet understand that when bullying has sexual overtones, it becomes sexual harassment — a federal crime.

Lisa Soronen, a staff attorney at the National School Boards Association, thinks increased attention to sexual-harassment issues in the workplace may have made parents less tolerant of sexual taunts directed at their children. "After the sexual harassment debate," she said, "we decided kids shouldn't have to tolerate nasty behavior."[62]

OUTLOOK

Going to Court

As recent lawsuits indicate, parents increasingly are suing their children's schools and school districts, contending they ignored parental complaints about bullies.

"It's every school administrator's nightmare," writes Santa Barbara, Calif., attorney Mary Jo McGrath. "The phone rings and on the other end of is an angry parent threatening to sue because his child was injured in a bullying incident that took place at school."[63]

The NEA's Newberry also expects more suits to be brought against the bullies themselves. "Boys will be boys, but a felony is a felony, and you can't hit someone or beat someone up without facing the consequences," he says. "That's the next step that we as a society have to take."

Barker, of the NEA's National Bullying Awareness Campaign, agrees. "Kids sometimes do things that adults are arrested and jailed for," she says. "If it gets to that point, you have to get the police involved."

Newman, of Fight Crime: Invest in Kids, says if the schools aren't responsive or the bullying amounts to physical assault, it's "perfectly legitimate" to file a lawsuit. "Assault is assault wherever it takes place."

However, he would prefer that the schools deal with the bullying long before the situation reaches that point. "Preventing kids from becoming bullies and intervening to get bullies back on track can not only protect children from the pain that bullying inflicts immediately but also can protect all of us from crime later on," he says. Newman and others believe strongly that education, training and "attitude adjustment" can solve the problem of bullying, even as serious and pervasive as it is.

"There's always more that can be done," says Feinberg of the National Association of School Psychologists. "We need to increase the basic anti-bullying message to every school district in the country, because I'm sure there are some who still believe the mythical notion that bullying is just a rite of passage that everybody goes through.

"But in general the message has been received, and people know that for it to be effective it has to be given to all the stakeholders involved — students, teachers, community leaders, administrators and parents — so they can all work collaboratively to eliminate, or at least reduce, the problem."

As to the future, he says, the biggest problem will be sustainability. "In our society, yesterday's news is old news. We have to make sure that our awareness of the problem doesn't fade because other things come into play."

Newberry hopes the rigorous new academic demands of the No Child Left Behind Act will not cause teachers and schools to lose their focus on social concerns. "That's going to be a kind of Catch-22," he says. "But, if you compare what's being done now with what was being done five or 10 years ago, I think we've made a gigantic leap in the right direction."

He also worries about the major changes occurring in students' home lives. "Twenty or 30 years ago, parents were able to spend two to three times as much time with their kids in the family room and at the breakfast or dinner table than they do now," he says. "We've lost the adult mentor for such things as social etiquette, manners, problem solving and communications skills, and as a result kids are not getting their emotional needs met at home. Look at the growth in gangs, which, by definition, are kids trying to create a family for themselves.

Indiana state Sen. Tom Wyss proposed anti-bullying legislation after seeing a television news investigation on school bullying in his state. "There was story after story of harassment of kids who are gay or effeminate," he recalls; "of kids getting beaten up; of girls saying things on the Internet like so-and-so is sleeping with so and so. I'm 62, and I was sitting there thinking, 'If I had bullied someone when I was a youngster, my parents would have gotten a phone call from school immediately, and they would have read the riot act to me.'"

"So the challenge for all of us is to create a team of parents, relatives, community leaders and schools who work together to help young people face adult responsibility and become adult leaders, and then good parents themselves," Newberry adds.

Davidson, the former North Carolina school board member whose son was bullied, advocates continual vigilance. "There are all sorts of reasons for tuning into this problem, because ultimately we will pay for it in some fashion if we don't. It's just the right thing to do: If a kid reaches out for help, we have to try to reach back."[64]

NOTES

1. Katy St. Clair, "The Bullying Industrial Complex Gets Touchy-Feely with Mean Girls and Boys," *East Bay Express*, June 16, 2004; see also Margie Mason, "Study: Anti-gay bullying widespread in America's schools," SFGate.com, Dec. 12, 2002.
2. Bob Gibson, "Student's suffering spurs two bully bills," [Charlottesville, Va.] *Daily Progress*, Jan. 18, 2005.
3. Heather Hollingsworth, "Parents turn to courts to stop bullying of their children by peers," The Associated Press, May 22, 2004.
4. Quoted in Michelle Boorstein, "In Suit, Va. Teen Accuses Schoolmates of Bullying," *The Washington Post*, Nov. 7, 2004, p. C1.
5. "Are We Safe?" National Crime Prevention Council, 2000.
6. T. R. Nansel, *et al.*, "Bullying behaviors among U.S. youth: Prevalence and association with psychosocial adjustment," *Journal of the American Medical Association*, April 25, 2001, pp. 2094-2100.
7. Jeff Kass, "Witnesses Tell of Columbine Bullying," *The Rocky Mountain News*, Oct. 3, 2000.
8. "Threat assessment in schools: a guide to managing threatening situations and to creating safe school climates," U.S. Secret Service and U.S. Department of Education, May 2002.
9. Linda Lumsden, "Preventing Bullying," ERIC Digest 155, Clearinghouse on Educational Policy Management, College of Education, University of Oregon, February 2002. The 16 states are: Arkansas, California, Colorado, Connecticut, Georgia, Illinois, Louisiana, Nevada, New Hampshire, New Jersey, Oklahoma, Rhode Island, Vermont, Washington, Oregon and West Virginia.
10. Sandra Feldman, "Bullying Prevention," Teacher to Teacher: Issues Affecting the Classroom Teacher, March, 2004, www.aft.org/teachers/t2t/0304.htm.
11. Peter K. Smith and Sonia Sharp, *School Bullying: Insights and Perspectives* (1994).
12. Robert Garofalo, *et al.*, "The Association Between Health Risk Behaviors and Sexual Orientation Among a School-based Sample of Adolescents," *Pediatrics*, Vol. 101, 1998; National Survey of Teens Shows Anti-Gay Bullying Common in Schools," U.S. Newswire, Dec. 12, 2002.
13. Patrik Jonsson, "Schoolyard bullies and their victims: The picture fills out," *The Christian Science Monitor*, May 12, 2004, p.1.
14. *Ibid.*
15. *Ibid.*
16. Nansel, *op. cit.*
17. Quoted on CBS News, "The Early Show," Oct. 17, 2000.
18. Ronald G. Slaby, "The Role of Bystanders in Preventing Bullying," *Health in Action* (forthcoming).
19. Hollingsworth, *op. cit.*
20. Boorstein, *op. cit.*
21. *Ibid.*
22. Bureau of Justice Statistics, www.atriumsoc.org/pages/bullyingstatistics.html.
23. U.S. Secret Service, *op. cit.*
24. Boorstein, *op. cit.*
25. Namsel, *op. cit.*
26. Bureau of Justice Statistics, *op. cit.*
27. Nickelodeon, Kaiser Family Foundation and International Communications Research, "Talking with kids about tough issues: A national survey of parents and kids," March 8, 2001.
28. Nansel, *op. cit.*
29. *Ibid.*
30. *Ibid.*
31. James Alan Fox, *et al.*, "Bullying Prevention Is Crime Prevention," Fight Crime: Invest in Kids, 2003.
32. National Association of School Psychologists, www.nasponline.org.
33. Jonsson, *op. cit.*
34. Jeff Holtz, "Parents File Lawsuit Over Bullying of Daughter," *The New York Times*, Jan. 9, 2005, Section 14CN, p. 2.
35. Jonsson, *op. cit.* (Davidson quote); Carolyn Norton, "Policy Against Bullying Drafted," *The Chapel Hill Herald*, Dec. 27, 2004, p. 1.

36. For background, see Kathy Koch, "Zero Tolerance," *The CQ Researcher*, March 10, 2000, pp. 185-208.
37. For background, see Kenneth Jost, "Testing in Schools," *The CQ Researcher*, April 20, 2001, pp. 321-344.
38. Quoted in Catherine Lee, "Getting Tough on Bullies," www.jrn.columbia.edu/studentwork/children/downlow/bullies.shtml.
39. Quoted in Andrew Baroch, "Legislators Try to Outlaw School Bullies," *Voice of America*, March 28, 2001 truthnews.net/culture/2001_03_bully.html.
40. American Psychological Association Monitor, www.apa.org/monitor/oct04/bullying.html.
41. Ken Rigby, *New Perspectives on Bullying* (2002).
42. *Ibid.*
43. Smith and Sharp, *op. cit.*
44. Rigby, *op. cit.*
45. Dan Olweus, *Bullying at School: What We Know and What We Can Do* (1993).
46. For background, see Kathy Koch, "Rethinking Ritalin," *The CQ Researcher*, Oct. 22, 1999, pp. 905-928.
47. Nansel, *op. cit.*
48. Jaana Juvonen, *et al.*, "Bullying Among Young Adolescents: The Strong, the Weak, and the Troubled," *Pediatrics*, December 2003, pp. 1231-1237.
49. Slaby, *op. cit.*
50. Juvonen, *op. cit.*
51. See Delwyn Tattum and Graham Herbert, *Bullying: A Positive Approach* (1990).
52. Andrea Cohn and Andrea Canter, "Bullying: Facts for Schools and Parents," National Association for School Psychologists, 2003.
53. Quoted in Baroch, *op. cit.*
54. Cathleen F. Crowley, "Board adopts new anti-bullying policy," *The Providence Journal*, March 10, 2004, p. C1.
55. Family Research Council, www.frc.org, Dec. 3, 2004.
56. Mary Ann Zehr, "Legislatures Take on Bullies With New Laws," *Education Week*, May 16, 2001.
57. Steven Dennis, "Bullying Bill Turns Into Gay Rights Flap," *The Gazette*, Feb. 21, 2003, www.gazette.net/200308/weekend/a_section/145455-1.html.
58. *Ibid.*
59. Matthew Mosk, "Ehrlich Vetoes Tuition Bill," *The Washington Post*, May 26, 2004, p. B1.
60. "What Does Gay Mean?" Teen Survey, National Mental Health Association, Dec. 12, 2002.
61. M. A. Cohen, "The Monetary Value of Saving a High-Risk Youth," *Journal of Quantitative Criminology*, Vol. 14, 1998, p. 5-33.
62. Hollingsworth, *op. cit.*
63. Mary Jo McGrath, "Capping the Heavy Price for Bullying," www.aasa.org/publications/sa/200304/focus_McGrath.htm.
64. Quoted in Jonsson, *op. cit.*

BIBLIOGRAPHY

Books

Hazler, Richard J., *Breaking the Cycle of Violence: Interventions for Bullying and Victimization, Taylor & Francis*, 1996.
A professor of counselor education at the University of Ohio in Athens looks at the problems faced by bullies and their victims and how these experiences color the rest of their lives.

Juvonen, Jaana, and Sandra Graham, eds., *Peer Harassment in School: The Plight of the Vulnerable and the Victimized, Guilford Press*, 2001.
Two University of California, Los Angeles (UCLA) professors have compiled essays by an impressive list of international contributors focusing on bullies rather than their victims.

Olweus, Dan, *Bullying at School: What We Know and What We Can Do About It, Blackwell Publishers*, 1993.
This definitive work is based on large-scale studies and other research by the author, who heads Norway's Research Center for Health Promotion at the University of Bergen.

Rigby, Ken, *New Perspectives on Bullying, Jessica Kingsley Publishers*, 2002.
An adjunct associate professor of social psychology at the University of South Australia and an oft-cited authority

on bullying draws on his extensive research into bullying in different countries, societies and social settings.

Smith, Peter K., Debra Pepler and Ken Rigby, *Bullying in Schools: How Successful Can Interventions Be? Cambridge University Press*, 2004.
This collection of studies by leading researchers examines the failures and successes of numerous anti-bullying efforts.

Smith, Peter K., and Sonia Sharp, *School Bullying: Insights and Perspectives, Routledge*, 1994.
A professor of psychology at the University of Sheffield (Smith) and an educational psychologist provide a good primer for understanding the causes of bullying and the scientific methodology used to study it.

Articles

"School Bullying is Nothing New, But Psychologists Identify New Ways to Prevent It," *Psychology Matters*, American Psychological Association Web site, www.psychologymatters.org/bullying.html.
The online newsletter provides a comprehensive overview of bullying and suggests ways to stop it.

Esplanage, Dorothy L., Ph.D., "Bullying in Early Adolescence: The Role of the Peer Group," *ERIC Clearinghouse on Elementary and Early Childhood Education*, November 2002.
Peers play an important role in perpetuating — and stopping — bullying, points out a well-known author in the field.

Jones, Adrienne, "Thwarting Bullies Proves Tough Work," *The Age, Ltd.*, Nov. 22, 2004.
Most anti-bullying programs achieve only modest improvements.

Makwana, Rachel R., "Bullying Victims Turn More to Courts," *The* [Conn.] *Record-Journal*, July 7, 2004.
Some parents have begun suing their children's schools, claiming they ignored repeated complaints about bullying and abuse.

Peterson, Karen S., "When School Hurts," *USA Today*, April 10, 2001.
U.S. schools, parents and government officials have slowly realized that bullying can cause long-lasting damage to children and bystanders.

Peterson, Karen S., "Net Broadens Reach of Kids' Rumors, Insults," *USA Today*, April 10, 2001.
Bullies have taken their vicious practices to the Internet.

Reports and Studies

"Bullying is Not a Fact of Life," *National Mental Health Information Center, U.S. Department of Health and Human Services*, www.mentalhealth.samhsa.gov/publications/allpubs/SVP-0052/.
This compact report includes information for parents and schools about bullying and how to deal with it.

"Hostile Hallways: Bullying, Teasing, and Sexual Harassment in School," *American Association of University Women, AAUW Educational Foundation*, May 2001.
Bullying is closely related to sexual harassment — a federal crime — if it is sexually based, according to the women's group.

Fox, James Alan, et al., "Bullying Prevention Is Crime Prevention: A Report by Fight Crime: Invest in Kids," 2003.
Preventing bullying at an early age is a cost-effective way to short-circuit a life of crime, according to this group of police, sheriffs, district attorneys and crime victims.

Nansel, T. R., et al., "Bullying Behavior Among U.S. Youth: Prevalence and Association with Psychological Adjustment," *Journal of the American Medical Association*, April 21, 2001, pp. 2094-2100.
This scientific paper based on research done in the two years just before Columbine was updated in 2003.

For More Information

American Association of School Administrators, 801 N. Quincy St., Suite 700, Arlington, VA 22203-1730; (703) 528-0700; www.aasa.org.

American School Counselor Association, 1101 King St., Suite 625, Alexandria, VA 22314; (703) 683-ASCA; www.schoolcounselor.org.

National Association of Elementary School Principals, 1615 Duke St., Alexandria, VA 22314-3483; (703) 684-3345; www.naesp.org.

National Association of School Psychologists, 4340 East-West Highway, Suite 402, Bethesda, MD 20814; (301) 657-0270; www.nasponline.org.

National Association of Secondary School Principals, 1904 Association Dr., Reston, VA 20191-1537; (703) 860-0200; www.principals.org.

National Mental Health Association, 2001 N. Beauregard St., 12th Fl., Alexandria, VA 22311; (703) 684-7722; www.nmha.org.

Parents, Families, and Friends of Lesbians and Gays, 1726 M St., N.W., Suite 400, Washington, DC 20036; (202) 467-8180; www.pflag.org.

7

Student Rights

Have Courts Gone Too Far or Not Far Enough?

Kenneth Jost

Getty Images/Mark Wilson

A supporter of the group Students for a Sensible Drug Policy demonstrates at the U.S. Supreme Court in March 2007 during arguments in the case of Alaska high-school student Joseph Frederick, who was suspended for displaying his "Bong Hits 4 Jesus" banner during a school-sponsored event off school grounds. In a 5-4 decision, the court upheld schools' power to punish students for advocating or promoting illegal drug use.

From *CQ Researcher*, June 5, 2009.

Savana Redding recalls it as "the most humiliating experience" of her life: the day she was forced to undress to her underwear at her school in Safford, Ariz., in what proved to be a fruitless strip-search for a prescription-strength pain reliever.

Authorities at Safford Middle School were on edge about drugs in fall 2003, partly because a year earlier a student had had a serious reaction to a prescription pill given to him by one of his schoolmates. So assistant principal Kerry Wilson reacted quickly on Oct. 8 when a student handed him what turned out to be a 400-mg ibuprofen tablet and told him the pills were being passed out for students to take at lunchtime.

The student's accusation led first to eighth-grader Marissa Glines, who was found to have several ibuprofen tablets in her wallet. Glines said she had gotten the pills from her classmate Redding. But when Wilson brought Redding to his office, she denied any knowledge of the pills.

A search of her backpack found nothing, but Wilson remained suspicious. He asked his administrative assistant Helen Romero to take Redding to the office of the school nurse, Peggy Schwallier, to look — as the school district's lawyers later put it — "for any pills that might be discreetly hidden in her clothes."

Redding, then 13, was directed first to remove her shoes and socks and then her shirt and pants. With nothing found, she was then told to shake the band on her bra and then the elastic on her underwear. Still nothing.

Redding was never touched, but, as she recalled later, she felt "violated" by the strip-search. Romero allowed her to get dressed and return to class, but the experience was so humiliating that

'Students Are Entitled to Freedom of Expression'

The U.S. Supreme Court's landmark decision in *Tinker v. Des Moines Independent Community School District* decision launched the student-rights era. The 7-2 ruling upheld the right of three middle- and high-school students to wear black armbands to signal their support for a Christmastime cease-fire in the Vietnam War.

"School officials do not possess absolute authority over their students. . . . In the absence of a specific showing of constitutionally valid reasons to regulate their speech, students are entitled to freedom of expression of their views."

Justice Abe Fortas, *Tinker v. Des Moines* (1969) (majority opinion)

"This case . . ., wholly without constitutional reasons in my judgment, subjects all the public schools in the country to the whims and caprices of their loudest-mouthed, but maybe not their brightest, students."

Justice Hugo L. Black, *Tinker v. Des Moines* (1969) (dissenting opinion)

Savana decided to transfer to another school. She says now she developed stomach ulcers as a result.

Nearly six years after the episode, Redding, now 19, sat before the nine justices of the U.S. Supreme Court on April 21 listening as they considered whether the strip-search violated her right under the Fourth Amendment to be free from "unreasonable" searches.[1]

In years past, Redding's grievance would have gone no further than the local school board — if she or her family had complained at all. But for the past 40 years, ever since a landmark Supreme Court decision, student-rights have been a staple on the dockets of state and federal courts up to and including the nation's highest tribunal.

The student-rights era began with a 1969 decision, *Tinker v. Des Moines*, that upheld the right of three middle- and high-school students to wear black armbands to signal their support for a Christmastime cease-fire in the Vietnam War. "It can hardly be argued," Justice Abe Fortas wrote, "that either students or teachers shed their constitutional rights to freedom of speech or expression at the schoolhouse gate."[2]

In the years since, "few realms of educational policy have escaped the courtroom," according to Frederick Hess, director of education policy studies at the American Enterprise Institute (AEI), a conservative think tank in Washington. The Supreme Court has established due process standards for student discipline and some limits on searches of students and their belongings. Today, lower courts are grappling with issues ranging from the free-speech rights of gay — and anti-gay — students and censorship of high-school newspapers to schools' efforts to police students' outside-school postings on the Internet. (*See sidebars, p. 158, p. 165, p. 170.*)

Four decades after *Tinker*, civil liberties advocates say the decision is one to celebrate. "The *Tinker* decision was a watershed moment," says Jamin Raskin, a professor at American University's Washington College of Law and editor of a book on student rights. "The Supreme Court essentially declared that education is about becoming a full-fledged citizen of democracy."[3]

"It seems a strange way to train children to be members of society to tell them that they have fewer rights than others," says Catherine Crump, a staff attorney in the First Amendment Working Group at the American Civil Liberties Union (ACLU). "That doesn't seem like a good way to turn kids into adults who are fully participating members of our democratic society."

Hess, who organized an AEI conference on education-related litigation in October 2008, agrees that recognition of student rights has had some benefits. "It's expected that adolescents will be more expressive," he says. "Bringing some of that into the school environment seems both inevitable and constructive."

On balance, however, Hess says the net impact of student rights has been "a substantial negative." The movement, he says, "has significantly curtailed the ability of educational leaders and classroom teachers to set expectations, enforce discipline or aggressively shape a school culture that is conducive to teaching and learning."[4]

Richard Arum, a professor of sociology at New York University, agrees. "The expansion of students' legal entitlements has not only had unintended consequences on the capacity of schools to socialize youth effectively," Arum writes, "but it has also increased the potential for student dissent in U.S. schools — whether of a political, religious or other ideological character."[5]

Without overruling *Tinker*, the Supreme Court has seemed more and more sympathetic to school administrators' concerns since the 1980s. In a pair of rulings under Chief Justice William H. Rehnquist, the court approved random drug testing for many high school students. And under current Chief Justice John G. Roberts Jr., the court in 2007 ruled that public schools can punish students for advocating or promoting illegal drug use.[6]

Student Speech Cannot Promote Illegal Drug Use

The Supreme Court's 5-4 decision in *Morse v. Frederick* (2007) upheld schools' power to punish students for advocating or promoting illegal drug use. Joseph Frederick, a high school student in Alaska, had been suspended for displaying off school grounds a banner reading "Bong Hits 4 Jesus."

"The question thus becomes whether a principal may, consistent with the First Amendment, restrict student speech at a school event, when that speech is reasonably viewed as promoting illegal drug use. We hold that she may."

Chief Justice John G. Roberts Jr., *Morse v. Frederick* (majority opinion)

"[T]he Court's ham-handed, categorical approach is deaf to the constitutional imperative to permit unfettered debate, even among high-school students, about the wisdom of the war on drugs or of legalizing marijuana for medicinal use."

Justice John Paul Stevens, *Morse v. Frederick* (dissenting opinion)

Representing Redding before the Supreme Court, Adam Wolf, of the ACLU's Drug Law Reform Project, acknowledges public concern about drug use by students. "We all want our schools to be safe and to be drug-free, but that does not give schools carte blanche to do anything they want," Wolf says. "Some policies just clearly cross the line and unreasonably invade student privacy."

But Matthew Wright, the Phoenix lawyer representing the school district, urged the justices to give schools flexibility in dealing with students suspected of using or distributing drugs. Schools are "in the untenable position of either facing the threat of lawsuits for their attempts to enforce a drug-free policy or for their laxity in failing to interdict potentially harmful drugs," Wright said in a statement prior to argument.[7]

As the justices deliberate over the strip-search case, here are some of the broad questions about student rights being debated by educators, parents and students themselves:

Do schools' anti-drug enforcement policies violate students' rights?

Parents in the small north Texas town of Lockney raised alarms in fall 1998 when authorities indicted 11 people for cocaine dealing. Even though none of the suspects was a student, the Lockney school board responded by instituting a program of mandatory drug testing for students in grades six through 12.

Out of 400 families, Larry and Traci Tannahill were the only parents to object to the testing program. On behalf of their then 12-year-old son Bradley, they sued the school district in federal court in Lubbock and won a court ruling in March 2001 barring the program as an unconstitutional invasion of students' rights against unreasonable searches. Judge Sam Cummings ruled the district had shown no special need for what he called an "intrusive" policy.[8]

Drug testing is one of the flash points between public school educators on one hand and student-rights advocates on the other. In Lockney, school officials — on

Are Students' Critical Blog Comments Protected?

Student-rights advocates and school administrators disagree.

Avery Doninger called Burlington, Conn., school administrators "douchebags" in a blog posting and urged readers to complain to the school superintendent. Katherine Evans created a Facebook page calling her English teacher in Pembroke Pines, Fla., "one of the worst teachers I've ever had" and invited other students to share their "hatred" of her on the page.

Both students ended up being punished for their Internet speech even though they wrote the postings off school campuses. Doninger was barred from serving on the student council, Evans suspended for three days and pulled out of honors classes. And both went to federal court, claiming that the disciplinary actions — even if relatively mild — violated their right to free speech.

The Internet had not been invented in 1969 when the Supreme Court issued its landmark decision in *Tinker v. Des Moines* protecting students' free-speech rights unless they disrupted the school or interfered with the rights of others. It was still in its infancy in the 1980s when the court narrowed students' rights by upholding educators' power to punish vulgar speech or to censor student newspapers that were part of the school curriculum.

Today, the Internet age has spawned social-networking sites such as Facebook and MySpace, which are especially popular among high-school students as forums for, among many other things, unfiltered news and comment about school life. And students' use of the sites has forced courts to reconsider the prior assumption that any power to punish student speech ended once students were past the schoolhouse gate.

School administrators say schools not only can but must punish disruptive Internet speech by students. "When there is an impact on the school environment, then I think the school has an obligation to act," says Francisco Negrón, general counsel of the National School Boards Association.

Student-rights advocates disagree. "Students cannot be punished for posting comments online from their home computers criticizing their teachers," says Maria Kayanan, associate legal director of the American Civil Liberties Union of Florida, which is representing Evans in her suit. "Absent a credible threat of harm, criticism is protected by the First Amendment."

Evans was a senior at Pembroke Pines Charter High School in November 2007 when she vented on Facebook about her English teacher, Sarah Phelps. The page drew favorable and unfavorable comments about Phelps until Evans removed it after three days. Evans, now a freshman at the University of Florida, sued to have the disciplinary record removed. She is seeking attorneys' fees but no damages.

City officials in Pembroke Pines have declined to comment on the pending litigation, but school officials in Broward County have generally defended the punishment. "When you start inviting people to say that they hate a teacher, that crosses the line," Pamela Brown, assistant director for the Broward County School District, told *The New York Times*. Pembroke Pines is in Broward County (Fort Lauderdale) and uses the Broward County disciplinary guidelines.[1]

advice of counsel — decided not to appeal the ruling. Instead, they trimmed the testing policy to apply only to students engaged in extracurricular activities. A year later, the U.S. Supreme Court upheld a similar drug testing policy adopted by a school district in Oklahoma.[9]

School officials say random testing helps deter drug use among students and amounts to only a minimal invasion of students' privacy. Anne Proffitt Dupre, a professor at the University of Georgia School of Law in Athens, says the Supreme Court decision validates the argument. "The Supreme Court has said that we can take judicial notice that we have a serious drug problem in our schools and that we can test students in that regard," she says.

The Supreme Court has never ruled on the constitutionality of schoolwide drug testing, but ACLU lawyer Wolf thinks the justices would strike down an unlimited policy. "When a school district tries to analyze the bodily fluids of any and all students, that violates the Constitution," he says.

Opponents add that the limited drug testing program is counterproductive because it may discourage some students from participating in extracurricular activities. "The best way to keep a kid from having a substance

Doninger was a junior at Lewis S. Mills High School in Burlington in spring 2007 when she fumed online about school administrators' decision to cancel a planned student festival. The school responded by barring Doninger from running for reelection as class secretary.

Opposing lawyers in her case take different views of the legal import of the new medium. Thomas R. Gerarde, who represents school officials, says that the online posting amounts to "the student talking to a full audience of the student body because he or she can reach every one of those students." But Jon L. Schoenhorn, Doninger's attorney, counters that the Internet is nothing more than "a bigger soapbox."[2]

Two lower courts sided with the school district. In its decision in May 2008, the Second U.S. Circuit Court of Appeals held that Doninger's posting could be punished because it "created a foreseeable risk of substantial disruption" at her school.

That decision appears to conflict somewhat with a ruling by a federal judge in Pittsburgh in 2007 that nullified a school's punishment of a student for an online parody of the school's principal. "The mere fact that the Internet may be accessed at school does not authorize school officials to become censors of the world-wide web," U.S. District Judge Terrence F. McVerry wrote.[3]

Experts appear to be as divided on the subject as judges. "If it affects what's going on in the school classroom, I think we would say that [schools] would be remiss if they didn't step in," says Anne Proffitt Dupre, a professor at the University of Georgia School of Law in Athens. But Jamin Raskin, a professor at American University's Washington College of Law, says school administrators are waging an impossible fight. "Censorship never works," Raskin says, "and it especially doesn't work in the age of the Internet."

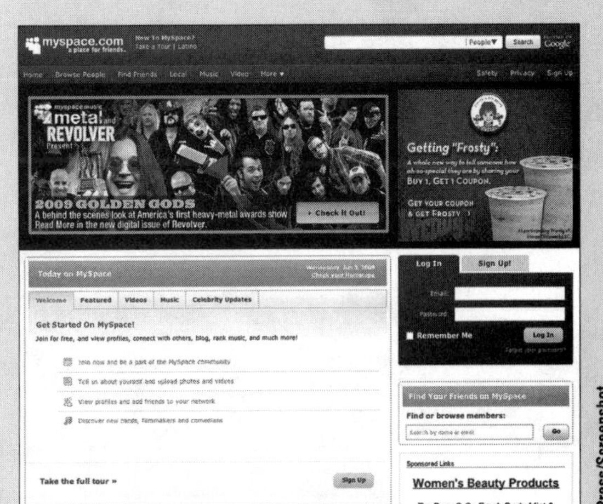

CQ Press/Screenshot

Students' use of social-networking sites such as MySpace has forced courts to reconsider the prior assumption that schools' power to punish student speech ended at the schoolhouse gate.

[1] Quoted in Carmen Gentile, "Student Fights Record of 'Cyberbullying,'" *The New York Times*, Feb. 8, 2009, p. A20. See also Jennifer Moody Piedra, "Student, suspended for blog rant, sues," *The Miami Herald*, Dec. 10, 2008, p. A1. The case is *Evans v. Bayer*, 08-CV61952 (S.D. Fla.); the complaint is on the ACLU-Florida Web site: www.aclufl.org/news_events/?action=viewRelease&emailAlertID=3689.

[2] Quoted in Arielle Levin Becker, "Web Speech: When May Schools Act?" *The Hartford Courant*, Feb. 1, 2009, p. A1. Some other background also drawn from story. The decision is *Doninger v. Niehoff*, 527 F.3d 41 (2nd Cir. 2008).

[3] The decision is *Layshock v. Hermitage School Dist.*, 496 F.Supp 2d 587 (W.D. Pa. 2007).

abuse problem is to keep them occupied [after school]," says Kris Krane, executive director of Students for Sensible Drug Policy. "If they're unsupervised and unoccupied, they're much more likely to get involved in substance abuse."

Krane also criticizes the zero-tolerance policies adopted in many school districts — policies that in some cases prescribe suspensions for seemingly minor drug-related violations.[10] "Zero-tolerance policies break down trust between students and their superiors at schools," says Krane, who joined the 10-year-old organization in 2006 after having previously worked with the National Organization for the Reform of Marijuana Laws (NORML). The policies, he says, "discourage students from talking with teachers, principals, guidance counselors."

"Some local communities prefer zero-tolerance policies, some do not," says Francisco Negron, general counsel of the National School Boards Association. "What is clear is that schools need to have a tool to ensure the safety of their kids."

Many experts, however, think schools go too far with their anti-drug policies. "I can understand why schools would adopt some policies to try to prevent dangerous

To Bong or Not to Bong

Joseph Frederick (above), a student at Juneau-Douglas High School in Alaska, was given a 10-day suspension for displaying his "Bong Hits 4 Jesus" banner on Jan. 24, 2002 (top). In a 5-4 decision in 2007, the Supreme Court upheld schools' power to punish students for advocating or promoting illegal drug use.

activities," says Joshua Dunn, an assistant professor of political science at the University of Colorado in Colorado Springs. "But when you hear about students being suspended for bringing in [some non-prescription medication], that sort of thing is excessive."

An official with the National Association of Secondary School Principals agrees. "Zero-tolerance policies need to be administered with good judgment," says Richard Flanary, senior director for leadership programs and services for the Reston, Va.-based association. "There are some documented cases where that has not been the case."

Other experts, however, say that educators deserve more support because of the difficulties they face in dealing with student drug use. "We don't realize what an impossible situation we put teachers and principals in," says the AEI's Hess. "If there are drugs in school, the public is going to come down hard on the schools for not doing enough to prevent drugs in the schools."

Despite that view, Hess says he considers the strip-search in Redding's case to have been "inappropriate." Flanary is similarly critical. "I could never envision doing a strip-search of a student under those circumstances," says Flanary, who was a middle-school principal in Virginia for 12 years before assuming his current post.

School boards association counsel Negrón disagrees. "The principal acted in a way that was very measured," he says. "It was done in a way to protect the integrity of the student."

Do schools improperly limit students' free-speech rights?

The dress code at Waxahachie High School, in suburban Dallas, proscribed all-black outfits and T-shirts with any writing other than school- or college-related insignia. So Paul "Pete" Palmer knew on the morning of Sept. 21, 2007, that he was pushing the envelope when — after being admonished for wearing all black — he accepted his father's suggestion to wear an "Edwards '08" T-shirt instead.

But the Edwards T-shirt did not pass muster either, and Palmer, then 15, was kept out of class until his mother brought an acceptable shirt. A month later, Palmer's attorney father filed a federal court suit on his son's behalf, challenging the school's dress code as a violation of student-speech rights guaranteed by the Supreme Court's landmark 1969 *Tinker* decision.

In her ruling, however, U.S. District Judge Barbara Lynn upheld the dress code, applying a lesser standard from another Supreme Court decision that allows some restrictions on speech if they further a substantial government interest, such as maintaining discipline. Lawyers for Liberty Legal Institute, a pro-Christian public-interest law firm representing Palmer, are now preparing to challenge the decision before the federal appeals court in New Orleans.[11]

The case exemplifies the continuing disputes over student speech despite the *Tinker* decision. A range of student-speech advocacy groups, including both traditional civil liberties organizations and more recently established religious-rights groups, continue to pepper federal and state courts with suits challenging school administrators' restrictions on students' expression.

Lawyers with those groups say courts are increasingly inclined to side with educators and against students in those cases. "It's hard to feel optimistic about where student free-speech rights are going in this country," says the ACLU's Crump. David Cortman, a lawyer with the pro-Christian Alliance Defense Fund, agrees that free speech for students is in jeopardy. "It's our concern that that right is slowly, and I would say rather quickly, being eviscerated by the courts," he says.

Some educators and experts, however, applaud what they see as the courts' evolving recognition of schools' need to limit speech that distracts from students' learning. "Adults in school settings are operating *in loco parentis* [in the place of parents]," says the AEI's Hess. "They're responsible as stewards for students for seven to eight hours per day" throughout the school year.

In its most recent decision, the Supreme Court in 2007 upheld a high-school principal's decision in Juneau, Alaska, to suspend a student for displaying a banner — "Bong Hits for Jesus" — that she interpreted as promoting the use of illegal drugs.[12] In arguments before the court, lawyers for the school district argued for a broad standard to permit restrictions on any speech inconsistent with a school's "educational mission." In a pivotal concurring opinion in the case, however, Justice Samuel A. Alito Jr. said such a sweeping standard would have given school officials too much discretion to limit student speech.

Crump says the court's decision has eroded student rights, but some experts disagree. "I don't think the right of students to freedom of expression has been fundamentally altered," says New York University's Arum. The most recent ruling, he says, "was not a fundamental change in the right of political expression."

Dupre, at the University of Georgia School of Law, says, however, that the decision has not resolved uncertainty about student-speech rights in the lower courts. "The courts are reeling from one side to another," says Dupre, author of a recent book on student-rights litigation. "There is no standard that seems to give guidance in many of these situations."[13]

http://granby01033.blogspot.com

Avery Doninger was a high-school junior in Burlington, Conn., when she blogged that school administrators were "douchebags" for canceling a planned student festival. The school responded by barring Doninger from running for reelection as class secretary. In May 2008, the Second U.S. Circuit Court of Appeals said Doninger could be punished because her posting "created a foreseeable risk of substantial disruption" at her school.

Dress codes are one of the difficult-to-chart areas, even though the *Tinker* decision upheld students' right to wear a political symbol — specifically, black armbands to protest the Vietnam War. Among the recent court cases is one from the federal appeals court in St. Louis rejecting an Arkansas school's decision to discipline students for wearing black armbands to protest the school's uniform policy.[14]

"Most schools do have dress codes," says Flanary at the principals' group. As in Waxahachie, the codes are aimed in part at barring "pictures or slogans that are provocative, offensive, sexual or suggestive in nature, vulgar, lewd or obscene." A post-*Tinker* decision by the Supreme Court upholds school authorities' power to punish sexually suggestive speech.[15]

Flanary says students' actions testing the dress codes are "inevitable," but can be minimized by developing the codes in collaboration with students and with using "good judgment" in dealing with exceptions. And he says teaching about student rights is part of a school's responsibility. "We educate kids to thrive in the real world," he says. "We have to be mindful of the world in which they live, and that is a part of it."

Do schools improperly limit students' religious freedoms?

Fifth-grader Joel Curry made candy-cane-style Christmas ornaments for a classroom project at Handley Elementary School in Saginaw, Mich., in December 2003. At his father's suggestion, Joel attached a card to the ornaments linking the candy cane to the story of Jesus. After consulting with an assistant superintendent, however, the school's principal, Irene Hensinger, decided that Joel could not use religious items as part of the classroom exercise.

With the religious messages removed, Joel received an A for the assignment. Even so, his parents filed a federal court suit on his behalf, saying that the school's actions violated Joel's freedom of religious speech. In January 2008, the federal appeals court in Cincinnati rejected Paul and Melanie Curry's suit, saying the school had "legitimate pedagogical concerns" for barring the religious-themed messages from the classroom project.[16]

The episode illustrates what Alliance Defense Fund (ADF) attorney Cortman calls "an increasing hostility toward religious speech in public schools." (Other attorneys from the group represented the Currys in the case.) "It seems they have an allergic reaction any time that religious speech occurs in the public-school setting even if it's engaged in by the student," Cortman says.

Church-state separation advocates, on the other hand, worry that some schools run afoul of Supreme Court decisions that bar any officially sponsored religious activities. "There are schools where there are regular invitations to outside clergy to come to schools to talk to students or where there are what appear to be officially sanctioned prayers," says Barry Lynn, executive director of Americans United for Separation of Church and State. A primer from the American Jewish Congress criticizes schools that invite "para-church groups."[17]

For his part, school boards association counsel Negrón says schools generally respect student rights while steering clear of giving any official imprimatur to religious activities. "Schools are aware that students have the right to engage in religious expression as long as it's done in an appropriate way under the school's rules," he says.

The difficulties in the area stem from Supreme Court decisions dating from the early 1960s that prohibit school-sponsored religious exercises ranging from classroom prayers or Bible reading to officially organized prayers at graduation ceremonies or athletic contests. The schools' role in organizing or sponsoring the religious exercises runs afoul of the First Amendment's Establishment Clause, which prohibits government action amounting to "establishment" of religion.[18]

A separate line of decisions, however, also limits school officials' discretion to exclude religious speech in situations where other forms of speech are allowed. Pro-Christian law firms such as ADF and Liberty Legal have aggressively used these free-speech rulings in support of students seeking to distribute religious materials at schools. But some school administrators fear religious solicitations can raise legal concerns, distract from classwork and offend or intimidate students of other faiths and non-believers.

The seemingly conflicting court decisions and the opposing points of view leave principals with "some uncertainty as to what they can and can't do," according to the University of Colorado's Dunn. "They legitimately live in legal fear of antagonizing one side or the other," he says.

Congress acted to strengthen religious rights in one area with the 1984 Equal Access Act, requiring any federally funded schools to allow student religious clubs to meet outside classroom time on the same basis as other extracurricular organizations. Cortman says the law is clear, but disputes continue. "We still to this day are getting cases denying equal access to religious groups, including pro-life groups," Cortman says. "We obviously win all of those cases, but it's extremely surprising that we have to bring them at all."[19]

Marc D. Stern, acting co-executive director of the American Jewish Congress, says the group had misgivings that the law would lead to active proselytizing of non-Christian pupils. But he says those fears have not come to pass. "The courts have reached a fairly good balance on what constitutes state-endorsed religious speech in schools and what's private speech," he says.

Stern says he has little concern about Christian messages attached to Christmas candy canes or Valentine's Day cards, but Lynn is "skeptical" of the practice, especially in elementary schools. He says teachers' involvement in holiday observances risks creating "an appearance of favoritism."

The AEI's Hess calls existing law "reasonably workable" but thinks religion has been unduly marginalized. "I worry that we try to enforce education and discipline while we divorce these from the Judeo-Christian traditions or Islamic tradition," he says. "I worry that it's destructive of the ability to develop really effective, culturally powerful schools."

"Tolerance and respect are sometimes hard to come by when these issues arise," says Flanary of the principals' association. "Trying to find that common ground is important."

BACKGROUND

Schools' Missions

For much of U.S. history, public-school students were expected to be seen but not heard from. The schools' prescribed curricula and strict discipline left students only limited room to shape their educational experiences. Progressive reforms in education beginning in the early 20th century placed greater emphasis on students' self-expression. Around the same time, courts began to intervene in some educational policy disputes. Only in the 1960s and '70s, however, did the Supreme Court recognize affirmative free-speech rights and due process protections for students in public schools.[20]

The public-school system that began to evolve in the early 19th century inherited from English common law the view that schools acted *in loco parentis* ("in the place of parents"), with all the authority over students in school that parents held over them outside the school. Courts gave teachers and principals a wide berth. In a Vermont case, for example, the court in 1859 found no fault with administering corporal punishment to a student who used a mocking nickname for his teacher. The teacher's power to punish disruptive speech, the court wrote, was "essential to the preservation of order, decency, decorum and good government in schools." Later 19th-century cases similarly upheld punishments for profane or disruptive comments and even a student's warning about unsafe conditions at the school.[21]

The progressive movement in education associated with the American philosopher John Dewey questioned schools' authoritarian approach to learning and discipline and gave students a more active role in their education. Overly rigid discipline, Dewey wrote in 1916, served "to cow the spirit, to subdue inclination" and to "increase indifference and aversion" to schools.[22] As the progressive movement advanced, public schools also found themselves embroiled in court cases challenging policies given to them under state laws. In 1923, for example, the Supreme Court invalidated a Nebraska law that forbade the teaching of foreign languages in public schools before the eighth grade. The law interfered with the rights of both teachers and parents, the court said. Two decades later, the court struck down on free-speech grounds a West Virginia law requiring teachers and students to salute the flag and recite the Pledge of Allegiance each day. The law impinged on "intellectual individualism" and "cultural diversities," the court explained.[23]

In a more dramatic intervention, the Supreme Court in 1954 outlawed the then prevalent practice of racial segregation in public schools. The court's historic ruling in *Brown v. Board of Education* capped a decades-long campaign by African-American students and families coordinated nationwide by the NAACP and its legal arm, the NAACP Legal Defense and Educational Fund. The ruling marked the beginning of decades of still continuing judicial supervision of efforts to promote racial diversity and equality in public schools. It also served to validate a litigation model for other students, families and groups to use in challenging school policies or decisions.[24]

The court opened the door to student-speech lawsuits with its 1969 ruling in the *Tinker* case. Three teenaged students in Des Moines — Christopher Eckhardt and John and Mary Beth Tinker — had been suspended for wearing black armbands to their schools in December 1965 to protest the government's policy in Vietnam. The school board, which learned of the plans beforehand, had issued an edict prohibiting the symbolic protest. In a ruling in September 1966, U.S. District Judge Roy Stephenson said the school board's authority to maintain order outweighed any free-speech rights the students might enjoy. The Supreme Court, however, disagreed. In the majority opinion, Fortas said schools could censor student speech only to prevent "substantial disruption" or to protect the rights of other students. In an angry dissent, Justice Hugo L. Black said the ruling "ushers in . . . an entirely new era in which the power to control pupils . . . is . . . transferred to the Supreme Court."[25]

CHRONOLOGY

Before 1960 *Student rights unrecognized in 19th century; Supreme Court enters field in 20th century.*

1960s-1970s *Supreme Court recognizes students' rights to free speech, due process.*

1969 Supreme Court overturns disciplinary actions against three students for wearing black armbands to protest Vietnam War; 7-2 ruling in *Tinker v. Des Moines* permits restrictions on speech only to prevent disruption or protect rights of others.

1972 Title IX prohibits discrimination based on sex in schools receiving federal funds.

1975 Supreme Court says schools must provide some procedural rights before disciplining students; 5-4 ruling in *Goss v. Lopez* requires notice of charge, explanation of evidence, opportunity to respond.

1977 California passes law protecting student journalists' freedom of expression; seven other states have similar laws by 2009, but California's remains broadest.

1980s-1990s *Supreme Court backs schools on anti-drug policies; drugs, violence in schools lead to "zero tolerance" policies.*

1984 Equal Access Act requires schools to give equal access to facilities for extracurricular groups, including religious clubs; Supreme Court upholds law in 1990, expands reach in 2001.

1985 Schools can search student lockers, Supreme Court rules.

1986 Schools can punish "vulgar" speech, Supreme Court rules.

1988 Schools can censor student newspapers if part of the school's curriculum, Supreme Court rules; decision prompts more states to pass student-press rights statutes. . . . First gay-straight alliance established at private Concord Academy in Massachusetts; by 2009, more than 4,000 such clubs are in schools.

1994 Gun Free Schools Act requires one-year suspension of any student found with a firearm.

1995 Supreme Court rules, 6-3, that schools may require random, suspicionless drug testing of student athletes.

Late 1990s Many school districts adopt zero-tolerance policies requiring discipline of students even for minor drug violations or other misconduct.

1999 Twelve students, one teacher killed in shooting at Columbine High School in Colorado; student shooters commit suicide at scene.

2000-Present *Bush administration pushes accountability, school choice; Supreme Court backs vouchers, limits racial diversity policies.*

2001 President George W. Bush pushes No Child Left Behind Act through Congress; law requires schools to raise student performance, sets financial penalties for "failing" schools.

2002 Supreme Court permits schools to require random drug testing for all students engaged in extracurricular activities. . . . Justices uphold school vouchers; challengers said aid to parochial students violated separation of church and state.

2006 U.S. Department of Education modifies sex discrimination rules to permit school districts to establish single-sex classes, schools. . . . Federal appeals court upholds ban on student's anti-gay T-shirt; Supreme Court erases ruling in 2007.

2007 Supreme Court rules, 5-4, that schools can punish students for advocating or promoting illegal drug use. . . . Justices also vote 5-4 to limit school districts' racial diversity policies; race-based pupil assignments held to violate equal protection principles. . . . School districts in Connecticut, Florida punish students for postings on social networking sites; court rulings on issue in conflict.

2009 Supreme Court weighs drug enforcement, student rights in Arizona strip-search case; ruling due by end of June.

Student Articles on 'Hooking Up' Lead to Crackdown

Flap reflects tenuous state of students' free-press rights.

The Jan. 30 issue of *The Statesman*, the student newspaper at Adlai Stevenson High School in Lincolnshire, Ill., flew off the lunchroom and hallway tables.

The sudden interest among the school's 4,600 students was easy to explain. A two-page inside spread examined "hooking up," complete with first-person accounts and an hour-by-hour timeline for how to score in today's dating scene.

"A lot more kids were reading the paper," recalls Jamie Hausman, a graduating senior and the paper's design editor. "They were excited about it."

Parents and school administrators, on the other hand, were less than thrilled. Jim Conrey, director of public information at the suburban Chicago school, faults the articles for having no interviews with students in favor of abstinence or with any of the school's health-education teachers. As for the timeline, Conrey, a former journalist, calls it "a how-to guide for a sexual predator."[1]

Controversy about the issue flared at a packed school board meeting. *The Chicago Tribune* weighed in with a favorable editorial, while the Illinois Family Institute countered that sex should be off-limits for a school newspaper.

Now, the flap has resulted in a new policy requiring pre-publication review by the director of the communications arts program and other administrators and the resignation of the newspaper's longtime adviser, Barbara Thill. She will continue to teach English but not journalism at the school.

Conrey says the new policy brings the newspaper in line with the collaborative philosophy of the rest of the curriculum. But Evan Ribot, a copy editor, said the policy has resulted in more "trepidation" and less time for reporting, editing and layout.[2]

The episode illustrates the tenuous state of free-press rights for journalists in public high schools. In the governing decision, the Supreme Court in 1988 upheld the power of school administrators to censor student newspapers if they were part of the school's curriculum. "A school must be able to set high standards for the student speech that is disseminated under its auspices," Justice Byron R. White wrote for the 5-3 majority in *Hazelwood School District v. Kuhlmeier.*[3]

The impact of the ruling has been weakened somewhat by laws on the books in seven states that generally give newspaper editors at high schools and public colleges the final say on editorial content. In California — the first state to adopt such a law — a court has gone so far as to say that a principal improperly intimidated a student author by post-publication criticism of a column he had written opposing immigration.[4]

But Frank LoMonte, a lawyer and executive director of the Student Press Law Center, says school administrators "are taking full advantage of the latitude" they have under *Hazelwood* to control the content of student newspapers. "Any kind of content that might cause the principal's phone to ring with complaints is too disruptive to be published," he says.

At Stevenson, Conrey insists the school administration is merely trying to instill professional journalistic standards at the student newspaper. He notes, for example, that the newspaper sought to conceal the identity of students interviewed by using only their first names, but that some of them were easily identifiable anyway. He also says the administration had previously complained about a story concerning a student's later-disavowed claim to be selling drugs at the school.

"The writing was on the wall," Hausman acknowledges. She agrees that the date timeline may have gone too far, but generally defends the rest of the issue as informative for students and parents alike. "Our parents' generation was so different from ours," says Hausman, who plans to study journalism at the University of Missouri beginning in the fall. "We decided to explore that a little bit."

"There's no doubt that it raised the level of discussion about the topic," replies Conrey. "It's good in the aggregate, but just because you talk about something doesn't make it a valid discussion."

---

[1] For background, see Jane Friedman, "Teen Sex," *CQ Researcher*, Sept. 16, 2005, pp. 761-784; and Kathy Koch, "Encouraging Teen Abstinence," *CQ Researcher*, July 10, 1998, pp. 577-600.

[2] Quoted in "School paper loses adviser over sex edition," Chicago Breaking News Center, April 1, 2009. See also "Stevenson High School adviser resigns position after prior review policy enforced," Student Press Law Center, April 21, 2009.

[3] The citation is 484 U.S. 260 (1988). For background, see Susan Phillips, "Student Journalism," *CQ Researcher*, June 5, 1998.

[4] The decision is *Smith v. Novato Unified School Dist.*, 150 Cal.App.4th 1439 (Cal. Ct. App. 2007), cited in Frank D. LoMonte, "Student Journalism Confronts a New Generation of Legal Challenges," *Human Rights*, Vol. 35, No. 3 (summer 2008).

Mary Beth Tinker and her brother John were suspended from classes at North High School in Des Moines, Iowa, in 1965 along with three other students for wearing black armbands to mourn Vietnam War dead. In 1969 the Supreme Court upheld a suit filed by the Tinkers and a third student, Christopher Eckhardt, arguing they had a right to display such political symbols. "It can hardly be argued," Justice Abe Fortas wrote, "that either students or teachers shed their constitutional rights to freedom of speech or expression at the schoolhouse gate."

In a lesser known but arguably more important ruling, the court effectively established minimal procedural rights for students nationwide before any disciplinary suspension, even for as little as one day. The 5-4 decision in *Goss v. Lopez* (1975) invalidated an Ohio law permitting suspensions of up to 10 days without any hearing. Instead, Justice Byron R. White wrote, school authorities must give a student "oral or written notice of the charges," "an explanation of the evidence" and "an opportunity to present his side of the story." The "rudimentary precautions," White said, were "less than a fair-minded school principal" would adopt. In dissent, Justice Lewis F. Powell Jr., a former school board president, called the decision "an unprecedented intrusion into the process of elementary and secondary education."[26]

Schools' Concerns

The Supreme Court's solicitude for student rights began with *Tinker* and peaked with *Goss.* Beginning in the 1980s, the justices evinced greater concerns for the difficulties that educators faced on such issues as drugs, sex and offensive or hate speech. Major Supreme Court decisions in the decade upheld schools' anti-drug policies and narrowed protections for student speech. The trend continued in the 1990s, even as many school districts adopted zero-tolerance policies that called for disciplining students even for minor infractions.

In the first of the rulings, the court in *New Jersey v. T.L.O.* (1985) extended Fourth Amendment protections to students with one hand but narrowed them with the other.[27] A teenaged student in Piscataway, N.J., who had been caught smoking cigarettes with a classmate, challenged the principal's subsequent search of her purse, which uncovered marijuana. The court upheld the search in a 6-3 decision. Instead of applying the traditional probable-cause requirement, Justice White said that accommodating "the substantial need of teachers and administrators for freedom to maintain order in the schools" called for permitting searches of students and their belongings based on "the reasonableness" of the search "under all the circumstances."

A year later, the court invoked *Tinker*'s exception for "disruptive" speech to significantly narrow protections for students. Matthew Fraser, a high school student in Washington state, had been suspended for three days and barred from election as commencement speaker after using what the court called "an explicit, graphic sexual metaphor" in a nominating speech for a student council candidate. The court's 7-2 decision in *Bethel School Dist. No. 403 v. Fraser* (1986) upheld the school's power to discipline students for comments "disruptive to the educational process." As Chief Justice Warren E. Burger explained, "It is a highly appropriate function of public-school education to prohibit the use of vulgar and offensive terms in public discourse."[28]

Two years later, high-school journalists suffered a setback when the court upheld school administrators' power to censor student newspapers, at least when the newspapers were part of the school's curriculum. The 5-3 decision in *Hazelwood School District v. Kuhlmeier* (1988) upheld the decision by a principal in a suburban St. Louis high school to delete two pages of a student newspaper because of articles dealing with teenage pregnancy and divorce.[29] For the majority, White treated the school-financed newspaper as part of the school's curriculum and found no obligation to allow students to publish articles that conflicted with the school's "legitimate pedagogical goals." Citing *Tinker*, dissenting justices said the articles should have been allowed because they did not disrupt classwork or invade the rights of other students.

Meanwhile, however, Congress had strengthened the rights of student organizations to use school facilities outside class hours. Religious groups originally pushed what became the Equal Access Act of 1984 in response to actions by school administrators and rulings by some federal and state courts preventing student Bible clubs from meeting on campus. The final bill applied more broadly to require equal access for any voluntary extra-curricular group. The Supreme Court in 1990 voted 8-1 to uphold the law as constitutional.[30] The immediate impact was to give a green light to Christian student groups, but over time the act was also used to force some reluctant school administrators to allow students to form gay-straight alliances — or, in some instances, to disband extracurricular clubs altogether to prevent them.

Student rights receded as an issue in the 1990s as educators and the public alike grew increasingly concerned about such behavioral issues as violence, drugs, gang activity and bullying.[31] Zero-tolerance policies prescribed mandatory discipline for various offenses, often with little regard for the severity of the misconduct. A federal law passed in 1994 required a one-year suspension for any student found in possession of a firearm on campus. Security and discipline codes were tightened nationwide after the deadly shootings at Columbine High School in Colorado in 1999 when two heavily armed students killed 12 students and one teacher before committing suicide themselves.

The get-tough atmosphere also gave birth to drug-testing policies that a handful of school districts adopted to try to detect students using illegal drugs. Twice, the Supreme Court upheld the policies against claims that random, suspicionless testing violated students' Fourth Amendment rights against unreasonable searches. In the first ruling, the justices in 1995 voted 6-3 to uphold an Oregon school district's policy requiring random drug testing of all student athletes. For the majority, Justice Antonin Scalia said schools' interest in protecting athletes' safety and deterring drug use among perceived role models outweighed the "negligible" impact on privacy. Seven years later, the court in 2002 voted 5-4 in an Oklahoma case to extend the rationale to permit drug testing of students in any extracurricular activity. Despite the rulings, there appeared to be no rush by school districts across the nation to institute drug testing.[32]

Standards and Choice

Under President George W. Bush, the federal government put its weight behind a view of student rights embodied in standards-based accountability for schools and enrollment choices for students and families dissatisfied with individual schools. The No Child Left Behind Act required annual standardized testing of public school students and gave students the right to transfer out of "non-performing" schools. The administration joined school-choice advocates in winning a pivotal Supreme Court decision upholding the constitutionality of publicly funded vouchers for students to attend private, including religious, schools. Later, Bush's two appointees to the Supreme Court provided critical votes for a ruling somewhat limiting student-speech rights and a separate decision limiting school districts' ability to engineer racial diversity in enrollment.

Bush pushed No Child Left Behind through Congress in his first months in office in 2001.[33] The law — which came to be known in educational circles as the pronounceable acronym "nicklebee" — requires school districts receiving federal funds to raise performance levels for students, especially minority or other disadvantaged students. Schools that fail to meet the standards must provide students transfers, tutoring or other supplementary services and face the threat of "restructuring" or closure. Passed with wide bipartisan support, the law proved controversial in its implementation. Teachers, administrators and school board members criticized standards as inflexible and federal funding to meet the goals as inadequate. The administration made some changes over time but continued to defend the law throughout Bush's eight years in office.

A year after the law's passage, the Supreme Court in June 2002 gave the administration an important legal victory by ruling, 5-4, that state and local governments can provide vouchers to students to attend parochial schools without violating separation of church and state.[34] The decision upheld a voucher program in Cleveland, established pursuant to a state law, that provided up to $2,250 for students to use for tuition at private schools. The vast majority of students attended parochial schools. Despite the ruling and the Bush administration's continued support, voucher programs failed to advance as much as supporters hoped. Teachers' unions strongly opposed the programs, and courts in some states — notably Florida — ruled vouchers unconstitutional on state law grounds.

Getty Images/Jerry Laizure

High-school students Lindsay Earls and Daniel James of Tecumseh, Okla., sued in 1999 to overturn their school's policy of mandatory drug testing for students participating in extracurricular activities. Two Supreme Court rulings in 1995 and 2002 approved random drug testing for many high-school students.

The Bush administration also gave its support to a different form of school choice by adopting rules to allow single-sex education in public schools. The rules, approved by the Department of Education in October 2006 after a two-year period of comment and deliberation, allowed voluntary single-sex classes or schools despite the federal law known as Title IX that generally prohibits sex discrimination in public schools. Single-sex education was touted by proponents as improving education for boys and girls alike and criticized by women's groups, among others, as ill suited to preparing students for the real world. By 2009, advocates were counting some 95 single-sex schools and 445 single-sex classes nationwide.[35]

In another clash with public school lobbies and traditional civil rights groups, the Bush administration sided with white families in a critical Supreme Court case challenging racial diversity policies in local school districts. The policies in Seattle and Louisville-Jefferson County, Ky., assigned some pupils to out-of-neighborhood schools in order to have some degree of racial balance at individual schools. White families in both districts challenged the policies as unconstitutional race-based discrimination. The court in June 2007 agreed, with Bush's two Supreme Court appointees — Chief Justice Roberts and Justice Alito — helping form the 5-4 majority. The ruling barred individual race-based assignments, but in a pivotal concurring opinion Justice Kennedy said school districts could use other policies, such as magnet schools or new school-site selection, to promote racial balance.[36]

Three days earlier, Roberts and Alito had also provided critical votes in the 5-4 decision upholding schools' power to punish students for advocating or promoting illegal drug use. Joseph Frederick, a student at Juneau-Douglas High School in Alaska, had been given a 10-day suspension for displaying his "Bong Hits 4 Jesus" banner off school grounds on Jan. 24, 2002. Principal Deborah Morse viewed the banner as pro-drug advocacy, while Frederick depicted it as nonsense. "The First Amendment does not require schools to tolerate at school events student expression that contributes to [the] dangers" of drug use, Roberts wrote for the majority. For the dissenters, Justice John Paul Stevens warned the ruling would limit student debate about drug policy.

Meanwhile, Savana Redding's strip-search case was moving toward the high court. Redding's mother April originally filed a civil rights damage suit on her daughter's behalf in Arizona state court against principal Wilson, his assistant Romero and nurse Schwallier. The Safford School District removed the case to federal court, where U.S. Magistrate Judge Nancy Fiora ruled that the strip-search satisfied the two requirements established under the Supreme Court's *T.L.O.* decision: justified at its inception and permissible in scope.

A three-judge panel of the Ninth U.S. Circuit Court of Appeals agreed in September 2007, but Redding won a hearing before a panel of 11 judges, who divided 6-5 in her favor on July 11, 2008. "Common sense informs us that directing a 13-year-old girl to remove her clothes, partially revealing her breasts and pelvic area, for allegedly possessing ibuprofen, an infraction that poses an imminent danger to no one, and which could have been handled by keeping her in the principal's office until a parent arrived or simply sending her home, was excessively intrusive," Judge Kim McLane Wardlaw wrote for the majority. The court said the principle was so well established that Wilson — though not Romero or Schwallier — could be ordered to pay damages for the search. Safford appealed both holdings to the Supreme Court, which agreed on Jan. 16 to hear the case.

CURRENT SITUATION

Deferring to Educators

State legislatures and federal courts alike appear to be leaning away from expanding student rights and toward giving greater deference and stronger legal protections to school administrators and teachers alike.

The trend can be seen in the enactment of laws in at least eight states to strengthen teachers' legal protections against damage suits for disciplinary actions against students. It can also be seen in recent federal appeals court decisions that the Supreme Court left standing favoring teachers or administrators in student discipline incidents.

Indiana became the most recent state to enact a so-called teacher protection law when Republican Gov. Mitch Daniels signed a bill on May 11 to give teachers "qualified immunity" from suit if they act in good faith under school policy in disciplining students or breaking up fights.[37] Daniels endorsed the proposal in campaigning for re-election to a second four-year term in 2008 and included it in the legislative program he submitted to the GOP-controlled legislature.

The bill was sponsored in the legislature, however, by a Democrat: state Rep. Clyde Kersey of Terre Haute. Kersey, a former teacher, said the bill "will restore order and discipline in the classroom that we haven't had in a long time because of the courts." The head of a local teachers' union also said the measure was needed. "Teachers have to be reasonably certain that they're not going to be sued for every frivolous case that comes up," Al Wolting, president of the Indianapolis Education Association, told the *Indianapolis Star.*

Daniels' office said seven other states had enacted similar laws: Alabama, Arkansas, Georgia, Minnesota, Mississippi, Texas and Wyoming. Legislatures in at least two other states — Missouri and South Carolina — considered similar proposals this year. The proposals are modeled after provisions that Congress included in the No Child Left Behind Act in 2001.

The federal Teacher Protection Act protects a school employee from civil liability if a student is injured in an attempt to discipline or control a student. But the immunity does not apply if an employee violated federal, state or local law; committed a sexual offense; or was guilty of gross negligence, reckless conduct or conscious indifference to the student's rights or safety.

Even without such legislation, federal appeals courts have recently been ruling in favor of teachers or administrators in suits, according to cases compiled on The School Law Blog by *Education Week* reporter Mark Walsh.[38]

In one case, the federal appeals court in Cincinnati rejected a suit filed on behalf of a seventh-grade student charging the Grant County (Ky.) Board of Education and various officials with violating her constitutional rights by questioning her about her actions in giving a prescription medication to a fellow student. The student argued that the school principal's actions in summoning her to his office and requiring her to write out an explanation of the incident that he later turned over to the local sheriff's office violated her rights under the Fourth and Fifth Amendments.

In a unanimous decision, however, a three-judge panel of the Sixth U.S. Circuit Court of Appeals ordered the suit dismissed, saying the principal had not acted at the behest of law enforcement. The U.S. Supreme Court declined on April 27 to hear the student's appeal of the ruling.

In an earlier case, the federal appeals court in New Orleans rejected a suit against a San Antonio charter school in connection with the paddling of an 18-year-old high school senior in 2004. Jessica Serafin claimed she was restrained by two school employees while principal Brett Wilkinson paddled her for leaving the school campus to buy breakfast, in violation of school rules. She was treated at a hospital emergency room for injuries to her hand sustained while trying to block the blows.

In defending against the suit, the school noted that an enrollment form signed by Serafin's guardian included permission for corporal punishment. In a brief and unsigned ruling in October 2007, the Fifth U.S. Circuit Court of Appeals said it was "well settled" that corporal punishment violates a public-school student's rights only if it is "arbitrary, capricious, or wholly unrelated to the legitimate state goal of maintaining an atmosphere conducive to learning."

The Supreme Court declined to hear Serafin's appeal in June 2008. The high court has not revisited the issue of corporal punishment since a closely divided decision in 1977 that upheld the practice and rejected any need for school administrators or teachers to give a student procedural rights before administering such punishment.[39]

Experts on both sides of the student-rights issue agree on the trend toward greater deference to educators. "We're

Gay-Rights and Christian Groups Embrace *Tinker* Decision

Courts generally side with students, not school officials, on speech rights.

Eighth-grader Chris Quintanilla started wearing a rainbow-colored wristband with the inscription "Rainbows Are Gay" to Parkridge Elementary School in Peoria, Ariz., in February. Principal David Svorinic took a skeptical look at the wristband and two days later called Chris' mother, Natali, to either suggest or demand that Chris stop wearing it or at least turn it over to conceal the pro-gay message.

As Natali recalls the conversation, Svorinic said the wristband was offending some of the teachers at the suburban Phoenix school and causing a disruption. A spokeswoman for the school says Svorinic never forbade Chris from wearing the wristband, but she acknowledges the principal observed that Chris was "putting his sexuality out there" by wearing it.

Natali contacted the Arizona affiliate of the American Civil Liberties Union (ACLU), which sent a sternly worded letter in March to Superintendent Denton Santarelli accusing the school of violating Chris' free-speech rights under the Supreme Court's landmark decision *Tinker v. Des Moines*. A month later, the ACLU reported the incident closed, with an assurance from the school that it would not prevent Chris from wearing the wristband in the future.

"I'm very proud of my son for standing up for his rights," Natali was quoted as saying in an ACLU press release, "and we both hope this means that other gay students won't be silenced at his school in the future."

The modern gay rights movement was only beginning to emerge when the Supreme Court issued the *Tinker* decision in late February 1969. (The "Stonewall" riot in New York City occurred four months later.) But today the debate over homosexuality is one of the most frequently litigated topics in student free-speech cases.

Students on both sides of the debate run afoul of school administrators at times, but courts generally side with the students. In July 2008, the ACLU got a federal court to nullify a decision by a principal in northern Florida to ban students from displaying pro-gay slogans. A few months earlier, the Alliance Defense Fund, a Christian public interest law firm, won a ruling from the federal appeals court in Chicago guaranteeing a student's right to wear a "Be Happy, Not Gay" T-shirt.[1]

In one notable exception, the federal appeals court in California upheld a decision by a principal in San Diego County to prohibit anti-gay students from wearing T-shirts proclaiming "Homosexuality Is Shameful" on the same day as the school's gay-straight alliance sponsored a day of silence. The 2-1 decision by the Ninth U.S. Circuit Court of Appeals in April 2006 held that the First Amendment does not protect "derogatory and injurious remarks directed at students' minority status such as race, religion and sexual orientation."[2]

In a case brought by a Christian public-interest law firm, a federal court in Chicago in 2008 said a student could wear an anti-gay shirt.

The Supreme Court effectively erased the decision in March 2007 by vacating the ruling and directing the case be dismissed as moot because the plaintiff had graduated. The Alliance Defense Fund, which represented the student, applauds the end result. "What a person may be offended by is too fluid for constitutional purposes," says David Cortman, a senior legal counsel with the Alliance Defense Fund, which litigated the case.

The ACLU also favors students' right to wear anti-gay T-shirts despite what Catherine Crump, a staff attorney with its First Amendment Working Group, calls its "strong support" for equality for gay students. "The traditional answer to [offensive] speech," Crump says, "is more speech."

The ACLU and other gay-rights groups have also enjoyed general success in safeguarding the right — guaranteed under the federal Equal Access Act — to form gay-straight alliances in schools and in winning gay couples the right to attend school proms. In a recent dispute, the ACLU challenged the use in Tennessee schools of a computer software filter that blocked gay news sites but not Web sites maintained by anti-gay groups.

For its part, the Gay, Lesbian, and Straight Educational Network (GLSEN) says free-speech disputes detract from the more tangible problem that LGBT students face in school: name-calling, bullying and harassment. "The real core issue is that words like faggot and dyke are still ubiquitous in the hallways," says executive director Eliza Byard. "Before we work on the fine points, I would like to see everyone come together and deal with the bullying and harassment that is so clearly unacceptable."

---

[1] The decisions are *Gillman v. School Bd. for Holmes County, Florida*, 567 F.Supp.2d 1359 (N.D.Fla.2008); *Nuxoll v. Indian Prairie School District*, 523 F.3d 668 (7th Cir.2008).

[2] The decision is *Harper v. Poway Unified School Dist.*, 445 F.3d 1166 (9th Cir. 2006). For later developments, see "Anti-gay challenge to dress code is rejected," The Associated Press, March 6, 2007.

AT ISSUE

Do student rights interfere with teaching in public school?

YES

Frederick M. Hess
Director, Education Policy Studies American Enterprise Institute

Written for *CQ Researcher*, June 1, 2009

We have unwittingly transformed K-12 schools from places where educators are expected to shape character, set boundaries and foster respect to ones where they are hesitant and unsure of their authority.

The greatest effect has been what former San Diego superintendent and California Secretary of Education Alan Bersin has termed "the anaconda in the chandelier" — the looming fear that a misstep could lead to lawsuits or grave professional consequences. The survey firm Public Agenda has reported that 47 percent of superintendents would operate differently if "free from the constant threat of litigation" and that 85 percent of teachers indicate that "most students suffer because of a few persistent troublemakers."

Fully 77 percent of teachers report that "if it weren't for discipline problems, I could be teaching a lot more effectively."

The most effective schools have always been unapologetic about setting norms and disciplining misbehavior. Journalist David Whitman, in his acclaimed 2008 book *Sweating the Small Stuff*, argues that the key to the success of high-performing charter schools like the KIPP Academies is their willingness to tell students exactly how they are expected to behave, with rewards for compliance and penalties for breaking the rules. Whitman shows how teachers ceaselessly monitor conduct and character to ensure that students act respectfully, develop self-discipline, work hard and take responsibility for their actions.

Thanks to more than a generation of court rulings, lawsuits and learned timidity, most schools shy from such muscular norms. The result is that educators have less authority, schools less discipline and students less opportunity to learn. Ironically, this all matters most in schools serving at-risk students, who start with fewer advantages and are most likely to be stuck in chaotic school environments.

Scholars Scott Carrel and Mark Hoekstra have documented the ill-effects of lax discipline, reporting that adding a single disruptive student to a class has a statistically significant negative effect on their peers' reading and math achievement.

It is too easy, of course, to blame the current state of affairs on the judicial process. Nations wind up with the schools they desire and deserve. In an era of confessional television and helicopter parents lobbying college professors for paper extensions, it is little wonder that schools have been buffeted by an insistence that they understand rather than discipline. Putting educators in a position to educate is not just a matter of law, it is also a question of character.

NO

Jamin Raskin
Director, Program on Law and Government, Washington College of Law, American University

Written for *CQ Researcher*, May 28, 2009

Ever since the Supreme Court struck down compulsory classroom prayer, group Bible readings and religiously inspired bans on teaching evolution, the defense of student rights has always meant improved teaching and learning in our schools. The deployment of the Establishment Clause in school cases has made it possible for science teachers to teach science and students not to be anxious all day because they pray differently or — God forbid — not at all.

The whole point of Justice Abe Fortas' landmark decision in *Tinker v. Des Moines* is that the free-speech rights of students are not an impediment to the learning process but a crucial ingredient of it. "In our system, state-operated schools may not be enclaves of totalitarianism," he wrote, and "students may not be regarded as close-circuited recipients of only that which the state chooses to communicate." Each student has something precious to offer the others, and "intercommunication among the students" is "an important part of the educational process."

It is the Supreme Court's determined retreat from this vision of student rights that has undermined learning. In *Hazelwood v. Kuhlmeier* (1988), the Court broke from *Tinker* and upheld a principal's censorship of two articles written by students for their school newspaper that had been enthusiastically approved by their journalism teacher. One concerned the impact of parental divorce on students, the other the problem of teen pregnancy as seen through the experiences of three students. The school thus squashed mature and thoughtful student expression about issues of profound importance to young people.

To be sure, the post-Columbine massacre era is a scary time to go to school. But that is because of the absurd availability of guns everywhere, which has nothing to do with student rights. (Why should students lose their First Amendment rights because adults refuse to face their Second Amendment responsibilities?) Students have lost every school drug-testing case that has gone to the Supreme Court, and no lawsuit has ever stopped a school from using a metal detector.

If students have been able to maintain a shred of privacy and personal liberty during this age of "zero tolerance" authoritarianism, then more power to them — they may get a taste of what it is like to live in a free society. More likely, they encounter random drug tests for extracurricular activities, humiliating strip searches for Midol, knee-jerk censorship of the school paper and yearbook and a relentless regime of testing.

going to see a continuing deference to schools when it comes to questions of safety," says school boards association counsel Negrón.

American University law professor Raskin views the trend less positively. "We have just had a strong judicial tilt away from liberty and toward authority," he says.

Debating a Strip-Search

Supreme Court justices are weighing how to prevent drug use while protecting student rights as they consider whether administrators at an Arizona middle school went too far in strip-searching a teenaged girl while looking for a commonly used pain medication.

Liberal justices pressed the attorney for the Safford school district to justify the strip-search of Savana Redding during the opening half-hour of oral arguments on April 21. But some of them appeared to join conservative justices by the end of the hour in giving greater weight to the need to give school authorities considerable leeway in investigating reports of unauthorized drugs on campus, even commonly available pain pills.

"Better embarrassment than violent sickness or death," the generally liberal Justice David H. Souter remarked near the end of Redding's lawyer's time. "What's wrong with that reasoning under the Fourth Amendment?"

Representing the school district, Phoenix attorney Wright opened by stressing that principal Kelly Wilson had reason to suspect Redding of possessing unauthorized pills that constituted a health and safety risk. With an enrollment of 400, the school had rules prohibiting students from possessing any medication — over-the-counter or prescription — without approval from the school nurse.

School authorities have "custodial and tutelary responsibility" for students, Wright explained. The court, he argued, "should defer to their judgment when they believe that certain rules are important and not second-guess those rules."

Wright encountered skepticism from justices across the ideological spectrum. Chief Justice Roberts and fellow conservative Justice Scalia pressed Wright on how far authorities could go. What about body cavity searches? Scalia asked. Wright ruled them out.

Liberals Souter and Justice Ruth Bader Ginsburg followed by questioning the details of the investigation. Did administrators have any reason to suspect Redding other than the accusation from her classmate who herself was caught with the unauthorized extra-strength ibuprofen? Ginsburg asked.

In his turn, Souter suggested it was "silly" to lump all unauthorized medications together. "If your rule . . . would put aspirin in the contraband category and justify the kind of search that went on here, I think we've reached the questionable point," Souter said.

Representing the Bush administration, assistant solicitor general David O'Neil argued that what he called "intrusive body searches" required "greater justification" than the reasonableness standard applicable, for example, to a search of a student's locker. Searching a student's underwear, he said, required specific information that the student was hiding drugs there. And in Safford's case, O'Neil explained, the school had no information or experience that students were doing that.

For Redding, the ACLU's Wolf echoed O'Neil's argument that school officials should have "location-specific" information before strip-searching a student. "The Fourth Amendment . . . does not countenance rummaging on or around a 13-year-old girl's naked body," Wolf said.

Wolf met resistance, however, from Roberts and the moderate-conservative Justice Anthony M. Kennedy, who asked whether a strip-search would have been justified if Redding had been suspected of having a more dangerous drug, such as heroin or methamphetamine. When Wolf said it would not have made a difference, Kennedy appeared dubious. "You don't mind our deciding the case as if this were a search for meth that was going to be consumed at noon?" Kennedy asked pointedly.

Later, liberal Justice Stephen G. Breyer raised doubts whether the search was as intrusive as Wolf was depicting. "I'm trying to work out why is this a major thing to say strip down to your underclothes, which children do when they change for gym, they do fairly frequently?" Breyer asked.

Ginsburg jumped in before Wolf could answer. "It wasn't just that they were stripped to their underwear," Ginsburg said, referring to the searches of both Redding and her accuser. "They were asked to shake their bra out, to shake, stretch the top of their pants and shake that out."

In a brief rebuttal, Wright acknowledged that some school districts have rules prohibiting strip-searches of students. But he used the concession to emphasize the argument for leaving the issue up to local officials' discretion. Administrators need "a bright-line rule," he said, permitting them to search any place where contraband might reasonably be hidden.

The justices are due to decide the case before they begin a summer recess at the end of June. The court could avert the main issue by dismissing Redding's suit on the ground that school officials had no reason to know the search was unconstitutional. But all three lawyers appeared to favor the justices ruling on the merits of the dispute.

OUTLOOK

Changing Times

As she looked forward to the 40th anniversary of the Supreme Court's decision in her case, Mary Beth Tinker acknowledged that the ruling gives school administrators a lot of leeway to censor student speech. But she said she planned to celebrate "a Supreme Court that stood with young people to affirm their rights." And she urged students themselves to celebrate "by becoming engaged in issues that are important to their lives."[40]

Tinker, her brother John and their friend Christopher Eckhardt decided on their act of defiance in an era when principals and teachers enjoyed largely unquestioned authority in their schools, and students had no recognized legal rights enforceable in courts. With the divisions over Vietnam beginning to emerge, Eckhardt worried that pro-war classmates might beat him up; but in fact no disruption or violence occurred at any of the three schools that he and the Tinkers attended.

More than 40 years later, public schools in the United States have been transformed — in many ways, for the better; in some ways, not. Legally enforced racial segregation has ended, though most students still attend racially identifiable schools. Students with disabilities have a federally guaranteed right to an "appropriate" public education. Teachers have been encouraged to adopt interactive, collaborative instructional methods. And students generally do not risk derision or discipline for questioning authority.

Yet school life is far more troubled in some ways today than it was in the supposedly tumultuous '60s. Bullying once confined to the classroom or playground now becomes far more hurtful when posted — often anonymously — on the Internet for all to read and see. Deadly school shootings have combined with the daily fear of weapon-carrying students to make metal detectors commonplace in inner-city, suburban and rural schools alike. The drug problem has grown from an occasional pot-smoker to more widespread use of marijuana, other illegal drugs and unauthorized prescription medications. And many principals and teachers say they live and work with the fear of physical violence from students and legal rebukes from the courts.

With the changing times, courts are changing too. "A pattern is developing that in terms of dangers that are serious and palpable, there is some duty and obligations [on the part of] the schools to do what they have to do to make the kids safe," says school boards association counsel Negrón. New York University's Arum sees "hints" of greater deference to educators in court rulings as well in public discussion of school policies.

In past rulings such as *Tinker*, the Supreme Court "imposed some liberty restraints on what schools can do," says American University law professor Raskin. "Now there are judges who essentially tell us that children should be seen and not heard."

The Supreme Court's role in creating the trend can be seen in its most recent decisions rejecting lower court rulings that backed student-rights pleas in the Oklahoma drug testing case in 2002 and the "Bong Hits 4 Jesus" case in 2007. "There are five votes on the court now for trying to pull back," says R. Shep Melnick, a professor of political science at Boston College.

Melnick says, however, that the changes are less than a complete reversal. "It will be around the edges," he says. In fact, the court shows no inclination to reconsider *Tinker* despite a strongly argued call by Justice Clarence Thomas in the 2007 decision to overrule it. No justice joined Thomas's opinion.

For now, educators and student-rights advocates alike are awaiting the court's latest pronouncement on the issue in Savana Redding's strip-search case, with a decision due by the end of June. Despite criticism of the Safford principal's actions in the incident, even from some educators, the justices' decision is hard to predict.

Redding, now 19 and a college freshman, attended the arguments and had mixed reaction to the proceedings. "It was pretty overwhelming," she told reporters assembled on the Supreme Court plaza after the session. "Some things made me mad, and other things I was glad to see that the judges could comprehend."[41]

NOTES

1. The case is *Safford Unified School Dist. No. 1 v. Redding*, 08-479. For documents in the case, see SCOTUSWiki, www.scotuswiki.com/index.php?title=Safford_United_School_District.
2. *Tinker v. Des Moines Independent Community School District*, 393 U.S. 503 (1969). For a full account of the case, see John W. Johnson, *The Struggle for Student Rights:* Tinker v. Des Moines *and the 1960s* (1997).
3. See Jamin B. Raskin, *We the Students: Supreme Court Cases for and about Students* (3rd ed., 2008).
4. See "From *Brown* to 'Bong Hits': Assessing a Half Century of Judicial Involvement in Education, American Enterprise Institute, Oct. 15, 2008, www.aei.org/event/1746. See Mark Walsh, "Scholars Weigh Court Influence Over School Practices, Climate," *Education Week*, Oct. 22, 2008, p. 9.
5. Richard Arum and Doreet Preiss, "Still Judging School Discipline," in Joshua Dunn and Martin R. West (eds.), *From Schoolhouse to Courthouse: The Judiciary's Role in American Education* (2009, forthcoming).
6. The drug testing decisions are *Vernonia School Dist. No. 47J v. Acton*, 515 U.S. 645 (1995), and *Board of Education v. Earls*, 536 U.S. 822 (2002). The more recent decision is *Morse v. Frederick*, 551 U.S. 393 (2007).
7. Quoted in Arthur H. Rotstein, "Supreme Court to Get Ariz. Teen Strip-Search Case," The Associated Press, April 19, 2009.
8. The case is *Tannahill v. Lockney Independent School District*, 133 F.Supp. 2d. 919. (N.D.Tex. 2001). For coverage, see David Stevens, "Drug-testing policy is struck down," *Dallas Morning News*, March 3, 2001, p. 33A. A documentary on the case, "Larry v. Lockney," premiered on PBS in July 2003.
9. The case is *Board of Education v. Earls*, 536 U.S. 822 (2002).
10. For background, see Thomas J. Billitteri, "Discipline in Schools," *CQ Researcher*, Feb. 15, 2008, pp. 145-168; and Kathy Koch, "Zero Tolerance," *CQ Researcher*, March 10, 2000, pp. 185-208.
11. The case is *Palmer v. Waxahachie Independent School District*, 08-10903. The earlier Supreme Court decision, *United States v. O'Brien*, 391 U.S. 367 (1968), upheld a conviction for burning a draft card. The court held that the government can restrict so-called expressive conduct if the restriction furthers an important or substantial government interest, is unrelated to suppression of speech and prohibits no more speech than necessary to further that interest.
12. The case is *Morse v. Frederick*, 551 U.S. 393 (2007).
13. Anne Proffitt Dupre, *Speaking Up: The Unintended Costs of Free Speech in Public Schools* (2009).
14. The case is *Lowry v. Watson Chapel School District*, 540 F.3d 572 (8th Cir. 2008). The Supreme Court declined to review the decision. For coverage, see Alberto D. Morales, "Appellate Court Rules School District Violated First Amendment Rights of Students Who Wore Black Armbands to Schools," Student Press Law Center, Sept. 8, 2008, www.splc.org/newsflash_archives.asp?id=1803&year=2008.
15. The case is *Bethel School Dist. No. 43 v. Fraser*, 478 U.S. 675 (1986).
16. The case is *Curry v. Hensinger*, SB F.3d 570 (6th Cir. 2008). The U.S. Supreme Court declined to review the decision. For coverage, see LaNia Coleman, "Candy-cane case dies at high court's door," *The Saginaw* (Mich.) *News*, Dec. 10, 2008.
17. See "Religion and the Public Schools: A Summary of the Law," *American Jewish Congress*, February 2009, www.ajcongress.org/site/DocServer/2009_RPS_-_February_09_Revision.pdf?docID=3421.
18. For background, see Patrick Marshall, "Religion in Schools," *CQ Researcher*, Jan. 12, 2001, pp. 1-24.
19. For background, see Kenneth Jost, "Religion in Schools," *CQ Researcher*, Feb. 18, 1994, pp. 145-168.
20. Background drawn in part from Dupre, *op. cit.*; Raskin, *op. cit.* For an up-to-date, one-volume history, see William J. Reese, *America's Public Schools: From the Common School to "No Child Left Behind"* (2005).
21. Justice Clarence Thomas collected the cases in his concurring opinion in *Morse v. Frederick*, 551 U.S. 393 (2008).

22. John Dewey, *On Democracy and Education: An Introduction to the Philosophy of Education* (1916), p. 129, quoted in Richard Arum, *Judging School Discipline: The Crisis of Moral Authority* (2003), p. 32.
23. The cases are *Meyer v. Nebraska*, 262 U.S. 390 (1923), and *West Virginia State Board of Education v. Barnette*, 319 U.S. 624 (1943).
24. For background see Kenneth Jost, "Racial Diversity in Public Schools," *CQ Researcher*, Sept. 14, 2007, pp. 745-768.
25. For background, see H. B. Shaffer, "Discipline in Public Schools," in *Editorial Research Reports*, Aug. 27, 1969, available online at CQ Press Electronic Library, http://library.cqpress.com/cqresearcher/cqresrre1969082700.
26. The citation is 419 U.S. 565 (1975).
27. The citation is 469 U.S. 325 (1985).
28. The citation is 478 U.S. 675 (1986). The school is in Spanaway, 10 miles south of Tacoma.
29. The citation is 484 U.S. 260 (1988).
30. The decision is *Westside Community Schools v. Mergen*, 496 U.S. 226 (1990). See also *Good News Club v. Milford Central School*, 533 U.S. 98 (2001).
31. For background, see these *CQ Researcher* reports: Thomas J. Billitteri, "Discipline in Schools," Feb. 15, 2008, pp. 145-168; John Greenya, "Bullying," Feb. 4, 2005, pp. 101-124.
32. The decisions are *Vernonia School Dist. No. 47J v. Acton*, 515 U.S. 645 (1995), and *Board of Education v. Earls*, 536 U.S. 822 (2002). For coverage, see respective editions of *Supreme Court Yearbook* (CQ Press). Also see Kathy Koch, "Drug Testing," *CQ Researcher*, Nov. 20, 1998, pp. 1001-1024.
33. For background, see Barbara Mantel, "No Child Left Behind," *CQ Researcher*, May 27, 2005, pp. 469-492. Also see Kenneth Jost, "Testing in Schools," April 20, 2001, *CQ Researcher*, pp. 321-344.
34. The decision is *Zelman v. Simmons-Harris*, 536 U.S. 639 (2002). For coverage, see Jost, *Supreme Court Yearbook 2001-2002*, *op. cit.* Also see Kenneth Jost, "School Vouchers Showdown," *CQ Researcher*, Feb. 15, 2002, pp. 121-144; and Kathy Koch, "School Vouchers," *CQ Researcher*, April 9, 1999, pp. 281-304.
35. See Jennifer Medina, "Boys and Girls Together, Taught Separately in Public Schools," *The New York Times*, March 11, 2009, p. A24. For background, see Kenneth Jost, "Single-Sex Education," *CQ Researcher*, July 12, 2002, pp. 569-592.
36. The decision is *Parents Involved in Community Schools v. Seattle School District No. 1*, 551 U.S. – (2007). For coverage, see Kenneth Jost, *Supreme Court Yearbook 2006-2007, op. cit.*
37. Background from Andy Gammill, "Teachers shielded from suits," *The Indianapolis Star*, May 12, 2009, p. 15A.
38. The cases discussed are *S.E. v. Grant County Board of Education*, 6th Cir., Oct. 10, 2008, and *Serafin v. School of Excellence in Education*, 5th Cir., Oct. 30, 2007. See The School Law Blog, http://blogs.edweek.org/edweek/school_law/.
39. The Supreme Court decision is *Wright v. Ingraham*, 430 U.S. 651 (1977).
40. See "A Conversation with Mary Beth Tinker," *Human Rights*, Vol. 35, No. 3 (summer 2008), p. 6.
41. Quoted in Joan Biskupic and Greg Toppo, "Girl's strip search argued in court," *USA Today*, April 22, 2009, p. 3A. See also Jesse J. Holland, "Justices hear arguments over school strip search," The Associated Press, April 22, 2009.

BIBLIOGRAPHY

Books

Law of the Student Press (3rd ed.), _Student Press Law Center_, 2008.
The 402-page compendium provides comprehensive coverage of general media-law topics such as libel, privacy and copyright as well as legal developments specifically relating to student print, broadcast and online media. Includes chapter notes, appendix materials.

Arum, Richard, _Judging School Discipline: The Crisis of Moral Authority_, _Harvard University Press_, 2003.
A professor of sociology at New York University and a former public-school teacher uses extensive empirical

research to argue that U.S. public schools face "a crisis in the legitimacy of school discipline." Includes extensive research data, notes.

Dunn, Joshua, and Martin R. West (eds.), *From Schoolhouse to Courthouse: The Judiciary's Role in American Education, Brookings Institution Press/ Thomas F. Fordham Institute*, 2009.
Ten experts from law, education and political science examine school-related litigation in such areas as desegregation, high-stakes testing, school finance, discipline, special education, school choice, religious freedom and student speech. Dunn is an assistant professor of political science at Colorado State University; West is an assistant professor of education at Brown University.

Dupre, Anne Proffitt, *Speaking Up: The Unintended Costs of Free Speech in Public Schools, Harvard University Press*, 2009.
A professor at the University of Georgia School of Law critically examines the impact of free-speech rulings, which she says have "dramatically changed the way public schools operate." Includes notes.

Johnson, John W., *The Struggle for Student Rights:* Tinker v. Des Moines *and the 1960s, University Press of Kansas*, 1997.
A history professor at the University of Northern Iowa provides a detailed account of the landmark *Tinker* case from the Des Moines students' initial decision to wear black armbands to school protest the Vietnam War through the Supreme Court decision upholding their free-speech rights and the aftermath of the ruling. The ruling, Johnson says, "will be remembered as long as students demand the right to be heard as well as seen." Includes a five-page chronology of the case and a short bibliographical essay.

Olivas, Michael A., and Ronna Greff Schneider (eds.), *Education Law Stories, Thomson/West*, 2008.
The book recounts the stories of a dozen landmark education-related cases in such areas as religion, school finance, race, gender and disabilities. Olivas is a professor at the University of Houston Law Center, Schneider a professor at the University of Cincinnati College of Law.

Raskin, Jamin, *We the Students: Supreme Court Cases for and about Students* (3rd ed.), *CQ Press*, 2008.
The high school text includes excerpts from and discussion of major decisions affecting students from the U.S. Supreme Court and other federal and state courts. Raskin is a professor at American University's Washington College of Law. Includes glossary, five-page bibliography.

Reichman, Henry, *Censorship and Selection: Issues and Answers for Schools, American Library Association*, 2001.
The longtime editor of the American Library Association's *Newsletter on Intellectual Freedom* gives practical guidance for school administrators, librarians and teachers on free-speech rights affecting school curricula, student newspapers and library acquisition policies. Includes notes, summary of major legal decisions and seven-page bibliography. Reichman is also professor of history at California State University, East Bay.

Valente, William D., with Christina M. Valente, *Law in the Schools* (6th ed.), *Merrill Prentice Hall*, 2005.
The textbook's nine chapters cover a full range of legal issues for public and private schools, including issues of student rights and discipline. Includes notes, select table of cases and glossary. William Valente is professor emeritus at Villanova University School of Law; his wife assisted on the book.

Articles

"Student Rights," *Human Rights*, Vol. 35, No. 3 (summer 2008), www.abanet.org/irr/hr/summer08/.
The nine articles in this issue of the quarterly journal of the American Bar Association's Section on Individual Rights and Responsibilities examine such topics as the impact of *Tinker*, student journalism and educational access for women and girls and for LGBT students.

On the Web

***The School Law Blog*, http://blogs.edweek.org/edweek/school_law/.**
The blog provides news and analysis on legal developments affecting schools, educators, students and parents. Author Mark Walsh is a contributing writer to *Education Week* who has covered education-related issues in the courts for 17 years.

For More Information

Alliance Defense Fund, 15100 N. 90th St., Scottsdale, AZ 85260; (800) 835-5233; www.alliancedefensefund.org. Legal alliance defending the right to speak about the Bible.

American Civil Liberties Union, 125 Broad St., 18th Floor, New York, NY 10004; (212) 607-3300; www.aclu.org. National organization advocating for individual rights via litigation, legislation and education.

American Enterprise Institute, 1150 17th St., N.W., Washington, DC 20036; (202) 862-5800; www.aei.org. Public policy research institute focusing on issues relating to government, politics and social welfare.

Americans United for Separation of Church and State, 518 C St., N.E., Washington, DC 20002; (202) 466-3234; www.au.org. Nonpartisan organization working to preserve church-state separation in order to ensure religious freedom.

Gay, Lesbian and Straight Education Network, 90 Broad St., 2nd Floor, New York, NY 10004; (212) 727-0135; www.glsen.org. National education organization striving to eliminate discrimination in schools based on sexual orientation and gender identity.

National Association of Secondary School Principals, 1904 Association Dr., Reston, VA 20191-1537; (703) 860-0200; www.principals.org. Organization of school principals promoting excellence in school leadership.

National School Boards Association, 1680 Duke St., Alexandria, VA 22314; (703) 838-6722; www.nsba.org. Represents state associations of school boards to foster excellence and equity in public education.

National Youth Rights Association, 1101 15th St., N.W., Suite 200, Washington, DC 20005; (202) 296-2992; www.youthrights.org. Youth-led nonprofit organization fighting for civil rights and liberties of young people.

Student Press Law Center, 1101 Wilson Blvd., Suite 1100, Arlington, VA 22209; (703) 807-1904; www.splc.org. Advocates, litigates and disseminates information relating to student free-press rights.

Students for a Sensible Drug Policy, 1623 Connecticut Ave., N.W., Suite 300, Washington, DC 20009; (202) 293-4414; www.ssdp.org. International grassroots network of students pushing for more sensible drug policies.

8

Juvenile Justice

Are Sentencing Policies Too Harsh?

Peter Katel

AP Photo/LM Otero

Alice Smith takes her son Erik home after his release from a juvenile prison in Corsicana, Texas, last year. She said Texas Youth Commission prison guards stood by while he was physically abused by other inmates. Last year the Dallas Morning News revealed brutality, sexual abuse of inmates and cover-ups at several commission facilities. Abuses have also been revealed at juvenile correctional facilities in California, Maryland and other states in recent years.

From *CQ Researcher*, November 7, 2008.

Washington, D.C., lawyer Matthew Caspari has developed some strong feelings about punishing teenage criminals since last August. That's when he wrestled with a knife-wielding 17-year-old who'd been harassing one of his neighbors on Capitol Hill.

Caspari had been taking a walk with his wife and their 6-month-old daughter when he saw a neighbor in trouble. As he was calling 911, the young man threatened him, and they began to fight. When Caspari's dropped cell phone picked up his wife's screams, police raced to the scene and arrested the man.

But what happened afterwards was equally disturbing, Caspari told a City Council hearing in October. After a Family Court judge released the youth while he awaited sentencing, he was back on the street hanging out with a tough crowd, Caspari said. That's why he said he opposed legislation to rescind the U.S. attorney's sole power to try teenagers 15 and older in adult court for violent crimes.

"Family Court is no deterrent," said Caspari. "Punishment and consequences are simply not taken seriously by the offenders. If you want to instill a sense of accountability in these teens and provide therapy and services — there's no reason why you can't provide that in the adult system — while protecting the community."

Democratic Councilman Phil Mendelson, who is co-sponsoring the proposal to reign in the U.S. attorney, says statistical evidence shows adult-court prosecution tends to reinforce — rather than diminish — young offenders' criminal tendencies.

"The inclination is, if somebody commits a crime, particularly a violent crime, then lock 'em up," Mendelson told the

Cut-Off Age for Juvenile Courts Is Typically 17

Children through age 17 must be tried in juvenile court in 39 states and the District of Columbia. The cut-off age is 16 in nine states and 15 in two — New York and North Carolina.

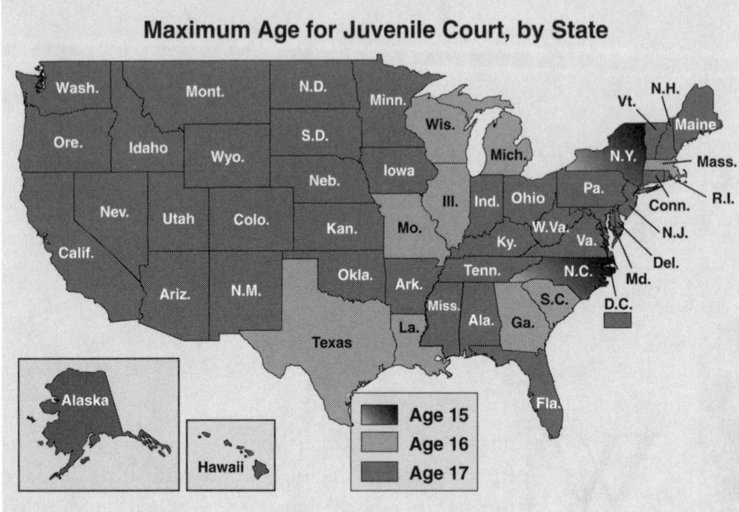

Source: Sarah Hammond, "Adults or Kids?" State Legislatures, April 2008

hearing. "And the research shows that is statistically counterproductive."

Mendelson's comment echoed the views of a growing number of juvenile justice experts and activists. With violent juvenile crime trending downward for the past 13 years, they say it's time to replace the tough sentences that state lawmakers enacted in the 1980s and '90s and handle more youth cases in juvenile court. The hard-line policies reflected skyrocketing juvenile crime and the prediction — later proved baseless — that violent, young "superpredators" would take over the nation's inner cities. (*See "Background," p. 187.*)

The get-tough measures eased the transferring of juveniles to adult courts where they faced tougher sentences. Some states allowed prosecutors to "direct file" juvenile cases in adult court; others left the decision to a judge, or made transfers automatic for certain charges.

But standards differ on when courts legally recognize that adulthood begins. In most states — especially those striving for more rehabilitation — 18 is the threshold age. In 10 states — Georgia, Illinois, Louisiana, Massachusetts, Michigan, Missouri, New Hampshire, South Carolina, Texas and Wisconsin — teens become adults at 17; in New York and North Carolina, it's 16.

Experts say they haven't determined how many convicts are serving time for crimes committed before they were 18. But the Campaign for Youth Justice, a Washington-based advocacy group, estimates that on any given day 7,500 youths under 18 are in jail or awaiting trial or transport to prison or juvenile detention.

Adult court sentences often are tougher than those in juvenile courts. Until 2005, they could include the death penalty, which the U.S. Supreme Court then banned for anyone who committed a capital crime before turning 18.

The backdrop to that decision was a decline in youth crime, and the drop continues. According to the most recent statistics, the 2007 arrest rate for youths ages 10-18 was down to fewer than 300 per 100,000 — the same level as in 1982.[1]

To counter assertions by prosecutors that tougher laws brought crime rates down, opponents of harsh penalties point to studies showing that juveniles tried as adults come out of prison more dangerous than when they went in, and hence more prone to become adult criminals. A nationwide Task Force on Community Preventive Services, appointed by the U.S. Centers for Disease Control and Prevention, concluded in late 2006: "Overall, available evidence indicates that use of transfer laws and strengthened transfer policies is counterproductive for the purpose of reducing juvenile violence and enhancing public safety."[2]

Indeed, at a recent conference on juvenile rehabilitation at the Brookings Institution, Bart Lubow, director of programs for high-risk youth at the Annie E. Casey Foundation, said the punitive laws of the 1980s and '90s had "resulted in the criminalization of delinquency." The Baltimore-based nonprofit is advising 100 cities and counties on how to reorganize their juvenile systems so that they rely less on incarceration.

Many prosecutors say they also want to channel more juveniles into detention alternatives — but not all of them.

In Oregon, says Clatsop County District Attorney Joshua Marquis, "We went from an extreme — 'everyone needs a hug and cup of Ovaltine' — to a more nuanced system. Delinquents who need a minimum of incarceration and a maximum amount of structure get treated one way. And then there are the young criminals who for all intents and purposes are young adults — they don't act like children, don't respond like children and you can't treat them like children."

Oregon voters approved the present system in 1994, when the tough-on-crime approach was sweeping the nation. Measure 11 stiffened sentences for certain violent offenses and applied them to defendants as young as 15.

By 2003, 31 states had passed laws requiring juveniles charged with certain crimes to be tried as adults. Also during the '90s, 13 states lowered the top age for juvenile court jurisdiction to 15 or 16. As a result, the number of inmates serving life without parole for crimes committed when they were under 18 began climbing; today 2,484 youthful offenders are serving such sentences.[3]

Youths Get Life in Prison in 31 States

Judges in 31 states must sentence juveniles to life in prison without parole (LWOP) if they are convicted of first-degree murder or certain other offenses; judges in 14 states have sentencing discretion. Five states and the District of Columbia do not permit juvenile LWOP. Pennsylvania has 444 youths serving life without parole — more than any other state.

* Ban on sentencing to LWOP is under court challenge

Source: "The Rest of Their Lives," Human Rights Watch, May 2008

But rollback advocates have scored a few successes. Connecticut last year raised its age threshold for adult court from 16 to 18. In 2006, Colorado abolished juvenile life without parole. In addition, several states have restricted adult-court transfers, and advocates are readying legislation for introduction in other states next year (*see p. 182*).[4]

Hard-liners can claim some victories as well. This year, a California proposal to abolish life without parole for juveniles failed to get the required two-thirds majority needed for passage. And in Colorado, Democratic Gov. Bill Ritter Jr., a former district attorney, vetoed a bill that would have stripped prosecutors of their sole authority to charge juveniles in adult court.[5]

"They wanted to take away our discretion — there's still a movement in our state to do that," says Denver District Attorney Mitch Morrissey. "They wanted to have more hearings and more experts and cost a lot more money."

Morrissey and other supporters of tough laws argue that prosecutors use them sparingly. In the suburbs of Minneapolis-St. Paul, Dakota County Prosecutor James C. Backstrom tells of resisting heavy pressure in 2006 to press for life without parole for two 17-year-olds who gunned down one of the boys' parents in cold blood. Instead, the prosecutor accepted pleas to a charge that didn't carry the no-parole proviso, giving them a chance to apply for release after 30 years.

"They knew right from wrong; there was no question they should be convicted of first-degree murder," Backstrom says, "but they had no criminal history whatsoever. I just did not feel that locking them up for the rest of their natural lives was the right thing to do. They'll have a chance to salvage some part of their lives. There were some strong disagreements, even from the victims' family."

AP Photo/Waco Tribune-Herald/Duane A. Laverty

Texas state Rep. Paula Pierson talks with an inmate at the Texas Youth Commission facility in Marlin in March 2007 in the wake of a scandal involving the sexual abuse of incarcerated youths.

Prosecutors everywhere can recall horrendous cases that warranted tough sentences. But rollback advocates argue such cases tend to obscure the fact that more than half of juvenile cases that end up in adult court don't involve crimes against people.

"You could certainly say that when you expand the use of adult court transfer you are likely to capture more serious offenders," says Jeffrey A. Butts, a research fellow at the University of Chicago's Chapin Hall Center for Children. "But it's a blunt instrument, so you pull a lot of youth into that pathway in the attempt to grab all serious offenders."

According to the Justice Department's Office of Juvenile Justice and Delinquency Prevention (OJJDP), about 51 percent of all 6,885 juvenile cases transferred ("waived") to adult court in 2005 (the most recent figures available) involved "person" offenses — that is, crimes against individuals. The rest were property crimes (27 percent), drug offenses (12 percent) and public order violations (10 percent), such as weapons, sex or liquor violations.[6] (*See graph, p. 184.*)

No national statistics exist on the total number of juveniles tried in adult court. The closest estimate, based on calculations by Butts, is 200,000 a year.

To be sure, statistics don't capture the nitty-gritty of crime in the streets. Lawyer Caspari says the teen who pulled a knife on him wasn't eligible for transfer to adult court because Caspari was never cut or stabbed. But he could have been.

That's why Caspari opposes allowing judges — instead of prosecutors — to send cases to adult court. The relative speed of the present system, he says, tells young offenders that they'll be held accountable quickly. "The practical reality is the defendant's lawyer can gum up the system by requesting it go back down to juvenile court, and that's another nine months," he says. "Is that the message you want to send to these kids?"

As prosecutors and experts debate the nation's juvenile justice policies, here are some of the key questions:

Should states roll back their tough juvenile crime laws?

When youth crime skyrocketed in the late 1980s and early '90s, legislatures across the country took a new approach toward handling young people charged with crimes. Lawmakers carved out major exceptions to practices designed, broadly speaking, to rehabilitate rather than to punish.

"Today we are living with a juvenile justice system that was created around the time of the silent film," Sen. John Ashcroft, R-Mo. (later U.S. attorney general in the first George W. Bush administration), complained to the Senate in 1997, reflecting a widely held sentiment. It's a system "that reprimands the crime victim for being at the wrong place at the wrong time, and then turns around and hugs the juvenile terrorist, whispering ever so softly into his ear, 'Don't worry, the State will cure you.' . . . Such a system can handle runaways, truants and other status offenders, but it is ill-equipped to deal with those who commit serious and violent juvenile crimes repeatedly."[7]

The new get-tough approach, adopted with variations in all states and Washington, D.C., focused on easing the process by which juveniles accused of homicide and other violent offenses could be tried in adult court. In some states, those convicted would do their time in adult institutions.

At least two states turned the corner ahead of the others. In New York, following two random murders by a 15-year-old in the New York City subway in 1978, the legislature gave automatic jurisdiction to the adult court system in violent crimes involving defendants as young as 13. Three years later, Idaho enacted a law that automatically sent youths 14 to 18 to adult court for murder and four other violent crimes.

Arrest Rate Declining for Juveniles

The arrest rate for violent crimes committed by juveniles has steadily declined since peaking in 1994. The rate in 2007 roughly equaled the level 25 years earlier. Prosecutors say crime is down because laws are tough. Youth advocates say crime in general has been dropping and that harsh laws only cause more recidivism.

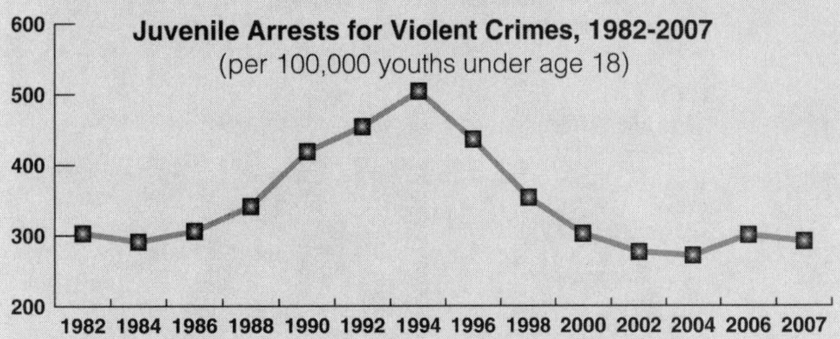

Source: Jeffrey A. Butts, "Juvenile Arrest Rates 1982-2007," presentation at the University of Chicago, September 2008

A drop in violent crime by both adults and juveniles that began in the early 1990s and continued into the new century seemed to validate the hard-line laws. Yet, criminologists argued that the drop would have happened anyway for a variety of reasons, including the waning of the crack boom.

"Most systematic analyses show that the crime rate is much less sensitive to crime policy than most people think," says Laurence Steinberg, a psychology professor at Temple University in Philadelphia and a specialist in adolescent development. In any event, he and others have said, juveniles handled in adult courts were more likely to return to crime upon release than those handled in juvenile court.

The effects of old-school confinement for young people is also being questioned in states that run juvenile institutions patterned on adult prisons. In California, a state judge in February ordered the Corrections Standards Authority to improve its reporting on conditions at the institutions, which failed to cite beatings and other mistreatment that federal investigators had uncovered. And in Texas, a major scandal over sexual and other abuses led to enactment of a new law that imposes new standards on youth prisons, including removing juveniles charged with misdemeanors from the institutions.[8]

Studies of juvenile recidivism often focus on adult court transfers. In a Justice Department-funded study in Florida, researchers reported in 2005 that 49 percent of juveniles transferred into the adult court system committed new crimes after release, compared with only 35 percent of the offenders who were kept in the juvenile system. Among violent offenders, recidivism ran to 24 percent and 16 percent, respectively.

"Juveniles exiting the adult criminal justice system are more likely — not less likely — to re-offend than juveniles who committed the same crimes and had comparable criminal histories," Steinberg says. "And those coming out of the adult system re-offend sooner and more seriously."

Young convicts who return from prison have serious effects on communities, Steinberg says. "Juvenile offenders have a lower success rate in the transition to adulthood than any other group of disadvantaged individuals," he says. "Our current policy, which presumably is supposed to reduce crime, actually makes our neighborhoods more dangerous."

But Oregon District Attorney Marquis says that juvenile advocates who focus on recidivism overlook a key fact — imprisoned criminals don't hurt anyone while locked up. "Incapacitation" is the law-enforcement term for that outcome, and, "That's not a small thing," says Marquis, a member of the National District Attorneys Association's Executive Committee.

Oregon's Measure 11 requires long prison sentences for 16 violent and sex-related crimes for all perpetrators age 15 and older. "The most effective thing that is done, realistically, is incapacitation," Marquis says. "In Oregon they actually counted up the number of people not raped, beaten or robbed as result of Measure 11." According to Crime Victims United, a citizens' group, the measure prevented 67,822 robberies, aggravated assaults, forcible rapes, manslaughters and murders through 2006.[9]

However, a 2004 Justice Department-funded study by the nonprofit RAND Corp. concluded the

Many Youths Land in Adult Courts for Committing 'Non-Person' Crimes

Half of the juveniles referred to adult criminal courts in 2005 were charged with property, drug and so-called public order offenses, or roughly the same percentage referred for crimes against persons.

Referral Offenses for Juveniles, 2005
(by percentage referred to adult courts and number of offenses)

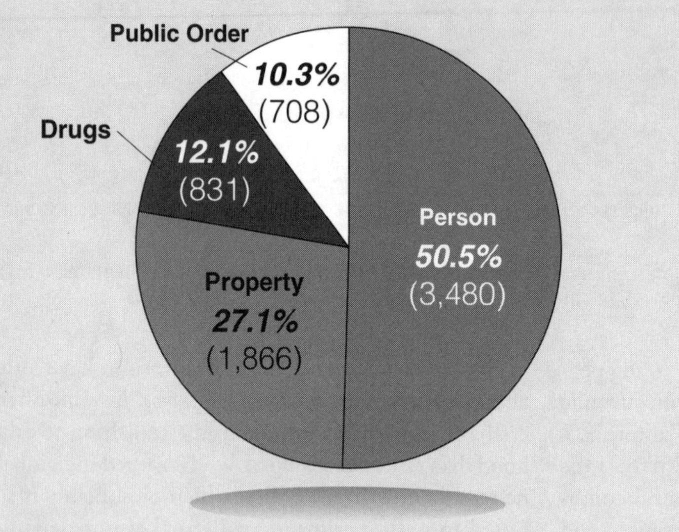

Source: "Easy Access to Juvenile Court Statistics: 1985-2005," National Center for Juvenile Justice, 2008; Office of Juvenile Justice and Delinquency Prevention

incapacitation effect was lessened because more small-scale offenders were being imprisoned along with violent criminals. In 1994, 24 percent of the defendants sent to prison for the crimes that would later be covered by Measure 11 had clean records. In 1999, when the law had kicked in, 36 percent had no prior offenses.[10]

Some leaders of the rollback movement favor certain exceptions. "I'd have no hesitancy even today to send some kids to adult court," says Shay Bilchik, a former Miami prosecutor who now directs Georgetown University's Center for Juvenile Justice Reform. "But that's a small minority of cases, probably less than 5 percent of kids who get transferred."

Prosecutors typically argue that a greater share of young offenders deserve transfer. "The changes incorporated in the juvenile codes in the early-to-mid-'90s were long overdue," says Minnesota prosecutor Backstrom. "In most Minnesota jurisdictions, 1-2 percent end up in adult court."

Did tough laws lower crime rates?

Juvenile crime began falling nationwide just as the last states to enact measures treating some juveniles as adult criminals were falling into line with the national trend.

The juvenile violent crime boom hit its peak in 1994. From that year to 1996, juvenile arrests for violent crimes declined by 12 percent, according to the Justice Department. Overall, juvenile arrests increased by 3 percent from 1995-1996, to 2.8 million, but drug crimes along with curfew violations and other "status" offenses largely accounted for the increase.[11]

To be sure, the pattern didn't hold true throughout the country, as is typical of all crime trends. And juvenile crime in the late 1990s remained far above its early-1980s level. Violent crime arrests began climbing steadily in 1988 — just as a virulent crack cocaine epidemic began hitting the nation's inner cities — from about 350 per 100,000 10-to-17-year-olds in the population to a peak of about 525 per 100,000 in 1994.[12]

But the decline in juvenile crime continued well into the new century. In 1995-2004, arrests of suspects age 18 and under fell 22 percent. (Adult crime remained essentially flat, registering a 1 percent drop, during the same period.)[13]

As early as 1996, Georgetown's Bilchik, then head of the Justice Department's Office of Juvenile Justice and Delinquency Prevention, noted that forecasts of an ever-rising wave of juvenile violence had been wrong. Instead, the crime numbers had started heading down. "The predictions of an onslaught of violent crime have been proven wrong two years in a row," he wrote in the department's annual statistical report, in a tacit swipe at the "superpredator" thesis.[14]

As violent juvenile crime continues to decline, however, hard-liners cite the downward trend as evidence that the tough laws of the 1980s and '90s delivered on their promise.

But even as the punitive approach took hold, some cities and counties used the flexibility in some laws to channel delinquents into rehabilitation-oriented programs. The outcomes have been positive, says the Annie E. Casey Foundation's Lubow. "Nobody's suffered, there's been no great public safety risk."

But backers of the tougher approach argue that juvenile crime responded to tougher laws just as adult crime trended downward in states that adopted laws requiring prison time after a third felony conviction.[15]

"You can compare the result to adult crime after we passed the three-strikes law in California," says Nina Salarno-Ashford, a former prosecutor who headed California's Office of Victims' Services. "We're taking the worst off the streets, and it does lower re-offending. Some do recidivate, but the heavier sentences for top-end offenders help in the decline." Salarno-Ashford's family founded Crime Victims United after her older sister was murdered in 1979.

Rollback supporters note that, despite the tougher laws, an uptick of violent crime from 2004-2006 briefly interrupted the downward slide. "I would venture that few of these get-tough reformers are willing to take credit for the increase in crime that has taken place in the last several years," Temple University's Steinberg told the Brookings youth rehabilitation conference.

Some on the law-enforcement side of the debate agree that simple explanations for crime upsurges and declines should be treated with some skepticism. But supporters of the tougher laws say they're willing to accept some uncertainty about what brought crime down — as long as it went down.

"Something's working," says Denver District Attorney Morrissey. "If it is because these laws got passed, and we treated violent offenders differently, I think that's good to see. Fewer people are getting victimized."

Morrissey says it would take a thorough statistical analysis to identify a direct connection between declining crime and a 1987 Colorado law that expanded prosecutors' power to transfer juveniles to adult court. Just as important, he suggests, are Colorado's rehabilitative programs for juveniles in detention institutions. "They tend not to go to prison" as adults, he says.

Crime-trend analysts on the youth advocate side of the debate have been arguing for years that the causes of crime surges and declines have little to do with law and policy changes. "If we go back to the 1970s and '80s, when New York was expanding the use of adult courts and prisons for juveniles, do you see a corresponding decline for youth crime in New York? No," says the University of Chicago's Butts, summarizing research by criminologist Simon Singer of Northeastern University.

Conclusive cause-and-effect evidence is virtually impossible to find, Butts says. "You'd need a study that is impossible to do — take a big sample of youth who don't know anything about criminal justice and expose some of them to information about adult transfer, and keep the others in a bubble," he says. Tracking the number from each group who got into trouble with the law would provide definitive statistics, he says.

Does the prospect of facing the adult court system deter juveniles from crime?

A key argument for tougher laws holds that many young, potential criminals are scared "straight" at the thought of going to adult court — and possibly adult prison.

"Proponents of the latest reform proposals espouse a philosophy of retribution and punishment — insisting that the juvenile court and its sanctions do not deter juvenile crime," the Office of Juvenile Justice and Delinquency Prevention said in summarizing a 1996 conference in Washington.[16]

In Idaho, the main author of a 1995 state law proclaims that the deterrent effect of his state's tougher approach is palpable. "Before, it was no big deal to go to juvenile court," says Republican state Sen. Denton Darrington. "Now, kids don't like to go before a judge who has control over their lives. He has a lot of options at his disposal: He can bind them over to adult court. He can put them in a local juvenile detention center. He can put them on probation and dictate the terms."

While the Idaho law stepped up penalties and eased the transfer of juveniles to adult court, it also expanded or created treatment programs for juveniles who weren't sentenced to detention.

Darrington, who logged 33 years as a junior high school history teacher, says he's certain young peoples'

After a Youth's Death, Who Pays?

Would jail help rehabilitate a young shooter?

Like his father before him, Airrion "Ali" Johnson was in the wrong place at the wrong time. The 16-year-old Washington, D.C., youth was hanging out with some friends late one night last year during the Labor Day weekend. He had his mother's permission to be out, but he wasn't where he said he'd be.

Instead of his best friend's apartment, Johnson and his pals were at another, unsupervised apartment, and one of the teenagers there, 18-year-old David Williams, had a pistol. Playing around, a 15-year-old girl grabbed the gun and — thinking it was unloaded — pulled the trigger.

"My mom is going to be so mad," Johnson said just after the bullet hit him in the chest. He was pronounced dead a little while later.

Johnson's mother was angry indeed. But Theresa Norville reserves her strongest outrage for the city's Department of Youth Rehabilitation Services (DYRS), which she says has failed to provide long-term supervision and counseling for the girl who fired the fatal shot.

"I'm in therapy once a week, and I know that there's no way this child could be rehabilitated in six months," says Norville, 35, an account analyst at Children's Hospital. She thinks the girl should be incarcerated — for her own good — not out walking around. "Rehabilitation can't be roaming the streets," Norville says, noting that Williams, the gun owner, pleaded guilty to manslaughter and is serving a 36-month sentence.

In fact, DYRS statistics show that young people who don't serve time at detention facilities but are supervised in "community-based placements" — which can include remaining at home — had a recidivism rate of 28 percent in fiscal 2007. By comparison, the recidivism rate for young people who had been confined was 16 percent.

Johnson's death provides a window into the real-life circumstances that lie behind arguments about punishment versus rehabilitation. Though Norville's criticism of the youth agency might have been expected from a victim's mother, she insists that she's not out for vengeance. What she says she wants is intensive counseling and monitoring for the girl, pointing out that only confinement would ensure that she gets help.

Indeed, Norville has visited Williams in prison and says he's gotten better rehabilitative attention behind bars than the girl has received from the DYRS.

Norville tells of hugging the girl after she broke down in the courthouse shortly after the shooting. "I told her, 'I don't hate you, I don't want you locked up for the rest of your life, but you did what you did, and everybody has to pay for their actions in life.' "

Shootings in Washington are often deliberate, so Johnson's accidental death wasn't a typical crime. But it did stem from possession of a handgun — which was illegal in Washington at the time. Williams had been carrying the pistol, he said, for protection from enemies in the often rough Shaw neighborhood, Norville says.

That same neighborhood, in fact, is where Johnson's 26-year-old father, also named Airrion, died in 1997 after being hit by a stray bullet fired during a shootout between rival gangs. A *Washington Post* report on the trial of some of the accused shooters confirms Norville's account of her husband. "He had a son, Ali, whom he adored, and a job working construction. He had nothing to do" with the gangs, the newspaper reported.[1]

Covering the trial three years later, reporter Neely Tucker wrote that immediately after being shot, Airrion "sat on the pavement saying, 'I'm okay. No, really, hey, I'm all right.' Then he died."

"Ali was six or seven at the time," Norville says. "We talked about it often." She used his father's death, she says, as a lesson about the importance of trying to be in the right place at the right time.

[1] See Neely Tucker, "Revenge on Trial," *The Washington Post*, April 6, 2000, p. A1.

determination to avoid the expanded juvenile system has played a major part in the juvenile crime decline. From 1994 through 2004, Idaho's juvenile arrests fell 27 percent — from 23,170 to 16,747 — even as the under-17 population grew 8 percent — from 158,005 to 170,936.

The rollback advocates don't quarrel with some aspects of the Idaho program and others that resemble it. But Idaho also allows imprisoning youths in adult prisons if they're convicted in adult court, though that step isn't mandatory.

But youth advocates draw the line at confining youths with adults, arguing that no deterrence or other purpose is served. "The more punitive the response, the more juvenile offenders re-offend," says Temple University's Steinberg. "Most crimes committed by juveniles are impulsive, stupid acts that occur when they're with their friends, not calculated decisions. To be deterred by the prospect of a long sentence or incarceration or transfer into the adult system, an adolescent needs to think like an adult." (*See sidebar, p. 190.*)

Deterrence, however, isn't the only rationale for keeping extremely severe penalties on the books. "With kids, the deterrent factor is less than with adults," says Minnesota prosecutor Backstrom, accepting a main argument of youth advocates. "A lot of kids don't think before they act."

However, Backstrom says, where violent crime is concerned, "There needs to be accountability," including any punishment short of the death sentence. "Life without parole for a kid would be used in a very limited set of circumstances, but there might be a case where it's warranted. To remove the possibility would be wrong. Juveniles have tied up and tortured elderly people — I don't agree with those who want to argue that people who do that shouldn't be locked up for life."

Some rollback proponents concede that some adolescents should be locked up, even in adult institutions. But focusing on extreme and relatively rare cases obscures a more important question: "The issue is whether the system is smart enough to distinguish high-risk kids from run-of-the-mill delinquents," says Lubow at the Annie E. Casey Foundation.

"About a quarter-million kids whose offenses were committed under the age of 18 are prosecuted annually in the adult system," Lubow says. "These are not, by and large, gang-banging, gun-wielding baby rapists. Are we better off for doing this? Do we deter kids from committing serious crimes?" The Centers for Disease Control study, among others, makes clear that the answer is no, he says.

But Oregon prosecutor Marquis says his contacts with adolescents leave no doubt that they're well-informed about the law change. "I am astounded at how many kids know about this. Over and over I have heard, 'They have a really tough law here in Oregon — you use a gun in a robbery, you get Measure 11.' "

The evidence is conclusive, Marquis says. "Juvenile crime has had a huge drop in Oregon." Statistics on the juvenile crime rate before and after Measure 11 took effect weren't available. But adult crime (which, under the new law, includes serious offenses committed by anyone 15 and older) did drop by 27 percent from 1995 and 1999. By 2006, violent crime in Oregon had decreased to less than 300 crimes per 100,000 persons.[17]

BACKGROUND

Separate System

America's young cities began growing in the early 1800s, largely because of waves of immigration. Given the desperate circumstances in which they arrived, and the long hours they worked, immigrants had little choice but to let their children roam the streets unsupervised. Not surprisingly, some got into trouble.

Alarmed at what they were seeing, early urban reformers established the forerunners of today's juvenile detention institutions. The New York House of Refuge, founded in 1824, was the first. A group of prominent citizens established the Society for the Reformation of Juvenile Delinquents and persuaded the state legislature to create the facility for "boys under a certain age who become subject to the notice of our police, either as vagrants, or homeless, or charged with petty crimes." They would be put to work, and given a basic education, "while at the same time, they are subjected to a course of treatment, that will afford a prompt and energetic corrective of their vicious propensities."[18]

Other cities, including Boston, Philadelphia and Baltimore, followed suit, but hope that "refuges" would put a big dent in juvenile crime proved ill-founded. The explosive growth of poor, often desperate, urban populations far surpassed the institutions' capacities.

Some cities and states concluded they needed another way to house wayward children. The first "reform school" opened in Massachusetts in 1849, but such institutions also proved ineffective.

Meanwhile, civic reformers perceived another problem — children convicted of serious crimes were being imprisoned with adults because adult courts and prisons were the only institutions available. Pressed by concerned citizens who argued that government had a

CHRONOLOGY

1800s *Civic reformers develop private institutions to help youths in trouble.*

1824 Civic leaders found New York House of Refuge to care for young vagrants, petty criminals.

1849 Massachusetts opens "reform school" for young people who hadn't committed crimes but weren't enrolled in school.

1899 Illinois Legislature creates nation's first juvenile court system to handle growing number of youths being tried and sentenced as adults.

1960s-1980s *Youth advocates successfully challenge the constitutionality of juvenile court proceedings nationwide, but liberalization wave ebbs as youth crime skyrockets.*

1966-1970 Supreme Court's *Kent, Gault* and *Winship* decisions extend constitutional due-process rights to defendants in juvenile courts.

1974 Congress amends Juvenile Crime and Delinquency Prevention Act of 1968 to ban detention for "status offenses" — curfew-breaking, cigarette purchasing and the like, which only apply to juveniles — for states receiving grants under the law, and to require separation of juveniles from adults in jails and prisons.

1978 Random murders by 15-year-old self-proclaimed "monster" Willie Bosket, spark tough, new juvenile crime law in New York.

1982 Supreme Court's *Eddings* decision limits death penalty for juveniles.

1987 Beginning of crack cocaine epidemic sees youth murder arrests climb to about 10 percent of all arrests, up from 6 percent in 1984.

1988 Supreme Court's *Thompson* decision prohibits capital punishment for juveniles convicted of crimes committed when they were 15 or under.

1990s *Legislatures nationwide respond to juvenile crime wave by toughening laws and easing the transfer of juveniles to adult court, usually in cases involving violent crime.*

1994 Violent juvenile crime nationwide reaches all-time high of 500 arrests per 100,000 under-18s in population . . . . Oregon voters pass Measure 11, requiring long prison sentences for certain serious crimes for offenders 15 and older.

1995 Twenty-one states require juveniles to be tried in adult court for certain serious crimes.

1996 Violent juvenile crime declines 6 percent from previous year. . . . Juvenile courts handle 1.8 million cases, quadruple the 1960 number. . . . Princeton University sociologist John DiIulio and fellow conservatives predict wave of "superpredator" youths.

1997 Forty-five states and Washington, D.C., have made it easier to transfer juvenile defendants to adult court.

2000s *Decline of juvenile violent crime continues; youth advocates seek to roll back hard-line measures.*

2001 DiIulio repudiates "superpredator" thesis.

2004 Violent crime arrests for juveniles fall 22 percent below 1995 level.

2005 Supreme Court in *Roper v. Simmons* abolishes death penalty for defendants under 18 when they committed their crimes; cites brain studies showing adolescents' capacity for judgment not fully developed.

2006 Colorado ends life without parole sentences for juveniles.

2007 Connecticut raises the age at which youths can be tried as adults from 16 to 18. . . . Move to abolish juvenile life without parole in California fails. . . . *American Journal of Preventive Medicine* reports "insufficient evidence" that transferring juveniles to adult court prevents violence.

2008 Gov. Bill Ritter, D-Colo., vetoes legislation to abolish prosecutors' authority to file charges against juveniles directly in adult court. . . . High-profile juvenile justice conference planned on Nov. 6 at Georgetown University to reform harsh laws on youth crime.

special duty to help juveniles mend their ways, the Illinois legislature in 1899 established the nation's first juvenile court in Chicago. Later that year, Colorado lawmakers took the same step in Denver.

Illinois and Colorado also created a category of juvenile offenses seen as gateways to the criminal life, such as "truancy" and "growing up in idleness."[19]

Unlike in adult courts, lawyers and constitutional protections weren't required in juvenile courts since judges would be acting in the juveniles' best interests. Moreover, the courts' stated goal wasn't punishment but rehabilitation.

Judges essentially had unfettered discretion to devise "treatment plans" for juveniles that could leave them confined until they were classified as cured, or they turned 21.

New Standards

By the 1960s, the juvenile court model was coming under growing challenge from liberals, who complained that young offenders not only were being denied legal representation but also other rights that adult defendants enjoyed.[20]

Some of these concerns were addressed in a string of U.S. Supreme Court decisions beginning in the mid-1960s. Starting with the basic questions of young peoples' due-process rights in juvenile courts, the high court eventually found itself grappling with perhaps the weightiest criminal-law issue of all for juveniles — the death penalty.

Before reaching that question, the court in 1966 laid the groundwork for extending adult rights to juveniles. The "essentials of due process" had to be provided to young people, the court said in its landmark *Kent v. United States* ruling. In his majority opinion, Justice Abe Fortas warned that juvenile courts were failing on all fronts: "There may be grounds for concern that the child receives the worst of both worlds: that he gets neither the protections accorded to adults nor the solicitous care and regenerative treatment postulated for children."[21] The following year, the court's *In re Gault* decision laid down specific requirements for juvenile court hearings in which defendants faced commitment to a detention center. In such cases, courts had to grant adequate notice of specific charges, notice of right to a lawyer, the right to confront witnesses and the right against self-incrimination.

Supreme Court decisions found an echo in Congress. The Juvenile Delinquency Prevention and Control Act of 1968 recommended — but did not require — that children charged with "status offenses" be dealt with outside the court system. Status offenses are acts that are illegal only for young people — buying cigarettes, for instance, or violating curfews.

Lawmakers toughened the law in 1974, making states' eligibility for federal grants contingent on removing status offenders from detention, and on physically separating juvenile offenders from adults in jails and prisons. Congress amended the law in 1980 to require that juveniles be removed from all adult jails.

The Supreme Court, meanwhile, continued addressing juvenile justice issues. In its 1970 *In re Winship* decision, justices required states to prove delinquency cases beyond a reasonable doubt — the same standard required in adult criminal convictions. *Breed v. Jones*, in 1975, established that transferring juveniles to adult criminal court after they have been adjudicated in juvenile court constitutes double jeopardy — the unconstitutional practice of trying someone twice for the same crime.

But in 1984, in *Schall v. Martin*, the court approved pretrial, or "preventive," detention. Holding a juvenile defendant thought to pose a risk of committing another crime isn't a punishment, the justices concluded. Procedures were in place, they said, to protect young defendants from improper detention.[22]

A 1985 Supreme Court decision (*New Jersey v. T.L.O.*) loosened Fourth Amendment protections for high school students, allowing school personnel to search students' lockers and belongings if "reasonable grounds" exist to believe that a student has violated school rules or the law. In other circumstances, the search standard is "probable cause."

But the high court began in the 1980s to take up the most morally and emotionally charged juvenile justice issue of all — the death penalty. Finally, following two decisions that limited capital punishment for juveniles, the court in 2005 banned the death penalty for defendants who were under 18 when they committed a capital crime.

Toughening Up

A wave of sensational crimes committed by young offenders — followed by skyrocketing street violence spawned by a crack cocaine boom that began in the 1980s — sparked a new era in juvenile justice in the 1990s.[23]

From 1975 to 1987, the number of juveniles arrested for violent crimes hovered around 300 arrests per 100,000

Should Adolescents Be Treated Like Adults?

Youth advocates and prosecutors square off.

Medical science is playing a key role in the debate over whether juveniles accused of serious crimes should be treated as adults. By scanning the brain in far more detail than ever before, researchers are providing data supporting a key argument by those who advocate rehabilitation rather than jail. They say juveniles shouldn't be treated like adults because the brain scans show they don't think like adults.

That position played a central role in the U.S. Supreme Court's 2005 *Roper v. Simmons* decision banning the death penalty as unconstitutional for juveniles who were under 18 when they committed the crime. Christopher Simmons, a high school junior in Missouri, broke into a house with a friend, with burglary and murder in mind. "Simmons said he wanted to murder somebody," Justice Anthony Kennedy wrote in the majority opinion in the 5-4 decision. Simmons had said they'd get away with the crime because they were minors.[1]

Shirley Crook, 46, was home alone, her husband away on a fishing trip. With duct tape, Simmons and his friend bound her hands and covered her eyes and mouth. They drove her to a railroad trestle at a state park, reinforced her bindings with electrical wire and threw her into the Meramec River.

Notwithstanding the facts of the case, Kennedy accepted evidence that adolescents' capacity for judgment remains immature. "The reality that adolescents still struggle to define their identity means it is less supportable to conclude that even a heinous crime committed by a juvenile is evidence of irretrievably depraved character," Kennedy wrote.[2]

For youth advocates, the decision represented a major breakthrough in their effort to gain acceptance for evidence that teenagers' brains haven't developed sufficiently for them to deserve the full weight of judicial penalties.

Outside the capital-punishment realm, however, youth advocates are still trying to make that case. Earlier this year, the American Bar Association adopted a resolution urging that judges take adolescent maturity levels into account.

"Youth are developmentally different from adults," the resolution says, "and these developmental differences need to be taken into account at all stages and in all aspects of the adult criminal justice system."[3]

The National District Attorneys Association is fighting to overturn the resolution. "We do not believe it is appropriate to take language articulated in a U.S. Supreme Court decision concerning whether or not to impose the death penalty on juvenile murders and apply the same logic in a completely different conceptual framework," the prosecutors said.[4]

In any event, the prosecutors remain skeptical of the adolescent brain studies. "Some of that is hocus pocus,"

youths ages 10 to 18 in the population. But in the following seven-year period, 1987-1994, the rate rose by more than 60 percent, to about 500 arrests per 100,000.[24]

Juvenile crime fell again, starting in 1994. By 2004, the juvenile arrest rate for violent crimes had dropped to 271 per 100,000. However, the new hardline laws remained in place. In 1996, juvenile courts handled about 1.8 million delinquency cases — more than four times the 400,000 cases in 1960.[25]

The rapid adoption of the tougher approach reflected not only rising juvenile crime but the fear that far worse was coming. By the mid-1990s, some politically conservative academics attracted considerable publicity and political influence by declaring that a new breed of young "superpredators" was developing. John DiIulio, then a political science professor at Princeton University, coined the term, which soon gained currency.

"Based on all that we have witnessed, researched and heard from people who are close to the action," DiIulio and two co-authors wrote in 1996, "here is what we believe: America is now home to thickening ranks of juvenile 'superpredators' — radically impulsive, brutally remorseless youngsters, including ever more preteenage boys, who murder, assault, rape, rob, burglarize, deal deadly drugs, join gun-toting gangs and create serious communal disorders." DiIulio's co-authors were John P. Walters, now director of the Bush administration's Office of National Drug Control Policy, and William J. Bennett, a prominent conservative who was Education secretary in the Reagan administration, and White House drug policy says Joshua Marquis, a district attorney in Oregon. "Some people mature early."

For his part, James C. Backstrom, the prosecutor in Dakota County, Minn., accepts the brain studies and even their possible relevance at sentencing. But, he adds, "There is a complete disconnect if you say that is a basis why they shouldn't be prosecuting kids as adults. I think a 16- or 17-year-old youth is fully capable of understanding right from wrong, and understanding that it's wrong to murder, rape or torture someone."

Backstrom was echoing an argument by Supreme Court Justice Antonin Scalia. In his dissent in *Roper*, Scalia quoted from an earlier decision in which the court wrote that it was "absurd to think that one must be mature enough to drive carefully, to drink responsibly, or to vote intelligently, in order to be mature enough to understand that murdering another human being is profoundly wrong, and to conform one's conduct to that most minimal of all civilized standards."[5]

Some medical professionals on the liberal side argue, in effect, that biology can trump morality. In the often chaotic circumstances in which most crimes take place, doctors say that the state of adolescent brains is highly relevant to the issue of how to hold juveniles accountable for actions that they don't control in the same ways that adults are capable.

"When children find themselves in emotionally charged situations, the parts of the brain that regulate emotion, rather than reasoning, are more likely to be engaged," said Physicians for Human Rights, a Cambridge, Mass.-based advocacy group, in a brief in the *Roper* case, "[6]

According to the group, brains scanned using magnetic image resonance — the same technology used to detect tumors and other abnormalities — show that adolescent behaviors are largely controlled by parts of the brain's limbic system, which is part of the so-called primitive part of the brain. It includes the amygdala, specifically important in adolescents' actions, which regulates fear, aggression and impulse. Only when the prefrontal cortex matures — usually when a person is in his 20s — do reasoning and understanding of consequences develop fully, the group said.[7]

The Supreme Court didn't delve into brain structure, but Justice Kennedy did explore the psychological dividing line between adolescence and adulthood, noting that parents are well aware of the differences. "Retribution is not proportional," he wrote, "if the law's most severe penalty is imposed on one whose culpability or blameworthiness is diminished, to a substantial degree, by reason of youth and immaturity."[8]

---

[1] *Roper v. Simmons*, 543 U.S. 551 (2005), www.oyez.org/cases/2000-2009/2004/2004_03_633/.

[2] *Ibid.*

[3] "American Bar Association — 105C," Adopted by the House of Delegates, Feb. 11, 2008, p. 5, www.abanet.org/leadership/2008/midyear/updated_reports/hundredfivec.doc.

[4] "State of the National District Attorneys Association in Response to the Proposed ABA Resolution Concerning Sentence Mitigation for Youthful Offenders," May 4, 2007, www.ndaa.org/ndaa/capital/capital_perspective_july_aug_2007.html.

[5] "Scalia, J. dissenting," *Roper v. Simmons, op. cit.*

[6] "Adolescent Brain Development, a Critical Factor in Juvenile Justice Reform," Physicians for Human Rights, undated, http://physiciansforhumanrights.org/juvenile-justice/factsheets/braindev.pdf.

[7] *Ibid.* See also, "Teenage Risk-taking: Teenage Brains Really Are Different From Child or Adult Brains," *Science Daily*, March 30, 2008, www.sciencedaily.com/releases/2008/03/080328112127.htm.

[8] *Roper v. Simmons, op. cit.*

director under President George H. W. Bush.[26] Five years later, however, DiIulio retracted the entire thesis, prompted by a downturn in juvenile crime — exactly the opposite of what he had predicted. DiIulio, who was then director of the White House Office of Faith-Based and Community Initiatives, said that he had a moment of revelation on the issue in 1996.

"I knew that for the rest of my life I would work on prevention, on helping bring caring, responsible adults to wrap their arms around these kids."[27]

Liberal youth advocates held DiIulio and his collaborators greatly responsible for the get-tough approach that prevailed in the '90s. But it had been foreshadowed in the late 1970s in New York City by a teenager who seemed to fit the "superpredator" archetype.

In 1978, 15-year-old Willie Bosket robbed and murdered two subway passengers. Under state laws at the time, he was sentenced to five years in detention — the maximum he could receive in Family Court, where all defendants under age 16 were automatically sent.

State lawmakers quickly enacted the Juvenile Offender Law, which gave the state Supreme Court (equivalent to district courts in other states) original jurisdiction over 13-, 14- and 15-year-olds charged with violent crimes, with no exceptions.

Bosket, who called himself a "monster" created by the criminal justice system, was released from juvenile detention and later returned to prison for assault. There, he earned two life sentences for crimes committed behind bars, including the stabbing of a prison guard.

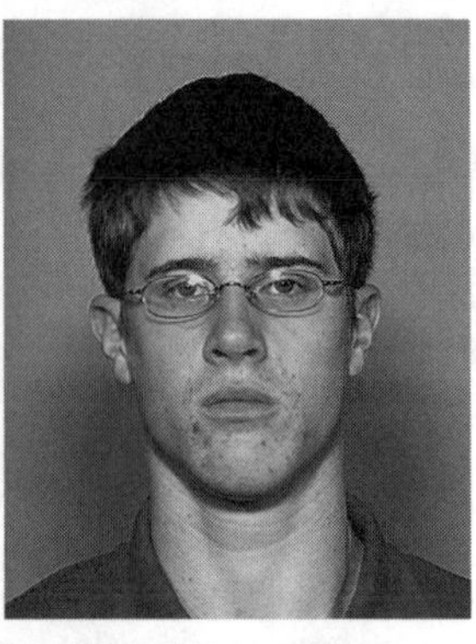

AP Photo/Dakota County Sheriff

Minnesota teenagers Matthew Niedere, left, and Clayton Keister, both 17, were convicted of shooting and killing Matthew's parents. Supporters of tough laws for juveniles say the boys' sentences support their argument that such laws are applied sparingly. Prosecutor James C. Backstrom resisted heavy pressure to seek life without parole for the pair, giving them a chance to apply for release after 30 years in prison. "I just did not feel that locking them up for the rest of their natural lives was the right thing to do," he says.

New York's Juvenile Offender Law, enacted years before other states toughened their juvenile crime laws, remains the nation's toughest, according to Jeffrey Fagan, a professor of law and public health at Columbia University. "The new law signaled a broad attack on the structure and independence of the juvenile court," he wrote this year, "a major restructuring of the border between juvenile and criminal court that was repeated across the nation in recurring cycles for more than two decades."[28]

Other states that revamped their "transfer" laws took a variety of approaches. Fourteen states and Washington, D.C., allowed prosecutors to file charges directly in adult court, without judicial approval, for serious felonies, typically including murder and other "person" crimes — in which a human being, rather than an institution, is the victim.

Studying the Fallout

Virtually as soon as tougher laws took effect, academics and policy makers began researching how effective they were. Focusing on the expanded use of adult court for juveniles, nearly all the researchers concluded that the laws were counterproductive.[29]

Fagan, now co-director of Columbia University's Crime, Community and Law Center, conducted a study published in 1995 that compared re-arrest statistics of youths picked up for robbery and burglary in New York and New Jersey, where adult-court jurisdiction laws differed. He concluded that the New Yorkers, who had been transferred to adult court, were 39 percent more likely to be re-arrested for a violent crime than the New Jersey juveniles, who had been handled in juvenile court.

And among the New Yorkers who'd been sentenced to prison for more than a year, their recidivism rate for violent crime was twice that of the juvenile-court comparison group from New Jersey.

A study published in 2002 by the Florida Juvenile Justice Department found similar results when comparing youths transferred to adult court and those retained in the state's juvenile system. The transferred juveniles showed a 34 percent higher recidivism rate.

Most other studies yielded similar data. But there were exceptions. Another Florida study published in 1997 found that youths transferred to adult court on property crime charges showed lower recidivism than counterparts arrested for similar crimes and kept in the juvenile system.

Overall, however, the Task Force on Community Preventive Services, appointed by the U.S. Centers for Disease Control, concluded: "The weight of evidence shows greater rates of violence among transferred than among retained juveniles; transferred juveniles were approximately 33.7 percent more likely to be re-arrested for a violent or other crime than were juveniles retained in the juvenile justice system."[30]

The various studies form a key part of rollback advocates' argument that emphasizing adult-court prosecution is counterproductive.

Skeptical prosecutors have faulted the studies, or at least questioned the relevance of a New York-New Jersey study to, say, Washington, D.C. "Are you going to use these statistics as a guide for your jurisdiction?" asks Patricia A. Riley, special counsel to the U.S. Attorney's Office in Washington, which is fighting a rollback proposal. (*See "Current Situation," p. 193.*)

And she questions the validity of studies conducted within one state, because juveniles who are transferred are — by definition — more serious offenders, hence more likely to recidivate.

Researchers did try to adjust for that factor. But Butts of the University of Chicago, who specializes in juvenile crime statistics, acknowledges that it's impossible to completely control for differences between juvenile defendants.

But he adds that on further reflection, he thinks the realities of juvenile justice can produce counterintuitive results. Property crime, for instance, can be dealt with more leniently by adult court judges and juries, which are used to older and tougher defendants who've done worse. "A jury doesn't want to send a 14-year-old to prison," he says. "But in the juvenile system a 14-year-old defendant can look like a serious case. There are a lot of things about this business that don't hold up when you start looking at them."

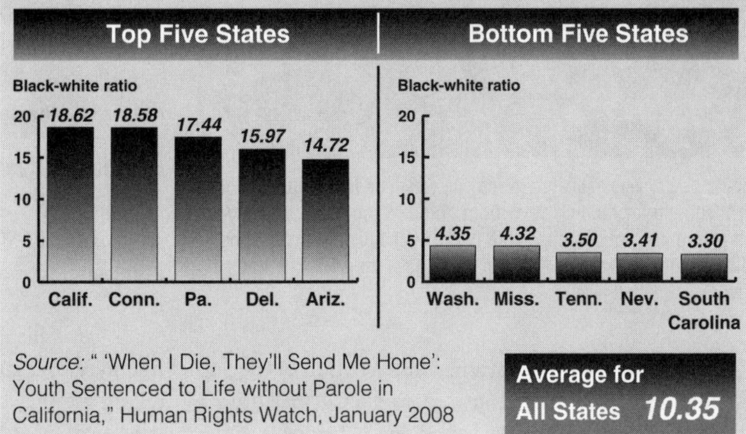

CURRENT SITUATION

State Campaigns

Advocates for change in the juvenile justice system are taking the fight to state legislatures. So far, efforts have been mounted in only a handful of states, but the campaigners are planning to expand their efforts.

Major targets are laws authorizing life-without-parole (LWOP) sentences for defendants who were under 18 when they committed their crimes.

In California, state Sen. Leland Yee, D-San Francisco, is planning to renew his efforts to prohibit juvenile LWOP, says a spokesman, Adam Keigwin. California approved juvenile LWOP as part of a sweeping 1990 tough-on-crime ballot initiative. Yee introduced an anti-juvenile LWOP bill this year but didn't take it to the full Senate because he lacked the two-thirds majority necessary to overturn a measure passed by referendum.

Alison Parker, deputy director of U.S. programs for Human Rights Watch, a New York-based global human-rights monitoring organization, says anti-juvenile LWOP campaigns may be mounted next year in Florida, Louisiana, Michigan, Washington state and Nebraska. Colorado in 2006 became the first state in the nation to abolish juvenile LWOP.

Human Rights Watch has made juvenile LWOP one of its major U.S. issues. Parker, who wrote exhaustive reports in 2005 and 2008 on the issue, reported this year — citing the Center for Global Law and Justice at the University of San Francisco — that the United States is the only country in the world in which juveniles are serving LWOP sentences. According to the center, at least 135 countries have explicitly prohibited juvenile LWOP.[31]

Nevertheless, prosecutors and other hard-liners argue that LWOP for juveniles should stay on the books. "We just believe that some crimes, even if committed by juveniles, deserve a life sentence," says Nina Salarno-Ashford, the California victims' rights advocate and ex-prosecutor. "Heinous murder, kidnap, torture — these are the kinds that get the life sentence. There are those who, in our view, will never be candidates for rehabilitation."

In 2005, Parker's research of juvenile LWOP cases found that most defendants were convicted of murder but that 26 percent "were convicted of felony murder where the teen participated in a robbery or burglary during which a co-participant committed murder, without the knowledge or intent of the teen." Sixteen percent of the juvenile LWOP convicts were 13-15 at the time of their crimes.[32]

AP Photo/Andy Carpenean

Raine Lowry was a juvenile when she was held in an adult facility in Wyoming for running away from home. Wyoming is the only state that has not complied with the federal Juvenile Justice and Delinquency Prevention Act, in part because the state still holds juveniles in adult jails.

Even so, says District Attorney Josh Marquis of Clatsop County, Ore., juveniles sentenced to LWOP make up a "tiny fraction" of youths tried as adults. "They tend to tug at the heartstrings of people who can't accept that there are people so damaged that they're never going to be safe to release."

Those seeking to change juvenile laws also are focusing on laws that require juveniles to be prosecuted as adults for certain crimes, or that make it easy to transfer juveniles into adult court.

"We know so much more about what works, and what doesn't work," says Liz Ryan, president and CEO of Campaign for Youth Justice, a Washington-based advocacy organization. She cites projects such as the Annie E. Casey Foundation's Juvenile Detention Alternatives Initiative, in which authorities in about 100 localities are cooperating. Except in exceptional cases, she says, "Kids can be safely supervised in the community. We don't have to lock up all those kids in detention facilities."

Many youth advocates cite a study earlier this year that compares the Missouri and Maryland juvenile justice systems. Missouri, which has embarked on a rehabilitation approach known as the "Missouri model," complete with dorm-style rooms in treatment centers and an emphasis on education, registered an 8 percent recidivism rate over three years. Maryland showed a 30 percent recidivism rate for youths coming out of its detention-oriented juvenile program.[33]

Elsewhere, Illinois repealed a law in 2005 that automatically transferred to adult court any juvenile charged with drug offenses in or near public schools or housing projects. Data showed that two-thirds of those transferred were low-level lawbreakers. Judges now decide on transfers.[34]

North Carolina and Illinois are also considering following Connecticut's 2007 move to raise the age of juvenile court jurisdiction to 17 — meaning that 16-year-olds could no longer be sent to adult court.[35]

Conflict in Washington

A debate on whether to limit the transfer of juveniles to adult court in Washington, D.C., shows the intensity of opinions, emotions and racial tensions that juvenile crime issues can arouse.

"I was still bleeding from the scrapes as they pushed my body back and forth, going through my pockets and telling me they were going to kill me," Chandler Goule, who lives on Capitol Hill, told a D.C. City Council hearing in October. The 31-year-old staff director of a House Agriculture subcommittee said one of his three attackers held a gun to his head. The 17-year-old gunman — the only one of the three to be arrested — pleaded guilty in adult court and was sentenced to 48 months in prison. If he successfully completes five years of "supervised release" after prison, his conviction will be expunged from his record.

The bill that Goule was testifying against would not have prevented that transfer to adult court, but it would have shifted the authority to order the transfer from the U.S. attorney (who prosecutes serious local crimes in Washington) to a judge. Youth advocates have argued for some time that the transfer decision should rest with a neutral overseer rather than with one side in a criminal proceeding.

"Why would you, the D.C. Council, give an unelected prosecutor appointed by the president the right to exclusively decide what happens to D.C.'s youth without even so much as a hearing?" Ryan of the Campaign for Youth Justice asked the two council members who held the hearing.

The U.S. Attorney's Office says its standards keep the number of juvenile adult-court cases low. "We do not take every eligible 16- or 17-year-old who commits these offenses,

AT ISSUE

Should state laws that facilitate prosecuting juveniles in adult court be changed?

YES

Liz Ryan
President and CEO,
Campaign for Youth Justice

Written for *CQ Researcher*, November 2008

When criminologists predicted in the 1990s that a new generation of youthful "superpredators" was on the horizon, state officials responded by passing laws to make it easier to try youths as adults. They intended, understandably, to make their communities safer. However, the latest research suggests the opposite effect: Youths prosecuted as adults are much more likely to re-offend.

For example, in August, the Department of Justice's Office of Juvenile Justice and Delinquency Prevention released a report — "Juvenile Transfer Laws: An Effective Deterrent to Delinquency?" — which found that prosecuting youths as adults has little or no deterrent effect on juvenile crime. In fact, it said, youths prosecuted as adults are more likely to re-offend than youths handled in the juvenile justice system. And late last year the federal Centers for Disease Control and Prevention released a report that showed virtually identical results.

Polling shows the public rejects punitive approaches and supports rehabilitation and treatment for youth, which is virtually non-existent in the adult criminal justice system. Two recent MacArthur Foundation polls showed that 89 percent of Americans agreed or strongly agreed that rehabilitative services and treatment would help reduce crime.

States have different laws for transferring youth under age 18 to adult court. In 44 states and the District of Columbia juvenile court judges under certain circumstances may send a youth to adult court, and 14 states and D.C. allow the prosecutor to directly file cases in adult court. Thirteen states prosecute 16- or 17-year-olds in adult court for any offense. Connecticut, New York and North Carolina try all 16- and 17-year-olds as adults. Connecticut recently raised the age of juvenile court jurisdiction to 18, beginning in 2010.

Many of the youth prosecuted as adults are placed in adult jails pretrial, where they are at risk of harm, abuse and suicide. A November 2007 report released by the Campaign for Youth Justice showed that up to 7,500 youths are in adult jails on any given day, but half to a third of these youngsters are ultimately sent back to the juvenile justice system or not convicted at all, suggesting that their offenses did not merit placement in the adult criminal justice system.

Based on this new research, several states have begun to re-examine and even reverse these harmful statutes. Other state officials should seriously re-examine their state policies governing the trial, sentencing and incarceration of youths as adults.

NO

James C. Backstrom
Dakota County Attorney, Hastings, Minn.;
Member, Board of Directors, National
District Attorneys Association

Written for *CQ Researcher*, November 2008

Prosecuting juvenile offenders in adult court is appropriate and necessary in certain cases to protect public safety and hold youths appropriately accountable for their crimes. Contrary to opponents' claims, this sanction is not being overused by prosecutors. Few jurisdictions prosecute more than 1-2 percent of juvenile offenders as adults. This is a tool reserved for the most serious, violent and chronic offenders, who should face more serious consequences for their crimes than those available in juvenile court.

Don't be misled by claims that large numbers of youths are being prosecuted as adults for low-level offenses, because these statistics come from the 13 states where laws classify 16- or 17-year-olds as adults for purposes of any prosecution. This has nothing to do with transferring juveniles to adult court.

Recent scientific studies have shown that the brain is not fully developed until the early to mid-20's and that the last portion of the brain to reach full maturity is the frontal lobe governing impulse control. While this may explain why some youths lack the reasoning ability to fully appreciate the consequences of their actions, it does not mean they should not be held accountable for their crimes. The vast majority of teenagers understand the difference between right and wrong and know it is wrong to torture or kill someone. This is why our laws rightfully allow adult prosecution for these and other violent crimes.

Juveniles who commit serious and violent crimes, particularly older youths, should face potential adult court sanctions. So, too, must this remedy be available for youngsters who have a long history of convictions for less serious felonies for which juvenile court disposition has not been effective. About one-third of our states also utilize "blended sentencing" models that combine both juvenile and adult sanctions for serious, violent or habitual juvenile offenders whose crimes have been determined not to warrant prosecution in adult court.

Prosecutors and judges thoughtfully and professionally enforce juvenile codes with fairness and impartiality every day, taking into consideration both mitigating factors — such as a juvenile offender's age, maturity and amenability to treatment and probation — and aggravating factors, such as the severity of the crime, the threat to public safety, the impact upon the victim and the offender's criminal history. After properly weighing these factors, the difficult decision to prosecute a juvenile offender as an adult is warranted in some cases.

even though we are importuned to take more of them than we do," Patricia A. Riley, a special counsel to the U.S. attorney, told the hearing.

From 1999 to Oct. 15 of this year, the office prosecuted 428 16- and 17-year-olds in adult court. During most of those years, prosecutors tried about 2,200 to 3,000 juvenile cases a year. "A juvenile who has an extensive and/or violent juvenile record is more likely to be prosecuted as an adult than one who does not," Riley said.

But the juvenile crime debate opens up issues that go far deeper than statistics and prosecutorial versus judicial authority. Witnesses at the hearing also included Jauhar Abraham and Ronald Moten, co-founders of Peaceoholics, a nonprofit that works to quell violence in the District.[36] They questioned why interest in crime prevention seems to be lower when African-American teenagers are the predominant victims, as well as offenders.

"We've been coming here for years complaining about the same type of homicides, and there ain't been an issue," Moten said, suggesting that the upsurge in interest came about because "all of a sudden our city is changing," as traditionally African-American neighborhoods gentrify.

In one horrific case, a 56-year-old man, Mark Kenneth Blank, died from a "severe head trauma" after being robbed and beaten by a trio of youths — ages 13, 14 and 15.

"I guarantee you a couple of those robbers were on drugs," Moten said. "For the last 20 years this government has done nothing to address the youth drug problem. There's more young'uns on PCP committing heinous acts in this city than ever before. We have turned our back on these children, and now the chickens are coming home to roost!"

Moments later, he was pounding the witness table in frustration.

OUTLOOK

Watching the Trends

Experts and activists on both sides of the juvenile justice divide have been analyzing the near-term possibilities as they awaited a change of administration in Washington. State governments are where the action is for juvenile crime laws. But veterans in the field say the federal government can play a big part in influencing policy nationwide.

"Given the problems that any new administration is going to have to take on, none of us would be naïve enough to think that juvenile justice is going to rise above the economy or Iraq or a lot of other things," says Lubow of the Annie E. Casey Foundation. Yet simply appointing the right OJJDP administrator, he says, could make a big difference, because administrators can use federal grant-awarding power to steer states toward a more rehabilitation-oriented approach.

In fact, says Bilchik of Georgetown University's Center for Juvenile Justice Reform, who once held the OJJDP job, the past several years represent a missed opportunity. Money saved as a result of fewer juveniles being arrested could have gone "to known, proven prevention programs and lessened even more the flow of kids into the juvenile justice system. It's mind-numbing to think about the lost opportunity."

The unknowns of a new administration aside, juvenile justice experts are unsure how long the declining crime rate will endure. If the country's ever-worsening economic conditions bring a significant increase in adult and juvenile crime, interest in rolling back some of the get-tough laws could wane.

"Periods of crisis are the absolute worst times in which to discuss crime policy," said Steinberg of Temple University, speaking to the Brookings-Princeton conference. "Panic trumps prudence, and policy gets made on the basis of fear rather than foresight."

On that score, Denver District Attorney Morrissey, whose views on crime and punishment tend to differ from Steinberg's, agrees. "If we continue to take the approaches we take, I hope we'll continue to see violent juvenile crime decline in Denver," Morrissey says. But, he adds, "If it goes up 1 percent, I know we're going to see a headline." And headlines will bring cries for crackdowns, he says.

A counterweight, points out Butts of the University of Chicago's Chapin Hall Center for Children, is the vastly expanded state of knowledge about juveniles and effective programs.

"It has been helpful to show decision makers that there is verifiable, quantitative evidence that young people make decisions differently from adults. You can't estimate someone's level of cognitive development based on his birthday."

Another factor that could moderate any increase in juvenile crime is demographic reality, says Minnesota prosecutor Backstrom. "We are seeing a declining population of juveniles across America overall," he says. "As the population declines, I think the crime rate is going to continue to go down."

That overall trend may not apply everywhere, but it's certainly the case in Backstrom's suburban-and-rural territory. "Our population is dropping in every category, except that when you get to 50 and older it skyrockets. They're not too prone to commit crimes."

But Backstrom says lawmakers shouldn't respond to the downturn the way the youth advocates are proposing. "When serious crimes are committed by youths, they need to be dealt with appropriately, with significant consequences. If we roll back the clock, we're going to be harming our society."

In Washington, at least one recent crime victim is optimistic. "In 10 years, it will be better," he says. "Property values in D.C. are going to continue to rise." Street criminals, he says, will "move on."

As for the social inequalities that underlie at least some D.C. crime, Caspari hopes better schools will provide improved opportunities for young people whose hopes for the future are stunted.

But one major characteristic of juvenile justice is unlikely to change — whatever the future holds. The field is complicated by so many issues of adolescent physiology, family values and local politics that laws and policies don't always determine what happens to individuals caught up in the system.

"It's much easier to articulate sound policy," says Lubow of the Annie E. Casey Foundation, "than it is to implement it."

NOTES

1. See Jeffrey A. Butts, "Juvenile Arrest Rates 1982-2007," Sept. 15, 2008, www.jbutts.com/onlinepps/ucr2007.ppt.
2. See Angela McGowan, *et al.*, "Effects on Violence of Laws and Policies Facilitating the Transfer of Juveniles from the Juvenile Justice System to the Adult Justice System," *American Journal of Preventive Medicine*, Dec. 3, 2006.
3. See Richard E. Redding, "Juvenile Transfer Laws: An Effective Deterrent to Delinquency?" *Juvenile Justice Bulletin*, Office of Juvenile Justice and Delinquency Prevention, U.S. Department of Justice, August 2008, www.ncjrs.gov/pdffiles1/ojjdp/220595.pdf. Also see Michelle Leighton and Connie de la Vega, "Sentencing Our Children to Die in Prison: Global Law and Practice," Center for Global Law and Justice, University of San Francisco School of Law, November 2007, www.usfca.edu/law/home/CenterforLawandGlobalJustice/LWOP_Final_Nov_30_Web.pdf; and "The Rest of Their Lives: Life Without Parole for Youth Offenders in the United States in 2008," www.hrw.org/backgrounder/2008/us1005/us1005execsum.pdf.
4. See Sharon Cohen, "States Rethink Charging Kids as Adults," The Associated Press, Dec. 2, 2007, www.washingtonpost.com/wp-dyn/content/article/2007/12/01/AR2007120100792_pf.html.
5. See "Gov. Ritter Veto Message on HB 08-1208," Colorado Governor's office, May 22, 2008, www.colorado.gov/cs/Satellite/GovRitter/GOVR/1211447629095.
6. "Easy Access to Juvenile Court Statistics: 1985-2005," Office of Juvenile Justice and Delinquency Prevention, U.S. Department of Justice, http://ojjdp.ncjrs.gov/ojstatbb/ezajcs/asp/display.asp.
7. *The Congressional Record — Senate*, Jan. 21, 1997, Sen. John Ashcroft, http://bulk.resource.org/gpo.gov/record/1997/1997_S00145.pdf.
8. For background, see Peter Katel, "Prison Reform," *CQ Researcher*, April 6, 2007, pp. 289-312. Also, Elizabeth Hernandez, "Perry signs TYC reform bill into law," *TheMonitor.com* (McAllen, Texas), June 8, 2007, www.themonitor.com/onset?id=2955&template=article.html; Michael Rothfeld, Jurist orders state to beef up monitoring of youth facilities, ending lawsuit," *Los Angeles Times*, March 13, 2008, p. B5.
9. See "Oregon Violent Crime and Measure 11," Crime Victims United, updated June, 2008, www.crimevictimsunited.org/measure11/presentation/index.htm.
10. See Nancy Merritt, Terry Fain and Susan Turner, "Oregon's Measure 11 Sentencing Reform: Implementation and System Impact," RAND Corp., December 2003, pp. 87-88, www.ncjrs.gov/pdffiles1/nij/grants/205507.pdf.

11. See Howard N. Snyder, "Juvenile Arrests, 1996," Office of Juvenile Justice and Delinquency Prevention, U.S. Department of Justice, November 1997, www.ncjrs.gov/pdffiles/arrest96.pdf.
12. *Ibid.*
13. See Jeffrey A. Butts and Howard N. Snyder, "Too Soon to Tell: Deciphering Recent Trends in Youth Violence," Chapin Hall Center for Children, University of Chicago, November 2006, p. 4, www.jbutts.com/pdfs/toosoon.pdf.
14. Snyder, *op. cit.*
15. For background see Patrick Marshall, "Three-Strikes Laws," *CQ Researcher*, May 10, 2002, pp. 417-432.
16. "Juvenile Justice at the Crossroads," conference proceedings, Dec. 12-14, 1996, reported in "Juvenile Justice," Office of Juvenile Justice and Delinquency Prevention, U.S. Department of Justice, May 1998, http://ojjdp.ncjrs.org/conference/plenarybig.html.
17. See Merritt, Fain and Turner, *op. cit.*, p. 84. Also, "Oregon Violent Crime and Measure 11," *op. cit.*
18. Quoted in Randall G. Shelden, "Delinquency and Juvenile Justice in American Society," 2006, pp. 21-22.
19. *Ibid.*, pp. 30-31.
20. Unless otherwise indicated, material in this subsection is drawn from "Juvenile Justice: A Century of Change," Office of Juvenile Justice and Delinquency Prevention, U.S. Department of Justice, December, 1999, www.ncjrs.gov/pdffiles1/ojjdp/178995.pdf; and Howard N. Snyder and Melissa Sickmund, "Juvenile Offenders and Victims: 1999 National Report, Office of Juvenile justice and Delinquency Prevention, U.S. Department of Justice, September 1999, Chapter 7, www.ncjrs.gov/html/ojjdp/nationalreport99/toc.html.
21. Quoted in Robert E. Shepherd Jr., "The Juvenile Court at 100 Years: A Look Back," Juvenile Justice, National Criminal Justice Reference Service, December, 1999, www.ncjrs.gov/html/ojjdp/jjjournal1299/2.html. The case is *Kent v. U.S.*, 383 U.S. 541 (1966).
22. The case is *Schall v. Martin*, 467 U.S. 253 (1984).
23. Unless otherwise indicated, material in this subsection is drawn from Jeffrey Fagan, "Juvenile Crime and Criminal Justice: Resolving Border Disputes," in "Juvenile Justice" issue of "The Future of Children," Woodrow Wilson School of Public and International Affairs, Princeton University, and the Brookings Institution, Fall, 2008, pp. 81-118; Jan Hoffman, "Quirks in Juvenile Offender Law Stir Calls for Change," *The New York Times*, July 12, 1994, p. B1. For background, see Craig Donegan, "Preventing Juvenile Crime," *CQ Researcher*, March 15, 1996, pp. 217-240.
24. Butts and Snyder, *op. cit.*, p. 4.
25. *Ibid.*, and Snyder and Sickmund, *op. cit.*, p. 141.
26. Quoted in Elizabeth Becker, "As ex-Theorist on Young 'Superpredators,' Bush Aide Has Regrets," *The New York Times*, Feb. 9, 2001, http://query.nytimes.com/gst/fullpage.html?res=9A03EED91531F93AA35751C0A9679C8B63. Also, "Biography, William J. Bennett," BennettMornings.com, undated, www.bennettmornings.com/agnosticchart?charttype=minichart&chartID=22&formatID=1&useMiniChartID=true&destinationpage=/pg/jsp/general/biography.jsp.
27. *Ibid.*
28. See Fagan, *op. cit.*
29. Unless otherwise indicated, material in this subsection, including summaries of other scholars' studies, is drawn from McGowan, *et al.*, *op. cit.*, and Jeffrey A. Butts and Ojmarrh Mitchell, "Brick by Brick: Dismantling the Border Between Juvenile and Adult Justice," Urban Institute, July 1, 2000, www.urban.org/UploadedPDF/1000234_brick-by-brick.pdf.
30. *Ibid.*, McGowan, p. S14.
31. See "The Rest of Their Lives," *op. cit.*, and Leighton and de la Vega, *op. cit.*, p. 4.
32. Ibid., "The Rest of Their Lives," pp. 1-2.
33. See Nancy Cambria, "Teen Offenders Get Help," *St. Louis Post-Dispatch*, Sept. 14, 2008, p. C1.
34. See Douglas W. Nelson, "A Road Map for Juvenile Justice Reform," Annie E. Casey Foundation, 2008, p. 15, www.kidscount.org/datacenter/db_08pdf/2008_essay.pdf.
35. *Ibid.*
36. See Peter Katel, "Fighting Crime," *CQ Researcher*, Feb. 8, 2008, pp. 121-144.

BIBLIOGRAPHY

Books

Bennett, William J., John J. DiIulio and John P. Walters, *Body Count: Moral Poverty . . . And How to Win America's War Against Crime and Drugs, Simon & Schuster*, 1996.
In a revealing look at the political atmosphere surrounding crime during the get-tough years, three leading conservatives sound a warning over a continued increase in juvenile crime — an increase that was ending as their book was published.

Butterfield, Fox, *All God's Children: The Bosket Family and the American Tradition of Violence, Vintage Books*, 2008 (originally published in 1996).
A veteran *New York Times* reporter traces the troubled history of one of New York's most notorious young criminals.

Shelden, Randall G., *Delinquency and Juvenile Justice in American Society, Waveland Press*, 2006.
A veteran criminologist at the University of Nevada examines the history and practice of juvenile justice, with a critical eye toward bias and unfairness that he finds pervasive.

Zimring, Franklin E., *American Juvenile Justice, Oxford University Press*, 2005.
In a series of long essays, a University of California-Berkeley law professor and a leading criminologist makes an extended argument for treating juveniles differently than adult offenders.

Articles

Cambria, Nancy, "Teen Offenders Get Help," *St. Louis Post-Dispatch*, Sept. 14, 2008, p. C1.
Cambria reports on a sophisticated rehabilitation program for juvenile offenders.

Casillas, Ofelia, "A teaching moment for troubled youths," *Chicago Tribune*, Aug. 27, 2006, p. C1.
A newly created Juvenile Justice Department in Illinois has been emphasizing education and therapy.

Cohen, Sharon, "Rethink Charging Kids as Adults," *The Associated Press*, Dec. 2, 2007.
An early report on the movement to turn back some of the hard-line policies of the high-crime years.

Hernandez, Raymond, and Christopher Drew, "It's Not Just 'Ayes' and 'Nays': Obama's Votes in Illinois Echo," *The New York Times*, Dec. 20, 2007, p. A1.
When the Illinois legislature expanded criminal court jurisdiction over some juveniles, state Sen. Barack Obama criticized the measure but voted "present," apparently because voting no would have been politically risky.

Weinstein, Henry, "Focus on Youth Sentences; California has sent more juveniles to prison for life than any other state except one, a report says," *Los Angeles Times*, Nov. 19, 2007, p. B4.
Weinstein reports on a major recent study of a controversial aspect of sentencing law.

Zezima, Katie, "Law on Young Offenders Causes Rhode Island Furor," *The New York Times*, Oct. 30, 2007, p. A16.
Rhode Island lawmakers reconsider the wisdom of their move to drop the age of criminal court eligibility from 18 to 17.

Reports and Studies

***Juvenile Offenders and Victims: 2006 National Report, Office of Juvenile Justice and Delinquency Prevention, U.S. Department of Justice*, March 27, 2006, http://ojjdp.ncjrs.org/ojstatbb/nr2006/.**
The most recent national report provides a wealth of statistics and data analysis.

Backstrom, James C., and Gary L. Walker, "The Role of the Prosecutor in Juvenile Justice: Advocacy in the Courtroom and Leadership in the Community," Dec. 20, 2005, www.co.dakota.mn.us/NR/rdonlyres/0000094a/nkahigkxbxrixmxnjvvvlrmismbxwnmr/RoleProsecutorAdvocacy CtRmLeadershipCommunity 122005FinalVersion.pdf.
Two experts in juvenile prosecution urge their counterparts to involve themselves in programs aimed at spotting and helping troubled youth before they get into more trouble.

Butts, Jeffrey A., and Ojmarrh Mitchell, "Brick by Brick: Dismantling the Border Between Juvenile and Adult Justice," *Urban Institute*, July 1, 2000, www.urban.org/UploadedPDF/1000234_brick-by-brick.pdf.
Two juvenile justice experts succinctly analyze the complicated ties between the parallel, age-defined justice systems.

McGowan, Angela, *et al.*, "Effects on Violence of Laws and Policies Facilitating the Transfer of Juveniles from the Juvenile Justice System to the Adult Justice System," *U.S. Centers for Disease Control and Prevention*, Nov. 30, 2007, www.cdc.gov/mmwr/preview/mmwrhtml/rr5609a1.htm.

A study frequently cited in the juvenile justice debate analyzes the evidence on the effects of juvenile transfer to adult court.

Parker, Alison, "The Rest of Their Lives: Life Without Parole for Child Offenders in the United States," *Amnesty International, Human Rights Watch*, 2005, www.hrw.org/reports/2005/us1005/ (updated May, 2008), www.hrw.org/backgrounder/2008/us1005/us1005execsum.pdf.

Human-rights professional offers meticulous documentation on the effects of the harshest sentence that juveniles can receive.

For More Information

Campaign for Youth Justice, 1012 14th St., N.W., Suite 610, Washington, DC 20005; (202) 558-3580; www.campaign4youthjustice.org. Opposes treatment of youths under 18 as adults in trials, sentencing and incarceration.

Center for Juvenile Justice Reform, Georgetown University, 3300 Whitehaven St., N.W., Suite 5000, Washington, DC 20057; (202) 687-0880; http://cjjr.georgetown.edu/index.html. Trains juvenile system administrators and advocates policies and laws that focus on rehabilitation.

Crime Victims United of California, 1346 N. Market Blvd., Sacramento, CA 95834; (916) 928-4797; www.crimevictimsunited.com. A prosecution-oriented victims' rights organizations advocating on issues of national relevance, including life without parole for juveniles.

National Council on Crime and Delinquency, 1970 Broadway, Suite 500, Oakland, CA 94612; (510) 208-0500; www.nccd-crc.org. A nonprofit think tank and advocacy organization promoting alternatives to incarceration.

National Juvenile Justice Prosecution Center, 44 Canal Center Plaza, Suite 110, Alexandria, VA 22314; (703) 549-9222; www.ndaa.org/apri/programs/juvenile/jj_home.htm. A research and training organization of the National District Attorneys Association.

Office of Juvenile Justice and Delinquency Prevention, 810 Seventh St., N.W., Washington, DC 20531; (202) 307-5911; http://ojjdp.ncjrs.org. A Justice Department agency that provides data on all aspects of juvenile justice.

9

Child Welfare Reform

Will Recent Changes Make At-Risk Children Safer?

Tom Price

AP Photo/Joel Page

Sally Ann Schofield was sentenced in Augusta, Maine, to 20 years in prison for killing her 5-year-old foster child in 2002. Logan Marr suffocated after being bound to a highchair with 42 feet of duct tape. More than 900,000 children were abused or neglected in the United States in 2003 and 1,390 died. Today about a half-million children live in foster homes under the jurisdiction of state child welfare agencies.

From *CQ Researcher*, April 22, 2005.

Daisy Perales, a 5-year-old San Antonio girl, died on Dec. 1, 2004, a week after she was found unconscious and bleeding, with head trauma, bruises, a fractured rib and a lacerated spleen. She weighed just 20 pounds.

Texas Child Protective Services had investigated her family seven times. Daisy was one of more than 500 Texas children to die of abuse or neglect from 2002 to mid-2004. The agency had looked into at least 137 of the cases.[1]

At the beginning of 2003, in Newark, N.J., police entered a locked basement to find Raheem Williams, 7, and Tyrone Hill, 4. Both were starving and covered with burns and excrement. The next day, police found the body of Raheem's twin, who had been dead for more than 30 days. The state Department of Youth and Family Services had received repeated warnings that the children were being abused.[2]

"Our system is broken, and we need to make monumental changes," New Jersey Human Services Commissioner James Davy declared a year later, after more scandals surfaced.[3]

A decade earlier, police in Chicago had discovered 19 children, ages 1 to 14, living in a filthy two-bedroom apartment with a half-dozen adults. Police described a horrific scene of dirty diapers, spoiled food, roaches and dog and rat droppings. One child had cigarette burns, cuts and bruises. The Illinois Department of Children and Family Services had been in contact with six of the children. [4] Following the discovery, the department placed the children with various caregivers, later admitting it had lost track of them. The department eventually confessed it had a backlog of

U.S. Probe Faults State Programs

No state child welfare programs fully comply with federal child safety standards, according to a three-year investigation by the Bush administration. Sixteen states did not meet any of the seven federal standards (below) used to assess children's programs, and no state met more than two of the standards.

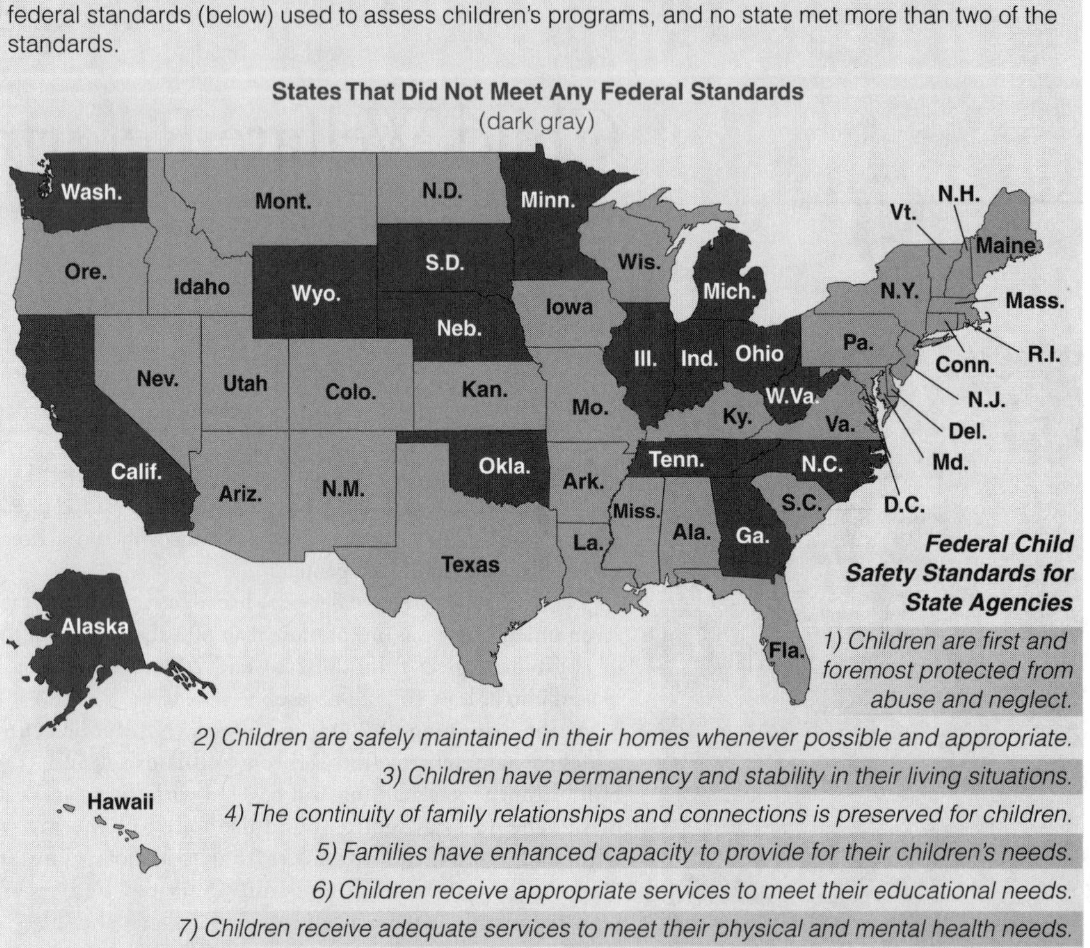

Source: U.S. Department of Health and Human Services

4,320 uninvestigated complaints of abused or neglected children.

But then consider these hopeful signs of reform:

- Legislation being considered in Texas this year would increase spending on child welfare programs, improve training for caseworkers and encourage the administration to reduce caseloads. Republican Gov. Rick Perry calls reform an "emergency issue."[5]
- New Jersey is planning to hire hundreds of new child welfare workers, speed investigations and reduce caseloads to no more than 25 children or 15 families per worker — down from the current maximum of more than 40 children and 20 families. Children who have lived in institutions for 18 months or more will be moved into "familylike" settings. An independent committee of child welfare experts, appointed in a lawsuit settlement, has approved the plan.[6]
- And Illinois has been transformed into "sort of the gold standard" for child welfare, in the words of Sue Badeau, deputy director of the Pew Commission on Children in Foster Care, a bipartisan group of political

leaders and child welfare experts that promotes child welfare reform. After the state's child welfare scandal in the mid-1990s, new leadership and a new philosophy have turned the Illinois system around, says Mark Testa, co-director of the University of Illinois' Children and Family Research Center and former research director of the state children's services department.

The department reduced caseloads and focused on keeping families together or quickly placing children in alternative permanent-living situations. It obtained federal waivers from regulations preventing subsidies for placements with relatives, such as grandparents or aunts and uncles. As a result, Illinois has reduced the number of children in foster care from 52,000 in 1997 to fewer than 17,000 today, according to Testa.

Nearly 1 Million Children Are Maltreated

More than 900,000 children in the United States were victims of abuse or neglect in 2003, about a 5 percent increase over the 1990 total. Most of the cases involved neglect, but 19 percent involved physical abuse and 10 percent sexual abuse.

Abused or Neglected American Children, 1990-2003*

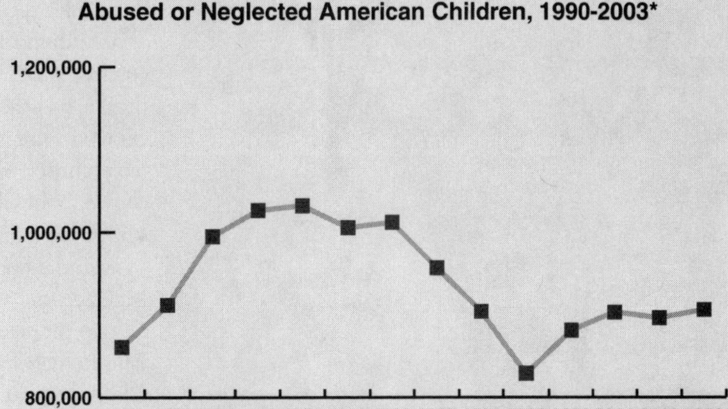

*2003 is the most recent year for which data are available

Source: Child Trends Data Bank, based on Department of Health and Human Services Reports, 1990-2003

So it goes in the American child welfare system: Scandal triggers public outrage which spurs reform, leaving children's advocates and child welfare workers constantly ricocheting between hope and despair. Meanwhile, more than 900,000 American children age 17 and younger were abused or neglected in 2003.[7]

"Reading the newspapers of late has been more like reading a horror novel, with case after case of abuse and neglect," said Texas state Sen. Jane Nelson, reflecting the nationwide despair generated by the unending reports of children who were mistreated while supposedly being protected by state agencies charged with doing so.[8] But, as the Republican author of reform legislation, Nelson also represents the potential for improvement that gives advocates hope.

Not a single state received a passing grade last year when the U.S. Health and Human Services Department (HHS) completed its review of state and local child welfare systems, and 16 states did not meet *any* of the seven federal child-care standards used to evaluate the programs. But the first eight states given follow-up reviews met all their initial targets for improvement, says Wade F. Horn, the department's assistant secretary for children and families.*[9]

State and local officials throughout the country agree on the need for substantial improvements in their child welfare systems, and even critics acknowledge that significant improvements are under way. Private organizations are adding to the ferment, from public-interest law firms demanding reforms in court to foundations that are supporting innovation. The Bush administration has offered up its plan for restructuring federal funding of child welfare, and both Republicans and Democrats in Congress agree not only on the need for reform but also on how that reform should be carried out.

"The consensus is: Where we can, we should protect the family," says Fred H. Wulczyn, an assistant professor at the Columbia University School of Social Work and a research fellow at the University of Chicago's Chapin Hall Center for Children. "Where we need to place kids in

---

* The states are: Arizona, Delaware, Indiana, Kansas, Massachusetts, Minnesota, Oregon and Vermont.

Getty Images/Melanie Stetson Freeman

Foster child Daphane Irvin, a senior at Chicago's South Shore High School, hopes to become an actress. Only 2 percent (1,900) of all foster care adoptions in 2002 were older teens, ages 16 to 18. Another 19,500 teens "aged out" of foster care without being adopted and must face the transition to adulthood alone.

foster care, we should proceed to permanent placement — such as with adoptive parents — as soon as possible."

Child welfare workers, government officials and children's advocates agree that it's best for children to live with their parents in healthy families, and that agencies should help families stay together. When children must be removed from their parents because of abuse or neglect, it's best to quickly return the children home safely or to place them permanently with adoptive parents or relatives.

Failure to do so can have disastrous consequences, as Maryland residents learned in early April.

Maryland houses 2,700 children in 330 privately operated group homes that are not adequately supervised by state agencies, according to an investigation by *The Baltimore Sun.*[10] In some of those homes, children have been denied needed medical treatment, served inadequate food, assaulted by employees and even supplied by employees with illegal drugs. At least 15 group home residents have died since 1998.

Children often are placed in group homes — which cost the state far more than foster family homes — when there is no other place for them. "There were some providers who were good, but there were others who we would have chosen not to be bothered with, but we had no choice," said Gloria Slade, former child placement supervisor for the Baltimore Social Services Department.

Maryland Human Resources Secretary Christopher J. McCabe said the state will recruit more foster parents to reduce the need for group homes. But Charlie Cooper, who manages the Maryland Citizens' Review Board for Children, said the state must offer a wider range of children's services.[11]

"You have a lot of things going on at the same time" to improve services to children, says Susan Notkin, director of the Center for Community Partnerships in Child Welfare, a nonprofit organization that funds and consults with agencies implementing innovative programs. "A lot of innovation is being tested. There's a lot of interest in looking at the financing."

Madelyn Freundlich, policy director for Children's Rights, a New York-based advocacy organization, agrees. "There is a lot of energy in the field right now," she says. "There has been a joining together of public agencies and the private sector to really look at foster care, and there is a growing awareness among the general public about foster care and the support needed to provide the right services for kids and families."

But the challenge is complex. And the road from good intentions to effective accomplishments is neither short nor straight. There are stark disagreements about how much spending should be increased (or whether it should be increased at all), how much federal control should be exercised over federally funded state and local programs, and which reform proposals are most likely to be effective.

Widespread agreement on the need for reform represents just "superficial consensus," says Douglas J.

Besharov, director of the American Enterprise Institute's (AEI) Social and Individual Responsibility Project and a former director of the U.S. Center on Child Abuse and Neglect.

"The Democrats who say they want to give states more flexibility want to make it open-ended [entitlement] spending," Besharov, a University of Maryland public affairs professor, says. "This is just an excuse to put in more money, while Republicans say they're looking for ways to cap expenditures. It's just like we're all in favor of long life and fighting cancer, but getting from here to there requires a lot more agreement than what I see."

As the nation struggles to help children from troubled families, here are some of the questions child welfare experts are trying to answer:

Do state and local governments do enough to keep families together?

Most headline-grabbing child welfare horror stories spring from parents mistreating children whom the system has failed to protect. But many child welfare experts believe the more common problem stems from agencies removing children from parents too frequently. It's not that the children didn't need protection but that agencies failed to provide early services that could have kept the kids safe and at home.

In fact, concern about taking children from their parents is so prevalent that a common measure of agency success is reducing the number of youngsters removed from their homes. Several private organizations are promoting reforms designed to improve services to troubled families before the children have to be removed. But there's still a long way to go.

Illinois' newfound reputation for quality stems in part from cutting its foster care population by two-thirds since the mid-1990s and removing fewer than half as many children from their parents each year, Testa says. Improvement in New York City's system is marked by a foster care caseload that dropped from just under 50,000 in the mid-1990s to just below 20,000 today, according to Columbia University's Wulczyn.

Nationwide, the foster care caseload also is declining, but it did not peak as early and is not falling as rapidly as in Illinois and New York. In 1999, nearly 570,000 American children lived in foster homes — an historic high. That number dropped to just above 520,000 in 2003, the most recent figure available. But the dip wasn't because fewer children were removed from their homes; it was because states did a better job of returning foster children to their parents or placing them in other permanent homes.[12]

Because child welfare systems differ from state to state, Wulczyn says, "it's hard to come up with one overarching statement about where the system is, except to say that it's not as good as it should be, but it's better than it was."

Illinois succeeds, Testa says, because it is "doing a better job making family assessments, working with families who can take care of their kids in the home and not putting those children unnecessarily into foster care." Child welfare experts would like to see that approach expanded throughout the country.

"Most places do not have the services and support that families need, so they would never get put into the child welfare system in the first place," says Judy Meltzer, deputy director of the Center for the Study of Social Policy, who serves on panels monitoring court-ordered reforms in New Jersey and Washington, D.C. "The infrastructure does a really bad job of being able to reach out and work with families before they get to the point where crises occur and kids have to be removed from their homes."

Meltzer and others say that even the best child welfare agencies can't provide those services by themselves. "If we think child welfare agencies alone will do it, we will always be stuck," says Wanda Mial, senior associate for child welfare at the Annie E. Casey Foundation, a leading operator and funder of programs for disadvantaged children.

"Government can't do it alone," either, says Notkin, whose Center for Community Partnerships promotes cooperation among many public and private organizations.

Parental substance abuse causes or exacerbates 70 percent of child neglect or abuse incidents, says Kathryn Brohl, author of the 2004 book *The New Miracle Workers: Overcoming Contemporary Challenges in Child Welfare Work.*[13] Abuse also stems from poverty, poor housing, ill health, lack of child care, parental incompetence, domestic violence, arrest and imprisonment, Brohl adds. Some children enter the child welfare system because they run afoul of authorities by committing a crime or frequently skipping school, says Mial, a former child welfare worker in Philadelphia.

Judges' Hearings Help Kids Feel Loved

"So, I [see] you want to be a cosmetologist," Judge Patricia Martin Bishop said to the teenager sitting before her. "What's that?" the girl asked.

"Someone who fixes your hair, does your nails — things like that," Bishop replied.

"I can't even do my own hair," the girl exclaimed. "I want to be a lawyer."

Bishop, the presiding judge in the Child Protection Division of Cook County Circuit Court in Chicago, looked at the girl's caseworker, who explained why she had changed the girl's answer on a questionnaire about her future. "I changed it to cosmetologist because she's reading at such a low level she'll never be a lawyer."

But Bishop quickly set the caseworker straight: "I'm not convinced she can't become a lawyer until we help her get through high school and give her the support she needs to get into college and get her through college and get her through law school. Until we've made some concerted effort to help her achieve her dreams, I'm not prepared to channel her to our dreams for her."

That moment, Bishop says, demonstrated exactly why she created "benchmark hearings" for teenagers.

Since 1997, Illinois has reduced its foster care rolls from 52,000 to fewer than 17,000, thus reducing demands on the court. Bishop was able to relieve Judge Patricia Brown Holmes of her regular caseload, and now they both conduct special hearings for unadopted teens about to leave foster care for independence.

The benchmark hearings are held when the child is 14, 16 and 17½. The children, as well as their caseworkers, teachers, doctors, coaches and other adults with whom they have important relationships, attend the meetings, which can last up to two hours. "I require the psychiatrist to face me and tell my why this kid's on meds," the judge explains. "I make the basketball coach come in and tell me how basketball helps or hurts this kid."

Every Illinois foster child attends a juvenile court hearing every six months, but they can be brief, Bishop says. The benchmark meetings tend to be longer because the judges want to get a clear picture of the child's capabilities and needs.

"The idea is to look at kids more holistically," Bishop explains, "to coordinate with the agencies, to help [the teens] for the present and for their dreams for the future. If there are unresolved issues after a benchmark hearing,

To avoid removing children from their parents in these circumstances, Brohl and other experts say, child welfare workers must be able to call on other agencies to address such problems as soon as they are discovered — or even before.

According to social psychologist Kristin Anderson Moore, who heads the Child Trends research organization, the most effective ways to deter child abuse and neglect include "helping people establish healthy marriages before they have children, helping teenagers delay child-bearing and helping parents delay having second births."

Some "very rigorous studies" have shown that starting home-visitation programs shortly after birth can reduce abuse and neglect by 50 percent, says Shay Bilchik, president of the Child Welfare League of America. A visiting nurse trains new parents, monitors the well being of the child and arranges for additional services needed by the family. "If you track those babies 15 years down the road," Bilchik says, "home visitation has been shown to reduce those babies' entering into the criminal world."

Rep. Wally Herger, R-Calif., chairman of the House Ways and Means subcommittee that oversees child welfare, noted that the federal government spends 10 times as much on state and local foster care and adoption services as it does on programs designed to hold families together.

"As a result," he said, "rather than focusing on the prevention of abuse and neglect, today's funding structure encourages the removal of children and breakup of families. That is unacceptable."[14]

There are deep disagreements about how that problem should be fixed, however.

"I don't have any doubt Wally cares about kids," says Rep. Jim McDermott of Washington, the ranking Democrat on Herger's subcommittee. "It's a question of how you do it."

I keep it on my benchmark calendar and have follow-up hearings."

The needs for follow-up can vary widely. "A girl came to one of my benchmarks wearing sandals and a short skirt in dead of winter," the judge says. "She had moved from one group home to another, and her allowance hadn't kept up with her so she couldn't buy the things she needed. I kept the case on my benchmark hearing calendar until we were able to resolve the allowance problem."

At another hearing, Bishop discovered that a boy had maintained a relationship with his mother, whose parental rights had been terminated years before — a not uncommon occurrence. "His mother had continued drugging," Bishop says. "My position was, if he's maintained this relationship it's incumbent upon us to make it work as best we can. We put the mother back into [drug-treatment] services. She got clean. We sent this kid back home before he turned 18."

Cook County Courthouse

Presiding Judge Patricia Martin Bishop of Chicago created "benchmark" hearings to protect teens' rights — and their dreams.

Adolescents need relationships that will help them make the transition to adulthood when they leave foster care, Bishop explains. Sometimes the relationship can be as unlikely as with a drug-addicted mother who had lost her parental rights. Sometimes it can continue to be the child welfare system.

Bishop is authorized to keep a foster child within the jurisdiction of the Department of Children and Family Services until age 21. And, using private donations, the department can even provide higher-education assistance until age 23.

Bishop doesn't have empirical data to establish the value of benchmark hearings, but she has heard encouraging anecdotes. "Lawyers who didn't want to do this now are requesting that I extend this down to age 12," she says. "Kids come and say, 'I want Judge Holmes to have my case, or Judge Bishop to have my case.'

"The state is such a poor parent. We [judges] can look a child in the eye and talk about what he or she hopes to do in the future. They feel as if they're heard. They feel as if they've gotten attention. They feel loved."

Does the federal government give state and local child welfare agencies enough financial support and flexibility?

As they lobbied on Capitol Hill last month, volunteers from the Child Welfare League of America boldly proclaimed their top legislative priority on oversized campaign buttons pinned to their lapels: "No caps on kids!"

The slogan is shorthand for their opposition to President Bush's proposal to convert the main source of federal child welfare funding — the foster care entitlement — into a flexible, capped block grant, or a single grant that the states can spend in various innovative ways with less federal control.

Under current law, states are entitled to federal reimbursement for every foster child whose parents would have qualified for welfare under the old Aid to Families with Dependent Children program in 1996. Overall, the federal government pays about half the nation's $22 billion child welfare bill, according to an Urban Institute study, while the rest comes from state and local governments.[15]

The welfare league argues that not only should the existing entitlement regime be preserved but also that the federal government should increase spending on various child welfare programs.

However, HHS Assistant Secretary Horn says groups like the Child Welfare League "live in a dream world where money grows on trees," adding that he himself prefers to live "in the world of the achievable."

Both sides agree that child welfare agencies should be able to spend more federal money on helping families stay together and on alternatives to traditional foster care, which receives the bulk of federal aid today. The administration contends this can be accomplished by letting states spend their existing federal foster care allotment for other activities, such as helping troubled families or supporting guardians. But many child welfare

Number of Foster Kids Has Declined

The number of foster children began declining after peaking in 1999, due largely to a rise in adoptions. Even so, more than a half-million American children were in foster care in 2003, a 31 percent increase over 1990.

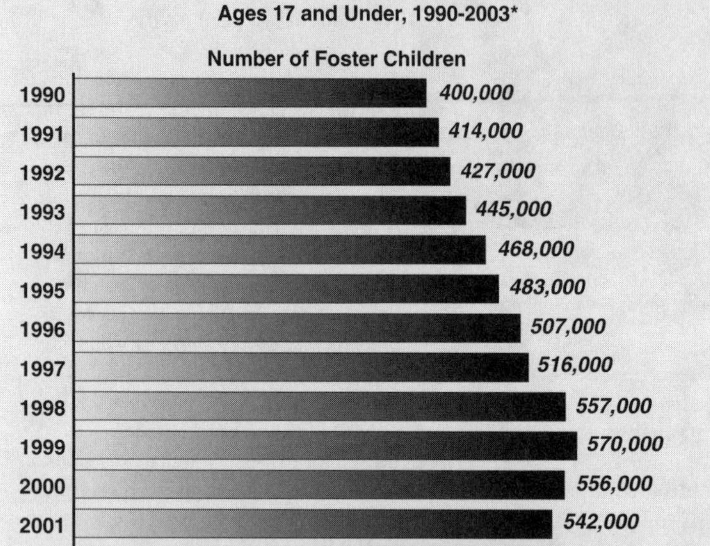

* *2003 is the most recent year for which data are available*

Source: Child Trends Data Bank, based on Department of Health and Human Services Reports, 1990-2003

advocates argue that the agencies need more money and warn that eliminating the entitlement could leave them with less in the long run.

The administration proposes giving states the option of accepting a block grant that could be spent on foster care and other services. Unlike the entitlement, the grant would not rise and fall with changes in the foster care caseload. For the first five years, each state would receive the same amount it would have received under the entitlement program based on the caseload change during the previous five years. That means states that had declining caseloads would receive less federal money. After five years, Congress would decide how to continue to fund the program.

Some states have implemented well-regarded innovations by obtaining waivers from federal regulations, leading administration officials to contend that allowing flexibility works. Pointing to the drop in welfare rolls that followed similar welfare reforms in the mid-1990s, the administration also argues that flexibility allows the states to be more effective while cutting costs.[16]

"We think if states are better able to focus money on prevention — which is cheaper than intervention — there would be less need for expensive out-of-home-care, in the same way that when states focused on work instead of simply cash, welfare caseloads declined," Horn says.

States would be hard pressed to shift money from foster care to other services, however, because child welfare systems already are underfunded, contends Liz Meitner, vice president for government affairs at the Child Welfare League. "We think a better strategy is to increase investments for prevention that will ultimately reduce the number of kids in foster care," Meitner says.

The Pew Commission on Children in Foster Care proposed maintaining the entitlement and beefing up federal aid while increasing flexibility.[17]

The commission calculated it would cost $1.6 billion annually just to extend federal aid to all foster children. Acknowledging the pressure to contain federal spending, the commission proposed extending aid to all but cutting the amount given for each child, so total federal aid would not rise. The commission suggested hiking other, more flexible, federal grants by $200 million the first year and by 2 percent above inflation in later years.

"Every child who experiences abuse or neglect deserves the protection of both the federal and state governments," said commission Chairman Bill Frenzel, former Republican representative from Minnesota, making a key argument against ending the entitlement.[18]

"Child welfare has traditionally been the safety net for vulnerable children and families," Freundlich of Children's Rights says. "It does not have waiting lists. It's had to be there for the children."

Block grant opponents point to the crack cocaine epidemic that devastated many families and caused child welfare caseloads to soar in the 1980s and '90s. Without the entitlement, states would have had to spend much more of their own money or agencies could not have cared for all the children coming through their doors. Many warn methamphetamine abuse could become the next crack. They also note that, over time, block grant programs haven't kept pace with inflation, and funding for some has declined.

The Social Services Block Grant, for example, dropped from $3 billion in 1981 to $1.7 billion in 2003, according to the Child Welfare League. Had it tracked inflation, she says, it now would total more than $6 billion.

But Assistant HHS Secretary Horn replies that if states reduce foster rolls they would receive more money through a block grant program than through an entitlement program. That's because the entitlement, which is based on the number of children served, would drop if the rolls dropped, while the block grant would not. If caseloads rise significantly, he adds, the administration plan includes an emergency fund that states could tap.

The federal government can't afford to give states both flexibility and an entitlement, the American Enterprise Institute's Besharov argues. "The only way to give states flexibility in a federal grant program is to cap it. Otherwise, they will steal you blind."

Besharov suggests extending the waiver option, which gives the states supervised flexibility, and "tying it to rigorous evaluations" to document what works best.

Testa, of the Children and Family Research Center, also supports more waivers, although he doesn't share Besharov's fear of entitlements. "We have to invest a lot more in demonstrations that will prove what works," he says. "We should be giving states permission to innovate but requiring them to demonstrate that what they're doing is working."

Because states have to match the federal funds under current law, he adds, they will not be motivated to spend more than they need.

Does the child welfare system prepare foster adolescents for adulthood?

Mary Lee's foster care judicial reviews always seemed the same. She'd wait for hours in the courthouse, then have what felt like a one-minute session during which the judge would "pat me on the back and say everything's great."

Then, when she was 16, a judge actually asked: "Mary, what do you want for your life?" And she told him.

"I said I want a family," she recalls. "I want to be adopted. I want to know that when I go to college I'm going to have a family to come home to, that I'm going to have a dad to walk me down the aisle and grandparents for my children. And if I stay in foster care, when I leave I'm not going to have anything. I'm going to be totally on my own."

A week before her 18th birthday, after five years in foster care, Mary was adopted by Scott Lee, her caseworker, and his wife in Montgomery County, Tenn. Now 23, Mary has graduated from Vanderbilt University and plans to attend law school. She traces her good life and bright future to that moment the judge asked her about her dreams.

"Adoption is not about your childhood," she explains. "It's about the rest of your life. You always need a mom and a dad. You always need your grandparents. You always need the family support."

Mary's happy-ending story is, unfortunately, rare. According to the latest available statistics, 92,000 teens ages 16 to 18 lived in foster homes in 2002 — 17 percent of the total foster population. Just 1,300 of them were adopted that year — 2 percent of all foster care adoptions. That same year, 19,500 teens "aged out" of foster care, usually by turning 18, and many of them faced the transition to adulthood the way Mary Lee feared she would face it — alone.[19]

Four years after leaving foster care, nearly half of these older teens had not graduated from high school, a quarter had been homeless, 40 percent had become parents and fewer than a fifth were self-supporting, according to the Jim Casey Youth Opportunities Initiative, which works with those young people.[20]

"Effective middle-class families parent their kids into their 20s, and these kids are cut off at 18," Moore of Child Trends notes. "From age 18 to 24 is a time kids need contact and care and monitoring from adults."

CHRONOLOGY

1800-1900 *Charitable organizations open "orphan asylums." Courts allow child protection societies to remove children from homes. Later, child-protection organizations pay families to take in homeless children.*

1853 Children's Aid Society of New York is founded and begins sending homeless children to Western families on "orphan" or "baby" trains in 1854.

1872 New York Foundling Asylum begins putting unwanted infants and toddlers on westbound "baby trains."

1900-1930s *First juvenile courts created. Child welfare agencies increase supervision of foster homes.*

1912 U.S. Children's Bureau established.

1935 Social Security Act provides federal funds for rural children's services, social-worker training.

1960-1970s *Federal role expands, focus intensifies on preserving families and alternatives to adoption.*

1961 Federal aid extended to poor foster children; more children's services are offered in urban and rural areas.

1962-69 Child-care professionals are required to report suspected abuse.

1974 Child Abuse Prevention and Treatment Act provides federal funds for protecting endangered children.

1976-79 Child welfare agencies try to reduce need for foster care. California, New York and Illinois subsidize adoptions.

1977 Foster care caseloads total about 550,000.

1980s-2000 *Single-parent households, unmarried births, child abuse and neglect reports all soar. Demands for reform increase. Lawsuits force improvements in state and local child welfare systems.*

1980 Congress creates federal adoption-assistance program. Social Security Act becomes main source of federal child welfare support.

1986 Foster caseload drops below 300,000; crack cocaine epidemic soon causes foster care rolls to soar.

1993 Federal government grants waivers for states to test innovative child welfare services.

1993-94 Discovery of 19 children living in squalor, death of another, spur shakeup of Illinois child welfare system.

1995 Foster caseloads hit nearly 500,000.

1997 Adoption and Safe Families Act increases federal support for adoption, family preservation.

1999 Foster caseloads peak at 570,000. Federal government increases aid for youths aging out of foster care.

2000s *Courts get federal money to reduce abuse and neglect backlogs, improve information technology.*

2001 Federal government offers new education assistance for aging-out youths.

2002 Authorities report 900,000 confirmed cases of child abuse or neglect nationwide, including 1,390 deaths.

2003 Foster rolls decline to 525,000. General Accounting Office says high caseloads and low salaries inhibit recruitment and retention of effective child welfare workers.

2004 Concern arises that a methamphetamine epidemic could raise foster care rolls. Pew Commission on Children in Foster Care argues that states need more child welfare money and flexibility. About 20 states receive waivers to offer support services not normally funded by federal programs.

2005 President Bush asks that federal foster care funding be converted to block grants. Illinois, now representing child welfare's "gold standard," cuts foster care population by two-thirds since mid-1990s and reduces average caseload from more than 50 to fewer than 20.

After Chris Brooks left foster care in Nevada at age 19, he slept in a car and on friends' couches. At age 18, Terry Harrak figured out how to sleep and scrounge food amid the bustle of a busy hospital in Northern Virginia.

But both Chris' and Terry's stories have happy endings, thanks to serendipitous relationships with caring adults. A professor studying homeless youth "took me under his wing" and "became kind of like an uncle," Chris says. Now 23, he attends college in Las Vegas and mentors homeless youth. While living in a shelter, Terry met a Child Welfare League staff member who was looking for homeless young people to testify before Congress. Now 25, she attends college and works as the league's youth leadership coordinator, staffing an advisory council on which Chris and Mary serve.

Chris and Terry both say they were ill-prepared for independent living. And both cite the need for ongoing relationships and training in such basic skills as balancing a checkbook, filling out a tax form and applying for college aid.

"Historically, in child welfare we never thought about the permanent lifetime relationships that these kids need," says Gary Stangler, head of the Casey program for older teens and former director of the Missouri Social Services Department. "If we got them to age 18 alive, we did our job.

"Adoption, especially the older you get, is difficult and uncommon. So the solution was training for independent living, which is the opposite of permanent lifetime relationships."

Stangler has observed "an awakening to the fact that we were doing a very poor job for kids once they left the foster care system without the support we take for granted for our own kids." Slowly, he says, things are getting better.

Legislation passed in 1999 provides federal aid for housing and education for former foster youths, but many young people do not know how to apply for it. States are allowed to keep them on Medicaid beyond age 18, but most don't. Private organizations and some states are helping older teens build the adult relationships they need. And a few courts are institutionalizing the kind of court procedure that turned Mary Lee's life around.

In Chicago, the Cook County Circuit Court's Child Protection Division conducts "benchmark hearings" when foster children turn 14 and 16 and six months before they age out. (*See story, p. 206.*) The hearings can last up to two hours. Participants include the most important individuals in the children's lives, such as caseworkers, teachers, doctors and adults with whom the children have or might build long-lasting relationships.

"All of us were grappling with how could we, the court, get a handle on this road to being independent," says Patricia Martin Bishop, the division's presiding judge, who established the hearings. "The thought was, if we had more time to concentrate on each of these kids, we'd get a better handle on what needs they have that aren't met."

Among the questions Bishop requires the children to answer during the hearings: "What do you want to do when you get out of school? What do you intend to do with your life?"

BACKGROUND

Orphan Trains

In the beginning, America's child welfare system provided a kind of residential vocational education: Families took in needy children, then fed, clothed and trained them in a trade. Such apprenticeships were common, even for youngsters who were not parentless or poor. But it was considered an especially attractive way to place orphans and other children whose parents couldn't care for them. The child got a home and learned a trade; the host family benefited from the child's work.[21]

In the early 19th century, religious and charitable organizations began opening orphan asylums, which became the most common means of caring for children without parents between 1830 and 1860.

Also in mid-century, Charles Lorring Brace organized the Children's Aid Society of New York, which created the "orphan train" or "baby train" movement. Urban centers like New York attracted hordes of immigrants who took difficult, dangerous and sometimes deadly jobs. Diseases like typhoid, diphtheria and cholera also hit the poor especially hard. Deceased adults left orphans or

How Illinois Reformed a Broken System

Clearer information is needed

Three times, the Illinois Children and Family Services Department took Joseph Wallace away from his mentally ill mother, and three times the youngster was returned to her. There was no fourth time, because on April 19, 1993, she tied an extension cord around the 3-year-old's neck and hanged him from a transom in their Chicago apartment.[1]

Early the next year, Chicago police discovered 19 children living in a squalid, two-bedroom apartment with a half-dozen adults. Again, the department knew about six of the children but had left them with their mothers.[2]

Although the tragedies were only tiny tips of an enormous iceberg of bureaucratic failure, they shined a media spotlight on the Illinois child welfare system and outraged the public. In the end, they spurred dramatic reforms in the system, making it a font of successful innovation.

"They've addressed preventing kids from coming into foster care in the first place, as well as strengthening reunification for children who return home safely and strengthening alternative forms of permanency through subsidized guardianship and adoption," says Sue Badeau, deputy director of the Pew Commission on Foster Care, who says the system is now the "gold standard" of child care.

The Illinois system was "sort of average" in the 1980s, became "a mess" by the mid-'90s and now is one of the best, says Jill Duerr Berrick, associate dean of the School of Social Welfare at the University of California, Berkeley. "We've seen tremendous innovation coming out of Illinois."

Illinois probably ran America's worst child welfare system in the mid-1990s, says Mark Testa, co-director of the University of Illinois' Children and Family Research Center. It had the nation's highest prevalence of children in foster care — 17.1 per 1,000 — where they remained in care longer than children in other states. The total foster care rolls soared from 20,000 in the late-'80s to 52,000 in 1997. But when horror stories repeatedly hit the media, public outrage triggered changes.

Feeling intense pressure from the public, the state legislature and a lawsuit by the American Civil Liberties Union, Republican Gov. Jim Edgar appointed a new department director, Jess McDonald. He launched a comprehensive overhaul of the system and hired Testa as in-house research director.

"Lawsuits are critical to reform," says Marcia Robinson Lowry, executive director of Children's Rights, a New York organization that sues local and state governments to get them to improve child welfare systems. "There is sustained pressure for reform because of a court order."

McDonald and Testa discovered a system engaged in self-destruction. It was taking custody of thousands of children who didn't need to be removed from their homes, which limited caseworkers' ability to take care of children who really were in danger.

"The state was stepping in and taking these kids into protective custody because they were living with someone other than their parents — grandmother, aunt, uncle — even

single parents who couldn't support their children. And as immigrants or the offspring of immigrants, many of the children had no extended families they could turn to for support.

Besides worrying about the children's well being, Brace warned they might grow up to be violent criminals, referring to them as the "dangerous classes." He convinced businessmen to support shipping the children west, where they presumably would live healthy and wholesome lives on farms.

The first orphan train carried children to Dowagiac, Mich., in 1854. Over the next 80 years, some 150,000 to 200,000 children were shipped to states in the West. In 1872, the New York Foundling Asylum, which took in unwanted babies, began putting infants and toddlers on the trains, a practice that lasted into the 20th century. As in colonial days, the farmers benefited from the labor of the children they took in.

In the 1870s growing public concern about child abuse and neglect spurred the founding of societies for the prevention of cruelty to children, and courts began to empower them to remove children from neglectful homes.

What we now know as foster care took root in the last two decades of the 19th century, when some child protection organizations began to pay families to take in homeless children so the children would not have to work.

though they were living safely," Testa explains. "Children were building up in long-term foster care because there were no pathways for moving kids into more permanent homes, and folks weren't asking the relatives if they were willing to adopt. There was this myopia of only recognizing nuclear families, and if you're not in a nuclear family you're taken into the child welfare system."

The new managers forced the department to stop taking children who were living safely with relatives and start offering those families services available to nuclear families. "That reduced the number of kids coming into foster care right off the bat," Testa says. "But large numbers were still remaining in long-term foster care, so moving kids out needed attention."

The Illinois child welfare system delivers most foster care services through private contractors rather than local government agencies. "The financial incentives were all geared toward keeping kids in foster care," Testa explains, because they were paid only for foster children. "There was no reward for moving kids into permanent homes."

The state began paying incentives for adoption and reunification with parents, and the foster rolls dropped again.

The state also sought a waiver from federal rules in order to use some of its federal foster care funds to subsidize guardianships. Guardianship does not require termination of parental rights as adoption does, but it creates a permanent relationship between the child and the guardian and removes state supervision. Many relatives willing to care for children do not want to adopt, Testa says, because that would require termination of the biological parents' rights.

Since obtaining the waiver in 1997, Illinois has moved more than 8,000 children from foster care to guardianship, Testa says, reducing state costs and freeing caseworkers to concentrate on families that really are in trouble. During the decade of reform, the average worker's caseload has dropped from more than 50 cases to fewer than 20, Testa says.

"Illinois takes far fewer kids into foster care than many other states," he explains, "because we're doing a better job making family assessments and working with families who can take care of their kids with some help."

Now the department's biggest challenge is helping older adolescents who remain in foster care and are less likely to be adopted. "The solution is to attach every child as early as possible to a permanent family, a mentor, someone who's going to care about them," Testa says.

One hurdle to adoption is that older adolescents lose foster services that help in the transition to adulthood. The department has obtained a new federal waiver to extend those services after adoption or while the child is in guardianship. The department also is working with universities to support former foster children while they're in school. And it's developed a program to recruit families to host college students during vacations and to maintain connections with them during the school year.

"The Illinois system has not achieved perfection," Berrick says, "but it's certainly made a remarkable turnaround."

[1] Phillip J. O'Connor and Zay N. Smith, "Woman Charged In Son's Hanging," *Chicago Sun-Times*, April 20, 1993, p. 3.

[2] Phillip J. O'Connor and Ray Long, "Police Rescue 19 Kids In Filthy Apartment," *Chicago Sun-Times*, Feb. 2, 1994, p. 1; Colin McMahon and Susan Kuczka, "19 Kids Found In Filth," *Chicago Tribune*, Feb. 2, 1994, p. 1.

As the century neared its end, states began to organize charity boards that tended to favor home placements over institutional care.

The modern child welfare system began taking shape in the early 20th century. In 1912, the federal government created the U.S. Children's Bureau, now part of the Health and Human Services Department, to conduct research and distribute information to state children's agencies. States began to create separate juvenile court systems, which ordered more children into government care. In the 1920s, child welfare agencies began to exercise greater supervision of foster homes. And the New Deal brought federal money into the picture.

The Social Security Act of 1935 made the Children's Bureau responsible for administering the new Aid to Dependent Children program, later known as Aid to Families with Dependent Children, or AFDC. Congress intended the program to preserve poor families that otherwise might not be able to afford to keep their children at home. Aimed primarily at widowed mothers, it supported state aid programs for children living with a parent or other relative. States also received federal assistance to establish or strengthen children's services in rural areas and to train child welfare workers.

The federal government didn't extend aid to foster children and to urban services until 1961. To receive that

AP Photo/Steve Nesius

Linda and Mike Hurley and adopted daughter Courtney pose for their first family photo after signing adoption documents in Tampa on June 4, 2004. Child welfare agencies around the nation are seeking adoptive parents or guardians to help older foster children make the transition to adulthood.

aid, the foster child had to come from a family with income low enough to qualify for AFDC. Assistance also was offered for a broader range of child services, including family preservation.

Child Abuse and Crack

Also during the early 1960s, Denver physician Henry Kempe called public attention to the "battered child syndrome," revealing that many hospitalized youngsters whose injuries had been attributed to accidents actually had been abused by a parent or other caregiver. Before the decade ended, all 50 states passed laws requiring doctors, teachers and other child-care professionals to report suspected abuse. Congress followed suit in 1974 with the Child Abuse Prevention and Treatment Act (CAPTA), which provided federal funds for child protection services, including procedures for reporting and investigating abuse and protecting endangered children.

During the late-'70s, child welfare agencies began focusing on moving children from foster care into permanent homes and on helping families avoid the need for out-of-home placements in the first place. Advocates of the shift in focus said it was better for children and would cost less than foster care.

Congress established a national adoption-information exchange program in 1978. California, New York and Illinois became the first states to subsidize adoptions in order to counteract the financial penalty suffered by foster parents who lose their foster payments when they finally adopt their foster children.

In 1980, Congress created a federal adoption-assistance program and merged it with the old AFDC foster care funds. Known as Title IV-E of the Social Security Act, it is now the main source of federal support for child welfare. The law required states to make "reasonable efforts" to keep children with their parents or return them as soon as possible. When families couldn't be reunited, the law declared placement with relatives or adoption to be superior to long-term foster care.

These efforts collided with the crack cocaine epidemic and other social pathologies from the mid-1980s through early-'90s.

From 1980 to 1994, single-parent households increased from 22 percent to 31 percent of all families. Births to unmarried teens soared from 27.6 per 1,000 females in 1980 to 44.6 in 1992. In 1993, 2.9 million child abuse and neglect reports were filed, up from 1.7 million in 1984.[22]

Foster caseloads — which dropped from a little more than 500,000 in 1977 to fewer than 300,000 in 1986 — soared back to nearly 500,000 by 1995.[23]

Federal and state governments, with support and prodding from private organizations, continued to press for family preservation and adoption as better alternatives to foster care.

In 1993, Congress authorized $1 billion over five years to help states strengthen troubled families. More federal money was distributed to help courts improve their handling of foster care and adoption cases. Congress gave the Health and Human Services secretary authority to grant waivers so states could use federal child welfare grants to finance innovative programs.

President Clinton declared adoption to be a national priority in 1996, saying "no child should be uncertain about what 'family' or 'parent' or 'home' means." The 1997 Adoption and Safe Families Act provided more incentives for adoption and family preservation. The Foster Care Independence Act of 1999 increased federal funding for counseling and other services for youths making the transition from foster care to adulthood. The money could be used for housing and other living expenses, and states could extend Medicaid coverage beyond the youths' 18th birthday.

In 2000 Congress authorized federal aid to help courts reduce backlogs of abuse and neglect cases and improve information technology systems. New federal educational assistance for so-called aging-out youths — those leaving the system — was authorized in 2001.

CURRENT SITUATION

Rigid Rules and Budgets

When Katie Sutton's grandchildren wanted to sleep over at a friend's house, Philadelphia child welfare caseworkers had to investigate the friend's family first. If she wanted to take a child to the doctor, she had to get a caseworker's instructions. When she wanted to take them across the nearby border into New Jersey, she had to get a caseworker's permission.

To Sutton, who had custody of five grandchildren as a foster parent, this was more than a nuisance.

Investigating a friend's family felt like "a way of invading their privacy and just automatically assuming that they have a bad background," she explained. For the grandchildren, the frequent involvement of caseworkers sent the message that "we're foster care kids, we don't belong anywhere, we have a label and we're different from everyone else."[24]

The children don't feel different anymore, because Sutton has become their permanent legal guardian, and they have left government supervision behind them. She hadn't wanted to adopt because she didn't want to terminate her son's parental rights. He's not a bad father, she said, just immature and emotionally and financially unable to care for his offspring. She couldn't afford to keep them outside the foster care system until Pennsylvania offered to subsidize her guardianship.

Her story encapsulates the state of the U.S. child welfare system today. Rigid rules and tight budgets make it difficult for agencies to tailor services to the specific needs of individual children and families.

Caseloads Are Double Recommended Levels

The average American child welfare caseworker oversees two-dozen or more children — twice as many as child advocate and accreditation organizations recommend. Some caseworkers manage as many as 110 cases.

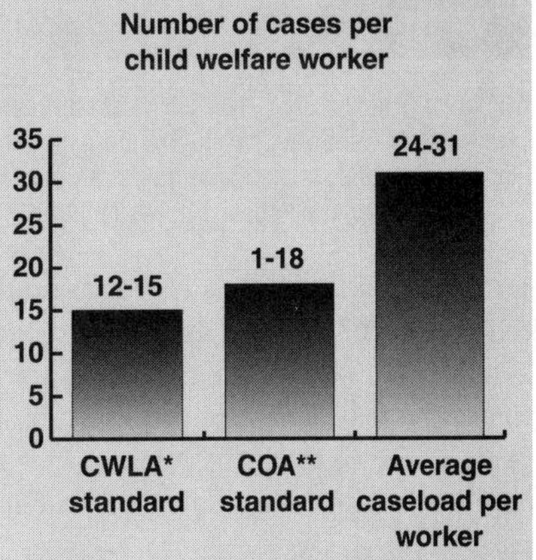

Number of cases per child welfare worker

	Number of cases
CWLA* standard	12-15
COA** standard	1-18
Average caseload per worker	24-31

* Child Welfare League of America

** Council on Accreditation for Children and Family Services

Source: "HHS Could Play a Greater Role in Helping Child Welfare Agencies Recruit and Retain Staff," U.S. General Accounting Office, March 2003

But federal, state and local governments — often in cooperation with private organizations — are moving toward more flexible policies that emphasize holding families together and placing children in alternative permanent homes when that's not possible.

It's common for relatives not to want to adopt, even when they're willing to make permanent homes for grandchildren, nieces or nephews, Testa at the University of Illinois says. "They don't want to get embroiled in an adversarial battle with a daughter or sister," he explains. "Many of them feel it's odd that they'd have to adopt someone to whom they were already related."

Getty Images/Chris Hondros

Stephen McCall of Brooklyn, N.Y., has been a foster parent for five years for, from left, Marshawn, Maleek, Brandon and Marcus. New York's child welfare agency is encouraging more potential foster parents to take adolescent and special-needs children.

In Sutton's case, Pennsylvania uses state funds to help her give the grandchildren a stable home. Sixteen other states do the same, while nine redirect surpluses from their share of the federal welfare program. Another nine have negotiated waivers with the HHS to spend some of their federal foster-care funds on subsidies for guardians.[25]

Waivers have become an important vehicle for reform of the child welfare system, just as they were for welfare reform in the mid-1990s. About 20 states have used them in varied ways, including for guardian assistance, drug-abuse treatment for parents, training of staff in private and public child services agencies, adoption promotion and other services to children and families not covered by federal foster care assistance.[26]

Whole Child Approach

Some state and local agencies have teamed up with private organizations and volunteers to improve the way they do business.

Some 70,000 volunteer court-appointed special advocates — or CASAs — represent the interests of children under court supervision throughout the country, for instance. Started in Seattle in 1976, the CASA movement has grown to 930 local programs that are united in the National Court Appointed Special Advocate Association. [27] The volunteer builds a relationship with a child and tells the court whether the child is receiving the care and services the judge has ordered.

Child welfare workers often don't have enough time to keep close watch on the children in their charge, says Kenneth J. Sherk, who helps lead an organization that supports CASAs and children in the Phoenix-area child welfare system. "They're overworked and underpaid and all bogged down in red tape, and often as not things just don't get done for these kids," Sherk explains. "The CASAs tell the court and the Foster Care Review Board here when a child needs counseling, dental work, new clothes, school books — the basic needs."

In 2002 child welfare agencies in St. Louis, Louisville, Cedar Rapids, Iowa, and Jacksonville, Fla., agreed to work with the Center for Community Partnerships in Child Welfare. The center funds and advises efforts to bring a broad array of public and private organizations and individuals together to help troubled families. It's now working in 80 communities, Director Notkin says.

"The problems of families at risk of child abuse and neglect are complex," Notkin explains. "Therefore, it's necessary to develop a neighborhood network of services and support that involves public agencies, private agencies, nonprofits, the business community, the faith community, neighbors and relatives."

The center also stresses creation of a unique plan for each family, Notkin says. "If substance abuse is a problem, make sure someone from substance-abuse treatment is at the table," she explains. "If job training is needed, the job-training folks need to be there."

A key component is the participation of neighborhood volunteers who may tutor the parents in the skills of parenting, help to care for the children and help integrate the family into the community. "Our fundamental principle is that in order to have safe children we need strong families, and strong families need healthy communities that they're connected to," Notkin says.

Comprehensive approaches must be advocated, says Rosemary Chalk, director of the National Academy of Sciences Board on Children, Youth and Families, because "there's no sense of overall accountability for the whole child within the child welfare system."

"We know these kids are in bad shape and in many cases may have serious health problems or serious educational deficits," she explains. "But no one is stepping up and saying we're prepared to deal with the whole child."

Such services work, child welfare experts say, but the demand exceeds the supply. In a study of mothers who

AT ISSUE

Should states be allowed to convert federal foster care funds into capped block grants?

YES

Wade F. Horn, Ph.D.
Assistant Secretary for Children and Families, U.S. Department of Health and Human Services

Written for *The CQ Researcher*, April 2005

States should be allowed to convert the Title IV-E foster care entitlement program into a flexible, alternative-financing structure. President Bush's proposed Child Welfare Program Option would allow them to do that. But the president's proposal is not a block grant. Its very name, Child Welfare Program Option, says it all: It is an option. If a state does not believe it is in its best interest to participate in this alternative, it may continue to participate in the current title IV-E entitlement program.

The states for many years have criticized the Title IV-E program as too restrictive. For instance, it only provides funds for the maintenance of foster children who have been removed from a home that would have been eligible for assistance under the old welfare program and for child welfare training. Under current law, Title IV-E funds cannot be used for services that might prevent a child from being placed in foster care in the first place, that might facilitate a child's returning home or that might help move the child to another permanent placement.

Under the proposed Program Option, states could choose to administer their program more flexibly, with a fixed allocation of funds over a five-year period. States would be able to use funds for foster care payments, prevention activities, permanency efforts, case management, administrative activities and training of child welfare staff. They would be able to develop innovative systems for preventing child abuse and neglect, keeping families and children safely together and quickly moving children toward adoption and permanency. They also would be freed from burdensome income-eligibility provisions that continue to be linked to the old welfare program.

Although states would have greater flexibility in how they use funds, they would still be held accountable for positive results. They would continue to be required to participate in Child and Family Services Reviews and to maintain the child safety protections, such as conducting criminal-background checks and licensing foster care providers, obtaining judicial oversight for removal and permanency decisions, developing case plans for all foster children and prohibiting race-based discrimination in placements. States also would be required to maintain their existing level of investment in the program.

Thus, the proposal allows — but does not force — states to enhance their child welfare services while relieving them of unnecessary administrative burdens. This option for flexible funding represents good public policy.

NO

Shay Bilchik
President and CEO, Child Welfare League of America

Written for *The CQ Researcher*, April 2005

It is too common an occurrence to read a newspaper or listen to the news and learn about yet another seriously abused or neglected child or a child welfare system struggling to protect the children in its care. Recently, every state, the District of Columbia and Puerto Rico had the performance of their child welfare system measured as a part of a federal review. States fell short in a variety of areas, including having excessive caseloads, inadequate supervision, inadequate training and lack of treatment services.

Each of these shortcomings relates to a failure to provide resources that would support high-quality performance — resources that should be provided through investments made by the federal, state and local governments responsible for protecting abused and neglected children.

Yearly, states confirm nearly 900,000 reports of abuse and neglect. There are more than 550,000 children in the nation's foster care system. Too many of these children stay in foster care far longer than necessary because of the lack of appropriate support services. In fact, nearly 40 percent of abused and neglected children don't receive treatment to address the emotional trauma they have experienced. In addition, much of this abuse could have been avoided through prevention services.

There is indeed a need for greater flexibility in the use of federal funds to help address these service gaps. Proposals that condition flexibility on capping federal funding, however, are shortsighted and reflect a lack of responsiveness to the results of the federal review. While it may seem difficult to argue against an option being presented to the states that trades funding level for flexibility, it actually is quite easy when it is being presented as the federal government's solution to the problems facing our nation's child welfare system. Such a proposal is tantamount to a freeze on the federal commitment to protecting children and contradicts the vital role that the federal government plays in keeping children safe.

Flexibility is needed, but new federal investments are also needed so that fewer children are hurt and more parents can safely care for their children. The federal review clearly tells us that this is the case. It seems a fair demand, therefore, that our federal leaders bring forward a reform proposal that presents serious solutions to the trauma and horror that confront our abused and neglected children — and no less.

AP Photo/Elise Amendola

A mourner leaves the funeral service of Dontel Jeffers, 4, in Boston's Dorchester section on March 16, 2005, wearing a photo of the abused child on his shirt. Dontel died in a foster home where he had been placed by the Department of Social Services. The boy's relatives claim his foster mother beat him.

received drug abuse treatment, for example, slightly more than half had custody of their children before entering treatment while three-quarters had custody six months after completing treatment, the Child Welfare League reported. Three-quarters of parents with children in the child welfare system need treatment, the league said, but only a little more than 30 percent receive it.[28]

In 2003 authorities received about 2 million child abuse or neglect reports involving more than 3 million children. Agencies found that more than 900,000 of the children had been neglected or abused and that 1,390 had died. Most of the confirmed cases involved neglect, but 19 percent involved physical abuse and 10 percent sexual abuse.[29]

Although most agencies prefer to keep children with their parents, about 525,000 lived in foster homes in 2003, a number that has steadily declined since peaking at 570,000 in 1999. The Congressional Budget Office estimates that the number of federally supported foster care children will drop from 229,000 this year to 225,000 next year and 162,000 by 2015. Because federal aid goes only to children from families with very low income, only about half of the foster caseload receives a federal subsidy.[30]

Many child welfare workers complain that this caseload exceeds the capabilities of the work force, and the Government Accountability Office (GAO) has endorsed that view. "A stable and highly skilled child welfare work force is necessary to effectively provide child welfare services," Congress' nonpartisan investigating arm said in a 2003 report.[31] However, workers' salaries tend to be too low to attract and maintain a well-qualified staff, and caseloads tend to be higher than those recommended by widely recognized standards, the agency found. (*See graph, p. 215.*)

"Large caseloads and worker turnover delay the timeliness of investigations and limit the frequency of worker visits with children," the GAO said.[32] In reviewing the performance of state child welfare agencies, HHS attributed many deficiencies to high caseloads and inadequate training.[33]

The Child Welfare League suggests a caseload of 12 to 15 children per worker, and the Council on Accreditation for Children and Family Services recommends no more than 18, GAO said. [34] Actual caseloads last year ranged from nine to 80, with medians ranging from 18 to 38 depending on the type of cases a worker was handling, according to a survey by the American Public Human Services Association.[35]

Beginning caseworkers earned a median salary of about $28,500 in 2002, and the most experienced workers about $47,000, the Child Welfare League reported.[36] Child welfare administrators complain about losing workers to jobs in schools, where the workers can continue to work with children while earning more in a safer environment.[37] Child welfare staff turnover ranges from 30 to 40 percent annually.

To induce workers to stay in their jobs, Rep. Stephanie Tubbs, D-Ohio, has introduced legislation to forgive their college loans. Ohio Republican Rep. Mike DeWine introduced a similar bill in the previous Congress but had not done so again this year.

OUTLOOK

Hope and Fear

Children's advocates view the future of child welfare with optimism and concern. Their hope springs from the reform movements spurring changes in many state and local programs, the trends in child welfare policies that seem to be moving in effective directions and the agreement among liberals and conservatives that more attention must be focused on early services to troubled families and speedy placement of foster children into permanent homes.

They worry that the federal financial squeeze might strangle child welfare funding and that a threatened increase in methamphetamine addiction could imitate the devastating crack cocaine epidemic of the 1980s and '90s and cause caseloads to soar once more.

"You have a lot of things going on, a lot of innovation being tested, a lot of interest in looking at the financing," says Notkin, of the Center for Community Partnerships in Child Welfare. "You also have, in the last few years, some really horrific stories coming to the attention of the public that dramatize the crisis in child welfare.

"The question is whether there will be enough political will to honestly confront the problems of the child welfare system, which are reflective of and connected to other problems in our society."

The Child Welfare League's Bilchik foresees "a three- to five-year window where we're going to see tremendous change in practice and a continuing push for reduction of federal support. Either states are going to ratchet up their support in tough economic times or we're going to see a reduction in the level and quality of care.

"I think we're going to go through another cycle where they push for less investment, which will result in more harm for children and that will lead to recognition that more resources are needed," he says. "At the same time, good practices will be adopted as we get better at keeping kids closer to home, reducing the number of times they move and placing them more often with kin."

Columbia University's Wulczyn predicts foster care rolls will shrink because "we're doing a better job of providing appropriate services," but he adds a caveat: "as long as we don't experience an unexpected social upheaval that mimics the crack cocaine epidemic."

The Casey Foundation's Stangler expects agencies to do "a much better job of promoting permanency arrangements for older youth. And I expect states to get better at connecting the dots between emancipating youth, education and the work force."

He looks to expansion of current programs through which families volunteer to provide home-like relationships to former foster children, offering them a place to come home to during college vacations, for instance, and adults to whom they can turn for parent-like guidance year-round.

An important challenge, says Meltzer, of the Center for the Study of Social Policy, is getting other parts of society to solve problems that shouldn't have been left to child welfare agencies to fix. "Ultimately, the child welfare systems have become services of last resort for a lot of problems related to poverty, mental health and substance abuse," she explains. "Figuring out how you build up resources so fewer kids and families need child welfare intervention is where you want to go."

HHS Assistant Secretary Horn is confident that the government and child welfare community know more today than 15 years ago about how to prevent child abuse and neglect. "I'm very encouraged by the renewed focus on helping families form and sustain healthy marriages," he adds, "because two parents in a healthy marriage don't come home one day and decide to abuse and neglect their children. Parents in unhealthy, dysfunctional and violent households do."

Rep. McDermott concedes the possibility of "some improvements here or there. But, if you're digging the kind of debt hole we've created, the first ones who are sacrificed into the hole are the kids."

"Republicans and Democrats do care a lot about kids," says Mial of the Casey Foundation. "What it comes down to is how well connected are they to what's happening."

Research and education are needed, for child welfare workers as well as for politicians, she adds.

And despite Horn's optimism about knowledge gained in the last 15 years, she says, "We know how to send kids to adoption. We don't necessarily know how to keep kids in a family or how to reunite them with their family."

NOTES

1. Lomi Kriel, "Bill to Overhaul Kid Agency Is Filed," *San Antonio Express-News*, Feb. 4, 2005, p. A8. And

Robert T. Garrett, "New bill on child abuse proposed; Police would become involved in most reports of juvenile injuries," *The Dallas Morning News*, Dec. 2, 2004, p. A4.

2. Suzanne Smalley and Brian Braiker, "Suffer the Children," *Newsweek*, Jan. 20, 2003, p. 32.
3. Leslie Kaufman, "State Agency For Children Fails Its Tests, U.S. Says," *The New York Times*, May 22, 2004, p B5.
4. Phillip J. O'Connor and Ray Long, "Police Rescue 19 Kids In Filthy Apartment," *Chicago Sun-Times*, Feb. 2, 1994, p. 1; Colin McMahon and Susan Kuczka, "19 Kids Found In Filth," *Chicago Tribune*, Feb. 2, 1994, p. 1.
5. Michelle M. Martinez, "Senators Giving CPS Reform Bill a Thumbs up," *Austin American-Statesman*, March 3, 2005, p. B1; "Senators Approve Protective Services Bill," *Austin American-Statesman*, March 4, 2005, p. B6.
6. Richard Lezin Jones, "Child Welfare Plan Approved," *The New York Times*, June 13, 2004, Section 14NJ, p. 6; Jones, "Monitor Approves Child Welfare Plan," *The New York Times*, June 10, 2004, p. B4; Jones, "New Jersey Plans to Lighten Load for Child Welfare Workers," *The New York Times*, June 9, 2004, p. B5; Jones, "Plan for New Jersey Foster Care Removes Many From Institutions," *The New York Times*, Feb. 16, 2004, p. B1.
7. "The Number and Rate of Foster Children Ages 17 and Under, 1990-2003," Child Trends Data Bank, available at www.childtrendsdatabank.org.
8. Robert T. Garrett, "Changes Urged for Care Agencies," *The Dallas Morning News*, Dec. 8, 2004, p. 4A.
9. "Trends in Foster Care and Adoption," U.S. Department of Health and Human Services, Administration for Children and Families, August 2004, available at www.acf.dhhs.gov/programs/cb/dis/afcars/publications/afcars.htm.
10. Jonathan D. Rockoff and John B. O'Donnell, "State's Lax Oversight Puts Fragile Children at Risk," *The Baltimore Sun*, April 10, 2005, p. 1A. Additional stories in the series, "A Failure To Protect Maryland's Troubled Group Homes," published April 11-13.
11. Rockoff and O'Donnell, "Leaders Vow To Fix Group Homes," April 14, 2005, p. 1A.
12. Child Welfare League of America press release, 2004.
13. House Ways and Means Committee, Human Resources Subcommittee, "Hearing to Examine Child Welfare Reform Proposals," July 13, 2004, transcript and documents available at http://waysandmeans.house.gov/hearings.asp?formmode=detail&hearing=161&comm=2.
14. Roseana Bess and Cynthia Andrews Scarcella, "Child Welfare Spending During a Time of Fiscal Stress," Urban Institute, Dec. 31, 2004, available at www.urban.org/url.cfm?ID=411124.
15. "Budget in Brief, Fiscal Year 2006," U.S. Department of Health and Human Services, pp. 6 and 98, available at http://hhs.gov/budget/06budget/FY2006BudgetinBrief.pdf.
16. For background, see Sarah Glazer, "Welfare Reform," *The CQ Researcher*, Aug. 3, 2001, pp. 601-632.
17. "Fostering the future: Safety, Permanence and Well-Being for Children in Foster Care," Pew Commission on Children in Foster Care, May 18, 2004, available at http://pewfostercare.org/research/docs/FinalReport.pdf.
18. House Ways and Means subcommittee hearing, *op. cit.*
19. "The AFCARS Report" (Adoption and Foster Care Analysis and Reporting System), U.S. Department of Health and Human Services, August 2004, available at www.acf.dhhs.gov/programs/cb/publications/afcars/report9.pdf.
20. www.jimcaseyyouth.org/about.htm.
21. Except where noted, information for this section is drawn from these sources: Rachel S. Cox, "Foster Care Reform," *The CQ Researcher*, Jan. 9, 1998. Kasia O'Neill Murray and Sarah Gesiriech, "A Brief Legislative History of the Child Welfare System," Pew Commission on Children in Foster Care, available at http://pewfostercare.org/research/docs/Legislative.pdf; Mary-Liz Shaw, "Artist Recalls the Rough Rumbling of the Orphan Trains," *Milwaukee Journal Sentinel*, Feb. 2, p. E1; Mary Ellen Johnson, "Orphan Train Movement: A history of the Orphan Trains Era in American History," Orphan Train Heritage Society

of America, available at www.orphantrainriders.com/otm11.html.

22. "National Study of Protective, Preventive and Reunification Services Delivered to Children and Their Families," U.S. Department of Health and Human Services, 1994, available at www.acf.hhs.gov/programs/cb/publications/97natstudy/introduc.htm#CW.

23. Margaret LaRaviere, "A Brief History of Federal Child Welfare Legislation and Policy (1935-2000)," the Center for Community Partnerships in Child Welfare, Nov. 18, 2002, available at www.cssp.org/uploadFiles/paper1.doc.

24. Press conference, Washington, D.C., Oct. 13, 2004, transcript, pp. 7-9, available at www.fosteringresults.org/results/press/pewpress_10-13-04_fednewsbureau.pdf.

25. *Ibid.*, p.12, for updated waiver figure. Also: Mark Testa, Nancy Sidote Salyers and Mike Shaver, "Family Ties: Supporting Permanence for Children in Safe and Stable Foster Care With Relatives and Other Caregivers," Children and Family Research Center, School of Social Work, University of Illinois at Urbana-Champaign, Oct. 2004, p. 5, available at www.fosteringresults.org/results/reports/pewreports_10-13-04_alreadyhome.pdf.

26. "Summary of Title IV-E Child Welfare Waiver Demonstration Projects," U.S. Health and Human Services Department, May 2004, available at www.acf.hhs.gov/programs/cb/initiatives/cwwaiver/summary.htm.

27. "History of CASA." Available at www. casanet.org/download/ncasa_publications/history-casa.pdf.

28. "The Nation's Children 2005," the Child Welfare League of America, pp. 2-3.

29. *Ibid.*, p. 1. Also: "Child Maltreatment 2002," Health and Human Services Department, available at www.acf.hhs.gov/programs/cb/publications/cm02/summary.htm.

30. Child Trends Data Bank, *op. cit.* Also: "CBO Baseline for Foster Care and Adoption Assistance," Congressional Budget Office, March 2005, available at www.cbo.gov/factsheets/2005/FosterCare.PDF.

31. "HHS Could Play a Greater Role in Helping Child Welfare Agencies Recruit and Retain Staff," General Accounting Office, (now called the Government Accountability Office) March 2003, available at www.gao.gov/new.items/d03357.pdf.

32. *Ibid*, pp. 3-4.

33. *Ibid*, p. 21.

34. *Ibid*, p. 14.

35. "Report From the 2004 Child Welfare Workforce Survey: State Agency Findings," American Public Human Services Association, February 2005, p. 22, available at www.aphsa.org/ Home/Doc/Workforce%20Report%202005.pdf.

36. Child Welfare League of America National Data Analysis System, available at www.ndas.cwla.org/data_stats/access/predefined/Report.asp?ReportID=86.

37. General Accounting Office, *op. cit.*, pp. 3, 11.

BIBLIOGRAPHY

Books

Brohl, Kathryn, *The New Miracle Workers: Overcoming Contemporary Challenges in Child Welfare Work*, *CLWA Press*, 2004.
A veteran child welfare worker and family therapist explains new challenges facing workers and administrators, including meeting legislature-imposed timelines for case management, working collaboratively with clients, understanding diverse cultures and nontraditional families, keeping up with research, improving pay and training and overcoming worker burnout.

Geen, Rob, editor, *Kinship Care: Making the Most of a Valuable Resource*, *Urban Institute Press*, 2003.
A collection of essays edited by an Urban Institute researcher examines how child welfare agencies are using relatives as foster parents, how this differs from traditional foster care, and how the caregivers describe their experiences.

Shirk, Martha, and Gary Stangler, *On Their Own: What Happens to Kids When They Age Out of the Foster Care System*, *Westview Press*, 2004.
A journalist (Shirk) and the former director of the Missouri Social Services Department (Stangler) who now runs a program for older foster children offer alternately inspiring and heartrending stories of 10 young

people who must leave foster care and learn to live on their own without the family and community relationships that most young people lean on as they make the transition from teen to adult.

Articles

Campbell, Joel, "Encourage Access to Juvenile Courts: The Time Is Right for Lifting Juvenile Court and Child Welfare System Secrecy," *The Quill*, Aug. 1, 2004, p. 36.
A leader of the Society of Professional Journalists' Freedom of Information Committee argues that one way to improve the child welfare system is to let the news media into juvenile courts.

Colloff, Pamela, "Life and Meth," *Texas Monthly*, June 2004, p. 120.
Methamphetamine is destroying families in East Texas — an epidemic child welfare authorities worry could spike foster care rolls nationwide.

Humes, Edward, "The Unwanted," *Los Angeles Magazine*, Jan. 1, 2003, p. 64.
The reporter exposes a dysfunctional Los Angeles children's home.

Rockoff, Jonathan D., and John B. O'Donnell, "A Failure to Protect Maryland's Troubled Group Homes," *The Baltimore Sun*, April 10-13, 2005.
In a four-part exposé, the authors reveal child abuse, neglect and even death within Maryland's state-supervised group homes for children.

Reports and Studies

"Fostering the Future: Safety, Permanence and Well-Being for Children in Foster Care," *the Pew Commission on Children in Foster Care*, May 18, 2004, available at http://pewfostercare.org/research/docs/FinalReport.pdf.
This influential report by a blue-ribbon panel headed by two former U.S. representatives — Republican Bill Frenzel of Minnesota and Democrat William H. Gray III of Pennsylvania — explores the need to improve the child welfare system. The commission argues for more flexibility and more federal funds while acknowledging need to moderate federal spending.

"HHS Could Play a Greater Role in Helping Child Welfare Agencies Recruit and Retain Staff," *General Accounting Office* (now the Government Accountability Office), March 2003, available at www.gao.gov/new.items/d03357.pdf.
A report by Congress' nonpartisan investigating arm presents evidence that child welfare agencies' effectiveness suffers because caseworkers are underpaid and given too many cases to manage.

Testa, Mark F., "Encouraging Child Welfare Innovation through IV-E Waivers," *Children and Family Research Center, School of Social Work, University of Illinois at Urbana-Champaign*, January 2005; http://cfrcwww.social.uiuc.edu/briefpdfs/cfrc.
An academic study by the former research director of the Illinois Department of Children and Family Services examines how states have used waivers of federal regulations to spend federal funds on innovative programs and suggests how to use waivers more effectively. Testa is co-director of the University of Illinois' Children and Family Research Center.

Vandivere, Sharon, Rosemary Chalk and Kristin Anderson Moore, "Children in Foster Homes: How Are They Faring?" *Child Trends Research Brief*, December 2003; www.childtrends.org/files/FosterHomesRB.pdf.
An analysis of surveys of children and families concludes that foster children are less healthy than other children, have more developmental and behavioral problems and often have problems in school.

For More Information

Annie E. Casey Foundation, 701 St. Paul St., Baltimore, MD 21202; (410) 547-6600; www.aecf.org. Advocates, conducts research and supports programs to benefit disadvantaged children and families; known for its Kids Count Data Book, an annual compilation of state-by-state statistics.

Child Trends, 4301 Connecticut Ave., N.W., Suite 100, Washington, DC 20008; (202) 572-6000; www.childtrends.org. Conducts research about children and publishes reports and statistics on its Child Trends Data Bank.

Child Welfare League of America, 440 First St., N.W., Washington, DC 20001; (202) 638-2952; www.cwla.org. America's oldest and largest child welfare organization advocates, suggests standards and educates welfare workers.

Children and Family Research Center, University of Illinois, 1203 W. Oregon St., Urbana, IL 61801; (217) 333-5837; http://cfrcwww.social.uiuc.edu. Leading university-based institution for studying children, families and child welfare services.

Children's Bureau, 370 L'Enfant Promenade, S.W., Washington, DC 20447; (202) 205-8618; www.acf.hhs.gov/programs/cb. Agency of the U.S. Health and Human Services Department that supports states' delivery of child welfare services, publishes reports and data on its Web site, maintains hotlines for reporting child and domestic abuse and runaway, missing or exploited children (1-800-4ACHILD).

National Court Appointed Special Advocate (CASA) Association, 100 W. Harrison, North Tower, Suite 500, Seattle WA 98119; (800) 628-3233; www.nationalcasa.org. Provides leadership, consultation and resources for more than 900 CASA programs across the country whose nearly 70,000 volunteers serve as advocates for 280,000 abused or neglected children.

Pew Commission on Foster Care, 2233 Wisconsin Ave., N.W., Washington, DC 20007; (202) 687-0948; www.pewfostercare.org. Blue-ribbon, bipartisan panel that proposed more federal funding and more flexibility for states to spend it.

10

Teen Pregnancy

Does Comprehensive Sex-Education Reduce Pregnancies?

Marcia Clemmitt

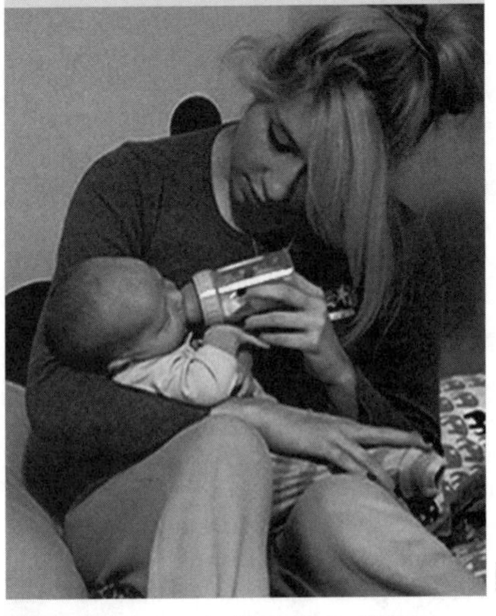
MTV

Nikkole feeds two-week-old Lyle on the MTV show "16 and Pregnant," featuring real teen mothers and their daily struggles. Forty percent of all American mothers today, and most teen mothers, are single when they give birth. While birth rates for girls 15 and younger are dropping, political debate remains sharp over the best approach to reducing teen pregnancy: comprehensive sex education or abstinence-only programs.

From *CQ Researcher*, March 26, 2010.

In September 2008, shortly after her nomination as the Republican Party's vice presidential candidate, Alaska Gov. Sarah Palin announced that her 17-year-old daughter, Bristol, was five months pregnant and would soon marry the baby's father, 18-year-old Levi Johnston.[1]

By March 2009, however, the couple had ended their engagement, and Bristol faced a future as a busy single mother — like at least eight out of every 10 teen girls who give birth. "It's just, like, I'm not living for myself any more. It's . . . for another person. . . . You're up all night. And it's not glamorous at all," Palin recently told Fox News' commentator Greta Van Susteren.[2]

Bristol Palin is not the only young celebrity swept up by the recent flood of media attention to teen motherhood. Tabloid magazines breathlessly chronicled the pregnancy of actress Jamie Lynn Spears, 17-year-old younger sister of pop star Britney Spears, who gave birth to a daughter in 2008.[3] Also in 2008, *Time* caused a sensation when it first reported that 17 girls at Gloucester High School in Massachusetts may actually have made "a pact to get pregnant and raise their babies together." The magazine later reported growing skepticism about the alleged deal.[4]

In fact, last year MTV launched a reality-television show, "16 and Pregnant," in which girls from around the country live out their pregnancies, childbirth dramas and struggles as teen mothers in front of the camera.

But while the media visibility of teen moms may be higher than ever, real-world statistics reveal a more complicated picture.

After plummeting by a third between 1991 to 2005 — a period when teen abortion rates and rates of sexual intercourse also

Teen Birth Rate Is Near All-Time Low

Teen birth rates shot up in the postwar Baby Boom years as American soldiers returned home from World War II. Rates then returned to more typical, lower levels, and in the 1990s plummeted as women pursued education and careers in a strong economy, and condom use increased as a result of HIV/AIDS fears. From 2005-2007, birth rates for older teens moved upwards slightly, partly because of a drop in contraceptive use.

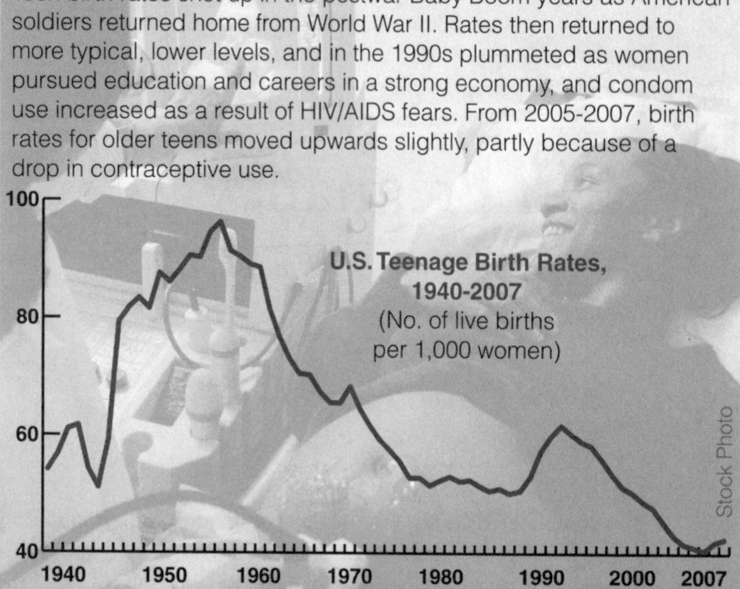

Source: "National Vital Statistics Reports," Centers for Disease Control and Prevention, National Center for Health Statistics, Sept. 25, 2001, Jan. 7, 2009, March 18, 2009

declined — birth rates among overall U.S. teens began rising slightly in 2005, according to the federal Centers for Disease Control and Prevention (CDC), but most of the increase was among older teens.

The overall birth rate rose by about 5 percent between 2005 and 2007, reaching 42.5 births for every 1,000 teen girls in 2007. But a breakdown of the statistics showed that the rates rose 4 percent for 18- to 19-year-olds and 3 percent among 15- to 17-year-olds between 2005 and 2006. Then they slowed a little, rising only another 1 percent for both age groups from 2006 to 2007.[5] But for younger girls — under age 15 — the rates continued their steady decline during the two-year period, dropping 14 percent.

Thus, in the average year, the vast majority — about three-quarters — of teen births are to women ages 18-19, while only a very tiny proportion of teen births occur among girls under age 15.[6]

"There are a lot of different factors at play" in the birth-rate increase, "from less use of contraception, maybe because of less fear of AIDS, to our anything-goes culture, where it's OK to get pregnant and have a baby in your teens," said Sarah Brown, CEO of the National Campaign to Prevent Teen and Unplanned Pregnancy.[7]

Before the uptick, teen births and pregnancies had been declining since 1957, when they peaked at 96.3 births for every 1,000 girls. Back then, most teen mothers quickly married. But teen weddings are much less common today, and most women get married later in life. Unmarried parenthood — both among teens and adults — also is less stigmatized today: Forty percent of all American mothers today, and most teen mothers, are single when they give birth. In addition, the long fall and recent rise in teen birth rates aren't unique to teens: They closely mirror birth trends for adult women.[8]

Against the backdrop of generally encouraging long-term statistics, however, political debate remains sharp over the best approach to sex education — the main tool the federal government has used to lower teen birth rates.

In late 2009, President Barack Obama and the Democratic Congress approved a major change in federal sex-education funding, declaring that federal funds now will be awarded mainly to programs proven to be effective at averting teen pregnancies or for research and development on programs that show "promise" in reducing teen pregnancies. The change marks the first time in nearly 30 years that the federal government will fund any school sex education other than so-called abstinence-only programs. Since the late 1990s, the federal government has spent nearly $2 billion on such programs, despite there being little or no scientific evidence that they were effective. (The federal government has funded public-information campaigns on contraception, however.)[9]

Advocates of comprehensive sex education — which discusses the benefits of delaying or forgoing sex but also provides substantial information on contraception — argue that research has clearly demonstrated that abstinence-only education does not effectively change teens' behavior.

While "many . . . abstinence programs improved teens' values about abstinence or their intention to abstain," those improvements "often did not translate into changes in behavior," wrote Douglas Kirby, a senior researcher at ETR Associates, a nonprofit reproductive health research group in Scotts Valley, Calif. In an analysis for the National Campaign to Prevent Teen and Unplanned Pregnancy, Kirby concluded that research on abstinence curricula has "not produced sufficient evidence to justify . . . widespread dissemination" of the programs.[10]

"Ten years ago the evaluations weren't there, but now they are, and they say that programs that talk both about abstinence and proper contraceptive use" are most effective, says Heather Boonstra, a senior public policy associate at the Guttmacher Institute, a policy-analysis group in New York City specializing in sexual health. Meanwhile, "the evidence is not there" to show that abstinence-only programs are effective, she says.

For the first time, earlier this year a rigorous study by John B. Jemmott III, a professor of psychiatry and communication at the University of Pennsylvania, found that a specific abstinence-only program helped delay the first sexual experience for a group of mostly 12-year-old African-American students in urban schools.[11] Jemmott said that while he is not an expert on the wide range of abstinence-only programs that exist, he believes the program he studied differs from many of the others. For example, in contrast to some abstinence programs, the curriculum he studied contained "no preaching" and was "not moralistic," he said. But in many abstinence programs, students are reminded repeatedly that condoms are not 100 percent effective in preventing pregnancy or sexually transmitted diseases (STDs), a message Jemmott worries might lead them to believe that using condoms is a waste of time.[12]

Teen Pregnancy Highest in U.S.

Teen birth rates are significantly higher in the United States than in Europe. The disparity is especially pronounced in France, Germany and the Netherlands, which provide easier access to sexual health information and services. The U.S. rate is nine times higher than in the Netherlands. The higher U.S. birth rate also reflects less consistent use of contraception and condoms by U.S. youths than their peers in Europe. Dutch young women were almost six times as likely as Americans to have been using contraceptive pills at last intercourse.

Teen Birth Rates and Contraceptive Use by Sexually Active 15- to 19-Year-Olds (2007)

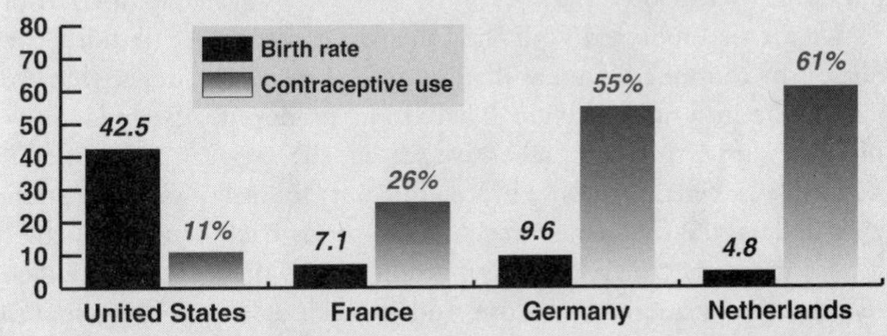

Source: "Adolescent Sexual Health in Europe and the U.S. — Why the Difference?" Advocates for Youth, September 2009

Most advocates of providing contraceptive information in sex-education courses hail the Obama approach as a welcome embrace of sound science and sensible public policy.

"Federal funding for sex education has undergone a sea change in the past six to eight months" away from the abstinence-only approach, says Bill Albert, chief program officer of the national campaign to prevent teen pregnancy. "Now the administration and Congress are saying that in the abstinence versus contraceptive-information battle, we are landing squarely on the side of science," Albert says.

Biology dictates that most "teens are going to be sexual" at some point, says Frank F. Furstenberg, a University of Pennsylvania professor of sociology and author of the 2007 book *Destinies of the Disadvantaged: The Politics of Teenage Childbearing.* Thus, "the true problem with the abstinence-only approach is that it's very hard to get teenagers to go four or five years" to abstain from sex, from the onset of puberty at 12 or 13 until the late teens, when youths are realistically likely to marry, he says.

But abstinence-only proponents say their programs get a bad rap, mainly because critics define them inaccurately. Our "most successful programs" do include education about condoms, for example, says Valerie Huber, executive director of the National Abstinence Education Association.

When parents are polled, they generally "assume abstinence education is 'just say no,' " but when the public understands that courses actually include discussion of topics such as sexually transmitted diseases (STDs), healthy decision-making, how to escape from an unhealthy relationship and many other topics, "we see a huge switch to support," she says.

"We are disappointed with the Obama change in policy," she continued. Studies that the federal government has deemed rigorous enough have so far produced only data supporting comprehensive sex ed, she says. "And while we certainly believe in accountability for taxpayer dollars, the Obama approach could set us back because there are clearly other important things that aren't being considered" in those studies, such as an appreciation for the inherent value of stressing "primary prevention" — abstinence as the only 100-percent foolproof way to prevent pregnancy and transmission of STDs, Huber says.

Even as debate continues over sex education, researchers are developing a more nuanced picture of who is most likely to become a teen parent and the long-term consequences of teen parenthood. On most measures of well-being, including education, workplace attainment and wage levels, the statistics are "very stark" for teenage mothers, says Boonstra. For example, only 2 percent of teen mothers get a college degree, compared with about 27 percent of Americans overall, according to the Census Bureau.[13]

Nevertheless, some studies now show that "many disadvantaged teens reorganize their lives and priorities around . . . mothering," and thus improve their lives, in at least some ways, after giving birth, wrote Lee I. Smith, a professor at the Saint Louis University School of Nursing. Upon having a child, "many teens recommit to school, realizing that a high school degree is a prerequisite to college and job opportunities," although college plans don't necessarily come to fruition, due to "the daunting challenge of combining school, work and mothering with unreliable child care," she said. Nevertheless, "a significant proportion of girls return to school during pregnancy or become more engaged with school after giving birth."[14]

As lawmakers, educators and families mull the best way to avert teen pregnancies, here some of the questions being asked:

Are abstinence-only sex-education programs ineffective?

Over the past few years, the first large-scale, federally funded analyses of abstinence-only sex-ed programs have emerged, and by and large the news has been complex and not terribly encouraging.

Studies overwhelmingly have found little or no evidence that abstinence-only courses change teen sexual behavior in ways that would avert pregnancies or the spread of STDs. But abstinence-education supporters say most studies take a too-narrow view of what constitutes reliable evidence. Some research, they say, has found good effects from abstinence-only programs.

Recent research clearly "shows that the Bush-era approach of abstinence-only funding is dead," says James Wagoner, president of Advocates for Youth, a Washington, D.C.-based nonprofit group that supports strong informational programs to improve adolescent sexual health.

For example, in 2007 a congressionally mandated study of four federally funded abstinence-only programs, conducted by Mathematica, a Princeton, N.J.-based research company, found that abstinence programs did not prevent children in elementary and middle school from changing behaviors that raise teens' risk of pregnancy. Specifically, it found that upper-elementary and middle-school students who completed abstinence programs were no more likely than those who didn't take the classes to abstain from sex, delay sex or have fewer sexual partners. The result was the same both in schools where there was little information available on sex and contraception outside of the abstinence program and in schools where students got a great deal of such information, in health classes and elsewhere.[15]

In November 2009, the Task Force on Community Preventive Services of the federal Centers for Disease Control and Prevention (CDC) reported after analyzing more than 40 abstinence-only strategies that there is "insufficient evidence to determine" whether "group-based abstinence education" effectively prevents pregnancies or STDs.[16] By contrast, the task force found that evidence shows comprehensive sex education does reduce the number of teens who have sex and the frequency that sexually active teens have sex, their number of partners and their risk of STDs, the panel said.*

The task force explicitly recommended that comprehensive sex-ed be "delivered to adolescents to promote behaviors that . . . reduce the risk of pregnancy" and STDs instead of abstinence-only programs.[17]

Randomized control trials like the Mathematica study — in which some students were randomly assigned to a specific sex-ed course while another randomly chosen "control" group did not take the course — are considered the gold standard of scientific evidence. But social conservatives who say abstinence-only education is the only morally responsible approach to sex education argue that social-science questions are driven by such diverse multiple factors that randomized trials cannot possibly capture all of the value provided by abstinence education. Other types of research have found significant merit in abstinence education, they say.

"I started with a very skeptical attitude, thinking how in the world could [abstinence education] work, given the culture and the society that kids live in," said Stanley Weed, founder and senior fellow at the Salt Lake City-based Institute for Research and Evaluation, a nonprofit organization that has analyzed many abstinence-only curricula. But "since that time I have learned that it can work. Not all [abstinence programs] do, but many of them do, and we have learned which ones do, and why."[18]

Weed said his analyses found that abstinence programs used in several states substantially decrease the number of students who began having sex within a year after completing the course. In one Virginia district, nine percent of students began having intercourse a year after they finished the abstinence program that Weed studied, compared to an average of 16.4 percent of students in that district who would have been expected to initiate sex by that age, for example.[19]

Of the many analysts who commented on their research to the CDC task force, two found "serious limitations" in the panel's conclusions about abstinence-only programs. Notably, the panel unfairly ignored findings that abstinence programs reduce teens' sexual activity because the results didn't come from randomized control trials, wrote Irene Ericksen, a researcher at the Institute for Research and Evaluation, and Danielle Ruedt, a public-health programs coordinator in the Governor's Office for Children and Families in Georgia. And the panel's report also implied that sex ed focusing on contraceptive information "is a superior approach," a conclusion they said was "not supported by the evidence" examined by the task force.[20]

Earlier this year, a randomized control study for the first time showed significant positive results for an abstinence-focused program, according to research led by the University of Pennsylvania's Jemmott. He found that a specific abstinence-only program helped delay the first sexual experience for a group of mostly 12-year-old African-American students in urban schools. Only about a third of the program participants began having sex within the next two years, compared to 42 percent of those who attended a safe-sex program.[21]

"This is a rigorous study that means we can now say that it's possible for an abstinence-only intervention to be effective," said Jemmott.[22]

"We now have, for the first time, news that an abstinence intervention can help," says Albert, of the National Campaign to Prevent Teen and Unplanned Pregnancy. "This course did take an approach that is different" from more traditional abstinence-only programs, he explains. "It did honestly answer questions about contraception, and it did not say 'delay until marriage.' " Perhaps because of that difference, it "did not reduce condom use."

Rebecca A. Maynard, a professor of education and social policy at the University of Pennsylvania Graduate School of Education, says the main takeaway from all the recent studies should be that, generally speaking, "abstinence education does no better and no worse than comprehensive" sex education. In fact, neither has been shown to strongly affect teens' behavior, she concludes.

The Mathematica study, for example, showed that "abstinence-only education didn't hurt kids," she says, while comprehensive sex-ed proponents had long argued that it would, by decreasing condom use. But

---

* Comprehensive sex-education — the alternative to abstinence-only curricula and sometimes called abstinence-plus or comprehensive risk reduction — recommends delaying sex but focuses strongly on informing students about condom use and contraception.

Older Teens Have Higher Birth Rates

The birth rate for American teenagers ages 18-19 is more than three times the rate for those 15-17. The rate for youths 10-14 is less than one birth for every 1,000 women. Rates for women in their late 20s are highest of all age groups.

U.S. Birth Rates by Age
(births per 1,000 women)

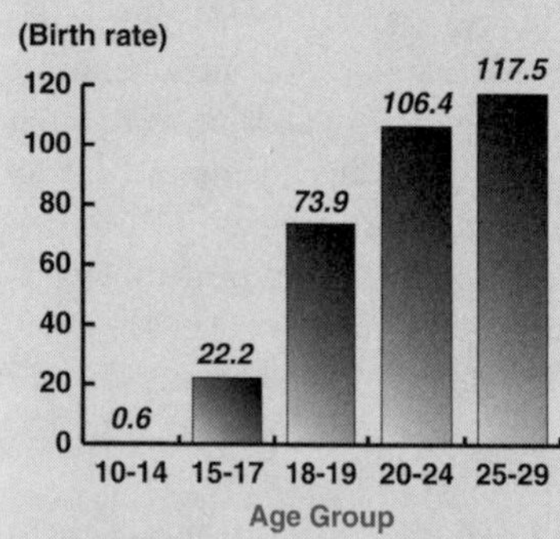

Source: "Births: Preliminary Data for 2007," National Vital Statistics Reports, Centers for Disease Control and Prevention, National Center for Health Statistics, March 18, 2009

abstinence-only sex ed also wasn't "the solution to the problem." In essence, she says, the body of research now available shows "no significant difference" between abstinence-only and abstinence-plus (comprehensive sex education) programs.

That's not surprising, she explains. The content of most abstinence-only programs "overlaps greatly with abstinence-plus" programs. The best courses of both varieties "all have a core of things about values, peer pressure and good decision-making," while they "diverge only in saying 'you may not ever' [in the case of abstinence-only courses] or 'you may not want to' [in abstinence-plus]."

Critics' complaints about both kinds of courses are largely caricatures. "Very, very few curricula say, 'God will strike you dead if you have sex,' or, on the abstinence-plus side, " 'Just go have fun, and don't think about the consequences,' " Maynard says.

Will Obama's plan to fund only evidence-based sex-ed programs work?

In 2009, President Obama proposed ending the practice of federally funding abstinence-only sex education programs. (Congress approved Obama's plan last December but this month voted to continue providing some abstinence-only funds for five years.) Now most federal sex-ed dollars will go only to programs scientifically proven effective at averting teen pregnancy and to a small number of programs that look "promising."

The Obama plan to fund evidence-based programs over pre-selected programs is a huge step in the right direction, says the National Campaign's Albert. "If we could just get people's feelings out of this," the most effective programs would eventually dominate the system because rigorous research can show that a program "either works or it doesn't."

Obama's approach is "an element of new hope," says Wagoner, at Advocates for Youth. The Democratic majority has said, "We're not going to fall into the old screaming-match model," in which comprehensive sex-ed advocates battle abstinence-only proponents for winner-takes-all. "They're trying to get at a higher altitude for the conversation, above the old food fights. And while the 25 percent [of funding being reserved] for 'promising programs' opens up the door to approaches I wouldn't agree with, that's fine." In the long run, Wagoner says, only programs shown effective through evidence will be disseminated around the country.

The Obama language is broad enough to allow funding for a variety of programs with some evidence behind them, and that's what's needed for tackling a complex social problem like teen pregnancy, says Ann L. O'Sullivan, a professor of primary-care nursing at the University of Pennsylvania School of Nursing and a pediatric nurse practitioner at the Children's Hospital of Philadelphia. "It's erroneous any time a society puts all its money into one program" to solve a complicated problem, she says.

"We don't want to make the same mistake we did with D.A.R.E." — the Drug Abuse Resistance Education program — which the federal government has "funded over and over and over" to the exclusion of other anti-drug approaches, despite numerous studies questioning its effectiveness, O'Sullivan says.

Although abstinence programs can apply for funding that will cover research on "promising" programs, abstinence-only proponents fear that even their best programs will be left unfunded. "There's a big difference between having the opportunity to apply and getting priority," says the National Abstinence Education Association's Huber.

She is also concerned that existing abstinence programs will be defunded at a time when rates of some STDs are at very high levels among teens, and teen birth rates are beginning to inch upward. "What rationale can be given for immediately eliminating the valuable abstinence skills currently received by 2.5 million students under currently funded" programs? Huber asked.[23]

About a quarter of teenage girls have an STD, or about 65 percent of teen girls who have had sex, according to a CDC study released in 2008. Human papillomavirus, associated with genital warts and potential development of cervical cancer, is the most common disease found, infecting 18 percent of girls, while chlamydia, which can cause long-term damage to reproductive organs, is the second most common, infecting 4 percent of girls ages 14-19.[24]

Robert E. Rector, a senior research fellow at the Heritage Foundation think tank, a strong supporter of abstinence-until-marriage education, predicts the new approach "will ultimately backfire" because it will fund programs that include "outrageous" suggestions, such as that teens fondle each other while putting on condoms. Comprehensive sex education "only survives by obscuring what they're actually teaching" from the public, since most curricula include at least some discussion of topics like masturbation or physical sexual relationships between teenagers, which most parents find offensive, says Rector.

South and Southwest Have Most Teen Mothers

The estimated proportion of females who will become teen mothers decreased nationwide from 25 percent in 1991 to 18 percent in 2006. But the estimates vary widely from state to state. In Mississippi 30 percent of the females are expected to become teen mothers, the highest among all states. Other states with high rates are primarily concentrated in the South and Southwest. Rates are lowest in New England, where several states are below 10 percent.

Top 10 States With Highest Percentages of Females Expected to Become Teen Mothers		Top 10 States With Lowest Percentages of Females Expected to Become Teen Mothers	
Mississippi	30%	New Hampshire	8%
New Mexico	29%	Vermont	9%
Arizona	28%	Massachusetts	9%
Texas	28%	Connecticut	10%
Arkansas	28%	North Dakota	11%
Nevada	27%	Rhode Island	11%
Oklahoma	26%	New York	11%
Kentucky	25%	New Jersey	11%
Tennessee	25%	Maine	12%
Georgia	24%	Minnesota	12%

Source: Kate Perper and Jennifer Manlove, "Estimated Percentage of Females Who Will Become Teen Mothers: Differences Across States," Child Trends, March 2009, based on 2006 data from "Vital Statistics Reports," National Center for Health Statistics

And while comprehensive sex-ed advocates say they favor curricula that discuss the value of abstinence, "that's really a joke," Rector charges. "Eight sentences in a text of 1,000 pages" does not constitute adequate attention to that vital principle, he says.

Furthermore, he says, the randomized, controlled research trials that federal funders will accept as evidence "are extremely expensive to run," and it's not clear how many will be conducted in the future. Thus, only programs that already have been deemed effective in existing trials will get funding, he says. "Only a very narrow set of curricula will be taught. Abstinence programs probably can't get in."

While advocates on the left believe the Obama plan is a significant improvement, some liberal groups are disappointed the funding is focused on teen pregnancy prevention rather than on comprehensive sex education, says Boonstra of the Guttmacher Institute. This could mean that programs will get funds even if they don't provide teens with enough information about issues like HIV/AIDS or homosexuality, for example, she says.

Even many who welcome the Obama funding plan caution that sex-ed programs alone will only change statistics at the margins. "You hope a program works, but a program is only a drop in the bucket" of what it takes to change behavior on the wide scale, says Boonstra.

For that, a wholesale change of "social norms" is needed, says the University of Pennsylvania's Furstenberg. "When you look at the last half-century, it's alarming how little progress we've made in narrowing the gaps" between U.S. teen pregnancy and the much-lower birth rates in other industrialized countries such as Canada, the United Kingdom and France, especially given the intense debate on the subject in the United States, he says.

The only approach that can accomplish large-scale change is for society as a whole — including schools, communities, families and the media — to send the message that it's vitally important for teens to be responsible about sex, which includes both delaying sex and using contraceptives, Furstenberg says. "But in this country there isn't a consensus that this should be done."

Does teen parenthood lead to a lifetime of hardship?

Teen mothers face a litany of well-documented problems, such as being more likely than their non-pregnant peers to drop out of high school and to live in poverty. And their children also start school at a disadvantage compared to their peers.

"Pick a statistic, and teen mothers are almost always worse," from their school dropout rates to the likelihood of receiving welfare or of having a low-paying job, says Leonard M. Lopoo, an associate professor of public administration at the Maxwell School of Citizenship and Public Affairs at Syracuse University.

But recent research adds nuances to the old picture of uniformly bad outcomes, suggesting, for example, that some problems once believed to be results of teen motherhood actually predate girls' pregnancies. And over the long haul, say some researchers, low-income teen mothers in particular may end up being not much worse off than their peers who did not give birth as teens.

Still, teen fathers and mothers both pay an "educational penalty" that puts them about two years behind their peers in school, says Stefanie Mollborn, an assistant professor of sociology at the University of Colorado at Boulder.

Only 51 percent of teen mothers earn a high school diploma before age 22, compared to 89 percent of women who did not give birth as teens, according to Child Trends, a nonprofit research group that studies child development issues affecting low-income families.[25]

The children of teen parents also face educational hurdles. Children born to teen mothers begin kindergarten with lower levels of school readiness, including lower scores on tests that measure math and reading readiness, language and communication skills, social skills and physical and social well-being compared to children born to women in their 20s, according to Child Trends and the National Campaign.[26]

Economic and other disadvantages for teen mothers and their children are more intense because very young fathers seldom help support the family, says Furstenberg. "The males don't have the same stake" in the baby when they are not married to the mother, he says. Despite "concerted efforts of various kinds to change this" over the past 20 to 25 years, there's been only a tiny amount of improvement in the amount of responsibility taken by young fathers. "Most people today are not going to start a decades-long relationship at 17 or 18," he continues, and "study after study shows the men don't hang around."

Yet, teen girls still think "the boys are going to step up," he says, so "we need to educate [them] about this. Young men in general are not going to step up." In reality, eight out of 10 teen fathers don't marry the mothers of their first children, and absent fathers of children born to teen mothers pay less than $800 annually, on average, to help with the child, according to the National Campaign.[27]

Several other factors make things even more difficult for young mothers today, says Mollborn. Welfare and federal housing assistance are harder to get than they were decades ago; the likelihood of marriage at a young age is diminishing; and some economists fear the U.S. job market may have permanently shrunk, leaving less opportunity for young parents and depleting the resources of parents and grandparents, who often help out young mothers. While it's hard to predict the future, "things are at least very bad in the short run" for teen mothers and their families, she says.

But new research is showing that some problems that have long been viewed as consequences of teen motherhood are now known to predate teens' pregnancies, says Mollborn. "We're seeing a whole lot of mental-health issues among teenage mothers and, yes, they definitely are at elevated risk for distress, but it doesn't seem to be caused by the experience of teen childbearing." More likely the "disadvantaged backgrounds that these girls are coming from" are causing problems like depression, not giving birth. Mollborn concludes that a combination of poverty and personal distress — such as depression — can often lead a girl to get pregnant in the first place. Low-income girls with psychological stress are much more likely to become teen mothers than either stressed wealthier girls or unstressed poor girls, she says.[28]

In some cases, parenthood spurs some unfocused teenagers to develop goals and a work ethic for the first time, Mollborn says. A child's arrival galvanizes some teen parents to undertake "concrete career plans" about the future, for the first time, she says. The young parent realizes that "I've got to be this child's role model."

Some academics who have followed groups of teen mothers for decades are finding that, years later, former teen moms and their children do about as well as their non-parenting teen peers who started out in similar circumstances. In the 1980s, analysts reported differences in life outcomes between teen mothers and other women that "were really very large and alarming," says Lopoo. "But now we're finding that they're not as large as was thought."

For example, "young mothers are less likely to complete high school on time, but now some research indicates that they make up for this when they're older. They have to do things in a different sequence," but as the decades pass many still do reach the achievement milestones that other people of similar background reach, Lopoo says.

"If you have your children young, then enter the labor force and never come out," for example, "that can often be beneficial for a woman" in the workplace because she won't lose her seniority or have to start over a second time at the bottom of the wage scale, as often happens to women who begin working, drop out of the workforce to have a child and then return to work, Lopoo points out.

It's having a second or third baby while still a teenager that does the most damage to a girl's future, says University of Pennsylvania nursing professor O'Sullivan, who since the late 1970s has studied teen girls at risk for having two or more teen births. "The first pregnancy does not destroy your life. It's the second and the third pregnancy that destroy your life."

BACKGROUND

Good News, Bad News

Despite the continuing hype surrounding teen pregnancy and birth rates, in recent decades teens have engaged in less sexual activity, gotten fewer abortions and used contraception more than they did in earlier decades. And teen births and pregnancies have been declining in the United States since the late 1950s.

Except for a few relatively short periods of increase — such as one that began in the late 1980s and continued until 1991 — U.S. teen birth rates have dropped continually since the peak year of 1957, when 96.3 out of every 1,000 teen girls gave birth.[29] In 2005, only 41 of every 1,000 teen girls gave birth — the lowest rate ever.[30]

The declining teen birth rates are not due to abortion, wrote John S. Santelli, a professor of clinical population and family health at the Columbia University Mailman School of Health, and Andrea J. Melnikas, a program coordinator at the New York City-based Population Council, a nonprofit that studies reproductive-health issues. Abortion rates for teens dropped continually beginning in 1988, even as both teen pregnancy rates and birth rates were declining.[31]

Some groups whose pregnancies were of particular concern saw the largest drops, according to Santelli and Melnikas. For example, younger teens — ages 10 to 17 — saw nearly twice the decline in birth rates as older teens in 1991 through 2005, while the African-American teen birth rate — which historically had been considerably higher than for other ethnic groups — dropped much more sharply than the birth rate for white and Hispanic girls.[32]

Experts also point out that those rates have closely tracked overall pregnancy and birth rates, says O'Sullivan of the University of Pennsylvania's nursing school. "Before you get all upset about teenage pregnancy, let's not forget that when teen mothers are having babies, all mothers

CHRONOLOGY

1950s-1980s *U.S. teen birth rates peak, but most teen mothers are married. Average age of marriage rises, and premarital sex becomes more common and accepted.*

1957 U.S. teen birth rate hits all-time high of 96.3 births per 1,000 women.

1960 Food and Drug Administration approves two powerful new contraceptives — the birth-control pill and the IUD (intrauterine device) — giving women and teen girls more say over their reproductive lives.

1972 Congress amends Social Security Act to declare that states must provide family planning services to sexually active minors. . . . Federal education law bans public schools from barring pregnant students and teen parents.

1981 Adolescent Family Life Act encourages young people to postpone sexual activity until marriage.

1987 Teen birth rates increase after long decline; increase continues until 1991.

1989 Supreme Court's *Webster v. Reproductive Health Services* decision makes it more difficult for teens to get abortions.

1990s *Teen pregnancies and birth rates plummet.*

1995 President Bill Clinton declares teenage pregnancy the nation's most serious social problem.

1996 New welfare law stipulates, for the first time, that to obtain funding abstinence-only sex education must meet an eight-point standard, including teaching that sexual activity outside of marriage is likely to have harmful psychological consequences.

1997 All 50 states apply for abstinence-education grants.

2000s *Birth rates for older teens begin rising mid-decade.*

2000 Ninety-two percent of middle schools have a required class teaching that abstinence is the best way to avoid pregnancy and sexually transmitted diseases (STDs); 62 percent have a class that teaches methods of contraception.

2005 Forty-one of every 1,000 teen girls give birth, the lowest rate in history.

2006 Teen birth rates rise for the first time since 1991, rising in 26 states, with biggest increases in South and Southwest and the smallest in the Northeast; birth rate for girls under 15 continues to decline, and the overall birth rate for all U.S. women reaches its highest level since 1971. . . . Department of Health and Human Services announces that federal abstinence-only funding can support programs aimed at encouraging abstinence for unmarried people in their 20s, as well as teens. . . . Forty-six states apply for abstinence-only funding.

2007 Teen birth rates continue to rise, although mostly among 18- and 19-year-olds. . . . . Large government-commissioned study finds that four federally funded abstinence-only programs don't affect the rates at which teens have sex or use condoms.

2008 Federal government allocates $176 million to three abstinence-until-marriage education programs. . . . Only about 28 states using federal abstinence-only funding.

2009 President Barack Obama proposes and Congress approves a funding switch from abstinence-until-marriage sex education to programs shown effective in lowering teen pregnancy rates. . . . Centers for Disease Control and Prevention task force reports evidence is still insufficient to determine whether abstinence-only education can prevent teen pregnancy and STDs and recommends that schools offer comprehensive sex education instead.

2010 Abstinence-only program for low-income, urban middle-schoolers is the first to be shown effective in a randomized, control study, causing students to delay their first time having sex. . . . The MTV reality-television program "16 and Pregnant" begins its second season. . . . In health-care reform legislation, Congress restores $50 million a year for abstinence education and adds $75 million for comprehensive sex education.

are having babies," so it makes little sense to consider the teen birth rate in a vacuum, she says.

The bad news, however, is that U.S. teen birth rates remain much higher than in many other industrialized societies, such as Canada and Western Europe. In 2007 Germany's rate was about one-quarter the U.S. rate, France's was one-sixth and the Netherlands' one-ninth.[33] (*See graph, p. 227.*)

Beyond those facts, however, matters grow murkier. For example, no one fully understands why rates fluctuate, such as they did in the late 1980s, which complicates efforts to cut them further, says Lopoo of Syracuse. "More liberal attitudes toward sex" were likely one factor driving the increase from 1986 to 1991, says Maynard, the University of Pennsylvania education and social policy professor. But sexual attitudes had been liberalizing for decades, both before and after that increase, and during most of that time birth rates have declined, says Lopoo.

"I've spent a considerable amount of time trying to understand it and have talked to the other people who've spent considerable amounts of time trying to understand it, but in the end none of us do understand," he says.

Experts feel they understand better why birth rates declined from 1991 to 2005 — and beyond for the under-15-year-olds. Strong social messages were widely disseminated at the time warning against welfare dependence and advocating condom usage to protect against HIV/AIDS. These helped to encourage teens to both delay sex and use contraception when they did have intercourse, says Maynard.

For example, between 1995 and 2002, the percentage of girls ages 15-19 who said they used a condom the last time they had intercourse increased from 38 percent to 54 percent, and the percentage who said they used a condom plus another form of contraception rose from 8 percent to 20 percent.[34]

In addition, "young people respond to their opportunities," says Lopoo, and with the economy booming in the 1990s and early 2000s, teens were "less inclined to choose" pregnancy.

Unmarried Moms

Most teen mothers — about six in 10 — are 18 or 19 years old when their babies are born —"legal adults in most states" — and hardly constitute the "epidemic" of "babies having babies" often depicted in the media and by advocacy groups, noted Kristin Luker, a professor of law and sociology at the University of California, Berkeley. In fact, the only real "epidemic" of teen births in American history, Luker said, occurred in "the 1950s, when teenagers were having twice as many babies as they had had in previous decades, but few people worried about them."[35]

It is clear, however, that a substantial change occurred between the 1950s and the 1990s, and it isn't primarily about teens having more sex, says the University of Pennsylvania's Furstenberg. "It's not like people in their teens didn't have sex all along," he says. "But they got married. And then, in the '60s, they started to not get married," and in the process substantially changed how society views teen — and, ultimately, even young-adult — sex. The non-marriage trend "started with African-Americans in low-income communities" and fairly quickly spread society-wide, Furstenberg says.

As a result, "sexual initiation is almost always non-marital today; likewise, teen childbearing has become predominantly non-marital," unlike in earlier decades, wrote Santelli and Melnikas.[36]

As the time between dawning sexual maturity and the age of socially approved marriage lengthened to well over a decade, the change spurred liberal groups to focus even more strongly on the need for sex-education courses to teach teens about contraception.

"While a 'wait until you're older' message is good for very young teens," ultimately "99 percent of Americans do have premarital sex" at some point, now that marriage is delayed longer, says Boonstra of the Guttmacher Institute.

Thus, in school sex-education courses, "you're training an adolescent who will one day soon be a 24-year-old" for whom the "wait until marriage" or "you're not ready for sex" messages are not appropriate, she says. "The teen years go very quickly, and not everyone goes to college," so middle- and high-school sex-ed courses are the last time everyone in the population can be reached with information about contraception, she says.

"Sometimes I think we are trying to repeal the law of gravity" by urging all young people in a society rife with sex-saturated media to remain abstinent, said former Rep. Christopher Shays, R-Conn. "There are natural instincts that young people have, and they are educated by their parents hopefully first to know proper conduct," but as a follow-up to parental conversations about values and

Views of Marriage Underlie Sex-Education Debate

Do liberals and conservatives have different goals about the future?

The liberal-conservative divide over teen pregnancy is often framed as a battle between education approaches: abstinence-until-marriage or comprehensive sex education. But the real issue runs deeper.

"This whole question of program effectiveness is a red herring," says Robert E. Rector, a senior research fellow at the Heritage Foundation think tank. "We're told we all share common goals, but that's not true." Liberals' goal is to decrease teen birth rates, Rector says, but conservatives have a bigger aim — relinking sex with marriage.

The Obama administration has taken funding for the Healthy Marriage program — formerly used to promote marriage in low-income communities — and diverted it to job training, says Rector.

That makes sense from the liberal point of view, since many left-leaning analysts argue that economic difficulties harm families and discourage poor people from marrying at the same time as they encourage teen girls who have no hopes for a good job to become mothers early. For social conservatives, however, the core problem for families is the lack of a two-parent commitment to raising children, Rector says.

"Simple messages could help reduce out-of-wedlock births because most women in low-income communities are, in fact, very pro-child, pro-family" and actually "overvalue marriage," construing it as a goal for later in life, Rector says.

Up to now, with single motherhood increasing, Healthy Marriage dollars have apparently had little effect. But "what do we do in other policy areas when a goal is hard to reach?" asks Rector. "Look at the school dropout rate. We don't just drop the goal. We keep on putting money into it." Democrats "are terminating the program because they don't agree with the goal," he says.

A growing economic divide in the United States between two different kinds of families has intensified the battle over marriage, argues June Carbone, a professor of law, the Constitution and society at the University of Missouri-Kansas City and coauthor of the 2009 book *Red Families v. Blue Families*, with George Washington University research professor of law Naomi Cahn.

When new, effective female contraceptives became available in the 1960s, there was broad bipartisan support for helping everyone get access to them, Carbone says. In 1970, for example, legislation to increase access to family planning was overwhelmingly passed by Congress and signed into law by Republican President Richard M. Nixon, who strongly backed it. At that point, "we were all in this together. College and working-class-women were getting pregnant without meaning to," and support for improved access to contraception bridged political divides, she says.

Carbone and Cahn argue that economic changes that put many working-class people in a more precarious financial situation, combined with improved contraception that freed women from unwanted childbearing, changed how Americans view marriage.

"The split goes back to the introduction of the [birth-control] pill," says Cahn. "That made it easier for more women to go to college and delay childbearing."

In addition, beginning as far back as 1945 and accelerating in the 1970s, there was "a huge expansion" in the kinds

good behavior, information is vital, Shays said. "We have had testimony in Congress where young people didn't realize that oral sex could transmit disease," a piece of missing information that could be literally life threatening.[37] Gonorrhea, HIV/AIDS, herpes and human papillomavirus are just a few of the many diseases that can be transmitted via oral sex.

But for social conservatives who believe sex outside of marriage is simply wrong, the fact that not only teens but also 20- and 30-somethings remain single makes instilling in teens the value of abstinence before marriage more vital than ever.

"Extreme interest groups believing in sexual freedom and sexual justice have denigrated the debate over abstinence education by turning it into a vehicle to promote their own ideological agenda of radical sexual autonomy," charged Rep. Mark Souder, R-Ind. "We ought not to be persuaded by these groups who, although adopting the of jobs, including "high-paying positions" open to women, says Carbone. As a result, more college-educated women waited longer to marry and, when they did, she says, they sought much more "egalitarian" marriages than in the past, or marriages in which husband and wife share more equally in wage earning, decision-making, housework and other similar matters.

At the same time, however, manufacturing jobs in the United States were disappearing, leaving blue-collar families in a precarious financial position that bred anxiety about a whole range of social changes, including the high-profile switch to egalitarian marriages by the middle class, says Cahn.

"The anxious group is not the college graduates, since they're continuing to make more money, but the ones who are losing ground" economically at the same time that the society around them is undergoing many changes, Cahn says. As a consequence, many working-class families have embraced ideals like abstinence-until-marriage sex education, which is based on principles that promise to be "eternal rather than contextual," she says. By contrast, the focus of comprehensive sex education on young people making their own decisions feeds into many people's anxieties about where society is heading, she suggests.

The hardening of social conservatives' opposition to contraception is evident in the reaction of some conservative communities to teen childbearing, says Stefanie Mollborn, an assistant professor of sociology at the University of Colorado-Boulder, who studies teen pregnancy. For example, many liberals were surprised when social and religious conservatives strongly supported former Alaska governor and Republican vice presidential candidate Sarah Palin when she announced her unmarried 17-year-old daughter's pregnancy.

But that's an increasingly common reaction, Mollborn says. "In politically conservative communities, what's often said now is that sex is a sin but a baby is a blessing," she says. "I grew up in such a community, and that was not part of the conversation," she recalls. But when Mollborn asked a teenage interviewee from a small, conservative Colorado mining town, "Who's really for teen pregnancy?" the girl answered, "The older people!"

Whatever drives the continuing divide over sex education, "in the end, much of the fight [is] about the moral worth of two different trajectories of human life," said Kristin Luker, a professor of law and sociology at the University of California-Berkeley. "Abstinence-until-marriage sex education presumes that people will marry relatively young and enhances the status of marriage by marking it as the only socially legitimate place to have sex. Comprehensive sex education, on the other hand, presumes that marriage will happen later in life, after people have prepared for a career."[1]

"We are stuck in a moral debate that other countries either haven't had or bypassed long ago," says Frank F. Furstenberg, a University of Pennsylvania professor of sociology. England, by contrast, also fiercely debated the morality of teen sex but ultimately "shifted and now looks at it as a public-health issue," after concluding that stopping teen sexuality was not feasible, Furstenberg says.

Some conservative commentators counter that the Western European approach of accepting teen sexuality and increasing contraceptive education is not the only path to lowering teen birth rates, saying that Japan has attained its low rates by promoting teen abstinence and strong marriages.

But Japan "is a very patriarchal model that is not relevant to us," says James Wagoner, president of Advocates for Youth, a Washington group that supports increased access to contraceptive education. "Is [the Christian group] Focus on the Family going to open up geisha houses" for unmarried men? Wagoner asks. "If you take one aspect of the culture, you have to take all of them, or your results will be very different."

— Marcia Clemmitt

[1] Kristin Luker, *When Sex Goes to School* (2006), p. 236.

language of science and reason" to promote contraceptive education, "are really just evangelists of a . . . tragically incorrect moral vision. We must . . . realize that this debate involves deep disagreements between competing values" about morality, said Souder.[38]

Welfare and Sex Education

While teen motherhood occurs in all socioeconomic and demographic groups, a very high proportion of teen births occurs in low-income families. This phenomenon has stirred most of the federal interest in the issue, since babies born to poor families are more likely to end up needing taxpayer-supported benefits, especially if their parents haven't completed their educations and face slim workplace prospects. Many conservatives argue that this fact constitutes a strong additional reason to spend government funds promoting both abstinence and the value of marriage.

Parental Involvement Can Make the Difference

"Kids want their parents to say, 'Don't have sex.' "

After studying teen pregnancy for half a century, Frank F. Furstenberg has distilled all his experience into one big insight: "If you had to take a pill 20 days in a row to become pregnant" — as required by the birth-control pill to ward off pregnancy —"there would be no teen pregnancies."

In short, teens don't intentionally become pregnant but mostly just allow it to happen, for a variety of reasons, simple and complex, says Furstenberg, a University of Pennsylvania professor of sociology and author of the 2007 book *Destinies of the Disadvantaged: The Politics of Teenage Childbearing*. Researchers like Furstenberg seek to uncover more of the causes that underlie unwanted pregnancies in an effort to reduce teen birth rates — which have dropped steeply over the past two decades — even further.

"There's no cheap, long-term solution," says James Wagoner, president of Advocates for Youth, a Washington group that supports so-called comprehensive sex education, which advocates the benefits of delaying or forgoing sex but also provides substantial information on contraception. But countries like the Netherlands have dramatically reduced teen births by making "an enormous sustained investment in young people," and the United States could do the same, he says.

Fostering the right kind of parental involvement is a major key, says Bill Albert, chief program officer of the National Campaign to Prevent Teen and Unplanned Pregnancy. "In surveys, teens say parents are the biggest influence in their decision-making about sex," a fact that many parents are surprised to hear, he says.

"When I talk to teenage mothers and fathers, they either say, 'Nobody talked to me about sex,' or 'I couldn't stay in my home' " because of family problems such as too much fighting, says Nicole Lynn Lewis, a Maryland-based motivational speaker for teens and a former teen mother of a now 10-year-old daughter. "What really started my situation and the break I had from my family is growing up with a lot of arguing and no talk about sex," says Lewis, who self-published a book about her own teenage life: *Glori: A Different Story*.

The parental conversation "can't be just one isolated" birds-and-bees discussion, says Lewis. "It has to be lots of conversations over time, helping the youngest kids feel comfortable talking about their bodies and their feelings," then moving on to what it means to have and be a good friend, not a bad one, for example, she says.

"Then, when they're old enough to have a girlfriend or a boyfriend, they'll already have thought about what makes someone a good person to have in your life and how to treat others," she says. "Kids want their parents to say, 'Don't have sex,' " says Lewis. "I would have liked my parents to have said, 'It's your decision, but we'd like you to wait.' "

"I believe that parents — even parents who were teen parents themselves — don't want to face the fact that

In a 2009 analysis, the National Campaign to Prevent Teen and Unplanned Pregnancy found that 28 percent of teen births occurred in families with incomes below the poverty line, although that group comprises only 13.2 percent of the population.[39] In the year of the study, the poverty level was around $14,800 for a one-parent/one-child family and $21,834 for a two-parent/two-child family. The study also found that 31 percent of teen births occurred in families with incomes ranging between the poverty level and twice the poverty level, which is still a lower-working-class income. Only 41 percent occurred in families with incomes that were more than double the poverty level.[40]

Federal welfare programs have focused on two main strategies for averting teen and other unmarried pregnancies: promoting abstinence until marriage and tightening the rules under which single and teen mothers could get government support for their families, thus removing government incentives to become a single mother.

Under the George W. Bush administration, the federal welfare program focused on averting teen pregnancies through abstinence-only education and reducing unwed pregnancies by promoting abstinence and the values of marriage, says the Heritage Foundation's Rector. By contrast, comprehensive sex-education advocates "do not talk about out-of-wedlock pregnancy." Or, if they do deal with it, they address it merely as an example of "unplanned" pregnancy, which is not the same issue at all since it

13-year-olds are sexually active," says Ann O'Sullivan, a pediatric nurse practitioner at the Children's Hospital of Philadelphia who has worked with pregnant teens since the 1970s. "Until we can change this perception," parents won't give their kids the right messages. "Remember those public service announcements that said, 'It's 10 o'clock. Do you know where your children are?' Well, we need new ones that say, 'It's 3 o'clock in the afternoon. Have you talked to your teen about avoiding an unwanted pregnancy?' "

Another widespread misperception is that it's the "wild girls, who call themselves hussies, run the streets and love parties" who are at highest risk, O'Sullivan says. In fact, "it's the quiet, meek daughter who sits on the porch who is the one that parents should worry about more," especially when it comes to the second and third teenage pregnancies that can truly devastate a girl's future, she says.

Nicole Lynn Lewis

Motivational speaker Nicole Lynn Lewis, a former teen mother, now urges teenagers to avoid pregnancy.

"Strong women like being girlfriends, they like going to school, partying," so while some have a first pregnancy, they are very careful to avoid a second, she says. "But the girls who liked being mothers better than they liked being in school, who didn't feel successful in school" or socially, are highly likely to have more than one teen birth. "We need to start in the sixth, seventh and eighth grade to find the girls who are not doing well in school and provide tutoring" to help them find successes to dissuade them from opting for teen motherhood, she says.

Some research shows that the extent to which parents are able to "monitor" their teens correlates strongly with pregnancy risk. "Do you know where your child is?" is a key question for families, since parents who don't ask are more likely to raise daughters who become teen mothers, says Anne M. Teitelman, an assistant professor of nursing at the University of Pennsylvania.

Research is also beginning to suggest that girls who grow up believing that boys should be the decision-makers when it comes to sex or who have boyfriends who wield the power in their relationships are at higher risk for early pregnancy, Teitelman says. "Teens will say things along the lines of, 'I thought that when he hit me, it was a sign that he cares about me; hitting was a sign that I engaged his emotions. And he's my boyfriend, so if he wants to have sex without a condom I should try to make him happy,' " she says.

Teens should be counseled repeatedly "to have a condom in your sock, if you're a boy, or in your bra, if you're a girl," says O'Sullivan. A tough and constant message all teens should hear is this: "If you are not planning to not have a baby, then you are planning to have a baby."

— ***Marcia Clemmitt***

doesn't speak to the value of having all children grow up in two-parent families, Rector says.

"Long ago, there was controversy over whether sex ed should even be taught," says the Guttmacher Institute's Boonstra. "But when AIDS came along, people said, 'Well, we've got to teach it,' and to reach kids where they are the venue had to be schools," she says. As a result, today most states require that schools teach at least a minimum of sex education, such as informing students about sexually transmitted infections including HIV.

Abstinence education began receiving federal funding as far back as 1982, in the Adolescent Family Life Act, signed into law by President Ronald Reagan, which promoted abstinence and disciplined decision-making among pregnant teens and teen parents. Federal funds for such programs rose steadily over the years.

In 1996, a new welfare law — the Personal Responsibility and Work Opportunity Reconciliation Act of 1996 — was passed during the Bill Clinton administration. It established the Title V program to provide up to $50 million a year in federal funding to states for abstinence-only education, and the amounts made available to these programs continued to rise. By 2009 President Bush's final budget allotted $204 million for abstinence education.[41]

Between 1997 and 2009, a total of around $1.9 billion in federal, state and local government funds had been funneled into abstinence-only education, with $1.5 billion of the total coming from the federal government.[42]

Getty Images/Jeff Fusco

A demonstrator at the National STD Prevention Conference in Philadelphia in 2004 criticizes President George W. Bush's plan to expand abstinence-only education, which many disease-prevention experts argued dangerously downplayed the effectiveness of condoms against sexually transmitted diseases. President Obama's new sex-ed funding plan focuses on preventing teen pregnancy through evidence-based programs, which urge sexually active teens to use condoms.

In 2006, the Bush administration's Department of Health and Human Services (HHS) issued a statement to clarify the administration's intention that abstinence education not be aimed only at young people in school but toward unmarried people up to age 29, through community and church groups, for example. "The message is, 'It's better to wait until you're married to bear or father children,' " and "the only 100 percent effective way of getting there is abstinence," no matter what one's age, said HHS assistant secretary Wade Horn.[43]

Liberal groups were dismayed at the announcement. "The notion that the federal government is supporting millions of dollars' worth of messages to people who are grown adults about how to conduct their sex life is a very divisive policy," said National Campaign CEO Brown. "If you use contraception effectively and consistently," problems of out-of-wedlock childbearing can be avoided.[44]

While federal support for an abstinence-until-marriage, pro-marriage message grew substantially over the past decade-and-a-half, state and local commitment to the idea began to wane by the end of the era.

In 2005, 46 states applied for federal abstinence-education money to fund programs in schools and community and religious organizations.[45] By 2008 only about 28 states were seeking the money. About 16 states that refused the funding specifically cited philosophical disagreement or lack of evidence that abstinence programs worked.[46]

In Idaho, for example, pregnancy rates rose among 15-to-19-year-olds between 2004 and 2006, after the state had been using federal abstinence funds. "There was mounting evidence that the abstinence programs weren't proving to be effective," said Elke Shaw-Tulloch, chief of the Bureau of Community and Environmental Health at the Idaho Department of Health and Welfare. The state decided in 2007 to stop applying for the funding.[47]

Large urban school districts have been heavy users of abstinence funds, partly because of their high rates of teen pregnancy and partly for financial reasons, says Wagoner of Advocates for Youth. With urban public schools under the gun to improve student performance in subjects like math and reading under the 2002 federal No Child Left Behind Act, many leapt at offers by abstinence-education groups to install ready-made sex-education programs, sparing schools the trouble of developing such courses and training teachers themselves, Wagoner says.

More recently, however, "you see big urban school districts like Pittsburgh, Cleveland and Chicago flipping to comprehensive sex ed, so you know that things are trending that way," Wagoner says.

CURRENT SITUATION

Birth Rates Rise

The administration's new framework for federal sex-education funding will shift most funds away from

AT ISSUE

Does the Obama administration have a good plan to fund evidence-based sex-education programs?

YES

Sarah Brown
CEO, National Campaign to Prevent Teen and Unplanned Pregnancy

Written for *CQ Researcher*, March 19, 2010

The new $110 million federal investment in preventing teen pregnancy is timely and important. Proposed by President Obama and passed by Congress, this initiative emphasizes good science, encourages research and innovation and underscores the need to tackle too-early pregnancy and parenthood. Equally important, the president's 2011 budget proposes higher funding for these investments.

The remarkable declines in U.S. teen pregnancy and childbearing — down 38 percent and 32 percent, respectively, since the early 1990s — represent extraordinary progress on an issue many once considered intractable.

Recent news, however, is discouraging. Teen pregnancy is up 3 percent (the first increase since 1990), and the teen birth rate has risen 5 percent over two years (the first increase since 1991). One of the great success stories of the past two decades is apparently in danger of unraveling.

Against this troubling backdrop, the new federal initiative is good news. Moreover, it is well-aligned with the public's growing realization that in this unforgiving economy, adolescence and young adulthood must be devoted to education and more education — high school and then some. Postponing families until completing school is now as much an economic and workforce imperative as it is a personal or family one.

The initiative is also historic — the first major commitment of federal funding for preventing teen pregnancy that places a premium on evidence-based, proven approaches. Although the public has long seen abstinence and contraception as complementary, the inside-the-Beltway battle has often set this up as an either/or choice. The new funding stream, by contrast, sidesteps this tiresome debate and focuses on what works. In the ongoing Washington battle pitting abstinence interventions against comprehensive sex education, this investment is firmly on the side of science. As the British are fond of saying, "Well done, all."

Also noteworthy, money is set aside for innovation and research. Although we don't yet know the precise criteria that will determine which programs are eligible for support, it is important to acknowledge that even effective programs can and should be improved. We must also look hard for new ideas. For example, could the parallel universe of electronic games that so many teens inhabit help tackle this issue? Might YouTube and Twitter become part of the solution?

How can effective programs developed a decade or more ago be adapted to meet the nation's growing cultural diversity? Stay tuned. . . .

NO

Christine Kim
Policy Analyst, The Heritage Foundation

Written for *CQ Researcher*, March 19, 2010

The Obama administration and Congress recently terminated federal abstinence-education programs, despite the fact that funding priorities already favor comprehensive sex education — and that social-science evidence supports abstinence.

In the last year of the Bush administration, the Department of Health and Human Services spent $4 on comprehensive sex ed and family-planning services targeting adolescents for every $1 it devoted to abstinence education. In all, nearly $786 million was spent addressing adolescent sexual activity.

By contrast, the Obama administration proposes spending an additional $130 million next year for "medically accurate and age-appropriate programs that reduce teen pregnancy." In short, more comprehensive sex ed. In theory, abstinence education could qualify for such funding. Evidence suggesting its effectiveness is building. Last month, the *Archives of Pediatrics and Adolescent Medicine* published a highly rigorous study that shows abstinence education can delay and reduce teen sexual activity.

Yet the Obama administration won't fund it, perhaps because opposition to these programs is often motivated by ideology, not science. At a 2008 hearing, for example, several medical and health experts were asked if they would support optional federal funding of abstinence education if they were provided evidence that these programs are as or more effective than comprehensive sex ed. Their reply? An unequivocal "no."

The debate about sex education is really about values. Authentic abstinence education teaches that school-age children should abstain from sex until they have at least graduated from high school; that sex should involve love, intimacy and commitment — qualities most likely to be found in marriage; and that marriage benefits children, adults and society.

Surveys show that nearly all parents want their children to be taught these messages. Yet in the classroom, the prevailing mentality often condones teen sexual activity as long as youths use contraceptives. Abstinence is usually mentioned only in passing, if at all. Many teens who need to learn about the benefits of abstaining from sexual activity during the teenage years never hear them, and many who choose to abstain fail to receive adequate support for their decisions.

Today's youth face enormous peer pressure to engage in risky behavior and navigate media and popular culture that endorse and glamorize permissiveness and casual sex. Sadly, the government implicitly supports these messages by spending hundreds of millions of dollars on programs that teach "safe sex" is sufficient.

Does Tough Love Reduce Teen Pregnancy?

More families today are confronting their pregnant teen daughters.

Is it counterproductive to offer too much help to teen moms? Affordable child care and financial support for career-training programs would help teen mothers reach educational and economic success and improve life for their children, some researchers say. But they also wonder where to draw the line between assistance that helps families and aid that may remove incentives for teenagers to avoid pregnancy in the first place.

Under current law, teen moms "can't get benefits while they're getting a 13th year of education" — such as completing a certificate program to become a medical office assistant — says Stefanie Mollborn, an assistant professor of sociology at the University of Colorado-Boulder. Current welfare law was specifically designed to bring more mothers into the workforce, so it's ironic that no support is provided for such 13th-year programs, which train people in specific job skills, she says. Indeed, many teen parents "say they'd especially like a short period of welfare support" for this purpose, Mollborn notes.

Another top priority for teen moms is access to affordable day care, which "is actually more beneficial to teen moms than it is to older moms" because many older mothers already have their high school diplomas or GEDs, while teen moms need extra support while they earn them, Mollborn says.

The best prescription for further lowering the teen and unwed birth rates in the United States is to articulate society-wide a firm, new norm that rejects unplanned pregnancies and teen motherhood as bad for individuals and society, many experts recommend.

Mollborn says her research is turning up evidence that at least some low-income communities that previously would have been non-judgmental about teen motherhood and offered whatever support they could are now taking a tougher line with young moms, partly for economic reasons.

In some low-income communities, becoming a mother as a teen actually reaped significant social rewards from family and neighbors, such as being treated like an adult while others one's own age were still treated as children, Mollborn says. Today, however, "fewer moms are getting any kind of social rewards for having a baby," and the struggling economy likely will push this trend further, she says.

More families today are confronting their pregnant teen daughters with tough questions, like, "Do you realize we have nothing to give you? Do you realize that we counted on you to finish school?" Mollborn says.

abstinence-only programs and toward comprehensive sex education. President Obama announced the new plan in 2009 and again in 2010. Congress, which must approve the federal spending plan each year in appropriations legislation, approved the plan late last year and is expected to do so again in 2010.

Currently, analysts and policymakers also are struggling to make sense of the new federal statistics — just beginning to be released and analyzed in 2009 and 2010 — showing the 5 percent uptick in teen birth-rates over two years in the mid-2000s.[48] While causes of the 2005-2007 increase aren't fully understood, it was not wholly unforeseen, and some of its contributing causes are known.

"The Hispanic population is growing," says Syracuse's Lopoo, "and among that population teen childbearing is high." In addition, the average age of the Hispanic population is younger, and any youth-heavy demographic will contribute disproportionately to birth rates.

Furthermore, CDC statistics show that contraceptive use was beginning to decline three or four years earlier, beginning around 2000 — clearly a significant harbinger that birth rates would soon rise, says University of Pennsylvania sociology professor Furstenberg.

Some commentators say federal funding for abstinence-only sex-ed programs has caused the decline in condom use, but many say that was far from the only factor. "Would I say these education policies have caused the break in the [overall downward] trend of teen births?" asks Furstenberg. "No." More germane, he says, is the fact that "the fear of AIDS has dropped," leading more teens to forgo condom use, he says.

Many blame a short attention span among policymakers and the public when it comes to chronic social issues. "This is a nation of problem solvers who want to solve social problems the same way we solve polio — once and for all," says Albert of the National Campaign. But social

Such increased social disapproval of teen motherhood "might backfire because when families are more ashamed" of a daughter's pregnancy, "they tend to be less willing to provide support," such as a place to live and child care, says Mollborn. The ultimate well-being of children born to teen mothers depends heavily on the young families having adequate finances in the early years, she says. On most measures of health and development, "if there are good resources in the family, by the time the child is 4 the child is doing about as well" as children who were not born to teen parents, she says.

To the extent that a tough stance against teen motherhood ends up hurting young children, it will certainly end up costing society more, says Frank F. Furstenberg, author of the 2007 book *Destinies of the Disadvantaged: The Politics of Teenage Childbearing.* Children with unmet early nutritional, medical, educational and other needs have their development stunted in many ways, he says. "You either pay now, or you pay later. If we put off costs, we'll just end up paying later in a different form."

But other analysts point out that being overly supportive of teen mothers can be a double-edged sword that incentivizes additional unplanned childbearing.

Research has shown that even unwed mothers who said that they didn't want second babies were more likely to become pregnant a second time anyway when they received benefits such as day care, baby showers or other kinds of nurturing social supports, says Rebecca A. Maynard, a professor of education and social policy at the University of Pennsylvania Graduate School of Education.

By contrast, mothers who are treated "with a no-nonsense approach — clearly informed about contraception and the negative impact of having a second child and then firmly told they must take responsibility for themselves and their families" — were less likely to have a second pregnancy, Maynard says her research found. The message of "You're having another baby, oh, how sweet" tends to lead to more ill-advised pregnancies, she says.

Facilitating life for girls who've had babies, such as by providing in-school day care, could incentivize further careless sex and more teen births, Maynard says.

The 1996 federal overhaul of welfare law was intended to diminish incentives for unwed pregnancies, and in at least one sense the law seems to have succeeded, says Mollborn. By 2001, only 17 percent of teen mothers she interviewed were on welfare, although many were low-income, she says. "We asked why, and they said 'There are so many strings attached.' "

The long-term effectiveness of welfare legislation in lowering teen birth rates is unclear, however. From 2005 through 2007, the latest years for which data have been analyzed, teen birth rates actually increased for the first time since 1991.

— Marcia Clemmitt

phenomena that are a risk for each subsequent generation "need constant attention."

For example, after the steep drop-off in teen births during the 1990s, private foundations that had funded anti-pregnancy programs shifted their money to other issues that were gaining more public attention, says O'Sullivan of the Children's Hospital of Philadelphia. "We did much better with this in the 1990s, but we've stopped thinking of it as an important problem."

It's not clear whether the 2005-2007 birth-rate increase is the beginning of a longer trend. For example, the steep decline of the 1990s and early 2000s may amount to the bottom of what's possible for U.S. birth rates under current conditions, says Maynard, "and now the numbers are just bouncing around a bit."

In any case, despite the increase, birth rates for teens under age 15 have actually continued to drop, and "most of the [2005-2007] increase is coming among women age 18 and older, with very little among teens younger than that," says the Heritage Foundation's Rector.

Nevertheless, with rates up nearly across the board, "this doesn't feel like an uptick," says Albert of the campaign to prevent teen pregnancy. "It feels like the beginning of a negative trend."

Evidence-Based Approach?

Last December, Congress approved the Obama administration's new plan for allotting $114.5 million to science-based sex education. Most federal funds will no longer be directed to abstinence-only-until-marriage programs but toward "medically accurate and age-appropriate programs that reduce teen pregnancy," which likely will include education both about abstinence and contraception.[49]

About three-quarters of the money will fund programs that "rigorous evaluation" has shown are effective at reducing teen pregnancy or "behavior risk factors" related to teen pregnancy. The rest will fund grants to develop and test additional strategies for teen-pregnancy prevention. In a conference report attached to the spending bill, Congress noted that these "development" funds are intended to go mainly to programs that stress abstinence while providing scientifically accurate, age-appropriate information about sex and contraception.[50]

"This bill marks the first time since 1981 that abstinence-only-until-marriage programs will not receive dedicated federal funding," said Jen Heitel Yakush, assistant director for public policy at SIECUS, the Sexuality Information and Education Council of the United States, a nonprofit group that promotes comprehensive sex education.[51]

But some abstinence-only funding is likely to find its way back into the budget after all. During the complex, year-long negotiating process over health-care reform, the Senate Finance Committee approved two pots of mandatory annual funding for sex education for the years 2010 through 2014, and that committee's version of health-care reform legislation was approved by Congress on Sunday, March 21. Under the panel's sex-ed compromise, for the next five years $75 million will go to evidence-based programs each year and another $50 million will be spent to continue the old abstinence-only grant program, explains the National Campaign's Albert. This money is in addition to any funds Congress may approve for sex education each year, such as the $114.5 million in 2010 funds that legislators provided last December for Obama's evidence-based sex-ed plan, Albert says.

The Obama administration is "axing" not just abstinence-only school programs but also the Healthy Marriage program, which promotes marriage in low-income communities, says the Heritage Foundation's Rector. The administration felt the funding would be more effective if spent on job training programs.

The cutback is occurring just at the time "the out-of-wedlock birth rate reaches 40 percent" of all births, Rector complains. That's a potentially disastrous decision, he says. Low-income families are much more likely to be living with a single parent, usually a mother, demonstrating that out-of-wedlock birth is a high risk factor for children to grow up in poverty, says Rector.

In 2008, 52 percent of all U.S. children in low-income families — with incomes of 200 percent or less of the federal poverty level — lived in single-parent households, compared to only 17 percent of children in families with moderate or high incomes.[52]

OUTLOOK

Births and the Economy

How the economy fares over the next few years will affect teen birth rates, experts say. But over the long term, they add, the best way to decrease teen pregnancies is to set strong social norms against teen childbearing in every community and communicate those norms consistently, while ensuring that as many young people as possible can envision prosperous futures if they wait to have babies.

The struggling economy "could affect what happens over the next several years," because "in a strong economy young people are more likely to see opportunities that education would allow them to take advantage of," says Lopoo of Syracuse University. "If I'm in high school and see that my older sister, who worked hard and finished school, is happy and succeeding, then I can feel confident that there'll be something out there for me and will be more likely to forgo having a baby," he says.

Although liberal and conservative analysts differ significantly on what the social norms on marriage and childbearing should be, most do agree that decreasing birth rates for teens and unmarried 20-something women much below current levels would likely require a society-wide commitment to sending the message that young, unmarried childbearing is unacceptable. Over the past several decades, public-health initiatives to drastically change social norms for behaviors like smoking and drunken driving demonstrate that, with concerted efforts, we can significantly change such social standards, many say.

"There was great skepticism that we could change the norms against smoking, but look where we are now," says Huber of the National Abstinence Education Association.

"We have 'no smoking' bars in a tobacco state like Virginia," says Wagoner of Advocates for Youth. "Once we thought that couldn't ever happen."

Advocates of establishing a more accepting attitude toward sexual activity among teens while promoting contraceptive use say that, even without a commitment to norm changing by the older generation, the future may hold such a norm change.

"The millennials" — the generation born in 1981 and after —"seem in surveys to be the most open on sexual health issues in history" and may eventually shift U.S. sexual norms to a "radical pragmatism" that accepts unmarried and teen sexuality as a biological given and focuses on contraceptive education to prevent pregnancy and STD transmission, says Wagoner. "In a society where 95 percent of people have sex before marriage, it's not clear what else makes sense," he says.

At present, however, "America has been so dysfunctional for so long in terms of sexual health that there are enormous gains to be made from low-hanging fruit," as a new Democratic majority in Washington gives renewed priority to contraception education and dissemination, says Wagoner. "Just by increasing delivery of condoms in urban areas, you could make major gains even in this economy."

NOTES

1. For background, see Nancy Dillon, Veronika Belenkaya and Tina Moore, "Bristol Palin's Pregnancy Was an Open Secret Back Home," *New York Daily News* online, Sept. 2, 2008, www.nydailynews.com.
2. Quoted in "Bristol Palin: Abstinence for All Teen's 'Not Realistic,' " CNN Politics.com, Feb. 17, 2009, www.cnn.com.
3. For background, see "Jamie Lynn Spears, Casey Aldridge Split," *US Magazine* online, Feb. 6, 2010, www.usmagazine.com/momsbabies/news/jamielynn-spears-casey-aldridge-split-201052.
4. For background, see Kathleen Kingsbury, "Pregnancy Boom at Gloucester High," *Time* online, June 18, 2008, www.time.com/time/world/article/0,8599,1815845,00.html; Kathleen Kingsbury, "Gloucester Pregnancy Plot Thickens," *Time* online, June 23, 2008, www.time.com/time/nation/article/0,8599,1817272,00.html.
5. Brady E. Hamilton, Joyce A. Martin, and Stephanie J. Ventura, "Births: Preliminary Data for 2006," *National Vital Statistics Reports*, Centers for Disease Control and Prevention, Dec. 5, 2007, www.cdc.gov/nchs/data/nvsr/nvsr56/nvsr56_07.pdf.
6. Hamilton, *et al.*, "Births: Preliminary Data for 2007," *National Vital Statistics Reports*, Centers for Disease Control and Prevention, March 18, 2009, www.cdc.gov/nchs/data/nvsr/nvsr57/nvsr57_12.pdf.
7. Quoted in Tamar Lewin, "After Long Decline, Teenage Pregnancy Rate Rises," *The New York Times*, Jan. 27, 2010, p. 14.
8. Hamilton, *et al.*, "Births: Preliminary Data for 2007," *op. cit.*
9. For background see Jane Friedman, "Teen Sex," *CQ Researcher*, Sept. 16, 2005, pp. 761-784, and Kathy Koch, "Encouraging Teen Abstinence," *CQ Researcher*, July 10, 1998, pp. 577-600.
10. Douglas Kirby, "Emerging Answers 2007: Research Findings on Programs to Reduce Teen Pregnancy and Sexually Transmitted Diseases," The National Campaign to Prevent Teen and Unplanned Pregnancy, November 2007.
11. For background, see Tamar Lewin, "Quick Response to Study of Abstinence Education," *The New York Times*, Feb. 2, 2010, p. A18, www.nytimes.com/2010/02/03/education/03abstinence.html.
12. Quoted in Faye Flam, "Study Offers Nuanced View of Abstinence Education," Philly.com, Feb. 17, 2010, http://m.philly.com/phillycom/db_/contentdetail.htm;jsessionid=1DF308091E4D61ED7D33C5836A7AA3B6?contentguid=D41gWkFI&full=true.
13. "Educational Attainment in the United States: 2007," Bureau of the Census, January 2009, www.census.gov/prod/2009pubs/p20-560.pdf.
14. Lee Smith, "Helping Teen Mothers Succeed," *The Journal of School Nursing*, June 2006, p. 130.
15. Christopher Trenholm, *et al.*, "Impacts of Four Title V, Section 510 Abstinence Education Programs," Mathematica Policy Research Inc., April 2007, www.mathematica-mpr.com/publications/pdfs/impactabstinence.pdf.
16. Quoted in Daniel J. DeNoon, "Expert Panel Rejects Abstinence-Only Sex Ed," *WebMD Health News* online, Nov. 6, 2009, www.medicinenet.com. The Task Force report has not yet been formally released by the Centers for Disease Control and Prevention.
17. Quoted in *ibid.*

18. Quoted in "Hearing on Domestic Abstinence-only Programs: Assessing the Evidence," transcript, House Committee on Oversight and Government Reform, April 23, 2008, http://oversight.house.gov/images/stories/documents/20080515131336.pdf.
19. Quoted in *ibid.*
20. Irene Ericksen and Danielle Ruedt, "A Minority Report: Fundamental Concerns About the CDC Meta-Analysis of Group-based Interventions to Prevent Adolescent Pregnancy, HIV, and Other STIs," Nov. 18, 2009, www.abstinenceassociation.org/docs/Minority_Report_CDC_Meta-Analysis_11-7-09.pdf.
21. For background, see Lewin, "Quick Response to Study of Abstinence Education," *op. cit.*
22. Quoted in *ibid.*
23. Valerie Huber, "President Obama Must Rethink His Stance Against Abstinence Education Funding," Lifenews.com, May 14, 2009, www.lifenews.com/nat5051.html.
24. Jacob Goldstein, "Teen STD Rates Cause for Concern, Not Panic," *The Wall Street Journal blog*, March 11, 2008, http://blogs.wsj.com/health/2008/03/11/teen-std-rates-cause-for-concern-not-panic/tab/article.
25. Kate Perper, Kristen Peterson, and Jennifer Manlove, "Diploma Attainment Among Teen Mothers," Fact Sheet #2010-01, Child Trends, January 2010, www.childtrends.org.
26. Elizabeth Terry-Humen, Jennifer Manlove and Kristin A. Moore, "Playing Catch-Up: How Children Born to Teen Mothers Fare," The National Campaign to Prevent Teen and Unplanned Pregnancy/Child Trends, January 2005.
27. Quoted in Kari Huus, "A Baby Changes Everything: The True Cost of Pregnancy's Uptick," The Elkhart Project, MSNBC.com, Feb. 19, 2010, www.msnbc.msn.com.
28. Quoted in Pauline Anderson, "Distress Combined With Poverty Increases Risk for Teen Pregnancy," *Medscape Medical News online*, July 31, 2009, www.medscape.com.
29. Stephanie J. Ventura, T. J. Matthews and Brady E. Hamilton, "Births to Teenagers in the United States: 1940-2000," *National Vital Statistics Reports*, Vol. 49, No. 10, Centers for Disease Control and Prevention, Sept. 25, 2001, http://cdc.gov/NCHS/data/nvsr/nvsr49/nvsr49_10.pdf.
30. "National Birth Rates for Teens, Aged 15-19," National Campaign to Prevent Teen and Unplanned Pregnancy, www.thenationalcampaign.org.
31. John S. Santelli and Andrea J. Melnikas, "Teen Fertility in Transition: Recent and Historical Trends in the United States," *Annual Review of Public Health 2010*, Dec. 9, 2009, pp. 17.1-17.13.
32. *Ibid.*
33. "Adolescent Sexual Health in Europe and the U.S. — Why the Difference?" Advocates for Youth, 2009, www.advocatesforyouth.org.
34. "Teenagers in the United States: Sexual Activity, Contraceptive Use, and Childbearing, 2002," Centers for Disease Control and Prevention, December 2004, www.cdc.gov/nchs/data/series/sr_23/sr23_024.pdf, p. 10.
35. Kristin Luker, *Dubious Conceptions: The Politics of Teen Pregnancy* (1997), p. 8.
36. Santelli and Melnikas, *op. cit.*, p. 17.5.
37. Quoted in "Hearing on Domestic Abstinence-only Programs: Assessing the Evidence," transcript, *op. cit.*
38. *Ibid.*
39. "Income, Poverty, and Health Insurance Coverage in the United States: 2008," press release, Bureau of the Census, Sept. 10, 2009, www.census.gov/Press-Release/www/releases/archives/income_wealth/014227.html.
40. "Socio-Economic and Family Characteristics of Teen Childbearing," The National Campaign to Prevent Teen and Unplanned Pregnancy, September 2009, www.TheNationalCampaign.org.
41. Tracy Hampton, "Abstinence-only Programs Under Fire," *JAMA* (*Journal of the American Medical Association*), May 7, 2008, p. 2013.
42. Sarah Kliff, "The Future of Abstinence," *Newsweek*, Oct. 27, 2009, www.newsweek.com.
43. Quoted in Sharon Jayson, "Abstinence Message Goes Beyond Teens," *USA Today*, Oct. 31, 2006, p. A1.

44. Quoted in *ibid.*
45. *Ibid.*
46. Kliff, *op. cit.*
47. Kevin Freking, "States Reject Abstinence-only Funding from Federal Government," The Associated Press, June 24, 2008, retrieved from *Huffington Post blog*, www.huffingtonpost.com.
48. "National Birth Rates for Teens, Aged 15 to 19," *op. cit.*
49. Rachel Larris, "Appropriations Bill Ends Abstinence-Only Funding, Increases Family Planning," *RH Reality Check online*, Dec. 15, 2009, www.rhrealitycheck.org.
50. *Ibid.*
51. Quoted in *ibid.*
52. "Demographics of Low-Income Children," National Center for Children in Poverty, Mailman School of Public Health, Columbia University, www.nccp.org.

BIBLIOGRAPHY

Books

Furstenberg, Frank F., *Destinies of the Disadvantaged: The Politics of Teen Childbearing, Russell Sage Foundation Publications*, 2007.
A University of Pennsylvania professor of sociology who has tracked teen motherhood among low-income urban families since the 1960s argues that both liberal and conservative advocates have often exaggerated or misrepresented facts about teenage motherhood to promote political agendas.

Luker, Kristin, *When Sex Ed Goes to School: Warring Views on Sex — and Sex Education — Since the Sixties, W.W. Norton*, 2007.
A professor of sociology and law at the University of California, Berkeley, traces the history of America's long-running battle over sex education and proposes explanations for the seemingly intractable nature of the liberal-conservative divide on the issue.

Regnerus, Mark, *Forbidden Fruit: Sex and Religion in the Lives of American Teenagers, Oxford University Press*, 2007.
An associate professor of sociology and religious studies at the University of Texas, Austin, examines influences on teenagers' sexual decision-making, especially their religious beliefs and parents.

Articles

Huus, Kari, "A Baby Changes Everything: The True Cost of Pregnancy's Uptick," *MSNBC.com*, Feb. 19, 2010, www.msnbc.com.
A 19-year-old father-to-be trades college for a job at a pork-packing plant, hoping to provide his girlfriend and their baby a more secure life than his single mother has had.

Jayson, Sharon, "Out-of-wedlock Births on the Rise Worldwide," *USA Today*, May 13, 2009, p. 10B.
Births to single mothers are rising worldwide, but European single moms are more likely than American moms to be living with their babies' fathers.

Kliff, Sarah, "The Future of Abstinence," *Newsweek*, Oct. 27, 2009, www.newsweek.com.
Over the past 15 years, a booming industry of abstinence-only education providers has developed around the country. Under new federal funding rules, the groups now wonder whether communities will continue to use the programs, and some contemplate developing compromise curricula that include more information on contraception.

Morris, Alex, "Truth and Consequences at Pregnancy High," *New York*, May 10, 2009, http://nymag.com.
Teen mothers in New York City's impoverished South Bronx struggle to complete their educations at Jane Addams High School for Academics and Careers, while their babies stay at an on-site day-care center. Nearly half the community's residents have incomes below the federal poverty level, and each year about 15 percent of neighborhood girls ages 15 to 19 become pregnant, far above the national average.

Reports and Studies

Bradley, Katherine, and Robert Rector, "How President Obama's Budget Will Demolish Welfare Reform," Web Memo No. 2819, *The Heritage Foundation*, Feb. 25, 2010, www.heritage.org.
Eliminating funding for marriage-promotion programs will increase single motherhood and, along with it, child poverty, say analysts from a conservative think tank.

Martin, Shanna, Robert Rector and Melissa G. Pardue, "Comprehensive Sex Education vs. Authentic Abstinence: A Study of Competing Curricula," *The Heritage Foundation*, 2004, www.heritage.org.
Abstinence-only courses teach that reserving sex for marriage strengthens people's marital happiness, while comprehensive sex-ed courses focus on tutoring students in the use of contraceptives and leave it to teens to establish their own principles about sex and relationship commitment, says an analysis by a conservative group.

Moore, Kristin Anderson, "Teen Births: Examining the Recent Increase," *Child Trends Research Brief #2009-08*, March 2009, www.childtrends.org.
The recent uptick in birth rates may have been driven by increasing economic disparity and fewer women reporting they've received formal training in contraceptive use.

Santelli, John S., and Andrea J. Melnikas, "Teen Fertility in Transition: Recent and Historic Trends in the United States," *Annual Review of Public Health 2010*, p. 17.1.
Improved contraceptive use accounts for most historical declines in teen pregnancy; lower contraceptive-use rates account for U.S. teen pregnancy rates being higher than in Europe.

Trenholm, Christopher, *et al.*, "Impacts of Four Title V, Section 510 Abstinence Education Programs," *Mathematica Policy Research, Inc.*, April 2007, www.mathematica-mpr.com/publications/pdfs/impactabstinence.pdf.
A government-commissioned report finds that four abstinence-only programs apparently make no difference in whether teens have sex or have unprotected sex.

For More Information

Abstinence Clearinghouse, 1300 Pennsylvania Ave., N.W., Suite 700, Washington, DC 20004; (202) 204-3055; www.abstinence.net. Promotes abstinence education.

Advocates for Youth, 2000 M St., N.W., Suite 750, Washington, DC 20036; (202) 419-1448; www.advocatesforyouth.org. Promotes comprehensive sex education for teens.

The Alan Guttmacher Institute, 120 Wall St., New York, NY 10005; (212) 248-1111; www.agi-usa.org. Research group that tracks and analyzes reproductive issues.

The Institute for Research and Evaluation, 6068 S. Jordan Canal Rd., Salt Lake City, UT 84118; (801) 966-5644; http://instituteresearch.com. Evaluates abstinence and pro-marriage programs.

MTV's "16 and Pregnant," www.mtv.com/shows/16_and_pregnant/season_2/series.jhtml. Web site of this cable TV reality show tracks the lives of several pregnant and parenting teens.

National Abstinence Education Association, 1701 Pennsylvania Ave., N.W., Suite 300, Washington, DC 20006; (202) 248-5420; www.abstinenceassociation.org. Promotes abstinence education through lobbying and public information.

National Campaign to Prevent Teen and Unplanned Pregnancy, 1776 Massachusetts Ave., N.W., Suite 200, Washington, DC 20036; (202) 478-8500; www.thenationalcampaign.org. Advocates of evidence-based programs for pregnancy prevention.

SIECUS (Sexuality and Information Council of the United States), 130 West 42nd St., Suite 350, New York, NY 10036; (212) 819-9770; www.siecus.org. Supports providing complete and accurate information on sexuality to teenagers.

11

Teen Spending

Are Teenagers Learning to Manage Money Wisely?

Pamela M. Prah

Joe Clark Photography

Running back Jerome Bettis of the Pittsburgh Steelers coaches a team of students in a game of "Financial Football" at Pittsburgh's Peabody High School. The animated money-management computer game incorporates lessons from Visa's Practical Money Skills for Life. Experts say teens are spending more than ever before but aren't learning how to use credit wisely.

From *CQ Researcher*, May 26, 2006

Eric Simmons' parents figured that giving him a debit card with a set limit was a good way for him to learn about managing money. So every month, the high school senior in Annandale, Va., gets $300 added to his debit card.

But Eric recently exceeded the limit on his debit card and then racked up hundreds of additional dollars on a credit card his mother got for him and his older sister for gas, school supplies and emergencies. And although Nancy Simmons discourages her son from buying online, he has spent hundreds of dollars on the Internet for shoes, clothes and accessories for his motorized scooter and remote-control car.

Simmons admits she "enables" her son's excessive spending by paying his bills and that she should have set stricter limits with him earlier. "I need to sit down and talk with him," she says.

Eric is part of the so-called Echo Baby Boomer Generation — the more than 75 million Americans, including at least 25 million teens, born between 1977 and 1994. Not since their baby boomer parents were teenagers themselves has a group of teens been so large and so coveted by product-pitching marketers. And they have an unprecedented amount of money to spend on whatever they want, from clothes to iPods to custom ring tones for their cell phones.

Many teens, like Eric, have access to debit and credit cards, a notion that just 20 years ago — when "plastic" was widely restricted to adults — was unimaginable. But critics say the industry has gone too far marketing to younger and younger kids, citing the Hello Kitty debit cards that Legend Credit Inc. launched in 2004 trying to attract the preteen set, often called the "tweens." (*See story, p. 260.*) "Don't think for a second the companies marketing these

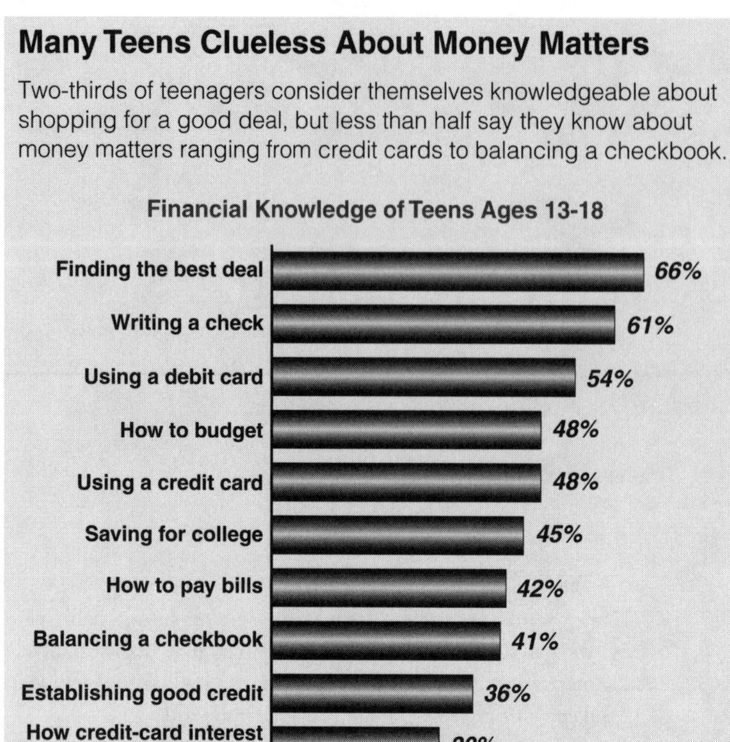

Many Teens Clueless About Money Matters

Two-thirds of teenagers consider themselves knowledgeable about shopping for a good deal, but less than half say they know about money matters ranging from credit cards to balancing a checkbook.

Source: "Teens and Money," Charles Schwab Foundation, April 19, 2006

cards have our children's best interests in mind," wrote *Washington Post* financial columnist Michelle Singletary in a recent column condemning the use of credit cards among young people. "They have one goal — to hook a customer as early in life as possible."[1]

Unfortunately, say consumer advocates, parents aren't teaching their kids how to use credit or debit cards or manage money. The average teen owes about $230, and about one-in-four youths ages 16-18 already is more than $1,000 in the red, says an April 2006 study from the Charles Schwab Foundation, a private, nonprofit organization created by the financial-services company.[2]

Many experts also worry about the long-term ramifications of young people not learning to save and going into debt at an early age. When today's young generation retires, the experts say, many employers will no longer be offering workers pensions, which provide a set amount of money each month. And with Social Security coffers quickly depleting, they say it is crucial for people today to begin saving for their own retirement.[3]

Estimates of how much American teenagers spend vary. Teenage Research Unlimited (TRU), a Chicago-based teen-marketing company, estimates that teens spent $159 billion last year, which is about $20 billion more than the entire 2006-07 Texas state budget.[4] The figure is up from $122 billion in 1997, the first year the company did the survey, says TRU Vice President Michael Wood, but down 6 percent from 2004. Wood attributes the dip to parents being skittish about the economy, making them more tightfisted, and rising gas prices. "Teens who drive are watching an unprecedented amount of their budget flowing directly into their gas tanks," he says. But teens are optimistic about 2006, with nearly half of the teens surveyed (47 percent) saying they think they'll spend more in 2006 than they did last year.

Today's teens are spending more because they have more money at their disposal, says Diane Crispell, executive editor of GfK Roper Consulting in New York, which has provided snapshots of U.S. teen spending habits since 1990 in the *Roper Youth Report.*

Traditionally, teens have received money for doing household chores (37 percent) or from their allowance (29 percent), says Crispell. Katy and Jenny Burgess, 14-year-old twins from Indianapolis, Ind., get most of their spending money from chores. "If we want something, we have to work for it," says eighth-grader Katy, whose family operates a farm.

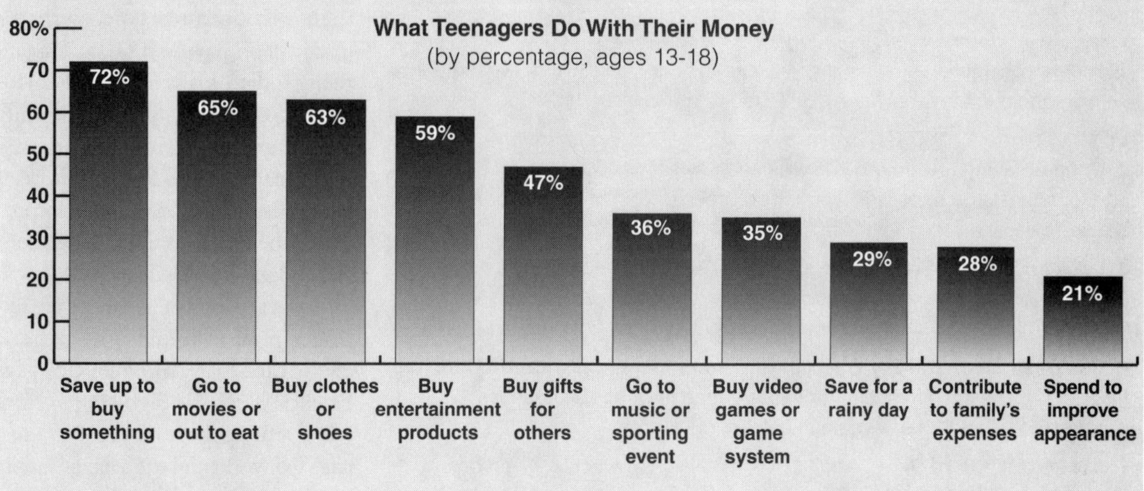

But in recent years a growing number of teens — about one-in-five today, and mainly girls — have been getting spending money simply by asking for it, Crispell says.

"If I need something, I ask for it," says Brittany Guenther, a ninth-grader at Bishop Ireton High School in Alexandria, Va. She typically garners about $50 per shopping spree.

Her friend Liz Guttman, on the other hand, negotiates. "I try to strike a deal; whatever they're willing to give, I take," she says. Both 15-year-olds recently were shopping for clothes — the most common item on a teen girl's shopping list — at Pentagon City Mall, outside Washington.

For boys, food and video games rank high, while CDs and personal-care products are popular among both boys and girls, the Roper survey shows. TRU's Wood says the technology category "has exploded" of late, with more teens buying video games and consoles, cell phones, wireless products and iPods.

Another new wrinkle on the teen-buying scene: Teenagers often don't have to wait until they have the money or their parents take them to the mall — They buy online with credit cards. Today's teen generation is the first to grow up shopping via the Internet.

"Everything has to be instantaneous," says Don Montuori, publisher of *Packaged Facts*, published by MarketResearch.com, a market research firm in New York City.

About 10 percent of teens have credit cards, and nearly twice that number have debit cards, says Wood. Visa USA, which has dubbed this younger set Generation Plastic or Gen P, estimated last year that payments via plastic — including online commerce — now account for about 53 percent of spending among 18- to 24-year-olds.[5]

While teens under 18 must have a parent co-sign for a credit card, there is no minimum age for debit or prepaid cards, explains Rhonda Bentz, vice president, Visa USA. Visa is among the companies that have developed cards especially for young people that parents can load with cash. Another is Payjr, which this summer plans to launch its version of a prepaid spending card exclusively for teens. Payjr President and Chief Executive Officer David Jones says the company is considering calling the card "scrilla," the rap term for money, in order to attract teens.

Financial Tips for Students

A money-management program co-founded by the U.S. Bankruptcy Court in Western New York offers 10 tips on staying out of debt, managing your finances and establishing a good credit rating.

1. Create a Budget: A realistic budget will identify exactly how you are spending your money — including your "needs" vs. your "wants" — and will help you budget the repayment of any debt you incur and how much you can spend on your "wants."

2. Open a Savings Account: You will need savings for both emergencies and for future large expenses. You will go broke relying on high-interest-rate credit-card loans to pay for these.

3. Look for Ways to Save Money: Buying at shopping clubs and with coupons, looking for the cheapest gas price, going to discount movie theaters and utilizing student discounts will help you save money.

4. Use Cash, Debit Card or Checking Account Instead of a Credit Card: People who use cash for their purchases spend less, so use cash if a purchase is under $20 or if you can eat it or drink it.

5. Avoid Credit Card Debt: Credit cards have high interest fees and often lead to late payments and over-limit fees. This means you will pay significantly more for everything you purchase. Remember, if you don't have any extra money in your budget to repay it within a reasonable amount of time with interest, you can't afford the purchase.

6. Pay Your Bills on Time: Paying your bills late, including credit card, rent, telephone, utility and cell-phone bills, hurts your credit rating.

7. Always Pay Debts Off as Quickly as Possible: Research the best credit card for rates and fees, and don't charge anything on it that you can't pay for at the end of the month. If you can't pay your credit card balance off in full, pay at least 10 percent of the balance. Never make just the minimum payment, and stop charging until you have paid off your balance.

8. Minimize Your Student-Loan Debt: Keep it to a minimum. Before choosing a college, ask yourself if the job you are likely to get after college justifies the loan debt you will incur at that institution.

9. Other Things to Avoid: Impulse shopping on the Internet, expensive behaviors like gambling and drugs, opening multiple store charge accounts, more than three-year car loans and pawn shops, rent-to-own and payday loan establishments. Also, don't open credit card accounts to get "free stuff." Those accounts will hurt your credit rating, even if you don't use them.

10. Remember the Consequences of Consumer Debt: Credit card and other consumer debt could hurt your future chances for a job, student loan, admission to graduate school, apartment or car loan. Today, everyone is pulling credit checks and using them to make decisions about your future.

Source: Credit Abuse Resistance Education (CARE), www.careprogram.us

Many teens get their first credit card just as they arrive at college or during their freshman year, and many run up credit card debt on top of their student loans. Some put their tuition on plastic, with the intention of paying it off, and spend their student loans and other financial aid on books, pizzas and daily living expenses. Today's typical undergraduate has four credit cards and owes more than $2,000, according to the Nellie Mae Corp., an education lender in Braintree, Mass.[6]

In fact, parents themselves are setting a poor example. The nation's credit card loan delinquencies have reached a record high, the savings rate is among the lowest in the industrialized world and the average family has $9,000 in credit card debt.[7]

"I don't think a lot of adults should have credit cards, let alone teens," says Dallas Salisbury, chairman of the American Savings Education Council, which sponsors the national "Choose to Save" campaign. Credit cards "lead people to overspend and run up debt."

Unless young people start to save more, "the end result will continue to be inadequate savings, overuse of credit and high rates of personal bankruptcies," says Salisbury who also is president and CEO of the Employee Benefit Research Institute.

About a dozen states now require schools to teach personal finance, but the Bush administration and some members of Congress are pushing for more financial literacy earlier in schools.

As policymakers, educators and parents debate the issues, here are some questions people are asking:

Are teens being taught to manage their money?

Many states today require students to take money-management courses. Seven states — Alabama, Georgia, Idaho, Illinois, Kentucky, New York and Utah — require students to take a personal-finance course before graduating from high school, up from two states in 2002, according to the National Council on Economic Education (NCEE). Nine states require that students be tested on personal finance.[8]

It is unclear, however, whether the courses change spending behavior, says NCEE President and CEO Robert F. Duvall. "We've only just begun to address that," he says.

In addition, the curriculum quality and difficulty of the financial-education requirements varies from state to state. Many of the state mandates are "relatively weak," says Stephen Brobeck, executive director of the Consumer Federation of America. For instance, some of the requirements can be met simply by attending three or four class sessions. Other states lack financial-education classes but cover some of the concepts in math, economics and social-studies classes, says Laura Levine, executive director of the Jump$tart Coalition for Personal Financial Literacy, a group of public and private organizations that promotes development of personal money skills. "Every state is so vastly different" in how it teaches teens to manage money, she says.

John Parfrey, director of the High School Financial Planning Program sponsored by the Colorado-based National Endowment for Financial Education (NEFE), speaks frequently with teachers and students who have participated in NEFE courses in financial planning, budgeting, savings, credit and insurance. Today's teens "have a lot of spending power but not a lot of sophistication about the basics," he says. For instance, they often are surprised to learn how setting aside a small amount when they are young can grow over time through compounding, and that the longer one waits to save, the harder it is to catch up.

"That's a real eye-opener" for teens, he says.

Parfrey says students who have participated in the NEFE financial-planning course appear to have changed the way they save and spend money. For example, three months after completing the course, about 60 percent said they were more focused on buying only things that they really need and trying to save more.[9]

Boston Bar Association

Students from South High School in Worcester, Mass., went to bankruptcy court to hear bankruptcy lawyer M. Ellen Carpenter, above, and Judge Joel B. Rosenthal discuss what happens when people spend beyond their means. The courtroom visit capped a financial-literacy program sponsored by the U.S. Bankruptcy Court for Massachusetts and the Boston Bar Association.

Judge John C. Ninfro II, chief judge of the U.S. Bankruptcy Court for the Western District of New York, has been visiting local schools since 1997, when he realized that many of the people in financial trouble who end up in his courtroom had never received financial-literacy education. "That is still true today," says Ninfro, who in 2002 formed the Credit Abuse Resistance Education (CARE) program (www.careprogram.us), which arranges visits by bankruptcy experts to high schools and colleges in 31 states to help students avoid credit problems.

"Our nation's high-school students are financially illiterate in too many ways, especially about credit cards," Ninfro says. For instance, kids are always shocked to discover that an $80 pair of running shoes can end up costing $120 if they are bought on credit and not quickly paid off in full, he says.

Recent surveys suggest that Scott Murray, a 16-year-old junior at Fairmount Heights High School in Prince George's County, Md., and his friends are typical teenagers when it comes to money matters. Although his mother talks to him about finances, he says he's not sure whether he has a credit or debit card. His friend Chris Grant, also 16 and a student at nearby Largo High School, says he thinks he has a savings account but is not sure. Neither of them is trying to save money.

"Most people I know don't save," says Murray.

Most teens say they recognize the importance of good money habits, including how to shop for deals and write a check, but less than half know how to budget money, use a credit card or save for college, according to the Charles Schwab Foundation's April survey.[10] And while one-third of teens owe money, only half say they are concerned about paying it back, the foundation found.

In the latest Jump$tart Coalition survey, the average high-school senior scored only 52 percent on a test of their knowledge of credit cards, saving and retirement.[11] The results were actually slightly worse than in 1997, when seniors scored 57 — an all-time high. "Our survey is fairly consistent in depicting the insufficient knowledge that young people have about money matters," says Levine.

A 2005 NCEE study gave high-school students an "F" on their understanding of basic financial concepts, such as annual percentage rates, inflation and interest.[12] Most didn't know, for example, that keeping cash in a piggy bank or under the mattress held a greater risk of losing value than investing the money in the stock market or mutual funds.

Many teens enter college without understanding the basics or the long-term consequences of poor money management. Researchers from Ohio State University found, for example, that 45 percent of college freshmen incorrectly thought their parents would be responsible for their credit card debts until age 21, and few were aware that late credit card payments could mean higher interest rates on car loans and mortgages.[13] The Government Accountability Office (GAO) found in 2005 that less than 20 percent of youths ages 18-24 knew their credit history could affect employment.[14]

Linda Sherry, who tracks credit and debit card issues for Consumer Action, a San Francisco-based consumer advocacy group, says many adults — not to mention teens — don't realize that a single late payment can allow a credit card company to impose much higher interest rates on the account. Even worse, some card companies routinely use credit reports to track customers' credit behavior on other credit cards. Here too, a single late payment on another credit card can lead a company to double or triple interest rates on their own card, even if the customer's payments on their card have been paid on time, she says. "People are always shocked" when they learn that, she says, and "most teens don't know about it."

Nancy Simmons says her son Eric thought his debit card simply would not work if his account ran out of money. He didn't realize he was racking up a slew of overdrawn penalties. She says the bank waved all but one $35 late fee after she and her son went in and talked with bank officials, but they made clear the bank wouldn't be as understanding the next time.

Should teens have credit cards?

Do credit cards teach teens about managing money or create the next generation of overspenders? Laura Fisher, a spokeswoman for the American Bankers Association (ABA), says teens can learn important lessons about budgeting and managing their money by using credit cards. They not only help teens establish credit but also give parents a sense of security from knowing their child has enough money during emergencies, she says.

"A secure card with set, low limits is a good way to get started," she says, suggesting a card with a $300 limit, the lowest that many credit card companies and banks offer.

But most card companies don't publicize their lowest-limit cards. When Nan Mead, a spokeswoman for the National Endowment for Financial Education, was shopping for a credit card for her son, she had to specifically ask for a lower limit on the card. "The credit card companies don't advertise that. Parents have to be proactive."

And giving a credit card to a teen is a double-edged sword, she says. A credit card can help develop a teen's credit, but if a parent doesn't provide the proper "context" youths often don't learn the dangers of running up high bills and paying only the minimum amount, she says.

Fisher agrees. "Education is key," she says. "Kids have to understand credit isn't magic money. They have to pay it back."

Banks and credit card companies have kicked off a credit education program that included, for example, 39,000 presentations by ABA members to 1.5 million teens in the past four years as part of the association's "Get Smart About Credit" program, Fisher says.

Pamela Erwin, senior vice president of the Wells Fargo Foundation, says credit cards are a good idea for teens but only if teens receive direction. Otherwise it is akin to handing over the car keys to a teen without any driving lessons. Cards are a way of life, she says, but "whether you are a teen or an adult, you still need a roadmap."

Nearly One-Third of Teenagers Owe Money

Nearly one-third of teens ages 13-18 owe money either to a person or a company (graph at left), and 34 percent of them owe more than $100 (graph at right). On average, older teens (16-18) owe $351 while younger teens (13-15) owe $84.

Amounts Owed by Teenagers Ages 13-18
(by percentage of teens in each category)

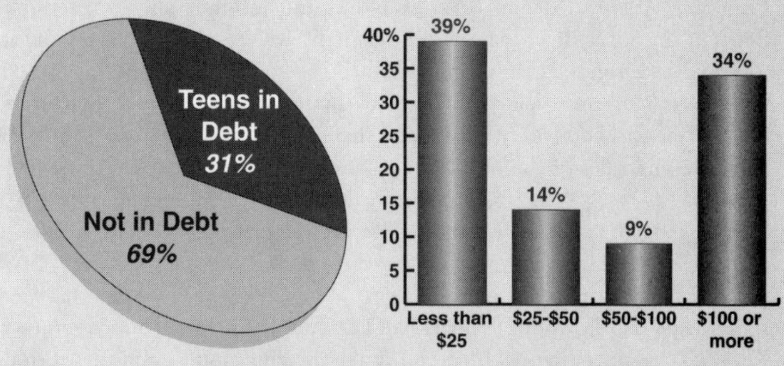

Source: "Teens and Money," Charles Schwab Foundation, April 19, 2006

No federal agency tracks how many teens have credit cards, and estimates from lenders and others vary widely, but as teens get older, clearly more get plastic. Only 5 percent of 13- to 14-year-olds have their own credit cards; by age 17, the percentage climbs to 9.8 percent and then doubles to 19.6 percent for teens 18 and older, according to an April poll by Junior Achievement, a Colorado organization that teaches young people about business.[15]

The poll found that more than 15 percent of teens with credit cards make only the minimum payment, which some teens don't realize means taking months or years longer to pay off the debt. The report notes it would take a teen making minimum payments more than nine years and almost $2,000 in interest fees to pay off a credit card with a $1,000 balance and 18 percent interest rate.

Teens who want and get their own credit card should also then have to pay the balance, says Mead. "Otherwise, they see no consequence of overspending, and that can lead to significant problems down the line."

"We do not encourage parents to give their children credit cards," says Brobeck of the Consumer Federation of America. The argument that they can help teens learn to handle money doesn't hold water, he says, because "most parents bail out their children, and the children don't learn the responsibility" of having and using credit cards.

Levine of the Jump$tart Coalition says there is no magic age for giving a teen a credit card; it depends on a teen's level of maturity. "There are a lot of young adults not mature enough to handle a credit card," she says.

Some consumer advocates argue that the credit card industry is more interested in roping in new customers at an early age than in teaching good financial skills.

Many teens get their first credit card as they head off to college. The latest Nellie Mae survey found that of the 76 percent of undergraduates in 2004 who had their own credit cards, 43 percent got it during their freshman year, and less than a quarter had the card before entering college.[16]

Marie O'Malley, vice president of marketing for Nellie Mae, said undergraduates are becoming more responsible in their use of credit. Five years ago, typical undergraduates owed nearly $3,000 on their credit cards; today it's just over $2,000, according to Nellie Mae. "The message of using credit responsibly is getting out," says O'Malley. Only 4 percent of students with credit cards said their parents paid their card bills, the survey found.[17]

But data from the federal government suggest many more parents are bailing out their kids' card debts. Jacqueline King, director of the American Council on Education's Center for Policy Analysis, says Department of Education data show that 56 percent of undergraduates had a credit card during the 2003-2004 school year, and 25 percent said parents helped pay the bill. The students polled included those at four-year universities as well as community and trade schools.

Salisbury of the American Savings Education Council says teens and credit cards are not a good mix. "A credit card doesn't teach you about money. It doesn't develop a sense of living within your means," he says. When he was in college, he says, he had $15 for food each week, "and when that cash was gone, it was gone." With credit cards, however, while there is a point in which card companies

Rappers, Contests Tout Wise Spending

In an effort to grab teenagers' attention, financial-literacy advocates are using online games, contests and celebrities to promote wise spending habits.

Visa USA, for instance, has recruited National Football League players — including the Denver Broncos' Jake Plummer, Atlanta Falcons' Warrick Dunn and Jerome Bettis of the Super Bowl champion Pittsburgh Steelers — to help get teenagers' attention. They visited classrooms in 17 cities last season to play an animated computer game called "Financial Football" with students that combines the structure and rules of the NFL with financial-education questions.[1]

Visa also offers two online games — "Smart Money Quiz Show" and "Road Trip to Savings" — geared to young, cyber-savvy teens (www.practicalmoneyskills.com).

Outside the classroom, rappers like LL Cool J, Alicia Keys and Nas plug financial literacy through the Hip-Hop Summit Action Network (HSAN), created by hip-hop pioneer Russell Simmons and veteran civil rights activist Benjamin Chavis Muhammad. The network in March kicked off the Hip-Hop Summit on Financial Empowerment's "Get Your Money Right" nationwide tour in Detroit, followed by shows in New York in April. The tour planned to open in Miami Gardens, Fla., in May where rappers Remy Ma, MC Lyte, Pitbull and Doug E. Fresh were scheduled to join experts from Chrysler Financial in urging fans to be financially responsible. Other hip-hop artists will be on hand this fall when the tour moves to Atlanta, Los Angeles and Dallas.

"The biggest misconception probably comes from the hip-hop community itself . . . that the money lasts forever," LL Cool J said at the New York summit. "You have to do the right thing with it."[2] HSAN offers a "Get Your Money Right" workbook on its Web site (http://hsan.org/).

A team of seniors from Blackman High School in Murfreesboro, Tenn., won a free trip to Washington, D.C., by turning a hypothetical $100,000 into $150,263 over 10 weeks as part of the "Capitol Hill Stock Market Game Challenge." Students nationwide played The Stock Market Game (www.stockmarketgame.org) developed by the Foundation for Investor Education. Teachers have used the game in classrooms since 1977 to teach young people about saving and investing and how the capital markets work.

Other financial companies and nonprofits offer various games and materials online, but the information is often difficult to find unless teens and parents know where to look. Here are links to some online resources:

- **Merrill Lynch** — Since launching its free "Investing Pays Off" program in 2001, the big financial-services

will stop approving purchases, that limit is typically thousands of dollars.

Janet Bodnar, a columnist for *Kiplinger's Personal Finance* magazine and author of *Raising Money Smart Kids*, advocates teaching money management a step at a time, first with cash, then with a checking account linked to a debit card and finally a credit card.

"Giving kids credit cards too early does more harm than good," she warned recently.[18]

Should teens be given prepaid credit cards?

Teens who don't have their own credit cards and can't use their parents' can still make purchases using prepaid cards, which some financial experts say teach teens how to manage their money. But critics say that many of these products come with high hidden fees.

Prepaid cards differ from regular credit or debit cards because they contain a set amount. Special prepaid cards for teens enable parents to determine how much money is on the card, track the teen's spending at anytime and "reload" the card with additional funds online or through an 800 number.

Bentz of Visa USA says parents love the prepaid cards because they teach their teens how to manage money, and teens love them because they give teens freedom, make them feel like adults and are easy to use for online purchases. Visa launched the program after parents asked for an alternative to other cards and because the company recognized that "the teen market is significant," says Bentz.

Visa estimates that "hundreds of thousands" of teens use the "Visa Buxx Cash Card," a prepaid card designed specifically for teens, says Bentz, who tracks teen issues for Visa.

But Sherry of Consumer Action prefers debit cards linked to a teen's checking account, because many prepaid products come with unusually high transaction fees or hidden charges. "I don't like them at all," she says.

company estimates it has provided its curriculum, which is broken down into courses for various age groups, to at least 1 million students, including many who are home-schooled. The company also has teamed up with "Sesame Street's" Elmo to teach younger children about the basics of saving, spending and planning. (www.ml.com/philanthropy/ipo/volunteer/curriculumletter.html).

- **National Endowment for Financial Education** — The nonprofit's online games and puzzles can be found at www.nefe.org/hsfppportal/index.html.
- **Wells Fargo** — The bank's "Hands on Banking" Web site (www.handsonbanking.org) has received 16 million visitors since it was launched in January 2004; at least 10 percent of the visitors clicked on the Spanish version. The company also has distributed more than 400,000 CDs and trained more than 5,000 Wells Fargo volunteers to assist in money-skill instruction for age groups ranging from fourth grade to adulthood.
- **U.S. Treasury Department** — The federal agency says it will soon add a youth link to its www.mymoney.gov Web site, which provides personal-finance information, including how to choose and use credit cards, get out of debt, protect credit records, start a savings-and-investment plan and understand Social Security benefits. In 2001 the government developed the Money Smart financial education program (www.fdic.gov/consumers/consumer/moneysmart/index.html), endorsed last year by the National School Boards Association and available in six languages.

Getty Images/Paul Hawthorne

Rapper Doug E. Fresh urges youths to be financially responsible.

[1] Visa/NFL press release, Dec. 6, 2005; www.practicalmoneyskills.com./english/presscenter/releases/120605.php.

[2] "Rappers urge financial responsibility," The Associated Press, April 23, 2006, and statement from Hip-Hop Summit Action Network at http://hsan.org/.

Bentz says the terms of using a Buxx Cash Card vary among the five banks that issue the cards. "We encourage parents to do the research," she says. Based on the banks' online disclosure notices, National City Visa Buxx cards have a $15 annual fee, a $1 fee for each ATM withdrawal and a $2.50 charge for loading the card if the money comes from a bank other than National City. Sandy Spring Bank's Visa Buxx card has a monthly service fee of $2, a $1 "inactivity fee" if the card is not used and a $15 penalty for overdrafts. Wachovia has a $12 one-time account-setup fee and a $1.50 charge if the teen withdraws cash from an ATM more than twice a month.

In July, Payjr plans to launch its version of a prepaid spending card that the company thinks may boost teen online shopping. "Until now, most teen spending was always done at the mall," says CEO Jones. Unlike other prepaid cards, he says, Payjr won't have excessive penalties if a teen spends more money than is in the account. "That is not teaching kids how to manage money, but taking advantage of them. We won't have abusive fees."

The company is still working on the details for its cards but says it envisions teaming up with MTV, Nickelodeon, Yahoo, Abercrombie & Fitch and other companies that Jones says are popular among teens. They're even considering allowing teens to upload their own photos and design their own cards. Payjr already offers a free online program that allows parents to manage their children's chores and allowances online, using instant messaging, e-mail and text messaging, for example, to notify teens when money has been deposited.

NEFE's Mead says prepaid cards can be a great way for parents to teach teens about fiscal responsibility, particularly if it is their first experience with "plastic." Teens can learn how to pace themselves and make sure they don't run

CHRONOLOGY

1940s-90s *Teenagers in the 1950s become the first generation to show economic and cultural clout. Over the decades, music, clothes and snacks top the list of "must-haves" for teens.*

1941 The word "teenager" is first cited in an article in *Popular Science* magazine to describe an age group that would soon became of keen interest to marketers.

1949 The Diners' Club card — the first universal credit card — is introduced, aimed at middle-class American adults.

1965 A survey by *Seventeen* indicates teenage girls spend $450 million a year for cosmetics and toiletries.

1980 Teenage shoppers pump $39 billion into the U.S. economy.

1990s *Credit companies begin to drop the requirement that anyone under 21 must have an adult co-signer to get a credit card. Teens begin getting their own cards.*

March 10, 1994 Aggressive marketing to college students by credit card companies prompts a House Banking, Finance and Urban Affairs panel to hold hearings on "kiddie" credit cards.

May 1997 The newly formed Jump$tart Coalition for Personal Finance Literacy tests high-school seniors, who correctly answer only 57 percent of financial questions. The coalition finds no improvement in students' scores over the next nine years.

June 1999 A controversial study by the Consumer Federation of America linking college students' debt with suicides draws widespread attention.

2000s *Rising levels of personal bankruptcies and concerns about easy access to credit cards prompt new education campaigns.*

2001 Treasury Department develops money-based math curriculum for use by schools to teach young people about personal finance.

May 2002 Nearly a third of youths ages 12-17 admit to feeling pressure to buy clothes and other products because their friends have them.

April 2003 Congress declares April as Financial Literacy Month.

December 2003 President George W. Bush signs the Fair and Accurate Credit Transactions Act into law, mandating creation of a Web site, toll-free hotline and national financial-literacy strategy.

October 2004 Treasury Department's Financial Literacy and Education Commission launches www.mymoney.gov and 1-888-mymoney to provide the public with information on personal-finance matters. . . . Hello Kitty debit cards are unveiled in a bid to attract preteens.

April 2005 President Bush signs Bankruptcy Abuse Prevention and Consumer Protection Act into law, which requires anyone filing for bankruptcy to get credit counseling. It also urges states to develop financial-literacy programs for elementary and secondary schools . . . . National Council on Economic Education (NCEE) gives high-school students an "F" grade for their poor understanding of basic financial concepts.

January 2006 For the first time since the Great Depression, Americans' personal-savings rate dips below zero into negative territory.

April 2006 Bush administration unveils National Strategy for Financial Literacy, a blueprint for improving Americans' understanding of issues such as credit management, retirement savings and home ownership.

May 2006 U.S. Senate Banking Committee holds hearing on financial literacy. Some senators express concern that the Bush administration's blueprint for financial literacy fails to provide a coherent strategy for getting more Americans financially savvy. Federal Reserve Chairman Ben Bernanke calls financial literacy vital for consumers and U.S. financial markets. He also promises to encourage banks that offer credit cards to include on consumers' monthly statements how many months or years it would take to pay off the full balance if a consumer only makes the minimum payment, a common practice for young people . . . . Securities and Exchange Commission launches podcasts to teach young people about investing and stocks on its Web site (www.sec.gov/investor).

out of money. And if the teen is responsible, she argues, buying online with a debit card is not much different from buying in a store. But if the parent is simply "pouring money into the debit account" without the teen tracking expenses or paying for it, then the lesson is lost.

Some critics, however, say allowing teens to buy online with plastic encourages overspending.

Clearly, teens today are not reluctant to purchase online, whether it's with their own credit card, their parents' card or a prepaid card. The April Junior Achievement survey found that nearly 60 percent of teens who have their own credit cards had bought items online with their cards.[19] Teenage Research Unlimited found that 42 percent of teens have made an online purchase, most commonly using their parents' credit cards. And 46 percent used other payment methods, such as prepaid cards and PayPal, an affiliate of eBay that lets anyone with an e-mail address send and receive online payments using a credit card or bank account.

Sherry says parents need to discuss the pros and cons of shopping at the mall vs. on the Internet and to make sure teens are aware of the penalties if they overspend. Levine of Jump$tart agrees. "It's not shopping online that is a problem, it's when it's unsupervised," she says. A debit card is a great tool for shopping online, "but with any tool, parental supervision and involvement are key."

BACKGROUND

Teen Market Emerges

While references to "teens" have been around for centuries, the word "teenager" was first cited in a 1941 article in *Popular Science* magazine to describe an age group that quickly became of keen interest to marketers.[20]

Until the Great Depression, many young Americans worked instead of attending high school. The Depression forced young Americans into schools so farm and factory jobs could go to adults. This shift created the first "teenage" generation.

"Teenagers occupy a special place in American life," journalist Thomas Hine writes in *The Rise & Fall of the American Teenager.* "They are envied and sold to, studied and deplored. . . . Some see these young people as barbarians at the gates, and others look forward greedily to large numbers of new consumers."[21]

Teen power began to grow in the 1950s — both culturally and economically — when marketers feared that adult demand for big-ticket items like cars, washing machines and other goods, which had been pent up during World War II, had been met and was coming to an end. But clean-cut '50s-era teenage girls clad in bobbysocks and poodle skirts were eager to buy, kicking off a teen spending spree.

Journalist Landon Y. Jones contends that youths born during the postwar baby boom were the "first generation of children to be isolated by Madison Avenue as an identifiable market. . . . From the cradle, the baby boomers [were] surrounded by products created especially for them."[22]

It didn't take long for advertisers to notice. Ever since, they have been trying to woo the 13-19 set, the vast group that has determined what is popular in music, movies, snack food and clothing — from the "flower children" of the 1960s to the disco and punk cultures of the '70s and '80s to rap of the '90s.[23]

Ad companies have tried various tactics to lure teens to spend, including using sex. But in the 1980s they began to pitch their appeal to younger markets, including the controversial Calvin Klein jean ads in 1980 featuring 15-year-old actress and model Brooke Shields, asking: "What comes between me and my Calvins? Nothing."[24]

That year teenage shoppers pumped an estimated $39 billion into the U.S. economy, according to a Rand Youth Poll, which also found that nearly 70 percent of young people surveyed said they spent money on things they later realized they did not want.[25] Calvin Klein, meanwhile, continued to push the envelope with controversial, sex-oriented ads.

Banking Deregulation

Deregulation of the banking industry in the 1980s and the prosperity of the '90s ushered in new ways for teens to spend money.[26] At the same time, credit card companies in the early 1990s dropped the requirement that youths under 21 needed a co-signer to get a credit card, explains Robert Manning, a finance professor at the Rochester Institute of Technology, in his 2000 book *Credit Card Nation.*[27]

When they were introduced in the 1950s, credit cards were typically geared for the middle class and — until the late 1970s — state usury laws prevented banks from charging excessive interest on the accounts. A 1978 U.S Supreme Court decision and banking deregulation in the 1980s, however, changed all that, allowing the banks to

How Marketers Woo Tweenagers

Audrey Sorensen celebrated her birthday with her "tween" friends, getting the Tutti-Frutti Manicure Delight at the CapeCodder Resort's spa in Hyannis, Mass. Meanwhile, in Washington, D.C., two 11-year-olds received prepaid credit cards for their birthdays.[1]

Some 29 million 8- to 12-year-olds — the so-called tweens — have emerged as a potentially lucrative consumer group that marketers are aggressively wooing. But critics worry the trend is encouraging young children to grow up too fast.

The tween market is far from being monolithic, says Don Montuori, publisher of *Packaged Facts*, published by Market Research.com, a market research firm in New York City. "There are nuanced differences," he says. He estimates that today's tween market includes 16.4 million 8-to-11-year-olds and nearly 13 million 12-to-14-year-olds and that their buying power totals $39 billion. But regardless of their chronological age, "everyone is trying to 'age up,' " he says. "The 12-year-olds want to be 14, and the 16-year-olds want to be 21."

Tweens generally have less money ($10 a week) than their older teenage siblings ($30), according to the 2005 *Roper Youth Market* report, published by GfK Roper Consulting. The 8-to-12-year-old set is more likely to plan for their "teen-type" purchases, such as video games for boys and clothing for girls, while buying snack foods is still the most popular way tweens spend their money on impulse, according to the report.[2]

According to Montuori's *Market Research* report, tweens say they get to choose "some or most" of the movies they see, the toys and dolls they buy, the brands of jeans and sneakers they wear and the fast-food restaurants they frequent.[3] "And when it comes to providing leeway to their kids as consumers, parents generally trust girls more than they do boys," Montuori says.

Tweens also spend more time playing video games and wanting the various accessories that go with them, such as lights, magnifiers, vibrating buttons, speakers, headphones and carrying cases. Kids in the 8-to-10-year-old age group spend about an hour and 25 minutes every day playing a video or computer game, while the slightly older 11-to-14-year-olds spend only an hour and nine minutes, according to a March 2005 Kaiser Family Foundation study.[4] Older teens ages 15-18 spend less than an hour playing video games.

Michele Stockwell, director of social and family policy for the Progressive Policy Institute, a liberal think tank, says marketers most often exploit tweens' strong desire to be older. Tween girls can now buy padded push-up bras, midriff-baring tops and high-heeled shoes in their sizes, she writes in a 2005 paper, "Childhood for Sale: Consumer Culture's Bid for Our Kids."[5]

By the time they're 12, both boys and girls are big consumers of hair-styling products, moisturizers and cologne to help them look and feel older. Most girls 12-14 are already using lipstick and lip-gloss (86 percent), nail polish (82 percent), eyebrow pencils (66 percent), eye shadow (80 percent) and mascara (53 percent), according to Marketresearch.com. In Hyannis, CapeCodder owner Deb Catania said she started offering manicure and spa treatments for tweens and teens because there was a demand.[6]

Tweens also are paying big bucks to redecorate their bedrooms, fueled in part, experts say, by the popularity of home-makeover TV shows. The average parent spent $76 over a three-month period on room decor and accessories for their tweenaged child, according to the New York market research firm NPD Group.[7] Jumping on the tween room-makeover bandwagon, movie stars Mary-Kate and Ashley Olsen — who have been acting since they were infants — now offer their own line of furniture and rugs.

Tweens also have clear brand preferences. "Today's tweens are the most brand-conscious generation in

charge high interest rates.[28] The high court followed up in 1996 with another decision lifting restrictions on the amount of late fees a card company could charge.[29]

Manning and other critics say the rulings encouraged card companies to specifically seek out high-risk, low-income customers, such as college students. Some companies charged interest rates as high as 30 percent to cover the risk of giving cards to young customers with little income or credit history. The campaigns often included offers of free gifts for college students and showed up unsolicited in their campus mailboxes.

The aggressive marketing to college students prompted Rep. Joseph P. Kennedy II, D-Mass., in 1994 to ask the House Subcommittee on Consumer Credit to hold hearings history," writes Juliet B. Schor, a sociology professor at Boston College, in her 2004 book *Born to Buy: The Commercialized Child and the New Consumer Culture.*[8] When 8-to-14-year-olds ask for something, more than 90 percent of their requests include a particular brand, according to Schor.

Marketers have discovered they must go where the kids are in order to tap into the tween market. Television outlets such as Viacom's Nickelodeon and Time Warner's Cartoon Network are trying to reach tweens with ads at theme parks, on Web sites and in magazines such as *CosmoGirl* and *Teen People.* "If we are really going to be a part of kids' lives, we've got to be with them wherever they go," a Nickelodeon executive told *Advertising Age* last year.[9]

Marketers say they must expand into non-traditional media because 60 percent of 12-to-14-year-olds say they fast-forward or skip commercials whenever possible. This indifference to traditional media requires new tactics, says Montuori, such as e-mail marketing, cell phone text-messaging, mall tours and Web-based sweepstakes. Data also suggest movie theaters are an effective way to reach this market: More than 40 percent of young teens say they notice ads when they are in the theater, according to Marketresearch.com.

Stockwell warns of the "unwelcome and unhealthy consequences for the children and families on the receiving end of all that marketing and consumerism."[10] Youths as young as 11 no longer consider themselves "children," according to Media Awareness Network, a Canadian nonprofit that says the Toy Manufacturers of America have changed their target market of birth to 14, to birth to 10 years of age.[11] Twenty years ago, the publisher of *Seventeen* magazine said its target audience was 16 years old, but now it caters to 11- and 12-year-olds.[12]

Schor says that too much consumerism at a young age can lead to major problems, including depression, anxiety and low self-esteem. "Day by day, marketers are growing bolder," she says, and year by year, "the harmful effects" mount.

Getty Images/Paul J. Richards

Youngsters take a dance lesson at Club Libby Lu at the Tysons Corner Mall in McLean, Va.

[1] Marie Ewald, "Facials for 13-year-olds? Spas target teens," *The Christian Science Monitor*, May 14, 2004; and Michelle Singletary, "Credit Cards for Kids? Not in My House," *The Washington Post*, April 2, 2006, p. F1.

[2] "Roper Youth Report," GfK Roper Consulting, September 2005.

[3] "The U.S. Tween Market," *Packaged Facts*, MarketResearch.com, May 2005.

[4] "Generation M: Media in the Lives of 8-18-Year-Olds," Kaiser Family Foundation, 2005; www.kff.org/entmedia/7251.cfm

[5] Michelle Stockwell, "Childhood for Sale: Consumer Culture's Bid for Our Kids," Progressive Policy Institute, August 2005.

[6] Ewald, *op. cit.*

[7] Erin Clark, "What a Tween Wants . . . Now," *Children's Business*, April 1, 2004.

[8] Juliet B. Schor, *Born to Buy: The Commercialized Child and the New Consumer Culture* (2004), p. 25.

[9] *Packaged Facts, op. cit.*

[10] Stockwell, *op. cit.*

[11] www.media-awareness.ca/english/parents/marketing/issues_teens_marketing.cfm.

[12] Robin Rauzi, "The Teen Factor: Today's Media-Savvy Youths Influence What Others are Saying and Hearing," *Los Angeles Times*, June 9, 1998, p. F1.

on "kiddie" credit cards. Officials from MasterCard and Visa defended their practices and detailed various programs they had instituted to educate young consumers.

"College students are adults and are treated as such by the bankcard industry," said Visa Senior Vice President and General Counsel Paul Allen, noting the average student used a credit card responsibly.[30]

Some of those students, however, were running up staggering debts with heartbreaking consequences. A 1999 study conducted by Manning and the Consumer Federation of America linked college students' suicides with their anxiety over high credit card debt, drawing widespread attention from the media and policymakers.[31] Among the students was Mitzi Pool, an 18-year-old University of

Oklahoma freshman who hanged herself after calling her mother and expressing remorse about losing her part-time job and maxing out three credit cards.[32]

In 2001, Iowa Attorney General Tom Miller lamented that "more and more students are slipping into high credit card debt with very serious long-term consequences" and quoted an administrator at Indiana University who said, "We lose more students to credit card debt than to academic failure."[33]

Between 1999 and 2001, at least 24 states considered — but only Arkansas and Louisiana approved — legislation to either study the effects of credit cards on college students or to limit credit card solicitation at institutions of higher education.[34]

The American Council on Education's King says that in the 1990s many parents were surprised their college-age students could get credit cards without their signatures and didn't know their kids were running up debt. Now, she says, some colleges ban credit card solicitation on campus, while others include financial-literacy information during orientation with freshmen and their parents.

Financial Literacy

Although Congress held several hearings in the 1990s on marketing credit cards to college students, it enacted no new laws. Sen. Christopher Dodd, D-Conn., a member of the Senate Banking Committee and a frequent critic of the credit card industry, has blamed the "very, very powerful" industry for blocking changes, including his proposal requiring anyone under 21 to prove they have the financial capacity to pay or have a parent co-sign when applying for a credit card.

"We've lost that every time I've offered it," Dodd said in a 2004 Public Broadcasting Service report, "Secret History of the Credit Card."[35]

In the early 2000s, however, growing concern prompted many banks and credit card companies to launch their own public-education campaigns to improve financial literacy. Many now offer free financial-literacy curricula for schools and online games (*see p. 256*).

The dot-com crash and the Sept. 11, 2001, terrorist attacks quickly ended the good times of the 1990s. But despite a recession, consumers — including teens — continued to buy, and often it was on credit. Rising levels of bankruptcies, including a troubling number of people under 25, and identity theft through credit cards prompted Congress in the 2000s to pass legislation calling for new efforts to teach young people about managing money.

The Fair and Accurate Credit Transaction Act of 2003 (FACTA), which primarily aimed to help consumers fight identity theft, also mandated creation of a Web site and a toll-free hotline directing consumers to personal-finance resources and a national financial-literacy strategy.

Congress also passed a resolution that year marking April as Financial Literacy Month, a move spearheaded by Reps. Rubén Hinojosa, D-Texas, and Judy Biggert R-Ill., and Sen. Daniel Akaka, D-Hawaii.

Two years later, the Bankruptcy Abuse Prevention and Consumer Protection Act of 2005 required that anyone filing for bankruptcy receive credit counseling and urged states to develop financial-literacy programs for elementary and secondary schools.

Akaka also added a provision to the Bush administration's landmark No Child Left Behind law setting aside $1.5 million to promote economic and financial literacy.[36] The National Council on Economic Education, which won the grants during the program's first two years, has provided subgrants to hundreds of local groups to bolster financial-literacy education.

CURRENT SITUATION

Wooing Youngsters

Politicians, business leaders, consumer groups and even pro football players and rappers are ramping up efforts to encourage teens to save and to spend their money wisely. But they are competing against a barrage of ads targeting teens as well as their parents, who are racking up billions in debt themselves.

"We have a long way to go," says Rep. Hinojosa, who frequently talks to parents and young people on money matters as co-founder and current co-chair of the House Financial and Economic Literacy Caucus.

Today's teens spend so much because they have been bombarded with ads to buy nearly since birth, say experts. The advertising industry spent $100 million pitching products to teens and kids in 1983, primarily through TV ads. But today, 150 times as much — $15 billion — is spent wooing young customers, according to a 2006 report from the Center for a New American Dream, a coalition of nonprofits that "helps Americans consume responsibly to protect the environment, enhance quality of life and promote social justice."[37]

Marketers today not only use TV and radio but also the Internet and the classroom to pitch their products — ranging from soft drinks and junk food to computers — to teens.[38] The Channel One television network, for example, provides video equipment to schools if classes watch daily news broadcasts liberally punctuated by promotional materials and commercials.[39]

"Contemporary American tweens and teens have emerged as the most brand-oriented, consumer-involved and materialistic generation in history," writes Juliet B. Schor, a sociology professor at Boston College, in her 2004 book *Born to Buy: The Commercialized Child and the New Consumer Culture.*[40] (*See sidebar, p. 260.*)

The perpetual advertising adds to teens' pressure to buy more things, says the Center for a New American Dream, which along with the World Wildlife Fund launched the "Be, Live, Buy Different" campaign calling on kids to be socially aware consumers. According to a 2002 poll conducted by the center, nearly a third of teens between ages 12 and 17 admitted to feeling pressure to buy things like clothes, shoes and CDs just because their friends had them, and more than half said they bought certain products to make them feel better about themselves.[41]

The center also found that kids asked for things, on average, nine times before they parents finally gave in. "As a result of unprecedented levels of advertising and marketing aimed at kids, our children feel intense pressure to try to bolster their sense of self-esteem at the mall, and they will go to incredible lengths to get their parents to give in," said Executive Director Betsy Taylor.[42]

Apparently, however, parents often give in to their kids' demands because they enjoy the products as much as their children, according a recent poll. This is a shift from generations past when parents and teens clashed over clothes and culture, said Yankelovich Inc., a marketing research firm, in its latest *Youth Monitor.*[43] Nearly 3-in-4 parents said they and their child had a lot in common when it comes to things they like to do and buy, ranging from the latest camera phones and iPods to blockbuster hits such as "Shrek 2."

"We have to remember that today's parents are, to a significant degree, the MTV, original 'Star Wars,' 'Star Search' generation," Yankelovich said. "So in some respects, the ruling pop culture of their youth is frequently echoed in today's pop culture."[44]

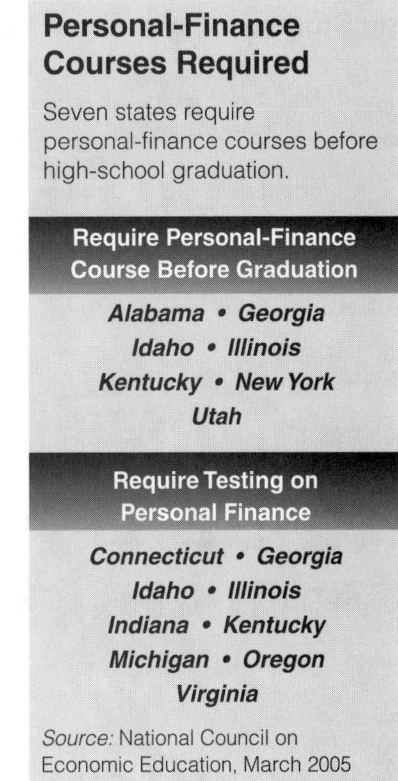

Personal-Finance Courses Required

Seven states require personal-finance courses before high-school graduation.

Require Personal-Finance Course Before Graduation

Alabama • Georgia
Idaho • Illinois
Kentucky • New York
Utah

Require Testing on Personal Finance

Connecticut • Georgia
Idaho • Illinois
Indiana • Kentucky
Michigan • Oregon
Virginia

Source: National Council on Economic Education, March 2005

National Strategy

While admitting that times have changed, Rep. Hinojosa wishes more parents emulated his own father when it comes to teaching money skills. As a 10-year-old growing up after World War II, Hinojosa was required to sock away a portion of his allowance and earnings into his piggy bank. When he earned $200, his father took him to the bank and opened a savings account. Hinojosa's own children got savings accounts when they were 12 and began investing in the stock market at 14.

"Young people can be trained to save early, and that continues through adulthood," he says.

But not enough teens and their parents are getting the message. "Most of our children haven't yet grasped the most basic financial and economic concepts that will enable them to prepare for their future," said Rep. Biggert, the other caucus co-chair, after the House approved a resolution

College Students Favor Debit Cards

Debit card use among college students surpassed credit cards and ATM cards in 2003. Today nearly three-quarters of college students use debit cards while less than half use credit cards.

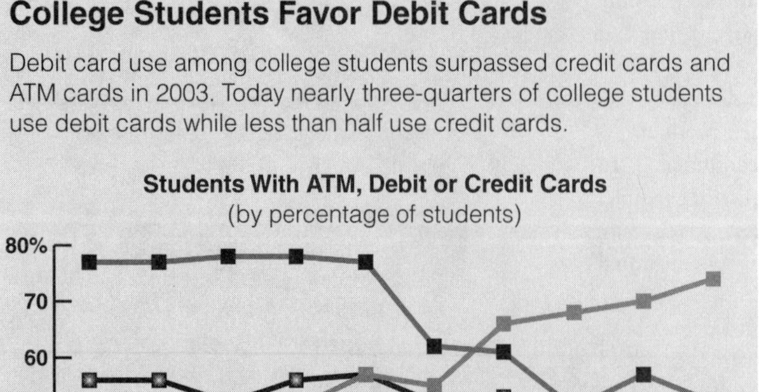

Source: Student Monitor LLC, 2006

for the third-straight year marking April as Financial Literacy Month.[45] As the leading congressional advocates for financial education, Biggert, Hinojosa and Akaka hosted a financial-literacy fair on Capitol Hill on April 25.

The Bush administration is also promoting financial literacy and trying to determine what works in the classroom, says Dan Iannicola, Jr., deputy assistant Treasury secretary for financial education, who participated in the department's recent 15-city tour touting Financial Literacy Month. Iannicola is surprised that so few young people seem to understand the consequences of using plastic, such as finance charges, compounding interest and fees. They also seem unaware that someone is watching how they use credit cards, and that their history shows up on a credit report. "I liken [credit reports] to a grade point average," a concept that students understand, he says.

He recently returned from Chicago with U.S. Treasurer Anna Escobedo Cabral, who was publicizing the National Strategy for Financial Literacy, a blueprint for improving Americans' understanding of credit management, retirement savings and home ownership.[46] The strategy describes programs the administration hopes communities will institute, including a money-based math curriculum developed by the Treasury Department in 2001 (www.publicdebt.treas.gov/mar/marmoneymath.htm) and a report on how schools can integrate financial education into their curricula (www.treasury.gov/financialeducation). The strategy also highlights programs that teach financial education to college freshmen, high-school dropouts seeking their GEDs and male juveniles in correctional facilities.

The 159-page strategy was developed by the Financial Literacy and Education Commission, made up of 20 federal agencies and headed by the Treasury Department, which was mandated by the Fair and Accurate Credit Transaction Act of 2003. By the end of this year, Iannicola expects to begin airing public-service announcements on credit literacy, another requirement of the law, which also mandated creation of a Web site (www.mymoney.gov) and toll-free hotline (1-888-mymoney).

Hinojosa and Biggert say the commission's report is a good start but doesn't go far enough. Biggert wants the commission expanded to include private-sector representatives; Hinojosa wants a hearing on the national strategy.

During a hearing on financial literacy held by the Senate Banking Committee on May 23, several senators expressed concern that the commission's report merely showcased some "best practices" but failed to provide a strategy to make more Americans financially literate. "The report is useful . . . but we need to do more," agreed Federal Reserve Chairman Ben S. Bernanke, who also is a member of the Financial Literacy and Education Commission. The Fed kicked off its "There's a Lot to Learn About Money" campaign in 2003 and provides information on personal finance, including resources for teachers, on its Web site (www.federalreserveeducation.org).

Sen. Richard Shelby, R-Ala., the committee's chairman, saying he was worried that young people were getting mired in credit card debt because they only pay the minimum amount listed on their statement, wondered if legislation was needed. Bernanke said the Fed was working on "guidance" to persuade banks that offer credit cards to include on each bill how many months or years it

AT ISSUE

Do credit card companies market too aggressively to youths?

YES

Travis B. Plunkett
Legislative Director, Consumer Federation of America

Written for *CQ Researcher*, May 2006

Many credit card issuers have targeted the least sophisticated and riskiest consumers in recent years, including young people, and encouraged them to run up high, often unsustainable levels of debt. This practice has proven to be very profitable for many credit card issuers, but it can have devastating consequences for consumers.

Starting in the early 1990s, card issuers targeted massive marketing efforts at college campuses across the country, resulting in a sharp growth in credit card debt among college-age and younger Americans. As a result, Americans under age 35 continue to show more signs of trouble managing credit card debt than any other age group.

Between the mid-1990s and 2004, the amount of credit card debt held by students graduating from college more than doubled, to $3,262. Americans under 35 are less likely to pay off their card balances every month than average Americans. They are paying more for debt obligations than in the past and are increasingly likely to pay more than 40 percent of their incomes on credit card debt.

Not surprisingly, more young Americans are declaring bankruptcy than in the past. Moreover, there is increasing evidence that credit card companies are now targeting high-school students with card offers. They are also marketing branded debit cards to adolescents, in part to encourage these young consumers to use similarly branded credit cards when they are older.

Young people are also financially vulnerable to the questionable pricing and business practices adopted by issuers to increase the profitability of lending to riskier customers. These abusive practices include "universal default," in which a consumer must suddenly pay a sharply higher interest rate on their outstanding balance with one credit card company because of a minor problem with another creditor.

Many creditors have also significantly increased their penalty fees, even for small transgressions like a payment that is made only a few hours late. Until recently, issuers also decreased the size of minimum payments that consumers had to pay, encouraging them to carry more debt for longer periods.

Several pieces of legislation have been introduced in Congress in recent years that would prevent credit card companies from targeting young people with unsustainable offers of credit and prohibit abusive fee and interest-rate practices. Unless credit card issuers adopt considerably more restraint in marketing and extending credit to less-sophisticated borrowers, the Consumer Federation of America will continue to urge Congress to adopt such restrictions.

NO

Louis J. Freeh
Vice Chairman and General Counsel, MBNA Corp.

From testimony before U.S. Senate Banking Committee, May 17, 2005

In discussing student marketing, it is important to note that we make every effort to ensure that credit card offers are not sent to people under the age of 18.

MBNA does promote its products to college-aged customers by partnering with more than 700 colleges and universities, primarily through the college alumni associations. By working closely with school administrators, we have earned the confidence and trust of most of America's premier educational institutions. . . .

Before granting credit to a college student, analysts familiar with the needs and abilities of college students review each application and decline more than half. . . . Most college student applicants report a separate income, and many already have an established credit history.

When evaluating an application, we consider the college students' projected performance as an alumnus, and when we grant credit, we typically assign a line of between $500 and $1,000. If a college student attempts to use his or her card beyond the credit line, we typically refuse the charge. And we do not re-price these accounts based on behavior.

Once a college student becomes a cardholder, MBNA delivers its "Good Credit, Great Future" brochure in a Welcome Package. The brochure highlights sound money-management habits, including guidance on how to handle a credit card responsibly. We also maintain a Web site aimed at college-aged consumers, highlighting many of the same tips. MBNA also conducts on-campus credit-education seminars, and we provide articles concerning responsible credit use for student and parent publications.

The performance of our college-student portfolio mirrors closely that of the national experience, as reported in [Government Accountability Office] reports and several independent studies. However, our accounts have much smaller credit limits and much smaller balances than the norm, our college student customers utilize their cards less often than the norm and these accounts are less likely to incur fees. Our experience has also been that college students are no more likely to mishandle their accounts than any other group of customers.

When we grant a card to a college student, we think of it as the beginning of what we hope will be a long relationship. . . . Given this, we have absolutely no interest in encouraging poor credit habits. In fact, everyone's interest is best served when college students make responsible use of credit. That is our goal in every situation, and certainly when dealing with college-aged customers.

JA Worldwide

The Junior Achievement program reaches 7 million K-12 students around the globe, including this youth at the A.H. Middle School in Richmond, Va. In-school and after-school programs cover financial literacy, career development, economics and related areas.

would take to pay off the full balance if a consumer only made the minimum payment.

The U.S. Securities and Exchange Commission, which regulates the stock markets, is trying podcasts to get the word out to young people about investing, SEC Chairman Christopher Cox told the Senate panel. The podcasts "Welcome to Your Money" and "Hot Stock Tips" are available on the SEC's Web site (www.sec.gov/investor).

Meanwhile, Sen. Akaka is pushing legislation that would create a pilot program requiring college students to get credit counseling and a financial-literacy program that gives grants to organizations that ban or discourage credit card marketing on campus.

Iannicola says states and schools should have the flexibility to figure out how best to integrate financial-literacy courses and that federal or state mandates may not be the best answer. But that is precisely the direction some states are taking. Seven states passed legislation in 2005 requiring financial education in schools, and New York and Illinois this year introduced measures to beef up their existing financial-education standards, according to a report from Citigroup.[47]

Shock Therapy

Some bankruptcy judges have turned to shock therapy to teach teens about the consequences of excessive debt. In March about 90 high-school juniors from Worcester, Mass., got a taste of the real world when they watched a mock consumer bankruptcy case in U.S. Bankruptcy Court in Boston.

"If many of the 25,000 debtors who filed for bankruptcy in Massachusetts last year better understood the risks of credit, they might have been able to avoid bankruptcy," said Chief Bankruptcy Judge Joan Feeney, who in 2004 created a task force with the Boston Bar Association to devise a financial-literacy curriculum.[48]

In Western New York state, Bankruptcy Court Judge Ninfro visits about 20 high schools and colleges each year, describing to students some of the cases he sees in his bankruptcy courtroom, such as the man who owed $20,000 on credit cards and lost his $60,000 job.

"Mounting credit card debt is a ticket to bankruptcy," he says. U.S. bankruptcy filings in the federal courts skyrocketed a record 30 percent in 2005, according to the Administrative Office of the U.S. Courts. More than 2 million individuals and businesses filed for bankruptcy in 2005, up from the 1.6 million the previous year and more than in any 12-month period in the history of the federal courts. Many people filed before the Bankruptcy Abuse Prevention and Consumer Protection Act of 2005 went into effect in October 2005. The act made it harder for people to file for bankruptcy.[49]

Many financial institutions today are trying to boost financial education. Citigroup, for example, has committed $200 million over 10 years to address financial literacy around the world.[50]

Meanwhile, the National Endowment for Financial Education (NEFE) plans to focus more attention on credit card fraud, Internet transactions and parental involvement. "The new materials will emphasize parents," NEFE's Parfrey says. "There's a real disconnect between parents and kids."

Experts agree that while it's important that teens learn about money in school, it's even more important for the lessons to begin at home. "By far, the largest influence on kids and how they behave financially is watching their parents," says Salisbury of the American Savings Education Council.

Parents are doing some things right, Salisbury says, just not enough. Most parents encourage their children to save, and eight out of 10 say they teach their kids to compare prices, he says, citing a 2001 council survey.[51] But only half the parents said they taught their kids how to track expenses and make a budget, and even fewer have taught them about different kinds of investments.

Even though the council's study is somewhat dated, Salisbury says the results are consistent with other reports showing that many parents carry large balances on their credit cards and don't have family budgets.

An overwhelming number of teens — 94 percent — say they are likely to go to their parents with money questions, but many are reluctant to sit down and talk with their kids about finances, especially those who feel their own habits are not exemplary, says Mead of the National Endowment for Financial Education. She urges parents to set aside a monthly "family money night" to discuss financial matters, such as the importance of saving, how to make a budget and what groceries and other necessities cost per week.

Levine of Jump$tart says that whether parents feel prepared or qualified to talk is beside the point, because it's not just what they say but what they do. "If you spend and charge too much, it's hard to expect that your teenage son or daughter won't," she says. "Parents have to set a good example."

OUTLOOK

Train Wreck?

Most financial experts are only cautiously optimistic that today's teens will be smarter than their parents about money, but others are downright bleak in their assessments.

"It's a train wreck waiting to happen," says Parfrey of the National Endowment for Financial Education.

The problem is that many of today's teens won't have pensions to fall back on when they retire, as their parents do. "Young people need to increase their financial IQ now if they are to survive in a world where there will be no Social Security, the costs of health care and college tuition for their kids will skyrocket, gas will be $5 to $6 a gallon and job security will totally be a thing of the past," says New York state Bankruptcy Judge Ninfro.

NEFE's Mead agrees. "Kids today are facing financial issues that their parents didn't," she says. "They will have to be much more financially savvy." Much depends on whether more schools teach financial literacy and whether the lesson is reinforced at home, she says; it may take "several generations."

Levine of the Jump$tart Coalition for Personal Financial Literacy predicts more states will require financial literacy in schools and hopes parents will reinforce the message at home. "It's so important that financial literacy become part of a child's formal education — in school, after school and at home.

"You wouldn't hand a kid a musical instrument and see if they can learn how to play it," she says. "Why would money be any different?"

But with young people being bombarded with ads that promote living rich and on credit, "We have a big challenge," says Duvall of the National Council on Economic Education.

Deputy Assistant Secretary of the Treasury Iannicola says the financial-literacy movement for both teens and adults is in its adolescence. "It's not new anymore, but it's not in full maturity," he cautions. And like any other social movement, it will take time before most Americans start changing their spending and saving habits, he says, citing the years of urging before Americans began using their seat belts and designating a non-drinking driver.

Ninfro likens today's spendthrift ways to the popularity of smoking in the 1950s, before the dangers were widely known. He predicts that just as millions of Americans have stopped smoking because of the cancer risk, they will, over time, stop running up thousands of dollars of debt once they realize the financial consequences.

Young adults who racked up debt and bad credit histories as teenagers are losing out on jobs, student loans, apartments, admission to graduate school and more because of their abuse of credit, he says. "We need to get young people the message," he says. "Education is really the only way."

NOTES

1. Michelle Singletary, "Credit Cards for Kids? Not in My House," *The Washington Post*, April 2, 2006, p. F1.

2. "Teens & Money 2006 Survey," Charles Schwab Foundation, April 2006.
3. For background see Alan Greenblatt, "Pension Crisis," *CQ Researcher*, Feb. 17, 2006, pp. 145-168.
4. Ann Holdsworth, "Teens Cash In," *Fiscal Notes*, Texas Comptroller, August 2005.
5. "Generation Fact Sheet," Visa USA Research, 2005.
6. "Undergraduate Students and Credit Cards in 2004," Nellie Mae Corp., May 2005.
7. Consumer Federation of America, 2005.
8. The nine states are Connecticut, Georgia, Idaho, Illinois, Indiana, Kentucky, Michigan, Oregon and Virginia, as reported in "Survey of the States," National Council on Economic Education, March 2005.
9. "Evaluation of the NEFE High School Financial Planning Program, 2003-2004," University of Minnesota.
10. "Teens & Money 2006 Survey," *op. cit.*
11. 2006 Jump$start Questionnaire; www.jumpstart .org.
12. "What American Teens & Adults Know About Economics," National Council on Economic Education, April 2005.
13. Creola Johnson, "Maxed Out College Students: A Call to Limit Credit Card Solicitation on College Campuses," *Journal of Legislation and Public Policy*, New York University Law School, Vol. 8, No. 2, p. 195, June 2005.
14. Government Accountability Office, "Credit Reporting Literacy: Consumers Understood the Basics but Could Benefit from Targeted Educational Efforts," March 2005.
15. Junior Achievement, "2006 Interprise Poll on Teens and Personal Finance," April 18, 2006.
16. Nellie Mae, *op. cit.*
17. *Ibid.*
18. Janet Bodnar, "Just Say 'No' to Plastic," *Kiplinger.com*, Aug. 11, 2005.
19. Junior Achievement, *op. cit.*
20. Thomas Hine, *The Rise & Fall of the American Teenager* (1999).
21. *Ibid.*
22. For background, see William V. Thomas, "Trends in Advertising," *Editorial Research Reports, 1981* (Vol. II) at *CQ Press Researcher Plus Archive*, CQ Electronic Library, http://library.cqpress.com.
23. For background, see Helen B. Shaffer, "Youth Market," *Editorial Research Reports 1965* (Vol. II) at *CQ Researcher Plus Archive*, CQ Electronic Library; http://library.cqpress.com.
24. Thomas, *op. cit.*
25. *Ibid.*
26. For background, see Richard L. Worsnop, "Consumer Debt," *CQ Researcher*, Nov. 15, 1996, pp. 1009-1032.
27. Robert D. Manning, *Credit Card Nation* (2000).
28. The Supreme Court case is *Marquette National Bank of Minneapolis v. First Omaha Serve Corp.* (439 U.S. 299).
29. The Supreme Court case is *Smiley v. Citibank (South Dakota), N.A.* (517 U.S. 735).
30. Transcript of House Banking, Finance and Urban Affairs Subcommittee on Consumer Credit and Insurance, March 10, 1994.
31. Robert D. Manning, "Credit Cards on Campus: The Social Consequences of Student Debt," Consumer Federation of America, June 8, 1999.
32. *Ibid.*
33. www.iowaattorneygeneral.org/consumer/press_releases/2001/campus_cc_debt.html.
34. General Accounting Office, "Consumer Finance: College Students and Credit Cards," June 2001, pp. 53-66. The office has since been renamed the Government Accountability Office.
35. www.pbs.org/wgbh/pages/frontline/shows/credit/.
36. For background, see Barbara Mantel, "No Child Left Behind," *CQ Researcher*, May 27, 2005, pp. 469-492.
37. "Tips for parenting in a commercial culture," *New American Dream*, April 2006.
38. For more background, see David Masci, "The Consumer Culture," *CQ Researcher*, Nov. 19, 1999, pp. 1001-1016.
39. For background, see Patrick Marshall, "Advertising Overload," *CQ Researcher*, Jan. 23, 2004, pp. 49-72.

40. Juliet B. Schor, *Born to Buy: The Commercialized Child and the New Consumer Culture* (2004), p. 21.
41. Center for a New American Dream, press release, 2002.
42. *Ibid.*
43. *Yankelovich Youth Monitor*, press release, June 2005.
44. *Ibid.*
45. Rep. Judy Biggert, press release, April 7, 2006.
46. www.mymoney.gov/ownership.pdf.
47. "The Drive for Financial Literacy," Citigroup, 2006. The seven states are Missouri, South Carolina, Texas, Virginia, Washington, West Virginia and Wyoming.
48. Boston Bar Association, press release, March 27, 2006.
49. www.uscourts.gov/Press_Releases/bankruptcy filings032406.html.
50. Citigroup, *op. cit.*
51. "Parents, Youth & Money Survey," American Education Savings Council and Employee Benefit Research Institute, April 2001.

BIBLIOGRAPHY

Books

Hine, Thomas, *The Rise & Fall of the American Teenager*, *Avon Books*, 1999.
A journalist traces the culture of youth in America, including what he calls the media-blitzed consumerism of today's teens.

Manning, Robert D., *Credit Card Nation*, *Basic Books*, 2000.
A finance professor at Rochester Institute of Technology examines how credit card companies targeted the college student market in the late 1980s and early 1990s and finds student credit card debt much higher than is commonly reported.

Schor, Juliet B., *Born to Buy: The Commercialized Child and the New Consumer Culture*, *Scribner*, 2004.
A sociology professor at Boston College says today's teens are the most brand-oriented, consumer-involved and materialistic generation in history and concludes that the onslaught of advertising aimed at children hurts kids' emotional and social well-being.

Articles

Bodnar, Janet, "Just Say 'No' to Plastic," *Kiplinger.com*, Aug. 11, 2005.
This column on teaching teens personal finance by the author of *Raising Money-Smart Kids* advocates teaching money management a step at a time, first with cash, then with a checking account linked to a debit card and finally a credit card.

Singletary, Michelle, "Credit Cards for Kids? Not in My House," *The Washington Post*, April 2, 2006, p. F1.
A *Washington Post* business columnist lambastes the credit card industry for marketing to young people.

Reports and Studies

"Credit Reporting Literacy: Consumers Understood the Basics but Could Benefit from Targeted Educational Efforts," *U.S. Government Accountability Office*, March 2005.
The congressional watchdog agency finds that less than 20 percent of 18- to 24-year-olds know their credit history can affect employment.

"Parents, Youth & Money Survey," *American Education Savings Council and Employee Benefit Research Institute*, April 2001.
The two sponsors of the national "Choose to Save" campaign find that only half of parents say they taught their kids how to track expenses and how to make a budget, and even fewer have taught their kids about different kinds of investments.

"Personal Finance 2006," *Junior Achievement*, April 2006.
An organization that educates young people about business and entrepreneurship finds that about 16 percent of teenage credit card holders make only the minimum payment.

"2006 Jump$start Questionnaire," *Jump$tart Coalition for Personal Financial Literacy*, April 2006.
The group's annual survey of high-school seniors finds that students earned an average score of only 52 percent on a test of their knowledge of credit cards, saving and retirement.

"Undergraduate Students and Credit Cards in 2004," *Nellie Mae Corp.*, May 2005.
The student-loan lender finds that of the 76 percent of undergraduates in 2004 who had their own credit cards, nearly a quarter had the card before entering college, while 43 percent got it during their freshman year.

"What American Teens & Adults Know About Economics," April 2005; and "Survey of the States," *National Council on Economic Education*, March 2005.
The first report from a network of state and university centers promoting the teaching of economics gives high-school students an "F" on their understanding of basic financial concepts; the second describes how each state deals with personal finance in the classroom.

"Youth Report," *GfK Roper Consulting*, September 2005.
A consulting firm finds that while the number of teens who get money from household chores and allowance has remained about the same in recent years, a growing number of teens get money simply by asking for it.

Johnson, Creola, "Maxed Out College Students: A Call to Limit Credit Card Solicitation on College Campuses," *Journal of Legislation and Public Policy*, New York University Law School, Vol. 8, No. 2, June 2005.
An Ohio State University researcher finds that few college students are aware that late credit card payments could mean higher interest rates on car loans and mortgages.

Manning, Robert D., "Credit Cards on Campus: The Social Consequences of Student Debt," *Consumer Federation of America*, June 8, 1999.
A controversial 1999 study links college students' debt with suicides, drawing considerable attention from the media and state and federal policymakers.

For More Information

American Savings Education Council, 2121 K St., Suite 600, N.W., Washington, DC 20037-1896; (202) 659-0670; www.choosetosave.org. A coalition of government and industry institutions to educate people on all aspects of personal finance.

Consumer Credit Counseling Service, 9009 West Loop South, Suite 700, Houston, TX 77096; (800) 873-2227; www.cccsintl.org. Helps people nationwide solve debt problems by providing counseling on personal finances.

Consumer Federation of America, 1620 I St., N.W., Suite 200, Washington, DC 20006; (202) 387-6121; www.consumerfed.org. A leading critic of credit card marketing to young people.

Credit Abuse Resistance Education (CARE), 1400 U.S. Courthouse, 100 State St., Rochester, NY 14814; (585) 613-4200; www.careprogram.us. A national program founded by Judge John C. Ninfro of the U.S. Bankruptcy Court in Western New York that provides resources, speakers and information to schools and colleges.

FederalReserveEducation.org. The Federal Reserve's online resource includes materials specifically geared toward teachers and high school and college students.

Jump$tart Coalition for Personal Financial Literacy, 919 18th St., N.W., Suite 300, Washington, DC 20006; (202) 466-8604; www.jumpstart.org. Regularly surveys high-school students' knowledge of basic money matters.

Junior Achievement, One Education Way, Colorado Springs, CO 80906; (719) 540-8000; www.ja.org. A nonprofit dedicated to educating young people about business and entrepreneurship.

National Council on Economic Education, 1140 Avenue of the Americas, New York, NY 10036; (212) 730-7007; www.ncee.net. A network of state and university centers that promote financial literacy in the classroom and track state developments.

National Endowment for Financial Education, 5299 DTC Blvd., Suite 1300, Greenwood Village, CO 80111; (303) 741-6333; www.nefe.org. Provides curriculum and materials for classrooms and researches financial-education issues.

Securities and Exchange Commission, 100 F St. N.E., Washington, DC 20549; 1-800-SEC-0330; www.sec.gov/investor.shtml. The federal agency charged with protecting investors provides information about saving and investing.

U.S. Financial Literacy and Education Commission (1-888-mymoney); www.mymoney.gov. Provides educational materials on financial issues.

12

Teen Driving

Should States Impose Tougher Restrictions?

William Triplett

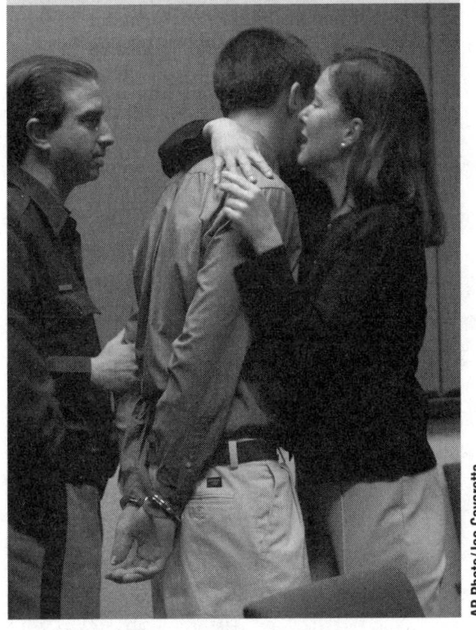
AP Photo/Joe Cavaretta

Sean Larimer, 16, of Las Vegas — who killed his three best friends when he crashed while driving drunk — is comforted by his mother after a court hearing on Jan. 5, 2004. He pleaded guilty to reckless and drunken driving and was sentenced to two years in a juvenile facility. Teen drivers are involved in more crashes than any other age group; deaths of drivers 15-20 years old have increased 13 percent since 1993.

From *CQ Researcher*, January 7, 2005

Police estimated that 16-year-old Lauren Sausville was driving nearly 60 miles per hour in a 35-mph zone in early December 2004 when her Ford Explorer ran off the road. The junior at Fairfax High School in Virginia overcompensated with a sharp turn that flipped the sport-utility vehicle (SUV) on its side, sending it careening into a car waiting at a stop sign.[1]

That car belonged to the friend she had been following, a 17-year-old boy who police said was legally drunk. He was not hurt, but Lauren was pronounced dead at the scene. Earlier, police said, she had persuaded a stranger at a convenience store to buy two six-packs of beer for her and her friends.

Another recent SUV accident in Virginia involved seven members of the women's crew team at T. C. Williams High School in Alexandria. They were traveling on I-95 near Springfield when the 17-year-old driver lost control of her Cadillac SUV and rolled. All survived except senior Laura Lynam.[2]

But no one survived when Weston Griggs, 17, drove his Volkswagen Jetta 70 mph in a 40-mph zone in Woodbridge, Va., shortly before 4 a.m. one October morning. He lost control and smashed into a telephone pole — snapping it into three pieces. Griggs and both his passengers, young men 18 and 22, were killed.[3]

Those were just a few of the recent accidents in suburban Virginia involving teenagers. In the last three months of 2004, at least 17 youths died in crashes in the Washington, D.C., area. Some had been drinking and driving; some made fatal rookie mistakes; and some were just along for the ride.

Accidents involving teenagers are disproportionately high throughout the United States. Drivers between ages 15 and 20

Most States Use Graduated Licenses

Most states and the District of Columbia limit teenagers' driving privileges by instituting graduated driver licensing (GDL) programs, which usually involve a learner's stage and an intermediate stage before an unrestricted license is permitted. GDL programs substantially reduce teen crash rates. Ohio, for example, reported that following its 1999 implementation of GDL laws, fatal crashes involving 16- and 17-year-old drivers dropped by 70 percent.

Types of Limits on Teen Licenses

	Learner's Permits		Intermediate Permits	
States	Adult supervision for six months	30-50 hours of adult supervision	No unsupervised night driving	Limits on teenage passengers
Alabama	x			
Alaska	x	x		x
Arizona				
Arkansas	x			
California	x	x		x
Colorado	x	x		
Connecticut				x
Delaware	x		x	
Dist. of Columbia	x	x		x
Florida	x	x		
Georgia	x			x
Hawaii				
Idaho		x	x	
Illinois				x

Continued⟶

Learner's Stage — Drivers must be supervised by adult driver for six months and must remain conviction-free during that period. In some cases, 30-50 hours of supervised driving with an adult driver are required.

Intermediate Stage — *Nighttime restrictions:* Unsupervised driving from 9 p.m. to 5 a.m. is prohibited. *Passenger restrictions:* Usually limit the number of teenage passengers without adult supervision; the optimal limit is one teenage passenger.

Source: Advocates for Highway and Auto Safety, "State Highway Safety Law Chart," October 2004

make up about only 6.4 percent of the nation's driving population, but for the last 10 years they have been involved in approximately 14 percent of all fatal car crashes.[4]

In 2003, nearly 7,900 teen drivers were involved in fatal accidents in the United States. Nearly half of them died, but most of the victims were passengers, drivers or passengers of other vehicles, or pedestrians. Another 308,000 teen drivers were injured in fatal crashes. About 6,000 teens died in automobile accidents in 2003, including 3,657 young drivers.[5]

Although those figures were down from the year before — when 3,838 teen drivers were killed — the trend over the last decade has been upward. Since 1993, deaths of drivers 15-20 years old have increased 13 percent.[6] Indeed, says Kristen Kreibich-Staruch, manager of safety programs and communications at DaimlerChrysler Corp., "traffic crashes are the leading cause of death" for teens of driving age. According to the Insurance Institute for Highway Safety (IIHS), motor vehicle crashes account for about 40 percent of adolescent fatalities.[7]

Moreover, teenage drivers are involved in more crashes — fatal and non-fatal — than any other age group. The Centers for Disease Control and Prevention (CDC) reports that in 2002 the motor vehicle death rate for teens (drivers as well as passengers) between ages 15 and 19 was 27.6 deaths per 100,000 population compared to 17.8 for people between 25 and 34 and 15.8 for those between 35 and 44.[8]

Jeffrey W. Runge, a physician who heads the National Highway Transportation Safety Administration (NHTSA), has described teen driving deaths in the United States as "an epidemic."[9]

Experts cite many reasons for the high toll. Driver education courses are being offered in only about half the nation's public high schools, many discontinued because of skyrocketing insurance costs. And even when courses are offered, they generally focus on helping students pass a driving test, not teaching them to drive defensively and safely, experts say. Commercial driving school programs have the same problem, they add, although driver education teachers — both public and private — disagree.

The mythical "invulnerability" of youth is also blamed: Teens by nature are risk-takers who rarely think about disaster, particularly when it comes to driving. For example, they are the least likely age group to use seat belts, and the most likely to drink and drive.

The CDC reports that 29 percent of teen drivers killed in auto crashes in 2002 had been drinking, and 77 percent were not wearing seat belts. Moreover, during the period from 1991 to 1997, more than one in three teens reported riding with a driver who had been drinking. And one in six admitted to drinking and driving.[10]

"Research continues to show that young drivers between 15 and 20 years of age are more often involved in alcohol-related crashes than any other comparable age group," says Mothers Against Drunk Driving (MADD).[11]

But there has been progress. The number of 15-to-20-year-olds involved in fatal crashes who had a blood alcohol concentration (BAC) higher than 0.08 g/210 liters of breath — the legal limit in most states — dropped 6 percent between 1993 and 2003, possibly due to the increased use of designated drivers.[12]

Nevertheless, teens tend to think of themselves as safe drivers.[13] Among 10 teens attending a recent class at the Northern Virginia Driving School in Arlington, Va., at least four had close friends who had been in serious accidents, but none thought the same could happen to them.

When asked why he drove fast, a student replied: "It's just the thrill of it, going fast!"

Types of Limits on Teen Licenses

	Learner's Permits		Intermediate Permits	
States	Adult supervision for six months	30-50 hours of adult supervision	No unsupervised night driving	Limits on teenage passengers
Indiana				x
Iowa	x			
Kansas		x		
Kentucky	x			
Louisiana	x			
Maine	x	x		x
Maryland		x		
Massachusetts	x			x
Michigan	x	x		
Minnesota	x	x		
Mississippi	x		x	
Missouri	x			
Montana				
Nebraska				
Nevada		x		x
New Hampshire				x
New Jersey	x			x
New Mexico	x	x		x
New York			x	
North Carolina	x		x	x
North Dakota	x			
Ohio	x	x		
Oklahoma	x			
Oregon	x	x		x
Pennsylvania	x	x		
Rhode Island	x	x		
South Carolina	x	x	x	
South Dakota			x	
Tennessee	x	x		x
Texas	x			x
Utah		x		x
Vermont	x	x		x
Virginia	x	x		x
Washington	x	x		x
West Virginia	x			
Wisconsin	x	x		x
Wyoming				

Some experts say that just because teens are allowed to drive at 16 (or even younger) does not necessarily mean they have the maturity to handle the physical or psychological challenges of driving, especially when egged on by their friends. For instance, a 16-year-old girl described as a model student and daughter died in

Fatalities Caused by Young Drivers

A majority (58 percent) of the people killed in crashes involving young drivers were not the young drivers but passengers, occupants of other vehicles and pedestrians.

Fatalities in Crashes Involving Drivers Ages 15-20

Year	Young drivers	Passengers of young drivers	Occupants of other vehicles	Non-occupants	Total fatalities
1999	3,564	2,578	2,245	752	9,139
2000	3,621	2,535	2,185	756	9,097
2001	3,617	2,529	2,172	746	9,064
2002	3,838	2,565	2,153	695	9,251
2003	3,657	2,384	1,979	646	8,666

Source: "Crash Stats," National Highway Traffic Safety Administration, November 2004

a crash while playing "road-hog" with a friend in another car.[14]

Inexperience is another factor: New drivers simply aren't aware of the many unexpected conditions they might confront, and they know even less about how to deal with them.

"They're always either understeering or oversteering, going off the road or hitting the curb, or turning too soon or too late," says Virginia driving school owner Larry Blake. "I've fought in two wars, and I can tell you, this is the most dangerous profession there is."

As Allan F. Williams, chief scientist for the IIHS, has put it, "You've got several things going on here — a risky driving style; inability to recognize or respond to dangerous driving situations and overconfidence in their abilities. When you put all those things together, you've got a pretty lethal combination."[15]

Some 45 states and the District of Columbia have responded to the problem by instituting graduated driver licensing (GDL) programs, which limit a new driver's privileges pending successful completion of phases involving increasing levels of risk exposure.

The Journal of Safety Research recently reported that GDL programs have helped reduce teen crash rates, but because of differences in state programs and evaluation methods, precise nationwide measures cannot be made.[16] And states don't enforce all parts of their GDL programs equally, making them less effective than they could be, advocates say.

But one factor clearly appears to help: raising the legal driving age. In England, where drivers must be age 17, and in Germany, where the age is 18, teens have lower fatality rates than in the United States.[17]

Some experts say more educational programs are needed; others contend they have little impact on teens. And still others argue for more parental involvement in teens' driving lessons. But a recent study by Liberty Mutual Insurance Co. and Students Against Destructive Decisions (SADD) indicated that more parental involvement actually can have a negative effect.[18]

Meanwhile, an upcoming explosion in the number of teenagers is putting new pressure on safety experts to improve teen driving. Reflecting a nationwide trend, the California Office of Traffic Safety recently released a study forecasting a one-third rise in the state's teen population by 2007. The increase will occur because the teenage children of Baby Boomers — who delayed having children to pursue careers — are reaching puberty.[19]

"Teenage traffic deaths could skyrocket over the next decade," California officials said.[20]

As parents, school officials and safety experts seek ways to better protect teen drivers, here are some of the key questions under debate:

Is driver education effective?

For many teens and parents, the value of driver education — behind-the-wheel experience bolstered by classroom instruction — seems self-evident.

However, some experts say formal evaluations of high school "driver ed" programs show they have little or no effect in reducing crashes.[21]

"Driver education programs are usually short-term, and only basic skills are learned," says Williams, of the IIHS. "There's not enough time to do more. To think this short-term course is going to make young people safe drivers is kind of unrealistic."

Having studied teen crash rates for 25 years, Williams concluded in a 2004 report: "There is no difference in the crash records of driver education graduates compared with equivalent groups of beginners who learned to drive without formal education."[22]

NHTSA Administrator Runge essentially concurs. "As it's currently configured, driver's education might make a difference in the first six months of driving," he said, "but after that, it doesn't matter much."[23]

Eric Skrum, communications director for the National Motorists Association (NMA), argues that current driver education programs don't put enough emphasis on behind-the-wheel experience. "Instead of telling kids about a skid, you need to get them into a skid," Skrum says. "Teach them how to handle the situation. The few hours that new drivers have now isn't training them for all situations they're going to be in."

While critics acknowledge that high school programs can teach good driving skills, they say the programs have little or no effect on teen attitudes. Indeed, the IIHS maintains that teenagers who have accidents are the least susceptible to behavior change through education.

Studies involving mostly young males have noted the "interrelationship among certain personality traits (rebelliousness, risk-taking, independence, defiance of authority), deviant driving practices (speeding, driving while impaired) and crashes and violations," the IIHS says. "The traits, values and peer associations of this high-risk group are such that changing their behavior through education is a difficult task."[24]

That is the very point that critics fail to understand, according to certified driving instructor Syed Ahmad, of Alexandria, Va. "When accidents happen, they always blame the driver's-ed classes," Ahmad says. "But the fact is, if your intention is to go out and party when you get your license, you're not going to make it."

Allen Robinson, chief executive officer of the American Driver and Traffic Safety Education Association (ADTSEA), says critics of driver education rely heavily — and inappropriately — on a 1974 study in DeKalb County (Macon), Ga. "When we planned the DeKalb study, we were too ambitious," he says. "We said we could reduce fatalities of 16-year-old drivers by 10 percent [through driver's education]. But we only achieved about a 4 percent reduction. So, it was unsuccessful in that respect. But today there isn't a single countermeasure — seat belts or anything — that can show a 4 percent reduction in fatalities."

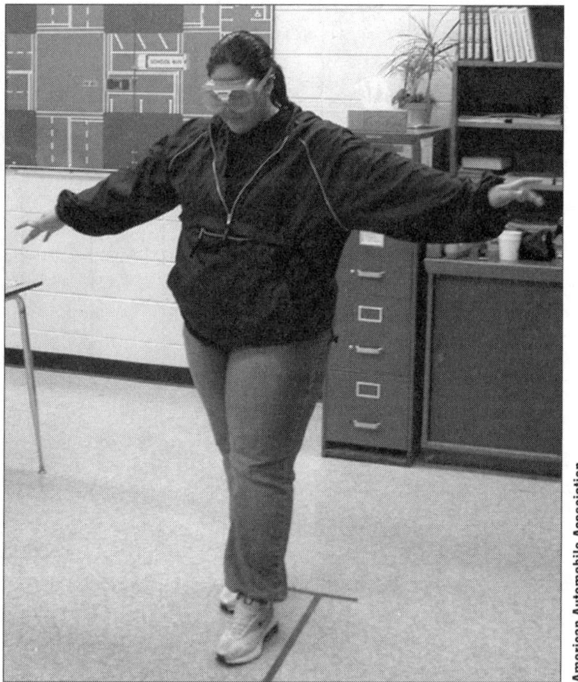

American Automobile Association

Wearing goggles that distort her senses as if she had been drinking, a driver education student tries, unsuccessfully, to walk a straight line — a common police test for drunkenness.

Yet critics continue to cite the DeKalb study, Robinson asserts, "as the benchmark for why driver's education 'doesn't work.' " Indeed, the study is one of the reasons many high schools discontinue their driver education courses.

However, Robinson says the Oregon Department of Transportation (ODOT) and the Center for Applied Research recently found "significantly lower rates of convictions, suspensions and crashes" for drivers who took a driver ed course versus drivers who learned through 50 hours of informal, supervised driving. An ODOT spokesperson says the report is still in draft form and under review, with no public release date set.

Driving school owner Blake (who says his pupils have included the daughters of former Presidents Richard Nixon and Gerald Ford), argues that not all schools evaluate students properly. In Virginia, he notes, instructors can waive a student's school road test if they feel the

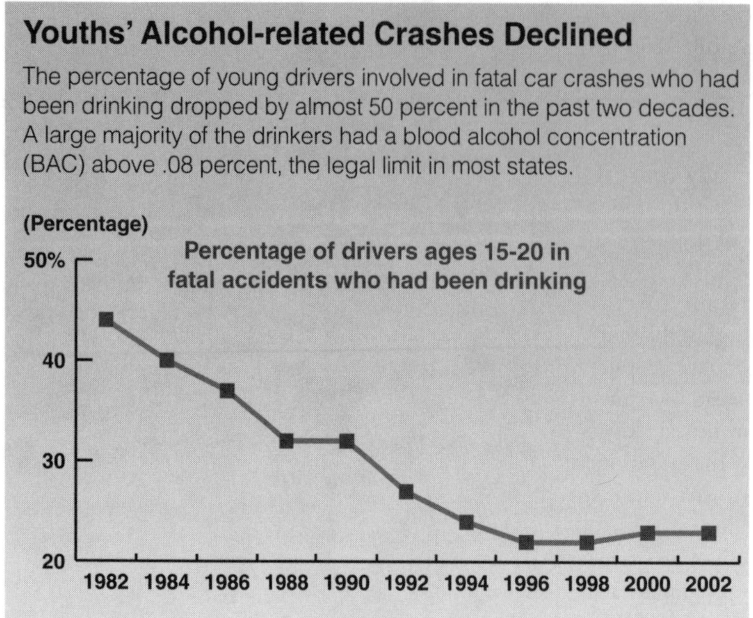

student has performed well during the course. Increasingly, though, commercial instructors are waiving their road tests for financial reasons, he says.

"When students find out an instructor is going to make them take the road test, they tell their friends, and those friends make sure they don't go to that driving school," Blake says. "More and more schools are waiving the road test because they're scared of losing business." If more schools enforced standards more rigorously, he claims, driver ed would be highly effective.

Indeed, some observers blame the lack of uniformity among driver ed curricula, not driver education per se. "It's all very uneven around the country," says Eileen Buckholtz, the mother of two young drivers and the administrator of the Web site teendriving.com, which advocates safe driving.

Stephen Wallace, chairman and chief executive officer of Students Against Destructive Decisions (SADD), adds, "There's a range of driver education programs out there, so a differing degree of effectiveness exists."

At a 2003 National Transportation Safety Board (NTSB) symposium on driver education, several safety experts argued for uniform, national standards for driver education. But Barbara Harsha, executive director of the Governors Highway Safety Association (GHSA), thinks that would be a mistake. "The states get no federal money for driver's education, so there's no way to make them comply with [national] standards." She favors encouraging states to adopt voluntary core requirements and guidelines for driver ed courses.

"Federal driver education standards would be a terrible idea," agrees Radley Balko, a policy analyst at the Cato Institute, a libertarian think tank. "Every state's driving is a little different — the skills you need to drive in Florida and in Alaska are quite different. States know better what's best for learning how to drive on their highways."

Yet, no one even knows how many states still offer driver's education in public high schools. "We know that about 55 percent of public high schools in the United States still offer it," Robinson of ADTSEA says, "but we don't know how many states."

Should more limits be imposed on teen drivers?

Graduated driver licensing (GDL) programs — used in some 45 states and the District of Columbia — are the most popular and widely used method of limiting teen driving. GDL programs generally feature three phases: a learner's permit, which allows driving only when supervised by a fully licensed adult; a provisional, or intermediate, license, which allows unsupervised driving under restricted circumstances and, finally, full licensure. The ages for each phase are usually 15, 16 and 17, respectively.

The first two phases require minimum training periods — varying from state to state — before the student can advance.

The theory behind GDL is simple. "By restricting when teenagers may drive, and with whom, graduated driver licensing allows new drivers to gain much-needed, on-the-road experience in controlled, lower-risk settings," according to NHTSA. "It also means that a teenager will be a little older and more mature when he or she gains a full, unrestricted license."[25]

New Zealand first introduced GDL in 1987, and three subsequent studies of the program showed positive effects.[26] In 1996, Florida became the first state to initiate a GDL program, and a subsequent evaluation showed that it substantially reduced teen deaths. So did later evaluations of GDL programs in California, Connecticut, Kentucky, Michigan, North Carolina, Ohio, Maryland and Oregon.[27] Ohio, for example, reported that following its 1999 implementation of GDL laws, fatal crashes involving 16- and 17-year-old drivers dropped by 70 percent.[28]

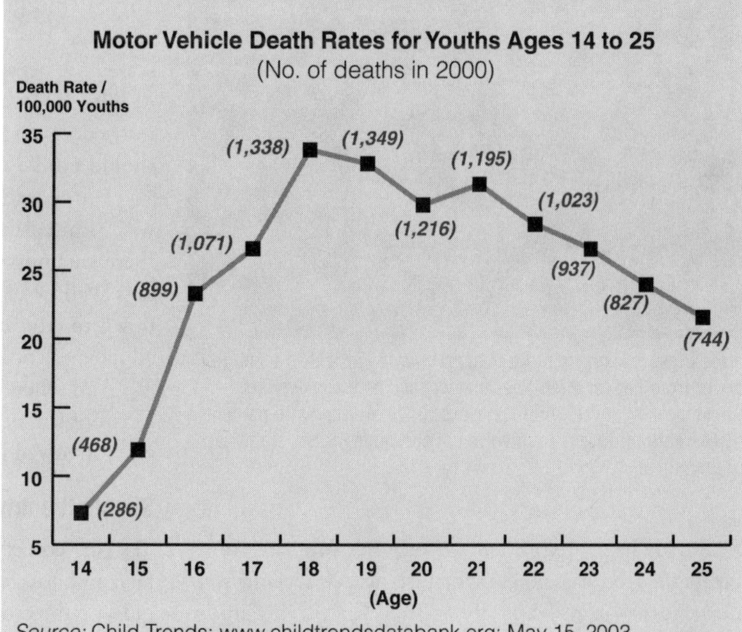

Source: Child Trends; www.childtrendsdatabank.org; May 15, 2003

While the collective fatality rates of 15-to-20-year-old drivers and passengers have been rising, statistics for specific ages support the effectiveness of GDL programs. For instance, the overwhelming majority of drivers in GDL programs are either 15 or 16. According to the CDC's National Center for Health Statistics, 491 15-year-olds died in motor vehicle accidents in 2000, but the death toll dropped to 422 in 2001. Motor vehicle deaths of 16-year-olds during the same period decreased from 933 to 908.[29]

But the next year, 2002, deaths in both age groups began creeping back up — to 479 for 15-year-olds and 1,046 for 16-year-olds.

Harsha of the GHSA suggests the increase was due to lax enforcement. Not all states enforce GDL laws equally, and some of the laws are weak. Harsha's group would like more states with GDL laws to limit nighttime driving and the number of passengers allowed in the vehicle with the teenage driver. "Research shows benefits of these things when they're enforced," she says.

Driving at night is generally more hazardous for all age groups. But for teens it can be especially dangerous. According to the *Journal of Safety Research*, many newly licensed drivers have had less practice driving at night than during the day. "Fatigue — thought to be a problem for teenagers at all times of the day — may be more of a factor at night; and recreational driving that is considered to be high risk, sometimes involving alcohol use, is more likely to take place at night."[30]

For 16-year-old drivers, the risk of a fatal crash is three times higher after 9 p.m. than during the daytime.[31] Overall, about 40 percent of teen motor vehicle fatalities occur at night.[32]

But most state GDL programs only impose a curfew on teen drivers after midnight or 1 a.m.[33] In any case, teen curfews are hard to enforce at any hour, according to Harsha, because police have little way of knowing whether a young person driving at night is underage.

The presence of teenage passengers also strongly increases crash risk for teenage drivers. Four studies have confirmed that the risk of an accident increases as more passengers ride with a teenage driver. One study demonstrated that just a single passenger nearly doubled the risk of a fatal crash, and two or more passengers raised the risk to five times that of driving alone.[34] Yet 29 states do not limit the number of passengers that can ride with teen drivers.

AP Photo/Jim Michaud

It took rescue workers more than an hour to extricate a teenage driver from her car after it became wedged between two large trucks near Andover, Conn., on Nov. 15, 2004. Nearly 20 percent of 16-year-old drivers are involved in accidents in their first year of driving.

Surprisingly, parents often oppose imposing more limits on teen passengers. For instance, Maryland state Del. Adrienne A. Mandel has tried for three years to enact legislation that would prohibit teenagers with provisional licenses from carrying any passengers under age 18 except family members. Her attempts have failed each time, she says, mostly because rural families oppose the measure.

"They say more young people will be on the roads if each one has to drive alone," Mandel says. But car-pooling could alleviate that, she points out. Parents in rural areas also complain that passenger limitations would be especially inconvenient in those areas where transportation options aren't abundant, Mandel says. "They're talking about inconvenience. I'm talking about saving lives," she says. Parents also opposed earlier curfews for teens because older teens often have jobs and need a way to get to work at night, she points out.

Teens themselves are often divided over limitations on driving, including GDL programs in general. In 1998, when Delaware was considering adopting a GDL system, a teenager unhappy with the idea wrote to the Web site teenink.com: "Getting a driver's license means freedom, and most of us can give you the number of years, months and days until that wonderful moment. You get to say good-bye to the yellow school bus, meet your friends or go to work."[35]

Yet, in early 2004 when South Dakota pushed back its curfew for teen drivers from 8 p.m. to 10 p.m., a 16-year-old girl who welcomed the later curfew still admitted that, "when I first started driving, it really scared me being out in the dark."[36]

The IIHS advocates earlier curfews and uniform restrictions on teen passengers, and the NTSB says teens should not be allowed to use cell phones while driving.

"Young and inexperienced drivers out late at night with limited practice and with other kids in the car — there are limits for those drivers that clearly make sense," says Wallace of SADD. "But to some degree, this comes down to education and practice. At some point, they're all inexperienced — they have to get out there and learn.

"And when they start, those are the ones we have to look out for, because nearly one in five 16-year-old drivers is involved in an accident in their first year."

Should the driving age be raised?

Teen drivers between the ages of 16 and 19 have the highest fatal and non-fatal crash rates in the country, but 16-year-olds are three times more likely to be involved in a crash than 19-year-olds. Every decade, more than 9,000 16-year-olds die in motor vehicle accidents in the United States.

Many safety experts blame the fact that states — including those with graduated driver licensing — grant unsupervised driving privileges at 16, which many safety advocates argue is too soon.

Besides being emotionally and psychologically immature, young, new drivers face other challenges when making decisions and judgments. Susan Scharoun, chairman of the psychology department at Le Moyne College, in Syracuse, N.Y., notes that biological factors influence teenage behavior, particularly when risk-taking is involved. Recent research shows that hormonal activity and incomplete development of the frontal lobe of the brain, which controls reasoning and memory, affect teen risk-taking behavior, according to Scharoun.[37]

Thus, 16-year-olds' emotional, psychological and biological immaturity — combined with their inexperience — explain why they have the highest percentages of single-vehicle crashes and crashes involving speeding and driver error, as well as the highest vehicle-occupancy rates, according to the IIHS.

CHRONOLOGY

1900s-1940s *Automobiles become cheaper due to mass production.*

1924 Henry Ford perfects the assembly line, making the Ford Model T the first successfully mass-marketed car.

1929 National car sales reach 27 million.

1950s *Postwar economic boom creates generation of teenagers who can afford cars. Rise of rock 'n' roll music both celebrates and fuels the growth of teen car culture.*

1955 In the movie "Rebel Without a Cause," hot cars and motorcycles symbolize youthful defiance.

1960s *Advocates and researchers begin to make automobile safety a national issue.*

1965 In his book *Unsafe at Any Speed*, consumer advocate Ralph Nader accuses U.S. automakers of marketing vehicles they know to be unsafe.

1966 President Lyndon Johnson signs National Traffic and Motor Vehicle Safety Act and Highway Safety Act.

1970s *Disturbing trends begin to emerge after federal government begins collecting detailed data on motor vehicle accidents.*

1970 National Highway Transportation Safety Administration (NHTSA) is established in the U.S. Department of Transportation (DOT).

1974 A study of driver education in DeKalb County (Macon), Ga., casts doubt on its effectiveness in preventing teen accidents.

1975 The DOT's Fatality Analysis Reporting System — in its first annual report on vehicle deaths by age group — reveals that more than 8,700 teenagers died on the nation's roads that year.

1978 The number of teens dying in car crashes peaks at 9,940.

1980s *Federal government tries to stop teen drinking-and-driving; teen motor vehicle deaths decline.*

1984 Congress passes National Minimum Drinking Age Act, setting 21 as the federal limit for drinking.

1990s *State governments search for ways to decrease the number of teen motor vehicle deaths. Many high schools stop offering driver education because of rising insurance costs and doubts about its effectiveness.*

1996 Florida becomes the first state to institute a graduated driver licensing (GDL) program. The following year, state authorities report a 9 percent reduction in fatal crashes among 15-to-17-year-olds.

1999 After starting GDL programs, Michigan reports a 25 percent reduction and North Carolina a 27 percent reduction in fatal crashes among 16-year-olds.

2000s-Present *Approximately 6,000 teens still die every year in motor vehicle accidents.*

October 2000 Congress establishes a .08 blood alcohol concentration as the national threshold for drunken driving and gives states four years to adopt it.

2004 Advocates and experts praise the increasing number of states with GDL programs but lobby for more restrictions on teen nighttime driving and the number of adolescent passengers a teen driver can carry.

August 2004 Liberty Mutual Insurance Co. and Students Against Destructive Decisions issue a report suggesting that teenagers learn some of their worst driving behaviors from their parents.

Fall 2004 At least 17 young people are killed on Washington, D.C.-area roads, one of the worst streaks of teen driving fatalities in the nation's history.

Teen Drivers and Alcohol: A Deadly Mixture

When I was in my 20s, I thought Jimmy had merely been unlucky, which he was. When I was in my 30s, I thought Jimmy had been foolish to drive after drinking, which he was. But when I was in my 40s, I realized that Jimmy had been misled by all of us — the alcohol industry, the fraternity culture, and we, his friends — to think that being young and having fun means drinking alcohol."

— ***William DeJong, MADD Victim's Tribute***[1]

William DeJong was a typical teenager with few worries and little sense of his own mortality. All that changed when his 19-year-old friend, Jimmy, died in an accident after driving drunk in Texas in 1971. Now a professor at Boston University, DeJong has spent his life researching student alcohol use for the Center for Alcohol and Drug Prevention and Mothers Against Drunk Driving (MADD).

"At first, I wasn't conscious that I was drawn to my work because of my friend," DeJong says. "But I think about him every time I hear about a student that dies from drunk driving."

The legal drinking age throughout the United States was raised to 21 in 1984, too late to have an impact on DeJong's friend. The number of alcohol-impaired teenage drivers involved in fatal crashes declined by 61 percent between 1982 and 1998, largely due to the law, but the decline has stalled in recent years.[2]

Alcohol is still a factor in nearly a third of all fatal crashes involving 15-to-20-year-old drivers, and that number is holding steady, says MADD President Wendy Hamilton. Alcohol is still a major contributor to the deaths of 15 teenagers a day from automobile accidents.[3]

Education and increased enforcement of underage drinking laws are key weapons in the fight to save teenagers' lives.

"The minimum-drinking-age law saves 900 teen lives each year, but if the law were better enforced, we know we'd save even more kids," Hamilton says, citing loopholes in some states that limit the prosecution of teens for purchasing, attempting to purchase or possessing alcohol and the apparent ease of acquiring alcohol by teens in many communities. For example, 14 states — Alaska, Arkansas, Delaware, Hawaii, Illinois, Indiana, Louisiana, Maine, Maryland, Mississippi, Nevada, New York, South Carolina and Vermont — do not prohibit attempts to purchase alcohol by those under 21 as long as they do not use fake identification.[4]

While the minimum-drinking-age law has helped reduce teen auto deaths due to drunken driving, it has not reduced teen alcohol use. Approximately 80 percent of students say they have consumed alcohol by the end of high school, and two-thirds of high school seniors report having been drunk, according to Students Against Destructive Decisions (SADD). And illegal alcohol use is all the more dangerous because it must be hidden, so underage drinkers often drink in vehicles or secluded areas, increasing the chances for drunken driving.[5]

Teens who drink and drive are more likely to participate in other dangerous driving behaviors, like driving too fast for the weather or traffic conditions and not wearing seat belts. Of the teen drivers who died in alcohol-related crashes in 2003, 74 percent were not wearing seat belts.[6]

Partly due to their inexperience and risk-taking behavior, young drivers make up 14 percent of all drivers drunk or sober involved in fatal crashes — even though they represent less than 7 percent of all licensed drivers.[7]

While parents often look to legislators, law enforcement and the community for answers, those groups continually cite parents' involvement as the best solution.

"Parents can have a substantial impact if they are willing to set boundaries," says Lucille Bauer, a public information officer for the police department in Montgomery County (Bethesda), Md., where more than a dozen fatal car accidents involving teens occurred in 2004. "Despite what they say, young people want limits, but unfortunately too many parents are afraid to set them. The police department wants to support parents in setting boundaries. We'd much prefer to prevent fatal collisions than to investigate them."

MADD's Hamilton agrees parents need outside support to protect their children. "Teens are getting mixed messages from the community, the entertainment industry and the

American teenagers are allowed to drive at younger ages than in most other countries. In Northern Europe, for instance, the minimum age for a beginning driver is typically 18; in England, it's 17. By contrast, an adolescent in Michigan can obtain a learner's permit at 14 years and nine months.

But the high crash rates of U.S. teenagers lead many — like Syracuse, N.Y., high school driver education instructor Ed Bregande — to recommend that states raise their minimum driving ages. He thinks learner's permits should not be issued to anyone younger than 17.

alcohol industry," Hamilton says. "As a country, we've got to start talking about this. We need to change the perception that drinking is a rite of passage, that every teenager is doing it. There are kids who don't drink."

But since statistics show that a large majority of teenagers will try alcohol well before leaving high school, many police departments try to inform young drivers about the serious consequences of mixing alcohol and driving.

Bauer's department recently introduced a program in which high school students drive a John Deere utility vehicle through an obstacle course while wearing special goggles that simulate the vision and balance of someone who is legally drunk.

"The students quickly realize how difficult it is to drive in an impaired state; it really seems to make an impact," Bauer says.

MADD, SADD, law enforcement and advocacy groups sponsor a host of other education programs targeting teens, but for the most part, their success rates are unknown.

Some advocates also suggest systemic changes, including graduated driver's licenses, driving curfews and crackdowns on selling or providing alcohol to teens. Bauer says adult prosecution is harder because some parents let their teenagers drink at home, thinking they are protecting their children by taking away their car keys. Bauer's department has a program, entitled "Parents Who Host Lose the Most," which reminds parents of the consequences of providing alcohol to minors: citations and fines for parents and physical harm for their children.

"The safest thing for parents is to not support any kind of alcohol use for their children because we know that besides drunk driving, it can lead to unwanted, unprotected sex; dangerous burns and falls and alcohol poisoning," Hamilton says.

Parents may not have convinced their kids to abstain from all alcohol, but they have generally succeeded in relating to their teens the concept that if they do drink when partying with their friends, they should choose "designated drivers" who will remain sober. American attitudes about drinking and driving shifted dramatically in the late 1980s, following a major publicity campaign by the Harvard Alcohol Project, which convinced U.S. adults that driving after drinking was irresponsible. Since the designated-driver campaign began in 1988, drunken driving deaths on U.S. roads dropped from 23,626 in 1988 to 16,580 in 1994.[8]

But according to a study conducted by DeJong, rather than completely abstaining from alcohol, teenage designated drivers often tend to be the group member who has consumed the least amount of alcohol or considers himself the least drunk. The study found that 40 percent of all designated drivers on college campuses — where most students are still underage — drink at least one alcoholic beverage before driving and more than 10 percent said they consumed five or more drinks and still drove home as the designated driver.[9]

Parents, however, can still have a substantial impact on their children's drinking and driving behaviors, according to a study by SADD and Liberty Mutual Insurance Co. The study found that parents who actively discourage their children from drinking are much more likely to raise substance-free teenagers. It also found that when parents talk to their kids about drinking, instances of drinking and driving decreased from 18 percent to 8 percent.[10]

"When parents commit to communicating with their children about this important issue, behaviors can change and lives can be saved," Liberty Mutual Executive Vice President John B. Conners said.[11]

— Kate Templin

[1] Mothers Against Drunk Driving (MADD), www.madd.org.

[2] *Ibid.*

[3] National Highway Traffic Safety Administration (NHTSA), www.nhtsa.dot.gov.

[4] MADD, *op. cit.*

[5] National Commission Against Drunk Driving, www.ncadd.com.

[6] NHTSA, *op. cit.*

[7] "Traffic Safety Facts 2003: Young Drivers," National Highway Traffic Safety Administration, www-nrd.nhtsa.dot.gov/pdf/nrd-30/NCSA/TSF2003/809774.pdf.

[8] http://www.hsph.harvard.edu/chc/alcohol.html.

[9] William DeJong and Jay Winsten, "The Use of Designated Drivers by U.S. College Students," The Higher Education Center for Alcohol and Other Drug Prevention, www.edc.org/hec/pubs/articles/des-drivers.pdf.

[10] "Teens Today," SADD and Liberty Mutual Insurance Co., www.saddonline.com.

[11] Liberty Mutual, www.libertymutual.com/personal/teen/2001_press-release.html.

"You hear talk of raising the age now and then," says Williams of the IIHS. "But the political reality is that whenever it has come up, it never goes anywhere."

"I think 16 certainly is too young to drive," concurs Harsha of the Governors Highway Safety Association. "But it's very difficult politically, especially in farm states, to raise the age. There's not enough public or political support yet for increasing the age. Possibly in the future."

Parents are often the biggest obstacle to raising the driving age. As one mother has put it, "When they get their license and they can drive themselves to practice and then drive home, for me, it was great."[38]

Some Cities Legalize Drag Racing

At Indianapolis Raceway Park, they call it "Midnight Madness." At Las Vegas Motor Speedway, it's "Midnight Mayhem." And at San Diego's Qualcomm Stadium, former home diamond of the Padres, it's simply "RaceLegal."

But in each venue the story's the same: Young men and women, mostly teenagers, competing in drag races to the cheers of friends and fans as police officers watch — or compete along with the kids.

Illegal drag racing has existed almost as long as automobiles. But ever since Hollywood began making movies about dragsters in the 1950s, fast cars have become a foundation of youth culture — spurring teens to see just how fast a car can go and striking fear in the hearts of parents and authorities.

Although no statistics exist detailing the extent and scope of illegal street racing in America, *The New York Times* recently reported that law enforcement officials across the country say "it has become a serious problem." Some authorities believe the popularity of two recent drag-racing movies — "The Fast and the Furious" in 2001, and its 2003 sequel, "2 Fast 2 Furious" — are at least partly responsible. For instance, in 1999 the Florida Department of Highway Safety and Motor Vehicles recorded 28 illegal street-racing accidents; by 2003 the number had climbed to 82.[2]

In recent years, some cities have begun channeling the racers off the public streets and into controlled environments. San Diego began suffering "an epidemic" of street racing in the late 1990s, said Stephen Bender, an epidemiologist and professor emeritus in the graduate school of public health at San Diego State University.[3] On any weekend night Bender said, more than 1,000 cars and 4,000 spectators would be involved in drag racing in the San Diego area.[4] In 2002, 16 teenagers were killed and another 31 injured in the illegal contests.[5]

With funding from the California Office of Traffic Safety, Bender started RaceLegal in 1998 as part of a university program at San Diego State. Competitors would have to wear helmets and submit their cars to a safety inspection prior to racing on a four-lane, eighth-mile (regulation length) strip inside Qualcomm Stadium. Drivers paid a $20 entry fee, spectators $5.

At first, drag racers tended to avoid RaceLegal — why pay for something they could keep doing on city streets for free? The San Diego government responded by ratcheting

Williams explains that parents face a dilemma: They want their kids to start driving as soon as possible so the parents don't have to chauffeur them around anymore. "But they also know it's dangerous for kids to drive," he says.

Teens are predictable on the issue. Asked if the minimum driving age should be raised to help reduce teen accident and fatality rates, a 16-year-old student at Northern Virginia Driving School answers for the entire class when he says, "Sure, right after they give me my license."

Others argue for raising the driving age because young minds are supposedly easily influenced by media images of speed. Last summer, for example, several highway and auto safety groups demanded that General Motors (GM) stop running a TV commercial during the Olympics that showed what appeared to be a 10-year-old boy — barely able to see over the steering wheel of a Corvette — driving wildly through a city. A voiceover in the ad called it "the official car of your dreams."

In a letter to GM Chairman G. Richard Wagoner, the groups wrote, "This ad is certainly among the most dangerous, anti-safety messages to be aired on national television in recent years. . . . Ads glorifying speed and high performance are common enough these days, but this is one of the . . . most reprehensible. Auto-industry ads promoting these illegal behaviors, especially in sports and other muscle-type cars, are suspect because they target young people, and this ad unabashedly sinks to a new low."

GM pulled the ad after receiving the complaint.

Some have argued that certain video games — like "Grand Theft Auto," which features reckless driving — have a similar negative influence on younger teens.

But Buckholtz of teendriving.com says, "I haven't seen any indicators that video games have that effect." Instead of raising the minimum driving age, she advocates a balance between needs and statistical reality. "A lot of kids at 16 and 17 have part-time jobs and need to go to activities. But that needs to be tempered by really good rules."

Teendriving.com recommends that teens be forbidden from carrying other teenagers as passengers for the first full year after obtaining a license.

up fines and penalties for illegal racing and then formed a special undercover police unit to enforce the new provisions. First infractions won racers a trip to jail in handcuffs, loss of vehicle for 30 days, $2,500 in fines and two points on their driver's licenses, which also were suspended for a full year. A second infraction caused complete forfeiture of vehicle and longer jail time. Spectators were fined $1,000.[6]

Street racers and their fans started to see the economic sense of going to RaceLegal. In 2001, San Diego prosecutors filed 290 illegal racing cases; in 2002 they filed 155, and in 2003 they filed only 60. Most important, Lydia DeNecochea, program director of RaceLegal, says that in 2004, only six illegal street racers died and 15 were injured.

"Our success is really a combination of all the efforts," DeNecochea says, referring to the city's toughened fines and penalties along with the police department's aggressive enforcement. "The alternative that RaceLegal offers is important, but if any of those other efforts were to weaken, I think we'd see a change in the statistics."

On a typical winter night, RaceLegal now attracts about 250 racers and 1,500 spectators, DeNecochea says. (In summer, 350 cars and 2,500 spectators.) Though police officers ensure that the races are organized and run properly, competitors sign a liability waiver. After showing a valid driver's license and passing a vehicle safety inspection, they then form two lines leading to the starting line of the drag strip.

The cars are all kinds — from Mustang Mach 1's and Chevelle sport coupes to Volvos and pickup trucks. Most of the racers are male, but females show up occasionally — and win. Sometimes police officers race, too, offering teenagers a chance to go head-to-head with a souped-up sheriff's cruiser.

DeNecochea says RaceLegal's insurer requires an ambulance during all racing heats. "In all the years we've been doing this," she says, "there've been only four crashes. Three drove away without a problem. One went to the hospital, but he was later released OK."

Allan F. Williams, chief scientist at the Insurance Institute for Highway Safety, acknowledges the growing popularity of programs like RaceLegal. But he isn't sure what the long-term impact might be. "I'm a researcher," he says. "There just isn't a lot [of data] on legal street racing yet."

[1] See George P. Blumberg, "Full Throttle and Fully Legal," *The New York Times*, Sept. 17, 2004, p. F1.

[2] *Ibid.*

[3] See Leonard Sax, "Teens Will Speed. Let's Watch Them Do It," *The Washington Post*, Nov. 28, 2004, p. B8.

[4] Blumberg, *op. cit.*

[5] "About Us," RaceLegal.com; www.racelegal.com.

[6] Blumberg, *op. cit.*

"Road Ready StreetWise" is a new video game thought to be having a positive influence on teen driving behavior. It is sponsored by RoadReadyTeens.org — a joint venture of DaimlerChrysler, AAA, National Safety Council, MADD, Hewlett Packard, WildTangent and Yahoo! Autos. The video allows teens to experience numerous driving hazards and emergencies in virtual reality.

"We've had over 3 million Web hits and 1.5 million game plays," says DaimlerChrysler's Kreibich-Staruch. "We're capturing kids' attention on average for 16 minutes."

More than 90 percent of teens who played the game said it made them more aware of risks they hadn't realized, and 60 percent said they would be more careful driving as a result, according to a University of Michigan study.[39]

"Whether that 60 percent has actually been more careful, we don't know," Kreibich-Staruch says. But agreeing that it's "impractical," as she puts it, to raise the driving age when so many parents want their teens to start driving as soon as possible, the key is more parental involvement in the early stages of driving, she says.

"Parents simply don't understand the risks," she says. "Even when they raise their awareness, which is good, parents don't think it'll happen to their kids. We had the father of a 16-year-old girl who'd had her license for three months and already had been in two crashes, and he still didn't think she was a bad driver."

BACKGROUND

The Teen Brain

Young people between ages 15 and 19 are three times more likely to die from all causes — primarily auto accidents, followed by homicide, suicide and drugs — than children ages 10 to 14.

Until recently, neuroscientists believed judgment-impairing surges of hormones in the later teen years were responsible for this difference.[40] Scientists had long known that neural connections form astonishingly quickly between birth and age 3, and that by age 6 the brain has already developed 95 percent of its adult structure. But new research shows that the human brain undergoes another period of major development between the onset of adolescence and roughly age 21.

"The biggest changes are occurring in the brain's prefrontal cortex, located right behind the forehead, which governs 'executive' thinking: our ability to use logic, make sound decisions and size up potential risks," the journal *Prevention* recently reported. The findings explain a lot about teen behavior and risk taking — particularly when driving is involved. "Knowing that this decision-making area is still under construction explains plenty about teens," the article continued. "Researchers have found that even among youths who generally show good judgment, the quality of decision-making fizzles in moments of high arousal. Emotion, whether happiness, anger or jealousy — particularly when teens are with their peers — overrides logic, making even the smart ones momentarily dumb."[41]

Researchers now believe the phenomenon helps explain teen behavior that seems to make no sense, such as when a good student who normally respects parents' rules ends up playing a fatal game of chicken on a dark road. Teasing by peers about being afraid, for instance, can temporarily short-circuit a teen's otherwise hardwired knowledge about what's wisely safe or stupidly dangerous.

Yet despite the wealth of statistics showing the frequency with which teens crash and the obvious roles that inexperience and immaturity play, little research exists on specific reasons why teen motor vehicle accidents occur. Bella Dinh-Zarr, director of traffic safety policy for AAA, told the House Committee on Transportation and Infrastructure in 2002 that data on crash causation for all age groups were at least 25 years old. Worse, the majority of the data focuses on factors relating to prevention of future injuries rather than crashes.[42]

The lack of data was most acute regarding teen drivers. While graduated driver licensing had been helping to reduce teen crashes, Dinh-Zarr said, more information is needed because teen crash rates remain disproportionately high. "Very little is known about the teenage driver," she said. "By targeting research to find better information about the cause of crashes — before, during, and immediately after they occur — we can design better interventions to protect young drivers."[43]

Further research into brain-development stages in late adolescence could help shed light on specific causes of crashes.

Car Culture

The most powerful influence on teenagers' relationships with cars has been American pop culture, which has always viewed cars as more than merely a means of transportation. When they first appeared, automobiles were expensive, putting them out of the reach of the average American. A car was a symbol of riches and fame.

That began to change with the advent of the first mass-produced automobile — the Ford Model T. During the first two decades of the 20th century, Henry Ford perfected the use of the assembly line and quickly brought the price of a car to within reach of almost any working family. By 1924, a Model T cost $290.

The American economy began to surge in the 1920s, and cars became the main symbol of growth. From 1916 to 1929, U.S. annual car sales tripled from 9 million to 27 million.[44] The American car culture was born.

The postwar boom of the 1950s spawned the teen car culture. As the economy once again surged — offering plenty of part-time jobs to students — teenagers could afford used cars of their own. And they made them a reflection of themselves.

"The ability to tune and soup-up muscle cars gave average Joes the opportunity to show off their power, their speed and their style in a way that personified the car as character," notes a history of the period.[45]

Hollywood added another layer of meaning: Movies like "Rebel Without a Cause" (1955) made dragsters and motorcycles a form of anti-establishment defiance for alienated youth. The film's wild popularity among teenagers spawned imitators like "Hot Rod Girl" (1956), "Hot Rod Rumble" (1957) and "Dragstrip Girl" (1957).

Such movies typically played at drive-in theaters, which made cars symbolically important — as the place where teen dating often began.

Driving was, in a word, cool. As a man in his 60s who fondly remembers those days has put it, "Between 1957 and 1959, my friends and I learned all the rituals that young boys needed to know concerning driving. We learned how important it was to be noticed behind the wheel of a fast car or with someone who had one. It was a time in our lives that we had looked forward to, having seen those slightly older than us doing the same things.[46]

At the same time, teens seemed to identify with rock 'n' roll music as much as they did with their cars. Rock music and cars seemed made for each other in the 1950s: Many music critics and historians have remarked that since its earliest days and even now, much of rock is about either cars or girls. Some of the first rockers on the scene, from Eddie Cochrane to the Beach Boys, often sang about both. And in cities and towns large and small across America, the songs could be heard blaring from teenagers' car radios.

Did You Know . . . ?

- Motor vehicle crashes are the leading cause of death for American teenagers.
- An average of 10 teen drivers a day were killed in fatal accidents in the United States in 2003. Another 308,000 were injured in fatal crashes.
- Young people ages 15-20 make up 6.7 percent of the total driving population but are involved in 14 percent of all fatal crashes.
- Nearly one in five 16-year-old drivers is involved in an accident in the first year of driving.
- Two out of three teenagers killed in motor vehicle crashes in 2002 were males.
- Since 1975, teen auto deaths have decreased more among males (40 percent) than among females (9 percent).
- 52 percent of teenage auto deaths in 2002 occurred between 9 p.m. and 6 a.m.
- In 2003, 25 percent of the young drivers killed in auto accidents were legally drunk.
- In 2003, 28 percent of the young, male drivers involved in fatal crashes had been drinking, compared with 13 percent of the young, female drivers involved in fatal crashes.
- 65 percent of young drivers who had been drinking and were involved in fatal crashes in 2003 were not wearing seat belts.
- 65 percent of teen passenger deaths occur when another teenager is driving.
- Nearly half of the fatal crashes involving 16-year-old drivers are single-vehicle crashes.

Sources: "Traffic Safety Facts 2003: Young Drivers," National Highway Traffic Safety Administration, 2003, and "Fatality Facts: Teenagers 2002," Insurance Institute for Highway Safety, 2002

Teen Slaughter

It wasn't until 1975 that the Department of Transportation's Fatality Analysis Reporting System began collecting basic data on highway accidents by age groups. Disturbing trends quickly emerged.

That year, more than 8,700 teens (ages 13-19) died on U.S. roads. More than likely, similar numbers had been dying in previous years because subsequent years witnessed a steady increase in teen highway deaths: from 9,356 in 1976 to 9,940 in 1978.[47]

During the 1980s, the number of teens killed in motor vehicle accidents fluctuated between a high of around 8,300 and a low of about 6,700.[48] Experts attributed the decrease in deaths from the previous decade to passage of the National Minimum Drinking Age Act (NMDAA) of 1984, which raised the drinking age to 21.

In 1982, for example, 41 percent of 16- and 17-year-olds and 57 percent of 18-to-20-year-olds who died in car crashes had blood alcohol content (BAC) of .08 or more. In 1985, the first year following enactment of NMDAA, the rates had dropped to 27 percent of 16- and 17-year-olds and 44 percent of 18-to-20-year-olds — the largest one-year drop in alcohol-crash-related statistics ever for those age groups.[49]

During the same period, media attention focused on the problem of teen drinking and driving as well, producing an additional positive effect, says Wallace of SADD.

Nevertheless, the number of teen deaths on highways still seemed extraordinarily high to some experts. "I've studied this problem for 25 years, and for a long time nobody paid attention to it at all," says Williams of the IIHS. "They sort of looked at [teen driving deaths] as collateral damage.

"In fact," he points out, "the idea of graduated licensing goes back to the 1970s. NHTSA tried to prompt states to adopt GDL programs, but no luck. It wasn't until the mid-1990s that it got started, and I don't know why. It's always been kind of a mystery."

Though variations in the different state programs and in methods of evaluating them made it impossible to assess the overall effectiveness of GDL, individual states could report their own results. For instance, in 1997, after the first year of its GDL program, Florida reported a 9 percent reduction in fatal crashes among 15-to-17-year-olds. In 1999, Michigan reported a 25 percent reduction in crashes among 16-year-olds, and North Carolina reported a 27 percent reduction.[50]

In fact, teen driving accidents have declined significantly over the last 25-30 years. In the 15-19 age group, deaths per 100,000 population dropped from 42 in 1980 to 25 in 1998.[51] And while in 1975 more than 8,700 13-to-19-year-olds died in motor vehicle accidents, by 2002 the number was down to 5,933.[52]

But the declines have slowed since the late '90s. The number of teen deaths per 100,000 population has remained at about 25 since 1998, and the number of 13-to-19-year-olds dying in crashes has been inching up since 1993, prompting the current concern and debate over what more can and should be done.

CURRENT SITUATION

Tougher GDLs?

Now that most states have GDL programs, the challenge is making them tougher. "In lots of places, the laws are weak," Williams says.

The IIHS and other groups, such as Advocates for Highway and Auto Safety (AHAS), call for tougher passenger restrictions and earlier curfews. In 2002, 87 percent of teenagers who died in crashes were passengers, and 41 percent died between 9 p.m. and 6 a.m., even though night driving accounted for only about 15 percent of the miles driven by teens.[53]

The AHAS recently asked state legislatures nationwide to pass new laws to help reduce all motor vehicle deaths, citing in particular the need to address teens' late-night driving. At the same time, MADD, DaimlerChrysler, the NTSB, NSC and AAA asked states to bar teens from carrying teenage passengers during their first six months of driving.[54]

Harsha of the Governors Highway Safety Association is urging states to develop programs that focus specifically on older teen drivers. "Older teens have three problems," she says. "They have the lowest seat belt use of any population," she says. "And they tend to speed and drive drunk. So you need underage-drinking programs and programs targeting teen seat belt use and speeding."

Parental — and, hence, state — resistance to passenger and nighttime restrictions so far haven't deterred some, like Maryland Rep. Mandel, who plans to reintroduce her bill restricting the number of passengers allowed in cars driven by Maryland teenagers. The Maryland Senate has passed a similar bill.

"My House colleagues just haven't focused on the issue," she says. However, she believes the recent deaths of at least 17 young people on Washington-area roads, including some in her district, may give impetus to the legislation.

Mandel hopes to follow the lead of Illinois state Sen. John Cullerton, who in 2003 sponsored a bill that prohibited any driver under 18 from driving with more than one passenger under 20, except for family members. Suburban mothers, who originally opposed the restriction because it would mean continued chauffeuring duties, finally supported the bill after learning about statistics suggesting the restriction could save lives. Their support convinced the legislature to enact the bill.[55]

But police officers can't tell by looking whether young drivers or their passengers are under the age limits. "It's hard for police to enforce these things," Williams says. "GDL laws are sometimes so complex that police don't even know what they are." Hence, many advocates insist that parents be the real enforcers of passenger restrictions and curfews.

The federal government, lacking any direct authority over motor-vehicle laws, concentrates on its Healthy People 2010 initiative, which aims to identify the most significant preventable threats to public health and establish national goals to reduce them. Some of the goals seek to reduce automobile fatalities; none focuses specifically on teens, but each involves particular issues that affect teens, such as speeding and alcohol.

Some observers speculate that Washington could link federal highway funding to state compliance with federal preferences for more state restrictions on teen driving — the same method by which the federal government convinced states to accept a national speed limit of 55 miles per hour (since repealed) and a 0.08 BAC rule.

But others don't like that idea. "I wouldn't want states to base teen driving restrictions on monetary incentives," Mandel says. "I'd rather they base them on wanting to

AT ISSUE

Are driver education courses for teenagers effective?

YES

Allen Robinson
CEO, American Driver and Traffic Safety Education Association

Written for *CQ Researcher*, December 2004

You have heard before that driver education is not effective. You will read in the opposing counterpoint that driver education is not effective. Why is that?

Part of the explanation is that researchers and traffic-safety professionals have used erroneous research design to evaluate driver education. Using fatalities as a comparison between trained and untrained drivers is an inappropriate approach. The reason they cannot be used in a random experiment is that there are too few fatalities to produce significant results.

The only valid, random evaluation of driver education has been the DeKalb study. When traffic crashes are used as a measure of effectiveness, the DeKalb study showed that, among those licensed to drive and who had taken driver education, accidents were significantly reduced during the first six months. The estimated magnitude of reduction ranges from 10-20 percent, depending upon control over outside variables.

Too often, comparisons are made of students who have not taken driver education with those who have taken driver education. Those who completed driver education obtained a license and were driving while those who did not complete a driver education program were not driving. When researchers do not control for exposure rates, how can you compare accident rates of two groups that are not equal that have different exposure rates?

The high initial rate of accidents is due to the inexperience of new drivers. The duration of benefit in the DeKalb study was limited to six months. The first six months of driving is the greatest risk for all new drivers and is where the accident experience is the highest. Studies conducted by the Insurance Institute for Highway Safety have demonstrated that the accident rate drops by two-thirds in the first 700 miles of driving.

If not driver education, then what? Without formal driver education meeting some specified set of requirements, instruction of new teenage drivers would be left to family, friends or schools operating under no specific requirements.

When asked, the majority of parents favor driver education. Driver education depends on well-prepared teachers teaching safe driving practices using the best available teaching techniques and curricula.

NO

Allan F. Williams
Chief Scientist, Insurance Institute for Highway Safety

Written for *CQ Researcher*, December 2004

Driver education for beginners might be a convenient way to learn basic driving skills, but it does not produce drivers less likely to be in crashes. This is not a matter of opinion. The best scientific evaluations of driver education all over the world come to this conclusion. The most recent review finds "little evidence that pre-license training per se reduces crash rates in the short or longer term."

Studies also have found an association between driver education and earlier licensure, which enhances mobility at the expense of safety. Moreover, research indicates that courses teaching advanced driving maneuvers — such as skid control — lead to more rather than fewer crashes by inspiring overconfidence and risk taking.

There is no mystery about why driver education fails to reduce crashes. Peer, parental, personal and other social influences that shape driving styles and crash involvement — which are largely beyond the reach of instructors — can readily overwhelm safety messages. As early as the 1970s, researcher Pat Waller noted the unrealistic expectations we have of driver education teachers, compared with teachers of other subjects. She asked, "Should the driver education teacher be responsible only for whether the student *can* drive adequately, or whether he *does* drive in this manner?"

No one expects a few hours of instruction in woodworking or culinary arts to produce skilled craftsmen or gourmet cooks, so why should we expect a few hours of driver education to produce skilled drivers? Even if it did, skilled drivers are not necessarily safe drivers.

Despite decades of research indicating that driver education does not reduce crashes among beginners, it continues to have tremendous popular appeal. There is great variation in the quality of driver education courses in the United States, so it is difficult to generalize about how well they teach beginners necessary skills. But even the best course is only a first step.

Experience and maturity are the keys to becoming a safer driver. In the United States we have recognized this by adopting graduated licensing, a main component of which extends the learner's period to maximize the amount of supervised driving by young beginners before they are licensed. Parents do most of the supervising. This is the best formula for preparing young beginners for the delights — and dangers — of driving.

save lives." Others, like Balko of the Cato Institute and Skrum of the National Motorists Association, oppose the idea because they feel that states are the best judges of their own driving restrictions.

Nearly all advocacy groups are seeking ways to develop or encourage parents to be more involved with teaching their teenagers to drive, particularly in supervising them during their first months of receiving a learner's permit.

"We advocate that parents log 100 hours minimum driving with their kids, taking them out in bad conditions, showing them the situations they may encounter and giving them a chance to practice," says Buckholtz of teendriving.com. "That's about the minimum you need before you can drive on your own."

> **"We advocate that parents log 100 hours minimum driving with their kids."**
>
> ***— Eileen Buckholtz, Administrator, teendriving.com***

Some states already have a parent-student driver requirement, but it is not known whether parents actually fulfill it. Maryland, for example, requires teenagers to log at least 40 hours of driving with their parents before applying for a provisional license. "But we have to go on the parents' word," says Jeff Tosi, a spokesman for the Maryland Motor Vehicle Administration.

Moreover, a recent study questions whether parents are the best driving instructors or role models. In 2004, SADD and Liberty Mutual Insurance surveyed some 3,500 middle and high school students. About two-thirds said their parents were or would be the greatest influence on their driving habits — the same percentage that said their parents talk on cell phones while driving. In addition, almost half said their parents speed, and 31 percent reported their parents didn't wear their seat belts.[56]

The parental habits were clearly reflected in the habits of the licensed drivers who were surveyed: 62 percent said they talk on a cell phone while driving; 67 percent were speeders, and 33 percent didn't wear a seat belt.[57]

"Parents have to lead by example," says DaimlerChrysler's Kreibich-Staruch. "There's no need to eat while driving, change clothes while driving, put on make-up or shave. Teens will think that's all OK."

She recommends that parents go to the RoadReadyTeens .org Web site, which has a portal dedicated to helping parents learn the most effective ways to positively influence their teenagers' driving.

Meanwhile, the American Driver and Traffic Safety Education Association continues to help states upgrade their driver education programs. For example, ADTSEA recommends that programs emphasize teaching student drivers to anticipate risky situations and how best to respond to them. Some states, like Michigan, have expanded driver education by requiring a preliminary, standard course for new drivers, then a second round of more detailed driver education after six months of driving with a restricted license.

"We're trying to increase the maturity and experience of young drivers," Robinson said.[58]

OUTLOOK

The Marijuana Menace

I hope teen accident rates go down," says Wallace of SADD, echoing the sentiments of all safety advocates.

But they'll need more than hope: Despite some lowering of teen deaths and injuries from motor vehicle crashes when GDL programs were first implemented, teen auto death and injury rates have either remained essentially unchanged or increased over the last several years, depending on how the data are analyzed.

Harsha, of the Governors Highway Safety Association, points out that every year more teenagers take to the roads as the teen population increases, and safety programs and initiatives take a while to have a significant impact. "So, for the foreseeable future we'll continue to see what we've been seeing," she says.

Wallace fears that teens driving under the influence of drugs may be the next obstacle to reducing accident rates. "It's the phantom menace that nobody's talking about," he says. In presentations at high schools around the country, Wallace has discovered that teens have three myths about marijuana: It doesn't impair driving ability; it's not harmful and it's not addictive.

"It is," he says.

Yet, while 30 percent of teenagers say they can't drink because they'll be driving, only 18 percent will say they can't use drugs because they'll be driving, according to the SADD-Liberty Mutual study. And the majority — 68 percent — of licensed teen drivers who use drugs regularly said they frequently drug and drive.[59]

SADD has joined with the White House Office of National Drug Control Policy to launch a "Steer Clear of Pot" campaign, Wallace says. The goal is to educate both parents and teenagers about the risks of marijuana use and driving.

He remains optimistic. "When you get people to focus on the problems," he says, "they start to respond."

RoadReadyTeens.org is hoping teens and parents will respond to a CD-ROM it plans to distribute in a trial with the state motor vehicle offices of California, Texas, Virginia, Pennsylvania and New York. It will include safety information and advice for parents as well the video game "StreetWise" for teens. When parents take their teenagers to apply for a license, "there's usually a long wait in DMV offices," DaimlerChrysler's Kreibich-Staruch says. "This will give them something to do. As we raise awareness, I think it'll filter down to teens, but I don't know when we'll see any big change in fatality rates."

Some businesses see a market in parents who may think the only way to make sure their teenagers drive safely is to watch them every time they drive. SmartDriver of Houston, Texas, and Road Safety International of Thousand Oaks, Calif., have created electronic monitoring devices that can be easily installed on newer model cars. The devices record various parameters of a vehicle in operation, including speed. One device can even sound an alarm if the vehicle exceeds a particular speed or if the driver does not wear a seat belt.[60]

But the effect that any measures — old or new — will have remains elusive. As Kreibich-Staruch observes, "It's tough to say what's going to happen. We can only hope that parents and teens will work together to solve this."

NOTES

1. See Tom Jackman, "Fairfax Girl, 16, Killed in Crash of SUV," *The Washington Post*, Dec. 5, 2004, p. C1.
2. See Fredrick Kunkle and Elizabeth Williamson, "As Dreams Die Young, Answers are Elusive; Teen Traffic Fatalities Spur Calls for Change," *The Washington Post*, Oct. 24, 2004, p. A1.
3. *Ibid.*
4. "Traffic Safety Facts 2003: Young Drivers," National Highway Traffic Safety Administration, 2004.
5. *Ibid.* See also, National Highway Traffic Safety Administration Office of Public Affairs, December 2004.
6. "Traffic Safety Facts 2003," *op. cit.*
7. "Q&A: Teenagers," Insurance Institute for Highway Safety, March 2004; www.iihs.org/safety_facts/qanda/teens.htm.
8. National Center for Health Statistics, Centers for Disease Control, December 2004.
9. "Teen Driving Death Rate Soaring," CBSNews.com, Oct. 21, 2004.
10. "Teen Drivers," Fact Sheet, National Center for Injury Prevention and Control, Centers for Disease Control, www.cdc.gov/ncipc/factsheets/teenmvh.htm.
11. Fact Sheet, Mothers Against Drunk Driving, www.madd.org/stats/0,1056,1807,00.html.
12. "Traffic Safety Facts 2003: Young Drivers," *op. cit.*
13. "Young Drivers: The High-Risk Years," video presentation, Insurance Institute for Highway Safety, 2002.
14. *Ibid.*
15. *Ibid.*
16. See James Hedlund, *et al.* "What We Know, What We Don't Know, and What We Need to Know About Graduated Licensing," *Journal of Safety Research*, Vol. 34, No. 1 (January 2003), pp. 107-115.
17. Patrick Welsh, "Sweet 16: Not for driving," *USA Today*, Nov. 29, 2004, p. 15A
18. "Teens 'Inherit' Parents' Bad Driving Habits; Annual Liberty Mutual/SADD Teen Driving Study Shows Parent Driving Behaviors Mirrored by Their Kids," press release, Aug. 10, 2004; www.libertymutual.com.
19. "A Youthquake is Coming! Increased Traffic Deaths Feared From Surge in Teen Population," American Driver & Traffic Safety Education Association, http://adtsea.iup.edu/adtsea/resource_library/young_driver_articles/youthquake.htm.
20. *Ibid.*
21. "Q&A: Teenagers," *op. cit.* See also Fredrick Kunkle and Elizabeth Williamson, "Safety Experts Doubt Benefits of Driver's Ed; Lots of Practice With Parent Seen as Surest Way to Learn," *The Washington Post*, Nov. 22, 2004, p. A1.

22. *Ibid.*
23. *Ibid.*
24. "Q&A: Teenagers," *op. cit.*
25. "Introduction: The Need for Graduated Driver Licensing," National Highway Transportation Safety Administration; www.nhtsa.dot.gov/people/injury/newdriver/SaveTeens/sect1.html.
26. Hedlund, *et al.*, *op. cit.*
27. "Q&A: Teenagers," *op. cit.*
28. Kunkle and Williamson, "As Dreams Die Young," *op. cit.*
29. National Center for Health Statistics, Centers for Disease Control, December 2004.
30. See Allan F. Williams, "Teenage Drivers: Patterns at Risk," *Journal of Safety Research*, Vol. 34, No. 1 (January 2003), pp. 5-15.
31. *Ibid.*
32. "Q&A: Teenagers," *op. cit.*
33. "Young Drivers: The High-Risk Years," *op. cit.*
34. See Allan F. Williams, "Teenage Passengers in Motor Vehicle Crashes: A Summary of Current Research," Insurance Institute for Highway Safety, December 2001.
35. "Teens and Driving," http://teenink.com/Past/1998/9586.html.
36. See Jon Walker, "Teen-driving bill convenient, but is it safe?," *Argus* (Sioux Falls, S.D.) *Leader*, Feb. 23, 2004, p. 1A.
37. See Jim McKeever, "Recent Deaths Raise Alarm About Teen Drivers; Hormones, Lack of Brain Development Put Them at Higher Risk for Accidents," *The* [Syracuse, N.Y.] *Post-Standard*, Oct. 24, 2004, p. A16.
38. "Young Drivers," Insurance Institute for Highway Safety, *op. cit.*
39. C. R. Bingham and J. T. Shope, "An Initial Evaluation of the Road Ready Teens Video Game: Final Report," University of Michigan, Ann Arbor, Transportation Research Institute, 2003.
40. See Sarah Mahoney, "What Was He Thinking? Don't Blame It All on Hormones. New Research Shows What Really Happened," *Prevention*, March 1, 2004, p. 158.
41. *Ibid.*
42. Bella Dinh-Zarr, testimony before the House Committee on Transportation and Infrastructure, June 27, 2002.
43. *Ibid.*
44. "U.S. Economic History," Microsoft Encarta.
45. "Car Culture in America — Captivating Generation After Generation," www.doityourself.com/auto/car-culture.htm.
46. See Russ Lancaster, "Cruising and Dragging: Teenagers and Their Cars," www.history. ilstu.edu/nhp/civilization/Site/car_cruising.html.
47. "Fatality Facts: Teenagers 2002," Insurance Institute for Highway Safety, www.iihs.org/safety_facts/fatality_facts/teens.htm.
48. *Ibid.*
49. *Ibid.*
50. "Fact Sheet: Graduated Licensing," Advocates for Highway and Auto Safety, July 2003, www.saferoads.org/issues/fs-GDL.htm.
51. "Motor Vehicle Deaths," Child Trends Data Bank, 2003, www.childtrendsdatabank.org.
52. "Fatality Facts: Teenagers 2002," *op. cit.*
53. "Q&A: Teenagers," *op. cit.* See also Teen Driver: A Family Guide to Teen Driver Safety, National Safety Council, 2004, p. 33.
54. See Rebecca Dana, "States Implored to Curb Teen Driving; Graduated Licensing, Limits on Passengers Urged by Safety Groups," *The Washington Post*, Dec. 17, 2004, p. B1.
55. See Melissa Savage, "Surviving Driving," *State Legislatures*, February 2004, p. 16.
56. "Teens 'Inherit' Parents' Bad Driving Habits; Annual Liberty Mutual/SADD Teen Driving Study Shows Parent Driving Behaviors Mirrored by Their Kids," press release, Aug. 10, 2004.
57. *Ibid.*
58. See Fred Bayles, "States Trying to Shift the Decline in Driver's Education," *USA Today*, Sept. 22, 2003, p. 3A.
59. SADD-Liberty Mutual study, *op. cit.*
60. See Jeanne Wright, "Black Boxes Can Monitor Teen Drivers," *Los Angeles Times*, Jan. 29, 2003, Part 7, p. 1.

BIBLIOGRAPHY

Books

Crossman, Donna R., and Richard Crossman, *Sixteen Is Too Young to Drive: Taking Control When Your Teen's Behind-the-Wheel, Footnote Publishing*, 2002.
Parents with 25 years of combined experience as defensive-driving instructors advise parents on how to safely manage their teens' efforts at learning to drive.

***Teen Driver: A Family Guide to Teen Driver Safety, National Safety Council*, 2004.**
American and foreign experts helped prepare this detailed, reader-friendly synthesis of the findings of a symposium on graduated driver licensing programs.

Articles

Durbin, Dee-Ann, "Uniform Driver Education Programs Needed for Teens, Experts Say," *The Associated Press*, Oct. 28, 2003.
The American Driver and Traffic Safety Education Association calls for national driver education standards so teenagers everywhere can receive uniform training.

Glasser, Debbie, "Parents, Teens Should Make Driving Contract; Positive Parenting," *The Miami Herald*, Oct. 28, 2004, p. SW4.
Parents should supervise their teen drivers by monitoring their behavior and setting restrictions, Glasser writes.

Gutierrez, Hector, "Teen Driver Limits Gain Support," *Rocky Mountain News*, Oct. 6, 2004, p. 10A.
As Colorado state legislators weigh a bill proposing teen passenger restrictions, parents urge the government to consider even more restrictions.

Kunkle, Fredrick, and Elizabeth Williamson, "As Dreams Die Young, Answers are Elusive; Teen Traffic Fatalities Spur Calls for Change," *The Washington Post*, Oct. 24, 2004, p. A1.
A recent spate of teen driving accidents in the Washington, D.C., area prompts experts and parents to question existing safety practices and standards.

Kunkle, Fredrick, and Elizabeth Williamson, "Safety Experts Doubt Benefits Of Driver's Ed; Lots of Practice With Parent Seen as Surest Way to Learn," *The Washington Post*, Nov. 22, 2004, p. A1.
Safety experts argue that driver's education does not reduce teen crash rates and that more direct parental involvement with their teens' driving is the key.

Mahoney, Sarah, "What Was He Thinking? Don't Blame it All on Hormones. New Research Shows What Really Happened," *Prevention*, March 1, 2004, p. 158.
New research reveals that children undergo a second period of significant brain development between the onset of adolescence and about age 21, suggesting that poor driving behaviors and decisions may be neurologically influenced.

McKeever, Jim, "Recent Deaths Raise Alarm About Teen Drivers; Hormones, Lack of Brain Development Put Them at Higher Risk for Accidents," *The* (Syracuse, N.Y.) *Post-Standard*, Oct. 24, 2004, p. A16.
The motor vehicle deaths of three area high school students cause parents to caution their teenagers about driving too many teen passengers.

Savage, Melissa, "Surviving Driving," *State Legislatures*, February 2004, p. 16.
Teen drivers continue to crash at disproportionately high rates, but states hold the power to bring the rates down through better enforcement of graduated driver licensing provisions and instituting further restrictions on teen drivers.

Reports and Studies

"Fatality Facts: Teenagers 2002," *Insurance Institute for Highway Safety*.
Data showing teen crash rates and some causative factors date back to 1975.

"Traffic Safety Facts 2003: Young Drivers," *National Highway Traffic Safety Administration*, 2004.
Annual compilation of statistics concerning motor vehicle accidents, deaths and injuries among teenagers.

Hedlund, James, *et al.*, "What We Know, What We Don't Know, and What We Need to Know About Graduated Licensing," *Journal of Safety Research*, Vol. 34, No. 1 (January 2003), pp. 107-115.
An interpretation and summary of the extensive research and data presented at a 2002 symposium sponsored by the National Safety Council on graduated driver licensing programs.

Williams, Allan F., "Teenage Drivers: Patterns at Risk," ***Journal of Safety Research*****, Vol. 34, No. 1 (January 2003), pp. 5-15.**
The chief scientist for the Insurance Institute for Highway Safety identifies patterns of teen driving risks.

Williams, Allan F., "Teenage Passengers in Motor Vehicle Crashes: A Summary of Current Research," ***Insurance Institute for Highway Safety*****, December 2001.**
A detailed overview of research showing clearly that as the number of teen passengers in a car increases, so does the chance for a deadly accident.

For More Information

Advocates for Auto and Highway Safety, 750 First St., N.E., Suite 901, Washington, DC 20002; (202) 408-1711; www.saferoads.org. A coalition of insurers, citizens' groups and public health and safety organizations.

American Driver & Traffic Safety Education Association, Highway Safety Center, Indiana University of Pennsylvania, R & P Bldg., Indiana, PA 15705; (724) 357-3975; www.adtsea.org. Works with driver's education instructors and state authorities to improve driver's education standards and practices.

Insurance Institute for Highway Safety, 1005 N. Glebe Rd., Suite 800, Arlington, VA 22201; (703) 247-1500; www.iihs.org. Researches highway safety and conducts crash tests on new cars and trucks; funded by auto insurance companies.

Mothers Against Drunk Driving, P.O. Box 541688, Dallas, TX 75354-1688; (800) GET-MADD; www.madd.org. With more than 600 chapters nationwide, fights drunken driving and supports victims of alcohol-related crimes.

National Highway Traffic Safety Administration, 400 Seventh St., S.W., Washington, DC 20590; (202) 366-9550; www.nhtsa.dot.gov. Issues vehicle safety standards, investigates safety defects and orders recalls when necessary.

National Safety Council, 1121 Spring Lake Dr., Itasca, IL 60143; (630) 285-1121; www.nsc.org. Conducts research and provides information on highway safety.

RoadReadyTeens, www.roadreadyteens.org. An online safety program for parents and teens sponsored by several corporate and nonprofit safety groups.

Students Against Destructive Decisions, P.O. Box 800, Marlborough, MA 01752; (877) SADD-INC; www.sadd.org. A peer-to-peer education organization with 10,000 chapters in middle and high schools.

13

Youth Suicide

Should Government Fund More Prevention Programs?

David Hosansky

AP Photo/Evan Vucci

Disturbing testimony on the possible link between youth suicide and antidepressants troubles Arizona parent Lorrie Weight during a hearing in Bethesda, Md., on Feb. 2, 2004. The hearing was held by a Food and Drug Administration scientific panel, which urged the FDA to issue stronger warnings to doctors prescribing antidepressants to anyone under age 18.

From *CQ Researcher*, February 13, 2004.

When his girlfriend broke up with him, 16-year-old Joe Muñoz was devastated. "I decided I'd show her; I'd kill myself," recalls Muñoz, now 42 and a Dallas freelance journalist.

But after taking two bottles of sleeping pills, the heartbroken teenager realized he had made a mistake. Instead of peacefully drifting into death as he had expected, his heart started painfully racing. Terrified, he told his younger brother to call the police. After being in a coma for two days, he found himself in the hospital — weak and frightened, but alive.

"You're a teenager, you've got hormones flooding your body, your girlfriend breaks up with you and all of a sudden it's the most horrible thing in the world, and you're never going to get better," he says. "You get so wrapped up in your teenage angst that it blinds you to everything else."

Muñoz' experience is not unusual. In recent years, about 2,800 young people between 10 and 21 have killed themselves annually, including about 1,600 in the emotionally volatile 15-to-19-year-old age group.[1] Millions more suffer from emotional problems and are at risk of suicide. In fact, every year more than 3 million high school students — one in five — consider or imagine committing suicide, according to the Centers for Disease Control and Prevention (CDC). About a third of those actually make an attempt, with some 400,000 requiring medical attention.

"If this were an infectious disease, we would call this an epidemic," said Joseph Woolston, chief of child psychiatry at Yale-New Haven Hospital.[2]

Recognizing Suicide Warning Signs

Suicidal tendencies among adolescents often go undiagnosed, in part because emotional instability is often misinterpreted as normal teenage mood swings. Here are some important warning signs to watch for among adolescents.

Makes suicide threats, direct and indirect
Is obsessed with death
Writes poems, essays or makes drawings about death
Exhibits dramatic change in personality or appearance
Shows irrational or bizarre behavior
Has an overwhelming sense of guilt, shame or reflection
Eating or sleeping patterns change
School performance shows severe drop
Gives away belongings

Source: National Mental Health Association

Suicide is a significant public health problem for all age groups, but especially among the elderly. Adults 65 and older have had the highest suicide rate of all age groups since 1933, when states began reporting suicide deaths.

While suicide is viewed as tragic at any age, it is perhaps more understandable among the elderly, who may be suffering from serious, end-of-life physical ailments. But when a young person commits suicide, experts say it is often because youths have trouble coping with both the rapid physiological changes that occur during adolescence and social pressures — such as dating, applying for college and possibly beginning to drink or take drugs.

"A lot of the kids are dealing with depression, loss, frustration, acute disappointment, rejection; sometimes they don't make the team, they break up with their boyfriend or girlfriend," explains David Fassler, a child psychiatrist in Burlington, Vt., and an associate professor at the University of Vermont. "You mix that kind of fairly common incident with impulsivity and substance abuse," and the result may be suicide.

Experts began seeing youth suicide as a major problem in recent decades, after the youth suicide rate nearly tripled between 1952 and 1996. Although the rate has decreased in recent years, suicide remains the third leading cause of death among 15-to-21-year-olds (after accidents and homicides). More American teens die at their own hands than from cancer, heart disease, AIDS, birth defects, stroke, pneumonia, influenza and chronic lung disease — combined.[3]

Similar high tolls overseas have caught the attention of the World Health Organization, which in 1996 urged member nations to address the suicide problem. In 1999 Surgeon General David Satcher called for a concerted effort to reduce suicide rates in the United States.

"The nation must address suicide as a significant public health problem and put into place national strategies to prevent the loss of life and the suffering suicide causes," Satcher said.[4]

But suicidal youngsters are difficult to identify and treat, and only limited government funds have been allocated for the problem. Few schools have programs to screen or counsel emotionally troubled students, rural areas often lack appropriate treatment facilities, and many states have not developed comprehensive suicide prevention plans.

Most suicidal teens have underlying emotional problems — especially depression — but parents, teachers and friends often miss the warning signs, thinking their moody youngsters are simply acting like normal teenagers.

"Many parents don't recognize when adolescents are depressed," says Lawrence Riso, a psychology professor at Georgia State University. "When their mood fluctuates quite a bit, they're seen as just being an adolescent. They may be depressed and one hour later look fine and go out and play basketball."

In contrast, he adds, "When you're an adult and you're depressed, you tend to not look good for weeks or months."

Contrary to popular belief, suicidal youngsters are often successful and full of energy. Laurie Flynn, director of the Carmel Hill Center for Early Diagnosis and Treatment at Columbia University, was shocked when

Experts Differ on Why Suicide Rate Is Declining

The number of youth suicides in the United States peaked in 1994 and has been declining ever since. Some experts say the rate has decreased because of a greater usage of antidepressants by youths, but new evidence indicates the new drugs may actually spur suicide attempts in younger patients.

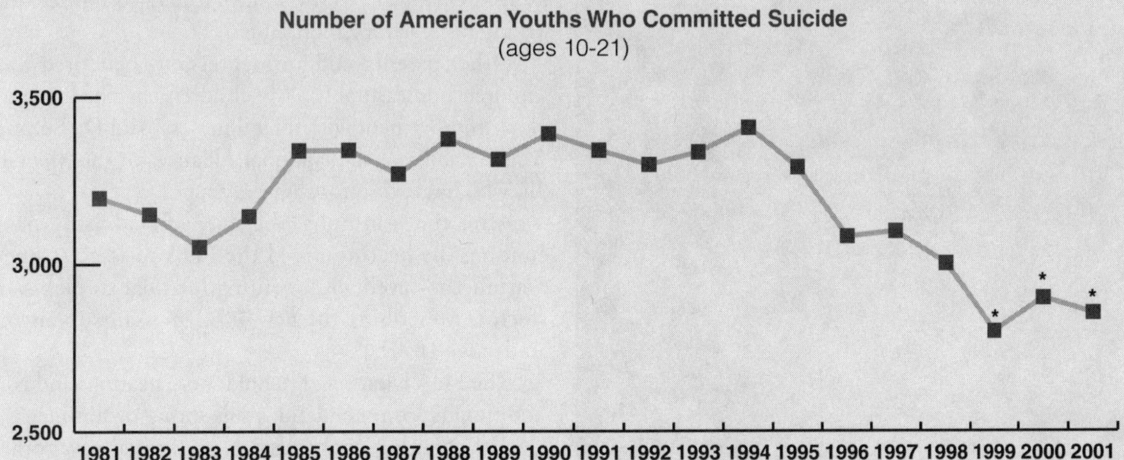

* The way in which suicide is recorded changed significantly in 1999, making it difficult to compare the number of deaths and death rates from 1998 and before with data after 1999.

Sources: Centers for Disease Control and Prevention, www.cdc.gov/ncipc/wisqars and National Center for Health Statistics, Vital Statistics System

her 17-year-old daughter, a top student, attempted suicide. "She was one of those kids who was a little star, active in the community," Flynn says. "I thought if she was depressed, I would see it. The truth is, you don't know."

Flynn later learned about a history of depression in the family. Her daughter has since graduated from college and is married.

Suicide rates are higher among whites — particularly white males — than among blacks. But certain minorities, such as Native Americans and Native Alaskans, have even higher rates. In fact, suicidal children come from all racial and socioeconomic backgrounds.

"This is an equal-opportunity event," warns child psychiatrist Harold Koplewicz, director of the Child Study Center at New York University.

Suicide is especially prevalent among youths in rural areas, perhaps because of widely scattered mental health services and the easy availability of firearms. Some experts argue that stricter gun control laws would help reduce the youth suicide rate, but others say youngsters would simply turn to other means to end their lives. (*See sidebar, p. 298.*)

Some research indicates that childhood emotional problems are on the rise.[5] An extensive analysis found that almost one in five children suffers from an emotional or behavioral illness. That's nearly triple the level of 20 years ago.[6] Experts are divided over whether the increase is due to societal changes — such as higher rates of substance abuse and fewer tight-knit families and communities — or to some other cause. Some studies indicate that kids who are bullied, gay or bisexual are particularly prone to depression and suicide.

Controversy also rages over the use of antidepressants to treat emotionally troubled and potentially suicidal teens. Doctors are writing 2 million antidepressant prescriptions a year for young people — sometimes in combination with therapy and sometimes without it. Some

AP Photo/Ralph Wilson

After three local teenage boys killed themselves recently, Judge John B. Leete of Coudersport, Pa., helped bring the Yellow Ribbon suicide-prevention program to town. Across the country, few schools have suicide screening or counseling programs, and many states lack comprehensive suicide-prevention plans. An estimated 1,600 youths ages 15-19 will take their own lives this year.

studies indicate that Paxil, Zoloft and other new-generation antidepressants may help reduce youth suicide rates, but other data indicate that such drugs may actually spur suicide attempts.[7]

Concerned by data linking the new antidepressants with suicidal thoughts and behavior in children and adolescents, British regulators in December warned doctors not to prescribe some of those drugs for young people.[8] The U.S. Food and Drug Administration (FDA) last year recommended that doctors refrain from giving them to children.

The FDA launched hearings on the highly charged issue on Feb. 2, 2004. Several bereaved parents urged officials to ban antidepressant use by children. "You have an obligation today [to prevent] this tragic story from being repeated over and over again," said Mark Miller of Kansas City, Mo., whose son Matt hanged himself after taking his seventh Zoloft tablet.

Other parents said antidepressants benefited their children immeasurably. "My children have had tremendous improvement with their illnesses," said Dr. Suzanne Vogel-Scibilia of the National Alliance for the Mentally Ill, who has two sons using the drugs.

After the testimony, the scientific advisory panel holding the hearing urged the FDA to issue stronger warnings — even while waiting for final studies — to doctors prescribing the new antidepressants to anyone under age 18.[9]

The FDA is expected to hold more hearings and issue additional recommendations this spring or summer.

Although less controversial, traditional psychotherapy sometimes doesn't work as well for teens, who tend to assert their independence from adults and thus may resist suggestions from a psychologist. In addition, troubled kids often live in dysfunctional families, which have trouble making sure the patient gets to psychotherapy sessions every week. Still, Riso says, psychotherapy can improve teens' moods and "decrease the frequency of suicidal behavior."

Unfortunately, most children never get the help they need. Mental health experts estimate that less than one-third of children with emotional problems — and as few as one-fifth of children with depression — receive treatment. "Earlier diagnoses and more vigorous treatment can lower the rate," says psychiatrist David C. Clark, director of the Center for Suicide Research and Prevention at Rush University Medical Center in Chicago. "Most people who die from suicide aren't getting psychiatric treatment."

To reduce the teen suicide rate, experts say it is vital to identify at-risk youngsters and get them into treatment. Several public schools have programs to train parents, teachers and students to spot potentially depressed children, and some experts say screening for suicidal tendencies should be as widespread as screening for hearing problems. (*See sidebar, p. 304.*)

However, the programs have earned mixed reviews, and officials in many schools are leery of raising the topic of suicide. Even mental health professionals who say school-based programs may help reduce the suicide rate say the topic needs to be approached carefully so as not to inadvertently spur suicide attempts and "clusters," in which several youths in the same community kill themselves.

"Teens are so impressionable that it's important that the information not be presented in a way that glamorizes suicide and makes a teen at risk consider suicide just because someone talks about it," says Lee Judy, certification coordinator of the American Association of Suicidology.

Meanwhile, few schools have counselors trained to help suicidal youngsters, and many regions lack counselors who specialize in emotionally troubled young people.

"It's a huge problem, and there aren't enough dollars," says Cheryl DiCara, coordinator of the Maine Youth Suicide Prevention Program.

Millions of dollars are spent each year on substance abuse prevention in schools, but youth suicide "is not getting the attention it needs as a public-health problem," says John Kalafut, a Rutgers University psychology professor and president of the American Association of Suicidology.

As society grapples with the problem of youth suicide, here are some questions it must address:

Is society to blame for youth suicide?

More than 20 years ago, when Kalufut began asking high-schoolers whether they knew anyone who had ever attempted suicide, 30 to 40 percent would raise their hands, the Rutgers professor recalls. "Now it's 100 percent," he says.

Rare from the time the government began compiling records in 1933 until the 1950s, youth suicide peaked in the early 1990s with the suicide rate for teens ages 15-19 reaching 11.1 per 100,000 population. Since then, the rate has declined significantly, to 7.9 per 100,000 in 2001. But that's still much higher than in 1950, when it was just 4.5 per 100,000.[10]

Moreover, suicide rates rose alarmingly in the 1990s for certain populations: The rate for youngsters 10-14 doubled between 1980 and 1996 — even though psychologists once thought children so young were immune to depression. The rate among that age group has been declining since it peaked in 1995, except for an increase in 1998. The rate for teenage girls stayed level in the mid-1990s after the rate for older boys began to decline, but the rate of girls' suicides has also begun to decline in recent years.

"For most people, [suicide] is probably a squeamish topic," said Dan Casseday, whose 16-year-old son committed suicide in 2002. "But if people understood the statistics about suicide, there'd be panic about [it]."[11]

No one knows what triggered the enormous jump in youth suicides, but many experts say societal changes could be a factor. The American Academy of Pediatrics, for example, lists four possible causes: easy access to firearms and other means of suicide; increasing pressures of modern life; stiff scholastic competition; and increased media violence.[12]

Other mental health professionals point to the breakdown of the nuclear family, manifested by higher divorce rates and more children living in single-parent households. Our increasingly mobile society also may play a role: Multiple changes of homes and schools can lead to emotional isolation, a key factor in youth suicide. Work demands keep many parents at the office until after dinnertime, or on their computers even after they come home, while neglected kids watch television or play video games.

"The reasons are probably broad societal types of things — people not living near extended families, less involvement in religion and other traditional supports," says David Brent, a professor of psychiatry, pediatrics and epidemiology at the University of Pittsburgh and a nationally recognized expert on youth suicide.

"I see a breakdown in the community's involvement in raising children," Kalafut adds. "The postwar generation of parents is the first in history to raise children without significant input from the community."

Others cite increased rates of alcohol and drug abuse, noting that many youths are impaired when they kill themselves. "From the 1960s forward, the biggest driver was the increasing availability of substances — drugs and alcohol," says the Carmel Hill Center's Flynn. "These substances allow youngsters to act on impulse because they take away inhibition."

A 1986 government survey found that half of the youths at risk of killing themselves cited family conflicts, more than one-third mentioned physical or sexual abuse and 17 percent blamed alcohol or drug abuse.[13] All three

Would Gun Control Reduce Suicides?

"Probably the single, most effective thing we could do to reduce the incidence of completed suicide is restrict access to firearms," says David Fassler, a child psychiatrist in Burlington, Vt., and an associate professor at the University of Vermont. "If you're impulsive and having thoughts about hurting yourself, you shouldn't be near them."

More than half of teen suicides are committed with guns.[1] Although girls are twice as likely to attempt suicide, boys are four times more likely to succeed in killing themselves, because they tend to use more lethal means, such as guns. According to a 1999 report by Surgeon General David Satcher, the increase in the rate of suicide during the 1980s and early '90s was almost entirely due to more young people using firearms to end their lives.

After his girlfriend broke up with him, 16-year-old Joe Muñoz, wanted to kill himself with one of his father's guns, but it was locked up. "Had his guns been out of the gun case, I would have shot myself," recalls Muñoz, now 42 and a freelance journalist in Dallas. Instead he took two bottles of sleeping pills, realized what he had done when his heart started palpitating and called for help.

"What I tell parents whose kids are at high risk of suicide is just get the guns out of the house for now," says John Kalafut, a professor of psychology at Rutgers University and president of the American Association of Suicidology. "I have sat with kids who said to me, 'If there had been a gun in my house a year ago, I wouldn't be talking with you today.' "

Although gun-control measures enjoy little political support in Washington, a few states have tightened controls. A new Maryland law requires guns to be sold with trigger locks and requires buyers to take a two-hour gun safety class. Last year, New Jersey passed a law that eventually will require guns to be sold with "smart gun" technology, which allows them to be fired only by an authorized user.

Other proposals — such as making it harder for people under 21 to buy or possess guns — are not getting much political traction.

The politically powerful National Rifle Association (NRA) and other advocates of gun ownership say the restrictions are misguided. The New Jersey law is flawed, they say, because the technology to create smart guns does not exist. And Maryland's restrictions will do little to prevent crimes and accidents with guns, in part because the safety locks are ineffective, they add.

David Eccles, an Annapolis gun shop owner who taught his 3-year-old son how a gun works, contends that it's more effective to explain guns to a child than to use safety locks. "It's not going to be any trick [for a child] to figure out where the keys are kept or how to rip the lock off," he said.[2]

The NRA supports educating children, rather than keeping them away from guns, using a mascot known as

problems became especially prevalent in the second half of the 20th century.

But other experts are not persuaded. Clark at the Center for Suicide Research and Prevention says the youth suicide rate waxed and waned even before the 1930s, when the government began keeping statistics. Although exact statistics are not available, evidence points to a particularly high rate around 1910, he says — a time when society was far different than it is today.

"None of the things we might point to today existed in 1910," he says, adding that more research is needed. "It really takes a major epidemiological study to tease this out. We have to look at thousands and thousands of cases."

Mental health professionals also caution that complex and poorly understood physiological factors should be taken into account, such as how chemical imbalances in the brain can lead to depression and suicide. A 1985 study even suggested that youth suicide victims tend to have mothers who received less prenatal care or smoked and drank during pregnancy.[14]

Others question whether suicide statistics are accurate. Some of the earlier increases could be due to society's greater acceptance today of recording deaths as suicides rather than as accidents. "Coroners were more likely to report suicides in the 1960s [than in earlier decades]," says Koplewicz of the Child Study Center.

Eddie Eagle to teach youngsters four basic steps to follow if they see a gun: Stop, don't touch, leave the area, tell an adult.

"The purpose of the Eddie Eagle Program isn't to teach whether guns are good or bad, but rather to promote the protection and safety of children," the NRA's Web site says. "The program makes no value judgments about firearms, and no firearms are ever used in the program. Like swimming pools, electrical outlets, matchbooks and household poison, they're treated simply as a fact of everyday life. With firearms found in about half of all American households, it's a stance that makes sense."[3]

But gun-control advocates cite a new study, published in the January issue of the journal *Pediatrics*, which found the gun lobby's educational programs were ineffective.[4] "They fail at keeping kids safe from guns," Mike Barnes, president of the Brady Campaign to Prevent Gun Violence United With the Million Mom March, says. "All they do is teach kids to recite the gun lobby's slogans. From an industry standpoint, it's a great marketing tool for introducing young people to guns."

Research on the issue is mixed. Last year, a Centers for Disease Control and Prevention (CDC) task force reviewed 51 studies of whether gun laws prevent violent crimes, suicides or accidents and concluded that the studies were contradictory, incomplete or poorly designed. It called for more research, concluding that there is "insufficient evidence to determine the effectiveness of any of the firearms laws."[5]

But the government is unlikely to conduct much research into the issue. In 1997 Congress forbade the CDC from promoting gun control, and the center's funds for gun research have been slashed from $2.6 million in 1995 to $400,000 in 2002.[6]

"No one knows if better gun control would reduce the suicide rate," says David C. Clark, director of the Center for Suicide Research and Prevention at Rush-Presbyterian-St. Luke's Medical Center, in Chicago.

He notes that some countries with strict gun-control laws, such as Canada, have youth suicide rates that are comparable to or even higher than those in the United States.

"People would shift to other means such as hanging and pills," he says, but he concedes, "We might make a small decrease in youth suicide."

Even though the evidence is mixed, he adds, it might be worthwhile trying to restrict guns and measure the impact on youth suicide. "I, for one, would love to see such an experiment."

---

[1] A report by the Child Trends DataBank concluded that firearms were used in 60 percent of teen suicides in 1999.

[2] Scott Albright, "Unlock and load: Handgun bill brings out emotions on both sides," *The* [Annapolis, Md.] *Capital*, April 9, 2000, p. A1.

[3] See http://www.nrahq.org/safety/eddie/

[4] Michael B. Himle, *et al.*, "An Evaluation of Two Procedures for Training Skills to Prevent Gun Play in Children," *Pediatrics*, January 2004, pp. 70-77.

[5] David Wahlberg, "CDC: Impact of gun laws cloudy," *Los Angeles Times*, Oct. 3, 2003, p. A1.

[6] *Ibid.*

Some experts say the jump in suicide rates was driven by a growing prevalence of emotional distress in the young. According to Koplewicz, more than 3 million American youths suffer from depression, even though childhood depression wasn't even recognized as a disorder until the last 25 years.[15] *The Journal of the American Academy of Child and Adolescent Psychiatry* concluded that increasing numbers of children are depressed and that they are showing more severe symptoms earlier in their lives. In Washington state, more children are hospitalized for psychiatric illnesses than for any other single reason.[16]

Children are aware of the pressures that can lead to emotional distress and even suicide. After the suicide of a 14-year-old student at Palo Alto High School in Silicon Valley, a third of the 756 respondents to a school newspaper poll said they felt very stressed, and an additional 44 percent said they were somewhat stressed.

"So many times we hear kids say, 'I can't go home tonight because I got a B+ on that test, and my parents will kill me,' " said Philippe Rey, associate director of Adolescent Counseling Services in Palo Alto, which works with area schools.[17]

But adults typically struggle to acknowledge or accept such distress in their own children. "We don't like to think of our children and our teenagers having mental disorders," Koplewicz says. "We think, 'What does a kid have to be sad about? It just doesn't make any sense.' "

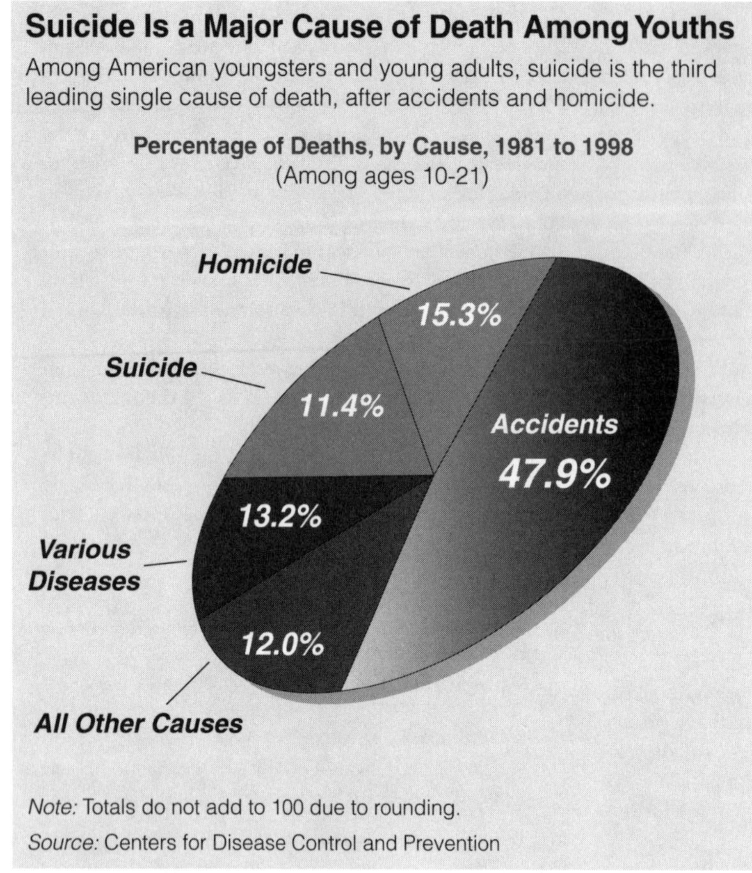

Suicide Is a Major Cause of Death Among Youths

Among American youngsters and young adults, suicide is the third leading single cause of death, after accidents and homicide.

Note: Totals do not add to 100 due to rounding.

Source: Centers for Disease Control and Prevention

Are schools and governments doing enough to prevent youth suicide?

Sue Eastgard is on a sometimes lonely quest. In Washington state, where an average of two youths a week commit suicide, she is both the director and sole full-time employee of the state Youth Suicide Prevention Program. With an annual budget of less than 25 cents per child, she can't reach most of the state's large schools and communities to help them with their programs.

"You can't do a program for $230,000 a year," says Eastgard, who sometimes has to drive three hours each way just to reach a single school. "We need funding to hire more people."

Maine faces a similar situation. The state won a three-year CDC grant to bolster crisis services and help school employees and students recognize at-risk youths in a dozen schools. The grant also pays for several other suicide prevention programs, including a statewide crisis hotline, an information resource center and various training programs. But the funding amounts to less than $300,000 a year, and it runs out next year.

"We want to continue doing this," says DiCara, of the Maine Youth Suicide Prevention Program. "But when this grant goes away, we won't have any money."

Such situations are common. Facing tight budgets and conflicting information about how best to reduce youth suicide rates, states and localities are devoting comparatively few resources to the issue. On the federal level, policymakers have focused more attention on the problem since a 1997 congressional resolution recognizing suicide as a national problem and Surgeon General Satcher's 1999 call for a national suicide prevention strategy.

In the last few years, federal grants for some state-based suicide prevention programs have increased slightly, and the government has helped fund the new national Suicide Prevention Resource Center in Newton, Mass.

States have stepped in as well. For example, nine states fund school-based mental health or suicide prevention programs. Oklahoma has created a Youth Suicide Prevention Council to help community anti-suicide efforts and make policy recommendations, and Washington funds a 24-hour crisis hotline.[18] But advocates warn that most states and communities still lack youth suicide prevention programs, and many people, especially in rural areas, cannot easily obtain counseling services.

"What is lacking is sufficient funding for program development, evaluation, training and initiatives," says Jerry Reed, executive director of the Suicide Prevention Action Network (SPAN). "A solid federal funding commitment to these efforts would undoubtedly reduce the suicide rate among our youth."

Depression Differs Among Adults, Youths

Major depression manifests itself differently in adults, adolescents and children. If a person exhibits four or more symptoms of depression for more than two weeks, experts say he or she should consult a physician.

Typical Signs of Depression:

Adults

Persistent sad or "empty" mood.

Feeling hopeless, helpless, worthless, pessimistic and/or guilty.

Substance abuse.

Fatigue or loss of interest in ordinary activities, including sex.

Disturbances in eating and sleeping patterns.

Irritability, increased crying, anxiety or panic attacks.

Difficulty concentrating, remembering or making decisions.

Thoughts of suicide; makes plans to commit suicide or attempts suicide.

Persistent physical symptoms or pains that do not respond to treatment.

Adolescents

Eating disorders.

Drug or alcohol abuse.

Sexual promiscuity.

Risk-taking behavior, such as reckless driving, unprotected sex or carelessness when walking across busy streets or on bridges or cliffs.

Social isolation, running away, difficulty cultivating relationships.

Constant disobedience, getting into trouble with the law, physical or sexual assaults against others, obnoxious behavior. Failure to care about appearance/hygiene.

No sense of self or of values/morals.

Inability to establish/stick with occupational/educational goals.

Dizziness, headaches, stomach aches, neck aches, arms or legs hurt due to muscle tension, digestive disorders.

Persistent unhappiness, negativity or irritability.

Uncontrollable anger or outbursts of rage.

Overly self-critical, unwarranted guilt, low self-esteem.

Inability to concentrate, remember or make decisions, possibly resulting in refusal to study or an inability to do schoolwork.

Slowed or hesitant speech or body movements, restlessness (anxiety).

Loss of interest in once-pleasurable activities.

Low energy, chronic fatigue or sluggishness.

Change in appetite, noticeable weight loss or gain, or abnormal eating patterns.

Chronic worry, excessive fear.

Preoccupation with death themes in literature, music and/or drawings; speaking of death repeatedly, fascination with guns/knives.

Suicidal thoughts, plans or attempts.

Children

School phobia or avoidance.

Social phobia or avoidance.

Excessive separation anxiety, running away.

Obsessions, compulsions or everyday rituals, such as having to go to bed at the exact time each night for fear something bad may happen.

Chronic illnesses (depression weakens the immune system).

Persistent unhappiness, negativity, complaining, chronic boredom, lack of initiative.

Uncontrollable anger with aggressive or destructive behavior, possibly hitting themselves or others, kicking, self-biting, head banging.

Harming animals.

Continual disobedience.

Easily frustrated, frequent crying, low self-esteem, overly sensitive.

Inability to pay attention, remember, or make decisions, easily distracted, mind goes blank.

Energy fluctuations from lethargic to frenzied activity, with periods of normalcy.

Eating or sleeping problems.

Bedwetting, constipation or diarrhea.

Impulsiveness or being accident-prone.

Chronic worry and fear, clingy, panic attacks.

Extreme self-consciousness.

Slowed speech and body movements.

Disorganized speech.

Dizziness, headaches, stomachaches, arms or legs ache, nail-biting, pulling out hair or eyelashes.

Suicidal talk or attempts.

Source: Suicide Awareness Voices of Education, www.save.org.

Suicide prevention programs are cost-effective, many experts say. Every emergency room visit for a suicide attempt costs taxpayers an average of $33,000.[19] In addition, untreated suicidal youths are more prone to other problems, including dropping out of school, abusing alcohol and drugs and committing violent crimes, including homicide.

"Every juvenile I've represented in a murder case has tried to kill himself," said William Lafond, a defense lawyer in San Diego. "Many of these kids feel helpless and depressed and don't understand why they did what they did. When they try to understand their feelings, they can't handle it."[20]

But even if the government provided more funds for youth suicide prevention programs, the evidence is mixed on how much can be achieved.

Some programs — such as Lifeline — strive to build communities in which at-risk youths are identified and guided into treatment. Designed by Rutgers' Kalafut and used in Maine and some jurisdictions in New Jersey, the program teaches parents, children, teachers and other school employees how to identify youths who appear troubled.

"The emphasis is building a community in which the leaders are committed to creating a safe and supportive environment," Kalafut explains. "Everybody feels responsible for everyone else and is competent to know how to get help for them."

Eastgard says it's important that kids know to look out for each other. She explains, "You say to your friend, 'You look down. Are you feeling so down you're thinking about suicide? Let's go talk to so-and-so' . . . The skills are not to be the junior counselor. The skill is to be comfortable to ask them the question and drag them to help. We're suggesting you don't have to have fancy psychological letters after your name to be an intervener."

There is some evidence such programs can be effective. Youth suicide rates in Bergen County, N.J., dropped by half over a 10-year period in which the local schools used the program, while the rest of the state showed no comparable decline, Kalafut said.

DiCara is heartened when she hears about troubled children who are identified and steered into counseling. "I know it's helping," she says. "We're hearing from a lot of people in these 12 schools that they're already getting kids into services. That's huge."

Other studies, however, raise serious questions about the effectiveness of school programs and even warn that talking about suicide may stir up suicidal thoughts in children. The National Institute of Mental Health (NIMH) concluded: "Many of these programs are designed to reduce the stigma of talking about suicide and encourage distressed youth to seek help. By describing suicide and its risk factors, some curricula may have the unintended effect of suggesting that suicide is an option for many young people who have some of the risk factors and in that sense 'normalize' it — just the opposite of the message intended," the report said. "Of the programs that were evaluated, none has proven to be effective."[21]

Experts particularly criticize the common tactic of having children attend a schoolwide talk after a student commits suicide. Such an approach, they say, can backfire by portraying suicide as a feasible option, sometimes inducing a cluster of suicides in a single school or community.

The University of Pittsburgh's Brant suggests that rather than focusing on suicide, "It's better to educate students more generically about mental health and substance abuse."

But counselors say children are already aware of suicide. Instead of avoiding the subject, they believe, schools should confront it in a sensitive way. "Most of the kids I've talked to were very relieved that suicide was discussed," says Margie Wright, executive director of the Suicide and Crisis Center in Dallas. "You can't plant that idea in someone's head. You're either suicidal or not. The more people are educated, the better off we'll be."

But all of the school programs in the world cannot help if there are insufficient counseling services for youngsters, critics say. Some school districts, especially in isolated areas, lack conveniently located counseling services, and there are only 7,000 board-certified child and adolescent psychiatrists in the United States and fewer than 6,000 child psychologists to treat the several million youths with diagnosable psychiatric disorders.[22]

"The schools can do whatever they want, but if there isn't adequate, competent treatment in the community, then the whole program won't achieve its own goals," Kalafut says. "Every piece has to be in place or the whole thing doesn't work."

CHRONOLOGY

1950s *Psychiatric researchers Leon Cytryn and Donald K. McKnew Jr., note that chronically ill and hospitalized children often exhibit symptoms of classical adult depression.*

1950 Youth suicide rate reaches about 4.5 per 100,000 population.

1960s *Youth suicide rate begins a decades-long climb. . . . Teens have more access to alcohol and drugs, and families appear more fractured. . . . First epidemiological study of a child population identifies depression in less than 1 percent of youngsters.*

1970s *Psychiatric researchers begin noting that depressed children present different symptoms than depressed adults. Cytryn and McKnew suggest three types of childhood depression: acute, chronic and masked.*

1980s *Youth suicide rate continues to climb, as childhood depression is recognized for the first time; schools begin establishing prevention programs.*

1980 Authoritative *Diagnostic and Statistical Manual on Mental Disorders* (*DSM-III*) recognizes depression in children and youths as a distinct disorder.

1983 California creates the first state-funded pilot programs to prevent suicide.

1986 Congress considers the Youth Suicide Prevention Act, which would have authorized the secretary of Education to make grants to local agencies and nonprofit organizations for suicide prevention programs. Instead, lawmakers roll the funding into a general program of state block grants. . . . Government survey of suicide experts finds that many at-risk youths cope with troubled families, physical or sexual abuse or alcohol/drug usage.

1987 Drugmaker Eli Lilly introduces Prozac, a powerful antidepressant.

1990s *Youth suicide rate peaks for various populations, reaching 11.1 per 100,000 for older teenagers before beginning to decline.*

1994 Food and Drug Administration (FDA) addresses concerns that untested drugs are being given to children by proposing that pediatric data be required on all drug products that might be prescribed for children "off-label," or for uses not originally intended.

1997 Congress passes a resolution recognizing suicide as a national problem.

1999 Concerns about youth violence are crystallized when two gun-wielding seniors at Columbine High School outside Denver on April 20 murder a dozen students and a teacher before killing themselves. . . . Surgeon General David Satcher declares suicide a public health problem and proposes initiatives to reduce the rate of suicides nationwide.

2000s *Researchers question safety of antidepressant usage among children.*

October 2000 A study in the *Archives of Dermatology* indicates that teenagers who take the acne drug Accutane are no more likely to attempt suicide than those who do not. Accutane has been associated with youth suicide and requires an FDA warning label.

2002 National Suicide Prevention Resource Center begins operation as part of a national suicide prevention strategy.

June 2003 FDA advises that antidepressant Paxil should not be prescribed for teens and younger children until further study.

Dec. 10, 2003 British health regulators warn doctors against prescribing most newer antidepressant drugs to children, arguing benefits are outweighed by risks of triggering suicidal thoughts, self-injury and agitation.

Feb. 2, 2004 FDA scientific advisory board opens hearings on the controversy over antidepressants and their possible role in youth suicide.

Summer 2004 FDA ruling on antidepressants is expected.

Screening Program Identifies Suicide-Prone Kids

American youngsters are checked for everything from flat feet and crooked teeth to tuberculosis and mumps, but few are screened for one of the most dangerous afflictions they could face — the impulse to take their own lives.

"You take your kids in for a physical checkup every year, but the chances of finding anything wrong in adolescents — who are in the best health they'll ever be in — is very remote," says Laurie Flynn, director of the Carmel Hill Health Center for Early Diagnosis and Treatment at Columbia University. "Yet we've got a half-million kids every year trying suicide seriously enough to warrant medical attention, and that's something to pay attention to."

Columbia's TeenScreen Program aims to change that. Developed by Columbia Professor David Shaffer and overseen by the health center, it uses questionnaires and interviews to identify youngsters who may be at risk for depression and suicide, as well as for eating disorders and substance abuse. The program is used in more than 100 communities in some 30 states.

Once parental permission is obtained, students fill out a brief survey that includes questions about depression, substance abuse and suicide. Students who score positive on any of the questions answer a series of questions designed to gain insights into their emotional well-being. The questions probe for possible signs of distress, such as, "Do you have trouble staying awake in school?" Each time the student answers "Yes," the program asks a follow-up question — for example, "Does it happen every day?"

Students are asked specifically if they have thought about committing suicide. If the answer is yes, the computer asks follow-up questions, such as, "This week?" "Have you made a plan?"

A health-care professional must be on site to assess the results and recommend appropriate action. About 10-15 percent of the youngsters tested have been referred for treatment.

Counselors give the program high marks and say the kids enjoy taking the test. "I think it's very effective," says Margie Wright, executive director of the Suicide and Crisis Center in Dallas, which has used the program in several schools. "Kids will tell computers things they don't tell people face to face."

The idea for the program arose from research indicating that the majority of teens who are at risk for suicide are never diagnosed. Shaffer and his colleagues, for example, investigated 120 teenage suicides over a two-year period and found that 90 percent had a mental disorder that had gone undetected. Although parents generally believe they can tell when their kids are depressed, many emotional problems are dismissed as typical adolescent mood swings.

"Teenagers go to great pains to hide emotional distress from their parents," Shaffer said.[1]

Wright says TeenScreen has shown that kids at greatest risk for suicide often appear relatively energetic or happy.

Are antidepressant drugs helping to reduce the suicide rate?

British health authorities grabbed the attention of medical professionals around the world in December when they warned against prescribing most of the newer antidepressant drugs to children. Britain's equivalent of the FDA said the benefits of popular medications like Zoloft, Celexa and Lexapro were outweighed by the risks that the drugs could cause harmful side effects, including suicidal thoughts, self-injury and agitation. Only with Prozac did the benefits outweigh the risks, they said.

"These medicines may do more harm than good in the treatment of depression in under-18s," the British agency warned.[23]

The FDA had previously cautioned doctors against prescribing the antidepressants to children. Now it is undertaking a more sweeping review of the safety of antidepressants for children, examining about 20 studies, both published and unpublished and mostly conducted by pharmaceutical companies, of children who took antidepressants.

But many psychiatrists say the drugs are essential for treating severely depressed young people, and may even be responsible for the recent drop in the overall youth suicide rate. "I tend to believe they're enormously helpful and save lives," says the Center for Suicide Research and Prevention's Clark. "Clinical depressions can be mild or moderate or severe. If it's severe, I'll always talk about medication."

The antidepressants under scrutiny are called selective serotonin reuptake inhibitors, or SSRIs. They are so popular that total worldwide sales in 2001 hit $15.9 billion, third behind ulcer medications and cholesterol and

This correlates with research showing that many youngsters who kill themselves are successful in their classes and relationships but often impulsive or predisposed toward depression.

"Kids who are depressed don't look like adults who are depressed," she explains. "They're doing well in school, doing well in sports. They may be popular kids. For some kids, enough is never enough. Some kids are beautiful, but they don't see themselves that way. Or they're not living up to their parents' expectations."

But experts warn that TeenScreen has several shortcomings. For one thing, some youngsters become suicidal very suddenly — and the danger signs may not be picked up by a test administered only infrequently.

"When it comes to psychopathology and mental health, a lot of the problems are on and off. You catch me this month and I'm depressed; you catch me next month and I'm not," says David C. Clark, director of the Center for Suicide Research and Prevention at Rush-Presbyterian-St. Luke's Medical Center in Chicago. "Some of the suicidal impulses that kill children can literally sweep in like a storm and take a kid who six weeks before was strong and sturdy."

Moreover, many localities lack appropriate care for those who test positive. When school officials in Florida saw a presentation on TeenScreen, they were impressed, but they worried about what would happen to the children after diagnosis. "We felt that we could not set up a system to provide the necessary services for students identified to need treatment," said Linda Jones, supervisor for Safe and Drug Free Schools in Pinellas County (St. Petersburg). "It's not a good idea to screen unless you can provide care."[2]

Money can also be a factor. Although TeenScreen software is provided for free, schools need to pay to implement the program and provide follow-up evaluations for youngsters who appear to be at risk.

Gwen Luney, assistant school superintendent for supportive services and federal programs in Hillsborough County (Tampa), estimated TeenScreen would have cost the school district about $200,000 a year. "We're hesitant to commit to a new program if there's a strong possibility [of budget] shortfalls. Also, are we going to find a place for this [diagnosed] child to go? If so, what if the child doesn't have insurance? Who picks up the cost?"[3]

TeenScreen has appeared on Washington's radar screen. Rep. Rosa DeLauro, D-Conn., has introduced legislation to create 10 federally funded TeenScreen demonstration projects. Some school officials are warming to the idea, in part because identifying at-risk youth early may help prevent problems down the road, including criminal behavior.

Flynn acknowledges the problems of implementing a successful screening and treatment program, but she asks if society has a feasible alternative. "Would we rather not do this and wait until the kids get worse?" she asks.

[1] Quoted in Carol Vinzant, "Suicide Mission; Teens Are Screened for Many Conditions, but Rarely for a Real Killer," *The Washington Post*, Feb. 25, 2003, p. F1.

[2] Eric Snider, "Climbing Out of Hell; We Could Do More To Help Kids Stay Alive," *Weekly Planet Tampa*, June 5-11, 2003.

[3] Quoted in *ibid.*

triglyceride reducers.[24] SSRI use has become increasingly widespread among the young, even though only Prozac has been approved for treating childhood depression (and some researchers even question Prozac's safety, noting that it has been linked to suicide attempts in adults).[25] About 2.1 million prescriptions were written for youths in 2002, compared to only 50,000 in 1992, according to a recent estimate.[26] Even though the drugs are recommended only for severe depression, more than half of American children being treated for depression are given antidepressants, according to a study published in December.[27]

Health experts have raised concerns about whether the drugs are being overprescribed, especially by pediatricians and general practitioners in managed-care plans. The drugs represent a less expensive alternative for treating depression than traditional therapy, which can cost more than $100 for a weekly visit and last for months or even years. A month's supply of Prozac, in contrast, costs about $140 (and as little as $20 for its generic version). Taking a pill is also easier for patients than driving to a therapist for a nearly hourlong session.

But some experts question whether the drugs are effective. One much-quoted study showed 69 percent of children improved while taking Zoloft, only slightly better than the 59 percent who improved while taking a placebo. Other studies, funded by the pharmaceutical industry, reportedly indicate that the drugs are no more effective than placebos — but those studies have not been published.[28] "Some people offer up these [medications] as a panacea," says the University of Pittsburgh's Brent. "They're better than nothing, but they don't work that well."

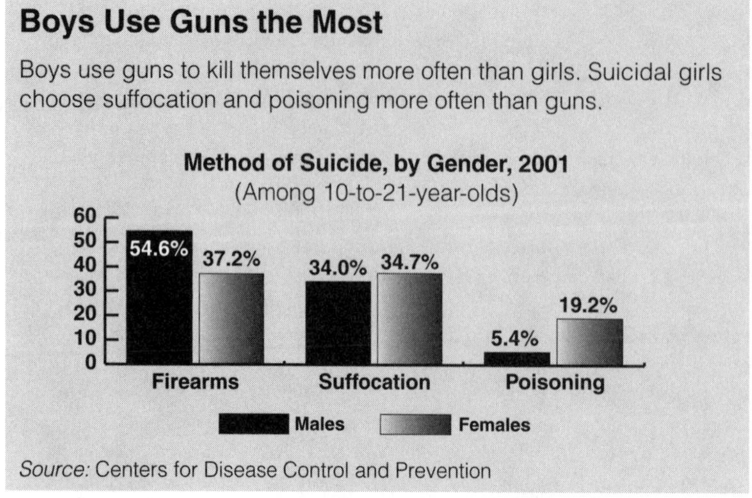

Still, some studies indicate SSRIs are reducing the youth suicide rate. *The Archives of General Psychiatry* reported in October that between 1990 and 2000 the increase in the use of antidepressants among children was associated with a decrease in teen suicides.

Mark Olfson, one of the study's authors, said that although it is too early to credit the antidepressants for the decrease, "It's a plausible hypothesis, and there's accumulating data."

Studies in Sweden and other European countries also have shown a correlation between antidepressant use and decreased suicide rates, but a study in Italy did not.

"These SSRIs can very possibly be lifesaving medicines," says Koplewicz of New York University's Child Study Center. "If someone really has depression, the first line of attack should be cognitive behavioral therapy.* It works in mild to moderate cases. Within 12 to 16 sessions, you're going to see a difference. If they don't get better, then adding medicine makes a lot of sense."

Although SSRIs appear to be safer than an earlier class of antidepressants known as tricyclic antidepressants, they still can have dangerous side effects. By boosting serotonin levels, they may cause physical and emotional agitation — a condition called akathisia. Some children can have a paradoxical reaction to the drugs, which causes them to become extremely restless or impulsive, and children with undiagnosed manic-depression can become unstable.

Some SSRIs are metabolized by the body very quickly and can cause a variety of reactions, including mood shifts, when abruptly halted. In three studies of Paxil examined by British regulators, 20 of 34 events "possibly related to suicidality" occurred during the 30 days after the children stopped taking the drug, compared with eight out of 17 in the placebo group in the same period.

Antidepressants are not the only drugs under scrutiny for links to youth suicide. A popular acne drug, Accutane, has been associated with suicide and requires an FDA warning label. The link, however, is not clear, and an extensive study published in the October 2000 issue of *Archives of Dermatology* indicated that teenagers who take Accutane are no more likely to try to kill themselves than those who do not.

Accutane is derived from vitamin A, which is involved with the growth and maintenance of skin. Some studies indicate that people who consume large amounts of vitamin A and related molecules suffer from depression, and concerns have been raised about individual cases of people taking Accutane who killed themselves.

Among the most publicized was the case of B.J. Stupak of Menominee, Mich., who shot himself in 2000. His father, Rep. Bart Stupak, D-Mich., has worked to publicize his son's story and others like it, and to have the drug taken off the market. Stupak said his son acted "out of the blue." The benefits of Accutane are "just not worth the side effects," he said.[29]

BACKGROUND

Studying Depression

Before the 20th century, youth suicide almost invariably was associated in literature with a traumatic event, such as the end of a relationship — perhaps most famously in

* In cognitive behavioral therapy, also called "talk" therapy, patients discuss their feelings with a psychologist or psychiatrist over a long period of time.

Shakespeare's *Romeo and Juliet.* It briefly took center stage in the 18th century with publication of Goethe's landmark novel, *The Sorrows of Young Werther.* The tragic tale of the doomed young man's unrequited love reportedly impelled dozens of young men throughout Europe to also commit suicide.[30]

Before the 1970s, youth suicide generally garnered little attention. In fact, many psychologists believed young people were incapable of long-term depression, although some psychologists had begun to discover signs of depression in children shortly after World War II. As early as 1946, Viennese psychiatrist Rene A. Spitz described what he called "anaclitic depression" in infants in orphanages, who failed to thrive when deprived of sufficient human contact. And, beginning in the 1950s, psychiatric researchers Leon Cytryn and Donald K. McKnew Jr. noted that chronically ill and hospitalized children often exhibited the same symptoms as classical adult depression, which had been recognized for millennia.

In the 1960s and '70s, several pioneering researchers attempted to differentiate between adult and childhood depression. Meanwhile, the first epidemiological study of a child population, in England in the mid-1960s, identified depression in less than 1 percent of youngsters. A 1967 report by the U.S.-based Group for the Advancement of Psychiatry asserted that depression in children often presented itself differently than in adults.

By the early 1970s, Cytryn and McKnew had suggested there were three types of childhood depression: acute, chronic and masked. But the psychiatric community was not ready to recognize childhood depression as a separate pathology. "The absence of a name for this entity [in diagnostic manuals] forces many professionals to misdiagnose their depressive patients," they wrote in the 1979 *Basic Handbook of Child Psychiatry.* "This in turn perpetuates the misconception that the condition does not exist."

Throughout the 1970s, a handful of psychiatrists began diagnosing depression in children more frequently, and doctors began to realize it had been underestimated in the past. In 1980, childhood depression finally was listed as a diagnosable psychiatric condition in the authoritative *Diagnostic and Statistical Manual on Mental Disorders (DSM-III).* By then, the youth suicide rate was rising dramatically — and mental health experts had become concerned that emotional problems in the young were a major risk factor.

Rising Toll

Modern thinking about suicide in general was largely shaped by Emile Durkheim, a French sociologist, and Sigmund Freud, the father of psychoanalysis. In *Le Suicide,* published in 1897, Durkheim listed three types of suicide: (1) altruistic suicide, where the customs and mores of a particular society dictate it (as with defeated warriors in certain cultures); (2) egotistical suicide, in which the victim is not sufficiently identified with the institutions of society and is forced to assume more individual responsibility than he can handle; and (3) anomic suicide, in which an individual's adjustment to society is suddenly broken or changed, as by financial reverses. To Freud, who wrote about man's inner destructivity, suicide represented the precocious victory of the inner drive toward death. None of these theories focused on youth suicide.

In 1933, the U.S. government began collecting statistics on morbidity. Although the data showed the nation's overall suicide rate remaining somewhat constant, the youth suicide rate increased dramatically after World War II with the emergence of the so-called Baby Boom generation. The rate of 4.5 suicides per 100,000 population in 1950 tripled over the next four decades. The trends initially coincided with a rebellious younger generation that was associated with drugs, sex and rock music.

But the alarming numbers persisted throughout the 1980s and even into the '90s, long after the turmoil of the '60s had subsided. Experts hypothesized about a variety of causes, including the breakdown of traditional families and communities, growing substance abuse and increasing violence — both in movies and rock songs and in real life. The increased suicide rate forced psychologists and policymakers in the 1990s to begin viewing mental health disorders in the young as a significant public health problem.

Meanwhile, mental health experts had become increasingly aware of the widespread problems of psychiatric disorders in the young. By then, an estimated 10 million children and adolescents had such disorders, according to Koplewicz of New York University. More than half of depressive adults said they had their first bout with the disease before age 20, a fact cited by many as proof of the urgency of catching and treating depression early in life.

Traditionally, mental health programs for the young in the United States have been the province of local care providers — churches, community mental health centers and private practitioners. But in 1983, amid rising concerns about teenage suicide, California created the first state-funded pilot programs to prevent suicide. High school teachers, administrators and students received instruction in sound decision-making, suicide warning signs, community suicide services, the relationship between substance abuse and suicide and how to improve interactions among students, teachers and school counselors.

Two years later, California expanded the pilot programs to encompass the entire state, and New Jersey launched its own program. Since then, about 15 other states have followed suit.

Federal Efforts

The federal government began to tackle the problem of mental illness — particularly the severely mentally ill — more aggressively in the 1960s. In February 1963, President John F. Kennedy asked Congress to adopt a "bold new approach" to those hospitalized with mental illness. Kennedy urged the creation of a nationwide network of community mental health centers to replace existing state mental hospitals. A shift to community-based care was widely seen as humane, since numerous abuses of patients had come to light at state-operated institutions.

Kennedy's goal of reducing mental hospital populations by half has been far exceeded: The number of hospital beds for the mentally ill has dropped from 550,000 in 1955 to only 40,000 today. But most of the money saved by shuttering state hospitals was not put back into the community mental health programs.

States continued to shutter hospitals, and by 1980, 2.4 million persons were receiving some sort of treatment at the nation's 750 mental health centers, 20 percent of which had been weaned off federal support. That same year President Jimmy Carter signed the Mental Health Systems Act, designed to boost funding for local treatment programs. But the following year, under the new administration of Ronald Reagan, the one-year-old law was repealed.

In 1981, as part of Reagan's proposals to curtail federal health programs, the Omnibus Budget Reconciliation Act restructured the nation's mental health system by shifting away from direct federal funding to a program of community block grants that states could apply to mental health treatment. Under the new system, funding for community mental health in 1982 dropped 30 percent below the previous year's level.[31]

In the 1990s, much of the national debate turned to the issue of "parity" — the concept that health insurance policies should cover mental health on a par with physical health. But the insurance industry has resisted the idea, which it warns would be costly and lead to higher premiums.[32]

In the meantime, government-funded research had begun shedding light on the causes of youth suicide. A 1986 survey of suicide experts found that many at-risk youths experienced troubled families, physical or sexual abuse, or alcohol or drug usage. The survey also pointed out that high achievers could also be at risk, because they tend to impose unrealistically high standards on themselves or feel a need to impress others.[33] Sexual orientation also appeared to play a role. A 1989 U.S. Department of Health and Human Services (HHS) study found homosexual teenagers were three times as likely as heterosexuals to attempt suicide.[34]

Even as youth suicide rates began to decline in the 1990s, several sensational school murder-suicides galvanized the nation's attention. Most dramatically, on April 20, 1999, two gun-wielding seniors at Columbine High School outside Denver murdered a dozen students and a teacher and wounded more than 20 others before killing themselves.[35] Many schools responded by establishing anti-bullying programs and trying to identify isolated or troubled students.

The same year, Surgeon General Satcher declared suicide a public health problem and proposed initiatives to reduce the rate of suicides nationwide, including youth suicides. The steps focused on increasing public awareness of suicide risk factors, enhancing services for potentially suicidal people and advancing research into suicide prevention. In 2001, Satcher unveiled the first installment of the national suicide prevention strategy, which focused on increased screening and increasing the number of states that require "parity" in health insurance — providing the same insurance coverage for mental health and substance abuse care as for regular health care.

Washington also has approved several grants for state and local suicide prevention programs, and for a nationwide toll-free suicide hotline (1-800-SUICIDE).

The Brain's Role

Research has shown a strong correlation between depression and suicide, and scientists are finding that some children are genetically predisposed to depression.[36]

Emotional disorder is often accompanied by abnormalities within and between the brain's neurotransmitters, composed of chemical compounds called amines. Neural impulses traveling in and out of the brain are accompanied by the release of these amines — manufactured and stored within nerve cells — which convey information from one nerve cell to another. Chemical messages from the neurotransmitters are passed along from cell to cell across the synapses, or small gaps between nerve cells.

An imbalance of brain amines — or an imbalance between the systems they are connected with — may impair the transmission of messages across the synapses, thus affecting the entire central nervous system and potentially producing symptoms of depression. Three amines in particular — dopamine, norepinephrine and serotonin — have been identified with depression.

In 1987, drug manufacturer Eli Lilly introduced Prozac, an antidepressant that increased levels of serotonin in the brain. Prozac proved highly popular among adults, and other SSRIs — including Paxil, Zoloft and Celexa — soon followed. With concern mounting about depressed children, doctors began prescribing the drugs for youngsters as well, even though the drugs' safety for use by children had never been tested.

From the start, some researchers worried about the new antidepressants' side effects. Some doctors noticed that their Prozac patients felt so uncomfortable they wanted to jump out of their skins. Controversies over the use of antidepressants for both children and adults has grown since then, culminating last year with the FDA warning for doctors not to prescribe Paxil to children and the British government cautioning against most popular antidepressants except Prozac.

CURRENT SITUATION

Federal Funds

Federal funding for youth suicide prevention has risen in recent years but still falls short of what's needed, advocates say.

Reed, of the Suicide Prevention Action Network, says funding has been on the upswing since 1997, when Congress passed a resolution recognizing suicide as a national problem. Since then, legislators have held three hearings on suicide prevention and authorized a suicide prevention resource center and a national hotline. The programs are slated to receive $3 million each in the omnibus appropriations bill for fiscal 2004, the same as last year.

Meanwhile, the Children's Mental Health Services Program — part of which goes to youth suicide prevention efforts — is set to increase by nearly $5 million in 2004, to $103 million.

"They've been very receptive," to our requests, Reed says. "They see that this is an important area to proceed on."

Appropriators also have ramped up funding for NIMH suicide research, increasing its appropriation by $2 million in fiscal 2003 and $1 million in the pending omnibus appropriations measure. NIMH is expected to receive $29.3 million for suicide research this year, $17 million of it targeted to youth issues.

And the CDC is expected to spend at least $2.8 million on suicide prevention in fiscal 2004, $2 million of it on research and $800,000 on data analysis and school-based suicide prevention pilot programs in Maine and Virginia, spokesperson Dagny Putman says.

Recent research suggests that school-based skills training and direct screening programs can increase coping skills and identify individuals at risk of committing suicide. Other studies suggest that programs aimed at training school personnel to recognize warning signs also may help reduce suicide risk.[37]

Additional funding for other school-based programs is provided in the Commerce, Justice and State department sections of the omnibus appropriations measure, as well as in the Labor, Health and Human Services portions of the bill. Among them are $150,000 for an online suicide prevention demonstration project in New York City and $1.1 million for prevention and awareness programs in Pennsylvania.

Still, mental health advocates did not get all they wanted from Congress. The Suicide Prevention Action Network was denied $8 million in grants to fund state and community suicide prevention plans, while the Mental Health Liaison Group — a nonprofit umbrella

AT ISSUE

Would stricter gun controls reduce the youth suicide rate?

YES

Mary Leigh Blek
President Emeritus, Million Mom March

Written for *CQ Researcher*, Feb. 3, 2004

After my son was shot and killed, I took a long hard look at how our nation protects our young people. We have a lot of work to do. When it comes to the very difficult issue of teenage suicide, there are fundamental truths that all parents know, but which policymakers typically ignore. A teenager's world is very different from an adult's.

One moment, young adults are soaring into the clouds, and the next they're crashing into the ground. Judgment and communication skills are still developing. As a mom and a former school nurse, I am intimately aware of the ups and downs that teenagers experience.

But I also know that it isn't always easy to learn when a teenager is having trouble.

Our job as parents is to show them our love and to offer them a safe environment. But we can't be everywhere, all the time. That's why we need a caring society and policymakers who are willing to help us build it.

I have often heard young adults say that if there had been a gun available to them, they would be dead. If we acknowledge that a teenager's world is different from our own, then we must make some choices about the world we both inhabit. It's the adult thing to do.

There are many issues concerning teenage depression and their mental well-being that must be examined by policymakers. But we do know that easy access to firearms greatly increases the risks of homicide and suicide.

A fleeting moment of despair combined with a teen's impulsivity and easy access to firearms is a recipe for disaster. The more lethal something is, the more likely death will occur. It's that simple. A recent study from the Harvard School of Public Health concluded that regions in the United States with higher levels of household handgun ownership experience higher suicide rates.

In many cases, technology holds the key. Cars are designed to be safer; guns should be, too. Technology that locks guns, or only permits the user to access it, offers policymakers opportunities to respect gun owners and safety. Many states have made the responsible decision to close loopholes in their laws that otherwise would allow young people to buy or possess guns.

It's time for Congress to act. We must also renew the ban on assault weapons and strengthen it. Sensible gun laws can help us prevent suicides, as well as homicides and injuries.

NO

John Lott
Resident scholar, American Enterprise Institute

Written for *CQ Researcher*, Feb. 5, 2004

Unfortunately, stricter gun-control laws will not reduce youth suicide. There are too many alternative ways for people to kill themselves. A few studies by economists and criminologists indicate that gun regulations may reduce gun suicides, but even they do not find evidence that total suicides decline.

In 2001, 90 American children under age 15 committed suicide with guns, and an additional 361 teens ages 15 to 17. With the National Institute of Mental Health estimating that more than 4.9 percent of 9-to-17-year-olds suffer severe depression during a six-month period, that makes gun suicide rare, even assuming that only the severely depressed commit suicide: The rate is about one in 10,000 of these depressed juveniles.

The problem with gun-control laws is the unintended drawbacks. Recent research in my book, *The Bias Against Guns,* covered juvenile accidental gun deaths and suicides for all the states from 1977 to 1998. I found that safe-storage laws had no impact on either type of death. In fact, in the states that adopted safe-storage laws, juvenile suicides using handguns actually rose very slightly relative to states without those laws.

In addition, law-abiding citizens were less able to defend themselves against crime. The 16 states that adopted these laws during the period faced more than 300 more murders and 4,000 additional rapes per year. Burglaries also increased dramatically.

Guns clearly deter criminals, with Americans using guns defensively over 2 million times each year — more than four times more frequently than the 500,000 times guns were used to commit crimes in 2001. Even though the police are extremely important at reducing crime, they virtually always end up at the crime scene after the crime has been committed. Having a gun is by far the safest course of action when confronting a criminal.

Locked guns (or gun-free households) mean that guns are not as readily accessible for self-defense. Moreover, many mechanical locks (such as barrel or trigger locks) also require that the gun be stored unloaded. Loading a gun obviously requires yet more time to respond to a criminal.

Even if one has young children, it does not make sense to lock up a gun if one lives in a high-crime urban area. Exaggerating the risks involved in gun ownership will make people lock up their guns or cause them not to own a gun in the first place, resulting in more, not fewer deaths.

group representing families, advocates and mental health providers — lobbied fruitlessly for funds for a suicide prevention program for children and adolescents. The program was authorized in 2000 as part of a broader children's health bill sponsored by Rep. Michael Bilirakis, R-Fla., but has never been funded.

Paul Seifert, director of government affairs for the International Association of Psychosocial Rehabilitation Services — representing agencies, researchers, educators, practitioners and administrators — blames the delay on competing priorities. "If they give money to fund [Bilirakis' bill], they will have to take it from somewhere else," he says.

But Julio Abreu, director of government affairs at the National Mental Health Association, says it's more a matter of misplaced priorities. "There has been a general lack of commitment to issues relating to mental health," he laments.

Funding for the mental health block grant is expected to drop by $22 million in fiscal 2004, to $415 million.

Meanwhile, advocates perennially have failed to pass a mental health parity bill, which would prevent health plans from charging higher deductibles, copayments and out-of-pocket expenses for the treatment of mental illness than for other illnesses. House Republican leaders, warning it would drive up health care costs, have blocked the bill.

But supporters counter that the bill could cut employers' costs by reducing absenteeism and disability claims. Reed's organization plans to renew lobbying for the bill this year.

In states and localities across the country, tight budgets are imperiling anti-suicide programs. Just last month, for example, Massachusetts Gov. Mitt Romney proposed eliminating $125,000 for suicide prevention.[38] Far to the west, cash-strapped city officials in Santa Fe, N.M., have shut down a program to help adolescents in crisis and cut back funding for suicide programs in schools. "It points to a downturn in the economy and a lack of adequate gross receipts that we depend on for our budget," said Santa Fe City Councilor Miguel Chavez.[39]

Suicide on Campus

Colleges and universities across the country are feeling the brunt of the increase in youth depression. From 1989 to 2001, the number of depressed students seeking help doubled, and those at risk for suicide tripled, according to a much-cited Kansas State University study.[40]

"No doubt, over the last 10 years people are coming in with more severe depressions," says Jaquelyn Liss Resnick, president the Association of University and College Counseling Center Directors. "The types of problems have not changed over time, but the severity has."

Suicide is the second-leading cause of death among college students, with an estimated 7.5 deaths per 100,000 students per year, according to a study of Big 10 campuses from 1980 to 1990. A nationwide study found that 9 percent of college students seriously considered suicide between one and 10 times in the 2002-3 school year, and just over 1 percent actually tried to kill themselves.[41]

Resnick and other experts say college students always have been under stress, due to academic and social pressures and being separated from their families. In addition, many are exposed to drugs and alcohol for the first time in college. Moreover, emotional vulnerabilities become more apparent during the intense work and sometimes sleepless nights typical of college life.

In addition, more children with serious mental illnesses today are being diagnosed and treated with antidepressants, which can enable some to attend and cope with college who years ago perhaps would not have even considered applying to college.

"All across the country, we're seeing a significant increase in people coming in who are on psychiatric medication," Resnick says.

The Miami Herald recently profiled one such woman, Caitlin Stork, who attempted suicide when she was 15, then tried again shortly after being discharged from the hospital. Doctors eventually diagnosed her as having a bipolar disorder and put her on the mood stabilizer lithium. Now a senior at Harvard, Stork also takes the anti-psychotic Seroquel.

"You would never believe how much I can hide from you," Stork wrote for a campus display on mental health. "I'm a Harvard student like any other; I take notes during lecture, goof off . . . but I never let on how much I hurt."

Some experts believe the situation is getting worse. "This is just the beginning," said Peter Lake, a professor of law at Stetson University who co-authored *The Rights and Responsibilities of the Modern University: Who Assumes the Risks of College Life?* He believes mental illness — particularly self-inflicted injury — will soon eclipse alcohol as the No. 1 issue on campuses.[42]

In response to growing needs, colleges have hired more psychiatrists, expanded the hours at counseling centers and instituted outreach programs. Teachers are being instructed to keep an eye on potentially overstressed students during exam times.

Congress also may step in. Last year, two House lawmakers introduced the Campus Care and Counseling Act, which would provide $10 million in fiscal 2005 for campus mental and behavioral health service centers.

Resnick believes campuses are a good place for troubled youths to get help, because they are tight-knit communities. "The vast majority of students come here to create a community," she says. "This allows for quite a bit of exposure to faculty and staff, campus ministers and other groups that can be on the alert for people who seem especially distressed. If you do a good job of outreaching, this can be a very good first-alert system."

But some students who need help sometimes don't know about the counseling services or are reluctant to use them because of the stigma attached to emotional problems. "A lot of students aren't that comfortable going up to a psychiatrist, and saying, 'Hey, I need some help,'" said Peter Maki, a University of Miami student and a member of a student outreach group.[43]

Seeking to close that gap, the nonprofit Jed Foundation last year launched a free Web site, Ulifeline.org, which links students to mental health centers, information about emotional problems and anonymous screening for depression, eating disorders and other problems. The foundation was founded by Donna and Phil Satow, whose son Jed hanged himself while a sophomore at the University of Arizona in 1998.

"The ability to access a Web site confidentially, in the privacy of your dorm room, has distinct advantages," said Morton Silverman, director of the National Suicide Prevention Center in Newton, Mass. "And university students today are very adept at using the information . . . so having a resource there to check on their mental health is an important thing."[44]

OUTLOOK

Positive Trends?

The youth suicide rate has dropped steadily in recent years. The rate for older adolescents (15-19), for example, has declined 29 percent since 1994, according to the National Center for Vital Statistics. But is it just a temporary downswing or a sign that society is finally finding solutions to the problem of youth suicide?

"It doesn't look like it's just a little blip," the Carmel Hill Center's Flynn says. "It looks like a trend, a very positive trend. The optimist in me believes we are beginning to get a handle on it."

In fact, she sees several positive trends, including improved treatment options such as antidepressants and a better understanding of the underlying factors that contribute to suicide.

The University of Vermont's Fassler also believes society may be turning the corner. "I am optimistic," he says. "We're having success in reducing the stigma associated with mental health treatment, and we're getting better at identifying kids earlier and making sure they get appropriate treatment."

Others are less optimistic about the future, warning that experts have yet to figure out precisely what drives the rate up and down. They also point out that rates have declined unevenly for different groups. For example, while the rate for those in the 10-to-14-year-old age group has dropped slightly in recent years, it is still more than double the 1970 rate.[45]

"It's like tides. The rates seem to go in and out," says Clark of Chicago's Center for Suicide Research and Prevention. "It's very hard to predict what's going to happen next."

He and others agree that many suicides are preventable with proper diagnosis and treatment. A major challenge remains in overcoming the stigma associated with mental illness and persuading those who need treatment to get it. But it can be an uphill battle, especially in small towns where traditional values hold more sway and people keep an eye on which cars are parked at the local crisis center.

"We have lots of people who would rather die than come and see a mental health professional," Clark says.

Other challenges include mobilizing societal resources by better equipping schools and local crisis centers to handle youth suicide and providing financial support for patients without insurance coverage. That could be an expensive proposition, especially in localities with high budget deficits. But failing to help troubled youths carries its own costs, mental health professionals note. Suicidal tendencies go hand-in-hand with other high-risk behavior, such as substance abuse, teen pregnancy and dropping out of school.

As Fassler puts it, treating youth depression is a "lot less expensive than dealing with the consequences and repercussions in the long run."

NOTES

1. U.S. Division of Vital Statistics data, www.cdc.gov/ncipc/wisqars.
2. Andrew Julien, "The Kids Are Hurting," *The Hartford Courant*, Dec. 15, 2002, p. A1.
3. These numbers, based on studies by the Centers for Disease Control and other agencies, were cited by then-Surgeon General David Satcher in a 1999 document, "The Surgeon General's Call to Prevent Suicide."
4. Satcher, *ibid.*
5. For background, see Kathy Koch, "Childhood Depression," *The CQ Researcher*, July 16, 1999, pp. 593-617.
6. Quoted in Julien, *op. cit.*
7. See Jane Tanner, "Mental Illness Medication Debate," *The CQ Researcher*, Feb. 6, 2004, pp. 101-124.
8. Shankar Vedantam, "Britain Warns Against Giving Newer Antidepressants to Kids; Only Prozac's Benefits Outweigh Risks, Health Officials Say," *The Washington Post*, Dec. 11, 2003, p. A2.
9. Lauran Neergard, "FDA hearing whether some drugs can trigger suicides by kids," The Associated Press, Feb. 2, 2004.
10. Division of Vital Statistics, *op. cit.*
11. Eric Snider, "Climbing Out of Hell; We Could Do More To Help Kids Stay Alive," *Daily Planet Tampa*, June 5-11, 2003.
12. The academy Web site is: http://www.aap.org/advocacy/childhealthmonth/prevteensuicide.htm
13. See Richard L. Worsnop, "Teenage Suicide," *The CQ Researcher*, June 14, 1991, pp. 369-392.
14. The 1985 study was led by Dr. Lee Salk, a family and child expert. It was cited by Bill Briggs in "Suicide: Isolation, access to guns tied to West's soaring rate," *The Denver Post*, Aug. 27, 2000, p. A1.
15. Harold S. Koplewicz, *More Than Moody* (2002).
16. Julien, *op. cit.*
17. Katherine Seligman and Diana Walsh, "Palo Alto High School Shaken by 2 Suicides; Students, Parents, Teachers Seek Help in Learning Signs of Distress in Teenagers," *San Francisco Chronicle*, Nov. 24, 2003, p. A1.
18. The states are California, Connecticut, Florida, Hawaii, Kentucky, Maryland, New Jersey, New York and Virginia. For background, see Julie Thomerson, "Violent Acts of Sadness: The Tragedy of Youth Suicide," *State Legislatures*, May 1, 2002, p. 30.
19. *Ibid.*
20. *Ibid.*
21. Carol Vinzant, "Suicide Mission; Teens Are Screened for Many Conditions, but Rarely for a Real Killer," *The Washington Post*, Feb. 5, 2003, p. F1.
22. Koplewicz, *op. cit.*
23. Vedantam, *op. cit.*
24. IMS Health, a pharmaceutical market research and business analysis firm; www.ims-global.com//insight/news_story/0204/news_story_020430.htm
25. Michael D. Lemonick, "Prescription for Suicide?" *Time*, Feb. 9, 2004.
26. Virginia Anderson, "Teens and Depression," *The Atlanta Journal and Constitution*, Oct. 19, 2003, p. 1LS.
27. Mark Olfson, *et al.*, "Outpatient Treatment of Child and Adolescent Depression in the United States," *Archives of General Psychiatry*, December 2003, pp. 1236-1242.
28. Anderson, *op. cit.*, and Shankar Vedantam, "Antidepressant Makers Withhold Data on Children," *The Washington Post*, Jan. 29, 2004, p. A1.
29. Quoted in Mary Duenwald, "Debate on Acne Drug's Safety Persists Over Two Decades," *The New York Times*, Jan. 22, 2002, p. F7.
30. For a good description of early attitudes toward youth suicide, see Worsnop, *op. cit.*
31. "Community Mental Health Centers at the 40-year Mark: The Quest for Survival," National Council for Community Behavorial Healthcare, 2003, p. 6.

32. For background, see Jane Tanner, "Mental Health Insurance," *The CQ Researcher*, March 29, 2002, pp. 265-288.
33. Worsnop, *op. cit.*
34. *Ibid.*
35. For background, see Kathy Koch, "School Violence," *The CQ Researcher*, Oct. 9, 1998, pp. 881-904.
36. See "Childhood Depression," *op. cit.*
37. Madelyn S. Gould *et al.*, "Youth Suicide Risk and Preventive Interventions: A Review of the Past 10 Years," *Research Update Review*, April 2003, pp. 394-396.
38. Scott S. Greenberger, "Romney Sets a $22.98B Blueprint," *The Boston Globe*, Jan. 29, 2004, p. A1.
39. Deborah Davis, "Budget Cuts Would Wound Crisis Response," *Santa Fe New Mexican*, Dec. 31, 2003, p. A1.
40. Sherry A. Benton, *et al.*, "Changes in Counseling Center Client Problems Across 13 Years," *Professional Psychology: Research and Practice*, Vol. 34, No. 1, 2003, pp. 66-72.
41. Daniela Lamas, "The Breaking Point: The Dark Side of College Life," *The Miami Herald*, Dec. 9, 2003, p. E11.
42. Quoted in *ibid.*
43. *Ibid.*
44. Shannon Dininny, "Colleges Sign on to Web Site Aimed at Reducing Youth Suicide," The Associated Press, Oct. 6, 2003.
45. Division of Vital Statistics, *op. cit.*

BIBLIOGRAPHY

Books

Fassler, David G., and Lynne S. Dumas, *"Help Me, I'm Sad,"* *Penguin*, 1997.
A child psychiatrist (Fassler) and writer (Dumas) examine the causes, symptoms and treatments of depression in youth, noting that young people often exhibit far different symptoms than adults. Includes first-person accounts from children and parents.

Koplewicz, Harold S., *More Than Moody*, *G.P. Putnam's Sons*, 2002.
A psychiatrist discusses childhood depression and suicide, including the diagnosis and treatment of college students suffering from emotional disorders.

Articles

Briggs, Bill, "Suicide: Isolation, Access to Guns Tied to West's Soaring Rate," *The Denver Post*, Aug. 27, 2000, p. A1.
The suicide rate in the Mountain States is up to triple the rate in Eastern cities or Southern agricultural areas. The article raises pertinent issues about how high suicide rates may be related to rural isolation and easy access to guns.

Goode, Erica, "British Ignite a Debate on Drugs and Suicide," *The New York Times*, Dec. 16, 2003, p. F1.
Regulators in Britain surprised many U.S. psychiatrists when they told British doctors to stop prescribing several common antidepressants for young people. The article discusses studies that indicate antidepressants may cause suicidal thoughts and behavior in the young, but also quotes experts who tout the drugs' benefits.

Harris, Gardiner, "FDA Intensely Reviews Depression Drugs," *The New York Times*, Oct. 28, 2003, p. F8.
The FDA is reviewing Paxil and similar drugs amid claims that they may increase the likelihood of suicide for teenagers and children.

Julien, Andrew, "The Kids Are Hurting," *Hartford Courant*, Dec. 15, 2002, p. A1.
Experts believe many children today are suffering from emotional and behavioral disorders because of unrelenting pressure to succeed and disintegrating families.

Lamas, Daniela, "The Breaking Point: The Dark Side of College Life," *The Miami Herald*, Dec. 9, 2003, p. E11.
Growing numbers of college students are coping with mental illness and suicidal tendencies, due to increased academic pressure, access to drugs and alcohol, and a greater number of adolescents using psychiatric drugs who now are able to graduate from high school and enroll in college.

Lemonick, Michael D., "Prescription for Suicide? British Authorities Say Some Antidepressants Can Be Deadly for Kids. Now the FDA Is Investigating," *Time*, Feb. 9, 2004, p. 59.
For years, a small but vocal group of patients and doctors has insisted that certain antidepressants, including Paxil, Zoloft, Prozac and other medications known as selective

serotonin reuptake inhibitors (SSRIs) carry an unacceptable risk of antisocial behavior and suicide. Now the U.S. Food and Drug Administration is about to hold hearings on the controversy.

Seligman, Katherine, and Diana Walsh, "Palo Alto High School Shaken by Two Suicides," *The San Francisco Chronicle*, Nov. 24, 2003, p. A1.
The authors examine the high levels of stress that afflict children in affluent areas of Silicon Valley.

Thomerson, Julie, "Violent Acts of Sadness: The Tragedy of Youth Suicide," *State Legislatures*, May 1, 2002, p. 30.
Suicide is the third-biggest cause of death among 15-to-24-year-olds. State legislators are trying to understand the reasons for this epidemic so they can design programs to help.

Vinzant, Carol, "Suicide Mission; Teens Are Screened for Many Conditions, but Rarely for a Real Killer," *The Washington Post*, Feb. 25, 2003, p. F1.
Columbia University's TeenScreen Program is designed to identify youngsters at highest risk of suicide so they can be steered into treatment.

Reports and Studies

Benton, Sherry A., *et al.*, "Changes in Counseling Center Client Problems Across 13 Years," *Professional Psychology: Research and Practice*, Vol. 34, Nov. 1, 2003, pp. 66-72.
A 13-year study of students seeking help at college counseling centers found the number of depressed students doubled, suicidal students tripled, and students seen after sexual assaults quadrupled.

Olfson, Mark, *et al.*, "Relationship Between Antidepressant Medication Treatment and Suicide in Adolescents," *Archives of General Psychiatry*, October 2003, pp. 978-82.
Researchers found a correlation between antidepressant prescriptions and lower suicide rates, although the correlation did not hold for girls or younger adolescents.

For More Information

American Association of Suicidology, 4201 Connecticut Ave., N.W., Suite 408, Washington, DC 20008; (202) 237-2280; suicide hotline 1-800-SUICIDE; www.suicidology.org.

National Institute of Mental Health, 6001 Executive Blvd., Suite 8235, Rockville, MD, 20852; (301) 443-3673; www.nimh.nih.gov.

National Mental Health Association, 2001 N. Beauregard St., Alexandria, VA 22311; (703) 684-7722; www.nmha.org.

Suicide Prevention Action Network USA, 1025 Vermont Ave., N.E., Washington, DC, 20005; (202) 449-3600; www.spanusa.org. An educational and advocacy organization that seeks to reduce the suicide rate.

Suicide Prevention Resource Center, 55 Chapel St., Newton, MA 02458-1060; (877) 438-7772; www.sprc.org.